TOURISM PLANNING
AND POLICY

TOURISM PLANNING AND POLICY

DIANNE DREDGE

GRIFFITH UNIVERSITY

JOHN JENKINS

THE UNIVERSITY OF NEWCASTLE

BICENTENNIAL
1807
WILEY
2007
BICENTENNIAL

John Wiley & Sons Australia, Ltd

First edition published 2007 by
John Wiley & Sons Australia, Ltd
42 McDougall Street, Milton Qld 4064

Offices also in Sydney and Melbourne

Typeset in 10.5/12 pt New Baskerville

National Library of Australia
Cataloguing-in-Publication data

Dredge, Dianne.
   Tourism planning and policy.

   Bibliography.
   Includes index.
   ISBN 9 7804 7080 7767.

   1. Tourism — Australia. 2. Tourism — Australia — Planning.
   3. Tourism — Government policy — Australia. I. Jenkins,
John M. (John Michael), 1961– . II. Title.

Cover images: © Peter Lik Publishing
Internal design images: © PhotoDisc, Inc.
Anniversary logo design: Richard Pacifico

Edited by Cathryn Game

Printed in Singapore by
Fabulous Printers Pte Ltd

10 9 8 7 6 5 4 3 2 1

CONTENTS

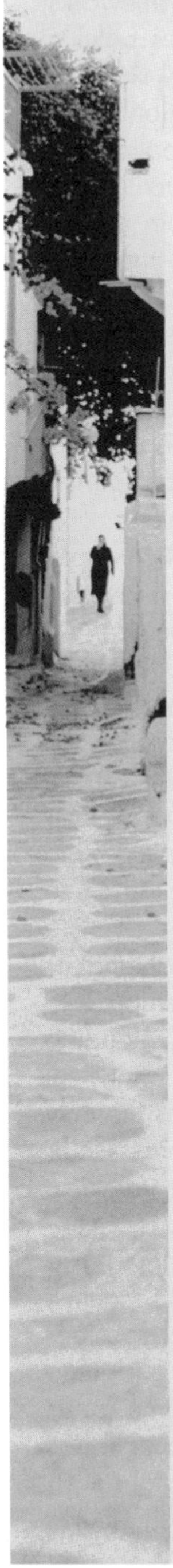

PREFACE ···

Informed tourism policy and planning is born of creative, strategic and resourceful individuals and agencies. It requires strong research, analytical and technical skills, and is based on an appreciation of theoretical frameworks, concepts, methods and approaches. On a practical level, it requires political sensitivity, thoughtful consultation and highly developed interpersonal skills. As tourism planning practitioners and researchers with extensive national and international experience, we believe that, on the whole, tourism policy and planning does not receive the critical attention it deserves. It is frequently seen as an outcome, an afterthought or a set of implications arising from tourism research. There is much talk about the policy implications of the impact of tourism or the need for government action to enhance the economic contributions of tourism. How the actions of governments, existing policy positions and policy-making processes contribute to these issues is often sidelined. With this book, *Tourism Planning and Policy*, we seek to promote critical and informed reflection of the way policy is made, the complex nature of tourism policy problems and issues, and the ideological and practical influences on tourism policy development.

Throughout this book we have attempted to integrate many different concepts, approaches, themes, theories and issues concerning tourism policy and planning. Of course, one cannot write a book that will be all things to all people. We have made choices about what to include and what not to include. Ultimately, the responsibility for building a deep appreciation of tourism policy and planning must be an individual commitment, so we encourage readers to look beyond this book, to engage with local case studies and reflect on their experiences. The aim of this book has been to help readers develop and enhance their skills and knowledge of tourism policy and planning processes, contexts and settings. Despite a keen focus on Australian settings, the theories and issues can be fruitfully employed in studies of other places.

By inviting other authors to contribute chapters on diverse spatial and/or contextual aspects of tourism policy and planning we have attempted to broaden the book's scope, enliven its content and to capture the understanding and knowledge of others. The authors contribute alternative analytical perspectives and diverse insights, but these should not be construed as the only explanations of tourism planning and policy processes and outcomes. Nor should their descriptions of particular case studies and institutional structures be considered best practice. They are simply alternative conceptions. Every chapter in the book demonstrates that tourism policy and planning are complex, dynamic, highly integrated with other fields, worthy of academic endeavour, informed by rigorous research in other disciplines and of substantial political relevance. It is also clear that tourism is a wonderfully intriguing mass phenomenon that is very difficult to manage successfully. In some areas tourism is a beast whose tentacles have wrought havoc; in other places it has been a wonderfully welcome addition to a region's economic and social development. Tourism has destroyed fragile environments while, conversely, it has contributed to the conservation of an enormous array of marine and terrestrial environments. It has destroyed some cultures and given renewed spirit to others. The challenge of tourism policy and planning research and practice is, therefore, to develop and implement informed policy processes and actions, and to critically evaluate, reflect on and improve outcomes and the inevitable impacts of tourism.

In writing this book, the authors have called upon the support of many agencies, institutions and individuals, whose diverse contributions have strengthened this book immeasurably.

Darren Taylor, Nina Crisp, Cathryn Game and others at Wiley have been highly supportive of the project from its inception and have helped us navigate this project from a few words over coffee to publication. Thank you. Without their support this book would not have been realised.

Dianne acknowledges the on-going support of her colleagues in the School of Environmental Planning, Griffith University, particularly Neil Sipe, Jenny Cameron, Eddo Coiacetto, Caryl Bosman and Lex Brown. Donovan Burton and Narelle Beaumont have provided significant research support while Meredith Lawrence, Jim Macbeth and Diane Lee have, perhaps unknowingly, provided inspiration and diverse opportunities for learning and reflection. John Jenkins, Michael Hall, Neil Leiper and Michael Fagence have, over the years, provided much appreciated feedback and critical commentary on various manuscripts for this and other publications. This feedback has strengthened and refined my understanding of tourism planning and policy enormously, and to these people I attribute my passion and enthusiasm for this exciting field of research and practice. The authors and publisher would like to thank reviewers Noel Scott, Justine Digance, Heather Zeppell and Leonie Lockstone for their involvement and feedback. Dianne also thanks Mary-Anne Smith for her assistance with the supplementary material.

John would like to thank the University of Newcastle for support in bringing this book to fruition. Thanks particularly, however, to great colleagues and friends Shane Homan, Kevin Lyons, Bill Mitchell and Kevin Markwell, and to colleagues elsewhere: Ralf Buckley, Richard Butler, Michael Hall, Dave Mercer, John Pigram, Rob Schaap, Tony Sorenson and Jim Walmsley. John also thanks Tina Montgomery for her assistance with the supplementary material.

Finally, this project would not have been realised without the support, encouragement and inspiration of some special people. In particular, Dianne would like to thank Deni, Jordi and Don, Shirley and Glen, Keith and Glenda, Leanne and Roz, and all those friends who continued to inquire kindly and enthusiastically about the progress of the book despite not being sure about its plot or characters! John would like to thank Hodgo, Maca and Phubb who provide the sparkle and reality checks in his life.

Dianne Dredge
John Jenkins
September 2006

ACKNOWLEDGEMENTS

The authors and publisher would like to thank the following copyright holders, organisations and individuals for their permission to reproduce copyright material in this book.

Images
• Routledge/Taylor & Francis Group, LLC: **95** © 1994 From Gunn, CA, *Tourism Planning*, Concepts, *Cases 3rd edition*; **321** © 1998 From Gunn, CA, *Tourism Planning 2nd edition*. Reproduced by permission of Routledge/Taylor & Francis Group, LLC • Oxford University Press: **165** adapted from *Studying Public Policy: Policy Cycles and Policy Subsystems*, 2nd edition by M Howlett and M Ramesh. Copyright 2003 Oxford University Press. Reprinted by permission of the publisher • John Wiley & Sons, Inc.: **197** from *Tourism Planning: An integrated and sustainable development approach*, Inskeep, E, 1991, John Wiley & Sons, Inc. reprinted with permission • Department of Sustainability and Environment, Victoria: **197** from 'Best Practice in Park Interpretation and Education', Victorian Department of Natural Resources and Parks Victoria (1999). Included with permission of Department of Sustainability and Environment, Victoria • Multilingual Matters: **199** from 'Public Choice and Tourism Analysis' by Ewen Michael, from *Current Issues in Tourism*, Vol. 4, Nos 2–4 2001; **343** from Newsom, Moore & Dowling, *Natural Area Tourism — Ecology, Impacts and Management*, p. 199, Channel View Publications. Included with permission of Multilingual Matters • © Western Australian Tourist Commission, included with permission of Tourism WA: **269**, **291** (both images) • Noosa Council: **312** from *Noosa Shire Council Corporate Plan 2003–2007* Appendix 1; **316** from *Noosa Community Tourism Board — Tourism New Development Project November 2002*, KPMG. Included with permission from Noosa Council • © Department of Conservation (New Zealand) www.doc.govt.nz: **346**.

Text
• Included with permission of Hon. Nick Greiner AC: **122–3** • Thomson Publishing Services: **126** from Elliot, *Tourism: Politics and Public Sector Management*, Routledge, London, 1997. Included with permission of Thomson Publishing Services • © Tom Ballantyne: **140–1** • *The Courier-Mail*/Lachlan Heywood: **162** • The Code of Conduct for the Protection of Children from Sexual Exploitation in Travel and Tourism © www.thecode.org: **166**. The Code is an organisation unto itself and is registered in Sweden. Partner organisations are ECPAT International — http://www.ecpat.net, the World Tourism Organization — www.world-tourism.org and UNICEF — www.unicef.org • © Gough Whitlam: **230–1** • © Commonwealth of Australia: **237** extracts from *Department of the Arts, Sports, the Environment, Tourism and the Territories Annual Report 1988–89*; **242–3** extracts from *Australian Tourism Commission Annual Report 1998–99*; **245** extracts from *Tourism Australia's Passport to Growth: A National Tourism Strategy*, June 1992, Commonwealth Department

of Tourism; **283**, **284** extracts from the *National Strategy for Ecologically Sustainable Development* from http://www.esd.gov.au/ reproduced by permission • Pearson Education: **239** from *Introduction to Tourism in Australia: Impacts, Planning and Development*, Colin Michael Hall, Longman Cheshire, 1991. Included with permission of Pearson Education • Adapted and included with permission of Parks and Leisure Australia: **259–61** • © Department of Conservation (New Zealand) www.doc.govt.nz: **346**, **347**, **354**, **356–7** • CABI: **367–9** adaptation of 'Ecotourism certification in New Zealand: Operator and industry perspectives', Rowe, T and Higham, JES in *Quality in ecotourism*, Black, R and Crabtree, A (Eds), CABI, 2006 included with permission.

Dianne Dredge and John Jenkins

CHAPTER 1

Introduction to *tourism policy and planning*

LEARNING OBJECTIVES

After studying this chapter you will be able to:

1 define the term 'policy' and explain the significance of policy analysis

2 explain the concept of 'planning' and discuss its relationship to policy

3 discuss the significance of such defining concepts as tourism, policy and planning with respect to tourism

4 identify and discuss the factors influencing tourism planning and policy

5 describe the philosophies and principles of tourism planning and policy.

This book aims to help students develop the skills and knowledge necessary to understand and critically analyse tourism public policy and planning processes, contexts and settings. The theoretical and applied emphases are on developed countries, and the case studies focus mainly on Australian situations. Some chapters briefly direct their attention to other countries such as New Zealand, but authors have generally linked concepts, theories and practice with familiar local and national circumstances. The strong focus on Australia, however, allows students to develop a sophisticated understanding of the different levels of policy-making and planning in contemporary society. For example, the links between different levels of government and between governments and business are explained in considerable detail. One of the benefits we see in the presentation of content in this book is that although it is structured in what appears to its editors to be a most logical sequence, individual chapters can be read 'selectively'. By this we mean that teachers could decide to present content in a different sequence — for instance, there's no foreseeable reason why chapter 5 could not follow chapter 3, but we feel the flow is better the way it is now. So readers will find some repetition as knowledge of policy and planning issues deepens through the book and as the examples and case studies used necessarily require reference to such issues on more than one occasion.

The book presents many examples of planning and policy theory and practice to explain how theories and concepts can be and have been applied and how policy-makers and interests (such as pressure groups or private sector entrepreneurs) can actively shape the policy-making environment. **Policy actors** and **agencies** can be creative and innovative in developing 'blueprints' for tourism development and in managing the most fragile tourist settings. Local communities can act persuasively to preserve local heritage and quality of life against aggressive and powerful developers and multinational corporations. Powerful private sector executives and board directors are members of the boards of statutory corporations, and it is difficult to see these people making decisions or fostering public policy that would negatively affect the profits of their companies and shareholders (so whose interest do they serve?). Ministers and bureaucrats can negotiate secretly and selectively with preferred interests or make decisions that serve their private agendas or serve the ideological thrusts of their political party. Occasionally, corruption does occur.

This chapter provides an introduction to the emergence of tourism as a legitimate and important area of planning and policy-making in contemporary society. Sections 1.2 and 1.3 discuss definitions and characteristics of policy and planning respectively. Section 1.4 explains how different views of or opinions about tourism influence the direction and approaches that governments adopt when dealing with tourism. Section 1.5 presents the conceptual framework for studying tourism planning and policy adopted in this book.

To assist you in acquiring an in-depth understanding of tourism policy and planning, this book is divided into three interrelated parts. The book's first part (chapters 1–6) is directed to planning and policy-making concepts, theories, philosophies and principles, and hence to the acquisition of historical and theoretical knowledge and frameworks necessary to understand and develop a critical awareness of policy and planning. For example, what is the role of the state in contemporary Australia? What systems of thought have influenced planning and policy-making in theory and in practice? Are any individuals or groups more powerful than others in relation to particular areas of tourism policy? What theories have been applied to help explain the distribution of power in tourism planning and policy-making? What is a pressure group? How do pressure groups operate? Are pressure groups important to policy and planning processes or are they a hindrance to 'good' policy? How have their roles, strategies and functions shifted over time? How is knowledge of policy and planning concepts and theories likely to help us understand policy-making in practice?

The second part (chapters 7–12) applies the knowledge acquired in the first section to case studies of tourism planning and policy-making at different scales and in different environments and settings. The first three chapters in this part look at national, regional and local tourism policy and planning respectively. The latter three chapters address protected lands, protected marine areas and indigenous tourism policy and planning. Again, the focus is mainly on Australia, except in the case of protected lands where, after a broad overview of internationally recognised issues, we consider the situation in New Zealand.

The book's third part (chapter 13) gives a brief review of what is canvassed in the book. This chapter also presents ideas for future research and suggests that despite extravagant accountability and managerial processes, the ever-widening availability of information and all the lessons of experience and practice, many events cannot be predicted, a good proportion of public sector decisions and actions are reactionary, and policy and planning processes remain a facet of life for which no defining model exists. There is as much art and craft to public policy-making and planning as there is to their analysis (Wildavsky 1979). Planning and policy-making are value laden, and we express great concern as to whether (1) the balance really has shifted towards sustainable tourism development, (2) governments are overly concerned with economic growth at the expense of the environment and people's quality of life in local communities and (3) whether many sectors of private industry really care about the state of the environment and are willing to trade short-term profits for environmental protection.

With these things in mind, our first task is to define such key terms as policy, planning and tourism.

1.2 WHAT IS POLICY?

Definitions in any discipline, field of study or activity have important roles. The task of defining policy has received a lot of attention, but no consensus has emerged (e.g. Howlett & Ramesh 1995; Colebatch 2002). Definitions clarify what it is we are looking at, and the process of arriving at definitions can be revealing. In the Parable of the Elephant, of which one can find variations, six blind men were led into a room in which there was an elephant. After inspecting a part of the elephant, each man emerged from the room with a different view of what an elephant is. One thought it was like a tree trunk; a second believed it was a fan; another thought it was a solid wall; another thought it was a spear; a fifth thought it was a rope; and the last person said it was just like a big snake. Different experiences led people to different perceptions. But piecing together their experiences would certainly give us a better perception of what an elephant is or might be, even if we could not see it or did not examine every aspect of the creature.

There is good reason to ask: what is policy? Is it evident only in government documents, budget papers, media releases or ministerial announcements? Is it always visible as a government action (e.g. a decision to spend money on roads or impose higher taxes on high-income earners)? How do we know whether what we are hearing from government or reading in a document is in fact a policy? Defining policy is not wasted effort. Clarifying what policy is, even if it is done from different perspectives, provides a means for people to understand what it is we are talking about, examining or researching. If such concepts were not clarified, it would not be possible for us to refer to any particular disciplines or fields of study and for bodies of knowledge to be developed. One could not develop a philosophy or set of principles for policy analysis if one could not define policy.

Without some overall picture of policy, it is difficult to understand how policy is formed, who influences policy and the outcomes and consequences of policy. That said, definitions can also limit 'deep' understandings about the factors that shape policy. If we place tight boundaries around what it is that is being researched, we limit the scope of a concept. If we were to consider policy as a document that records a government decision or action, then we would exclude verbal announcements by a premier or prime minister or decisions announced by a member of the government after cabinet meetings but not yet recorded in policy documents available to the public.

It is useful to examine definitions of policy and how they have evolved. The waves of theoretical development that have occurred in the social sciences during the last few centuries have had an important influence on how policy has been defined and conceptualised. So, too, have important shifts in the ways in which policy is actually made. The growth and influence of government business enterprises and multinational corporations have, for example, and as we shall see in later chapters, called into question the independence of government and other institutions of the state and substantially influenced the ways in which governments conduct their affairs.

■ *1.2.1* **The evolution** *of policy studies*

Policy, and hence politics, is not a new field of study. Since ancient Greek times, communities have been struggling with the organisation of political life and the roles and responsibilities of government. **Political realism**, for example, has a lengthy history. It evolved from the works of Thucydides, Machiavelli, Hobbes and others writing in different countries centuries ago. Political realism is characterised by competition between power bases, whether it be competition between nation states (at the global level) or competition between classes (as Marx would have had it). Even today, Machiavelli's *The Prince* (written around 1505 and published in 1515) is considered a classic description of how a monarch ought to act to stay in power. There is less concern with ideals. Maintaining power is paramount. Although princes must have virtues, they must avoid being hated. Machiavelli provides, for example, practical accounts of how a prince can exhibit virtues even when he is being deceitful and how a prince ought to be severe rather than merciful in dishing out punishment because severity will breed fear. And, according to Machiavelli, with fear comes power.

To cut a long story short, there is some consensus that modern policy studies started to gain substantial momentum during the 1940s (e.g. see Hogwood & Gunn (1984) and Bridgman & Davis (2004) for a detailed explanation). So it is from this point that our discussion will continue.

Around the 1940s and 1950s, the prevailing view was that governments had overarching knowledge about what was best for their citizens. Governments, significantly swayed by prevailing philosophies associated with modernism (which is discussed in section 3.4), were strong and dominant and wielded considerable control over policy development. In this context Thomas Dye originally defined policy as 'whatever governments choose to do or not to do' (Dye 1978: 3). This definition has provided an important historical basis for understanding policy because, apart from being broad and flexible, it implies governments make choices about what is important and unimportant and, therefore, which issues receive attention and resources and which issues do not. Some argue that Dye's definition is significant because it also suggests that even where a government chooses not to be involved (e.g. refusing to fund the development of regional tourism organisations and strategies), taking this position can also be construed as policy. However, Dye's definition is problematic because, among other things, it does not differentiate between trivial and significant actions and inactions of government (Howlett & Ramesh 1995). For example, if a government chooses staples or glue to bind its tourist brochures, is this policy? If a government chooses not to regulate dolphin-watching tours, does this constitute policy? Under Dye's definition both are policy, although logically we see the first as being trivial whereas the second is of much greater consequence but amounts to government deciding not to actively intervene. So policy is also about the position of government on significant issues.

Since Dye's definition gained widespread acceptance in the 1970s, the very nature of government and its relationship with society has changed considerably. In what is broadly known as postmodernism (discussed in section 3.4.3), postmodern, critical and feminist studies ignited a re-evaluation of relationships between the individual, civil society, government and business. Along with these changing relationships, conceptions of policy have also shifted dramatically. The growth of multinational corporations and the fluid movement of capital investment across international borders has meant that governments have become increasingly interested in creating the right conditions for attracting investment and maximising growth opportunities. In turn, government and business have become increasingly engaged in **collaborative planning and policy-making**, whereby business is driven to maximise positive economic outcomes and government has sought to achieve popular political objectives, such as increased investment and employment. As a result, relationships between government and business in some policy arenas have become so entwined that the distinction between public and private (sector) policy is not clear. Nevertheless, we should note that even where non-governmental actors and agencies contribute to policy-making, their decisions and actions are not public policy (Howlett & Ramesh 1995).

In addition to increased collaboration between governments and business in policy-making, communities are now also demanding greater input into planning and policy development. It has become increasingly evident that there is no singular public interest. There are communities of interest, each with different goals, issues, values and knowledge that contribute to policy dialogues and, in turn, affect decision-making. Accordingly, the traditional coupled notions that policy development was undertaken by government and in the best interests of a homogeneous public interest have also been dismantled.

As the study of public policy has matured, attempts to define policy reflect historical developments. Considine (1994: 4) for example, avoids referring directly to government in any authoritative sense and recognises that policy involves dynamic collaboration between policy actors with varying interests and the legitimisation of a common view by the **institutions of government**. Considine sees policy as the continuing work done by groups of policy actors who use available public institutions to articulate and express the things they value.

Alternatively, Bridgman and Davis (2004: 3) define public policy as 'the vehicle through which politicians seek to make a difference. Policy is the instrument of governance, the decisions that direct public resources in one direction but not another. It is the outcome of the competition between ideas, interests and ideologies that impels our political system.' In this definition, policy is inherently political, involving trade-offs between different issues and decisions about how scarce government resources will be directed. Moreover, Bridgman and Davis's definition suggests that policy problems are perceived and acted on by a range of interests. This aspect distinguishes this definition from older definitions, which were embedded with a strong, paternalistic government focus.

■ 1.2.2 **Contemporary** *definitions of policy*

Contemporary definitions of policy reflect a growing emphasis in the social sciences on the social construction of policy, on the interactions between actors and agencies and on the values brought to the policy process. Considine (1994: 3) states that traditional government-focused definitions provide 'a staging post from which intellectual provisions may be drawn for a further journey'. He finds these definitions lacking because they do not provide any information about how policy is formed.

Moreover, adopting these definitions could stymie inquiries into larger social questions about who wins and who loses in policy and how policy is formed from contests between values and ideas aligned with policy agendas, discussions and debates. From this viewpoint, there are those scholars who argue for a broader understanding of policy as a complex dialectical process between a range of actors inside and outside government (e.g. Forester 1989; Fischer & Forester 1993; Fenna 1998; Renn 2001), although the picture of who is inside and who is outside is blurred when one considers, for example, that bureaucrats could be members of interest groups (e.g. conservation-oriented organisations) and company executives, as members of statutory boards, drive decision-making for government business enterprises. What a statutory authority decides to do from day to day might well be dictated by a board more concerned with industry growth and profits than the broader public interest (i.e. with marketing and promotion and development than with residents' quality of life).

The importance of understanding the broader social processes that contribute to the way policy emerges or forms is highlighted in this book. From this perspective, then, the study of policy challenges students to turn their minds to critical consideration of alternatives, perspectives and ideas outside their own value systems and views of the world. Such a skill will foster a better understanding and deeper explanation of the causes and consequences of policy.

For the purposes of this book, and drawing on the earlier definition by Bridgman and Davis (2004), **policy** is defined as being a position, strategy, action or product adopted by government and arising from contests between different ideas, values and interests. As we shall see in later chapters, both the political and bureaucratic arms of government are important players in the policy development process, but policy also cuts across public/private sector boundaries and domains to include business and civil society. Any public policy also has inherent characteristics.

■ *1.2.3* **Characteristics** *of policy*

A policy has seven important characteristics.
1. Policy involves government, although the extent and nature of government involvement in policy-making varies dramatically from large-scale infrastructure funding and construction to minor 'watchdog' or monitoring status.
2. Policy is a stated intention or commitment to undertake a particular action or bring about change (Levin 1997). It involves a course of action that has been legitimated by government, even if government has not been wholly responsible for the development of that policy position.
3. Policy involves hypothesizing about future circumstances and what conditions might be best to achieve a certain outcome (Bridgman & Davis 2004). Implicit in this characteristic is the notion that policy involves choice and decision-making.

4. Policy is any action that brings about an effect or outcome or an allocation or redistribution of resources, and it involves an intervention of some kind (Levin 1997) or a decision not to intervene.
5. Policy is an organisational practice or response to an issue or situation. This organisational practice does not necessarily sit wholly within government and could involve government and non-government sectors in the collaborative processes of policy development.
6. Policy is fundamentally about the choices that are made by governments and their policy collaborators and the expression of that choice through policy documents and actions (Bridgman & Davis 2004).
7. Policy involves mediating the values and interests of a wide range of stakeholders with an interest in the policy issue and is inherently political. Accordingly, there is an element of **politics** in all policies (Colebatch 2002).

1.3 WHAT IS PLANNING?

Much like policy, there is no universal agreement on how to define planning. Definitions have highlighted common threads in what **planning** involves but, according to Gleeson and Low (2000: 12),

> planning is a dialectical concept rather than an 'analytical' one. An analytical concept is one that can be perfectly and finally defined in such a way that we can know what it is and what it is *not*. A dialectical concept, on the other hand, is one that overlaps with other concepts and even with its opposite. It (planning) is a concept, like 'justice' or 'democracy' or 'money', crucially important for social life, but one that can never be pinned down in a unique, perfectly encompassing definition [original emphasis].

Yet planning is a traditional and basic human activity. In its simplest form, planning is about identifying appropriate steps to achieve some predetermined goal. Although planning can occur across a wide range of issues (e.g. financial planning, career planning, social planning or business planning), the field of urban and regional planning has provided useful, in-depth analysis and discussion of what planning is in the context of government and people. It is from this literature that a range of definitions is drawn and from which a number of common themes arise:
• Planning is concerned with the future.
• Planning is about acquiring knowledge and investigating and identifying the best approaches for government intervention.
• Planning is about anticipating or forecasting change under conditions that are often uncertain.
• Planning is about developing a strategic vision.
• Planning is about evaluating different courses of action and facilitating political decision-making.
• Planning is value-laden and political.

1.3.1 Evolution *of planning*

Planning was certainly a function conducted in many ancient civilisations, but the birth of modern planning as a field of practice and theory emerged from the Industrial Revolution and growing concerns about the living conditions of an increasingly urban population in such countries as the United Kingdom (e.g. Campbell & Fainstein 1996). Environmental pollution generated by an industrialising economy, high levels of migration from rural to urban areas, increasing population densities and unsanitary slum development gave rise to serious diseases and illnesses (also see Hall 2002). As the social reform movement gained momentum its protagonists claimed that government action was needed to improve living conditions. In this context, planning emerged as a function of government (Hall 2002). Early notions of planning were that planning was an instrumental government activity concerned with the physical layout of urban and regional areas. Not surprisingly, early ideas about tourism and recreation planning tended to emphasise a physical–spatial approach (Costa 2001). Towards the middle of the twentieth century the ways in which planning was conceived began to acknowledge the politics of planning (e.g. clashes of values and interests), the role of government and the influences of actors, agencies and business in the planning process. In the latter part of the twentieth century, theory and practice have progressively been situated within planning's broader social setting.

In contemporary literature, planning is now understood to involve a dialogue between overlapping or complementary and competing interests. Planning has been increasingly framed as **communicative action** (Fischer & Forester 1993), collaboration and partnership building (e.g. Innes 1996; Healey 1997) and **capacity building** (e.g. Amin & Thrift 1994). These approaches assert the importance of the interactive qualities of planning, links and synergies between government, community and business and the building of social, intellectual and institutional capacity. In this view, planning is the activity and process of policy development and relationship-building between various actors, agencies and interests. Authority to plan and to make policy is therefore shared. This view of planning is far different from modernist approaches.

1.3.2 Who undertakes *planning and policy development?*

As the roles and responsibilities of governments change, as citizens and communities of interest become increasingly engaged in policy development and as policy expertise emerges inside and outside government, defining policy is much like trying to hit a moving target. Since the 1970s, the role of government and its relationship to business and community interests have evolved, and we no longer view policy simply as the actions and decisions of government. Business and community groups have become increasingly active in policy debates (Ryan, Parker et al. 2003). The appointment of industry and community representatives to boards and committees convened for the purposes of planning and policy-making is a case in point. Moreover, recent trends in public management since the 1980s have led to a sustained 'hollowing out' of government. The down-sizing, outsourcing and privatisation of many government functions and operations normally assumed by departments or government business enterprises means that many traditional areas of policy-making and imple-mentation have been assumed by, or granted to, non-government sectors: the private and volunteer sectors. These shifts make it increasingly difficult to define public policy simply as a function of government, especially when one considers, for example, the work of volunteers and religious organisations in welfare programs and the evolution of self-regulation and accreditation and certification programs in ecotourism.

The roles of planners and policy-makers warrant some consideration. Hall (2000: 7) observes that 'planning is a kind of decision-making and policy-making'. This is perhaps misleading because planners themselves generally do not have authority to make decisions about the position or intention of government policy. However, they are influential in acquiring and inter-preting information and deciding the characteristics of consultation and par-ticipation. They can be influential gatekeepers and disseminators or filters (acting justly or unjustly) of the knowledge that enters into debates. Planners are facilitators and active agents in political decision-making processes, and they have an important entrepreneurial role in framing issues and shaping planning and policy processes. Put simply, planners can shape many aspects of planning processes, debates and outcomes despite the fact that their involvement and influence are not always immediately evident.

■ 1.3.3 **Interrelationships** *between policy and planning*

The debate about what policy and planning are and what they are not demonstrates the strong link between policy as the formal manifestation of a government's position and the planning process that leads to the development of policy. Planning and policy both involve political debate about what the agenda is, what the issues are, who is involved or affected and the alternative courses of action available to address problems. This debate percolates through institutional structures and practices and through interagency relationships and is mediated or influenced by politics (Hall & Jenkins 1995).

In this view, political decision-making is an important key in understanding the difference between planning and policy. Planning is a process that occurs up to the point of decision-making. Policy denotes the formal adoption of a position by government. However, planning does not terminate at the point of decision-making and the adoption of policy. Planning is a continuous process that contributes to the refinement of policy. Although planning forms a foundation for policy-making, not all planning leads to decision-making or to formal stated intentions of government policy. Many plans are gathering dust on the shelves of local councils and government departments and will never see the light of day. Many plans and policies are abandoned when there is a change of government.

For the purposes of this book, planning is regarded as a process (sometimes systematic; sometimes logical; sometimes secretive and corrupt). Through this process, information is gathered, retained and analysed (perhaps even discarded) and alternative courses of action are identified and evaluated. If planners make choices, which they do, then planning is a value-laden process. Planners bring their values, world views, experience and past practice into the process, and trade-offs are made between competing values and interests. In other words, planning assists the decision-making process that takes place in a politicised environment. In this environment, it is the role of planners to inform and facilitate good decision-making. Planning is the process of connecting information and knowledge with decisions and actions (Wildavsky 1979: 127). Good decision-making, and therefore good policy, relies on rigorous and informed planning.

1.4 WHAT IS TOURISM?

Definitions of tourism are diverse and have been the subject of colourful and vigorous debates (e.g. Leiper 1979, 1990; Smith 1988, 1991, 1998). Although an overarching definition remains elusive, the common wisdom is that tourism is a complex phenomenon informed by, and itself informing, many disciplines (e.g. anthropology, sociology, geography, economics, geography, history) and fields of study (e.g. leisure and recreation studies). Definitions tend to be developed for specific purposes or to underpin particular studies or research activities. The perspective from which someone looks at tourism influences the way tourism is defined and vice versa.

1.4.1 Defining *tourism from different perspectives*

The ideas or notions that bureaucrats, politicians, academics, citizens and organisations hold about tourism have an important influence on the way tourism is defined. In academic circles, there are many definitions, some more conceptually robust than others. Pearce (1987) noted that tourism 'may be thought of as the relationships and phenomena arising out of the journeys and temporary stays of people travelling primarily for leisure or recreational purposes'. According to Leiper (2004: 44): 'Tourism can be defined as the theories and practices for being a tourist. This involves travelling and visiting places for leisure-related purposes. Tourism comprises the ideas and opinions people hold which shape their decisions about going on trips, about where to go (and where not to go) and what to do or not do, about how to relate to other tourists, locals and service personnel. And it is all the behavioural manifestations of those ideas.'

Each definition places leisure and recreation as central aspects of tourism and travel. However, other academics see tourism differently. For example, Weaver and Lawton (2000: 3) emphasise a stakeholder management perspective in their definition of tourism: 'Tourism is the sum of the phenomena and relationships arising from the interaction among tourists, the tourist industry, host governments, host communities, origin governments, universities, community colleges and non-government organisations, in the process of attracting, transporting, hosting and managing these tourists and other visitors.' In yet another example, Smith (1988) defines tourism in terms of no less than 53 Standard Industrial Classification codes. His purpose was to undertake a study of the extent of tourism's influence on the economy at different scales; an approach that has been adopted in the development of National Tourism Satellite Accounts across the world.

Governments also generate a range of definitions of tourism, but generally these are directed to capturing the economic significance of tourism (WTO 1994). Governments' definitions of tourism are generally driven by the need to collect and analyse statistical data for a range of purposes, including quantifying industrial production and consumption, balance of payments, current accounts, multiplier effects, employment generation, and travel and immigration. The expressed needs of tourism operators, industry organisations and governments for comparability of data throughout local, regional and national jurisdictions have stimulated the development of internationally recognised statistical definitions and classifications of tourism, tourists and excursionists. Such definitions and classifications have been applied by the World Tourism Organization (WTO). According to WTO (1994), tourism comprises the activities of persons travelling to and staying in places outside their usual environment for not more that one consecutive year for leisure, business and other purposes.

Not surprisingly, many government definitions conceptualise tourism as an industry or network of businesses and emphasise the consumer or the good or service being produced. In Australia, for example, 'the tourism industry embraces a diverse range of providers and users or a variety of goods and services and overlaps with many sectors of the economy' (Department of Industry, Tourism and Resources 2002: 4).

The ways in which tourism is conceptualised and defined have important implications for where tourism responsibilities and administrations are located in governments and the focus and shape of tourism policy and planning.

▪ *1.4.2* **Defining tourism** *in a policy and planning context*

As we have seen, defining tourism is problematic. Should and do planners and policy-makers share similar or markedly different academic definitions of tourism? Some academic definitions are conceptually and practically sound, but highlight particular aspects of tourism such as leisure and recreation, or stakeholders, or tourism's supply elements. Should planners and policy-makers therefore adopt definitions that capture a broader population of travellers (e.g. business travellers) and are statistically driven for the purpose of measuring visitation and economic performance? For the purposes of this book and in the context of developing good planning and policy, we, like Leiper and Pearce above, believe it is important to adopt a broader view of tourism. Tourism:

- involves the movement of people and resources
- is characterised by a collection of government, businesses, activities and processes that assist people to make decisions about travel
- involves the production and consumption of a range of tangible (e.g. tourism products) and intangible (e.g. sense of place) resources
- overlaps and intersects with the daily lives of local communities
- involves the production and consumption of tourist experiences
- produces a range of intended and unintended consequences and effects that need to be critically examined and managed.

By conceptualising tourism broadly, we begin to see that tourism policy and planning require attention in a number of policy areas and should not simply be cast as economic development activities aimed at growing supply and demand.

1.5 STUDYING TOURISM PUBLIC POLICY

Globally, academic research in tourism policy captured little attention until the late 1980s or early 1990s, and even then, given the scale of tourism in popular culture and society, there is far too little in-depth analysis of tourism policy-making. According to Jenkins (2001), perhaps this has much to do with the fact that few tourism researchers have backgrounds in political science, public policy and politics and hence a lack of critical engagement with public policy theory (notwithstanding overlaps between these disciplines or fields and, say, sociology and aspects of human geography and economics). Nevertheless, the study of tourism policy offers the opportunity to examine many topics that should be of interest not only to industry, government agencies and students but also to researchers working in and on the boundaries of many disciplines (e.g. economics, geography, history, sociology). These topics include:

- the history of tourism organisations and public administrations
- the role of the state in tourism policy-making
- the political nature of tourism policy-making processes
- public participation in tourism planning and policy processes
- the sources and distribution of power in tourism policy-making
- the influence of pressure groups on tourism policy-making
- leadership and the roles of significant individuals
- organisational behaviour and tourism policy-making
- the exercise of choice by public servants in complex policy environments
- the political economy of tourism
- international and interregional comparisons of tourism policy-making, and
- perceptions of the effectiveness of tourism policies.

The evidence in many tourism and leisure journals (e.g. *Annals of Tourism Research; Culture and Policy; Current Issues in Tourism; Environment and Planning D; Geojournal; Journal of Travel Research; Leisure Studies; Tourism Geographies; Tourism Management*), books, conference proceedings, websites and postgraduate theses testifies to the growing interest in diverse tourism public policy issues from an increasing variety of viewpoints.

■ *1.5.1* **The social construction** *of tourism policy and planning*

Our emphasis in this book is on understanding and interpreting planning and policy-making as dynamic, socially constructed activities that involve a wide range of agents and organisations characterised by varying degrees of interest and commitment to tourism. Tourism planning and policy development takes place in multi-actor settings, and it is important to understand how different conceptions of tourism and different values and ideas are mediated in planning and policy processes.

From the previous discussion it is evident that the term 'policy' means different things to different people depending on their position, values, experience and a range of other factors (Jenkins 1978; Wildavsky 1979; Davis et al. 1993; Considine 1994; Colebatch 2002). Definitions abound, and the models depicting policy processes present researchers with many choices in developing conceptual frameworks for research (Jenkins 1978; Wildavsky 1979; Majchrzak 1984; Morgan 1990; Parsons 1995; Levin 1997). There is no best way of approaching the analysis of policy that will reveal a higher order of truth. The different approaches available are the viewpoints from which 'reality' is constructed. This is generally known as a social constructionist approach to policy studies (Colebatch 2002: 4). Put simply, what is observed and explanations about 'what happened' will be influenced by many factors. These factors include: (1) the research methods employed by researchers (e.g. a deductive line of inquiry versus an inductive approach); (2) the theories, concepts and frameworks employed by researchers (e.g. the emphasis given to particular issues varies among theories of the role of the state); (3) the researcher's values and interests (i.e. whether the researcher is trained as an economist or a geographer, or whether the researcher is attached to a particular ideology).

■ *1.5.2* **Broad** *principles*

As we investigate many examples of tourism policy and planning in this book, we will see that the goal of sustainable tourism development is frequently claimed to underpin tourism policy and planning; that is, achieving tourism development that minimises negative effects and maximises positive effects and can be sustained over the long term is a stated fundamental goal for most agencies and communities engaged in tourism development and management. Whether they actively pursue genuine **sustainable development** principles is open to question. Whatever the case, tourism planning and policy must be sensitive to such factors as the local political climate, community expectations and aspirations, and organisational cultures if policy directions and measures are to be accepted and successfully implemented. In this sense, sustainable tourism development cannot be given local meaning and tangible direction unless it is constructed within a plausible understanding of the planning and policy environment. In what follows, broad principles and a framework for building understandings of tourism planning and policy environments are discussed.

In order to understand specific planning and policy-making environments, we need to be more precise about what the issues are and why they have become issues. In this regard, after an extensive review of public policy literature, Hall and Jenkins (1995) developed a broad conceptual framework for the study of tourism public policy. They identify four principles essential to the development of comprehensive analyses of tourism policy:

1. Tourism public policy should be studied at macro, meso and micro levels over time and space.
2. Historical underpinnings and understandings provide important contextual information.
3. The case study approach provides opportunities for an appreciation of particular policy problems and applications.
4. Integrated description, theory and explanation within an interdisciplinary framework and the explicit recognition of ideology and values provide important explanatory powers.

These principles are widely supported in the policy analysis literature (e.g. Davis et al. 1993; Healey 1997; Fenna 1998; Colebatch 2002).

This book builds on these principles by developing a specific approach to tourism planning and policy analysis that takes into account the particular characteristics of tourism and the complexity of the tourism public policy environment. We emphasise that tourism cannot be understood simply through the analysis of one community (the local) without reference to (say) global forces, or by isolating tourism as a particular policy sector independent from (say) transport and energy. The influences of the physical environment and social, economic, political and cultural factors (from the micro level to the macro) should be taken into account in order to identify forces that directly or indirectly influence tourism planning and policy-making.

Figure 1.1 shows the conceptual framework for the analysis of tourism planning and public policy-making adopted in this book. It clearly includes and acknowledges the principles identified by Hall and Jenkins (1995: 95). In this framework, the policy issues or items around which the analysis is based are not identified by the researcher alone. They are explored and constantly redefined throughout the course of the research. The researcher moves towards the centre of the diagram in an effort to understand planning and policy-making, oscillating between multiple levels of analysis, drawing from the contributions of different disciplines, examining particular cases and building integrated description, explanation and theory. The researcher also cuts across time and space to identify relations and events and to extract information that provides insights into the characteristics of tourism policy-making. This conceptual framework, therefore, has greater theoretical and practical utility than that of Hall and Jenkins (1995).

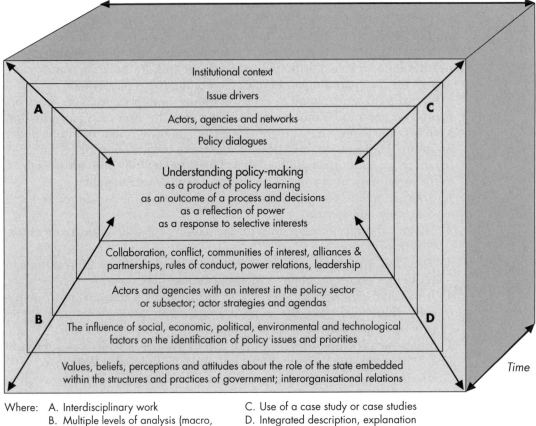

Space

A

C

Institutional context

Issue drivers

Actors, agencies and networks

Policy dialogues

Understanding policy-making
as a product of policy learning
as an outcome of a process and decisions
as a reflection of power
as a response to selective interests

Collaboration, conflict, communities of interest, alliances &
partnerships, rules of conduct, power relations, leadership

Actors and agencies with an interest in the policy sector
or subsector; actor strategies and agendas

The influence of social, economic, political, environmental and technological
factors on the identification of policy issues and priorities

B

D

Values, beliefs, perceptions and attitudes about the role of the state embedded
within the structures and practices of government; interorganisational relations

Time

Where: A. Interdisciplinary work
        B. Multiple levels of analysis (macro,
           meso and micro)
        C. Use of a case study or case studies
        D. Integrated description, explanation
           and theory building

■ **Figure 1.1**   *Conceptual framework for the study of tourism planning and policy*

■ *1.5.3* **Key** *dimensions*

On the basis of this framework (see figure 1.1), the overlapping and intersecting nature of five key dimensions are identified and discussed below.

Space and time

Policy is affected by events and circumstances at several intersecting scales
and changes over time (see figure 1.2). Broadly speaking, events and
circumstances at macro and middle levels can influence events and circumstances at micro levels. Similarly, micro events and circumstances are not
independent and can influence macro and meso events and circumstances.
For example, events in or caused by one country (e.g. stock market and
interest rate movements; terrorist attacks and the reactions of nation states;
industrial disputes; international marketing and promotion campaigns) will
influence tourism planning and policy-making in other countries. At a local
scale, events in one part of a country will influence other parts of the
country. For instance, the development of a resort in a local community

could influence tourist flows and local residents' quality of life; a decision to legislate for a bed tax in a particular city might shift some or most demand for accommodation to other cities and towns and influence (redistribute) supply; a new highway or international airport will dramatically alter tourist flows and regional multipliers. These examples illustrate the complexity of policy-making across space.

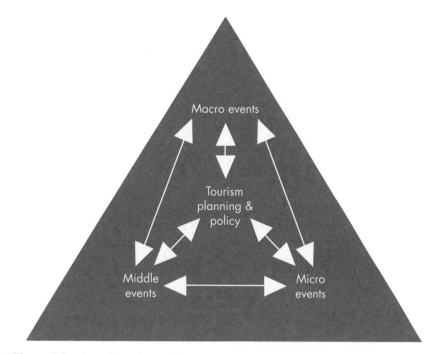

■ **Figure 1.2** *Interdependencies between public policy, events, time and space*

Events and circumstances change over time, as does the basis of knowledge. The terrorist events of recent years have in part served to redefine national approaches to tourism development and promotion. The importance of foreign income generation is now being evaluated against the increasingly important issue of homeland security. Although both these issues are important, the relative weights given to them in tourism policy-making have shifted. Economic conditions also change over time. Economic cycles and shifts in interest rates and unemployment rates have a significant effect on the level of government interest and involvement in tourism. Time affects the level of knowledge and expertise a community accumulates and, as a corollary, its ability to position itself strategically and to develop and promote tourism. Public policies have a history — they have been developed perhaps over the course of many years, might have involved contributions from literally thousands of people and agencies and have effects that could influence decision-making. History is everywhere, although its influence might not be immediately evident. Nothing can be understood without historical context.

Institutional context

Tourism planning and public policy-making take place in an institutional context. Healey (1998) suggests that the institutional context can be understood in terms of two components. First, the hard institutional structures are the formal frameworks and procedures for planning and policy-making. These hard structures provide the legal framework and define the rights and responsibilities of those who are involved in planning and policy-making. Second, the soft institutional structures include rules of conduct, conventions and social relations that are endowed with values, beliefs, attitudes and institutional knowledge. These soft structures can include written and unwritten rules of participation and the interests and values of agencies and individuals. These soft structures can have a profound influence on the ways individuals and agencies engage with the policy process, on the ways they engage with each other, on their capacity to learn and on their abilities to debate, bargain and negotiate in planning and policy processes. The hard and soft structures for planning and policy-making are interrelated and provide a politically charged environment for policy-makers and planners.

Issue drivers

A range of issue drivers direct governments' attention to and stimulate their interest in tourism planning and policy. **Issue drivers** are those internal and external factors that 'push' problems on to political agendas for resolution (Bridgman & Davis 2004). A range of internal and external drivers classified into six broad categories is shown in table 1.1. These drivers overlap and shape the way in which tourism planning and policy is conceptualised and undertaken.

Actors and agencies

The effects of time and space are interpreted and given meaning by actors and agencies. Planners and policy-makers carry attitudes, values and perceptions. Individuals from all walks of life have values, interests and world views linked to historical events, including education, personal experience and relationships. Agencies, for example, develop well-ingrained organisational cultures, routines and approaches; they develop ways of doing things that might be difficult to change.

Policy dialogues — mediating values and ideas

Institutions and individuals are infused with **values**. Critical understandings and evaluations about people and the institutions of tourism public policy are necessary to improve and inform tourism policy-making and planning. Examining the ways in which politicians, government departments and authorities, bureaucrats and interest groups interpret and act out their roles and responsibilities can illustrate complex cause and effect relationships and enhance our knowledge of the subtleties of tourism policy-making processes. Planning and policy-making cannot be separated. Planning is unavoidably political and constrained by the political systems in which it takes place (Allensworth 1975), and this situation highlights the salience of political economy perspectives to planning approaches, theories and practices.

DRIVERS	EXTERNAL	INTERNAL
Economic	Regional and rural decline Employment generation Add value to natural resources Economic measures (e.g. tax incentives, grants)	Factory closures in a particular locality Availability of local investment capital
Sociocultural	The valuing of indigenous cultures Drive to increase standards of living (through employment generation and increased economic activity) To promote skill development Population growth and patterns of population movement	Availability of skills and expertise in the local community Community support and interest Availability and marketability of local cultural resources
Environmental	Increasing consumer awareness of green issues Increased political pressure to protect and enhance natural environments Government commitment to environmental education, awareness and appreciation	Availability of unique or distinct natural resources in a locality Local developmental or environmental issues
Public administration	Implementation of neo-liberal public management ideas including downsizing, outsourcing, enabling, emphasis of cost-effectiveness and efficiency of government	Outsourcing of local destination marketing functions Local budgets
Political	International community pressures (e.g. international conventions) Interest group pressures (e.g. community groups, peak industry associations) Media coverage and commentary	The extent of tourism interests and support within a local community Political influence of tourism stakeholders
Technological	Advances in transport technology Advances in information dissemination (e.g. internet), booking services	Availability of technological advances in the local community

Political economy highlights the historical relations between organisations, individual actors, events, and broad social and economic conditions. The influence of economic, social and environmental contexts and institutional histories are emphasised. This concurs with Forester's view that 'planning conflicts often involve not only resources like money, but relationships that involve personality and politics, race, ethnicity and culture, too' (2000: 147). According to Sandercock (2003: 212–13), Forester

> was saying something with profound implications for how we think about and practise planning. If it is relationships between people that are driving a land use or resource management conflict, then something more than rational discourse among concerned stakeholders, or the usual toolkit of negotiation and mediation, is necessary to address what's really going on. Conflictual relationships involve feelings and emotions like fear, anger, hope, betrayal, abandonment, loss, unrecognized memories, lack of recognition and histories of disempowerment and exclusion.

Understanding policy and planning

Understanding tourism policy and planning requires an appreciation of the complex and ever-changing world in which policy is made and the different world views of those involved in the processes of investigating 'what happened'. It also requires the merging of substantive and procedural knowledge to enable a thorough and insightful understanding of how policy is made and what influences it. But the objective is not simply to understand policy and planning. In a reiterative process, this knowledge filters back into planning and policy processes so that creativity, learning and policy innovation occur as actors and agencies refine their strategies, modes of engagement and behaviour.

Our approach in this book is explicitly directed to the challenges of understanding and explaining tourism policy and planning in its broader social, political, economic, geographic and environmental contexts. It is also important to recognise the links between what happens at different spatial and sociopolitical scales and the influence of historical events and circumstances. Understanding tourism planning and policy requires a broad knowledge that cuts across a number of related disciplines and fields of study including economics, policy analysis, politics, planning, philosophy, geography, sociology, public administration and organisational studies. The following chapters draw from substantive theories about social, political and organisational life and procedural theories of how planning and policy processes work. Through this process it is possible to develop critical knowledge of tourism planning and policy processes that inspire innovative and creative planning and policy practice.

CHAPTER REVIEW

This chapter has provided an introduction to the theoretical landscape of tourism planning and public policy and sets the scene for further exploration of planning and policy theories and concepts contained in section 1 of this book. In this chapter, the evolution and characteristics of policy were discussed, and it was found to be dynamic, value-laden and political. For the purposes of this book, 'policy' was defined as a position, strategy or product adopted by government and derived from a contestation involving diverse values, interests and ideas.

Planning overlaps significantly with policy and has been defined as the process through which information is collected and analysed and through which various courses of action are identified and evaluated. The decisions and actions of government (i.e. policy) are derived from this planning process. It should therefore be evident that the characteristics of the planning process have direct implications for how well conceived and designed policy is. Critical analyses of planning and policy development are important in understanding how and why governments do what they do and how to improve on previous policy directions.

Conceptions of tourism were also discussed with a view to understanding tourism policy and planning. The term 'tourism' is open to interpretation depending on the context for which it is being defined or the viewpoint of the person or agency employing the term. Interestingly, individuals (e.g. Neil Leiper) and any number of organisations have changed their applied definitions of tourism, which highlights people's shifting understandings of a concept as well as, perhaps, the evolution of knowledge in search of truth. Specifically, however, tourism should be conceptualised broadly for the purposes of analysing tourism policy and planning because only then can interconnections between different policy sectors be explored and contributions from other disciplines and fields of study be drawn on.

We argue for a social constructionist view of policy, observing that tourism planning and policy cannot be separated from their historical contexts and spatial links. In this vein, a framework for studying tourism planning and policy was presented that serves as a basis for the remainder of the book. In this framework we argue that attention be given to the role of space and time; the nature of the institutional context; the influences generated by the social, economic, environmental and political context; the characteristics of actors, agencies and networks; and the nature of policy dialogues.

SUMMARY OF KEY TERMS

Agencies

'Agency' (agencies) refers to government departments and other bodies created to perform a government or quasi-government function. For the purposes of this book, agencies can include statutory corporations, ministries, departments and government research organisations.

Capacity building

'Capacity building' refers to the ability to develop, enhance and maintain different capabilities, skills, knowledge and expertise necessary for tourism planning and policy development.

Collaborative planning and policy-making

'Collaboration', and 'collaborative planning and policy-making' in particular, refers to cooperation, support and mutual assistance between actors and agencies in the pursuit of common interests.

Communicative action

'Communicative action' is a term originally derived from the works of the German philosopher Jürgen Habermas to denote the process of expressing, appreciating and processing others' views in an effort to arrive at an agreed solution or course of action.

Institutions of government

The term 'institutions of government' refers to organisational structures set up by government to achieve certain objectives. Institutions of government are often resilient because they have a long tradition and have established strength in their practices and routines. Institutions can change as a result of political pressures and shifting government philosophies; however, change is generally slow.

Issue drivers

'Issue drivers' are those internal and external factors that 'push' problems on to political agendas for resolution. The rise of the environmental movement, for example, has seen the mobilisation of conservation as a key political concern. Similarly, tourism issue drivers such as the World Tourism Organization or, in Australia, the former Tourism Council Australia, have been able to influence the political agendas of elected governments.

Planning

'Planning' is defined as strategic activity comprising a number of stages that lead to the determination of a course of action to meet predetermined goals. Planning is concerned with the future; is devoted to acquiring knowledge and identifying appropriate courses of action; is about anticipating change, developing a strategic vision and facilitating political decision-making; and is value-laden and political.

Policy

'Policy' is defined as being a position, strategy, action or product adopted by government and arising from contests between different ideas, values and interests.

Policy actors

'Policy actors' refers to individuals as active agents operating within planning and policy processes to pursue individual goals and objectives.

Political realism

Political realism gives prominence to power and the role of the nation state. Nation states are principally concerned with the 'national interest' and hence with such matters as its political autonomy and ability to defend itself and to compete with other nation states. The national interest could also include concerns about cultural, economic, environmental and political resources and hence decisions and actions concerning expansion of the nation state or enhancing quality of life in existing territorial regimes.

Politics

'Politics' has been defined in many ways. According to Heywood (1997: 410), politics is the 'activity through which people make, preserve and amend the general rules under which they live'. According to Davis et al. (1988: 61), 'Politics is the process by which the structure, process and institutions are brought to a decision [including non-decisions] or outcome. It is an endless activity; while politics operates, all decisions [and non-decisions and actions] are provisional.' So politics means that no decision or action is final. All decisions and actions of a government or institution of the state are open to question, debate and argument and are, ultimately, subject to change.

Sustainable development

The term 'sustainable development' was coined in the Brundtland Report, *Our Common Future* (World Commission on Environment and Development 1997) and is used to denote the idea that development should meet the needs of current populations within the ecological limits of the earth and without compromising the needs of future generations.

Values

'Values' are the beliefs, ideas and principles that underpin groups, societies and individuals. Values can be deeply embedded and unexpressed, or they can be overt. Actors and agencies in planning and policy use their value systems to determine which issues are deemed to be problems, which issues require attention and which issues do not.

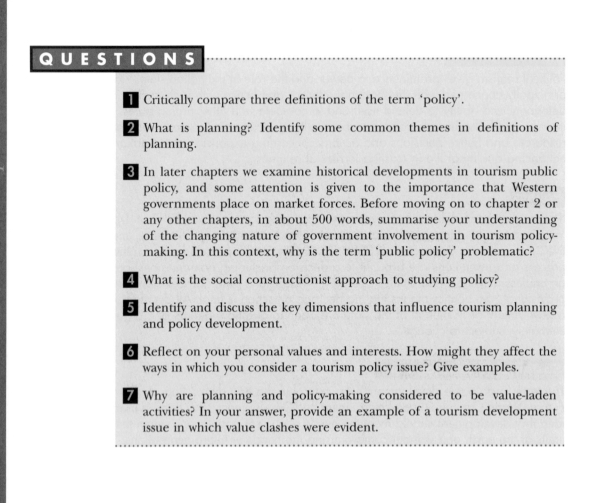

QUESTIONS

1 Critically compare three definitions of the term 'policy'.

2 What is planning? Identify some common themes in definitions of planning.

3 In later chapters we examine historical developments in tourism public policy, and some attention is given to the importance that Western governments place on market forces. Before moving on to chapter 2 or any other chapters, in about 500 words, summarise your understanding of the changing nature of government involvement in tourism policy-making. In this context, why is the term 'public policy' problematic?

4 What is the social constructionist approach to studying policy?

5 Identify and discuss the key dimensions that influence tourism planning and policy development.

6 Reflect on your personal values and interests. How might they affect the ways in which you consider a tourism policy issue? Give examples.

7 Why are planning and policy-making considered to be value-laden activities? In your answer, provide an example of a tourism development issue in which value clashes were evident.

EXERCISES

1 Using Factiva or another database of newspaper articles, over a period of three to four months collect media representations of tourism events (e.g. press releases and newspaper publications, radio transcripts, television documentaries or videos). Reflect on the extent to which tourism public policy and planning receives coverage at local to national levels. What are the major policy issues? Identify overlaps with other policy sectors.

2 Find three or four tourism policy documents or strategies. Ensure that your sample includes historical and contemporary documents. In each document, find definitions of tourism or extracts in which tourism has been conceptualised. Complete the following exercises:
(a) Compare and contrast the way in which tourism has been defined or conceptualised.
(b) On the basis of your reviews, how have definitions or conceptions of tourism evolved over time?

EXERCISES

(c) Identify in which portfolio tourism was situated. Discuss what might be the dominant viewpoint or interests driving tourism policy development in each document (e.g. economic development and growing markets, managing effects, sustainable development).

3 Find in a dictionary of etymology the origin of the following words: politics, policy and planning. Compare and contrast the meaning and significance of these terms.

FURTHER READING

Bridgman, P & Davis, G 2004, *The Australian Policy Handbook,* **3rd edn, Allen & Unwin, Sydney.** This book provides an introduction to policy analysis and includes good practical discussions about the development of policy studies, definitions and characteristics of policy. Although it focuses on the Australian context, the book provides practical examples and illustrates the process of policy development.

Colebatch, H 2002, *Policy,* **Open University Press, Buckingham, UK.** This book provides a good introduction to policy theory and practice and includes critical discussions of definitions and concepts.

Hall, CM 2000, *Tourism Planning: Policies, Processes and Relationships,* **Pearson Education, Harlow, UK.** *Tourism Planning* provides a brief but useful discussion of basic definitions and concepts of planning, policy and tourism.

Howlett, M & Ramesh, M 1995, chapter 1 of *Studying Public Policy: Policy Cycles and Policy Subsystems,* **Oxford University Press, Don Mills, Ont., pp. 3–17.** This book contains a useful, critical discussion of the historical development of policy studies, and it compares and contrasts various definitions of policy and different ways of understanding the policy-making process.

Jenkins, JM (ed.) 2001, *Current Issues in Tourism,* **Tourism Policy Making: Theory and Practice (special issue), vol. 4, nos 2–4.** This volume contains 13 detailed case studies that approach tourism policy analysis from a range of perspectives.

Wet Tropical rainforests, North Queensland

The Wet Tropics World Heritage Area in Northern Queensland, Australia, provides an example of the complex context in which tourism planning and policy-making occurs across spatial jurisdictions and over time. The range of intersecting issue drivers, the values and interests of the various stakeholders and the political struggles of the time illustrate that planning and policy development varies throughout time and space and is necessarily value-laden.

Background

In 1974 the Commonwealth Government signed the Convention for the Protection of World Cultural and Natural Heritage. In doing so, the Commonwealth accepted an international responsibility to identify, protect and manage sites of universal significance. The Commonwealth Government began the lengthy task of identifying, selecting and preparing nominations for World Heritage listing. The Wet Tropical rainforests had been identified as being significant some years earlier when environmental activists had attracted international media attention to their attempts to stop the development of a coastal road north of the Daintree River. The Commonwealth set about making a case for listing.

However, the Queensland Government believed that the Commonwealth was acting unconstitutionally because, under the Australian Constitution, responsibility for environmental and natural resource management rested with the states. The State Government believed that the Commonwealth was encroaching on its areas of responsibility and that, over the longer term, Queensland would lose control of and power over some areas of policy and planning. Bitter and protracted legal and media battles ensued. After a win in the High Court that legitimated the Commonwealth's right to be involved in environmental protection and management where it was deemed to be of national concern, the Wet Tropical rainforests were unilaterally nominated by the Commonwealth and later inscribed on the World Heritage Register in 1988. The Wet Tropics World Heritage Area (WTWHA) lies between Townsville and Cooktown and comprises more than 894 000 hectares included in a range of leasehold and freehold land tenures.

Inscription on the World Heritage Register effectively gave the rainforests iconic standing within the international community, stimulating significant interest in and visitation to the area. From a tourism perspective, the marketability of the area was further heightened because it is the only place in the world where two World Heritage areas—the Wet Tropics and the Great Barrier Reef—exist side by side.

Institutional context

A change of government in Queensland in 1989 brought a new phase of cooperation between the governments. Complementary legislation was passed by the Queensland Government (in 1993) and the Commonwealth (in 1994) to set up the Wet Tropics Management Authority (WTMA). The WTMA is a statutory corporation vested with responsibilities to develop policies, strategies and plans to protect, manage and promote the World Heritage values of the area. The WTMA has taken on an important strategic planning and tourism management role. Day-to-day management and implementation of WTWHA plans and policies are the responsibilities of the Queensland National Parks and Wildlife Service (QNP&WS). However, the *Environment Protection and Bio-diversity Conservation Act 1999* (Cwlth) requires that all activities likely to have a significant effect on areas of national environmental significance be referred to the Commonwealth for assessment.

Adding to this complexity, large tracts of land with significant environmental values were excluded from the listing because they were in private ownership. At the time of listing it was deemed politically too difficult to acquire all privately owned land, so only a small proportion of privately tenured land was included in the listing. This decision meant that land in public and private ownership came under different planning regimes and is subject to different policy frameworks. For example, responsibility for decisions about the use and development of private lands in the WTWHA falls to the local authorities included in the listed area. However, if the land is in public ownership or is leasehold, responsibility falls to the QNP&WS. For many of the local authorities covered by the Wet Tropics World Heritage Area, this created a vexed situation. Most were rural councils with small rate bases and limited funds for planning and management. As a result, the institutional context in which planning and policy development occurs in the Wet Tropics is characterised by a complex division of roles and responsibilities among Commonwealth, state and local governments.

Tourism planning and policy in the Wet Tropics

Tourism planning and policy in the Wet Tropics is complicated by the following two factors:
1 the different levels of government involved, and
2 the division of roles and responsibilities of various agencies that have an interest in tourism.

The WTMA is governed by a Ministerial Council with equal representation of Commonwealth and Queensland governments. The Ministerial Council appoints a board whose job is to prioritise the authority's objectives, strategies and policies. The authority is a small policy-focused organisation responsible for the development of plans, strategies and policies to guide the management of the Wet Tropics area within the guidelines provided by legislation. In August 2000 the authority released the Wet Tropics Nature

(*continued*)

Based Tourism Strategy, which outlines the approach to the management of tourism in the Area. The Wet Tropics Nature Based Tourism Strategy coexists with and complements other plans and policy work produced by the authority, including the Wet Tropics Conservation Strategy (2004) and the Wet Tropics Walking Strategy (2001). It also coexists with day-to-day management policies and decision-making frameworks of the QNP&WS.

Other policy and planning activities also influence the development and management of tourism in the Wet Tropics. For example, the authority also seeks to work collaboratively with the Queensland Department of Local Government and Planning on the Far North Queensland Regional Plan (FNQ2010). This regional plan seeks to manage growth and development and to prioritise infrastructure provision. In this context, tourism is one such issue driver, and collaboration needs to occur across these different planning and policy development exercises. Further, the activities and initiatives of tourism marketing organisations, such as Tourism Queensland and the regional organisation, Tourism Tropical North Queensland, also influence tourism growth, visitation and management of the WTWHA. The planning and policy activities of local governments included in the area also affect the provision and level of tourism infrastructure and services in certain locations.

This case study illustrates that the functions and activities of many agencies and organisations influence tourism planning and policy development in the Wet Tropics World Heritage Area. Moreover, without collaboration across these levels of government and among different agencies, it is possible that some planning and policy initiatives to manage tourism could contradict each other.

Questions

Consider the following dimensions of planning and policy:

1   List all the agencies involved in the case study and briefly describe their functions and responsibilities.

2   What might be the values and ideas of each of the governments and agencies? Briefly summarise any possible conflicts in their values and ideas.

3   What social, economic, political and economic issue drivers have influenced the development of this policy framework?

4   Explain why time and space are key dimensions in understanding how policy and planning occurs in the Wet Tropics.

References

Dredge, D & Humphreys, J 2003, 'Local government, world heritage and ecotourism: Policy and strategy on Australia's tropical rainforests', in DA Fennell & RK Dowling (eds), *Ecotourism Policy and Planning*, CABI Publishing, Wallingford, UK, pp. 121–40.

Far North Queensland Regional Plan 2006, 'Far North Queensland 2010 Regional Planning Project', viewed 29 March 2006, www.lgp.qld.gov.au/?ID=173.

MacDonald, G & Lane, M 2000, *Securing the Wet Tropics*, Federation Press, Sydney.

Wet Tropics Management Authority 2006, 'Managing a World Heritage Area', viewed 29 March 2006, www.wettropics.gov.au/mwha/mwha_index.html.

REFERENCES

Allensworth, DT 1975, *The Political Realities of Urban Planning*, Praeger, New York.

Amin, A & Thrift, N 1994, *Globalisation: Institutions and Regional Development in Europe*, Oxford University Press, Oxford.

Bridgman, P & Davis, G 2004, *The Australian Policy Handbook*, 3rd edn, Allen & Unwin, Sydney.

Campbell, S & Fainstein, S 1996, 'Introduction: The structure and debates of planning theory', in S Campbell & S Fainstein (eds), *Readings in Planning Theory*, Blackwell, Cambridge, UK, pp. 1–14.

Colebatch, HK 2002, *Policy*, Open University Press, Buckingham, UK.

Considine, M 1994, *Public Policy: A Critical Approach*, Macmillan, Melbourne.

Costa, C 2001, 'An emerging tourism planning paradigm? A comparative analysis between town and tourism planning', *International Journal of Tourism Research*, vol. 3, pp. 425–41.

Davis, G et al. 1993, *Public Policy in Australia*, Allen & Unwin, Sydney.

Department of Industry, Tourism and Resources 2002, *The 10-Year Plan for Tourism: A Discussion Paper*, Canberra.

Dye, T 1978, *Understanding Public Policy*, Prentice Hall, Englewood Cliffs, NJ.

Fenna, A 1998, *Introduction to Policy Analysis*, Longman, Melbourne.

Fischer, F & Forester, J 1993, *The Argumentative Turn in Policy Analysis and Planning*, Sage, Newbury Park, CA.

Forester, J 1989, *Planning in the Face of Power*, University of California Press, Berkeley, CA.

—— 2000, 'Multicultural planning in deed: Lessons from mediation practice of Shirley Solomon and Larry Sherman', in M Burayidi (ed.), *Urban Planning in a Multicultural Society*, Praeger, Westport, CT.

Gleeson, B & Low, N 2000, *Australian Urban Planning: New Challenges, New Agendas*, Allen & Unwin, Sydney.

Hall, CM 2000, *Tourism Planning: Policies, Processes and Relationships*, Prentice Hall, Harlow, UK.

Hall, CM & Jenkins, J 1995, *Tourism and Public Policy*, Routledge, London.

Hall, P 1980, 'Approaching the problem', in *Great Planning Disasters*, University of California Press, Berkeley, pp. 187–98.

—— 2002, *Urban and Regional Planning*, 4th edn, Routledge, London.

Healey, P 1997, *Collaborative Planning: Shaping Places in Fragmented Societies*, Macmillan, London.

—— 1998, 'Building institutional capacity through collaborative approaches to urban planning', *Environment and Planning* A30 1531–46.

Heywood, A 1997, *Politics*, Palgrave, New York.

Hogwood, BW & Gunn, LA 1984, *Policy Analysis for the Real World*, Oxford University Press, Oxford.

Howlett, M & Ramesh, M 1995, *Studying Public Policy: Policy Cycles and Policy Subsystems*, Oxford University Press, Toronto.

Innes, JE 1996, 'Planning through consensus building: A new view of the comprehensive planning ideal', *Journal of the American Planning Association*, vol. 62, no. 4, pp. 460–72.

Jenkins, J 2001, 'Editorial', *Current Issues in Tourism*, Tourism Policy Making: Theory and Practice (special issue), vol. 4, nos 2–4, pp. 69–77.

Jenkins, WI 1978, *Policy Analysis*, Martin Robertson, Oxford.

Leiper, N 1979, 'The framework of tourism: Towards a definition of tourism, tourist and the tourist industry', *Annals of Tourism Research*, vol. 6, no. 4, pp. 390–407.

—— 1990, 'Partial industrialization of tourism systems', *Annals of Tourism Research*, vol. 17, pp. 600–2.

—— 2004, *Tourism Management*, 3rd edn, Pearson Education Australia, South Melbourne.

Levin, P 1997, *Making Social Policy: The Mechanisms of Government and Politics and How to Investigate Them*, Open University Press, Buckingham, UK.

Majchrzak, A 1984, *Methods for Policy Research*, Sage, Newbury Park, CA.

Morgan, G 1990, 'Paradigm diversity in organizational research', in J Hassard & D Pym, *The Theory and Philosophy of Organizations*, Routledge, London.

Parsons, W 1995, *Public Policy: An Introduction to the Theory and Practice of Policy Analysis*, Edward Elgar, Aldershot, UK.

Pearce, D 1987, *Tourism Today: A Geographical Analysis*, Longman Scientific and Technical, New York and Harlow, UK.

Renn, O 2001, 'The role of social science in environmental policy-making: Experiences and outlooks', *Science and Public Policy*, vol. 28, no. 6, pp. 427–37.

Ryan, N, P Parker et al. 2003, *Government, Business and Society*, Prentice Hall, Sydney.

Sandercock, L 2003, *Cosmopolis II: Mongrel Cities in the 21st Century*, Continuum, London.

Smith, SLJ 1988, 'Defining tourism: A supply side view', *Annals of Tourism Research*, vol. 15, no. 2, pp. 179–90.

—— 1991, 'The supply-side definition of tourism: Reply to Leiper', *Annals of Tourism Research*, vol. 18, pp. 312–18.

—— 1998, 'Tourism as an industry: Debates and concepts', in D Ioannides & K Debbage, *The Economic Geography of the Tourist Industry*, Routledge, London, pp. 31–52.

Weaver, D & Lawton, L 2000, *Tourism Management*, John Wiley & Sons Australia, Milton, Qld.

Wildavsky, A 1979, *Speaking Truth to Power: The Art and Craft of Policy Analysis*, Little, Brown, Boston.

World Commission on Environment and Development (WCED) 1987, *Our Common Future*, Oxford University Press, Oxford.

World Tourism Organization 1994, *Compendium of Tourism Statistics*, Madrid, WTO.

Dianne Dredge and John Jenkins

CHAPTER 2

The state, *institutions and actors*

LEARNING OBJECTIVES

After reading this chapter you will be able to:

1 discuss theories about the role of the state and how they could influence government involvement in tourism

2 identify and discuss the institutions of the state and give examples of how they might affect tourism planning and policy

3 define the terms 'public interest' and 'civil society' and explain why these concepts influence planning and policy

4 describe the changing roles and responsibilities of the state, especially since the 1970s

5 identify and explain three approaches for understanding institutional arrangements.

Institutional arrangements are those frameworks within which planning and policy take place. They are sets of established rules, procedures, customs, laws, conventions and behaviours that shape the ways in which tourism planning and policy-making are undertaken. Institutional arrangements regulate, directly or indirectly, political and social life and are the frameworks through which issues and debates percolate and are turned into government policy and action. They are constantly changing shape; they are inherited, thought about and altered over time by a myriad of stakeholders, agencies and individuals seeking to achieve their individual and/or collective goals and objectives. Organisations and agencies, such as tourism bureaux and associations, lobby groups and government departments, perceive, interpret and give meaning to these institutional arrangements. Organisations and the professionals who work in them interactively constitute and reconstitute the rules, traditions, customs and processes that underpin tourism planning and policy-making. Their sheer 'slipperiness' makes institutional arrangements quite a fascinating aspect of tourism planning and policy-making.

This chapter examines fundamental concepts in planning and public policy, including the state, institutions and institutional arrangements and the relationships between the state, institutions and civil society. Following this introduction, section 2.2 discusses the concept of the state and identifies various theories that explain its role. Section 2.3 examines why institutional arrangements have an important influence on policy and vice versa. Section 2.4 explains the concepts of civil society and public interest in order to place previous discussions about the state and its institutions in context. Section 2.5 explores how the role of the state is changing and identifies challenges to the modern state. Finally, section 2.6 presents the reader with various frameworks or viewpoints for understanding institutional arrangements. These frameworks give the reader greater appreciation of the ways in which institutional arrangements affect planning and policy-making and provide some direction for those seeking to investigate particular arrangements.

2.2 $\mathcal{T}$HE STATE

■ 2.2.1 Conceptualising *the state*

The state shapes a nation's political culture and the nature and distribution of power that political and bureaucratic arms of government can exercise. The **state** refers to the full collection of institutions through which control is exercised and societal change is regulated. The state includes the legislature, various arms of the bureaucracy, the courts, military, police, regulatory authorities, government business enterprises and a full range of rules, regulations, laws, conventions and policies that shape the capacity of governments to govern (Ryan, Parker & Brown 2003).

The primary functions of the state include the making and implementation of laws and maintaining peace and order. The characteristics of the state and the institutional arrangements that shape its activities are generally determined by a constitutional framework. A **constitution** is a document or set of documents that set out the fundamental principles by which the state operates, including the form, character and powers of governments and the desired relationship between the people and the legislature, executive and judiciary. Constitutions can exist at many different levels, in supranational organisations such as the United Nations (UN) or the World Tourism Organization (WTO) and at national and subnational levels.

In Australia, the *Commonwealth of Australia Constitution Act 1900* is a single constitutional document that was created by an Act of the British Parliament. It establishes the roles and responsibilities of Commonwealth and state governments and embodies a separation of powers between the three independent arms of government:

• the legislature — which comprises elected representatives who debate and pass laws and provides a forum in which new issues and problems can be identified

• the executive — also referred to as the ministry or **cabinet**, which implements the laws, and

• the judiciary — the courts that interpret and apply the laws in specific circumstances.

In contrast, New Zealand does not have a single constitutional document but a set of documents, conventions and laws. The Treaty of Waitangi (1840) and the *Constitution Act (1986)* NZ provide important directions with respect to the system of government and the roles and responsibilities of public institutions in New Zealand. These are supplemented by statutes, case law and practices that set out the roles and responsibilities of government and the relationships between the legislature, the executive and the judiciary.

Although constitutions have significant authority, they are documents that require interpretation and refinement over time as a result of issues and problems not anticipated at the time of their writing. How, why and when a constitution has been adapted and interpreted throughout history by the judiciary and the bureaucracy also become important in understanding the roles and responsibilities of government. Tourism is a relatively recent social, economic and environmental activity and is a good example of a policy sector where government roles and responsibilities have emerged as a result of negotiation and compromise and not through constitutional provision (Dredge & Jenkins 2003).

State institutions exist at different geographical (or spatial) scales: national, regional and local (Ham & Hill 1993). In federal systems of government, such as in Australia, the USA, Canada and Germany, different levels of the state operate interdependently. The relationships between different levels of government are an important dimension of institutional arrangements. When considering the role and nature of the state and its effect on planning and policy-making, it is important to consider how different sets of institutional arrangements at different scales coalesce, collaborate, conflict or clash to shape policy and planning outcomes. These are referred to as **intergovernmental relations** (see the end of chapter case study on p. 63).

The role *of the state*

There are many theories of the state, but liberal democracy is the key context in which we analyse the role of the state (Dunleavy & O'Leary 1987: 4). Democracy, simplistically, means rule by the people (Heywood 1997: 66). Democracies vary around the globe, so different models of democracy have been described and variously praised and criticised. Models include classical, liberal, protective and developmental democracy. A broad consensus of democracy (liberal democracy) holds that represented governments are duly elected at regular intervals. Liberal democracies are characterised by electoral choice (more than one candidate from which to choose) and political parties (of which there might be few or many) (Heywood 1997: 27–8, 75). But in most democratic states far less than 100 per cent of eligible voters lodge votes, and large segments of the population might decide not to vote. In Australia and New Zealand voting is compulsory.

Any discussion of the state requires that the discussion be contextualised within society. Different views on the roles and responsibilities of the state are important statements about, among other things, society, systems of government and the historical development of a nation. Key questions for exploring the role of the state in any political decision or action that is taken include:

• Why should government and the wider state intervene?
• How should government and the wider state intervene?
• Who has influenced public policy and with what effect?
• What policies or programs are foregone in any decision or action (i.e. what are the opportunity costs)?
• What are the likely effects of the decisions and actions taken?
• Who benefits, wins or loses?
• What consequences arise from any form of government intervention?

For tourism, the development of legislation concerning visas, environmental assessment, the allocation and distribution of resources, such as national, regional and urban parks, walking tracks and the construction of transport infrastructure, such as airports and roads, can be highly political issues. Choices and decisions are made to allocate funds and other resources to particular policies, programs and projects at the expense of others. These are generally made in response to competing claims from affected individuals and agencies, consideration of related programs, party political ideology and resource constraints. There are winners and losers, and the distribution of power in democratic societies has been the subject of lengthy historical debate.

Rival theories of the state are plentiful and varied. Theoretical perspectives include pluralist (and neo-pluralist), elite, Marxist (and neo-Marxist) and Weberian (and neo-Weberian). In the space available, we will briefly describe and compare each of these theories of the state.

Pluralism

The origins of pluralist theories of the state 'can be traced back to the writings of seventeenth-century social-contract theorists such as Thomas Hobbes and John Locke' (Heywood 1997: 87). Pluralists argue that 'power in western industrialized societies is widely distributed among different groups' (Ham & Hill 1993: 28) and that the state is a more or less neutral body that arbitrates between the competing interests of society (Heywood 1997: 98). **Pluralism** is society-centred. The state, then, is considered a referee, with much attention given to government. It is not uncommon in the pluralist tradition 'for "the state" to be dismissed as an abstraction, with institutions such as the courts, the civil service and the military being seen as independent actors in their own right, rather than as elements of a broader state machine' (Heywood 1997: 86).

A more critical analysis of the state has been adopted in recent works under the labels of 'reformed pluralism' and 'neo-pluralism'. It is acknowledged that government and interest group relationships are frequently institutionalised and that certain groups could be excluded from policy agendas and debates. This is a more 'realistic' and applied perspective or view of the political system. Business, for instance, is a powerful political force and has a firm foothold in influencing government decision-making (see chapter 4) throughout the world. In addition, the state elite, which, ironically, includes government agencies and staff, is extremely influential. If we accept this view, then government itself might be considered a political actor and indeed a powerful interest group, although not in the traditional sense (see below).

Since the 1970s pluralism has been subjected to intensive criticism. Pluralist explanations neglect the persistent and sometimes powerful influence of business and corporate elites on policy-making and have a limited or narrow view of state action. Brian Head explained the significance of interest groups and electoral politics to policy-making processes, but criticised the traditional pluralist perspective. Head argued that pluralists generally fail to account for international and historical forces influencing public policy and the structural constraints affecting government activities. Further, the pluralist perspective lacks a coherent 'theory of the state apparatus as a set of structures distanced from both the government and from the economic groups' (Head 1983: 27).

Despite its limitations, pluralism's strong focus on the role of interest (pressure) groups in public policy processes is also something of a strength. Such a focus directs our attention, for example, to the extent and nature of political organisations in politics, to interest group competition and to the ways in which groups coalesce around a particular policy issue. However, pluralist perspectives of decision- and policy-making processes do not adequately explain how governments and the wider state actually work. Pluralist-based accounts are likely inadequate, for example, in explaining the widespread application of neoclassical economic agendas or ideas (and hence ideology) to drive political action, the power of multinational corporations in developing countries, or why sex tourism was for so long an economically 'respected' and 'successful' (or at least tolerated) industry in several countries in South-East Asia.

Elite theory

Elite theory is based on the premise that power (political or economic) is concentrated in a minority of the population. Public policy, then, reflects 'the values and preferences of a governing elite' (Anderson 1984: 16). Elitism is a belief in, or practice of, rule by an elite or a minority. 'Gaetano Mosca (1857–1941), Robert Michels (1876–1936) and Vilfredo Pareto (1848–1923) are widely credited with developing the concept as a central idea in the social sciences in the late nineteenth century' (Green 2003: 144). The term 'elite' 'has been used in conjunction with Marxist analyses of class and economic power, as well as in accounts of corporatism as a form of state and/or government/interest group intermediation. It is, therefore, difficult to provide one clear definition of elitism with which all would agree' (Green 2003: 144).

Power can be gained from one or more sources, including technical expertise (e.g. scientists), wealth (e.g. entrepreneurs), access to information or knowledge (business people with good networks and alliances in government), formal appointment to an office or executive position (e.g. chief executive officers) (Green 2003: 144). Elite theory sees an unequal distribution of power in society. Power is concentrated in the upper socio-economic classes, who seek to preserve a system that serves their values rather than those of the wider population; in essence, a few have power and many do not and the few are very influential (Dye & Zeigler in Anderson 1984: 16–17).

'Whereas classical elitists strove to prove that democracy was always a myth, modern elitist theorists have tended to highlight how far particular political systems fall short of the democratic ideal' (Heywood 1997: 76). In modern states, elite positions are closely related to command of economic resources and formulation of public policy and especially the development and expansion of large-scale organisations, which encompass the bureaucrats of large and powerful government agencies, multinational enterprises and the military (e.g. Mills 1956; Ham & Hill 1993). Elite theory is 'an important alternative to pluralism' (Ham & Hill 1993: 33). In recent times, neo-Marxists take the comparisons further. Ralph Miliband in his treatise on the role of the state in capitalist society, which is based on the ideas of Marx, seeks to show that the power elite is little more than a ruling or dominant class (Ham & Hill 1993).

Marxism

In the mid-nineteenth century, Karl Marx wrote *The Communist Manifesto* (with Friederich Engels), *Capital* and other works. Marx viewed and recounted history as a story of struggle: the struggle between social classes produced by the way a given society reproduces its existence year to year and day to day. **Marxism** is concerned with social class and 'who gets what'. It asks questions about how a capitalist society allocates labour and other resources and how consumption regulates and perpetuates differential relations in society. 'The relationship between capitalists and workers is an exploitative one — capitalists minimising the wages they pay and retaining maximum profits for themselves. The state in capitalist countries merely plays the role of propping up the exploitative system by curbing and regulating some of the worst excesses of capitalism and providing it with a "human face" '(Veal 2003: 300).

For Marxists 'the capitalist state's main function is to assist the process of capital accumulation' (Ham & Hill 1993: 33). Marxists argue essentially that the state 'is an instrument for class domination' (Ham & Hill 1993: 34), which maintains 'the class system by either oppressing subordinate classes or ameliorating class conflict' (Heywood 1997: 98). Hence the state is considered to be acting largely on behalf of the capitalist class. 'In terms of its world view, the Marxist perspective sees the antagonistic relationship between classes as the central fact of politics in all societies ... The overall pattern of public policy supports the general interests of capital' (Brooks 1993: 41).

The Marxist critique has been applied to the provision of leisure. 'It argues that by providing those leisure services which the market is incapable of delivering — such as parks, sports facilities, children's play facilities, quality arts output and conservation of the natural and historic heritage — the state provides capitalism with a civilized face. Not only does the state provide capitalism with a human face, it provides basic infrastructure at the public expense upon which the private sector builds profitable enterprises ...' (Veal 2003: 43). Unfortunately, especially given the salience of Marxist accounts to studies of political economy, the field of tourism studies has grossly neglected this complex view of the state.

Corporatism

Corporatism, like pluralism, recognises bargaining between competing interests. However, there is an important distinction in that corporatism sees the implementation of public policies and programs through interest groups and especially through corporate interests (e.g. corporatisation of government business enterprises) so that there are intricate and very direct links between business and the state. Max Weber argued that the notion of democracy known to Ancient Greeks could not be delivered in modern times, as politics and government were dominated by the professional elite of politicians and bureaucrats. He considered the modern era to be 'one of "party machine politics", in which the degree of participation of the ordinary citizen in the forging of political policies is strictly limited' (Giddens 1982: 91).

One way of understanding how corporate power is exercised and unfolds is to focus on an aspect of business interaction with government (e.g. see Richter 1989; Hall 1994; Jenkins 2001a, 2001b; Jenkins & Stolk 2003). What analysts might find are that there are many dimensions of economic or corporate power: the domination of the corporate economy by relatively few companies; high market concentration in specific industries; trade practices (e.g. price-fixing arrangements); interlocking company directors; and, ultimately, the extent and nature of the relationship between big business and the governmental processes (or, in other words, the relationships between economic and political power) (Wheelwright 1974). The brokering of deals around policies concerning taxes, subsidies and resort developments and other projects have been questioned in both developed and developing countries (e.g. see Richter 1989; Hall & Jenkins 1995: 61–3; Doorne 1998; Jenkins 2001a).

The field of tourism studies is giving greater consideration to the role of the state (e.g. Richter 1989; McMillan 1991; Hall 1994; Hall & Jenkins 1995; Elliott 1997; Jenkins 2001a). Nevertheless, in a review of four tourism economics books, Jenkins (1996) argued that each book was superficial in its contextual discussion of tourism (and leisure) economics because many key factors that influence, or are influenced by, economic policy were largely ignored. For instance, Bull's text, *The Economics of Travel and Tourism* (1995), does not discuss political economy transformations since the 1970s, yet such transformations have, among other things, shaped the roles of government generally and with respect to tourism specifically. No reference was made to the changing role of the state, especially in terms of changing macroeconomic and microeconomic regulatory functions. No mention was made of post–World War II commitments to Keynesian economic principles. In Australia high levels of immigration, the development of manufacturing industries, financial regulation and full employment were promoted and then replaced by neoliberal policies aimed at external balances and low inflation (see Bell 1995). At the micro level, high and extensive protectionism was abandoned and replaced by neoliberal commitment to free trade, but again such developments were given little attention. In short, critical links between domestic political economy transformations, changes in the world economy and economic policy were largely ignored. As Bell (1995: 2) pointed out:

> at the macroeconomic level, the pattern of change in Australia reflects global pressures towards neo-liberal policy convergence, driven in no small way by the power and policy preferences of global financial markets. Microeconomic reform has also been forced on Australia by changes in the world economy, but the choice of response has been more a domestic affair, driven in part by coalitional pressures reflecting the structure of the economy. Overall … these transformations in state function in the last twenty years reflect a significant weakening of state capacity *vis-à-vis* the domestic economy.

Clearly, the state merits attention and critical analysis because it is a central aspect of tourism planning and policy-making in developed and developing countries. The state performs many functions: as developer, interest protector, regulator and arbitrator, redistributor, facilitator and organiser (Davis et al. 1993: 26–7). Indeed, as Minogue puts it, 'any satisfactory explanatory theory of public policy must also explain the inter-relations between the state, politics, economy and society' (Minogue, n.d.: 5, in Ham & Hill 1993: 17).

2.3 INSTITUTIONS AND INSTITUTIONAL ARRANGEMENTS

> Institutional arrangements are … one of several important factors in the tourism public policy process. They are best viewed as a filter that mediates and expresses the play of conflicting social and economic forces in society. (Hall & Jenkins 1995: 18.)

Tourism planning and policy development, as with all public policy, takes place within a framework that is much larger and more complex than any one public sector organisational unit. In other words, in any discussion of the institutional framework in which policy is made, it is important to recognise that the public sector is not a monolithic structure but comprises a large number of intersecting and loosely related subsectors that cut cross public and private boundaries (O'Faircheallaigh et al. 1999). In many sectors including tourism, the increasing interdependence of one sector with another means that the institutional framework within which policy is formulated is fragmented, and opportunities occur for policy in one sector to be ignored, reinterpreted and even counteracted by other sectors. The challenge for any person working in the field of tourism policy is therefore to understand that these interconnections exist and to operate effectively and strategically to develop 'good' tourism policy that recognises broader influences.

Examples of this interconnectivity are everywhere. For example, a national government's initiative to list World Heritage areas for the purposes of conserving cultural and natural resources of international significance can also have a significant influence on the visibility of an international destination and on visitor numbers (see chapter 1). In turn, this listing process has implications for a range of local government activities, including visitor management and the provision and servicing of infrastructure. National economic policy, such as the setting of exchange rates, can have a profound influence on the relative attractiveness of overseas destinations compared to domestic destinations and can have important implications for the economic development and management activities of local councils and other levels of government. Foreign, immigration, trade and defence policies can all have important repercussions on levels of inbound and outbound tourism and have flow-on effects for regional and local conditions. Limiting immigration reduces the potential growth of the travel market associated with visiting friends and relatives. A government decision to deregulate financial markets will significantly reshape national and international investment patterns and ownership of capital.

A discussion of institutional arrangements for tourism planning and policy also needs to acknowledge that the collection of agencies and organisations responsible for the development and delivery of policy has expanded since the 1980s. This expansion is partially in response to the neoliberal push to debureaucratise and outsource and because of the increasing recognition given to the breadth and intricate nature of public issues. Governments are doing more with less, and the private and non-government sectors have expanded to fill the void (Davis & Weller 2001; Dredge & Jenkins 2003).

In tourism, this is illustrated by the increasing use of not-for-profit and semi-public organisations to operate many visitor information centres and destination marketing agencies. Once such operations were principally undertaken by governments and driven by a mandate to protect the **public interest**. However, the increasing use of these organisations, which are at 'arm's length' from government and are often created with a commercial mandate in mind, effectively place the importance of the 'public interest' behind profit and commercialisation.

Public management of tourism therefore is not simply a task of agreeing on a coherent set of policy solutions derived from a single public tourism agency. It is much more than this. A variety of different actors and agencies contribute to tourism planning and policy, but their goals, objectives, practices and procedures concerning any policy issue can be markedly different.

The institutional environment is characterised by a web of formal and informal structures, laws, rules, conventions, relationships, behaviour, values, ideas, processes and requirements known as institutional arrangements (Hall & Jenkins 1995: 19). Institutional arrangements are more than organisational structures and include ways of practice, values and ideas that are embedded in society and institutions and carried forward, re-evaluated and modified over time. In a functional sense, these institutional arrangements shape government actions, and they provide a steering mechanism to help identify possible courses of action. According to Considine (1994), institutional arrangements have an accumulated intelligence, often over generations, and this intelligence is transmitted in the form of rules, customs and routines that shape individual behaviour and relations with others. And, although in theory they provide stability and order, the disadvantage is that institutions of government have limited ability to respond quickly to new conditions and are often criticised for being unable to adapt and respond quickly to change.

■ 2.3.1   The legislature

The **legislature** is that arm of government with the power to make laws. In democratic societies, the legislature derives its authority from the electoral process, although the characteristics of election and representation vary from country to country. In Australia, New Zealand, the USA, the UK and many other Western democracies, government is characterised by a system of representative democracy whereby the people elect representatives to serve in parliament and to exercise power and participate in decision-making on their behalf. Elected representatives form government, and, through a process of debate and decision-making, policy development and implementation, governments pursue their objectives (Bridgman & Davis 2004). It is also important to note, however, that a legislature does not always comprise democratically elected representatives. The former Soviet Union, where representatives were appointed by the ruling Communist party, is a case in point.

It is important also to note that in democratic systems, elected governments represent the will of the people; however, citizens and elected representatives have very little direct participation in the process of policy development (Howlett & Ramesh 1995). Planning and policy-making is generally dominated by members of the executive or cabinet, by appointed committees and experts in the bureaucratic arm of government. Nevertheless, the legislature, together with its elected representatives, is an important forum for discussions about societal issues, policy process and policy content. The task of these elected representatives is to keep the executive accountable, to scrutinise proposed legislation, to undertake debate and to seek modification before legislation can become law. In theory, this process is intended to keep the system honest. However, in practice, individuals often require party support to be elected, and they usually remain loyal to their political party throughout their terms. Strong party affiliations mean that voting is often influenced by party positions and can therefore influence the nature of debate and the content of legislation passed into law.

■ *2.3.2* The executive

The **executive**, also known as the cabinet or ministry, is those individuals charged with delivering and administering the law. There are two main legislature systems in Western societies: the parliamentary system and the presidential system. In parliamentary systems, such as Australia, New Zealand and Canada, the legislature holds supreme power. The executive comprises representatives who are appointed from the legislature and whose responsibility it is to administer the laws made by the legislature. The parliamentary system is also termed **responsible government** because the executive is drawn from and accountable to the legislature. Under this system the prime minister and the executive can be removed from office by the legislature.

In presidential systems, such as the USA and Brazil, the executive and the legislature are completely separate. The president and the executive are elected by popular vote and are not members of the legislature. The executive and the legislature are considered two equal and independent branches of government, and each have responsibilities in terms of proposing legislation, making judicial appointments and entering into international treaties (Ryan et al. 2003). However, although the executive has full policy-making powers, it relies on the legislature to pass policy into law. At times difficult situations can arise when the president and the executive seek to do something but the legislature blocks such initiatives.

■ *2.3.3* The judiciary

The **judiciary**, as courts operating in various jurisdictions, has responsibility for interpreting the law as required. In essence the separation between the judiciary, the legislature and the bureaucracy is intended to allow the courts to apply the law independent of political interpretation or bias and to focus on issues of justice and equity in a particular issue or case. However, in reality, the judiciary and the executive are not necessarily completely independent. The executive can have a large influence on the functioning of the court system through budgetary controls and legislative reform processes. For example, the legislature can raise concern over the collective influence of judicial outcomes and identify a need for an inquiry or legislation to assess and address perceived trends.

In turn, the judiciary also has an important role to play in interpreting and giving meaning to laws. Sometimes these interpretations are not precisely what was intended by the original legislation. In the case of Australia, High Court interpretations of the Constitution, and particularly the notion of national interest, have been instrumental in opening up Commonwealth involvement in areas of policy once considered to be the sole domain of the states and territories. The progressive expansion of Commonwealth powers in environmental management and policy is a case in point. Arguing the international and national significance of environmental issues, the Commonwealth has been able to expand its range of concerns (Papadakis & Young 2000). The High Court of Australia reinforced this expansion in several landmark cases during the 1980s in which the Commonwealth Government's incursions into environmental protection and management were upheld.

In essence, then, the judiciary has considerable power to consolidate and reinforce government policy-making but also, where it does not agree with governments' interpretation of powers, the judiciary has power to overturn the actions of government (Ryan et al. 2003). This case law then becomes a significant dimension in shaping the roles and responsibilities of government.

■ 2.3.4 The bureaucracy

For the development and implementation of public policy, governments rely on the bureaucracy and its public servants. **Bureaucracy** denotes that arm of government characterised by an organised hierarchical structure, permanent employees and a set of procedures and routines that are used to support the legislature in their law-making. Traditionally, the powerful ideas of Frederick Taylor, John Milton Keynes and Max Weber (see chapter 3), which laid the foundation for the development and operation of bureaucracy during the twentieth century, have been increasingly challenged since the 1970s. In particular, public servants have historically been committed to a lifelong career in the public service and the concept of professional neutrality. They have conceptualised their role in terms of providing rational expertise to decision-making and executing administrative processes. However, recent reforms of public administration have branded traditional models of bureaucracy as wasteful, outmoded, ineffective and bloated (Considine & Lewis 2003). These criticisms have led to a push for greater transparency and accountability and have opened up debates about such matters as the values underpinning the public service as well as its size, composition, management and operations (Uhr 1995; Considine & Lewis 2003).

2.4 CIVIL SOCIETY, PUBLIC INTEREST AND THE STATE

■ 2.4.1 Civil *society*

Societies are defined by their sociocultural characteristics. 'Society' is broadly defined as a group of human beings who share common beliefs, values and culture and who are characterised by common patterns of communication (including but not limited to language) and interaction. Societies also have geographical boundaries, which most often correspond with the geographical boundaries of the state or territorial waters; islands off the mainland; federal, state or provincial and local government or council borders; and aerial limits. For example, in Canada, French and English societies coexist, and local and provincial boundaries do not demarcate these societal divisions.

In the context of the Western democratic societies that are the focus of this book, the notion of democracy is intimately connected with **civil society**. Classical conceptions of democracy uphold idealistic notions that citizens exert control over policy-making and that the legislature is responsible to the people, politics is open and honest, and policy-making is informed and rational (Huntington 1993). In this classical conception, civil society comprises various constellations of self-organised interests all of which have equal access to policy-making. However, democratic systems do not necessarily give equal weight to all members of society. Even the earliest conceptions of democratic systems in Ancient Greek and Roman times excluded women, slaves and alien residents, and the ruling bodies exhibited only limited responsibility for this citizenry. In other words, even in democratic societies there is inclusion and exclusion.

The notion of 'civil society' and relationships between the state and economic interests are of enduring interest in policy studies. Renewed interest in exploring the links between civil society, markets and the state has been driven by growing criticisms that state institutions alone do not necessarily ensure democratic policy-making for the public interest (Huntington 1993). Joseph Schumpeter, in *Capitalism, Socialism and Democracy* (1942), sought to dismantle the notion that there is indeed a common good. He argued that the public consists of individuals without the will, competence or power to address organised interests and that democracy allows the interests of the public to be registered but leaves policy-making up to those elites who are sufficiently qualified and experienced to make decisions (King & Kendall 2004). As a result, democratic systems in the late twentieth century have come to be viewed as democratic only 'to the extent that its most powerful collective decision-makers are selected through fair, honest and periodic elections in which candidates freely compete for votes' (Huntington 1993: 7).

Critics argue that after two decades of economic neoliberalism, market forces and commercial interests have gained unprecedented influence within the state apparatus. The notion that politicians and bureaucrats are contracted to act in the interests of citizens is increasingly questioned, and a crisis in the legitimacy of and trust in government has been identified (Putnam 2000; McAllister & Wanna 2001). At the same time the idea of public interest has been progressively interrogated to the point that it has become a 'labyrinthine' notion (Lane 2000); that is, the public interest comprises a variety of legitimate and potentially competing interests, it is ambiguous and its boundaries are fuzzy. In this context, it is worth while to consider how public interests are organised to influence policy development.

◼ 2.4.2 **Public** *interest*

The question of 'what is the public interest?' is a fundamental one for planning and public policy. Who is public policy made for, and what interests are served by public policy? These are not simple questions. In the strictest sense, the public interest is the 'interest of no one special'; the interest of any individual or group taken at random (Thomas 1994: 95). In this sense, public interests are not those of particular sectional groups in society but are, more fundamentally, about shared values about life and wellbeing and embody moral and ethical notions of what is just and right. Therefore public interests are those interests that can be potentially beneficial to all members of society; but as society is not homogenous, some policy decisions might be more or less beneficial to some individuals and groups. This, in effect, is a 'common interest' view of public interest.

Take the case of local government, whose primary responsibility is to manage the current and future needs of local communities. A local council that provides funding for the establishment of a destination marketing agency does so because it is deemed to be in the 'public interest'; that is, by promoting tourism the local economy will benefit, and all community members, to varying degrees, will benefit from this decision. The marketing might lead to more visitors and private investment in recreational resources, such as theme parks or pools. However, where the destination marketing agency is set up as a membership-based, semi-autonomous agency with a commercial mandate, the 'public interest' becomes less clear. The destination marketing agency undertakes its activities in response to the interests of its membership (i.e. tourism operators and service providers), and the wider 'public interest' becomes marginalised. Benefits accrue to the sectional interests of the local tourism industry while the local community, whose land taxes help subsidise the destination marketing agency, can become alienated or disenfranchised. The theme park and pools might be constructed, but they could be expensive, congested and noisy. They might not be a priority of many local residents.

Herein lies part of the difficulty of applying the concept of 'public interest'; it is a subjective notion that requires interpretation by planners and policy-makers. They are required to interpret and give meaning to 'the public interest' through their policy formulation activities, but they are inevitably influenced by their own value systems, ideas and beliefs, the institutional frameworks within which they work and the policy actors with whom they have contact. In other words, planners and policy-makers are not necessarily rational, autonomous agents, and the public interest is never clear-cut. Relationships between the state and business interests, too, for example, influence how the public interest is perceived and interpreted.

Other understandings of public interest differ from the above interpretation of common collective interest. According to utilitarian thinkers, such as the Enlightenment philosopher Jeremy Bentham, there is no such thing as a collective public, and the notion of a public interest is impossible to grasp without understanding those that comprise it. Under this assumption, public interest is the sum of all relevant individual interests. In this way, because an interest is not shared by a large number of people, it is possible to discount it. For example, the construction of an airport could bring widespread national economic benefit and might therefore be regarded as being in the public interest. Despite the enormous social and environmental costs or externalities (e.g. noise, sleep disturbance, air pollution, traffic congestion) that might arise, these are generally localised and can be minimised if the public interest is viewed as the sum of individual interests. For example, the Commonwealth or State Government decides to fund the instalment of double-glazed windows for local residents under the flight path and to undertake road building to ease congestion; arrivals and departures of aircraft are limited to particular times, say 6am to 10pm, although this would do little to satisfy shift workers.

In tourism, this is well illustrated generally by the use of economic multiplier effects and cost-benefit analyses to support public expenditure on tourism marketing and promotion. The argument goes that tourism activity has widespread positive economic consequences and contributes to community well-being and quality of life well beyond the economic benefits enjoyed by local industry. The negative effects of tourism tend to be localised and specific to individuals or small groups. In this view, then, where the public interest is deemed to be the sum of individual interests, the benefits to the wider community outweigh the negative consequences for those locals who are so affected.

A third interpretation of the public interest adopts a holistic, non-individualistic ideal. This view is adapted from the ideas of Hegel and argues that the public interest is some overall, unitary position derived from the essence, character and spirit of a society (Thomas 1994). The notion that tourism should be promoted because it represents a pathway to global peace and tolerance exemplifies this approach to public interest. Not surprisingly, this view is often criticised as lacking substance and is open to being manipulated by the particular group making policy.

PLANNING IN PRACTICE

Wilsons Promontory National Park

Wilsons Promontory National Park (50 460 ha) is located in Victoria at the southernmost point on Australia's mainland. 'The Prom', as it is called by many, is one of Australia's oldest national parks (initially established as a temporary reserve in 1898 and made permanent in 1905). It boasts spectacular coastal landforms and diverse plant and animal communities, and has important cultural and spiritual links with local Aboriginal groups. The park receives 12 000 day visits and more than 260 000 overnight visits per year (Parks Victoria 2002). The focus of overnight accommodation is at Tidal River, which is the principal node for visitor facilities and services.

The park is also closely associated with the European settlement of the area and is a particularly popular natural asset for many Victorians. Many campers have been holidaying at the Prom for generations, and it is not unusual to have up to 5000 campers at Tidal Creek in summer. This popularity and its historical association with the people of Victoria has meant that the park has come to be seen as an important and much-loved public asset (Slattery 2002).

The issues

In October 1996, the State Government released the Wilsons Promontory Draft Management Plan and the Tidal River Master Plan. Some 3256 submissions on the Draft Management Plan were received (Parks Victoria 1997). Proposals to change the mix of accommodation available by limiting camping and allowing further development of commercial accommodation were especially controversial (Slattery 2002). In particular, there was a proposal to develop a luxurious, privately operated hotel and a proposal to develop a 45-bed lodge and walkers' huts in little-developed parts of the park (Slattery 2002). An overnight visitor cap of 4000 was proposed, which effectively meant that the balance between campers and those in commercial accommodation would be altered by reducing the number of campers (Parks Victoria 1997: 22).

The public values that underpin national park planning processes are often not clearly articulated. In this case study it appears that the interests and values of government, pressure groups and broader societal interpretations were quite different, leading to conflict and disharmony. It appears that the Victorian Government's penchant for neoliberal public administration principles (see chapter 3) led to the idea that commercialisation of the national park would lead to more cost-effective park management: it would open up opportunities to wider and more lucrative markets and diversified local economic development would generate broader public benefits. The Victorian National Parks Association (VNPA) was the major pressure group involved in the campaign against the proposals, although other coalitions of interested parties also emerged (Slattery 2002). The VNPA's main focus was on the pursuit of effective conservation management, and, because at the time membership was made up of about 3000 families, it is fair to say that conservation management was and continues to be a major public interest (VNPA 2006).

Underpinning the controversy were the vexed questions: what are the public interests in this national park management process, and how should the variety of public interests over national parks be prioritised? Slattery (2002) analysed the values expressed in the submissions to ascertain how 'public interest' was conceptualised and to what extent consensus emerged about its meaning. This research found that 'deeply held philosophical values and spiritual beliefs' about the way this particular national park fulfilled broader health, wellbeing and environmental values were evident (Slattery 2002: 576). Indeed, values about public interest extended well beyond personal, contemporary self-interest to more fundamental moral concerns about the protection and use of natural resources. As a result of the negative debate, the Victorian Government abandoned plans for the luxury hotel, and a commitment was made to retain the current number of campsites at Tidal River (Parks Victoria 2002).

(continued)

Conclusions

This case is useful in considering the nature of public interest and how it is manifested and represented in the planning process. In this case, the role of government and its ideological commitment to reducing the public sector, encouraging privatisation and capitalising on publicly owned assets (i.e. the park) were also important values that underpinned the government's interpretation of the public interest. A strong public response, evidenced by more than 3200 submissions, yielded an alternative competing conception of public interest based on a variety of values (e.g. health, wellbeing, environmental conservation and spiritual, cultural and recreational considerations). Yet this conception of the public interest was underpinned by a moral obligation to protect and manage this park for a collective good that extended well beyond the government's utilitarian focus on financial gain and economic benefit.

This case illustrates the importance of explicitly considering the values, ideas and aspirations that underpin the 'public interest' in the planning process. In this case, long-held social and cultural values about an important — and perhaps even iconic — natural resource were challenged by a government seeking to adopt utilitarian neoliberal public management objectives. The result was to stimulate the emergence and strengthening of societal pressure groups, political controversy and the inevitable time and financial consequences of plan review and amendment.

References

Parks Victoria 1997, *Wilsons Promontory National Park Management Plan, July 1997*, Melbourne.
—— 2002, *Wilsons Promontory National Park Management Plan, March 2002*, Melbourne.
Slattery, D 2002, 'Resistance to development at Wilsons Promontory National Park (Victoria, Australia)', *Society and Natural Resources*, vol. 15, pp. 563–80.
Victorian National Parks Association 2006, 'The parks: History and development', viewed 29 March 2006, www.vnpa.org.au/theparks/history.htm.

■ 2.4.3 Implications *for the state*

Civil society is frequently used to denote broad-ranging self-organising communities of common interest. According to the London School of Economics Centre for Civil Society (2004):

> Civil society refers to the arena of un-coerced collective action around shared interests, purposes and values. In theory, its institutional forms are distinct from those of the state, family and market, though in practice, the boundaries between state, civil society, family and market are often complex, blurred and negotiated. Civil society commonly embraces a diversity of spaces, actors and institutional forms, varying in their degree of formality, autonomy and power. Civil societies are often populated by organisations such as registered charities, development non-governmental organisations, community groups, women's organisations, faith-based organisations, professional associations, trades unions, self-help groups, social movements, business associations, coalitions and advocacy groups.

The nature and extent of separation of the state from civil society has been a source of considerable philosophical and practical debate that can be traced back to two streams of eighteenth-century thought. The first, associated with John Locke, was to argue that society was a self-regulating economic and social entity with a degree of unity and coordination that exists separate from the political realm. In this way, public opinion was conceptualised as a legitimate and potentially powerful tool for countering state power. However, this separation between the state and society was criticised because it had the potential to promote anti-political sentiment and to reduce the state's legitimacy in addressing societal concerns.

The second stream of thought was influenced by the varied contributions of Montesquieu, Tocqueville, Hegel and others who argued that civil society could not and should not be conceptualised as a separate and autonomous entity. Such conceptualisations, they argued, open up the possibility that, in a strong, self-regulating economy, the state would become marginalised and that this self-regulation would potentially be disguised as the will of society. However, this self-regulation would be nothing more than the will of powerful interests.

Historical arguments about the relationship between civil society and the state aside, civil society and its networks of associations cannot exist separately from the state (Walzer 1995); that is, the state affects agents and groups within civil society in different ways and to different extents. Some groups will become institutionalised to varying extents (and might even go underground), and groups will develop different forms of communication and adopt different forms of behaviour in pursuit of their interests and in response to the state.

In order to bring societal interests back into policy-making, to redress waning trust and confidence in the state and to counter powerful market interests perceived to have captured policy-making, governments have been searching for alternative ways of accommodating public interests. Since the 1990s key institutional changes characterised by a shift from government to governance have been underway. Policy systems have been characterised by increasing constellations of interests and their power and influence on public policy. These changes will be further discussed in chapters 4 and 6. At this point it is useful to examine briefly the importance of interest groups as an organising mechanism in society.

■ 2.4.4 Interest groups, *activists and policy entrepreneurs*

Interest groups are formal or informal collectives of non-governmental actors and agencies organised around common interests. They are also referred to as pressure groups, interest groups and advocacy coalitions. Interest groups seek to shape government planning and policy through various forms of advocacy, negotiation and activism. Interest groups influence political debate whereas policy activists and policy entrepreneurs target their activities towards intervention in planning and policy-making processes (Yeatman 1998). All are important in democratic systems because they allow various collective interests to be raised and debated within policy debates, and they challenge the state to balance competing interests in a more explicit and transparent manner than would normally be the case in a closed bureaucratic policy-making system.

There are various frameworks for classifying interest groups according to the purpose of the group and depending on whether one takes a welfare state approach, a liberal approach or some other approach (see Ryan et al. 2003). This chapter cannot explore these classifications in depth (see chapter 4), but in an effort to better explain the role of interest groups we adopt the following broad groupings, which are not necessarily mutually exclusive because individuals and agencies can be members of more than one type of interest group:

- *producer interest groups* — groups that represent the interests of associations and sector groups, such as those identified in table 2.1
- *welfare state client interest groups* — appeal to all members of society and promote issues perceived to be in the general public interest, such as the Australian Council of Social Service (ACOSS)
- *spontaneously unorganised interest groups* — including demonstrations and movements of civil disobedience
- *non-associational groups* — groups drawn together by a common feature or characteristic, such as local quality of life, ethnicity or cultural heritage (e.g. Aboriginal groups; residents' action groups)
- *other professional groups* — groups characterised by a common professional foundation (e.g. Ecotourism Australia).

The reality of modern politics is that interest groups are becoming stronger and more vocal. But interest groups do not necessarily exhibit equal opportunity to participate in and influence government planning and policy-making. The role, influence and access of interest groups to the policy process is largely dependent on the organisational characteristics of the group and the resources they are able to garner (Howlett & Ramesh 1995). In other words, the nature of the membership base (i.e. narrow or diverse), the level of expertise and innovation present within the membership, access to financial and other resources, the strength of connections with the machinery of government and with other interest groups all have a significant effect on the power and influence of interest groups. Some groups form 'peak associations', which attract and marry the resources and power of their participating organisations and can become quite powerful advocates in policy-making. Well-resourced interest groups might be able to hire permanent staff, such as political advocates, researchers, community liaison officers and membership consultants, which provides a further benefit of being continually visible in the policy process and having an established and evolving platform of information from which to draw their position and arguments.

■ Table 2.1
*Some peak
tourism
industry
associations,
Australia and
New Zealand*

AUSTRALIA	
Australian Business Travel Association (ABTA)	A peak organisation with chapters in each state that focus on business travel management. ABTA provides professional development and promotes best practice and networking, which includes exchanging new ideas with International Business Travel Association partners in 14 other countries.
Australian Federation of Travel Agents (AFTA)	AFTA is the national peak body that represents the majority of travel agents in Australia, including retail outlets, industry organisations, hotels, wholesalers and tour operators.
Australian Hotels and Hospitality Association (AHHA)	Peak association representing hoteliers and the hospitality industry. AHHA provides advice on regulatory, industrial, legal, economic and commercial issues.
Australian Tourism Export Council (ATEC)	ATEC, previously the Inbound Tour Operators' Association, is the national peak industry organisation that represents inbound tourism operators and suppliers, including inbound tour operators, accommodation providers, attractions, airlines, cruise lines, transport and entertainment. ATEC lobbies government, provides marketing benefits and business advice, conducts workshops and facilitates the development of strong commercial relationships with distribution networks.
Tourism and Transport Forum (TTF)	Formerly the Tourism Task Force, TTF is an elite lobby group representing more than 200 large corporations — business interests in the tourism, property, infrastructure and transport sectors. TTF lobbies government and undertakes research and advocacy.
NEW ZEALAND	
Tourism Industry Association New Zealand (TIANZ)	TIANZ is a peak lobby group representing more than 3500 industry tourism businesses. Its core functions are networking, advocacy, industry development and membership services.
Travel Agents Association of New Zealand (TAANZ)	TAANZ is a trade organisation representing New Zealand travel agents. It promotes quality standards and professional conduct among its members.
Inbound Tourism Operators Council of New Zealand (ITOC)	ITOC is a trade association representing the New Zealand inbound tourism industry.
Holiday Accommodation Parks Association of New Zealand	HAPNZ represents tourism accommodation and park operator interests in New Zealand. HAPNZ focuses its activities on industry advocacy, industry development, membership services and the development of industry standards.

Community interests tend to be less well organised and in some destinations even quite fragmented, depending on the relative importance and diversity of issues. For example, small nodes of interest might form around specific issues such as the management of holiday rental accommodation, environmental issues or traffic management (see section 6.5). These interests compete for attention and available resources (e.g. time, expertise, money) within the community. At times they inhibit the synergy of community action because of the number of groups addressing specific matters. In these circumstances competing interests and fragmentation could tend to weaken the position of community groups engaging in planning and policy processes.

Interest groups usually seek to influence policy-making through lobbying members of the bureaucracy and elected representatives; however, they serve a number of important functions, which are not commonly recognised:

- operating as channels of communication between interest group members and the machinery of the state
- legitimising demands by reaching a consensus through internal debate, negotiation and compromise
- serving as a forum for regulating members' attitudes, values and behaviour
- assisting in administration by providing a channel for dialogue and communications between government and society, and
- promoting the views of organised sectors of the electorate (Pross 1986).

The above discussion points to the inescapable observation that the role of the state, its behaviour and responses are inextricably bound up with economic and societal interests. However, the modern state is increasingly subject to a range of challenges derived from changing ideas about the nature of relationships between business, societal interests and the state.

2.5 *R*ETHINKING THE ROLE OF THE STATE

■ 2.5.1 Challenges *to the modern state*

On the basis of the preceding discussion, it is possible to identify a number of interrelated shifts that have taken place in recent decades and have a profound influence on the institutional framework in which tourism planning and policy takes place. First, the traditional bureaucratic power bases of the state have been eroded. Keating and Weller (2000: 74) put it this way: 'The nature of the constituency is changing. People have become more sceptical, better informed, less trusting and still more demanding. Despite the comparative prosperity [compared to the 1950s and 1960s], expectations have generally run ahead of capacity. Even if governments can do more now than at any time in the past, they seem less able to meet *all* the demands [original emphasis].'

Second, the traditional 'tax and spend' model of government has become outmoded, and attitudes towards government spending have changed. Raising sufficient taxes to undertake an ever-expanding range of activities is challenging for governments. Moreover, the assumption that governments know best and can accurately and effectively target spending has been laid to rest. The idea that public spending is good has been widely rejected, which has had implications for the funding of infrastructure and other welfare goods traditionally provided by government. Tourism, which relies heavily on public goods (e.g. infrastructure, public services, protected areas and so on) has been affected by this shift as evidenced by the increasing adoption of user-pays schemes and problems with aging infrastructure.

Third, the notion of a collective public interest has broken down and individualism has increased (Giddens 1998; Hurst 2000). As a result, governments are no longer able to claim that they operate for a collective public interest, an understanding of which is derived from the overarching expert knowledge of its civil servants (Keating & Weller 2000). Instead, governments are increasingly faced with balancing different sets of competing values and making trade-offs about the public interest based on the more utilitarian view of benefit for the greatest number. In tourism, for example, the bewildering array of interest groups operating at all levels of government has created new political divisions and blurred the traditional divisions between public interests and capital. For example, ecotourism operators eager to maximise commercial potential in protected areas are increasingly engaging in the environmental policy arena, and environmentalists are expounding the virtues of tourism as a tool for environmental protection (see chapters 5, 7 and 8). In the case of Wilsons Promontory in Victoria, government policies seeking to increase commercial accommodation opportunities in the national park were justified as being in the public interest, yet community backlash was based on the argument that commercialising national parks negatively effected the park, which was not in the public interest (see Planning in Practice: Wilsons Promontory National Park on p. 46).

Fourth, the strength of the **institutions of the state** has been challenged by processes of globalisation. **Globalisation**, at the risk of oversimplification, is the transnational transformation of the economic system and its consequent effects on political and social systems (Ladeur 2004). It is characterised by the deregulation of financial markets and the increased flightiness of global capital to the point where any government's ability to manage their own affairs and maintain control over internal conditions have been undermined (Keating & Weller 2000). Although some argue that globalisation is a myth and that it is part of a larger set of trends, others argue that it is a reality with an important transformative effect on the state. Giddens (1998) rightly argues that the state will not disappear under globalisation but that its roles and responsibilities will shift to accommodate these new conditions. Governments will continue to exist:

• to provide a forum for the representation of diverse interests
• to reconcile competing claims

- to create and protect the public sphere in which debate about policy issues can occur
- to provide collective security and welfare
- to regulate markets in the public interest, foster competition and fairness
- to foster social peace through policing
- to promote education and human development, and
- to ensure an effective system of laws (Giddens 1998: 47).

These changes have dramatically altered relationships between the state, business and civil society and have stimulated new debates about the nature of exchange between business, the state and society in planning and policy. Conceptualising the policy arena as networks of policy actors engaged in debate, lobbying, negotiation, strategising, compromise and advocacy has gained increasing momentum.

2.5.2 Governance

New forms of interaction between the state and civil society with its multitude of interest groups have emerged. **Governance** refers to a new form of coordination and coherence among a wide range of actors, including political actors, bureaucracy, corporate interests and civil society, all of which are characterised by different objectives and interests (Pierre 2000: 4). Governance, therefore, involves the establishment and maintenance of new relationships between the state, civil society and economic interests and embodies a less state-centric conception of the role of the state in society. It also reflects a more active citizenry and a proliferation of interest groups engaging with more open and transparent government (Marsh 2002).

Models of governance have been driven by a range of intersecting factors, including:

- The increasing difficulty of demarcating the difference between public and private interests in particular policy issues.
- Criticisms that civil servants do not look after the public interest. Instead, public officials fulfil their duties on the basis of more personal objectives, such as reward, personal power, prestige and job security (Lane 2000). Accordingly, greater transparency and access to policy-making processes is required.
- Increasingly powerful criticisms that governments do not cater for a 'greater public good' and that powerful interests influence agendas and decision-making.
- The impossibility of separating the political and bureaucratic arms of the state. Politics and policy are inseparable, and policy-making needs to reflect these competing values and issues.

The increasing uptake of governance structures and processes is derived from the work of various critics seeking alternatives to the heavy hand of bureaucracy and the effects of an unconstrained market. This balance is encapsulated in a 'third way', which seeks 'a synergy between public and private sectors, utilising the dynamism of markets but with the public interest in mind' (Giddens 1998 in Considine & Lewis 2003: 132). In this way, strategic development of partnerships and alliances between public and private spheres gives rise to notions of policy communities and networks that reflect interdependencies among politicians, bureaucrats, members of society and businesses.

Before we move towards understanding networks and policy communities (see chapter 6), it is useful to consider the perspectives from which institutional arrangements can be understood.

2.6 UNDERSTANDING INSTITUTIONAL ARRANGEMENTS

The state and its institutions are an inevitable part of daily life, but it stands to reason that institutional arrangements for tourism planning and policy, as with other areas of policy, vary significantly from country to country, region to region and locality to locality. So how might we investigate and seek to understand the influence of government institutions on planning and policy? How do institutions shape policy dialogues, relationships between actors and the type of policy solutions that might be considered appropriate? Such research is inevitably pragmatic, and no single method or approach has attracted consensus. Nevertheless, it is important to understand the opportunities and limitations of institutions and how they set down 'pathways' for dialogue and action (Considine 1994). Three approaches to studying institutional arrangements are described below.

2.6.1 Traditional *state-centred approaches*

'Traditional' institutional studies conceptualise the state as having a central and pivotal role in planning and policy formulation. These traditional approaches to understanding the role of institutions are generally state-centred, focusing on descriptions of the structures, organisation, duties and functions of government. Yet within this broad approach little attention has been placed on the links between the nature of government institutions and their influence on policy content (Dye 1978). Criticism of this approach began to emerge from the 1970s onwards as a result of observations that the state was not an independent and all-powerful actor in the process of policy formulation but that the state was inexplicably tied to and a manifestation of political culture (see chapter 3).

2.6.2 Cultural *studies*

In response, a second general approach to the study of government institutions emerged: cultural studies. In this approach, political culture is thought to shape institutions and the boundaries and contexts in which institutions operate (Uhr 1995). In other words, cultures have a powerful effect in elevating some interests over others, in marginalising some interests and in establishing domination. The strength of this cultural approach, then, is to draw attention to the different interests and values that operate in institutions and to understand the way institutional rules and order are perpetuated by dominant cultures.

In tourism, this approach is well demonstrated by the work of Jennifer Craik (1991), who examined the cultural values embedded in the Queensland Government's approach to resort development in the 1980s. Although this case study is now somewhat dated, it remains a valuable historical account of the overwhelming economic development agenda and values of the Queensland Government of the time. Cultural studies can also be undertaken from a sectoral point of view. Jenkins and Wearing (2003) interrogate the values underpinning ecotourism policy development in Australia and find an alarming trend towards commercialisation of protected areas.

Both traditional state-centred and cultural approaches to studying institutions highlight important characteristics of institutions, but neither approach is adequate in providing a comprehensive understanding of the role and influence of institutions in planning and policy-making; that is, 'the relationship between political institutions and political culture is such that culture alone does not explain institutional behaviour and institutional literature does not alone explain culture' (Uhr 1995: 212). Institutions are alive with values, ideas, beliefs and interests that go well beyond dealing with the task or issue at hand (Wildavsky 1979; Selznick 1996). These values, ideas and beliefs play out to influence the way issues are dealt with and which solutions are identified. Institutions are both culture modifying and culture dependent (Uhr 1995).

■ 2.6.3 New institutionalism

New institutionalism is a perspective that has been couched in response to growing criticism of both the traditional state-centred and cultural approaches to the study of institutions. New institutionalism seeks to 'bring the state back in' and to conceptualise the state as a dependent variable in a complex system of interests and events (March & Olsen 1984; Immergut 1998).

Coinciding with the breakdown of overarching theories of public policy, there has been an increasing emphasis on connections between institutional structures, culture and organisational behaviour. Contemporary views of planning and policy embrace a discursive or communicative element in which policy-making is conceptualised as a dynamic process resulting from interaction between a range of policy actors (see chapter 6). Emerging from this conception of policy-making, increasing attention has been given to the ways power, politics and interest structures embedded in institutions influence planning and policy formulation and the ways institutions in turn change and adapt as a result of policy.

Discussions of the shortcomings of traditional views of rational scientific policy-making and centralised bureaucratic policy processes have fuelled the emergence of 'new institutionalism'. The new institutionalism position argues that traditional rational scientific models of policy-making conceive the state as a central and pivotal agent, but new communicative models of policy-making emphasise that the state is one actor and that a broader, more eclectic conception is required; that is, state actors and agencies can play a critical but not necessarily deterministic role in shaping policy discourses and policy outcomes (March & Olsen 1984). Moreover, policy cannot be wholly understood in terms of discourses generated among pressure groups and individuals, influenced by social forces and implemented by government officials with little autonomy. State officials carry with them institutional practices, ideas and values that variously influence the content and style of policy debates (March & Olsen 1984). Atkinson and Coleman (1992: 154) note that the state is not an inert entity shaped by historical struggles and liable to capture by society's strongest interests. Rather, the state is an active agent, moulding society and serving the interests of office holders sometimes as much as, or more than, the interests of citizens.

In this view, institutional arrangements are not impermeable, everpowerful superstructures within which individual actors and agencies operate to produce tourism planning and policy outcomes. Institutional arrangements can actually change over time, albeit slowly, and are continually shaped by the actors and agencies involved in tourism planning and policy.

In this context, Reich (2000) identifies four distinct forms of new institutionalism that have emerged to explain institutional behaviour:

- *historical institutionalism,* which seeks to relate the interplay of societal forces and institutional structures and processes over time
- *new economic institutionalism,* which focuses on explaining the nature, extent and balance of transactions among groups and the strategies, inducements and bargaining games played in the development of policy
- *institutions of cognitive frameworks,* which views institutions as sets of culturally specific practices, beliefs, rules and rituals that are adopted, implemented and reproduced by organisations
- *institutions as actors themselves,* which conceptualises institutions as a coherent set of state actors that pursue interests and actions as any other actor in the policy process.

None of these approaches can claim to have greater explanatory power than any other. Each form of institutional analysis delivers insights and no single viewpoint or approach provides a definitive explanation. If we share different views on the role of the state, the influence of pressure groups or the roles of the bureaucracy as a source of advice and action for democratically elected governments, then we will quite logically formulate different causes and effects of tourism policy and planning.

This chapter has discussed the role of the state and the nature of the institutional environment in which tourism planning and policy processes take place. There are various theories about the role of the state and the way it influences government involvement in issues of public concern. Pluralism, elite theory, Marxism and corporatism were discussed. These theories each provide explanations of the way interests are brought to bear in planning and policy-making and why certain groups of interests are more powerful and influential than others.

These theories about the role of the state are manifested through a full range of institutional structures and processes that characterise the state. These institutions include the legislature, the executive, the bureaucracy and the judiciary. Planning and policy-making can be considered products of the values and ideas embedded in these institutions about the role of the state and its relationship with economic and societal interests.

All these institutions of the state are usually funded through public revenue, and the main criterion for undertaking their activities is the public interest. However, the 'public interest' is a vexed term that can be defined in a number of ways. It can be defined as being a broad moral and ethical notion, a set of interests common to a section of society, or a utilitarian concept whereby public good is the sum of individual and often diverging interests. It is important to understand which values governments pursue in the public interest because they can open up critical thinking about the role of government and the way different policy decisions can be justified.

This chapter also discussed the changing role of the state and the challenges these present to modern government. In particular, the influence of globalisation and the move towards governance structures, which seek to bring civil society, its interest groups and the state into closer partnership, are important shifts. The chapter concludes with the exploration of three approaches that can be used to understand the influence of institutional arrangements and the role of the state in policy-making. These approaches are the traditional state-centred approach, cultural studies and new institutionalism. Each of these approaches can be used to build critical understandings about the causes and effects of tourism planning and policy.

SUMMARY OF KEY TERMS

Bureaucracy

Bureaucracy denotes the administrative or organisational arm of government and is characterised by an organised hierarchical structure, permanent employees and a set of procedures and routines that are used to support the legislature in its law-making.

Cabinet

Government ministers who have executive powers over a particular area of policy. In Australia's parliamentary system, ministers are members of parliament, and they are accountable to parliament and, by default, the people.

Civil society

Civil society denotes a broad range of self-organising communities of common interest, which could be formal or informal. It includes such organisations as registered charities, non-governmental organisations, community groups, women's organisations, faith-based organisations, professional associations, trades unions, self-help groups, social movements, business associations, coalitions and advocacy groups.

Constitution

A document or set of documents that sets out the fundamental principles by which the state operates, including the form, character and powers of governments and the desired relationship between the people and the legislature, executive and judiciary.

Corporatism

A theory of the state that recognises the bargaining between different interests in the policy process and that corporate interests have particular influence with the state.

Elite theory

A theory of the state based on the premise that power is concentrated in a minority of the population and that public policy reflects the values of the governing elite.

Executive

The executive, also known as the cabinet or ministry, is those individuals charged with delivering and administering the law.

Federalism

A system of government in which the central government is stronger and more powerful than the weaker provincial governments, such as in Australia.

Globalisation

Globalisation is the transformation of the economic system and its consequent effects on political and social systems. It is characterised by the deregulation of financial markets and the increased flightiness of global capital to the point where governments' ability to manage their own affairs has been undermined.

Governance

Governance involves the establishment and maintenance of new relationships between the state, civil society and economic interests, and it embodies a less state-centric conception of the role of state in society. It also reflects a more active citizenry and a proliferation of interest groups engaging with more open and transparent government.

Institutional arrangements

Institutional arrangements are the complex and overlapping webs of formal and informal structures, laws, rules, conventions, relationships, behaviour, values, ideas and processes. Institutional arrangements transcend organisational units and particular governments; they are ways of practice, values and ideas that are embedded in society and are carried forward, re-evaluated and modified over time.

Institutions of the state

Institutions of the state are the organisational structures and practices that allow societies to make policy and pursue society's objectives.

Interest groups

Interest groups are formal or informal collectives of non-governmental actors and agencies organised around common interests.

Intergovernmental relations

Intergovernmental relations refers to the relationships and nature of exchange between different governments. Intergovernmental relations can exist between different levels of government in a federal system or between nation states. In Australia, state and federal governments are sovereign entities, and intergovernmental relations refers to the full range of formal and informal mechanisms through which governments relate to one another.

Judiciary

The judiciary, made up of the courts and its officers, has responsibility for interpreting the law as required.

Legislature

The legislature is the institution given responsibility for making laws. The legislature is formed in different ways depending on the system of government adopted. In democratic systems, the legislature comprises representatives elected by popular vote who debate and make laws.

Marxism

Marxism is a theory of the state that is concerned with who gets what in society and the role of the state in regulating and perpetuating class relations. In Marxism the state is considered to work largely on behalf of the capitalist class in fostering capital accumulation and supporting the exploitation of workers. The state's role is to address only the worst excesses of capitalism to give it a 'human face'.

Pluralism

Pluralism is a society-centred theory of the state that sees the state as a more or less neutral body that arbitrates between competing interests of society.

Public interest

Public interest is a complex and controversial term generally used to denote the aggregate interests of a society, which are to be enhanced or protected by some form of government intervention. However, the notion of public interest sits in opposition to observations that societies are characterised by a range of competitive interests and values such that there can be no aggregation of individual needs and expectations.

Responsible government

Responsible government, also known as the parliamentary system, has the executive drawn from and accountable to the legislature. This contrasts with the presidential system whereby the executive and legislature are separate.

State

The state refers to the full collection of political institutions through which control is exercised and societal change is regulated. The state includes the legislature, various arms of the bureaucracy, the judiciary, military, police, regulatory authorities, government business enterprises and a full range of rules, regulations, laws, conventions and policies.

QUESTIONS

1 What are institutional arrangements? Explain why it is important that policy-makers and analysts understand them.

2 Identify and discuss the various theories about the role of the state. Discuss which theories tend to dominate contemporary tourism planning and policy practice.

3 Identify and discuss the institutions of the state, and give examples of how they might affect tourism planning and policy.

4 Define the concepts of civil society and public interest. Why are these concepts difficult to define but important for tourism planners to be aware of?

5 What are interest groups? Identify the roles that interest groups play in tourism planning and policy.

6 How has the role of the state changed over time? Give an example in relation to tourism.

7 Identify and describe three approaches for understanding the role of institutions in planning and policy-making. Give examples in tourism.

EXERCISES

1 Examine the values of the Australian and New Zealand public services, which are detailed on the following websites: Australian Public Service: www.apsc.gov.au/publications02/values.htm and New Zealand Public Service: www.ssc.govt.nz/coc. Compare and contrast the main principles and values on which each public service operates.

2 Examine the Tourism White Paper (Australia) available at: www.dist.gov.au/assets/documents/itrinternet/TourismWhitePaper2005 0209174539.pdf or the New Zealand Tourism Strategy available at: www.tourism.govt.nz/strategy/index.html. Divide the class into groups and allocate a section of the White Paper or Tourism Strategy to each group for review. Answer the following questions:

(a) Provide an overview of the section's content in 200 words.

(b) Identify the key words or phrases in each section that suggest the government's direction and perceived role (in a minimum of 10 words or phrases).

(c) Describe the role of state embedded in the Tourism White Paper or the Tourism Strategy.

(d) Compare and contrast the interests being represented.

(e) How is the public interest represented?

FURTHER READING

Davis, G & Wanna, J 2004, *The Australian Policy Handbook,* **Allen & Unwin, Sydney.** This text gives a useful introduction to the field of public policy. It provides an overview of the Australian state and the nature of its institutional arrangements.

Dredge, D & Jenkins, J 2003, 'Federal–state relations and tourism public policy, New South Wales, Australia', *Current Issues in Tourism,* **vol. 6, no. 5, pp. 415–43.** This article presents a detailed historical case study of intergovernmental relations between the Federal Governent and the New South Wales Government. It illustrates the dynamic nature of intergovernmental relationships and the influence of politics on the role of government in the context of tourism policy.

Hall, CM & Jenkins, J 1995, *Tourism Public Policy,* **Routledge, London.** This book is a good introductory text that outlines the institutions of the state and approaches to studying tourism public policy.

Ryan, N, Parker, R & Brown, K 2003, chapter 7, 'National institutions of governance' (pp. 95–117); chapter 8, 'The public service' (pp. 119–34); and chapter 12, 'Interest groups and society' (pp. 205–29), in *Government Business and Society,* **2nd edn, Prentice Hall, Frenchs Forest, NSW.** This book provides an excellent discussion of the institutions of the state and relationships between institutions and actors.

Intergovernmental relations and tourism in Australia

Australia's federal system of government was created in 1901 when each of the independent colonial administrations came together to establish the Commonwealth Government. The agreement reached was to create a dual system of sovereignty whereby this new Commonwealth Government was vested with a limited number of 'exclusive' powers relating to issues of national or international significance. The state and Commonwealth governments shared jurisdiction over some 'concurrent' powers such as defence, international trade, immigration and income tax collection. Those powers and responsibilities not mentioned in the Constitution became 'residual' powers, the responsibility for which fell to the states. It is noteworthy that each of the states had different origins and political underpinnings and were highly competitive. Debates about federation were often highly controversial with argument centring on division of responsibilities and balance of power between the future Commonwealth and state governments. The model that was eventually adopted was thought to ensure that the states retain both the balance of power and independence from the Commonwealth Government.

In Australia's federal system, neither state and territory governments nor the Federal Government are subordinate to each other. However, local government is a creation of the states and is not recognised in the Constitution. Its roles and responsibilities are set out by the relevant state legislation, and it is subordinate to the states. Different state governments have tended to intervene in local government affairs to varying degrees but, at the risk of oversimplification, there is a widespread traditional view that local government lacks expertise, is more open to corruption and is less capable. More contemporary views tend to acknowledge the important and expanding role of local government.

Tourism is a relatively new area of policy and was not mentioned in the Constitution, which was prepared at the turn of the nineteenth century. As a result, primary responsibility for tourism, as a residual power, has fallen to the states, although the increasing economic importance of tourism at an international level stimulated more committed and substantial Commonwealth Government involvement from the mid-1960s onwards. In 1976 an Intergovernmental Agreement on Tourism was signed, which set out the roles and responsibilities of the Commonwealth and the states or territories. However, this highly structured approach had a limited shelf-life because, as social, economic and political conditions change, so to do the issues relating to tourism's management and policy development.

(continued)

Studies of the influence of **federalism** on tourism policy formulation reveal that all levels of government are involved to varying degrees in tourism planning and policy (see figure 2.1). Involvement can be direct (e.g. providing tourism information and marketing services) or indirect (e.g. providing public toilets, parks and recreation infrastructure or surf lifesaving services). Roles and responsibilities are unclear, and there is considerable overlap and counter-vailing of policy solutions at various levels of government. Efforts to establish a shared position and a collaborative intergovernmental approach have been thwarted by disagreements between the state or territory governments and the Commonwealth, especially where different political parties have tended to adopt different preferred levels and types of intervention.

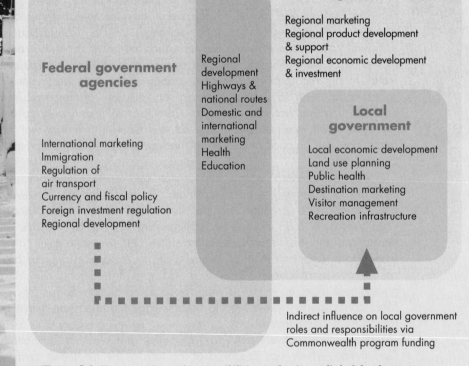

State government agencies

Regional marketing
Regional product development
& support
Regional economic development
& investment

Federal government agencies

Regional
development
Highways &
national routes
Domestic and
international
marketing
Health
Education

International marketing
Immigration
Regulation of
air transport
Currency and fiscal policy
Foreign investment regulation
Regional development

Local government

Local economic development
Land use planning
Public health
Destination marketing
Visitor management
Recreation infrastructure

Indirect influence on local government
roles and responsibilities via
Commonwealth program funding

■ **Figure 2.1** *Tourism roles and responsibilities under Australia's federal system*

Yet perhaps the most important implication of federalism for tourism policy and planning in Australia is vertical fiscal imbalance (VFI). During the twentieth century, changes to revenue-raising arrangements between the Commonwealth and states or territories have led to an acute vertical fiscal imbalance, which has had a major influence on policy development in all sectors. Vertical fiscal imbal-ance is the difference between revenue raising and constitutional spending responsibilities between the states and the Commonwealth. Put simply, under the

Constitution the states have a relatively large number of responsibilities to fund but possess limited revenue sources. The states also have a heavy responsibility in supporting local government, being a creation of the states. The gap between state-generated revenue on spending is filled by Commonwealth grants and transfers to the states but also opens the potential for political coercion by the Commonwealth. So the Commonwealth might agree to fund the states for specific programs against performance-based or other criteria.

VFI is exacerbated by the expansion of roles and responsibilities of governments during the twentieth century. Overlapping jurisdictions, administrative red tape and size and duplication of effort are some of the criticisms of federal systems in which power is shared and responsibilities for different levels are not clearly articulated. In the case of tourism, the need to combat this complexity and avoid duplication led to a Partnership Australia agreement between the Commonwealth and states and territories in 1994. Despite this agreement, however, the federal, state or territory and local governments have tended to deal with tourism in a relatively uncoordinated manner, and considerable overlap and disagreement remains in planning and policy initiatives among governments.

Questions

Consider the following dimensions of planning and policy:

1 How might the new institutional approach be relevant to understanding Australia's division of tourism roles and responsibilities in the case study?

2 What is vertical fiscal imbalance (VFI)? How might VFI influence tourism policy and planning at different levels of government?

3 Explain what is meant by exclusive, concurrent and residual powers in the context of the Australian Constitution.

4 What is meant by overlapping and countervailing policy? Give examples of where this might occur.

References

Dredge, D & Jenkins, J 2003, 'Federal–state relations and tourism public policy, New South Wales, Australia', *Current Issues in Tourism*, vol. 6, no. 5, pp. 415–43.
Hall, CM 2003, *Introduction to Tourism: Dimensions and Issues*, 4th edn, Hospitality Press, Frenchs Forest, NSW.

REFERENCES

Anderson, JE 1984, *Public Policy-making*, 3rd edn, Holt, Rinehart & Winston, New York.

Atkinson, M & Coleman, W 1992, 'Policy networks, policy communities and the problems of governance', *Governance: An International Journal of Policy and Administration*, vol. 5, no. 2, pp. 154–80.

Bell, S 1995, 'The transformation of the Australian state in comparative perspective', paper presented at the Public Policy Network Conference, University of Tasmania, Hobart, February.

Bridgman, P & Davis, G 2004, *The Australian Policy Handbook*, 3rd edn, Allen & Unwin, Sydney.

Brooks, S 1993, *Public Policy in Canada*, McClelland & Stewart, Toronto.

Bull, A 1995, *The Economics of Travel and Tourism*, Longman, Melbourne.

Considine, M 1994, *Public Policy: A Critical Approach*, Macmillan, Melbourne.

Considine, M & Lewis, J 2003, 'Bureaucracy, network or enterprise? Comparing models of governance in Australia, Britain, the Netherlands and New Zealand', *Public Administration Review*, vol. 63, no. 2, pp. 131–40.

Craik, J 1991, *Resorting to Tourism: Cultural Policies for Tourism Development in Australia*, Allen & Unwin, Sydney.

Davis, G & Weller, P 2001, *Are You Being Served? State, Citizens and Governance*, Allen & Unwin, Sydney.

Davis, G et al. 1993, *Public Policy in Australia*, 2nd edn, Allen & Unwin, Sydney.

Doorne, S 1998, 'Power, participation and perception: An insider's perspective on the politics of the Wellington waterfront redevelopment', *Current Issues in Tourism*, vol. 1, no. 2, pp. 129–66.

Dredge, D & Jenkins, J 2003, 'Federal–state relations and tourism public policy, New South Wales, Australia', *Current Issues in Tourism*, vol. 6, no. 5, pp. 415–43.

Dunleavy, P & O'Leary, B 1987, *Theories of the State: The Politics of Liberal Democracy*, Macmillan, London.

Dye, T 1978, *Understanding Public Policy*, Prentice Hall, Englewood Cliffs, NJ.

Elliott, J 1997, *Tourism Politics and Public Sector Management*, Routledge, London.

Giddens, A 1982, *Sociology: A Brief But Critical Introduction*, Macmillan, London.

—— 1998, *The Third Way: The Renewal of Democracy*, Polity Press, Oxford.

Green, M 2003, 'Elitism', in JM Jenkins & JJ Pigram (eds), *Encyclopedia of Leisure and Outdoor Recreation*, Routledge, London, pp. 143–4.

Hall, CM 1994, *Tourism and Politics: Policy, Power and Place*, John Wiley & Sons, Chichester, UK.

Hall, CM & Jenkins, J 1995, *Tourism and Public Policy*, Routledge, London.

Ham, C & Hill, M 1993, *The Policy Process in the Modern State*, 2nd edn, Harvester Wheatsheaf, Hemel Hempstead, Herts.

Head, BW 1983, 'State and economy: Theories and problems', in BW Head (ed.), *State and Economy in Society in Australia*, Oxford University Press, Melbourne, pp. 22–54.

Heywood, A 1997, *Politics*, Palgrave, New York.

Howlett, M & Ramesh, M 1995, *Studying Public Policy: Policy Cycles and Policy Subsystems*, Oxford University Press, Toronto.

Huntington, SP 1993, *The Third Wave: Democratization in the Late Twentieth Century*, University of Oklahoma Press, Norman.

Hurst, P 2000, 'Democracy and governance', in J Pierre (ed.), *Debating Governance: Authority, Steering and Democracy*, Oxford University Press, New York.

Immergut, E 1998, 'The theoretical core of the new institutionalism', *Politics and Society*, vol. 26, no. 1, pp. 5–34.

Jenkins, JM 1996, 'Book reviews: *The Economics of Leisure and Tourism: Environments, Markets and Impacts; The Economics of Travel and Tourism; Tourism Economics; Travel and Tourism in Australia: The Economic Perspective*', *Journal of Sustainable Tourism*, vol. 4, no. 4, pp. 229–35.

—— 2001a, 'Statutory authorities in whose interests? The case of tourism New South Wales, the Bed Tax and "the Games" ', *Pacific Tourism Review*, vol. 4, no. 4, pp. 201–19.

—— 2001b, 'Editorial', *Current Issues in Tourism*, Tourism Policy Making: Theory and Practice (special issue), vol. 4, nos 2–4, pp. 69–77.

Jenkins, J & Wearing, S 2003, 'Ecotourism and protected areas in Australia', in D Fennell & R Dowling (eds), *Ecotourism Policy and Planning*, CABI International, Wallingford, UK, pp. 205–33.

Keating, M & Weller, P 2000, 'Rethinking government's roles and operations', in G Davis & P Weller (eds), *Are You Being Served? State, Citizens and Governance*, Allen & Unwin, Sydney, pp. 73–97.

King, R & Kendall, G 2004, *The State, Democracy and Gloablization*, Palgrave Macmillan, Basingstoke, UK.

Ladeur, KH 2004, *Public Governance in the Age of Globalization*, Ashgate, Aldershot, UK.

Lane, J 2000, *The Public Sector: Concepts, Models and Approaches*, Sage, London.

London School of Economics Centre for Civil Society 2004, Definition of Civil Society, viewed 20 April 2006, www.lse.ac.uk/collections/CCS/introduction.htm.

March, JG & Olsen, JO 1984, 'The new institutionalism: Organizational factors in political life', *American Political Science Quarterly*, vol. 78, pp. 735–49.

Marsh, I 2002, 'Governance in Australia: Emerging issues and choices', *Australian Journal or Public Administration*, vol. 61, no. 2, pp. 3–9.

McAllister, I & Wanna, J 2001, 'Citizens' expectations and perceptions of governance', in G Davis & P Weller (eds), *Are You Being Served? State, Citizens and Governance.* Allen & Unwin, Sydney, pp. 7–35.

McMillan, J 1991, 'The politics of tourism in Queensland', in P Carroll et al. (eds), *Tourism in Australia*, Harcourt Brace Jovanovich, Sydney, pp. 97–113.

Mills, CW 1956, *The Power Elite*, Oxford University Press, New York.

O'Faircheallaigh, C et al. 1999, *Public Sector Management in Australia: New Challenges, New Directions*, 2nd edn, Macmillan, Melbourne.

Papadakis, E & Young, L 2000, 'Mediating clashing values: Environmental policy', in G Davis & M Keating (eds), *The Future of Governance: Policy Choices*, Allen & Unwin, Sydney, pp. 153–76.

Pierre, J 2000, 'Introduction: Understanding governance', in J Pierre (ed.), *Debating Governance: Authority, Steering and Democracy*, Oxford University Press, New York, pp. 1–10.

Pross, P 1986, *Group Politics and Public Policy*, Oxford University Press, Toronto.

Putnam, R 2000, *Bowling Alone: The Collapse and Revival of the American Community.* Simon & Schuster, New York.

Reich, S 2000, 'The four faces of institutionalism: Public policy and a pluralistic perspective', *Governance: An International Journal of Policy and Administration*, vol. 13, no. 4, pp. 501–22.

Richter, L 1989, *The Politics of Tourism in Asia*, University of Hawaii Press, Honolulu.

Ryan, N, Parker, R & Brown, K 2003, *Government, Business and Society*, Prentice Hall, Sydney.

Schumpeter, JA 1942, *Capitalism, Socialism and Democracy*, Allen & Unwin, London.

Selznick, P 1996, 'Institutionalism "old" and "new" ', *Administrative Science Quarterly* 41: 270–77.

Slattery, D 2002, 'Resistance to development at Wilsons Promontory National Park (Victoria, Australia)', *Society and Natural Resources*, vol. 15, pp. 563–80.

Thomas, H 1994, *Values and Planning*, Ashgate, Aldershot, UK.

Uhr, J 1995, 'Institutions in context: Reconstructing Aristotle's defence of cultural studies', *Australian Journal of Political Science*, vol. 30, pp. 211–27.

Veal, AJ 2003, 'Marxism', in JM Jenkins & JJ Pigram (eds), *Encyclopedia of Leisure and Outdoor Recreation*, Routledge, London, pp. 300–1.

Walzer, M 1995, *The Concept of Civil Society: Towards a Global Civil Society*, Berghahn Books, New York.

Wheelwright, EL 1974, *Radical Political Economy: Collected Essays*, Australia & New Zealand Book Company, Sydney.

Wildavsky, A 1979, *Speaking Truth to Power: The Art and Craft of Policy Analysis*, Little, Brown, Boston.

Yeatman, A 1998, *Activism and the Policy Process*, Allen & Unwin, Sydney.

Dianne Dredge and John Jenkins

CHAPTER 3

Historical *development*

LEARNING OBJECTIVES

After reading this chapter you will be able to:

1 explain why an understanding of tourism policy and planning history is important for contemporary research and practice

2 identify and discuss the major phases in social science thinking and how they have influenced the development of policy studies

3 describe the historical development of tourism, identifying those factors that have stimulated government involvement in tourism

4 identify and critically discuss broad approaches to tourism planning and policy

5 identify and discuss the stages in the tourism planning and policy development process.

*I*NTRODUCTION

Developing an understanding of the history of any subject is important. Through historical understandings it is possible to develop rich insights into the present, for 'Nothing in this world can be known or understood intelligently without some ideas as to its origin ... the present is, in its entirety, the outcome of the past and from that recognition should come a very lively and intelligent interest in the world around us' (Auchmuty 1955: 133, in King 1957: 9).

This chapter examines the history of tourism planning and policy. It is a brief Western, contemporary version. It draws on what we see as some, but certainly not all, of the ideas that have influenced thinking about the relationships between public and private spheres and the development of public policy. Mention is made of a number of influential economists, philosophers and planners, although such influential thinkers as Karl Marx and Adam Smith were as much political economists as they were philosophers.

The following section, section 3.2, explains why history is important, identifying factors that shape how and why history is reported. The fact is that 'every innovator with a bright idea staggers forward with and against a vast deadweight of accumulated practices and ways of thinking' (Heclo 1974: 17–18). Section 3.3 discusses shifts in social science ideas, philosophies and theories associated with the Enlightenment, and these are linked to past and present public management approaches. Section 3.4 discusses modernity and its influence on bureaucratic policy-making. Section 3.5 provides a brief historical overview of the development of tourism as an area of government concern. Section 3.6 traces the historical development of tourism planning and policy, and identifies and discusses major themes emerging in tourism planning and policy theory and practice. Section 3.7 outlines the shifting approach to tourism planning and policy processes.

*T*OWARDS A CRITICAL
3.2 HISTORY OF TOURISM
PLANNING AND POLICY

Compiling a history of tourism policy and planning is complex because stories of history are imbued with meaning; that is, the study of history is a means to identify and explain what issues, values and beliefs were important (or unimportant) at a certain time and how values and value systems influenced individuals', groups' and agencies' decisions, actions and events. History involves more than a chronology of events. Cultural history, for example, alerts us to the many angles or viewpoints from which history can be constructed. It identifies the risks of generalised or superficial versions of history and the inherent flimsiness of historical accounts that empower a single dominant perspective and reduce the significance of other (competing or alternative) perspectives. Cultural historians argue that acknowledging multiple viewpoints creates richer and more diverse accounts of history that, to some greater extent, enable 'silent' and disempowered (or weaker) voices to be heard. In this context, some cultural historians argue that the sources of information and the frameworks of understanding that are employed by historians should be clearly explained.

The history of tourism was explored in the seminal work of John Urry, a noted sociologist (1990, 1995). Urry traced the development of tourism in the context of the transcendental restructuring of social and economic systems over the last two centuries. Stephen Britton (1991), a geographer, explored the historico-spatial development of tourism with reference to social and economic processes. Davidson and Spearitt (2000), the latter a well-known historian, examined the development of tourism in Australia and drew together the cultural shifts taking place and the rise of increasingly powerful business interests in tourism. John Richardson (1999), a former tourism consultant, journalist and general manager of the Australian Tourist Commission, presented a 'history of the business of Australian travel and tourism'. Actually this description, which is by Richardson himself, probably does the book some injustice. In fact, it is broader in scope than business because, among other things, it does indeed amply demonstrate that 'The history of Australian tourism represents a significant contribution to the development of Australian nationhood' (Richardson 1999: 334). *Then There Were None*, a video written and directed by Elizabeth Kapuuwailani Lindsey, recounts how Hawaiians, on the verge of extinction, were displaced by outside influences and how the island and its culture have been 'sold off'.

Each of the above contributors or writers presented history according to their life and educational experiences and understandings. But these are only a few of many factors that influence the way history is presented. Here we discuss a further five factors that influence the way history is told.

◾ *3.2.1* Historical *settings and context*

The history of tourism planning and policy cannot exist outside its settings and context: society, politics, culture and economic systems are the 'superstructures' that support and give meaning to history (Gordon 2004). For example, dominating political platforms or themes shift and change over time so that a tourism project or policy initiative's acceptability can also shift and change in line with current thinking. Hence any examination of tourism planning and policy must be considered in the context of a rich history of ideas and influences that shape it and the setting and context in which planning and policy-making actually took place.

◾ *3.2.2* Constraints

There are many versions of history, but pragmatic boundaries are generally drawn around what is useful and relevant to present contexts. For example, given time and other constraints, it might be possible to present only a partial history that can contribute to, but not wholly explain, policy events and circumstances. Tourism policy analysts might choose a single and specific period to interrogate, or institutional boundaries might be used to define the study such as Peter Carroll's investigation of federal tourism agencies in Australia (Carroll 1991). Among many possible orientations, a history of tourism planning and policy could adopt one or more of the following perspectives:

- the practice of tourism planning and policy
- the theory of tourism planning and policy
- the nature of government involvement in tourism
- the process of planning and policy-making
- the roles of interest groups and significant individuals
- the nature of relationships between government, civil society and business, and
- the influence of academies and individual academics on planning and policy theory and practice.

■ 3.2.3 Values *and value systems*

The idea that there are several versions of history (or events) can be traced to people's values and value systems, their interests, their areas of expertise, the information to which they have access and whether or not they are motivated by a desire to interpret history in particular ways and give events particular meanings. As noted in chapter 2, one's 'attachment to' or preference for a particular theory of the state will influence explanations of 'what happened'.

■ 3.2.4 Inherent *bias*

Much of our information about what happened in the past comes from what was written, from individuals who might or might not still be around to give their versions of events, recordings of conversations, television documentaries, archaeological finds and other sources. Books, journals, diaries, committee minutes, cabinet documents and letters all carry meanings forward; all carry the inherent biases of their writers, as do art and music. How can we distinguish truth from fiction or right from wrong? Little wonder that our interpretations of history vary.

■ 3.2.5 History *as more than description*

History is not simply about description. History should seek to identify and interpret the meanings and influences of historical cues on current events and circumstances. In particular, the power and influence of ideas and knowledge about governments' roles and responsibilities and how governments should address tourism are important.

Tourism planning and policy history focuses on the positions, strategies, products or processes adopted by government to address diverse public issues associated with tourism. In this sense, the aim of this history of tourism planning and policy is to discuss both the substantive ideas and procedural directions that have been evident in government approaches to tourism over time. This history is set within a number of broader contexts and themes: theoretical developments taking place in political economy and the social sciences; broader sociocultural and economic processes; and shifts in political and public administration ideology that influenced what governments have done and how and why they did it. These contexts and themes are explored in more detail in later chapters. We now turn our attention to the history of thought that influences the social sciences and policy studies, beginning with the period known as the Enlightenment.

3.3 SOCIAL SCIENCES AND POLICY STUDIES

■ 3.3.1 The Enlightenment

The **Enlightenment**, also known as the 'Age of Reason', was an intellectual movement that occurred in Europe and spanned much of the fifteenth to the nineteenth centuries, although some scholars date it back further to the thirteenth and fourteenth centuries. Whatever the case, the term 'Enlightenment' denotes a scholarly breaking with the darkness of blind religious faith and ignorance to a new and enlightened truth based on science and scientific method. During the Enlightenment, dominating religious explanations of the world were rejected in favour of increasingly rational and scientific understandings of the social and physical worlds. The movement had, as a core tenet, that religion, superstition and ignorance were sources of human misery and that progress could be achieved only by applying scientific observation and objective reasoning (Hollinger 1994). Contributing to this scientific view of the world was a range of inventors, explorers and philosophers who argued for the application of mathematical or scientific methods to understand the natural world, for example Galileo (1564–1642) and Isaac Newton (1642–1727). Innovation and technology were consequences of this new paradigm of building knowledge.

■ 3.3.2 The Enlightenment *and the social sciences*

At the same time as the Enlightenment was challenging traditional understandings of the natural world in Europe, discoveries of new worlds and new cultures in the Americas and in Asia had a profound influence on the study of the social sciences. As part of this emergent interest in the social sciences, a number of Enlightenment thinkers devoted attention to age-old tensions between the public and private spheres. The struggle to understand the independence of 'public' and 'private' is central to the way governments conduct their business and what actions they take in planning and public policy formulation. Accordingly, the following discussion highlights the way philosophical argument about the extent and nature of government involvement in private matters has influenced broad shifts in policy-making and government action over time.

3.3.3 The Enlightenment: *politics, the economy and government*

Several philosophers of the Enlightenment influenced thinking about policy and government action. Table 3.1 summarises the contributions of a range of thinkers about social science, economics and the role of government from the Enlightenment onwards. The discussion below briefly elaborates on the development of critical thought with respect to power, politics and statecraft. These developments are important because they illustrate the range of critical ideas about relationships between politics, the economy and the role of government that developed during this period.

■ **Table 3.1**   *Influential thinkers in the social sciences, economics and government*

INFLUENTIAL THINKERS	DATES	MAIN CONTRIBUTION
Nicolo Machiavelli	1469–1527	Machiavelli, a politician and diplomat, is best known for his work *The Prince*, which is a practical guide to the exercise of power in Renaissance Europe. Machiavelli argued that deceit and judicious use of the truth were useful in maintaining power.
Francis Bacon	1561–1621	Bacon was a lawyer and philosopher. He developed the inductive method of inquiry, which ran contrary to prevailing beliefs in religious faith. Bacon coined the phrase 'knowledge is power'.
Benedict de Spinoza	1632–1677	Spinoza is best remembered for his work *Ethics*, which argues that God and nature are inseparable. He also argues that human behaviour is predictable because it is deterministic and hedonistic and that governments should seek to liberate people.
Jean-Jacques Rousseau	1712–1778	An important member of the French Enlightenment, Rousseau argued that liberty and equality should be the object of policy. Outraged by the inequalities of his own society, Rousseau believed that man's freedom lay in pursuing self-interest but that governments impeded this.
Jeremy Bentham	1748–1832	Bentham was a utilitarian philosopher, political economist, lawyer and legal reformer. His writings focused on the utilitarian ideal of a society whereby 'the greatest happiness' could be achieved by 'the greatest number'. He was enthusiastic about government efficiency, justice and democracy. He shared Adam Smith's views about individual economic freedoms and was critical of the rigid class structure that characterised the Britain of the day.
James Mill	1773–1836	With his good friend Jeremy Bentham, James Mill developed the utilitarian ideas about the 'greatest happiness for the greatest number'.
Auguste Comte	1798–1857	Often regarded as the 'Father of Positivism', Comte used observation and experimentation to develop knowledge. Comte believed that the key to social problems lay in developing a science of sociology.

INFLUENTIAL THINKERS	DATES	MAIN CONTRIBUTION
Karl Marx	1818–1883	Marx considered history to be a struggle between social classes. The struggle stemmed from the way society reproduced its existence from day to day. The way society allocates or distributes labour and other resources of production and precisely who gets what perpetuates differential relations. According to Marx, 'The executive of the modern state is but a committee for managing the common affairs of the whole bourgeoisie.'
Frederick Taylor	1856–1915	Taylor is best known for his work on the principles of scientific management (1911). Taylor's scientific studies of industrial production improved the efficiency of firms, and 'Taylorism' became a widely adopted management approach.
Thorstein Veblen	1857–1929	Veblen, an economist and sociologist, is best known for his satirical examination of American society in *The Theory of the Leisure Class* (1899). He argued that culture influenced economics and coined the term 'conspicuous consumption'.
Max Weber	1864–1920	Weber was a political economist and sociologist whose work examined the sociology of government and politics. He wrote of the bureaucratisation of society and the hierarchical structure of the civil service. His works were influential in the expansion and structuring of bureaucracy in the early twentieth century.
John Maynard Keynes	1883–1946	Best known for his work *The General Theory of Employment, Interest and Money*, Keynes argued that government policies could be used to promote demand at a macro level and to fight high unemployment and deflation. He argued against the prevailing liberalist philosophies of the time, which proposed that there was an automatic tendency in markets to move towards full employment and production.
Friedrich Hayek	1899–1992	Hayek's writings are grounded in works of Adam Smith, and he is widely regarded as responsible for the re-emergence of liberalism in the latter part of the twentieth century.
Karl Popper	1902–94	Popper was a Professor of Logic and Scientific Method at the London School of Economics. Popper argued that public policy should seek to 'minimise avoidable suffering', which represented a divergence from the utilitarian argument of the 'greatest happiness'. Popper argued for an evolutionary approach to understanding and that critical feedback and successive adjustments were necessary. This observation led to the notion of incrementalism.

Nicolo Machiavelli (1469–1527) and Francis Bacon (1561–1621) are often referred to as the philosophical fathers of policy studies. As noted in chapter 1, Machiavelli's *The Prince* (1515) made insightful observations about the working of politics, human behaviour, ethics and morals and, among his contributions, he argued that good leaders require cunning and deceit in order to do good. Even today, *The Prince* is considered to be a classic exposition of the way elites need to manipulate moral, theological and ethical codes in order to maintain power; after all, power is paramount. And, as Parsons (1995) so acutely observes, *The Prince* still resonates with modern politics and political method, or 'statecraft', today.

Francis Bacon, on the other hand, examined policy as a rational course of action. He argued that knowledge was power and that, in order to maintain power, leaders were required to build support and legitimacy by using knowledge. Knowledge, he believed, would be the cornerstone of a rational political order and, to this extent, his works were influential in the formation of universities and learned societies from the late seventeenth century (Parsons 1995).

Benedict de Spinoza (1632–1677) was a rationalist, believing in the power of knowledge. He believed that God was in nature; everything is God. Good and evil exist only in so far as an individual thinks good and evil to be; God loves or hates no one. Spinoza saw power (or rights) as the essence of government, which should seek to liberate people. Spinoza defended free speech and religious choice.

Philosophers in the latter part of the eighteenth century, influenced by **utilitarianism**, argued that the actions of government should be underpinned by the principle of maximising the best outcome for the largest number of people. Jean-Jacques Rousseau (1712–1778) wrote influential works, including *Social Contract* and *Discourse on the Causes of Inequality Among Men*. The former states, 'Man is born free, and everywhere he is in chains'. Rousseau's work over the term of his life was laced with contradictions concerning society and social order, yet this might also be an important characteristic of his work: bringing to life contradictions in society and social order. Rousseau considered all men to be equal but that society and its institutions negated their freedom and brought about inequality. He disputed notions of private property and believed that states should act morally and preserve the freedom of the people.

Heavily influenced by **scientific rationality**, such philosophers as Jeremy Bentham (1748–1832) and James Mill (1773–1836) believed it was possible to anticipate and measure policy outcomes and to choose courses of action on the basis of their expected outcomes. This thinking later gave rise to a rational logic approach that was used to evaluate different courses of action that could be taken by government and to aid in decision-making. In other words, good information should lead to good decisions, which should, in turn, lead to good consequences or outcomes (Parsons 1995).

Through Enlightenment, then, it was thought that knowledge, reason and science could liberate society, but there was disagreement in the detail. Into the philosophical debates, a range of economists contributed ideas about the nature and extent of government involvement in the pursuit of societal prosperity and freedom.

The Classical School of Economics has its origins in the mid-eighteenth century and contributes some powerful ideas about the interdependence of public and private interests. Early economists were influenced by the thinkers of that age: philosophers and those working in the natural sciences. The concept of an economic machine emerged. It possessed several key elements: everything is related to everything else; there are laws defining the operation of the machine; individuals coalesce in and around various groups or classes; barriers to trade should not exist and nations should be free to pursue their self-interest and maximise the world's wealth; individuals, too, ought to be able to pursue, without government regulation, their self-interests so as to maximise the economic welfare of society. This latter concept reflects the notion of the invisible hand, inspired by Adam Smith.

TOURISM PLANNING BREAKTHROUGH
Adam Smith's invisible hand

Adam Smith was a professor of philosophy, although his book, *An Inquiry into the Nature and Causes of the Wealth of Nations* (1776), is generally regarded as a work of economics. In this book he uses the metaphor of the 'invisible hand' to describe the unintended positive outcomes for society in which people work for their own benefit:

> . . . every individual necessarily labours to render the annual revenue of the society as great as he can. He generally, indeed, neither intends to promote the public interest, nor knows how much he is promoting it. By preferring the support of domestic to that of foreign industry, he intends only his own security; and by directing that industry in such a manner as its produce may be of the greatest value, he intends only his own gain and he is in this, as in many other cases, led by an invisible hand to promote an end which was no part of his intention. Nor is it always the worse for the society that it was no part of it. By pursuing his own interest he frequently promotes that of the society more effectually than when he really intends to promote it. I have never known much good done by those who affected to trade for the public good.

In 1776, Adam Smith (in his *Inquiry into the Nature and Causes of the Wealth of Nations*) argued against those (the mercantilists) who supported the idea that nation states should retain their wealth within their borders. Smith argued that states engage in trade and exchange. He praised the virtues of competition and highlighted the importance of manufacturing while challenging the primacy of agriculture. He noted the importance of specialisation and the division of labour, pointing out that productivity was linked to labour skills. Labour had an exchange value. Prices were determined by the interactions of supply and demand. Market economies left to themselves without government intervention (laissez-faire), tended to reach equilibrium. As capitalists pursued their interests, they contributed to the welfare of others, 'led by an invisible hand to promote an end which was no part of his intention'. In other words, public interest was most likely served when economic freedoms were allowed to operate unfettered. Public and private interests converged at this point. However, Adam Smith is sometimes misunderstood or misread. He criticised capitalism and did not advocate a completely free market. Smith criticised owners' retention of profits when they would not raise wages. He advocated taxes on wealth. Smith also believed interest rates ought to be regulated or limited and that some types of infrastructure ought to remain in public ownership.

Karl Marx (1818–1883) thought about the state very differently from Adam Smith and rejected the notion of free markets. Marx was concerned with the historical forces driving development and most particularly the significance of economics and economic life in the determination of the political administration and public interest. There was a clear and unambiguous division between the ruling class (the bourgeoisie who owned and controlled the means of production) and the people who worked for wages (the proletariat). These workers were alienated from what they produced, from other workers and from the entire work process. Marx and Engels wrote in *The Communist Manifesto* (1842: 79, 83, 85), 'The history of all hitherto existing society is the history of class struggles ... The need of a constantly expanding market for its products chases the bourgeoisie over the whole surface of the globe. It must nestle everywhere, settle everywhere, establish connexions everywhere ... The bourgeoisie, during its rule of scarce one hundred years, has created more massive and more colossal productive forces than have all preceding generations together.' Marx considered the economic base and the political base as intertwined. Civil society was dominated by class struggle and, more pointedly, the proletariat was dominated by the bourgeoisie. Marx believed that, ultimately, the class struggle would end by a proletarian revolution leading to the overthrow of the bourgeoisie.

It is worth noting that Karl Marx was practically ignored by his contemporaries, but has been highly influential, especially among the socialist movement. Instead, the liberal ideas of Adam Smith and his protagonists continued to dominate at a time when industrialisation was bringing transcendental changes to society.

3.4 *M*ODERNITY

■ 3.4.1 **Modernity** *and the social sciences*

Modernity is the term used to characterise the complex social, economic and political processes that, from the latter part of the nineteenth century to the mid-twentieth century, resulted from the intellectual and technological advances of the Enlightenment. Modernism is profoundly difficult to define and, despite having been the subject of considerable philosophical interrogation, it still remains unclear whether it is a period, a process, a style, a theme or a context (Rosenau 1992; Hollinger 1994).

At the risk of oversimplification, modernity's origins coincided with the Industrial Revolution, the predominance of classical economic theory, the rise of democracy and the emergence of leisure. The Industrial Revolution brought about a rapid rise in living standards, but this was by no means universal or spread equitably. Technological innovation and industrialisation stimulated mass production and the emergence of a class of industrialists possessing considerable political and economic power. Efforts to increase productivity and accelerate capital accumulation required increasingly organised and specialised workforces. The restructuring of work together with workers' lower levels or complete lack of direct contact with their bosses induced a loss of identity. Some workers and work groups were exploited and undervalued. Employees were no longer valued as individual creative talents involved in artisan work as they were in the Middle Ages. Mass production redefined workers as tradable commodities in the production process (Rojek 1993).

The Industrial Revolution was accompanied by social, environmental and economic impacts that accentuated differences between the 'haves' and the 'have-nots'. A growing number of philosophers, educated industrialists and philanthropists realised that the dominant laissez-faire, free market approach was having a negative effect on society in general and workers — the source of labour and production — in particular. A strong social welfare reform movement emerged, and Adam Smith's idea of the invisible hand was increasingly challenged.

Governments became more concerned with improving working conditions and creating healthy and productive environments for workers, thereby increasing productivity. Happy, healthy workers and prosperous industrialists were likely to return governments to office! Through collective action, organised workers gained political power to obtain improved working conditions and pay. Among many changes that took place between the mid-nineteenth and twentieth centuries, governments regulated working hours, agreed on minimum wages and legislated workers' rights to recreational leave. These events increased disposable incomes and fuelled consumption. Improved access to leisure time led to the development of service industries. Greater, although far from universal, public access to education, health and infrastructure was achieved. Larger numbers of workers could now travel to the seaside and the countryside, and it was not uncommon for large companies to sponsor picnic days at seaside or country destinations. These changes had a profound influence on patterns of leisure and tourism and gave rise to early forms of mass tourism that continued into the twentieth century (Soane 1993; Urry 1995).

Influenced by these massive changes, Thorstein Veblen, widely considered the father of 'institutional economics', wrote *The Theory of the Leisure Class* (1899). Veblen was interested in inequality and institutional and business behaviour. He sought to explain the ways these manifested themselves in society. Veblen was a strong opponent of industrial society. He believed it encouraged wasteful practices, was overly competitive and encouraged conspicuous consumption. Governments and authorities were more concerned with powerful businessmen and the profitability of their enterprises than with democratic principles and economic, social and political equality.

Veblen was writing in a period when expanding business empires and the accumulation of wealth were central to Americans. Veblen shunned their visible signs of success such as wasteful and lavish expenditure on expensive clothing and jewellery (which he termed conspicuous consumption). He criticised businessmen for making money out of unproductive enterprise and capitalistic 'sabotage', in which people were sacked or businesses closed if prices and/or profits fell too low.

Over time, it became obvious that the 'invisible hand' of the market could not bring equilibrium to public and private interests and liberate society. Government intervention was required. Along with technology and innovation, the dominance of classical economics had also brought with it an emphasis on individualism, consumerism, secularisation and capitalism. These and other 'isms' have had a profound and not necessarily wholly positive influence on contemporary societies, human rights and social justice. Moreover, critics question the claims of Enlightenment philosophers that a rational, objective society could liberate humanity, arguing instead that modernism has brought oppression and subjugation (Rosenau 1992).

3.4.2 Modernity *and the role of government*

Under modernity, links between emerging research in the social sciences and government became clearer as intellectuals grappled with the influence of modernity on society. As Hollinger (1994: 3) explains: 'The rise of the social sciences thus began with the need to understand modernization. The rise of market capitalism and the modern state and the growing influence of Newtonian physics, in all areas of life, called for understanding and also for prediction, because predictability meant some stability and control in tumultuous times.'

Attempts to understand the influence of modernity on social life were heavily influenced by positivism. **Positivism** denotes a commitment to rational scientific explanations of cause and effect and the belief that a single, real and objective truth exists. This paradigm, or predominating view, was widely held within the natural sciences and was perhaps first applied to the social sciences in the early nineteenth century (during the latter stages of the Enlightenment and the onset of modernism) by Auguste Comte (1778–1857). Interestingly, it was about this time that Marx was shaping and writing his political economic ideas.

By the late nineteenth century, debates started to emerge about the role of government in protecting public interests. Laissez-faire liberal economic development had brought with it many unintended social, economic and environmental consequences, and the private sphere had shown little interest in dealing with these issues. In the late 1880s Woodrow Wilson had argued that the role of bureaucracy was to defend public interests, that the public service was a professional career and that public servants required a moral code to undertake their duties. These ideas were later taken up and developed by Max Weber, with powerful consequences for the growth of bureaucracy in the twentieth century (see chapter 4 for a more detailed examination of Weber's ideas). For Weber, public administration was the best and most rational means of promoting the public interest. He believed that the division of the state into a political arm and a bureaucratic arm was the most effective way to achieve a strong and rational public administration. Furthermore, the hierarchical organisation of bureaucracy and divisions of roles and responsibilities into specialised jurisdictions was a technically superior approach that provided the opportunity for rational planning and management. Weber's ideas provided a powerful stimulus for the twentieth-century state eager to legitimate its role as a defender of public interests and to ameliorate the consequences of public problems. These ideas promoted the development of large bureaucracies during the early part of the twentieth century. However, Weber also noted that there were risks associated with bureaucracy, namely depersonalisation and bureaucratisation (Ham & Hill 1993).

In 1911, Frederick Taylor laid out a series of rational scientific principles for public administration that were to become known as Taylorism (see section 4.2.1 for a more detailed discussion of Taylor's contributions). These principles, summarised in table 3.2, became powerful organising principles for government and had a profound influence on theories of organisations, the nature of policy-making and the extent and nature of government involvement in public issues for most of the twentieth century (Hughes 2003).

■ Table 3.2
Shifts from public administration to public management

PRINCIPLE	PUBLIC ADMINISTRATION PRE-1970	PUBLIC MANAGEMENT POST-1970
Principle of bureaucracy	Governments should organise themselves according to classic principles of bureaucracy and hierarchy articulated by Max Weber.	Rigid bureaucracy was not the only approach.
Principle of administrative procedure	Administrative procedures could be set out in manuals that administrators could follow.	Not all public issues and problems required the same treatment; flexible management practices had advantages.
Principle of bureaucratic delivery	Principle of bureaucratic delivery meant that once involved in a policy area, governments would become the provider of goods and services.	Public bureaucratic delivery is not the only or necessarily the most efficient way of implementing policy.
Principle of separating politics and bureaucracy	Politics and public administration should be separated such that politics retained a decision-making function and public administration involved the implementation of that decision.	Politics and bureaucracy are intertwined and not easily separated.
Principle of public interest	Public servants would serve the 'public' interest and that the role of the bureaucracy was to serve the pubic objectively and selflessly.	Public servants can be motivated by other factors not necessarily in the public interest.
Principle of a professional bureaucracy	Public administration requires a specialised professional expertise that does not exist outside bureaucracy.	Expertise exists both inside and outside bureaucracy; contemporary public sector tasks involve managerial skills, not administrative or procedural skills.

Source: *adapted from Hughes 2003 and Ham & Hill 1993.*

Widespread adoption of Taylorist principles resulted in governments adopting rational comprehensive approaches to planning and policy-making. Issues were identified and analysed with clinical objectivity, and 'blueprint' solutions were developed and implemented by government. It was not until the mid-twentieth century that waves of criticism about scientific rationality and criticisms of bureaucratic principles began to emerge.

◼ 3.4.3 Postmodernism

By the 1960s, the well-established rational scientific paradigm was increasingly being criticised, and a new wave of social science development began to have far-reaching implications for understanding societal issues and problems (Giddens 1990). At the time, the emerging perspectives in the social sciences began to challenge disciplinary boundaries and to fuel growing suspicion of broad assumptions and overarching theories of cause and consequence that had previously dominated the social sciences under modernism. This movement has generally become known as postmodernism, a rather contentious term frequently criticised by many people whose work most closely aligns with the term. Important also is the notion that postmodernism is not a shift away from the rational and technical approaches of modernism, but rather a critique that has developed over the last 150 years and which gained prominence from around the 1960s.

Postmodernism is characterised by a rejection of overarching theoretical foundations in favour of free-floating and pragmatic approaches to understanding social change (Fraser & Nicholson 1988). It recognises that there are multiple ways of framing social issues and building understandings. There is no single overarching truth. Researchers often have deeply embedded ideas, beliefs and means of analysis from which to view a social problem. Hence they have the potential to neglect or prejudice other views and explanations of complex social issues.

William James (1842–1910) and John Dewey (1859–1952) contributed to the development of pragmatism, which has had an important influence on political science and policy studies. In the wake of Charles Darwin's *Origin of Species by Natural Selection* (1859), William James, a doctor with an interest in biology and adaptation, argued that it was important to open oneself to empirical knowledge and that it was possible to improve and adapt policies via reflection and empirical knowledge. Later, and among the many ideas Dewey contributed, he saw progress as a process of social experimentation and that societal problems could be solved by learning and testing. Both William James and John Dewey contributed significantly to the idea of **pragmatism** in the policy sciences, whereby democratic policy-making has been understood as a process of problem-solving based on empirical knowledge for societal progress and betterment.

The main interests of Karl Popper (1902–1994) were in the conflicts between science and politics, admonishing positivism and criticising rational scientific models of policy development. Popper believed that facts do not exist separately from perceptions and values; that politics was therefore inevitably involved in policy; and that social progress could not be made in large-scale change. He argued that change was a slow process of trial, error and learning, terming this idea 'piecemeal social engineering' (Parsons 1995: 49). Popper's piecemeal social engineering was accepted by postmodern policy analysts eager to demonstrate the incremental way policy-making occurs.

In the early part of the century, John Maynard Keynes revolutionised the way governments work and spend money with the publication of *A General Theory of Employment, Interest and Money* (1936). Keynes condemned laissez-faire economic policy as he encouraged greater expenditure by governments in order to promote growth. Keynes' ideas helped stimulate the development of large bureaucracies. Keynes helped return the attention of economists to macro issues and attacked Adam Smith's notion of the 'invisible hand'. He argued that unemployment was not voluntary, that it can 'drag on' and that governments should stimulate demand for economic reasons. Keynes' thinking inspired governments to invest heavily in order to stimulate employment by undertaking large-scale investment in public infrastructure and encouraging development by using incentives.

By the 1960s, big bureaucracy was increasingly under attack. Criticisms of the inefficiencies and ineffectiveness of large-scale public administration, lack of coordination between departments, divisions of departments and isolation from the public were emerging (see chapter 4). Ripples of support for principles of individualism and the benefits of market freedoms were emerging from members of the 'new right' (e.g. Friedrich Hayek and others). Inflation, rising unemployment and restructuring of industrial manufacturing were among a vast sea of conditions contributing to the re-emergence of ideas that the free market and competition would provide more effective solutions to societal problems, and that large government impedes creativity and problem-solving.

Against this background, Amitai Etzioni, a sociologist, contributed a number of important ideas to public policy. Among other things, Etzioni argued for **communitarianism** and hence a return to an emphasis on individual and community responsibilities in policy-making. Etzioni was convinced that neither market freedom nor government intervention were in and of themselves the answers to achieving public interest (Etzioni 1969, 1996).

■ *3.4.4* Contemporary *planning and policy*

These waves of development in the social sciences, combined with the massive restructuring of global social and economic systems since the 1950s, have had a profound influence on government approaches to planning and policy. Ostrom (1989) observed two opposing forms of public administration — bureaucracy and markets — and that, since around the 1930s, a gradual and significant shift in the public sector has taken place from bureaucracy to market management. Etzioni contributed a third form, that of communitarianism, which has formed the basis of efforts to reinsert social values into policy-making. The traditional bureaucratic model, articulated in the principles of Taylorism (see table 3.2), advocated heavy government involvement and intervention in issues of public significance. Under this model, bureaucrats have significant power to identify problems and solutions on the basis of the unquestioned expertise of the professional bureaucracy.

Since the 1950s, however, the principles of Taylorism have gradually been rejected in favour of a market-based approach to public management. This new approach has been characterised by a move towards a more participatory style of policy-making, which embraces many government and non-government actors and agencies.

From the shifts taking place in the social sciences, and the transformations in the way that governments perceived their roles and relationships with civil society and business, there has come a renewed interest in the liberal philosophies. **Neoliberalism**, as it has come to be known, is an influential political ideology that has enjoyed a revival in many Western economies since the 1970s. Its origins are found in the laissez-faire doctrines of the nineteenth century when governments embraced free market capitalism as a driver of economic and social growth and adopted a 'hands-off' approach to many areas of public policy. Neoliberalism is based on a premise that government intervention results in market inefficiencies and can impede market development and economic growth. However, it has misread the fathers of classical economics — Adam Smith in particular. Smith actually believed government intervention was needed. He did not, as some believe, adhere to notions of a completely free-market state. Neoliberals have a vulgar or mutated interpretation of classical economics. Indeed, when one reads or hears their utterances and interpretations of policy it seems that perhaps they have not interrogated Adam Smith's work closely enough but simply adopted the aspects that suit their purposes and interests.

As a political ideology, neoliberalism, which lacks a strong theoretical foundation, has had a profound influence on the way governments have defined their roles and executed their responsibilities since the 1970s. There has been a strong push in many countries to downsize government and to divest it of responsibilities to the private sector through corporatisation, privatisation and the shedding of 'non-essential' assets. This has resulted in a 'hollowing out' of government. A strong emphasis on the efficiency and effectiveness of policy has been accompanied by interrelated efforts to measure, benchmark and evaluate policy outcomes. With this general history of social sciences and policy studies in mind, we can now examine the development of various lines of thought in tourism planning.

3.5 TOURISM: A HISTORICAL OVERVIEW

It is important to understand the historical roots of tourism policy in order to understand the driving values and ideas that have led to contemporary tourism planning and policy issues and problems. Current policy issues and problems frequently have historical underpinnings.

3.5.1 Pre-modern *tourism*

Before the emergence of Neolithic settlements, nomadic lifestyles involved travel, but the idea of travel between origin and destination, as the basis of tourism, did not exist. The first permanent settlements started to emerge around 5000 BCE, and from that time people have been travelling and engaging in tourism. There is evidence that travel, predominantly for the purposes of trade, military activities, government administration and spiritual and family matters, was part of life in the Neolithic communities of Mesopotamia and China and later in the ancient civilisations of Greece, Egypt and the Roman Empire (Mumford 1961). In Greece, for example, there was much travel between Greek city states and trade locations surrounding the Mediterranean. The Olympic Games was also an important event that generated significant travel (Weaver & Lawton 2002).

In Ancient Rome, the push to colonise and expand the empire led to massive growth in travel. The Romans were also highly skilled engineers, so the development of extensive road networks, bridges and other public infrastructure facilitated the growth of travel. Resort towns were used to extend the colonisation process. Towns, characterised by the construction of significant public infrastructure, including baths and theatres, were located in places where people could take advantage of natural springs and where soldiers and wealthy Romans could seek rest and respite. Bath (UK), Tiberias (Israel) and Saint Rafael (France) are examples of Roman resorts that have remained popular visitor attractions. In brief, travel has been part of human activity since pre-modern times, but direct government involvement in tourism, and hence tourism planning and policy, is a relatively recent activity.

3.5.2 Industrialisation *and tourism*

The regulation of working hours and increased recreation leave, coupled with technological developments, such as the development of the steam engine and railways during the nineteenth century, meant that travel became less costly and more accessible to the masses. At the time, environmental problems associated with industrialisation and rapid urbanisation prompted a romanticised appreciation of the sea and countryside that was reflected in the poetry, literature, paintings and newspaper communications of the day. People flocked to the countryside and seaside as a way of escaping the smells and disease of the city, prompting the development of new resort towns such as those of Brighton (UK), Mornington and Manly (Australia), Rotorua (New Zealand) and Banff (Canada).

Governments responded by constructing railways to carry passengers to these destinations. This new appreciation of the environment also prompted the emergence of the bushwalking and conservation and national park movements. Governments allocated parkland, nature reserves and national parks in diverse locations across Europe, North America and Australia. These actions can be considered as some of the first types of government involvement in tourism and travel, although such involvement did not always directly refer to tourism *per se*.

During the turbulent years of land settlement in Australia in the nineteenth century, for example, there were significant developments on the recreation and domestic tourism front. The population swelled dramatically during the gold rush of the 1850s, recreation activities became increasingly diverse and demand for recreational areas grew. The pressures on the city of Sydney intensified because its sewerage disposal was inadequate (posing serious threats to people's health) and because of overcrowding. Many people wanted to escape the city, among other things, for their leisure.

By the late nineteenth century, public recreation encompassed a wide range of activities, including spectator sports (e.g. cricket, boxing and racing); shooting and fishing, which were popular among all classes; golf and bowls, which were popular among the wealthy; picnics, which were popular with families; boating and, later as it increased in popularity and respectability, bathing; cycling, which by the 1890s was 'all the rage'; and finally, walking and then hiking became popular 'as people broke from main roads and paths and struck out into the bush' (Pettigrew & Lyons 1979: 18). Growth in recreation participation and pressures on outdoor recreation resources was subsequently reflected in legislative and policy developments in New South Wales and other Australian colonies.

In 1863, the first laws to protect 'scenic areas' were passed in Tasmania; that same year Jenolan Caves, in the Blue Mountains, New South Wales, was set aside as a public reserve; and in 1872 Kings Park, Perth, Western Australia, was set aside for public use (Comben 1996). Australia's first national park, 'National Park' (renamed Royal National Park in 1954), was established in 1879, mainly through the efforts of the New South Wales Zoological Society (whose goals centred on the introduction and acclimatisation of birds and animals) and Sir John Robertson, an influential politician, former Minister for Lands and Premier of New South Wales (see Pettigrew & Lyons 1979). The park comprised 7300 hectares of land (expanded to 14 000 hectares in 1880), which were set aside for 'public recreation' under the provisions of section 5 of the New South Wales *Crown Lands Alienation Act 1861* (Black & Breckwoldt 1977). Originally, the provision of public recreation opportunities (as in North America) was the primary objective of national parks in Australia; more generally, 'to ensure a healthy and consequently vigorous and intelligent community ... all cities, towns and villages should possess places of public recreation' (John Lucas, MLA, to Legislative Assembly, 21 March 1879, in Pettigrew & Lyons 1979: 15).

Robertson's proposal for such a park is most likely to have been influenced by the establishment of large parks that were being created on the outskirts of the expanding London metropolis and used for a variety of recreational activities from the mid-nineteenth century (Pettigrew & Lyons 1979: 18). Royal National Park provided holiday accommodation, sporting facilities and picnic areas. The emphasis was clearly on human pleasure and amusement, and exotic flora and fauna (e.g. a deer park was established in 1885) were introduced into the park.

From this background, then, it is possible to argue government was involved in stimulating early forms of tour create conditions suitable for the development of tourism. that stimulating tourism was important for economic therefore, government investment was in the public tourism was not a direct or explicit area of governmen. tourism development fostered an emerging service sector and created interest from wealthy investors eager to capitalise on the growing leisure services sector.

By the mid- to late nineteenth century, governments in many countries were actively involved in tourism. For example, governments helped to establish accommodation and tourist facilities at hot springs in Canada, Europe and parts of Asia. The New South Wales Government established visitor facilities at the Jenolan Caves, and the New Zealand Government established the Waitomo Hotel near caves of the same name in 1908. During this period, however, government action in fostering tourism development focused principally on local investment in railways, accommodation and tourist infrastructure, such as tracks and guardrails. This was a supply-driven approach largely aimed at managing visitation.

3.5.3 **Contemporary** *tourism*

Throughout the early part of the twentieth century domestic tourism continued to increase. Rapidly modernising economies meant that people had more leisure time and more disposable income. Visits to the seaside and countryside at weekends and on annual leave became more common, and some communities were transformed from humble roots into thriving leisure destinations (e.g. Dredge 2001; Lynch & Veal 2001). Most local governments struggled to deal with the influx of visitors and the management problems that resulted. For example, some communities often came under significant environmental and social pressures during the holiday season when such problems as uncontrolled camping on coastal foreshores gave rise to crowding and the need to manage effluent and waste.

International tourism was more limited during the first part of the twentieth century. However, in the post-1945 period, developments in transport technology such as automobiles, high-speed trains and jet air travel stimulated massive increases in international and domestic travel around the world to ever more remote and sensitive settings (Hall 1998; Richardson 1999). Increases in travel created new management issues for central and local governments, including visa regulations and controls, customs and security, spread of pests and diseases, currency regulation, destination management, transport and visitor management.

After World War II tremendous economic, social and political changes took place in Australia and overseas. Immigrants flowed from Europe across the world. International tourism arrivals increased, and travel for the purpose of 'visiting friends and relatives' increased dramatically. In the immediate post-war period, however, many governments were focused on restructuring their economies from wartime to peacetime, and tourism remained a low priority. In 1950, 25 million international arrivals were generated worldwide; however, by 2004 the figure had grown to more than 750 million (WTO 2005). Globally, tourism accounts for an estimated 7 per cent of goods and services exported, and in 2004 tourism ranked fourth in terms of export earnings behind chemicals, automotive products and fuel (WTO 2005). The growth in tourism worldwide since the 1950s and its increased economic importance have stimulated governments to take a greater interest in tourism.

Before the emergence of mass tourism in the 1950s, tourism was generally not a significant area of policy for government. Most governments were focused on managing a range of domestic issues, such as rapid industrialisation, war-time production, international relations and provision of infrastructure. Tourism was not a significant economic activity, and it tended to be managed on an ad hoc basis as issues and problems arose. In other words, government made policies that affected tourism, but there was no overall attempt to manage the tourism phenomena. Such policies ranged from managing standards of public decency at swimming beaches by separating male and female bathers, to provision of parks and reserves and rail services to popular coastal resorts to immigration and issuing visas. That is not to say that tourism had not been recognised as a potential area of government involvement. Rather, the priorities of governments lay elsewhere, and tourism was not perceived to be important enough to warrant government attention or resources.

By the 1980s, the growth in tourism worldwide was sufficient to stimulate widespread government interest in tourism as a form of economic development. At a time when the agricultural and industrial sectors were declining in importance, tourism was perceived to be a potentially important tool for regional economic development. Tourism was seen as an economic replacement activity: a way of attracting investment and generating employment for declining agricultural and industrial sectors. Developing countries in the Asia Pacific region, Central and South America and Africa began to focus on using tourism as a way of attracting investment in infrastructure and improving export earnings. Tourism was also seen as an important tool for economic development in major metropolitan areas and in rural and remote communities. For example, urban regions and global cities such as Sydney, London or Hong Kong compete on a global scale for capital investment and export earnings. Tourism is a tool for promoting identity, raising awareness and competing on the global economic stage.

Since the 1980s, tourism has found its way on to the agenda of most governments worldwide. However, it is increasingly being recognised that tourism is not a panacea for economic development and investment attraction. Other areas of concern, for example environmental management, national security and community well-being, have emerged as politically important issues. The following sections review some key developments in the planning and policy approaches of governments.

Ideas about tourism policy and planning can be broadly divided into two categories: (1) substantive ideas that provide the direction and underpinning values embedded in tourism policy and planning; and (2) procedural ideas that outline how tourism planning should be conducted and how policy should be developed. Each of these strands has been broadly influenced by historical thinking in the social sciences and by shifts in public administration. These two broad sets of ideas overlap and should not be thought of as discrete areas of theoretical or practical endeavour. In recent years, and as discussed at the end of this section, these two bodies of thought have coalesced in the development of communicative and collaborative planning.

3.6.1 Substantive ideas *about tourism policy and planning*

Few attempts have been made to classify, categorise and characterise the development of tourism planning theory and practice. Getz (1986) identifies four traditions or approaches to tourism planning according to the values that underpin the planning or policy activity:

- boosterism
- economic
- physical/spatial
- community.

Getz observes that these traditions are not necessarily sequential, nor are they mutually exclusive. In other words, a tourism planning activity could exhibit more than one approach. To these traditions and building on an enormous wave of attention to sustainable development throughout the 1980s, Hall (1998) added an additional approach, sustainable planning.

These traditions and approaches identified in tourism planning literature are useful insofar as they allow researchers and practitioners to reduce complex and intersecting streams of literature into neat, easily identifiable approaches, yet there is danger in such a simplistic and reductionist approach. Tourism planning and policy theory and practice are informed by a range of cultures, disciplines, methods and frameworks over time and across space (Macbeth 2005). Classifying the rich literature in tourism planning and policy into time periods or simplifying underpinning values (e.g. economics, community) has the potential to obscure the richness and diversity of tourism planning as a whole process and as a substantive body of ideas about tourism as a human activity, as a private and public sector activity and specifically as an area of government involvement.

The main criticism of the above approaches is that the development of tourism planning thought and practice has not been contextualised against the transcendental shifts taking place in social science thought and public administration ideology. At any one time there are different, often conflicting, ideas behind policy development and decision-making, and it is only against the context of these ideas, existing in different scales and in different disciplines, that an understanding of tourism planning and policy processes can be achieved.

Put simply, it is important to understand the evolution of tourism planning and policy as a dialectical process that is filtered through institutional contexts, issue drivers, actors and agencies and policy dialogues; through broad ideological debates and local politics. Six substantive approaches underpinning government approaches to tourism planning and policy can be identified running through this history (see table 3.3). They are interwoven into a rich context that reflects the development of tourism, shifts in public administration approaches and broader thinking taking place in the social sciences. As the following discussion reveals, these themes are not mutually exclusive, and they have received differing degrees of attention throughout recent history. At times, different themes have been simultaneously promoted by different agencies and at different scales, thereby making it impossible to equate a single theme with any one period in history. Our substantive approaches below improve on earlier attempts to categorise tourism planning approaches, as they reflect theoretical and ideological foundations and not just the peculiarities of disciplines or personal values and place.

■ Table 3.3
Substantive approaches to tourism planning and policy

THEME	EXPLANATION	EXAMPLE
Industry development planning and policy	Characterised by financial measures and tools (e.g. incentives, tax breaks, subsidies, grants) to assist in strengthening industry capacity	Industry clustering Industry network development Partnership and alliance building
Market planning and policy	Characterised by the use of mechanisms, tools and approaches to promote the development and expansion of markets; assuming that market growth will lead to product development and diversification	Subsidies for cooperative marketing schemes
Spacio-physical destination planning and policy	Characterised by spatial destination planning, modelling of relationships between attractions, services, origins and destinations, transport routes and nodes, marketing and information	Destination models Resort morphologies
Conflict management planning and policy	Characterised by the identification of consequences and measures to mitigate the social, cultural, environmental and economic effects of tourism on local destinations	Mediation of visitor/resident conflict
Communicative tourism planning and policy	Characterised by the desire to establish collaborative dialogue in which multiple interests are represented	Collaborative planning, round tables, partnership
Crisis-response planning and policy	Characterised by need to address crises as they emerge; draws from all the above themes	Recovery strategies for terrorist attacks and natural disasters

The evolution of tourism planning and policy, as with other social sciences, is best understood in terms of the broader ideological shifts taking place and their influence on the public administration ideologies and the structures and practices of government. Table 3.4 summarises the shifts that have occurred in social science theory, public administration ideology and tourism planning and policy since the 1960s. The following discussion outlines the broad evolutionary stages that have taken place in tourism policy and planning and should be read in conjunction with table 3.4.

■ **Table 3.4**
Historical development of tourism planning and policy studies

PERIOD	THEORETICAL DEVELOPMENTS IN SOCIAL SCIENCES	PUBLIC ADMINISTRATION IDEOLOGY	EMPHASIS OF TOURISM PLANNING AND POLICY STUDIES
1960s	• Positivism	• Central government dominance • Planning and policy development as a technical, bureaucratic activity	• Tourism planning and policy as a tool for socioeconomic development • Spatial modelling of destinations; normative methods of vacationscapes (see Gunn 1994) • Tourism planning and policy as a means of minimising negative consequences of tourism
1970s	• Critiques of modernism and positivism emerge • Postmodernism gains momentum	• Relationship between government and civil society increasingly questioned	• Infrastructure (supply-driven) tourism planning and policy development • Rational comprehensive tourism master planning • Market-driven planning and policy development
1980s	• Dismantling the notion of homogeneous public interest • Post-positivist policy research gains momentum • Recognition of researcher as an active agent in planning and policy processes	• Neoliberalism • Shift from public administration to new public management	• Community tourism planning (Murphy 1988) • Spatial destination planning (see Gunn 1994)

(continued)

PERIOD	THEORETICAL DEVELOPMENTS IN SOCIAL SCIENCES	PUBLIC ADMINISTRATION IDEOLOGY	EMPHASIS OF TOURISM PLANNING AND POLICY STUDIES
1990s	• Critical studies, discourses and the argumentative turn • Feminist and gender studies	• Increasing emphasis on governance structures and private–public sector partnerships	• Institutional influences on planning and policy development (Pearce 1992) • Integrated sustainable tourism development (Inskeep 1991) • Power, influence and politics in tourism planning (Richter 1989; Hall 1998; Hall & Jenkins 1995)
2000s	• Post-postmodernism	• Post-neoliberalism	• Business–industry relationships, corporatisation (Jenkins 2001) • Collaboration, partnerships (Bramwell & Lane 2000) • Industry self-regulation (Jenkins & Wearing 2003)

■ 3.6.2 **Early** *ad hoc approaches*

The development of tourism planning and policy as a separate area of government concern emerged in the 1950s and 1960s, although there is evidence to suggest that governments and politicians were interested in the economic benefits of tourism well before this time. For example, an international peak body, the International Congress of Official Tourism Traffic Organizations (a forerunner of the World Tourism Organization) was set up in 1925 to represent the public and private groups with an interest in tourism and to lobby for improved conditions to facilitate the growth of tourism worldwide.

Evidence in Australia suggests that as early as the 1930s local governments were interested in the promotion of tourism in their localities and politicians were interested in using tourism as a tool for regional economic development (see Planning in Practice: 'Tourism planning and policy in 1926'). Before the 1950s, government responses to tourism were relatively fragmented and ad hoc, and little systematic analysis of tourism activity was undertaken.

By the 1960s, advances in transport and communications technology had transformed tourism from a local and regional activity into a more widespread, even global, activity, and governments had become increasingly interested in harnessing economic benefits. The forerunner of the WTO, the IUOTO, undertook several studies of tourism markets and growth potential, and the OECD commissioned studies to examine the constraints and opportunities for tourism development in a number of developing countries. At the same time, geographers, economists, anthropologists and sociologists began to undertake more rigorous and informed analyses about the consequences of tourism growth and development, especially in developing countries.

PLANNING IN PRACTICE

Tourism planning and policy in 1926

Conference of Councils Tourist Bureau

A conference of the municipal councils of Newcastle and Stockton and the Lake Macquarie Shire was held in the council chambers, Watt Street, last night. This has been convened for the purposes of considering the question of establishing a Tourist Bureau in Newcastle. Mr W. Tweedie, deputy town clerk, acted as secretary to the conference.

Alderman H. P. Cornish, Mayor of Newcastle, said that all were probably conversant with the reasons for the conference. They failed to get the Government to establish a branch of the Tourist Bureau in Newcastle, and it was decided to try and do something on their own account. Newcastle had been looked upon as a place where they could get coal and steel, but they had more. They had quite a lot of attractions, many of them unique and beautiful.

Mr H. J. Lamble, Director of the Government Tourist Bureau, Sydney, explaining the basis upon which this was established, said the resorts, such as Kosciusko, were all returning a profit to the State. To ask the Government to establish a branch just to spend money was asking too much. There were no assets in the Newcastle district to bring the Government Bureau any return, but Newcastle and the other council had assets. Their beaches were assets. What he would suggest was a local tourist bureau in Newcastle, to operate the assets along commercial lines as best they could. He outlined what had been done by the Blue Mountains Council, which had invited neighbouring councils and shires to join in what they had done. The development side of the bureau's work would be important, and there was the showing of the facilities of travel.

Councillor Hardy, president of the Lake Macquarie Shire, said there was the question of maintaining the bureau. He would like to know how that was done.

The Mayor said that he had gone into that with Mr Tweedie during the afternoon, and the conference would be given information on that aspect of the proposal.

Source: Newcastle Morning Herald and Miner's Advocate, *19 August 1926 (p. 7).*

Varied government responses to these antecedents to tourism planning and policy began to emerge depending on the social, economic and physical conditions at the destination. Initially, the prevailing views of the time were heavily influenced by a strong 'boosterism' development ethic, which had emerged as a result of industrialisation and modernisation over the first half of the twentieth century. Governments sought to promote tourism growth, regional economic diversification and employment creation.

By the late 1960s and early 1970s, however, the small number of academics who had emanated from diverse disciplines to specialise in the study of tourism was growing. Applying their own disciplinary perspectives, these writers were becoming increasingly critical of the dominant economic boosterism approaches to tourism that were being adopted by governments across the world. Such publications as the seminal texts of noted anthropologist Valene Smith (*Hosts and Guests*, 1978) and Luis Turner (*The Golden Hordes*, 1975) adopted an anthropocentric view of tourism and raised concern for the impact of tourism on indigenous cultures, the undelivered promises of economic growth and improved standards of living in developing countries and the processes of economic colonisation that were occurring as a result of tourism. However, there is little evidence that these debates occurring in literature had any direct or immediate influence on government approaches to tourism. Indirectly, information about and understanding of tourism were growing, but it would be some time before a critical mass of scholars and research emerged and began to influence tourism planning and policy visibly in substantial ways.

■ 3.6.3 Physical *supply-led approaches*

By the late 1960s, attention by professionals and academics applying a spatial approach for planning and managing tourism (e.g. geographers, landscape architects, planners, officers in parks and recreation agencies) stimulated the emergence of a range of spatial planning techniques, models and approaches for tourism. Spatial master planning was consistent with prevailing ideas about the bureaucratic role of government and models of government intervention (e.g. Gunn 1994; Kaiser & Helber 1978). Governments had a tendency to be paternalistic and were characterised by centralised, technical plan-making. Tourism planning focused on destination layout and design. In this approach, tourism was broken down into spatial units, such as land uses, or spatial elements, including nodes, precincts, gateways and transport corridors. Gunn's Regional Planning Concept (1994), although by no means the only model, exemplifies this approach (see figure 3.1).

The spatial or physical approach to tourism planning regards tourism as a form of land use to be managed using spatial strategies. The consequences of tourism could be addressed by the spatial separation of hosts and guests or resident and tourist activities. It was also underpinned by a supply-led approach based on the principle that a well-planned physical destination would attract visitors (Gunn 1994); that is, in a typical

■ Figure 3.1

■ Figure 3.1

*Gunn's
Regional
Planning
Concept*

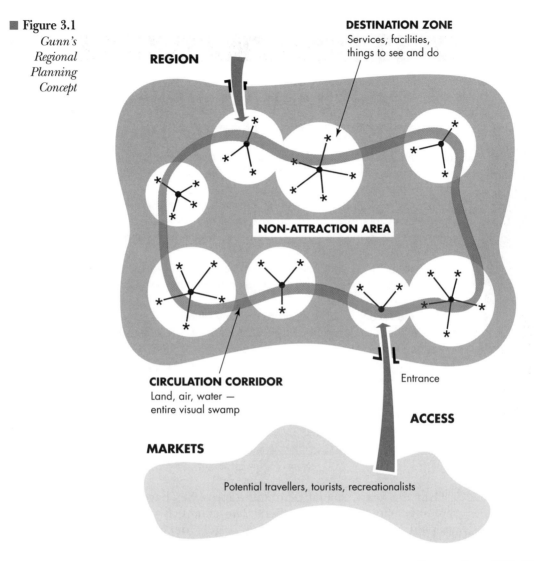

REGION

DESTINATION ZONE
Services, facilities,
things to see and do

NON-ATTRACTION AREA

CIRCULATION CORRIDOR
Land, air, water —
entire visual swamp

Entrance

ACCESS

MARKETS

Potential travellers, tourists, recreationalists

Source: *Gunn 1994: 126.*

cause-effect relationship that characterised positivist policy development, it was assumed that where tourism product existed, tourists would arrive! Typical of the time were idealistic planning processes, such as that profiled in Planning in Practice: 'County planner praised for scheme to attract tourists', p. 96.

An important criticism of this approach is that the ideals embodied in the models and concepts of the physical planning tradition tended to ignore complex political, cultural and economic forces that enable localities, regions and nations to transform into tourism destinations. In other words, tourism planning and policy-making does not occur in a vacuum, and it should not occur without contributions from business and the community.

County planner praised for scheme to attract tourists

The County Planner (Mr F. Stone) was to be complimented on the plans he had put forward for the tourist development of Newcastle and the surrounding district, the Lord Mayor (Ald. Quinlan) said today.

'It is just what Newcastle wants,' he said, 'and it is a plan which I feel all organisations interested in the promotion of this city will have to work for.

'However, to bring the scheme into being is going to cost a lot of money, and this fact is likely to delay it for many years.

'In spite of this, public men [sic] will now be guided by a definite scheme, and it is to be hoped that all steps taken from now on will be in accordance with it.'

Mr Stone's plan, which was presented to yesterday's County Council meeting, envisaged the development of a tourist centre at the eastern end of Newcastle containing a high-class tourist hotel of between 750 and 1000 bedrooms, high-density residential holiday flats, a cabaret and night club and parking facilities, as well as replanned and augmented amenities and facilities at Newcastle Beach.

In addition, it provided for the erection of tourist hotels in surrounding waterside suburbs and the development of other tourist centres in the district.

Source: Newcastle Sun, *25 July 1950 (page number unknown).*

Over the years, spatial planning approaches have been championed by some agencies more than others. The extent to which governments have adopted spatial tourism planning largely depended on the roles and responsibilities of government, regardless of whether this approach was suitable for addressing the perceived issues associated with tourism or whether the government had any jurisdiction over land use planning. For example, local governments generally exercised jurisdiction over land use planning and regulation and were therefore more likely to undertake spatial destination planning than higher levels of government (e.g. Dredge 1997). National governments generally do not have widespread and direct control over land use planning and decision-making, so it was much less likely that spatial planning was adopted at a national level.

■ 3.6.4 Building markets: *a demand-led approach*

Throughout the 1970s tourism was increasingly being cast as a business with enormous economic potential. At the time, global economic restructuring was resulting in the closure of large manufacturing enterprises and industrial production was being downsized and rescaled. Service industries such as tourism were championed as economic replacement activities in local communities that were subject to deindustrialisation. At the same time, criticisms of traditional bureaucratic planning and management were becoming louder, and governments began to take on a more bullish, market-driven approach to tourism planning and policy development. Sir Frank Moore, chairman of the Queensland Tourist and Travel Corporation, summed up this attitude: 'You should not deliver yourselves into the hands of bureaucrats. Bureaucrats create nothing. They live off everyone else, mostly by shuffling and administration, and they don't do it very well' (Moore in King & Hyde 1989: 28). Moore's comments lack substance.

Emerging from this changing focus, tourism planning and policy began to embrace a market-driven approach, which is characterised by stimulating and manipulating demand in a way that allows those sectors with potential for expansion to grow. Many contemporary governments, committed to neoliberal economic management, remain committed to this approach even today. This market-led approach is characterised by a range of planning and policy instruments that stimulate and promote the expansion of tourism markets. For example, cooperative marketing schemes are a popular policy tool for sharing the costs of marketing destinations. Another example was the holiday incentive program.

PLANNING IN PRACTICE

Australia's Holiday Incentive Program 2002

During the 2001–02 year, the government provided funds through the Holiday Incentive Program, to help the tourism industry overcome the effects of the Ansett collapse and the September 2001 terrorist attacks in the USA. The program formed part of a $20 million assistance package to the tourism industry, announced by the Federal Government in October 2001. A rebate of $150 was offered to people undertaking domestic holidays under certain prescribed conditions. A significant proportion of domestic tourism occurs in regional Australia. The program provided more than 29 000 households with the rebate, giving a major boost to tourism throughout regional Australia at a time when the industry was experiencing some difficulties (Commonwealth Department of Transport and Regional Services, Ministerial Budget Statement 2002–03).

Influenced by shifts occurring in public administration ideology, the market-driven approach was also consistent with moves to debureaucratise tourism agencies in the late 1970s and early 1980s. In many Australian states, tourism was removed from many government jurisdictions, where tourism development and growth were thought to be stymied, and it became the responsibility of a statutory corporation. Statutory corporations managed by industry representatives, it was believed, would improve market efficiency and be more responsive to the needs of the industry (Craik 1991) (see chapter 4). Curiously, there was no tourism research to validate this view.

■ 3.6.5 Building industry: *an industry-led approach*

Changing notions about the role of bureaucracy and government that began to take hold during the 1970s and 1980s were consolidated in the 1990s. Massive economic restructuring as a response to globalisation of trade and the consolidation of powerful global corporate interests led to a rethink about the role of government in tourism development. Governments increasingly adopted the complementary roles of 'enablers' and facilitators of economic growth and change and began to withdraw from direct involvement in many areas of policy, including tourism (Dredge 2005). Governments began to reassess the way they were involved in tourism and sought to reduce direct participation in favour of strategies that would stimulate industry and business to help themselves. In tourism, where a large majority of businesses are small operations or family-run, there can often be a lack of business expertise, knowledge and capacity to cope with business development and market change. As a result, governments' role in tourism shifted from direct provider of destination planning services to one of facilitating and building industry capacity. Cooperative marketing campaigns (in which industry funds are matched by government) and business planning and management were areas in which governments became more involved.

Academics and business groups influenced by neoliberal economic management principles have introduced and promoted a number of inter-related concepts and approaches that have proved to be powerful in recent debates about tourism planning and policy. These include:
- *Business or industry clusters* — an idea originally put forward by Harvard Business School economist Michael Porter, which stresses the need for industry members or operators to arrange themselves into clusters or networks of complementary activities, thereby increasing opportunities to share information and knowledge and develop innovation.
- *Strategic competitive advantage* — a concept that argues for the development of competitive advantage through the careful and systematic analysis of other competitive products and the strategic identification of gaps and opportunities in the marketplace.
- *Capacity building* — a concept that takes on many forms; its underpinning tenet is that governments should focus on helping communities and businesses to help themselves by developing their own institutional and social capacities.
- *New regionalism* — a concept heavily influenced by notions of clustering and competitive advantage. Proponents of new regionalism argue for selective regional development policies and programs and hence regional

variations and differentiation. Some regions, because of their comparative advantages in perceived areas, will be preferred over others.

• *Partnership building and collaboration* — concepts that are intended to
promote the strategic development of alliances, partnerships and other
relationships that enable exchange of ideas and innovations and help to
gain or consolidate competitive advantage.

■ 3.6.6 Discourses of power and communication: *a participation-led approach*

As industry-led and marketing approaches to tourism planning and policy
have consolidated, the quality of planning and policy processes has also
come under scrutiny. Three important influences in theoretical development emerged during the 1990s and influenced tourism planning and
policy thought. First, there was a growing awareness that planners were the
brokers of change, but were not responsible for initiating change, making
decisions or implementing urban transformation (e.g. Faludi 1987).
Second, it signalled the realisation that tourism was complex and dynamic,
influenced by a range of contextual parameters outside the direct influence
of planners and policy analysts. Planners were one set of actors who helped
to set the stage, who helped frame the issues and who brought critical
understanding to problems at hand. Third, the notion that there was a collective 'public interest' was dismantled. The idea that there were multiple
publics and communities of interest fuelled community planning and
consultation (e.g. Murphy 1988).

These new ideas in planning ideology emphasise collaborative planning
(e.g. Healey 1997), communicative processes (e.g. Forester 1989, 1993) and
consensus building (e.g. Innes 1996), from which collective approaches to
resolving problems and strategies can be identified. At the heart of all these
ideas is the notion that, by analysing the nature of social relationships and
information exchange, new ways of understanding issues and conflicts and
new ways of planning can be established. Healey (1997) asserts that new
understanding, cooperation and synergy building can enhance the social
and cultural qualities of the institutions in which public policy-making
occurs. As a result of this theoretical shift, new debates in planning theory
suggest that planning must stimulate open, intellectual dialogue between
cultural communities to develop new planning approaches, to manage
coexistence in shared spaces and to develop intellectual and social capacity.
According to Healey (1997: 71): '… planning efforts should be judged by
the qualities of the process, whether they build up relations between stakeholders … and whether the relations enable trust and understanding to
flow among stakeholders and generate sufficient support for policies and
strategies to enable these to be relevant to the material opportunities available and the cultural values of those involved and have the capacity to
endure over time'.

Paralleling the development of spatial tourism planning models and concepts there was a growth in interest in the characteristics and qualities of planning processes and decision-making procedures. The core approach adopted during the 1960s was the rational comprehensive planning process, which was influenced by rational decision-making models in policy analysis and planning literature (e.g. Chadwick 1971; Hogwood & Gunn 1984). This approach conceived tourism planning and policy-making as a rational comprehensive process that followed a number of logical stages. It has also become known as the 'stagist' approach to policy and includes the following steps:

1. problem identification
2. formulation of goals and objectives
3. information gathering and data collection
4. analysis and interpretation of data
5. development of alternative solutions or scenarios
6. choosing the preferred alternative
7. development of the final plan
8. implementation and evaluation.

By the mid-1970s, planning and policy scholars were well aware of the nature of planning processes as a technical exercise within a political setting. It was acknowledged that comprehensiveness was an ideal, but it was, in reality, unachievable. Planning and policy-making were necessarily bounded by a range of factors, such as what was feasible within the limitations of the process, the nature of the information available and the expertise of the personnel involved. Rational comprehensive models failed to acknowledge the political realities of planning, and a greater level of procedural sophistication was required. However, given that tourism was still a relatively new field of academic endeavour and that limited attention was being placed on tourism planning and policy development as a separate line of enquiry, the rational comprehensive model continued as the predominant procedural paradigm in tourism (e.g. Getz 1986; Mill & Morrison 1985).

By the 1980s, critiques of modernity and positivism had gained considerable momentum. Notions that there were overarching solutions were increasingly dismantled, and in their place researchers started to appreciate that tourism planning and policy development took place in a politically charged environment (Richter 1989). There was no universal tourism planning and policy process and no overarching solutions. Moreover, tourism planners and policy analysts became increasingly aware of their own values in framing issues and in identifying solutions. There was a shift away from developing model processes towards an examination of the way tourism planning and policy actually happened.

This shift in the planning literature is best demonstrated in the work of Bramwell (2004), Bramwell and Lane (2000) and Jamal and Getz (1995, 1999) among others. Using rich case studies, these authors demonstrate that communicative planning is a difficult process; power varies among individuals and groups; there are different frames or ways of understanding any issue; barriers to knowledge and learning and conflict enhance and empower some interests over others. The role of planners and policy-makers is to be aware of these nuances, to manage the process and to ensure as far as possible that their decisions and actions are reflective and proactive.

This chapter provides an overview of the way shifts in the social sciences and public administration ideology have shaped development of tourism policy and planning thought and practice. The shifts and changes can be situated in the context of broad social science philosophy, in the changing nature and role of government and in the growing importance of tourism as an economic, social and cultural activity. An appreciation of these historical ideas provides insights that explain why previous decisions have been taken and the cause and consequences of various policy actions. Learning from past events and actions enriches planning and policy debates about the future.

In this chapter, major shifts in social science thinking were discussed, starting with the Enlightenment, or the 'Age of Reason'. The Enlightenment brought with it critical ideas about the relationship between power, politics and the role of government and its relationship to business and societal interests. Modernity refers to the processes of intellectual and technological change that resulted from the Enlightenment. Modernity's main influence on policy and planning was to stimulate thinking about the role of government in moderating the effects of social, economic and technological change. During this period, bureaucracy grew in size and a rational scientific management paradigm began to dominate. Postmodernism brought with it a critical and reflective edge to policy and planning. The existence of different and equally plausible causes and consequences of policy became acceptable. Big bureaucracy and government intervention came under attack as ideas about individualism and market freedoms flourished. Contemporary ideas about tourism policy and planning have continued to dismantle the idea that government knows best, and attempts to build partnerships between government, industry and community are increasing.

In the context of these shifts in social science thinking, tourism has grown to become a major social, cultural, economic and political phenomenon. Government involvement in tourism has shifted during this time from basic infrastructure provision and the material development of attractions to a role of enabling and facilitating business and communities to manage tourism.

During this time, approaches to tourism planning and policy have also changed. In this chapter we discussed five broad approaches: ad hoc tourism planning and policy development; physical destination planning — a supply-led approach; building markets — a demand-led approach; building industry — an industry-led approach; and discourses of power and communication — a participation-led approach. Each approach is not necessarily mutually exclusive, and elements of each and any approach could be present in a particular tourism planning and policy exercise.

Finally, this chapter discussed tourism planning processes and the need to understand that tourism planning and policy development is a dynamic process comprising interrelated stages set in the context of a continued dialogue between actors and agents. Understanding tourism planning and policy development processes in this way can highlight ways in which tourism planners can operate as innovative and active policy entrepreneurs.

SUMMARY OF KEY TERMS ....

Communitarianism

An ideology that emerged in the late twentieth century and criticises classical liberalism and capitalism. It emphasises notions of civil society, the individual's responsibility to the community and the importance of the family to society. Communitarian philosophy asserts the importance of social capital and human rights.

Enlightenment

The Enlightenment, also known as the 'Age of Reason', was an intellectual movement that occurred in Europe and spanned much of the fifteenth to nineteenth centuries. The term is generally used to denote a rejection of religious explanations of the world in favour of increasingly rational and scientific explanations of natural and physical worlds.

Modernity

Modernity denotes a period in the history of Western culture when traditional societies were transformed from small, religious, authoritarian communities by the growth of the science and rationality associated with the Enlightenment. The modern period generally includes the seventeenth to late nineteenth centuries and traverses the Renaissance to the Industrial Revolution.

Neoliberalism

A contemporary interpretation of economic liberalism that emerged in the 1970s. Neoliberalists argue that government interventions results in market inefficiencies and can impede market development and economic growth. They support free trade and open markets as measures to improve corporate efficiencies.

Positivism

Positivism denotes a commitment to rational scientific explanations of cause and effect and the belief that a single, real and objective truth exists.

Postmodernism

Postmodernism is characterised by a rejection of overarching theoretical foundations in favour of free-floating and pragmatic approaches to understanding social change. It recognises that there are multiple ways of framing social issues and building understandings and that there is no single overarching truth.

Pragmatism

Pragmatism is understood as a process of problem-solving in which solutions are developed and tested, and empirical knowledge is in turn fed into the process of change for societal progress and betterment.

Scientific rationality

Scientific rationality is founded on rational and logical notions of cause and consequence. In this view, it is possible to anticipate and measure policy outcomes and choose courses of action on the basis of their expected outcomes. This thinking later gave rise to a rational logic approach, which was used to evaluate the different courses of action open to decision-makers.

Utilitarianism

Originally advocated by Jeremy Bentham, utilitarianism is the belief that achieving the greatest happiness of the greatest number should guide government decisions.

QUESTIONS

1 Identify and discuss five factors that influence the way history is presented. Give examples.

2 What were the main contributions of Enlightenment thinkers to public policy ideology?

3 How did the social and economic changes of nineteenth-century industrialisation influence thinking about the role of government?

4 Explain the broad principles of Taylorism on which public administration was based and how these have changed as a result of the shift to public management.

5 What effect did postmodernism have on the policy sciences?

6 Identify and briefly discuss broad phases in the historical development of tourism.

7 Discuss the shifts occurring in government approaches to tourism since the rise of leisure and tourism in the late nineteenth century.

8 Discuss what is meant by substantive and procedural ideas about tourism planning and policy development. Give examples.

9 Identify and discuss five approaches to tourism planning and policy.

10 Identify and discuss the stages involved in policy development.

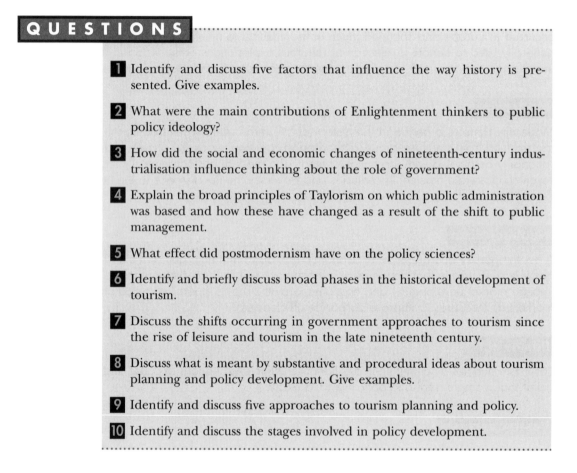

EXERCISES

1 Examine one of the three Planning in Practice textboxes in this chapter: Tourism Planning and Policy in 1926; County Planner Praised for Scheme to Attract Tourists 1950; or Holiday Incentive Scheme 2002. Discuss the various ideas and values that influenced government approaches to tourism planning and policy development at this time.

2 Choose a period in the historical development of tourism (e.g. pre-1850, 1850–1950, post-1950) and answer the following questions:
   (a) What social and other forces influenced tourism planning and policy in that period?
   (b) Which individuals were influential in the areas of economic thought, social planning and philosophy?
   (c) How did wider developments in thinking affect tourism policy and planning structures, processes and actions?

3 From table 3.1 choose three influential thinkers who have contributed to philosophies of the social sciences. Research their contributions and explain in your own words the contributions of these thinkers and their influence on modern policy studies and public administration.

FURTHER READING

Costa, C 2001, 'An emerging tourism planning paradigm? A comparative analysis between town and tourism planning', *International Journal of Tourism Research*, vol. 3, no. 6, pp. 425–41. This article compares the historical development of town planning and tourism planning theory and identifies parallels between the two fields.

Hall, CM 2000, chapter 2, 'The changing dimensions of tourism planning', *Tourism Planning: Policies, Processes and Relationships*, Pearson Education, Harlow, UK. This chapter provides a good overview of the development of tourism policy and planning in an historical context. It identifies important themes that emerge in the theoretical literature and their implications for tourism planning practice.

Ham, C & Hill, C 1993, *The Policy Process in the Modern Capitalist State*, 2nd edn, Harvester Wheatsheaf, New York. This book provides an invaluable introduction to the ideological struggles that underpin relationships between public and private spheres of interest and the influence of these struggles on policy-making and the role of the state.

Weaver, D & Lawton, L 2005, *Tourism Management*, 3rd edn, John Wiley & Sons Australia, Brisbane, pp. 55–89. This book contains a detailed examination of the emergence of tourism from pre-modern times, including a discussion of the economic, social, demographic, technological and political factors that stimulated the emergence of contemporary tourism.

Tourism planning and policy development, Lake Macquarie 1950–2000

Historical processes of tourism planning in Lake Macquarie illustrate changing ideas and approaches towards tourism planning and management since the mid-twentieth century. These shifts, typical of changes in government approaches to tourism development in Australia and internationally, have been driven by shifting contexts, changing values and the ideological shifts outlined in this chapter.

In 1950, a tourism master plan was prepared for the County of Northumberland, a New South Wales Government administrative region that encompassed the Lower Hunter Valley. The county's land use planner had prepared the plan, proposing a range of accommodation and attraction developments throughout the region. The plan was quite typical of the physical master planning approach that dominated land use planning practice at that time and embodied the view that the state was the principal agent in tourism development. But such plans cannot guarantee that a proposed development will happen or that tourist facilities will be built in a proposed location. In other words, this physical master planning approach existed outside the realities of the market-based land development process that operates in Australia.

In the 1970s, a range of recreation plans, foreshore studies and a local environmental plan for Lake Macquarie, still influenced by the prescriptive methods and approaches of physical land use master planning, was prepared. These plans and policy documents adopted standards for the provision of open space and recreation facilities and identified sites for recreation and tourism development. Again, little could be done to guarantee their development.

In 1977, the Lake Macquarie City Council formed a Lake Macquarie Tourist Facilities Development Panel, the task of which was to identify and develop the tourism capacity of the local area. At the time, the State Government had adopted boosterist regional development policies and had identified tourism as a sector of potential growth. Lake Macquarie City Council was also keen to boost tourism through the appointment and work of the panel. The panel focused on one task: to identify and investigate sites of potential tourism development and to advise on how tourism development might be achieved. In presenting its findings to the council, the panel claimed that although environmental and social impact studies had not been carried out, it could 'reasonably be assumed that the tourism facilities proposed are based on planning and economic grounds and that there would be no untoward environmental or social consequences' (Minutes of Ordinary Council Meeting, 6 November 1978). This style of planning was consistent with the bureaucratic, rational scientific approach to planning at the time and the dominant supply-led approach to tourism planning and policy development. The proposals led to public outcry, and concerns were raised about the lack of public consultation and the transparency of the planning process.

By the 1980s, tourism had become an important economic activity in many regional areas of Australia. Strong growth in international visitation, particularly from Asian and North American markets, drove a push to build tourism resorts and to increase yield by building integrated products and experiences. Integrated resort developments stimulated property speculation in many coastal areas. These resort developments were usually characterised by high financial risk and long lead times before financial returns could be made and were targeted at international markets sensitive to international economic conditions (i.e. outside the control of governments and corporations).

In Lake Macquarie, a major integrated resort and residential proposal was proposed at Caves Beach. Council planners saw the potential local economic benefits and championed the proposal. However, economic conditions weakened (most notably, interest rates rose and investor confidence weakened), market demand fluctuated and the developer went into receivership before the proposal received final approval. Throughout this time, the local community became increasingly frustrated and angry at the lack of consultation with local residents. Council did not have an overall strategy or approach to tourism development and dealt with issues and individual projects on a case-by-case basis.

After a period of disinterest in planning for tourism, in the early 1990s the council renewed its commitment to addressing tourism in a more strategic manner. It hired a tourism officer, and a tourism planning strategy was prepared by a consultant, the Hunter Valley Research Foundation. The strategy sought to develop a strategic outlook for tourism and have this integrated with the local area plan (i.e. strategic land use plan). However, the departure of the tourism officer a short time later meant that responsibility for and commitment to the document was lost. The new tourism officer who was appointed sought to consult with industry as his first priority. He set about building networks of industry contacts and empowering industry to build a competitive and synergetic product. The tourism strategy was shelved, becoming little more than a background information document rather than the living strategy and vision it was intended to be.

During the 1990s, industry disharmony was evident. The tourism industry itself was fragmented, and networks of competing interests began to emerge or consolidate based on geographic localities around the lake. Council resources were limited, expertise among industry stakeholders varied and debates about which issues should be prioritised became heated. The Local Tourism Association was disbanded on two occasions and reformed. The council did not replace the tourism officer after his departure (which was owing to high stress and lack of organisational support) and, as a result, there was very little communication between the Local Tourism Association and the council during this time.

In 1996 the council undertook a major strategic planning exercise called Lifestyle 2020. The project was an ambitious attempt to develop a vision for the future of Lake Macquarie and to integrate policy directions among all sectors and responsibilities of the council. This reflected the emergence of new

(continued)

approaches to planning, which emphasised collaboration, communication and partnerships between government, community and business. Through this process it was recognised that tourism represented a potential economic development opportunity, especially since the Hunter region was experiencing an uncertain economic future as a result of the downsizing and closure of many industrial operations in the 1990s. However, tourism, leisure and lifestyle are inextricably linked, and the community had to be consulted about the future direction and extent of tourism development in the city. Extensive public consultation exercises were held throughout the city, and goals and objectives linking tourism, leisure and lifestyle were identified and built into the overall strategic vision for the future. An important element of the continued implementation of this vision is that the council has a productive partnership with the Lake Macquarie Tourism Association. The development of council policy direction on tourism-related issues requires positive consultation with the peak body and with the wider community.

Questions

1 Identify and briefly outline instances when each of the following approaches to tourism planning and policy were adopted in Lake Macquarie:
   (a) physical destination planning — a supply-led approach
   (b) building markets — a demand-led approach
   (c) building and empowering industry — an industry-led approach
   (d) policy dialogues, communication and participation.

2 Are each of these approaches mutually exclusive or can they coexist?

3 What are the advantages and disadvantages of each of these approaches in the case of Lake Macquarie?

REFERENCES

Black, A & Breckwoldt, R 1977, 'Evolution of systems of national park policy-making in Australia', in DC Mercer (ed.), *Leisure and Recreation in Australia*, Sorrett, Melbourne, pp. 190–9.

Bramwell, B 2004, 'Partnerships, participation and social science research in tourism planning', in AL Lew, CM Hall & AM Williams (eds), *A Companion to Tourism*, Blackwell Publishing, Oxford, pp. 541–54.

Bramwell, B & Lane, B (eds) 2000, *Tourism Collaboration and Partnerships: Politics, Practices and Sustainability*, Channel View Publications, Clevedon, UK.

Britton, S 1991, 'Tourism, capital and place: Towards a critical theory of tourism', *Environment and Planning D*, vol. 9, pp. 451–78.

Carroll, P 1991, 'The Federal Government and tourism 1945–90', in P Carroll et al. (eds), *Tourism in Australia*, Harcourt Brace Jovanovich, Sydney, pp. 68–81.

Chadwick, GA 1971, *A Systems View of Planning: Towards a Theory of the Urban and Regional Planning Process*, 2nd edn, Pergamon, Oxford.

Comben, P 1996, 'Evolution of Australia's parks', *Australian Parks and Recreation*, Spring, pp. 10–11.

Commonwealth Department of Transport and Regional Services 2003, Ministerial Budget Statement 2002–2003, www.dotars.gov.au/dept/budget/regional/2002_2003/strengthening_sector_specific.aspx#7.

Craik, J 1991, *Government Promotion of Tourism: The Role of the Queensland Tourist and Travel Corporation*, Research Paper No. 20, February, Centre for Australian Public Sector Management, Griffith University, Brisbane.

Davidson, J & Spearitt, P 2000, *Holiday Business: Tourism in Australia Since 1870*, Miegunyah Press, Carlton, Vic.

Dredge, D 1997, 'Land use planning policy: A tool for destination place management', *Australian Journal of Hospitality Management*, vol. 5, no. 1, pp. 41–50.

—— 2001, 'Leisure lifestyles and tourism', *Tourism Geographies*, vol. 3, no. 3, pp. 279–99.

—— 2005, 'Local versus state driven production of "the region": Regional tourism policy in the Hunter, New South Wales, Australia', in A Rainnie & M Grobbelaar (eds), *New Regionalism in Australia*, Ashgate, Aldershot, UK, pp. 302–20.

Etzioni, A 1969, *The Active Society: A Theory of Society and Political Processes*, Free Press, New York.

—— 1996, 'The responsive community: A communitarian perspective', 1995 Presidential Address, *American Sociological Review*, vol. 61, pp. 1–11.

Faludi, A 1987, *Planning Theory*, Pergamon Press, Oxford.

Forester, J 1989, *Planning in the Face of Power*, University of California Press, Berkeley, CA.

—— 1993, Critical Theory, *Public Policy and Planning Practice: Toward a Critical Pragmatism*, State University of New York Press, Albany, NY.

Fraser, N & Nicholson, L 1988, 'Social criticism without philosophy: An encounter between feminism and postmodernism', *Theory, Culture and Society*, vol. 5, nos 2–3, pp. 374–94.

Getz, D 1986, 'Models in tourism planning: Towards the integration of theory and practice', *Tourism Management*, vol. 1, pp. 21–32.

Giddens, A 1990, *The Consequences of Modernity*, Stanford University Press, Stanford, CA.

Gordon, A 2004, 'Introduction: The new cultural history and urban history—intersections', *Urban History Review*, vol. 33, no. 1, pp. 3–8.

Gunn, C 1988, *Vacationscape*, Van Nostrand Reinhold, New York.

—— 1994, *Tourism Planning: Basis, Concepts, Cases*, 3rd edn, Taylor & Francis, Washington, DC.

Hall, CM, 1998, *Introduction to Tourism: Development, Dimensions and Issues*, 3rd edn, Longman, Melbourne.

—— 2000, *Tourism Planning: Policies, Processes and Relationships*, Pearson Education, Harlow, UK.

Hall, CM & Jenkins, J 1995, *Tourism and Public Policy*, Routledge, London.

Ham, C & Hill, C 1993, *The Policy Process in the Modern Capitalist State*, 2nd edn, Harvester Wheatsheaf, New York.

Healey, P 1997, *Collaborative Planning: Shaping Places in Fragmented Societies*, Macmillan, London.

Heclo, H 1974, *Modern Social Politics in Britain and Sweden: From Relief to Income Maintenance*, Yale University Press, New Haven, CT.

Hogwood, BW & Gunn, LA 1984, *Policy Analysis for the Real World*, Oxford University Press, Oxford.

Hollinger, R 1994, *Postmodernism and the Social Sciences: A Thematic Approach*, Sage, Thousand Oaks, CA.

Hughes, OE 2003, *Public Management and Administration: An Introduction*, 3rd edn, Palgrave Macmillan, Basingstoke and New York.

Innes, JE, 1996, 'Planning through consensus building: A new view of the comprehensive planning ideal', *Journal of the American Planning Association*, vol. 62, no. 4, pp. 460–73.

Inskeep, E 1991, *Tourism Planning: An Integrated and Sustainable Development Approach*, Van Nostrand Reinhold, New York.

Jamal, TB & Getz, D 1995, 'Collaboration theory and community tourism planning', *Annals of Tourism Research*, vol. 22, pp. 186–204.

—— 1999, 'Community roundtables for tourism-related conflicts: The dialectics of consensus and process structures', *Journal of Sustainable Tourism*, vol. 7, no. 3/4, pp. 290–313.

Jenkins, JM 2001, 'Statutory authorities in whose interests? The case of Tourism New South Wales, the bed tax, and "the Games"', *Pacific Tourism Review*, vol. 4, no. 4, pp. 201–19.

Jenkins, J & Wearing, S 2003, 'Ecotourism and protected areas in Australia', in D Fennell & R Dowling (eds), *Ecotourism Policy and Planning*, CABI International, Wallingford, UK, pp. 205–33.

Kaiser, C & Helber, L 1978, *Tourism Planning and Development*, CBI Publishing Company, Boston.

King, B & Hyde, G 1989, *Tourism Marketing in Australia*, Hospitality Press, Melbourne.

King, CJ 1957, *An Outline of Closer Settlement in New South Wales*, Part 1, Division of Marketing and Agricultural Economics, Department of Agriculture, Sydney, NSW.

Lynch, R & Veal, AJ 2001, *Australian Leisure*, 2nd edn, Pearson Education Australia, Frenchs Forest, NSW.

Macbeth, J 2005, 'Towards an ethics platform for tourism', *Annals of Tourism Research*, vol. 32, no. 4, pp. 962–84.

Marx, K & Engels, F 1967 (originally published 1842), *The Communist Manifesto*. With an introduction by AJP Taylor, Penguin, Harmondsworth.

Mill, RC & Morrison, AM 1985, *The Tourism System: An Introductory Text*, Prentice Hall, Englewood Cliffs, NJ.

Mumford, L 1961, *The City in History*, Penguin, London.

Murphy, P 1988, *Tourism: A Community Approach*, Methuen, London.

Ostrom, V 1989, *The Intellectual Crisis in American Public Administration*, University of Alabama Press, Tuscaloosa.

Parsons, W 1995, *Public Policy: An Introduction to the Theory and Practice of Policy Analysis*, Edward Elgar, Aldershot, UK.

Pearce, D 1992, *Tourism Organizations*, Longman Scientific and Technical, Harlow, UK.

Pettigrew, C & Lyons, M 1979, 'Royal national park—a history', *Parks and Wildlife*, vol. 2, nos 3–4, pp. 15–30.

Richardson, JI 1999, *A History of Australian Tourism and Travel*, Hospitality Press, Melbourne.

Richter, L 1989, *The Politics of Tourism in Asia*, University of Hawaii Press, Honolulu.

Rojek, C 1993, *Ways of Escape: Modern Transformation of Leisure and Travel*, Macmillan, Basingstoke.

Rosenau, PM 1992, *Post-Modernism and the Social Sciences: Insights, Inroads and Intrusions*, Princeton University Press, Princeton, NJ.

Rousseau, JJ 1968 (originally published 1762), *The Social Contract*. Trans. and introduced by M Cranston, Penguin, Harmondsworth.

Soane, JV 1993, *Fashionable Resort Regions: Their Evolution and Transformation with Particular Reference to Bournemouth, Nice, Los Angeles and Wiesbaden*, CAG International, Wallingford, UK.

Smith, A 1976 (originally published 1776), *An Inquiry into the Nature and Causes of the Wealth of Nations*, Oxford University Press, Oxford.

Smith, VL 1978, *Hosts and Guests: The Anthropology of Tourism*, Basil Blackwell, Oxford.

Turner, L 1975, *The Golden Hordes: International Tourism and the Pleasure Periphery*, Constable, London.

Urry, J 1990, *The Tourist Gaze: Leisure and Travel in Contemporary Societies*, Sage, London.

—— 1995, *Consuming Places*, Routledge, London.

Veblen, T 1973 (originally published 1899), *The Theory of the Leisure Class* (with introduction by John Kenneth Galbraith), Houghton Mifflin, Boston.

Weaver, D & Lawton, L 2005, *Tourism Management*, 3rd edn, John Wiley & Sons Australia, Brisbane.

World Tourism Organization 2005, 'About the World Tourism Organization (WTO–OMT)', www.world-tourism.org/aboutwto/aboutwto.htm, viewed 7 June 2006.

John Jenkins and Dianne Dredge

CHAPTER 4

Trends, *perspectives and practice*

LEARNING OBJECTIVES

After reading this chapter you will be able to:

1 discuss how various historical paradigms or frameworks are used to understand the organisation and operation of public administration

2 explain the importance of organisational culture and its influence on policy-making

3 identify and discuss the role and impact of strategic and corporate planning

4 discuss the advantages and disadvantages of statutory corporations

5 discuss the advantages and disadvantages of self-regulation

6 explain the features of pressure groups and their influence on policy-making

7 discuss the role of multinational corporations in policy-making

8 describe the influence of these trends and perspectives on particular tourism sectors, such as ecotourism and nature-based tourism and other niche areas.

This chapter critically examines trends and perspectives influencing contemporary tourism planning and practice. It necessarily retraces some of the ground of the previous two chapters, but expands on their key themes and issues. The trends, perspectives and practices here include:

- the creep of entrepreneurial and neoclassical imperatives, ideas and values into decision- and policy-making processes of public sector tourism organisations
- the rise of strategic and **corporate planning** and enterprise and the emergence of organic organisational structures involving various blends of public and private input
- the growing importance of deregulation, privatisation and self-regulation in tourism industry activity, especially in supposedly sustainable nature-based tourism and ecotourism initiatives
- the extent and nature of business–government relations
- the rise of pressure groups and industry associations and their subsequent consolidation and relations with government, and
- the nature of multinational corporations and their influences with respect to tourism policy and planning.

Examining these trends helps us gain insights into tourism planning and policy processes. In previous chapters, the focus has been on macro elements: globalisation, institutional arrangements and the role of the state. This chapter's focus on what amounts to micro and middle-level issues broadens our understandings of some neglected factors in research on tourism planning and policy processes. For instance, we will see that business–government relations are now so deeply embedded in and fundamental to tourism policy-making and planning that they are central to our understandings of the distribution of power in planning and policy processes and to what is now a hotly contested landscape of policy-related activity.

Section 4.2 gives a brief overview of organisation theory and practice, which was touched on in chapter 2. After all, any public decision involves organisations of people, resources and activities: government departments, statutory authorities, political parties, lobby groups and other institutions. Section 4.3 examines the influence of organisational culture, and section 4.4 explores strategic and corporate planning as important focus of public policy. Section 4.5 examines government enterprises as a means of public policy delivery and the implications these have had on the focus and content of tourism policy. Section 4.6 discusses self-regulation and accreditation schemes in the tourism industry, especially those affecting ecotourism operators. Section 4.7 examines political lobbying as an important feature of liberal democracies and the impact lobby groups have had on tourism policy development. Section 4.8 examines the impact of multinational corporations and the influence they wield in tourism policy.

Organisations involve a grouping of people and resources around some common idea, action or issue. Schools of thought about organisations have evolved over time, and ideas about organisations can be traced back many, many centuries. There is no consensus about best practice organisational structures, behaviour or operations, but various schools of thought have been prominent at different times. As Bolman and Deal (1984) put it, 'within the social sciences, major schools of thought have evolved, each with its own views of organizations, its own well defined concepts and assumptions and its own ideas about how managers can best bring social collectives under control'.

Organisational theory is characterised by a lack of consensus about the best way to structure and manage organisations. So it comes as no surprise that several scholars and practitioners have attempted to group schools of thought, trace their origins and explain their interrelationships and hence arrange them into some coherent collective, chronologically and/or thematically (e.g. see Shafritz & Ott 1992). This section presents a selective and generalised overview of some popular theories about the ways in which organisations have evolved in terms of their structures, functions and operations and the influence of streams of thought on how they are managed and the ways they (or their members) actually conduct themselves. These theories are then linked to developments in public sector tourism organisations in Australia.

4.2.1 Scientific management *and the concept of bureaucracy*

More than two centuries ago, with the onset of the Industrial Revolution and dramatic changes to the production of goods and services, owners and managers of organisations confronted a series of rather unfamiliar problems and questions. Organisations grew and required much greater interaction between people, resources and information over ever-increasing distances. Patterns of trade were changing. Charles Babbage gave an indication of what was to come by way of the scientific management movement when he wrote *On the Economy of Machinery and Manufactures* in 1832. Frederick Winslow Taylor subsequently developed his philosophy of **scientific management** in the 1880s, which was published in *The Principles of Scientific Management* (1911). Taylor's studies of time and events in organisations provided the impetus for and basis of models and theories about how to structure or redesign work environments to increase workers' output and wages. Work was to be designed to promote efficiency (one best or specific way of doing each activity or task), and workers were often closely watched over in many aspects of their work. Separation between operators of plant machinery and managers and planners became fashionable, but not without some resistance from those workers on the manufacturing floors who became increasingly alienated from decision-making. In other words, a hierarchical and bureaucratic structure gradually became more entrenched in organisations.

The classical school (e.g. Babbage 1832; Fayol 1956; Taylor 1947) dominated organisation theory until around the 1930s (Bolman & Deal 1984, 1991; Ham & Hill 1993; Harmon & Mayer 1986; Shafritz & Ott 1992). That school is still influential, but remains rooted both in the Industrial Revolution of the eighteenth century and the professions of mechanical engineering, industrial engineering and economics (Shafritz & Ott 1992). The fundamental tenets of the classical school are that:

- organisations exist to accomplish production-related and economic goals
- there is one best way to organise production and that way can be found through systematic, scientific inquiry
- production is maximised through specialisation and division of labour, and
- people and organisations act in accordance with rational economic principles (Shafritz & Ott 1992: 27).

The Weberian concept of bureaucracy was, in part, a response to an increase in the size and complexity of units of administration. 'Bureaucratisation is the development of large systems of hierarchically structured and functionally inter-dependent offices used to manage extensive and complex operations' (Britton 1991a: 54). Government departments have long been structured along similar lines to Weber's notions of a modern bureaucracy (see table 4.1).

■ **Table 4.1**
Weber's concept of the bureaucracy

I	There is the principle of official jurisdictional areas, which are generally ordered by rules; that is, by laws or administrative regulations.
II	The principles of office hierarchy and of channels of appeal (*Instanzenzug*) stipulate a clearly established system of super- and sub-ordination in which there is a supervision of the lower offices by the higher ones.
III	The management of the modern office is based on written documents (the 'files'), which are preserved in their original or draft form and on a staff of subaltern officials and scribes of all sorts. The body of officials working in an agency, along with the respective apparatus of material, implements and the files, makes up a bureau.
IV	Office management, at least all specialised office management — and such management is distinctly modern — usually presupposes thorough training in a field of specialisation.
V	When the office is fully developed, official activity demands the full working capacity of the official, irrespective of the fact that the length of his or her obligatory working hours in the bureau might be limited.
VI	The management of the office follows general rules, which are more or less stable and more or less exhaustive and which can be learned. Knowledge of these rules represents a special technical expertise that the officials possess.

Source: *Weber 1968: 956–8.*

■ 4.2.2 The machine *bureaucracy*

For Weber, the aims of bureaucratic structures are precision, reliability and efficiency. Building on Weber's work, Mintzberg (1979, in Britton 1991b: 9) recently developed the concept of the 'machine bureaucracy', which possessed the following fundamental characteristics:

- highly specialised organisation
- routine operating tasks
- formalised operating procedures
- a proliferation of rules and regulations
- highly formalised communication channels (usually upward)
- centralised power and decision-making, and
- an elaborate administrative structure with a sharp division of labour between line and staff.

Mintzberg asserted that an underlying assumption of organisational design has been that organisations require articulated objectives, sharp divisions of labour, clearly defined tasks, well-developed hierarchies and formalised systems of control, which amounts to rational authority (Britton 1991a). This 'desirable' configuration of elements, which conforms to the ideal-type, machine-like bureaucracy defined by Weber, was a predominant and overt theme in the structure and functions of government departments in Australia and elsewhere until the 1970s.

Ham and Hill (1993) noted that a second important theme derived from Weber's work, yet one that is based on a misunderstanding of his approach, concerns the relationships between rationality and rigidity. A machine-like bureaucracy is an effective structural form in closed, stable or protected environments with authoritarian management (Britton 1991a). Legal and rational authority prevails in bureaucracies because in theory such authority is seen to be the most efficient means to an end. However, rational frameworks or structures are not well adapted to some tasks, and hence some organisations have developed more fluid structures, which nevertheless show strong evidence of hierarchical frameworks.

■ 4.2.3 Mechanistic *and organic systems of management*

Burns and Stalker (1961) drew a distinction between mechanistic (bureaucratic or rational) and organic management systems. **Mechanistic systems**, on the one hand, involve structures broadly comparable to the Weberian model and are most suitable for stable tasks and stable public policy arenas. On the other hand, Burns and Stalker considered **organic systems** were better adapted to unstable conditions. In these cases, problems requiring decisions and actions often arise, but cannot be broken down and distributed among specialists within a clearly defined hierarchy. Individuals must thus perform tasks in the light of their knowledge of the functions and operations of the firm as a whole. Communication between people of different ranks tends to resemble lateral forms of consultation rather than vertical command (Burns & Stalker 1961).

These theories of organisations were limited but useful. The limited explanatory powers of the classical and 'modern' structural and systems schools of organisation theory in interpreting events and the ways things are and should be done in organisations are now well documented. The modern structural school, which is grounded in the classical school, places much importance on legitimate authority (authority that flows down through the organisational hierarchy) and formal rules (promulgated and enforced by those in authority) in ensuring that organisational behaviour is directed towards the attainment of organisational goals and clearly specified objectives (Shafritz & Ott 1992). However, the modern structuralists, including Burns and Stalker (1961), Blau and Scott (1962) and Mintzberg (1979), 'also have been influenced greatly by the neoclassical, human relations-oriented and systems theorists of organisations' (Shafritz & Ott 1992: 201).

The primary question for the classical and 'modern' structural school's organisation theory has been how best to design and manage organisations to achieve their declared purposes effectively and efficiently. The personal preferences of organisational members are assumed to be restrained by systems of formal rules, authority and norms of rational behaviour (Shafritz & Ott 1992). This is a major shortcoming in the explanatory powers of those theories, because lower-level actors, including 'street level bureaucrats' (Lipsky 1980), acquire decision-making and policy-making power and use that power in many ways. The power they exercise might not be obvious. However, even the most basic interpretations of a person's application for a visa or a recommendation from a local planner to a developer to follow a course of action concerning a tourism development proposal involve a policy-based decision or interpretation of policy by someone at the 'lower level' (or 'coalface'). The planner might be responding to an inquiry for which there is no specific instruction and only broad rules. Indeed, there might even be confusion as to when a direction from a government minister to an organisation has been received or as to precisely when it takes effect (the case study 'The Western Australian Tourism Commission, Eventscorp and the 1995 Global Dance Foundation "affair"' on p. 148 provides a good example). This observation leads us to a need to explain the relevance of other models or schools of organisation theory (e.g. power and politics schools) as well as theories concerning organisational culture and the ways organisations actually perform their tasks.

■ 4.2.4 **Power,** *authority and bureaucracy*

The framework for Weber's conception of bureaucracy is to be found in his ideas on power, domination and authority. Power is a key political issue, 'but on its own is an inadequate explanatory notion because it leaves out the social meanings which people attach to its use' (Self 1985: 11). To have power is to be able to get desired things done, to effect decisions, actions and outcomes (Britton 1991a). The distribution and use of power in organisations has been advanced by such prominent authors as Mechanic (1962), Cohen and March (1986), Clegg and Dunkerley (1977, 1980), Pfeffer (1981), Mintzberg (1983) and Harmon and Mayer (1986).

According to Aldefer (1979) and Brown (1983), power will be highly concentrated in tightly regulated organisations and diffuse in loosely controlled organisations. So power can be deliberately and formally concentrated in organisations by the use of highly structured and regulated systems of management. Yet even 'When power is concentrated at the top of a highly regulated system, politics does not disappear, but it is often forced underground' (Bolman & Deal 1991: 188). Crozier (1964), for instance, recognised that those with power are not limited to those with hierarchical authority; the powerful are not necessarily those with authority. 'Politics inevitably intrudes into policy formulation because the instruments of power — information, resources and authority — are not centralised in the hands of a minister but fragmented across parties, departments, community groups and clients.' Policy must be negotiated (Davis & Weller 1987: 386).

Policies reflect the distribution of power in decision-making and policy-making. For example, the government of the day and the chief executive officer of a state tourism organisation (e.g. Tourism NSW) might prefer a tourism marketing and promotion model based on a regional approach in which regional tourism organisations are strongly supported. If there is a change of government and/or CEO, there could be a major paradigm shift to an approach that does not support regional organisations but which promotes carefully targeted products. Funding might be unexpectedly withdrawn from regions as specific products throughout the state (say, wine and special events) are promoted as opposed to regions (say, the North Coast of New South Wales or the Hunter Valley) (see Dredge & Jenkins 2003). Nevertheless, the ways departments and agencies decide and act in these and other circumstances are also reflected in their organisational cultures, which manifest and cement themselves over time and which are resistant to change. Hence, a deeply embedded organisational culture might see a tourism agency responsible for funding regional organisations resist the idea that regions be abolished, especially if they have been part of the institutional framework for many years.

4.3 ORGANISATIONAL CULTURE

An organisation's culture is one expression of its 'personality': its characteristic way of doing things (Jacques 1951, in Jans & Frazer-Jans 1991: 336). The term 'culture' has been applied to organisations since the 1930s (e.g. Arnold 1938; Selznick 1957; Bower 1966; Barnard 1968; Schein 1985). Schein (1985: 9) defined **organisational culture** 'as a pattern of basic assumptions — invented, discovered, or developed by a given group as it learns to cope with its problems of external adaptation and internal integration — that has worked well enough to be considered valid and, therefore, to be taught to new members as the correct way to perceive, think and feel in relation to those problems'. Bower (1966) defined culture more concisely as 'the way we do things around here'. In other words, an organisation's culture is the unique style of a group of people, which incorporates the informal practices and coping strategies considered necessary to carry out the tasks and functions required by an organisation. In any organisation, then, there is usually some system of shared beliefs or meaning about the organisation and its function that distinguishes it from others. With this in mind, organisational culture could be considered akin to the glue that binds the formative parts of the organisation together (Britton 1991b: 2). An organisation's culture will significantly affect the way it grapples with policy and planning issues — from the way it detects and receives policy problems to the way it reacts and monitors and perceives its influence.

The organisational culture or symbolic management perspective is far removed from the mainline structural and systems schools. 'It assumes that many organisational decisions and actions are almost predetermined by the

PLANNING IN PRACTICE ··············

The 'top-heavy' Australian Tourist Commission needs a restructure

In the section of the Report of the Australian Government Inquiry into Tourism (1986) titled 'ATC options for management structure' (appendix 28), the committee indicated that it had examined the submission from ATIA [Australian Tourism Industry Association] with regard to the ATC's organisational structure. The committee recommended two possible options:

Option I

In line with current management theory, there are too many levels creating a steep hierarchy ...

There is no relationship between the structure and the programs the Commission undertakes. The Committee feels strongly that the structure must reflect the strategy of the organisation, which in turn is reflected in its programs. In this regard, the Committee also noted that the operations area has no marketing thrust ...

In line with ATIA's view that the current organisation is top heavy, the Committee considers there are too many branches and too many positions at the Class II level. Some rationalisation could be obtained, e.g. combining Directors Advertising and Publications/Information; Program Planning and Strategy and Planning and abolishing Director National Tourism (corresponding to the revised Corporate mission).

Under Option II it was noted: 'Again, the structure does not appear to reflect the marketing thrust of the Commission.'

patterns of basic assumptions that are held by members of an organization' (Shafritz & Ott 1992: 48). Those patterns of assumptions continue to exist and to influence behaviour because they repeatedly lead people in that organisation to make decisions that 'worked in the past'. With repeated use, the assumptions might slowly drop out of people's consciousness but continue to influence organisational decisions and actions, even when the organisation's environment changes (Shafritz & Ott 1992). Ultimately, the culture of an organisation affects its behaviour and 'can block an organization from making changes that are needed to adapt to a changing environment' (Shafritz & Ott 1992: 482).

Since the 1970s organisations, both public and private, have had to learn to adapt to changing, sometimes volatile, environments. Organisations have been variously reduced in size, restructured, had activities and functions outsourced, reviewed their missions and foci and shaped themselves to deal more effectively with their internal and external environments (see Planning in Practice: 'The "top-heavy" Australian Tourist Commission needs a restructure', p. 119). There is also a hint of the influence of pressure groups (e.g. the Australian Tourism Industry Association — ATIA), which is discussed later in this chapter.

Much of the criticism of bureaucracies has ironically stemmed from the private sector (where, along with its successes, there is now much evidence of corruption, failure, deceit, self-interest and bankruptcy). Interestingly, too, many private companies are often structured along traditional bureaucratic (and hierarchical) lines, which have rules and conditions controlling behaviour, channels of communication and staff dress and presentation.

Organisations are not isolated or self-contained (Burns & Stalker 1961). Organisations must be seen as an open system, as must nation states and local and regional economies (see chapters 1 and 2). Organisations depend on others for resources: people, goods, services, infrastructure, protection, knowledge and information. Developments in organisation theory and behaviour reflect these developments. Structure and culture are only two important elements in the functions and operations of an organisation, but structure in particular has been used as a major means of reframing Australian and overseas tourism organisations. Other means relate to the development of strategic and corporate plans, processes and accountability.

4.4 STRATEGIC AND CORPORATE PLANNING

Governments' interest in **strategic planning** took on renewed emphasis in the late 1960s and early 1970s. Strategic management emerged as the result of concerns about such matters as:
• increased globalisation and more open economies/nation states
• increased organisational size and complexity — from small-sized firms to multinational corporations embodying diverse functions
• increased turbulence in business environments

- greater propensity for markets to change
- intense competition and more detailed consumer knowledge
- massive growth in advertising, marketing and promotion
- rapid technological advancements in such areas as communications, transport and service provision.

In the public sector we can also point to:

- international influences from other countries, such as the USA
- tendencies towards reduced government intervention, and
- the influence of powerful bureaucrats, government advisers and other interests (e.g. Viljoen & Dann 2003).

In 1973, global economic crises followed closely on the heels of massive increases in world oil prices. Governments in developed countries, including Australia, suddenly found themselves exposed to strong and at times unpredictable global forces largely beyond their control (Alaba 1994). Government responses were complicated by other forces.

The fact is that the 1970s was a watershed for the bureaucracy and government institutions of Australia because it was a period during which dramatic economic and social shifts significantly influenced the processes of government administration. According to Alaba (1994), in Australia, the 1970s were a period of large-scale changes in lifestyles and values — a change both in 'the ideals of the middle-class culture from those of the puritan work ethic to those of the hedonist ethic of a consumer society' (Horne 1980: 3) and changes in society's environmental concerns. Government administrations were required to address these matters.

Some bureaucracies were not well placed or organised to address these concerns. As Alaba noted in the Australian context, compounding 'the effect of the economic crisis and the new demands and complexities of modern government were the examples set by overseas countries which had reviewed their public administrations during the previous two decades' (Alaba 1994: 51). Overseas administrative reform inquiries dating from the 1950s 'drew attention to the reform inquiry as an instrument for improving Australian systems of government administration within international and national environments where resources were [supposedly] becoming less available to support the bureaucratic [s]tate' (Alaba 1994: 52; also see Parker 1979).

Although 'Signs of over-reliance and over-dependence on bureaucratism appeared perhaps for the first time in Australia in the 1890s' (Caiden 1980: 443), in the 1970s there were concerns that the 'public bureaucracy had grown too fat during the good years, that its managerial elite had lost touch with reality and that public sector performance was just not good enough and had to be improved' (Caiden 1980: 443; also see Emy & Hughes 1988). As a result, several Australian governments commissioned inquiries to advise them on such matters (Caiden 1980). Indeed, four major reform inquiries were undertaken in Australia in the mid-1970s (Wilenski 1986; Alaba 1994). The results illustrate Australian governments' move towards corporate planning and the adoption of business principles. In this sense, corporate planning undertaken by governments embraces concerns for business planning, resource allocation, and managing and accounting for performance.

The reform inquiries in conjunction with other developments produced major shifts in public administration and policy-making. Peter Wilenski (1986) provided a concise overview of these reforms, which were directed to:

- *Achieving a more democratic administration,* reinforcing principles of 'ministerial control of and responsibility for, the public service' (Wilenski 1986: 193). One of the key ways of facilitating this was to open up the appointments of senior executive officers. These people could be recruited from inside or outside the public service on contracts for specified periods. These reforms were introduced to ensure that the public service was 'responsive' to elected government demands and to improve performance of public sector managers.
- *Introducing program budgeting.* A more efficient administration was sought through the Financial Improvement Management Program, 'designed to encourage program managers to specify objectives clearly, measure resources, develop performance indicators and assess the effectiveness of programs and to focus on results' (Wilenski 1986: 195).
- *Seeking a more equitable administration* through affirmative action plans and equal employment opportunity, including the setting of targets for appointment of women, Aborigines and other groups.

In summary, the adoption of corporate planning principles by governments illustrates moves towards smaller government, improved efficiency and effectiveness, improved responsiveness and a reduction in government expenditure and improved accountability (Dunford, Bramble & Littler 1998, in Viljoen & Dann 2003: 29) have been key forces for public sector reform. They were reflected in tourism administrations (see Tourism Planning Breakthrough: 'Premier criticises tourism bureaucracy and bureaucrats').

TOURISM PLANNING BREAKTHROUGH
Premier criticises tourism bureaucracy and bureaucrats

A Coalition Government will place tourism where it correctly deserves to be — not as an opiate of the masses but as an integral part of the state's future growth strategy. We will create a Ministry of Economic Development and Tourism, thus liberating your industry from its current poor cousin status. This senior Ministry will play a coordinating role, at the macro-economic level, of the development initiatives of all portfolios.

The vital role of tourism as the only labour-intensive, decentralised and expanding industry of the post-industrial age will be recognised in its inclusion in this key Ministry.

The Minister will have an efficient and commercially literate department that will have as its principal role the creation of an economic climate to allow all viable industries to prosper. Within this framework the tourism industry will be predominantly developed and controlled by the private sector without any unwarranted intrusion or fettering by government ...

The principal agency to implement the government's tourism policy will be a rethought and restructured New South Wales Tourism Commission.

I am on record as wishing to create a new culture within the public service that will reward initiative, provide incentive and create opportunities for self-development to the same extent as is provided in the private sector.

The New South Wales Tourism Commission will be the flagship for the demonstration of that new approach.

... possibly because it was one of the last organisations to change from a department to a commission, it is generally perceived in the industry as still demonstrating many of the negative characteristics of the bureaucracy. It unfortunately has not developed sufficiently the private sector approach demonstrated by the more robust and aggressive Western Australian Tourism Commission and the Queensland and Tourism Travel Corporation.

The New South Wales Tourism Commission will need to be dynamic, creative, innovative, marketing oriented, motivated by free enterprise and run on business-like lines.

Its role will be limited to that required by the private sector and its staff will possess the same level of competence and dedication as the private sector tourist industry they will serve.

Many within the existing Commission do possess those qualities. I am sure they will be happy to be surrounded by more of their kind.

Source: *N Greiner, n.d., circa 1988, 'The tourist and hospitality industry —
A liberal perspective', a speech by Nick Greiner, MP, Leader of the Opposition
in New South Wales to the Hospitality Management Guild, Sydney Hilton
Hotel, 2 September.*

Tourism Planning Breakthrough: 'Premier criticises tourism bureaucracy and bureaucrats' indicates developments projected for tourism administrations in New South Wales, but they were also evident in other states and territories and at the federal level. In the Commonwealth Department of the Arts, Sport, the Environment, Tourism and Territories 1988–89 Annual Report, it was stated: 'The Department embarked on a corporate management style, established an executive management committee (EMC) of senior staff chaired by the Secretary (today's equivalent of Director-General), an audit committee, an information technology steering committee, a corporate planning steering committee and a national consultative council (NCC).' The EMC met regularly to oversee 'day-to-day management and policy issues'. *Program budgeting* meant that corporate objectives would be pursued by devolution of management of resources to line managers responsible to Divisional Heads. The Department refined its program objectives to 'take account of the *Government's social justice objectives*'. *Performance indicators* were refined. The NCC was 'supported by four subcommittees with responsibility for *industrial democracy, equal employment opportunity,* occupational health and safety and accommodation' (pp. 4–5; our emphasis).

Soon after Nick Greiner became Premier in 1988, he set about restructuring many New South Wales public administrations. One of these administrations was the New South Wales Tourism Commission, which the New South Wales Office of Public Management investigated in detail and which was the subject of a (then) confidential report released in February 1993. The review noted that the commission lacked a clear focus and strategic direction and that it tried 'to be all things to all people' (p. 8). The review put this down in part to the historically overwhelming influence of the *Tourism Commission Act 1984* (NSW). 'This Act sets the very general, all embracing, objective for the Commission to "achieve economic and social benefits for the people of NSW through the development of tourism"' (p. 8). The commission's corporate plan for 1992–95 lacked 'quantifiable measures of performance and outcomes' (p. 9) and, ultimately, clear directions as activities were conducted in an ad hoc fashion and effectiveness was impeded (p. 10). It came as no surprise when, in June 1994, after many months of internal review and debate, the New South Wales Tourism Commission adopted a new name, Tourism New South Wales, and a new logo to boost the organisation's profile as an aggressive marketer of New South Wales holidays. Tourism New South Wales's mission was 'advancing the cultural, environmental and social benefits of tourism in New South Wales' (Tourism NSW 1994: A2). Tony Thirwell, the general manager and chief executive of Tourism New South Wales, stated: 'Our new identity projects New South Wales as an innovative, responsive and customer-focused organisation leading the development and marketing of tourism across the State' (Tourism NSW 1994: A11).

These directions in public administration were among many examples of a streamlining of the public service, the provisions for greater accountability and the conduct of government 'business' in an efficient and business-like manner, like the private sector. Interestingly, Considine's (1990) research indicated that corporate planning, program budgeting and performance indicators in public service organisations yielded modest results. Senior and middle-level managers in the public services of South Australia, Victoria and the Commonwealth criticised these reforms and could see few gains (Considine 1990). Interestingly, too, even by this time, there was no evidence that private sector organisations performed any better or more efficiently than public sector administrations.

Indeed, the idea that private sector organisations and their employees are more efficient than public sector administrations is a great myth. The public (or civil) service notionally serves the government of the day; does not have clearly defined links between budgets, activities and performance; pursues activities prescribed by laws and legislation, and these, as we have seen, might be broad and vague and involve red tape supported by parliamentarians to regulate the private sector; regulates market activity because of externalities and so is vitally concerned with operating in arenas where market failure is evident (e.g. environmental protection and management, welfare, education, health); and has a prime purpose that is not competitively driven (e.g. Viljoen & Dann 2003). Policies do not always meet their intended aims. But government agencies in one form or another do survive. That said, throughout Australia's history governments of all persuasions have selectively and purposefully established business enterprises that do act in more business-like manner. These are often called statutory authorities or organisations, government business enterprises or Crown corporations. In Australia, such authorities are now prominent in federal, state and territory government tourism administrations.

4.5 GOVERNMENT ENTERPRISE: STATUTORY CORPORATIONS

Tourism statutory authorities are established for many reasons and by governments of all persuasions in several countries. Their strategic directions are clearly oriented to commercial activities and marketing (see for example Craik 1991a). These authorities are an interesting and often controversial form of public administration.

Australian state and federal governments and (perhaps more to the point) cabinets have formal control over a large number of **statutory corporations** and **agencies** that operate with varying degrees of independence and whose employees are not always public servants as defined by relevant Public Service Acts. Statutory corporations are not part of the conventional public service, but they do fall within ministerial portfolios. In brief, they are more independent of cabinet control than are departments and are established by legislation to function independently of government departments (Davis 1991).

Governments establish public corporations primarily as an institutional mechanism for combining two features (see tables 4.2 and 4.3): (1) public control to protect the public interest and (2) managerial autonomy to operate commercial enterprises (Mascarenhas 1982). The decision to establish a statutory authority rather than having the same function performed by a department typically is justified by the need for impartiality in decision-making. Market failure is frequently offered by economists as an explanation for public ownership (Mascarenhas 1996). However, other motives for creating statutory corporations include 'political and ideological pressures to redistribute wealth, balance social and commercial costs, exploit natural resources, create employment, promote regional development, rescue declining industry, promote indigenous industry, promote national prestige and develop new technology' (Zeckhauser & Horn 1989: 14, in Mascarenhas 1996: 66). Statutory authorities as a form of organisation have several advantages over the departmental form (Spann 1979: 118–19) (see table 4.2).

To illustrate the application of these advantages of statutory organisations, examples of typical foci of corporate objectives and key roles of tourism statutory corporations are outlined in table 4.3. From these corporate objectives and key roles it is possible to discern a corporation's alignment with industry and commercial interests and its distance from bureaucratic management.

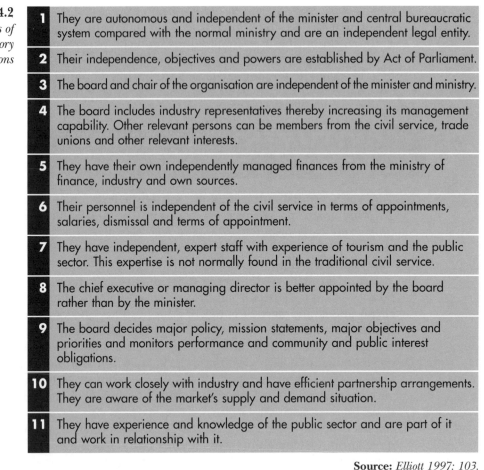

■ Table 4.2 *Advantages of statutory organisations*		
1	They are autonomous and independent of the minister and central bureaucratic system compared with the normal ministry and are an independent legal entity.
2	Their independence, objectives and powers are established by Act of Parliament.
3	The board and chair of the organisation are independent of the minister and ministry.
4	The board includes industry representatives thereby increasing its management capability. Other relevant persons can be members from the civil service, trade unions and other relevant interests.
5	They have their own independently managed finances from the ministry of finance, industry and own sources.
6	Their personnel is independent of the civil service in terms of appointments, salaries, dismissal and terms of appointment.
7	They have independent, expert staff with experience of tourism and the public sector. This expertise is not normally found in the traditional civil service.
8	The chief executive or managing director is better appointed by the board rather than by the minister.
9	The board decides major policy, mission statements, major objectives and priorities and monitors performance and community and public interest obligations.
10	They can work closely with industry and have efficient partnership arrangements. They are aware of the market's supply and demand situation.
11	They have experience and knowledge of the public sector and are part of it and work in relationship with it.

Source: *Elliott 1997: 103.*

■ Table 4.3 *Key roles and corporate objectives of Tourism New South Wales*		
CORPORATE OBJECTIVES	Corporate objectives of Tourism New South Wales are: • to build and convert awareness of New South Wales destinations in target markets • to develop private and public sector partnerships to grow and manage tourism • to share knowledge to improve industry effectiveness and stimulate investment • to foster a dynamic organisational culture built on strategic thinking, resource management, teamwork, proactive communication, innovation and creativity • to demonstrate the organisation's effectiveness to government.
KEY ROLES	Tourism New South Wales promotes and supports the development of New South Wales destinations by: • marketing New South Wales destinations • working with and providing advice to industry, government agencies and other key stakeholders about the development of sustainable destinations.

Source: *New South Wales Department of Tourism Sport and Recreation 2005: 5.*

Tourism statutory corporations are generally structured and linked to the broader machinery of government in one of two ways. First, the statutory corporation can be situated as a stand-alone (autonomous) agency, whose board is responsible to the Minister for Tourism (see figure 4.1a). The second and more complex structure (shown in figure 4.1b) is one in which the agency is part of a larger department whose functions and branches traverse one or more additional portfolios such as small business, regional development, sport and recreation. The tourism corporation retains considerable autonomy because of the legislation governing its functions and operations while the board continues to report directly to the minister. However, ministerial responsibilities and reporting requirements will require the corporation to work closely with and consult other branches (e.g. regional development or small business).

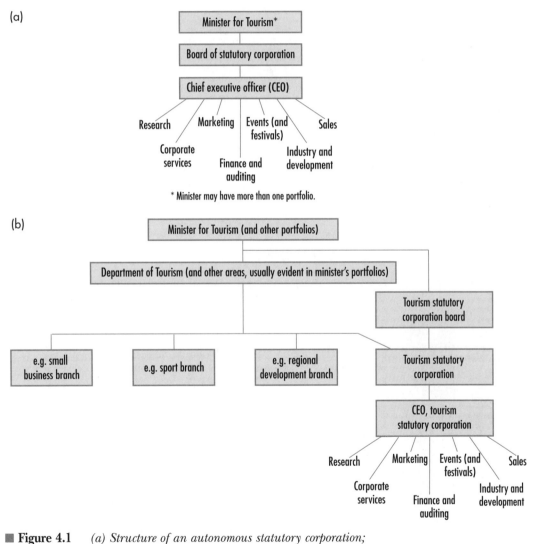

■ **Figure 4.1**   *(a) Structure of an autonomous statutory corporation;*
(b) structure of a corporation that belongs to a large department

■ Table 4.4 *Tourism New South Wales board members and their affiliations in 2006*

MAURICE NEWMAN AC, FSIA CHAIRMAN	Maurice Newman joined the board as chairman in 2002; his current term expires in May 2008. Maurice is the current chairman of the following organisations: the Australian Stock Exchange, the Sydney Convention and Visitors Bureau, the Federal Treasurer's Financial Sector Advisory Council, the Australian Father's Day Council and the Council of Governors and Patrons of the Taronga Zoo Foundation. Maurice is the co-chairman of the Singapore-Australia Business Alliance Forum. He is a director of the Queensland Investment Corporation, a patron of the Committee for Economic Development of Australia (CEDA), an adviser to the Marsh Group of Companies, and a member of the Business Council of Australia's Chairmen's Panel. In 2002, Maurice was appointed Chancellor of Macquarie University.
LESLIE CASSAR, AM DEPUTY CHAIRMAN	Appointed to the board in 2004, Leslie's current term expires in November 2007. Leslie was appointed deputy chairman in December 2005. He serves as chairman of the Tourism and Transport Forum (TTF Australia) and is a director of World Aviation Systems, Malta (WAS). Additionally, he is a director of AC Cars, manufacturer of the AC Cobra sports car. Previously he enjoyed a long and successful career with Qantas Airways in Australia and overseas, and then with the Concorde International Travel/World Aviation Systems Group in Australia prior to the company being sold to ABNAMRO in 2002.
RUTH FAGAN	Appointed to the board in 1998; Ruth's current term expires in August 2007. Ruth is presently the Cowra Tourism Manager and a councillor of the Cowra Shire. She was the chairman of the Board of Cowra Tourism for 10 years and formerly operated a motel in a vineyard in Cowra.
NARENDRA KUMAR	Appointed to the board in 2005, Narendra's current term expires in November 2008. Narendra is the Executive General Manager Regional Airlines with Qantas Airways. He has held previous roles at Qantas as Executive General Manager Subsidiary Businesses and Group General Manager Commercial Services. He has also held various senior management positions with Air Pacific in Fiji and is currently a director of Harvey Holidays Pty Ltd.
JOHN O'NEILL, BA (HONS)	Executive Director and General Manager, Tourism NSW — John commenced with Tourism NSW in October 2003. He is a director of the Australian Tourism Data Warehouse, a director of the Sydney Convention and Visitors Bureau, a member of the National Online Strategy Committee and a board member of Tourism Snowy Mountains Inc and the Northern Rivers Tourism Regional Tourism Organisation. In 2003–04 John chaired the Australian Standing Committee on Tourism (ASCOT) and chaired ASCOT's Intergovernmental Agreement Working Party. Previously he was a part owner and chief executive of a niche media company, the ticketing communications manager for the Sydney Organising Committee for the 2000 Olympic games and the winner of various awards during a 15-year career in media working for country, metropolitan and national newspapers, magazines and national television networks.

NICHOLAS PAPALLO OAM, LLB	Appointed to the board in 2002; Nicholas' current term expires in April 2007. Nicholas is a solicitor with a city practice, which he established in 1965. He is a director of the following organisations: Mondo Pacific Pty Ltd, APC Socotherm Pty Ltd, G&N Management Pty Ltd and Magaldi Power Australia Pty Ltd. Nicholas is the honorary trade and investment envoy for New South Wales to Italy.
DENIS PIERCE	Appointed to the board in 2000; Denis' current term expires in December 2006. Denis is the managing director of ATS Pacific Pty Ltd. He is a director of the following organisations: Encore Business Tourism, Present Australia, Grida Investments Pty Ltd, Coalaa Pty Ltd, Tane Mahuta Pty Ltd, Labasa Pty Ltd, Stonebridge Forest Ltd. He is a board member of the regional tourism organisation Tourism Tropical Queensland and the International College of Tourism and Hotel Management at Manly, NSW. Denis is a former chairman of the Inbound Tourism Organisation of Australia and a recipient of the 2000 ITOA Award of Excellence for Outstanding Individual Contribution to the Australian inbound industry.
JOHN THORPE	Appointed to the board in 2002; John's current term expires in April 2007. John is the president of the Australian Hotels Association (NSW) and president of the National Australian Hotels Association. He is also the owner of the Harbord Beach Hotel. John was awarded the 2003 Centenary medal in recognition of his support and service to the community.
CHARLOTTE VIDOR PHC MPS, MUrbStud (Macq)	Appointed to the board in 1996, Charlotte's current term expires in February 2007. Charlotte is a director of Toga Hospitality, which includes Medina Apartment Hotels, Vibe Hotels and Travel Lodge Hotels. Charlotte is also the licensee and manager, Robert Edwards Real Estate Pty Ltd.
ROBERT (BOB) ADBY	Director-General, NSW Department of Tourism, Sport and Recreation (TSR); Bob commenced with TSR in November 2004. He is also the chief executive officer of the Sydney 2009 World Masters Games with responsibility for establishing the structures and processes for planning and implementing the Games. Bob attends Tourism NSW Board meetings as an observer.

Source: *Tourism New South Wales, www.tourism.nsw.gov.au.*

In most states and territories both structures have been applied by governments since the 1980s. Movements between them occur with shifts in thinking about whether small autonomous operating units are more efficient and effective than larger groupings of related portfolios. Inevitably, questions arise as to whether monolithic organisations covering several portfolios or small, tightly focused organisations are better positioned to address tourism and other issues. There are arguments to support and oppose both options. Small units with a tight focus and a clear charter may be easier to manage, particularly in terms of limiting bureaucratic discretion, and for statutory corporations, tight foci and clear charters are essential. However, many small autonomous operating units without formal charters may result in overlapping legislation, policy and administrative practices (e.g. sport, recreation, tourism, leisure and events). Many small units will also result in increased competition for scarce government resources while history suggests that individual government agencies will grow over time. Conversely, large organisations encompassing several branches responsible to a single minister could be designed to reduce the need for several administrations with high-level staff, diverse legislation and policy development. This reduces the likelihood of several ministers speaking on overlapping matters. That said, large organisations may become bogged down in their administration, inefficiencies may be difficult to detect, and leadership may be constrained by administrative tasks.

Under both of these structures, statutory corporations generally have a given number of 'independent' (e.g. private sector) board members or commissioners, who wield considerable power and who are appointed for a given term to administer the corporation (see for example Jenkins 2001). Parliament fixes the structures, functions and powers of statutory corporations and the means of government control in legislation (Warhurst 1980). Government is responsible for the actions of statutory corporations and exercises its power in various ways. Government can vary legislation that governs the operations of statutory corporations and their operations and controls their budgets, as well as appointments to their boards and to senior staffing positions. Cabinet gives directives or policy statements to statutory corporations, but it might struggle to force an agency to decide or act immediately in a particular way, especially where corporations are not answerable to the minister but to parliament (Mascarenhas 1996).

There are many problems associated with the establishment and operations of statutory authorities. Widespread problems include: high costs of operating and supporting boards, the potential for conflict between boards and the government, and the difficulty of clearly defining powers that match the corporation's responsibilities. Public corporations must 'reconcile the conflicting demands of operating like a private enterprise while having to be accountable to the public through the legislature' as with varying degrees of success they attempt to 'bridge the demands of politics with business and [try] to combine business objectives with social purposes' (Mascarenhas 1996: 63). As will be seen below, there are also times when the private interests of board members of statutory corporations are clearly in conflict with government policies and actions and perhaps with the 'public interest'. As Warhurst (1980: 151) noted, after governments establish statutory corporations they often are left to 'lament the lack of control which they are able to exercise over them'.

In his 1997 report into the corporate governance of public sector authorities, the New South Wales Auditor-General, Tony Harris, launched a trenchant attack on the performance of authorities. Harris concluded there was no evidence that 440 boards added value to the government authorities (a comment that curiously attracted little publicity) and highlighted the dilemmas of boards of corporatised entities, which supposedly operate at arm's length from elected politicians. 'There is still confusion about who is running the entities — the minister or the board ... Even when it should clearly be the board there are still signs that ministers believe it is they who should be running the entities ... You can see it in announcements by ministers: "Ministers have decided that ..."' (Harris, in Washington 1999: 28). A vivid demonstration of this potential overlap and confusion was in the appointment of Michael Knight as Minister for the Olympics and later as president of the Sydney Organising Committee for the Olympic Games (SOCOG). Knight conceded that it was a high-risk strategy for him to have the two jobs: 'Some of my colleagues have said: "Gee, if you become President and Minister then the Government owns all the problems and can't distance itself from SOCOG's failures." [But] I don't see the fate of the Government riding on my shoulders . . . The Government was always in the Olympic tent — it took Cabinet and the IOC and the community a long time to come to terms with me doing the two jobs but when it actually happened there was pretty much a consensus view . . . it doesn't matter how many nice things are said or how many statutory positions I hold' (Mitchell 1996: 20).

In Australia, tourism statutory corporations in the states and territories have been established for a host of reasons, with their respective foci coming to rest mainly on the marketing of their respective tourism destinations and a range of commercial activities (Craik 1991a; Hall 1998). Critical examinations about what tourism statutory corporations have been and ought to be doing have been raised by several writers (e.g. Industries Assistance Commission [IAC] 1989; Craik 1991a, 1991b, 1992; Jenkins & Stolk 2003; Elliott 1997). Few, however, have explored the relationships between the public and private sectors and the role of statutory corporations, such as Tourism NSW, as institutions of the Australian state (for earlier critical analyses of the situation in Queensland, see McMillen 1991 and Craik 1991a, 1992).

According to Wettenhall, statutory corporations breach the traditional chain of responsibility fashioned in the Westminster system, as an appointed commission is elevated and on it is conferred far more decision-making autonomy than 'enjoyed by public servants in orthodox departments' (1990: 10; also see Warhurst 1980). Statutory corporations are more independent of cabinet control than are departments and are established by legislation to function independently of government departments. There is an enormous body of literature concerning the roles and activities of statutory authorities and public enterprise, much of which focuses on the justification or non-justification for such bodies' existence and accountability (Davis 1991). 'Commentators on the role of statutory authorities and public enterprise have correctly identified the central dilemma as "freedom versus accountability" ' (Davis 1991: 98). In fact, serious doubts have been cast on government and bureaucratic integrity and accountability with regard to tourism statutory authorities (see the case study 'The Western Australian Tourism Commission, Eventscorp and the 1995 Global Dance Foundation "affair" ' on p. 148).

Industry (read 'capital') wants government intervention only where it suits its needs and will often exploit situations for its own benefit to the detriment of the wider community. One way industry can minimise government intervention is via **self-regulation**. The area of self-regulation is an interesting and controversial one. A discussion of self-regulation might begin with the questions: why don't some areas of the tourism industry want laws and legislation governing access to and use of resources in natural environments, and why should businesses coalesce and go out of their way to develop their own industry guidelines? Self-regulation in ecotourism is a valuable contemporary example for highlighting such issues.

Ecotourism is a substantial and growing part of the tourism industry. It is a significant factor in the positioning and branding of Australia as an attractive tourist destination. Ecotourism is also an important economic activity. For example, ecotourism businesses are estimated to employ the equivalent of 4500 full-time staff (Cotterill 1996). Ecotourism in Australia's protected areas presents great challenges to diverse interests, including governments and managers of protected areas, ecotourism operators and local communities. There is an urgent need to balance ecotourism's economic development with the environmental sustainability of protected areas. Ecotourism frequently takes place in fragile ecosystems, and their susceptibility to increasing tourism and other pressures is threatening their ecological integrity.

Three basic principles underpin most definitions of ecotourism: (1) ecotourism is nature-based; (2) ecotourism is associated with sustainability and seeks to minimise tourism's negative effects; and (3) ecotourism has an educational component designed to motivate positive changes in people's attitudes and behaviour regarding environmental conservation (Buckley 2001; Weaver 2001a). Ecotourism has been defined in Australia as 'Ecologically sustainable tourism with a primary focus on experiencing natural areas, that foster environmental and cultural understanding, appreciation and conservation' (EA 2005), but there is no consensus on its precise meaning (Weaver 2001b).

As many protected areas experience pressures of increasing tourism demand and use becomes more intensive, the potential for conflict between maintaining environmental quality, maximising recreational accessibility and satisfaction and promoting economic development is enhanced. Governments and tourism industry operators have been seeking to create circumstances in which market forces, or non-governmental institutions such as industry bodies, perform regulatory functions. Self-regulation and accreditation in the tourism industry is one such example and is receiving international coverage (e.g. Issaverdis 2001; Weaver 2001a, 2001b; Buckley 2002). Ecotourism Australia (EA) is the Australian ecotourism industry's peak representative body. EA's vision is 'to be leaders in assisting ecotourism and other committed tourism operations to become environmentally sustainable, economically viable and socially and culturally responsible' (EA 2005). One of EA's largest and most significant projects is the National Ecotourism Accreditation Program (NEAP). NEAP is an industry-driven eco-certification scheme or program, which EA claims enables industry, protected area managers and consumers to identify 'genuine' ecotourism products.

The concepts of accreditation and certification are gaining some reluctant acceptance in the tourism industry, but are considered a means of enhancing tourism product standards and contributing to environmental sustainability and organisational marketing profiles (McKercher 1998; Harris & Jago 2001; Issaverdis 2001). Recent figures suggest there are approximately 3000 nature and ecotourism operators in Australia (ABS 2003), of which more than a thousand are licensed to operate in national parks (Buckley 2003). Yet a recent list of accredited products reveals only 240 companies and agencies with at least one product certified through NEAP. A number of factors are, however, providing further impetus to accreditation: 'the increasing expectation of standards and awareness of service quality by customers, the increasing expectation by travel intermediaries that the product will be safe and environmentally responsible, an increased industry awareness of sustainable business practice and a growing interest in [tourism] research' (Issaverdis 2001: 582; also see Fennell 1999; Weaver 2001a, 2001b).

Assessments of ecotourism accreditation in Australia and overseas are far from conclusive about its merits and about accredited operators' attitudes and perceptions of related schemes. According to Fennell (2002: 214), 'the jury is still out on the success of Australia's accreditation process'. This view was reflected during the Ecotourism Australia-Wide Online Conference, a project of the Australian Heritage Commission and the former Ecotourism Association of Australia, which noted that opinion is still divided on the merits of accreditation (www.ecotourism.org.au/products.asp.

Buckley (2001; 2002: 183, 185) argued that 'ecolabels and environmental accreditation are controversial topics in tourism' because they can be used by regulatory agencies to grant permits and because their main function is to act as a 'market mechanism'. He proposed that 'the most basic test of a tourism ecolabel (e.g. Advanced Accredited Ecotourism operator) is whether it is accepted by tourists as meaningful, reliable and useful in choosing individual products' (2002: 185). Essential components of an ecolabel program are, therefore, 'transparent criteria and procedures with detailed information readily available to the public as a backup for the labels themselves' (2002: 186). To be effective and reliable, ecolabel schemes need adequate accreditation criteria, clearly defined procedures for assessment and auditing and penalties for non-compliance. Furthermore, information on each of these aspects of the schemes needs to be available to prospective tourists and members, and the ecolabels must be recognised by the target market.

Weaver (2001a: 158) stated that the self-funded NEAP scheme has led to Australia being regarded as 'the world leader in ecotourism accreditation'. However, Weaver also notes that the NEAP scheme has a number of limitations: (1) the initial application's reliance on self-assessment by the operator could result in misleading submissions being accredited and not exposed until an on-site audit is undertaken; (2) the integrity of the auditing process is questionable because the paper audit is based on a self-assessment by the operator; and (3) operators are notified 60 days before on-site auditing and, as auditors must be allowed free entry, the audited operator is aware of precisely when the audit takes place. Since Weaver made these observations, changes have been made to certification processes, but operators are still notified at least 21 days before on-site audits (see NEAP 2003). In short, in Australia, there is no independent on-site auditing of accredited and non-accredited ecotourism products, and EA has given no indication as to how often any particular operator is audited other than to signal a commitment to eventually audit all accredited operators and that a percentage of operators will be audited each year (NEAP 2003). Yet, according to Jean-Pierre Issaverdis (2001: 580), who at the time of his writing was a board member of EA, auditing is the necessary component to ensure that applied concepts of benchmarking, accreditation and best practice 'are valid and that reliable measures of performance are defined'.

Weaver also indicates that Australia is likely to provide leadership in ecotourism quality control, quality systems management and comprehensive mandatory certification. However, such a position could not be achieved and sustained unless present practice is thoroughly and independently investigated. Despite the widespread promotion and encouragement of ecotourism as a sustainable form of tourism by public and private sector agencies, 'Ecotourism has a shortage of sound empirical data' (Fennell 2001: 639).

Recent research has examined operators' motivations and satisfaction with regard to NEAP programs and consumer motivations and preferences with respect to NEAP products (e.g. Tourism Queensland 2000a, 2000b). Other research has investigated tourists' attitudes to ecotourism and ecotourism accreditation (Nielsen, Birtles & Sofield 1995) and accreditation for adventure tourism products (Bergin & Jago 1999).

Mayes, Dyer and Richins (2004) compared the perceived effects of dolphin–human interaction programs on the pro-environmental attitudes, beliefs, intended behaviour and intended specific actions of participants. At the two Queensland destinations they investigated, the researchers found great variations among the products across a wide range of variables, such as participant numbers, interpretive material, hygiene, and touching and feeding of dolphins. Despite the important contributions of these and other studies, no independent research provides detailed evidence of the extent to which accredited and non-accredited ecotourism products comply with accreditation guidelines and park permit conditions or compare in their operations. Furthermore, no independent study has thoroughly investigated operators' attitudes to and perceptions of NEAP, park permit conditions and other means of industry regulation in Australian states and territories.

The issue of accreditation was raised in the Commonwealth Government's Tourism White Paper (2003), and $2 million was allocated to the development of a national accreditation program. There were no indications as to how ecotourism accreditation principles and practices could be improved, but many constraints to tourism accreditation were noted. The White Paper listed 'major constraints' to tourism accreditation, including the 'failure of current arrangements to convince many businesses that the benefits of accreditation outweigh the compliance costs . . . ; concerns about the way in which some programs are designed or administered . . . limited or infrequent auditing and standards that do not set a high enough hurdle' (pp. 32–3). The White Paper also acknowledges that 'there are a number of accreditation programs currently operating in Australia . . . With limited resources these programs are often unable to adequately promote the benefits of tourism accreditation to businesses and consumers and cannot provide independent, rigorous and cost effective auditing procedures . . .' (pp. 32–3). Two core components of Ecotourism Australia's Accreditation Program are 'environmental sustainability' and 'contribution to conservation'. A question that ought to be asked is: how can operators whose actions may have a negative effect on the life of marine species such as dolphins obtain ecotourism accreditation?

Strong support for self-regulation in tourism has come from many quarters, although often from those with vested interests, such as the operators and their organisations (e.g. Ecotourism Australia, an organisation run by mostly private sector operators). A particularly important aspect of influence has been the growth of pressure (i.e. lobby or interest) groups.

PLANNING IN PRACTICE

Who's really taking care of the dolphins?

For more than 20 years, Indo-Pacific Humpback dolphins have been fed at Tin Can Bay. Mayes, Dyer and Richins (2004, pp. 40–1) made some telling observations, including:

- no limits were placed on how many people were permitted to feed the dolphins
- during holiday seasons and other periods of high visitor numbers, up to a hundred people were in the water and could remain until the dolphins departed
- people touched dolphins
- feeding was not controlled or monitored. 'Indeed, the amount of food per dolphin appeared to vary and after the feeding session, the practice was to feed all remaining defrosted fish to the dolphin(s) and/or to the cormorants and pelicans that had become a nuisance for both visitors and dolphins. Hygiene levels and practices at Tin Can Bay appeared to be minimal compared to those at Tangalooma.'

In October 2005 a ban was placed on dolphin feeding at Tin Can Bay. However, although locals and visitors defied the ban, the Queensland Minister for the Environment, Desley Boyle, decided not to pursue legal action enforcing the ban. In an ABC interview, Tin Can Bay café owner Steve Walker, who organises daily feedings and earns a dollar or two from the activity, stated that 'people power' had 'swayed the Queensland Environment Minister to allow feeding to continue'. This was a surprising move.

The previous owners of the café had been told to stop feeding the dolphins. According to an agreement that ended in March 2005 when the signatories departed, feeding of the dolphins was to be phased out. The Hon. Desley Boyle MP, Minister for the Environment, Local Government, Planning and Women (2005), stated, 'I offered the new owners of the café the opportunity to put to me a proposal for this phase-out to be completed in a way that considered their business interests. I was shocked to receive a submission that not only proposed perpetuating the feeding but to expand the exploitation of these rare, wild animals. Clearly the new owners are only interested in these dolphins as a drawcard for their own commercial gain and have no regard for the dolphins' safety. I have no choice but to reject this submission and call an end to feeding at Tin Can Bay (Boyle 2005).'

(continued)

Among several incidents highlighted by the minister, it was noted that dolphins learn to follow boats, are injured by boats, suffer injuries from fishing lines and are exposed to contaminated food, diesel spills, discharges, and cold and flu germs. Feeding could contribute to deaths of infant dolphins. 'Draft national guidelines, developed by the Commonwealth and States, say wild dolphins should not be fed and there should be no expansion of existing authorised programs. With the exceptions of Tangalooma and Sea World, in Queensland waters wild dolphins live in their natural environment. These amazing creatures should be viewed with wonderment and awe from a safe distance.'

References

Mayes, G, Dyer, P & Richins, H 2004, 'Dolphin–human interaction: Environmental attitudes, beliefs and intended behaviours and actions of participants in interpretation programs: A pilot study', *Annals of Leisure Research*, vol. 7, no. 1, pp. 34–53.
Ministerial Statement: the Hon. Desley Boyle MP, Environment, Local Government, Planning and Women, 2005, 'Dolphin feeding over at Tin Can Bay', 28 September, viewed 29 March 2006, http://statements.cabinet.qld.gov.au/cgi-bin/display-statement.pl?id=8709&db=media.
Queensland Department of Environment 2001, 'Conservation and management of whales and dolphins in Queensland 1997–2001', viewed 29 March 2006, www.epa.qld.gov.au/publications/p00524aa.pdf/Conservation_and_management_of_whales_and_dolphins_in_Queensland_19972001.pdf.

Further reading

'Dolphin-mania: A study guide', viewed 29 March 2006, http://abc.net.au/programsales/study-guide/StGd_Doplhin_Mania.pdf.

4.7 *P*OLITICAL LOBBYING AND LOBBY GROUPS

Two important features of liberal democracies are organised pressure groups and political lobbying. The term 'pressure group' is most often used interchangeably with the terms 'interest group' or 'lobby group'. A **pressure group** can be defined as any association or organisation that makes a claim, either directly or indirectly, on government so as to influence public policy without itself being willing to exercise the formal powers of government (Matthews 1980, in Hall & Jenkins 1995). Several features of pressure groups can be observed:

- They have a legitimate right to operate and represent sectional interests, who in fact authorise them to do so.
- They attempt to influence governments, but do not seek to gain government.
- Not all activities need be or indeed are political. Activities variously include provision of financial advice to members; the conduct of field

trips, seminars and conferences; research; contributions to training and education packages; and contacts for developing networks and alliances.

- They often seek to influence government policy indirectly by attempting to shape the demands that other groups and the general public make on government, for example through the conduct of public relations campaigns.
- They are central to our political systems. They are important sources of information and alternative advice for governments (political parties, parliamentarians, their advisers and senior bureaucrats) and provide a means for private individuals and agencies to influence the policy process.
- Contrary to much opinion, they are not too powerful, can be screened and filtered by government officials (or bureaucrats), political parties and parliamentarians, and in fact ultimately do make an important contribution to peaceful democratic processes and help relative to other parts of the world (see for example Hall & Jenkins 1995).

Well-organised pressure groups are important to politicians and bureaucrats. In the tourism policy and planning arenas, lobby groups have had a chequered history, but are becoming increasingly prominent.

The Australian National Travel Association was founded in 1929. ANTA was based in Melbourne and launched with a budget of £70 000 for five years. Its main functions were to promote Australia overseas, to stimulate domestic travel, to enhance accommodation and infrastructure, particularly in rural areas, to help coordinate operators and tourist bureaus, to disseminate information and to educate Australians about the benefits of attracting overseas visitors (Richardson 1999; Leiper 1980). In the late 1950s ANTA initiated moves to establish a statutory authority in order to increase its financial security and enhance its ability to influence policy processes. In 1964 ANTA commissioned Harris Kerr & Foster and J. Stanton Robbins Inc. to conduct a detailed survey of the Australian tourism industry. Their recommendations were that the Australian Government establish the Australian Tourist Commission to promote the Australian tourism industry overseas. This was a pivotal moment in federal tourism policy and administration (Leiper 1980; Richardson 1999).

The Australian Tourist Commission (ATC) was established as a statutory authority in 1967 around the existing ANTA offices and staff. The general manager of ANTA, Basil Atkinson, was the commission's first general manager. With the ATC in place, ANTA reoriented itself to become concerned mainly with domestic matters (Richardson 1999). In the mid-1970s ANTA made submissions to government on matters relating to depreciation on hotels and motels, appeared before the Industries Assistance Commission (IAC) during IAC's inquiries into tourist accommodation and export incentives and made a major contribution to the establishment of the National Tourism and Hospitality Industry Training Committee (Richardson 1999).

In 1979, ANTA became the Australian Travel Industry Association (ATIA), establishing itself as the industry's voice and representative on a range of policy matters. By the early 1980s, however, ATIA was in financial crisis, and it was restructured and renamed Australian Tourism Industry Association. In the early 1980s ATIA released *Australia — Tourism in the 80s*, indicating the need for a coordinated approach to achieving the benefits of tourism through a framework for collective action by industry and government, with encouragement for joint public–private initiatives.

The chairman of ATIA's board of 1985 was Sir Frank Moore. Other board members included senior executives of Lend Lease, Trans Australian Airlines, Qantas, UK-Australia-New Zealand British Airways, the Queensland Tourist and Travel Corporation and Captain Cook Cruises. ATIA established a strategy and policy forum (ATIA Council), produced its first newsletter (*ATIA NOW*), transferred its national office from Sydney to Canberra, expanded its membership to include the Australian Hotels Association, the Australian Automobile Association, large (multinational) corporations and state and regional tourism organisations. ATIA, whose chairman had close political affiliations with the National Party, was building political clout and making representations to government on all major matters concerning tourism, supported by visions of tourism through national strategies such as Tourism 2000, the establishment in partnership with the Australian Federation of Travel Agents of the first Chair of Tourism and Centre for Tourism Studies at James Cook University and the holding of the first National Tourism Conference in Canberra. It made major representations to the Kennedy Inquiry into tourism and went about aggressively promoting itself as the body that could unite the industry and speak as the industry's voice.

By 1990 ATIA, still chaired by Sir Frank Moore, had an operating revenue of $3.9 million and 413 members, turned a profit of $156 000 and had accumulated substantial assets. It launched *ATIA's Strategy for the 1990s*, which 'set out the long-term policy objectives for ATIA and the Australia tourism industry and identifies shorter term actions which ATIA needs to address' (p. v).

ATIA, however, met with competition from an unexpected source: John Brown, the former federal (Labor) Minister for Tourism, who had been forced to resign his portfolio in December 1987. In an announcement in which he launched a new tourism lobby group, Tourism Task Force (TTF), Brown stated, 'I feel almost like Lazarus ... Here I am, rising like a phoenix from the ashes' (cited in Lane 1989: 6) as chairman of the TTF.

There was much criticism and debate of TTF among industry representatives, by ATIA, the Inbound Tourism Organisation of Australia, government ministers and others. Concerns were raised that the industry was becoming more splintered amid claims by John Brown that other industry associations had not been doing their jobs properly (e.g. Ballantyne 1989). TTF was launched in the shadow of the 1989 air pilots' dispute. A survey by Deloitte, Haskins & Sells uncovered a plethora of agencies representing tourism businesses, with the main agencies being identified as ATIA, TTF, AHA, ITOA, AFTA and the Catering Institute of Australia. It was argued that there was confusion as to whom government should listen to and that there should be an umbrella organisation with several chapters. Indeed, both ATIA and TTF separately sought funding from government for the tourism industry in the wake of the 1989 pilots' dispute. Others, such as the Melbourne-based consultant Geoff Hyde, doubted that the then federal Labor government would work with Frank Moore, who had strong and lengthy links with the National Party.

At its September 1994 Annual Tourism Conference, ATIA announced that it would be restructured and reconstituted to form Tourism Council Australia in order to raise the industry's profile, establish a stronger membership base and broaden its collaborative networks. 'We continued to represent the widespread interests of the tourism industry in an aggressive and comprehensive manner, stepping up membership development and increasing demands for input and representation at Parliamentary inquiries, specialist committees, industry forums and international affairs' (TCA 1994: 3). TCA increased its membership base to more than 600 organisations, representing 30 000 affiliated bodies. In July 1995 Bruce Baird, former New South Wales Minister for Tourism, was appointed as TCA's first managing director. Baird had also served the former New South Wales coalition government as Minister for the Olympics Bid and Minister for Roads. This type of movement from politics to private industry associations and interest groups is not at all unusual. Indeed, Baird soon re-entered politics, winning pre-selection for the seat of Cook in 1998 and being voted into parliament as the Member for Cook the following year.

TCA returned its headquarters to Sydney. According to Richardson (1999: 299): 'TCA saw its chief role as leading the policy debate and to that end its 1997–98 figures indicate the scale of its effort — it made more than 60 submissions to governments and departments, it put out 200 media releases and Baird made more than 150 speeches to various audiences. In that year it also inaugurated a Prime Minister's lunch.'

Brown's TTF lobby group attacked the Australian Tourist Commission and lobbied government to restructure the organisation and to devolve some of its functions and responsibilities to TTF (Moffet 1991). Within days, several lobby groups, including ATIA, AHA, AFTA and ITOA, responded and slammed TTF's proposals. In February 1992 AFTA quit TTF; other organisations feeling the pinch of the recession were reluctant to pay their fees; and soon after Brown declared TTF would probably need to be disbanded (see Tourism Planning Breakthrough: 'Brown took pay cut of $100 000 in tourism job').

After a shaky start, TTF gradually reignited itself and went from strength to strength but was bathed in controversy for several years. In 2002 it was renamed Tourism and Transport Forum, and its members now include organisations ranging from major commercial transport companies to multinational corporations, financial advisers, state tourism corporations such as Tourism NSW to universities and the Cooperative Research Centre for Sustainable Tourism.

TTF, a not-for-profit company, is governed by a board of directors. TTF's website states that it 'is the peak industry group for the tourism, transport and infrastructure sectors. As a national, member-funded CEO forum, TTF advocates the public policy interests of the 200 most prestigious corporations and institutions in Australian tourism, transport, property, infrastructure and investment' (www.ttf.org.au/about/about.htm). The organisation's influence is recounted by Warwick Smith, executive director, Macquarie Bank, who states: 'TTF Australia successfully brings together the major players in transport, tourism and property and gives voice to their political and commercial aspirations. During my time as Deputy Chair of TTF and as a former Federal Minister, I was witness to TTF's ability to access and influence public policy — across the country and across the political spectrum — to the benefit of its national Members' (www.ttf.org.au/about/pdf/TTF_Our_Members.pdf).

TOURISM PLANNING BREAKTHROUGH
Brown took pay cut of $100 000 in tourism job

The former Federal Minister for Tourism, Mr John Brown, has revealed that he took a $100 000 pay cut last year in his $250 000-a-year job as chairman of the controversial Tourism Task Force. He voluntarily trimmed his salary after the group lost several members whose own businesses went broke, while others were unable to pay annual fees because of the recession. The task force, which mainly lobbies government for a bigger tourism budget, operates on money raised through $15 000 annual fees from its more than 60 members. Mr Brown, who will still earn $150 000 a year from the task force, also disclosed that it will continue to exist despite reports of its imminent closure.

He put a motion to about 40 task force members last month to wind up the company, partly because some were failing to pay fees. He also argued that the task force had achieved its objectives. But it was decided at a second meeting on Thursday that the group would continue 'in a modified form'. Operating costs will be cut by 25 per cent, from $400 000 a year to $300 000. Staff will be reduced from four to two.

Speaking for the first time about the crisis, in an exclusive interview with the Herald, Mr Brown said he took the pay cut in June last year because of the prevailing conditions, despite having 'a contract which was viable'. 'It's still a highly paid position but try and get a consultant to do the hours that I do at an hourly rate and see what you get,' he added. He told members he wasn't prepared to spend the rest of his life chasing people to pay their fees and neither should his staff.

Tourism is the nation's largest export earner, worth $6.5 billion annually and the biggest employer, providing some 600 000 jobs, with prospects of creating another million by the end of the decade.

'We will now restrict our activities in some areas but basically to lobbying,' he said.

Mr Brown has agreed to stay on only until the end of this financial year. 'If the members want to go on from then they will have to tell me. I've been more than chuffed by the support that was evident from the members. When I said we were going to close the place down they were really shocked and there was a constant thread through that meeting that no, this should not be allowed to happen.'

News that the task force was considering closure had been welcomed with glee in some quarters. Since its formation three years ago it has been the target of industry attacks, mostly voiced in private. Amongst the complaints were that the former minister was making a 'power grab' to control the tourism industry and that the existence of several other major industry bodies made it unnecessary. But Mr Brown argues that his value lies in the lobbying power he wields through close political contacts. 'Members of this organisation are also members of other lobby groups … they formed this group simply because they believed these other groups, while they deal with their own charter and do a good job, don't have the capacity to lobby governments as we have,' Mr Brown said.

The task force's membership reads like a who's who of the tourism, banking, building and business sectors. While it is confidential, the *Herald* has obtained a copy.

Among those listed are the ACTU president, Mr Bill Kelty, Ansett joint chairman, Sir Peter Abeles, the Federal Airports Corporation chief, Mr Bill Swingler, Radio 2UE broadcaster Mr Alan Jones and the Qantas chief executive, Mr John Ward.

'We have no difficulty at all with the political parties and never will have … it is totally apolitical and our members realise we are the only major group that is seen as apolitical and has the capacity to knock on every door and gain admittance,' Mr Brown said.

Had his political lobbying power and value to the task force been weakened by the departure of the former Prime Minister, Mr Hawke, a close personal friend? 'Rubbish. I still have the same close association with Keating as I had with Hawke. Keating and I have been friends a lot longer than Hawke and I. 'Griffiths [the present Federal Minister for Tourism] is a very close friend. Jull [Mr Jull, the Opposition tourism spokesman] and Hewson [Leader of the Opposition] I count as friends,' said Mr Brown. 'I have really good relations with people in the tourism industry right across the board so I don't have any reservations about knocking on any political party's door and being admitted, simply because they see me and they see this organisation as being someone without a political axe to grind and we haven't.'

He rejects criticism that the task force has achieved little, pointing out that in the five years he was Minister for Tourism the budget to the Australian Tourist Commission went from $9 million to $38 million. 'In the three years I wasn't around it went from $38 million to $40 million,' he said. 'Since we have been back here as a tourism task force it has gone from $40 million to $78 million. It's not coincidental. It happens to be a fact.'

Source: *Ballantyne 1992.*

TTF now boasts of its role in influencing a range of tourism and related policies. Although some policy initiatives are aligned with TTF goals and ideas, TTF cannot lay claim to being the major influence. Moreover it is now a lobby group with a broad focus, and it is not likely to be able to represent the grass roots of the tourism industry — the small to medium-sized operators — when it is governed and driven by a wealthy elite.

Some questions concerning the membership of TTF are warranted. Some universities (La Trobe, University of New South Wales, University of Technology, Sydney) and the Sustainable Tourism Cooperative Research Centre are members of TTF. Do these education and research-based institutions, heavily funded by the public purse, endorse TTF's policies? Should they be members of a lobby group that is a voice for powerful corporations, many of which are multinational? Why are these institutions members? What expenses (e.g. costs of membership) do they incur? Are they given priority for research projects conducted by TTF? These questions would be an interesting frame of reference for research into public–private collaborations and alliances.

4.8 MULTINATIONAL CORPORATIONS

Multinational corporations are corporations whose business is conducted internationally in at least two countries or nation states. They have become an enormously powerful aspect of contemporary society, significantly influencing public policy either directly or indirectly through pressure groups such as Tourism and Transport Forum (see TTF's website www.ttf.org.au for membership). Multinational corporations have executives and directors with strong political connections and political savvy, and indeed some corporations have specially resourced units or branches to broker and negotiate with bureaucrats and government ministers. Multinational corporations are practically everywhere, and people in Western nations are now quite accustomed to them. They have brought about tremendous shifts in the geographical location of tourism production and the characteristics of international tourism trade and economic activity (Bull 1995).

Businesses expand by many means, such as creating new branches or subsidiaries (and franchises and alliances are increasingly critical elements in this process) or through vertical and horizontal integration by way of partial acquisitions of companies, mergers and takeovers (Sinclair & Stabler 1997). The means of expanding a business can occur domestically (locally) or internationally (globally). Meethan (2004: 110) makes the important distinction between 'earlier forms of transnationalism and contemporary globalization' and 'the apparent erosion of the autonomy of the nation-state'. He highlights financial deregulation, the development of high-speed communication technology, the post-Fordist organisation of companies, labour force mobility and flexibility, global marketing and decentralisation as major aspects of the geographical spread of multinational corporations, their products and brand reach. Many of the previous constraints to the growth of multinational corporations (e.g. slow communication technology; difficulties and slowness in transferring funds and capital; difficulty in monitoring offshore activities; tight regulatory controls) have been ameliorated. According to Meethan (2004: 117): 'Globalization then appears to pull in two ways, both towards the creation of MNCs [multinational corporations] by the extension of operations through take-overs, the formation of strategic alliances or franchising agreements, and, in terms of consumption, towards more localized or regional branding and niche marketing. In addition, we also see that the extension of services cuts across "traditional" sectoral boundaries, so that convergence at one level is complemented by divergence at another.'

Profit growth, investment returns, market share and product diversification are important business motivations in the travel and tourism industry (Meethan 2004). More specifically, businesses seek to become multinational corporations for many reasons, including the following:

- investment advantages as capital flows to countries with the highest marginal productivity
- securing production advantages over local industry as a result of innovations, superior technology, skills, knowledge and management. Some nation states offer taxation and other concessions or inducements for multinational corporations to establish themselves or to remain in a country. The latter might involve financial inducements because of concerns that the departure of an multinational corporation might result in massive multiplier effects, a loss of jobs and loss of important technology or resources on which a local economy was based (e.g. resorts and tourism, as in such countries as Hawaii and such Australian regions as the Gold Coast and Cairns)
- monopolistic advantages arising from horizontal and vertical integration, which is particularly prevalent in the tourism industry and other service sectors
- possible product life extension: as a market is exhausted in one country, there might be the opportunity to exploit a market elsewhere
- economies of scale can be applied internationally as exhibited by such companies as Club Med, Hertz, Accor and Hyatt. (Bull 1995: 193–5; see also Meethan 2004).

Accor is a multinational company with its origins in France (www.accorhotels. com.au). Accor operates more than 3500 hotels and resorts in almost a hundred countries. The company claims to employ about 158 000 people, and in Australia and New Zealand it has more than 110 hotels and backpackers, including the following brands: Sofitel, Novotel, Mercure, Ibis, Formule One and Base Backpackers. Accor also owns the Sydney Convention and Exhibition Centre, Blue Line Cruises and one of Sydney's best-known restaurants, the Summit. Executives of this group, Thakral Holdings and other large corporations have held influential positions with Tourism NSW and various pressure groups and industry associations, such as TTF and Australia Hotels Association respectively.

Multinational corporations have an enormous influence on economies and wield tremendous power. In smaller, less developed countries they are able to control resources and manipulate governments with the promises of international tourism partnerships and alliances and the importation of knowledge, skills and job creation. Conversely, they are able to avoid high levels of taxation by international financial and capital transfers, and environmental and social consequences of their activities are also well documented (e.g. Richter 1989). The contribution of multinational corporations to sustainable tourism and the conservation of natural and cultural heritage is questionable. Their histories, structures and operations lead us to wonder how much public interest can be expected from corporations that are responsible to their shareholders, whose principal concerns include maximising market shares, revenues and profits, and which frequently achieve their aims by mergers and take-overs and by squeezing out small local operators. Some multinational corporations have laudable goals and socially responsible policies, but many seek competitive advantages, market share and growth at the expense of local cultures and lifestyles.

CHAPTER REVIEW

This chapter has addressed several trends in approaches and perspectives on tourism planning and policy. Many other trends are also critical to sustainable tourism planning and development, but those mentioned here clearly highlight the way the boundaries between the public and private sectors are becoming increasingly blurred. There are risks in this development. There is no guarantee that industry will do what is in the 'public interest' when its principal interests are revenues, profits, market share and growth. The discussion and cases in this chapter indicate a need to critically question the roles of self-regulation and accreditation schemes, statutory corporations, pressure groups and the power of multinational corporations. Those who operate accreditation schemes will laud their credibility, yet their claims are porous. Adoption of accreditation and certification has hardly been widespread, and the ecotourism accreditation and certification process has major flaws.

Governments have yielded to the private sector too much discretion for making decisions that affect the public interest. The drive to do so has been ideological and far too hasty, with the branches of government trees being shaken by concentrated sources of power to which few small businesses and less wealthy individuals have access. It seems, too, that now even publicly funded institutions such as universities see fit to join forces with private interests in supporting the activities of powerful interest groups. The fact is that corporatism is writ large, and it's dressed up as collaboration and partnership. Tourism presents some classic cases.

SUMMARY OF KEY TERMS

Corporate planning

Corporate planning is a process in which decisions are made systematically with reference to their costs, associated risks and effects. Corporate planning implies that decision-making has a carefully devised and ordered structure and that the performance of any decisions, actions and programs are thoroughly monitored and evaluated in a timely manner.

Ecotourism

Ecologically sustainable tourism with a primary focus on experiencing natural areas, which fosters environmental and cultural understanding, appreciation and conservation.

Mechanistic systems

Mechanistic systems are stable systems of a hierarchical and well-defined order in which authority flows through predetermined lines, usually from the top down.

Organic systems

Organic systems are systems of management that allow people to deal with matters as they arise. People are not limited to highly specialised tasks and move fluidly between tasks of sometimes a markedly different nature.

Organisational culture

Organisational culture is a catch-all term that describes the way things are done in a work environment. It is commonly applied to indicate that the way people do things has a pattern that has developed over time. So it can encompass such matters as standards of dress, ways of addressing people, lines of responsibility, record-keeping and file management, inductions and codes of behaviour.

Organisational theory

Organisational theory is concerned with the best way to structure and manage organisations. In organisational theory several schools of thought trace the origins of organisations and explain interrelationships among components of an organisation and its outside environment and hence arrange them into some coherent collective, chronologically and/or thematically.

Pressure group

Pressure groups (also known as lobby or interest groups) are associations or organisations that represent particular interests and seek to influence policy and planning processes. These groups might be large and have lengthy histories, or they might rise in response to specific development or other issues and hence have specific foci and lead a short life.

Scientific management

Scientific management is a school of management theory and approaches first developed by Frederick Winslow Taylor to facilitate factory production. The work environment is designed in a manner that promotes efficient resource use and task specialisation to maximise output while reducing staff effort.

Self-regulation

Self-regulation can take many forms and is evident in many policy and planning arenas. Self-regulation, in theory, seeks to encourage people to meet a non-enforced set of standards, operational criteria or processes. It involves the assumption that people and groups can work together. Non-government organisations often set up codes of behaviour and standards for industry, but there is no compulsion for individuals or companies to comply with them.

Statutory corporations or agencies

Statutory corporations or agencies are not part of the conventional public service, but they do fall within ministerial portfolios. In brief, they are more independent of cabinet control than are departments and are established by legislation to function independently of government departments.

Strategic planning

Strategic planning involves a process of preparing short- to long-term strategies to meet business and corporate objectives. Strategic plans typically define an organisation's mission and values; critically examine its strengths, weaknesses, opportunities and threats; analyse the human and other resources available to an organisation; indicate the organisation's potential strategic directions — objectives and key result areas — after consultation with stakeholders; indicate possible options; ensure a program of implementation, monitoring and evaluation exists; and presents scenarios based on estimates of change in factors influencing an organisation.

QUESTIONS

1 Briefly define the terms 'bureaucracy' and 'organisational culture'. Why are these concepts important in the analysis of tourism policy and planning?

2 Outline the principles underlying Weber's concept of bureaucracy.

3 Briefly describe mechanistic and organic management systems and identify their strengths and weaknesses.

4 Define 'strategic planning' and 'corporate planning'. What influence have the principles underpinning these concepts had on tourism public policy-making?

5 What is an interest or lobby group? What functions does such a group perform? Should universities and the Sustainable Tourism Cooperative Research Centre be members of such a group as TTF?

6 Discuss the advantages and the disadvantages of tourism statutory corporations.

7 What are self-regulation and accreditation? What are the advantages and disadvantages of self-regulation and accreditation schemes to government, to industry and to consumers?

8 Scour the web and academic articles online for examples of criticisms of self-regulation in tourism by industry operators or such organisations as Ecotourism Australia or Tourism and Transport Forum, then summarise these arguments and give examples.

9 Does Ecotourism Australia conduct adequate auditing of accredited ecotourism operators? How often should auditing be conducted? Should operators be notified when an audit will take place? Why?

10 Do multinational corporations exhibit too much power? Discuss this question, giving examples from tourism.

EXERCISES

1 Select a tourism organisation. Examine its most recent annual report. Briefly review its missions, values and objectives. Note the language used in the report. After completing this task, review the annual report of the same organisation (or its successor) from 10 years ago. What, if anything, has changed with regard to the organisation's mission, values and objectives? In reading only the introduction of each report, can you see any signs of shift in corporate language or the style of reporting the organisation's business over the 10-year gap?

2 Statutory corporations generally have a given number of 'independent' (e.g. private sector) board members or commissioners, who wield considerable power and who are appointed for a given term to administer the corporation. Go to the website of Tourism Australia or a state or territory tourism organisation (e.g. Tourism NSW). Briefly describe the structure of that organisation. Now list the members of the board and briefly describe their backgrounds on the basis of information provided at the corporate website. Do a further search through databases and the web to build a profile of one or more board members. Why do you think this person was appointed to the board? Does he or she have any connection with the political party currently in power?

3 Where is self-regulation evident in the tourism industry? Why might the private sector support self-regulation initiatives? Can the private sector be relied on to initiate and maintain high environmental standards in the industry? If self-regulation fails, what might responsible governments do?

4 Examine the Tourism and Transport Forum website. Should state tourism organisations and publicly funded universities and research centres be members of powerful lobby groups and pay to be members of such organisations? What happens when a lobby group supports the development of policy that is contrary to the views of some of its members?

Websites

Australian Conservation Foundation, www.acfonline.org.au/default.asp?section_id=0.
Australian Government's Tourism White Paper and associated sites, www.tourism.australia.com.
Ecotourism certification (NEAP program), www.ecotourism.org.au/EcoCertification3.pdf.
Hunter Region Strategic Tourism Plan, www.huntertourism.com.au/plan.pdf.
Sustainable Tourism Stewardship Council (STSC), www.rainforest-alliance.org/programs/tourism/initiatives/stewardship-council.html.
Tourism NSW, www.tourism.nsw.gov.au/home.
Tourism Queensland, www.tq.com.au.
Tourism and Transport Forum, www.ttf.org.au.
Tourism Victoria, www.tourismvictoria.com.au.
Tread Lightly, www.treadlightlyaustralia.com.au/index.asp.

....

The Western Australian Tourism Commission, Eventscorp and the 1995 Global Dance Foundation 'affair'

In May 1995, the Western Australian Government via Eventscorp, an arm of the Western Australian Tourism Commission (WATC, a statutory government agency) contracted Global Dance Foundation (GDF) to host a World Dance Congress in Perth in August 1997. The congress was to be an eight-day festival of dance planned for 6–13 August and a four-day leadership conference from 5 to 8 August. Peter Reynolds, chairman of the non-profit Global Dance Foundation Inc., was to be the event organiser. WATC signed a contract with GDF 'to provide funding to assist the foundation in holding the Dance Congress (WA Parliamentary Debates, 19 March 1997: 591; West Australian, 10 May: 3). State Parliament was advised that a feasibility study (which was never tabled in Parliament) was carried out, but 'no credible WA Dance Company or association had been consulted about the proposal' (WA Parliamentary Debates, 19 March 1997: 591). The study claimed that the congress would provide a $6m boost to the state. The World Dance Congress never eventuated. The government's funding was never repaid.

In early 1994, Peter Reynolds approached the Western Australian Minister for Tourism, Treasurer and Premier, Richard Court, at a function at Swanbourne Senior High School. At that function, Reynolds, a friend of Court's father, Sir Richard Court, informed the Premier, Minister for Tourism and Treasurer of his plans to hold a Global Dance Festival in Perth (WA Parliamentary Debates 1998: 4156). Court passed the idea to the WATC and Eventscorp, both of which considered the event an enterprising opportunity. However, 'progress was slow. Reynolds got back to the Premier and said they were a mob of donkeys at the Tourism Commission; they did not have the brains to assess his marvellous idea properly and he wanted a bit of action' (WA Parliamentary Debates 1998: 4157). Subsequently, the Premier organised a meeting on 22 December 1994, which he, Mr Crockett (head of Eventscorp), Peter Reynolds (head of GDF) and a ministerial adviser all attended. During this meeting the Premier apparently made it clear that the event was to go ahead. Immediately following the meeting, Crockett had a meeting with the Crown Solicitor's Office to commence drafting the contract, but with no review clauses tied to payments to GDF. Crockett considered that Richard Court's approval signified a ministerial direction.

Premier Court approved the congress despite Reynold's strict confidentiality provisions and advice from the state's leading dance body that it had never heard of GDF or Reynolds before. Indeed, it was later found that GDF had been set up only to access government funds and that GDF received a large sum from the government before the contract was signed and before GDF was incorporated (*West Australian*, 21 March 1997: 6; 5 July: 12). In 1998 the WATC's Sponsorship Agreement with Global Dance Foundation Inc. was investigated by the Western Australian Public Accounts and Expenditure Review Committee (PAERC).

The review began after months of debate and argument about the decision-making processes concerning the awarding of funding in the GDF contract and the involvement of Premier Richard Court, whose father had provided a supporting reference for his friend Peter Reynolds. Premier Court is portrayed in Hansard reports and by the media as the architect of the whole affair, acting against the wishes and advice of Eventscorp, WATC, Treasury and Crown Solicitors, who apparently recommended a more considered approach to supporting the proposed congress (WA Parliamentary Debates, 17 June 1998: 4132; *West Australian*, 13 March 1998: 6).

'Senior state officials contradicted the Premier's evidence given at the inquiry. Officers from Treasury, the WA Tourism Commission and the Crown Solicitor's Office told the inquiry they raised concerns about the financial risk and accountability of the $430,000 deal' (*West Australian*, 5 July 1997: 6). The Premier overrode those concerns and ignored Treasury and expert advice. He supported GDF's chief, Peter Reynolds, who complained that Eventscorp was being 'stupidly pedantic' in its evaluation of the proposal. This was a curious assertion given the confidentiality agreements limiting Eventscorp's access to Reynolds' submission to the Premier (WA Parliamentary Debates, 17 June 1998: 4132).

The PAERC's findings were extensive. According to Finding 35 of the PAERC, 'The credentials of the Global Dance Foundation and Mr Reynolds' companies were not scrutinized sufficiently.' The WATC erred by signing a contract with a non-incorporated body (GDF), which did not consult the dance community and whose credentials (along with Reynolds' other companies) were not widely known. Problems in the structure and content of the contract between the WATC and GDF diminished the ability of WATC to obtain information from GDF, while 'the contract did not specify clearly the respective obligations of the parties with regard to the performance of their obligations' (Finding 28) (also see *West Australian*, 5 February 1998: 8; 13 March: 6).

The committee criticised the Premier, saying he should have been aware of the serious doubts expressed by officials towards the planned dance event. It also said that Premier Court faced a conflict of interest in authorising, as both Treasurer and Minister for Tourism, $430 000 in partial government funding of the World Dance Congress. The committee found Court's claim that the event had general government support hard to corroborate (also see *West Australian*, 13 March 1998: 6). Indeed, the Assistant Director of Treasury, Garry Hall, had advised Premier Court against allocating $430 000 to the project (*West Australian*, 13 March 1998: 6). Among other things, the committee recommended that all requests by ministers to statutory authorities should be put in writing, that the Treasurer should not be allowed to authorise supplementary funding for another of his portfolios without Cabinet's approval and that

(*continued*)

ministers issue formal written directions if public servants disagreed with government decisions. Premier Court formally rejected the inquiry's recommendations on the basis that its findings were flawed but offered little insight into his reasoning. Shane Crockett, executive director of the WATC and general manager of Eventscorp, denied responsibility, arguing that it was the WATC board that had statutory responsibility. Crockett also argued that responsibility could not be attributed to the then chief executive of the WATC, Kevin Harrison. The matter of the GDF contract was referred to the Crown Solicitor's Office and the Western Australian Government considered suing GDF's 'promoter', Peter Reynolds.

The GDF involved a complex web of networks and alliances, including a statutory corporation (the WATC and its Eventscorp arm), parliamentary figures (i.e. ministers, the Premier), bureaucrats, and private sector individuals and agencies. There was confusion in what should be interpreted by bureaucrats as a ministerial direction. There was well documented criticism about the number and nature of portfolios held by a minister and by Premier Richard Court. Event-based proposals to the WATC were not adequately evaluated. If the GD 'affair' could be considered a case of bad governance, weak public administration and failure to adequately address the complexities of blending economic and political power in public enterprise, this should come as no surprise. The standards of performance of statutory corporations have been uneven, occasionally because of sheer bad management or deliberately debilitating political action, but more often because of confusion and error stemming from inadequate understanding of the character, problems and needs of public enterprise management' (Wettenhall 1969: 631).

Questions

1 What cultural and organisational imperatives occurring over the last 20 years contributed to the Global Dance Foundation Affair?

2 Identify the actors and agencies involved in the Global Dance Foundation Affair, their affiliations and responsibilities. Why is it difficult to identify who is responsible for the misuse of public funds?

3 Explain in terms of this case study Davis and Weller's observation: 'Politics inevitably intrudes into policy formulation because the instruments of power — information, resources and authority — are not centralised in the hands of a minister but fragmented across parties, departments, community groups and clients' (1987: 386).

References

Gallop, G 1998, 'The state as market—Western Australia in the 1990s', Essay 10 in G Gallop (ed.), *A State of Reform: Essays for a Better Future*, Helm Wood Publishers, Wembley, UK.

Peachment, A 1991, 'WA Inc.', in A Peachment (ed.), *The Business of Government: Western Australia 1983–90*, Federation Press, Leichhardt, NSW.

Royal Commission into Commercial Activities of Government and Other Matters 1992, *Report of the Royal Commission into Commercial Activities of Government and Other Matters*, Perth, WA.

Sheil, C 1997, *Turning Point: The State of Australia and New Zealand*, Evatt Foundation and Allen & Unwin, St Leonards, NSW.

West Australian 1997, 'Dance probe powerless to call on Court', 5 July, p. 12.

—— 1997, 'Officials put Court on spot', 5 July, p. 6.

—— 1997, 'State was dancing on thin ice', 21 March, p. 6.

—— 1998, 'Taxpayers back loser', 10 May, p. 3.

—— 1998, 'Court was warned on dance contract', 13 March, p. 6.

—— 1998, 'Dance row puts focus on secrecy', 5 February, p. 8.

Western Australian Parliamentary Debates, various years.

Wettenhall, R 1969, 'Public ownership and public service', in H Mayer (ed.), *Australian Politics: A Second Reader*, Cheshire, Melbourne.

REFERENCES

Accor undated, viewed 29 March 2006, www.accorhotels.com.au/corporate/accorhotels.asp and www.accorhotels.com.au/hotdeals/faq.asp.

Alaba, R 1994, *Inside Bureaucratic Power: The Wilenski Review of New South Wales Government Administration*, Hale & Iremonger, Marrickville, NSW.

Aldefer, CP 1979, 'Consulting to underbounded systems', in CP Aldefer & C Cooper (eds), *Advances in Experimental Social Processes*, vol. 2, John Wiley & Sons, New York.

Arnold, TW 1938, *The Folklore of Capitalism*, Yale University Press, New Haven, CT.

Australian Bureau of Statistics 2003, *Year Book Australia*, ABS, Canberra.

Babbage, C 1963, *On the Economy of Machinery and Manufactures*, 4th edn (originally published 1832), Kelley, New York.

Ballantyne, T 1989, 'Fear and loathing mark Brown's entrance into tourism rescue efforts', *Sydney Morning Herald*, 22 November, p. 17.

—— 1992, 'Brown took pay cut of $100 000', *Sydney Morning Herald*, 7 September: 4.

Barnard, C 1968 (first published in 1938), *The Functions of the Executive*, Harvard University Press, Cambridge, MA.

Bergin, S & Jago, L 1999, 'Accreditation of adventure tour operators: The consumer perspective', in J Molloy & J Davies (eds), *Delighting the Senses: Proceedings of the Ninth Australian Tourism and Hospitality Research Conference*, Council of Australian University and Hospitality Educators Conference, Adelaide, pp. 305–16.

Blau, PM & Scott, WR 1962, *Formal Organizations: A Comparative Approach*, San Francisco, Chandler.

Bolman, LG & Deal, TE 1984, *Modern Approaches to Understanding and Managing Organizations*, Jossey-Bass, San Francisco.

—— 1991, *Reframing Organizations: Artistry, Choice and Leadership*, Jossey-Bass, San Francisco.

Bower, M 1966, *The Will to Manage: Corporate Success Through Programmed Management*, McGraw-Hill, New York.

Britton, N 1991a, 'Constraint or effectiveness in disaster management: The bureaucratic imperative versus organisational mission', *Canberra Bulletin of Public Administration*, vol. 64, pp. 54–64.

—— 1991b, 'The culture of emergency services: some relevant considerations', paper prepared for the Emergency Service Librarians Workshop, Australian Counter Disaster College, Mount Macedon, Victoria, 8–13 September.

Brown, LD 1983, *Managing Conflict at Organizational Interfaces*, Addison-Wesley, Reading, MA.

Buckley, R 2001, 'Environmental impacts', in DB Weaver (ed.), *The Encyclopedia of Ecotourism*, CABI Publishing, Wallingford, UK.

—— 2002, 'Tourism ecolabels', *Annals of Tourism Research*, vol. 29, no. 1, pp. 183–208.

—— 2003, *Case Studies in Ecotourism*, CABI Publishing, Wallingford, UK.

Bull, A 1995, *The Economics of Travel and Tourism*, Longman, Melbourne.

Burns, T & Stalker, GM 1961, *The Management of Innovation*, Tavistock Publications, London.

Caiden, G 1980, 'Administrative reform', *Australian Journal of Public Administration*, vol. 39, nos 3/4, pp. 437–53.

Clegg, S & Dunkerley, D 1977, *Critical Issues in Organisations*, Routledge & Kegan Paul, London.

—— 1980, *Organisation, Class and Control*, Routledge & Kegan Paul, London.

Cohen, MD & March JG 1986, *Leadership and Ambiguity: The American College Presidency*, 2nd edn, Harvard Business School Press, Boston.

Considine, M 1990, 'Managerialism strikes out', *Australian Journal of Public Administration*, vol. 49, no. 2, pp. 166–78.

Cotterill, D 1996, 'Developing a sustainable ecotourism business', in H Richins, A Crabbe & J Richardson (eds), *Proceedings of the 1995 Ecotourism Association of Australia Conference*, Bureau of Tourism Research, Canberra, & EAA, Sydney.

Craik, J 1991a, *Government Promotion of Tourism: The Role of the Queensland Tourist and Travel Corporation*, Research Paper No. 20, February, Centre for Australian Public Sector Management, Griffith University, Brisbane.

—— 1991b, *Resorting to Tourism: Cultural Policies for Tourist Development in Australia*, Allen & Unwin, St Leonards, NSW.

—— 1992, 'Australian tourism: The emergence of a state-coordinated consultative policy framework', in S Bell & J Wanna (eds), *Business–Government Relations in Australia*, Harcourt Brace Jovanovich, Sydney.

Crozier, M 1964, *The Bureaucratic Phenomenon*, University of Chicago Press, Chicago.

Davis, B 1991, 'Part-time policy-makers', paper presented at the Conference of the Structure and Organisation of Government Research Group of the International Political Science Association, University of Melbourne, 22–23 March.

Davis, G & Weller, P 1987, 'Negotiated policy or metanonsense? A response to the policy prescriptions of Murray Frazer', *Australian Journal of Public Administration*, vol. 46, no. 1, pp. 380–7.

Dredge, D & JM Jenkins 2003, 'Destination place identity and regional tourism policy', *Tourism Geographies*, vol. 5, no. 4, pp. 383–407.

Ecotourism Australia 2005, www.ecotourism.org.au.

Elliott, J 1997, *Tourism: Politics and Public Sector Management*, Routledge, London.

Emy, H & Hughes, O 1988, *Australian Politics: Realities in Conflict*, Macmillan, Melbourne.

Fayol, H 1956, *General and Industrial Management*, trans. C Storrs, Pitman, London.

Fennell, D 1999, *Ecotourism: An Introduction*, CABI Publishing, Wallingford, UK.

—— 2001, 'Areas and needs in ecotourism research', in D Weaver (ed.), *The Encyclopedia of Ecotourism*, CABI Publishing, Wallingford, UK.

—— 2002, *Ecotourism Programme Planning*, CABI Publishing, Wallingford, UK.

Hall, CM 1998, *Introduction to Tourism in Australia: Development, Dimensions and Issues*, 3rd edn, Longman, Melbourne.

Hall, CM & Jenkins, JM 1995, *Tourism and Public Policy*, Routledge, London.

Ham, C & Hill, M 1993, *The Policy Process in the Modern Capitalist State*, 2nd edn, Harvester Wheatsheaf, Hemel Hempstead, Herts.

Hansard *see* Western Australian Parliamentary Debates.

Harmon, MM & Mayer, RT 1986, *Organization Theory for Public Administration*, Scott, Foresman & Co., Glenview, IL.

Harris, R & Jago, L 2001, 'Professional accreditation in the Australian tourism industry: An uncertain future', *Tourism Management*, vol. 22, no. 4, pp. 383–90.

Horne, D 1980, *Time of Hope: Australia 1966–72*, Angus & Robertson, Sydney.

Industries Assistance Commission 1989, *Travel and Tourism*, Report No. 423, AGPS, Canberra.

Issaverdis, J-P 2001, 'The pursuit of excellence: Benchmarking, accreditation, best practice and auditing', in D Weaver (ed.), *The Encyclopedia of Ecotourism*, CABI Publishing, Wallingford, UK, pp. 579–94.

Jans, NA & Frazer-Jans, JM 1991, 'Organisational culture and organisational effectiveness', *Australian Journal of Public Administration*, vol. 50, no. 3, pp. 333–46.

Jenkins, JM 2001, 'Statutory authorities in whose interests? The case of Tourism New South Wales, the bed tax, and "the Games"', *Pacific Tourism Review*, vol. 4, no. 4, pp. 201–19.

Jenkins, JM & Stolk, P 2003, 'Statutory authorities dancing with enterprise: WA Inc., the Western Australian Tourism Commission and the Global Dance Affair', *Annals of Leisure Research*, vol. 6, no. 3, pp. 222–44.

Lane, B 1989, ' "Phoenix" Brown bounces back to sell Australia', *Australian Financial Review*, 10 November, p. 6.

Leiper, N 1980, 'An interdisciplinary study of Australian tourism: its scope, characteristics and consequences, with particular reference to government policies since 1965', unpublished Masters thesis, Department of General Studies, University of New South Wales, Kensington, NSW.

Lipsky, M 1980, *Street-Level Bureaucracy*, Russell Sage Foundation, New York.

Maclaren, F 2002, 'A strategic overview of ecotourism accreditation and certification: The road forward', http://72.14.203.104/search?q=cache: 7oBAJZWAeGoJ:www.milenio.com.br/ilhas/certification.htm+%22A+ Strategic+Overview+of+Ecotourism+Accreditation+and+Certification:+ The+Road+Forward%22&hl=en&gl=au&ct=clnk&cd=4.

Mascarenhas, R 1982, *Public Enterprise in New Zealand*, New Zealand Institute of Public Administration, Wellington.

—— 1996, 'The evolution of public enterprise organisation: A critique', in J Halligan (ed.), *Public Administration under Scrutiny: Essays in Honour of Roger Wettenhall*, Centre for Research in Public Sector Management, Canberra.

Mayes, G, Dyer, P & Richins, H 2004, 'Dolphin–human interaction: Changing perceived pro-environmental attitudes, beliefs, intended behaviours and intended actions of participants through management and interpretation programs', *Annals of Leisure Research*, vol. 7, no. 1, pp. 34–53.

McKercher, B 1998, *The Business of Nature-Based Tourism*, Hospitality Press, Elsternwick, Vic.

McMillen, J 1991, 'The politics of tourism in Queensland', in P Carroll, K Donohue, M McGovern & J McMillen, *Tourism in Australia*, Harcourt Brace Jovanovich, Sydney.

Mechanic, D 1962, 'Sources of power of lower participants in organizations', *Administrative Science Quarterly*, vol. 7, pp. 349–64.

Meethan, K 2004, 'Transnational corporations, globalization and tourism', in Lew, AA, Hall, CM & Williams, A (eds), *A Companion to Tourism*, Blackwell, Oxford, pp. 110–21.

Mintzberg, H 1979, *The Structuring of Organizations: A Synthesis of the Research*, Prentice Hall, Englewood Cliffs, NJ.

—— 1983, *Power in and Around Organizations*, Prentice Hall, Englewood Cliffs, NJ.

Mitchell, A 1996, 'Tourism and the party folk', *Sun Herald*, 3 October, p. 20.

Moffet, L 1991, 'Tourism Task Force's ATC move slammed', *Australian Financial Review*, 17 May, p. 26.

Morgan, DJ 2003, 'Self-regulation', in JM Jenkins & JJ Pigram, *Encyclopedia of Leisure and Outdoor Recreation*, Routledge, London, pp. 451–2.

NEAP 2003, *Nature and Ecotourism Accreditation Program*, 3rd edn, Ecotourism Association of Australia and Australian Tourism Operators Network, viewed 29 March 2006, www.ecotourism.org.au/EcoCertification3.pdf.

New South Wales Department of Tourism Sport and Recreation 2005 *Annual Report: New South Wales Department of Tourism Sport and Recreation*, Sydney. http://corporate.tourism.nsw.gov.au/scripts/runisa.dll? CORPORATELIVE.21562452:2COLUMN::pc=ROLE, retrieved 29 June 2006.

Nielsen, N, Birtles, A & Sofield, T 1995, 'Ecotourism accreditation: Shouldn't the tourists have a say?', in H Richins, J Richardson & A Crabtree (eds), *Ecotourism and Nature-based Tourism: Taking the Next Steps*, Proceedings of the Ecotourism Association of Australia (EAA) National Conference, Brisbane, pp. 235–42.

Office of Public Management, New South Wales Premier's Department 1993, *Review of the NSW Tourism Commission: Final Report*, OPM, Sydney.

Parker, RS 1979, 'The Wilenski Review', *Australian Journal of Public Administration*, vol. 38, no. 2, pp. 168–75.

Pfeffer, J 1981, *Power in Organizations*, Pitman, Marshfield, MA.

Richardson, J 1999, *A History of Australian Travel and Tourism*, Hospitality Press, Elsternwick, Vic.

Richter, L 1989, *The Politics of Tourism in Asia*, University of Hawaii Press, Honolulu.

Schein, EH 1985, *Organizational Culture and Leadership*, Jossey-Bass, San Francisco.

Self, P 1985, *Political Theories of Modern Government, Its Role and Reform*, George Allen & Unwin, London.

Selznick, P 1957, *Leadership in Administration: A Sociological Interpretation*, Harper & Row, New York.

Shafritz, JM & Ott, JS 1992, *Classics of Organization Theory*, 3rd edn, Brooks/ Cole, Pacific Grove, CA.

Sinclair, MT & Stabler, M 1997, *The Economics of Tourism*, Routledge, London & New York.

Spann, RN 1979, *Government Administration in Australia*, George Allen & Unwin, Sydney.

Sustainable Tourism Stewardship Council (STSC) 2002, viewed 20 January 2002, www.ra.org/programs/tourism/initiatives/stewardship-council.html.

Taylor, FW 1947, *The Principles of Scientific Management*, Norton, New York.

Tourism Council Australia 1994, *Annual Report*, TCA, Sydney.

Tourism New South Wales 1994, *Tourism New South Wales Annual Report 1993–1994: A Year to Write Home About*, Tourism NSW, Sydney.

—— 1996, *Regional Tourism Strategy 1997/98–1999/2000*, Tourism NSW, Sydney.

Tourism Queensland 2000a, *NEAP Consumer Survey* (August), Tourism Queensland, Brisbane.

—— 2000b, *NEAP Industry Survey* (August), Tourism Queensland, Brisbane.

Tourism and Transport Forum, viewed 29 March 2006, www.ttf.org.au/about/about.htm and www.ttf.org.au/about/pdf/TTF_Our_Members.pdf.

Tourism White Paper 2003, viewed 10 October 2005, www.industry.gov.au/content/itrinternet/cmscontentcfm?objectID=4E01EE73–65BF-4956-B057EC96612BDDCB.

Viljoen, J & Dann, S 2003, *Strategic Management*, 4th edn, Prentice Hall, Frenchs Forest, NSW.

Warhurst, J 1980, 'Exercising control over statutory authorities: A study in government technique', in P Weller & D Jaensch (eds), *Responsible Government in Australia*, Drummond, Richmond.

Washington, S 1999, 'This is no way to do business', *Australian Financial Review*, 5 August, p. 28.

Weaver, D 2001a, *Ecotourism*, John Wiley & Sons Australia, Milton, Qld.

Weaver, D (ed.) 2001b, *The Encyclopaedia of Ecotourism*, CABI Publishing, Wallingford, UK.

Weber, M (Roth, G & Wittich, C, eds) 1968, *Economy and Society: An Outline of Interpretive Sociology*, trans. E Fischoff et al., Bedminster Press, New York.

West Australian 1997, 'Court plays down losses in tourism', 16 May, p. 10.

Wettenhall, R 1969, 'Public ownership and public service', in H Mayer (ed.), *Australian Politics: A Second Reader*, Cheshire, Melbourne.

—— 1990, 'Australia's daring experiment with public enterprise', in A Kouzmin & N Scott (eds), *Dynamics in Australian Public Management: Selected Essays*, Macmillan, South Melbourne.

Wilenski, P 1986, *Public Power and Public Administration*, Hale & Iremonger in association with the Royal Australian Institute of Public Administration, Sydney, NSW.

Dianne Dredge and John Jenkins

CHAPTER 5

Policy instruments, *implementation and evaluation*

LEARNING OBJECTIVES

After reading this chapter you will be able to:

1 discuss what is meant by the term 'policy instrument'

2 identify and discuss the variety of policy instruments available to governments to address public issues

3 critically discuss factors that influence the choice of tourism policy instruments by planners and policy-makers

4 discuss the importance of implementation and identify the factors that influence the implementation of tourism policy

5 discuss the importance of evaluation and describe general approaches to the evaluation of tourism planning and policy.

ℐNTRODUCTION

In 1973, noted policy analysts Jeffery Pressman and Aaron Wildavsky published a book entitled *Implementation: How Great Expectations in Washington are Dashed in Oakland; or, why it's amazing that federal programs work at all, this being the saga of the economic development administration as told by two sympathetic observers who seek to build morals on a foundation of ruined hopes.* The title is exceedingly long but, more importantly, the book also became a seminal text, which demonstrates that greater attention needs to be paid to the role and importance of policy implementation and evaluation; that is, all the best intentions in the world can come unstuck as a result of poor choice of policy instrument and poor implementation structures and processes.

This chapter seeks to examine policy implementation and evaluation as important concepts in tourism policy-making. It also seeks to explore the barriers to and opportunities for implementation and evaluation in tourism. Tourism planners and policy actors need to place great attention on choice of instrument and be rigorous and thoughtful in the ways they identify and analyse available policy instruments. All too often, policy solutions are identified and implemented without a clear understanding of their advantages and disadvantages or what the best instrument would be, given the range of factors influencing the policy problem. Sometimes, the choice of policy instrument is driven largely by key actors' ideological preferences and personal perceptions rather than by diligent research. Moreover, the choice of instrument, such as the introduction of an operator tax, can be just as contentious as the policy problem itself and lead to problems of non-acceptance by the broader community of interests (see Planning in Practice: 'Introduction of the Reef tax').

PLANNING IN PRACTICE

Introduction of the Reef tax

Massive growth in visitor numbers throughout the 1980s placed significant pressure on the Great Barrier Reef Marine Park Authority's ability to keep up with growing management and enforcement costs. As a result, the Commonwealth Government introduced a compulsory tax on operators who held permission to undertake certain activities known as 'chargeable permissions'. This Great Barrier Reef Marine Park environmental management charge (EMC) was introduced in 1993 via Commonwealth legislation and supporting regulations. The environmental management charge was intended to provide additional financial support for the management of the park.

The fee is collected by operators who conduct activities in the park. These activities include tourism operators, boat charter and boat mooring operators, as well as pearl and clam farmers and operators of land-based sewerage outfalls. The EMC is payable by a tourism operator and is based on a fee per day for every tourist participating in their activities. On introduction of the legislation, the EMC was expected to raise an additional $1 million in 1993. It raised $6.6 million in the 1993 financial year.

The introduction of the tax was not supported by many of the operators, and it became quite controversial. They argued that they had no option but to pass on the tax to tourists and that the increased cost of tours and activities would likely have a negative effect on visitor numbers and business earnings. Moreover, the cost of collecting and administering the EMC unfairly burdened small operators, adding to their overheads and affecting profit margins. However, these consequences did not eventuate and tourism visitation continued to increase. Later, with the introduction of the Goods and Services Tax (GST) in 2000, an additional issue emerged that confused the application of the EMC. GST was not payable on the EMC if it was directly paid by the operator; however, it was payable where the tax formed part of the operators' ticket charges. Operators took different approaches; some levied GST on the EMC and others did not. Over time, these operators became concerned that they might become liable for outstanding GST and sought clarification from the relevant minister. In 2004 an amendment bill was passed that clarified the roles and responsibilities of operators and tourists. It said that GST was not payable on the EMC.

This case illustrates a number of salient points about implementation. First, implementation can be as controversial as the solution itself. Second, over time problems can emerge as policy in other areas is implemented (in this case the introduction of the GST). Implementation strategies might need to be clarified and reassessed periodically. Third, policy solutions rarely sit alone. Intersecting areas of policy (in this case the taxation policy and the EMC user-pays environmental management policy) meant that clarification was required.

Sources: *Great Barrier Reef Marine Park Authority 2005; Martyn 2004.*

In the next section, section 5.2, the tools of government, also known as policy instruments, are explored. In particular, policy instruments can be classified and understood in many ways: in terms of the type of resources used, how control over the issue is manifested and the level of government involvement. Understanding the types of instrument available is the first step in considering what instruments are best in particular circumstances. Section 5.3 discusses the nature of implementation. Implementation is an important component in the policy process as it enables governments to develop effective strategies for turning policy into action. Understanding the opportunities and constraints surrounding implementation is important in refining and delivering effective policy. Section 5.4 then considers evaluation and its role in helping governments improve and refine policy solutions.

According to Bridgman and Davis (2004: 69), 'policy instruments are the means by which governments achieve their ends'. Governments confront public problems using a range of instruments, programs, tools, approaches and techniques to achieve their goals. More than one instrument might be used to solve a problem, and all instruments have strengths and weaknesses. How various instruments work (or do not work) together is therefore important, but so too are understandings about the consequences of different **policy instruments** and hybrids thereof. Moreover, the choice of instrument depends on how policy problems are analysed and understood and the perceived repertoire of policy instruments available. So, as O'Toole (2004: 312) rightly observes, 'practitioners come in many flavours' and the success or otherwise of policy instruments and their implementation can also rest with the expertise and knowledge of those designing and implementing solutions.

Attention to the choice of instrument has become increasingly important since the 1980s as traditional modes of dealing with public issues have shifted; that is, in large modern bureaucracies, the traditional way of dealing with many problems was through government-centred methods, such as regulation or direct public provision of services. We see evidence of this in tourism where, in the late nineteenth and early twentieth centuries in Australia and New Zealand, governments opted to build and operate such facilities as guesthouses and attractions (see section 3.5.2). These were resource-intensive policy instruments in terms of both investment and continuing maintenance costs.

However, changes in approaches to public administration since the 1980s have sought to offset government's role by facilitating and enabling communities to help themselves and to reduce society's dependence on government-funded solutions (see chapter 4). As a result, a wider array of policy instruments and hybrid solutions devised from different policy instruments are being developed. Present evidence suggests that the withdrawal of governments from areas of health care, aged care, urban infrastructure, employment agencies and public education have been contentious.

■ 5.2.1 Types *of policy instrument*

In the broader policy sciences, since the 1960s considerable effort has been dedicated to identifying and classifying the different types of policy instrument available. However, these efforts have been plagued by problems because, although many policy instruments are available, there are also many hybrids of the instruments themselves. Different political contexts and different problems also influence the ways in which various policy solutions are constructed and implemented. Moreover, as O'Toole (2004) points out, normative 'on the ground' differences have made it difficult to develop overarching classifications of policy instruments and implementation procedures. As a result, there are as many instruments as there are policy problems, and it would be almost impossible to develop a definitive classification of available instruments. Further, the number and type of instruments will also vary according to the problem (e.g. economic, social or environmental), the level of government and the nature and availability of resources. The choice of instruments also needs to take local political conditions, community aspirations and expectations into account and be mindful of local organisational cultures and practices (see chapter 4).

There are a number of alternative ways of understanding the nature of policy instruments:

- Policy instruments can be conceived of and understood as manifestations of *the way government uses its resources* to address a policy issue or problem.
- Policy instruments can be categorised according to *who has the control and ability* to address the policy issue.
- Policy instruments can be broadly conceived in terms of *the nature and level of government involvement* in addressing the policy problem.

Each is discussed below.

Policy instruments as the use of government resources

In 1986, Christopher Hood argued that it made sense to understand policy instruments in terms of the resources that governments deployed rather than by making long lists of policy instruments (Hood 1986). Hood divided policy instruments into four groups organised around the nature of the resources used by governments to address policy problems:

1. information instruments — use information and knowledge to influence behaviour of public and private sector interests
2. treasury instruments — use government money and other resources to influence, coerce and manipulate behaviour
3. authority instruments — use legal and official powers of government to enforce behaviour, and
4. organisation instruments — use the organisation and actions of government agencies to shape behaviour.

Later, Bridgman and Davis (2004: 69) adopted these themes, renaming them to reflect contemporary influences:

1. advocacy — using information and education to manipulate behaviour
2. money — using financial incentives, spending and taxing
3. government action — delivering services directly, or indirectly facilitating their delivery, and
4. law — legislation, regulation and compulsory provisions to achieve compliance.

Planning in Practice 5.2: 'Auditor to probe grants program' demonstrates that the use of government resources, in this case a grant scheme, also could be influenced by political agendas and drivers that are not necessarily explicit. In the program described, funding, including for some tourism-related projects, was distributed in a manner that might have been used to procure political advantage.

Auditor to probe grants program

A new and potentially damaging probe by the Commonwealth Auditor-General will be launched into the Federal Government's controversial regional grants program.

Auditor-General Ian McPhee will investigate the administration of the $500 million grants scheme after a Senate inquiry last month found serious deficiencies in transparency and accountability.

The audit — to be carried out in the first half of next year — will pay special attention to several 'questionable' grants highlighted in the Senate report, including a failed tourist railway venture at Beaudesert in southeast Queensland and a milk-processing plant near Atherton in north Queensland.

Last month's report by the Labor-controlled Finance and Public Administration References Committee found that more than half of the grants in the 2004 regional partnerships program were awarded in the three months leading up to the last election, fuelling community perceptions of pork-barrelling.

Concerns were also raised about the government's $100 million Sustainable Regions Program, although that will not be included in Mr McPhee's audit.

A similar probe by the Auditor-General's office into alleged pork-barrelling in 1993 ended the ministerial career of the then Labor environment minister Ros Kelly. She was found to have interfered in the disbursement of community sporting grants so that Labor marginal seats received three-quarters of a $30 million program.

In contrast, the bulk of funding under regional partnerships was directed to Coalition-held seats.

Labor's regional development spokesman Kelvin Thomson, who complained to the Auditor-General's office in March that the scheme was a vote-buying slush fund, yesterday said an independent audit of the program was a victory for public accountability.

'Over a decade ago another auditor-general's report proved fatal for the political career of a minister named Kelly. It may be that history is about to repeat itself,' Mr Thomson said.

The bulk of grants last year were approved by former parliamentary secretary De-Anne Kelly.

A spokeswoman for Transport and Regional Services Minister Warren Truss — whose department oversees the scheme — said the check by the Auditor-General was a normal part of accountability within government.

'We are confident that the regional partnerships program will stand up to the test and we have no concerns,' she said.

Mr Truss announced earlier this month that regional partnerships would be streamlined to make a 'good program even better'.

'The changes will make the application process simpler and faster, and provide clearer guidance on what kind of projects will be approved,' he said.

Source: *Heywood 2005: 14.*

In tourism studies, there has been little in the way of structured attempts to organise and understand the wide array of policy instruments available to assist government achieve its tourism objectives. What little discussion there is tends to focus on discussing the advantages and disadvantages of approaches in single case studies or on evaluations of policy instruments employed in different subsectors such as ecotourism (e.g. Mihalic 2003) or marine tourism (e.g. Greiner et al. 2000). Table 5.1 lists the types of policy instruments that have been adopted in tourism. It is not intended to be a comprehensive list but rather to illustrate the number and diversity of instruments available.

■ Table 5.1

A selection of policy instruments in tourism

TYPE OF INSTRUMENT	EXAMPLES IN TOURISM
Advocacy	strategic tourism plans (with no statutory base) ecotourism guidelines accreditation schemes ecomarketing demonstration projects energy-saving principles environmental management community behaviour and tolerance encouragement of international investment
Money	tourist levies departure taxes accommodation levies user-pays charges licences and permits differential charges for tourists developer contributions tax rebates investment incentives loan guarantees tax relief direct and indirect subsidies fines penalties declaration of free trade and investment zones
Government action	infrastructure provision (e.g. airports, roads) resort development provision and management of attractions and services, such as hotels, museums interpretation facilities marketing and promotion education research
Law	zoning land use regulations building regulations public health and occupational health and safety fire and safety regulations foreign investment regulations

Policy instruments as control

An alternative to the above classification is that instruments can also be organised in terms of where the control lies in implementing policy. Ouchi (1980) identified three main mechanisms through which control is exercised to achieve policy outcomes:

- *Market forces* involve interventions that change free market pricing, so that the new prices motivate actors to change their behaviour. In tourism, levies, bed taxes, entrance fees and user-pays charges are examples.
- *Bureaucracies* exercise control through regulation. For example, in tourism, site licences, park permits for operators and visitor permits are ways of controlling the timing, levels and distribution of visitation in national parks.
- *Clans* allude to the control that can be exercised through self-regulation and because of the actors' belongingness to a community of interest. Accreditation programs, membership of industry associations, charters and codes of ethics are examples.

Ouchi's contribution is important because it helps us understand that there are different sources of power and that, ultimately, cooperative action is necessary between governments, markets and clans. Transactions or exchanges take place between markets, bureaucracies and clans. For cooperation to occur, each stakeholder has to think there is advantage in participation.

This line of thinking has been instrumental in the development of mixed instruments, such as ecoaccreditation programs, in tourism (see section 4.6). In this example, the market (tourism operators and suppliers) have substantial power to improve environmental management by adopting procedures and behaviour that foster environmental conservation. Collectively, through a peak body association (clan), accreditation standards are developed, which are then voluntarily adopted by suppliers and operators who seek a competitive marketing angle. The rise of networks of ecotourism operators and their adoption of accredited ecotourism practices is another example of the manifestation of the power to change things in a 'clan' or group of networked actors and agencies (see section 4.6). Moreover, clans and networks can have a powerful influence on whether (or not) government policy, such as managing the feeding of dolphins in Tin Can Bay, is implemented (see Planning in Practice: 'Who's really taking care of the dolphins?', pp. 135–6). The power of networks and their ability to accept, legitimise and implement government policy is also discussed in a case study of Scotland's tourism network on p. 185.

Policy instruments as the level of government involvement

Departing from the idea of a typology of policy instruments, Howlett and Ramesh (1995) argue that policy instruments can be usefully conceptualised as existing on a continuum of government involvement. At one end, voluntary instruments are characterised by low levels of government involvement and low dependency on government resources. At the other end of the continuum, compulsory and regulatory policy instruments require high levels of state involvement and high levels of government resourcing (see figure 5.1). This conceptualisation is useful for policy planners working within government, where the resources of government are an extremely important (but not the only) influence on policy instrument choice.

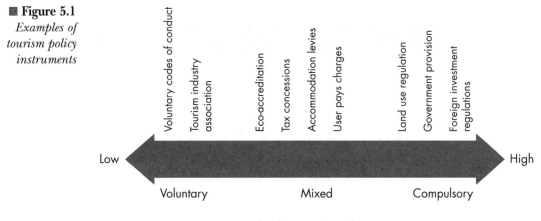

Level of state involvement

Source: *adapted from Howlett & Ramesh 1995: 82.*

Voluntary instruments

In tourism, the use of **voluntary instruments** designed to manage the effects of tourism and to influence tourist and operator behaviour is growing. These include self-regulatory codes of conduct for operators, tourists, businesses and self-imposed, industry-formulated performance standards (see chapter 4). As an example, Planning in Practice: 'Code of conduct — sexual exploitation', discusses an attempt to foster behavioural change among some tourism operators so that 'clan pressure' will reduce the sexual exploitation of children by tourists. In a context in which many countries and many tour operators are involved and there are no clear lines of agency responsibility, few resources and little opportunity to implement and police regulatory measures, voluntary instruments like this code of conduct can help to increase awareness and change operator behaviour.

The increasing adoption of voluntary instruments in tourism is driven partly by neoliberal ideology (see section 3.4.4), which has sought to reduce direct government involvement, and partly by the lack of direct statutory powers that many governments are able to exercise over tourism, tourism investors and operators and tourist behaviour.

In general, voluntary instruments are usually the most difficult to implement and anticipate the consequences thereof. This is because they rely on goodwill, altruism and commitment of business and civil society, which is uneven and not constant. Moreover, implementation is problematic because voluntary instruments need continuous commitment, which is often not forthcoming when political power, social conditions, industry competition and profitability factors change. And in any case, as we saw in section 4.6, accreditation guidelines often have little or no basis in law and hence cannot easily be enforced by government. Moreover, if businesses did not think there was economic benefit in the application of voluntary instruments many would likely not bother to comply.

Code of conduct — sexual exploitation

In 2004 ECPAT, a network of organisations and individuals working towards the elimination of child prostitution, pornography and trafficking, the World Tourism Organization and UNICEF developed a code of conduct for the suppliers of tourism services. This code, entitled the Code of Conduct for the Protection of Children from Sexual Exploitation in Travel and Tourism, seeks suppliers' commitment to developing ethical standards and practices in the conduct of their businesses. The code comprises six simple directives:

1 To establish an ethical policy regarding commercial sexual exploitation of children.

2 To train the personnel in the country of origin and travel destinations.

3 To introduce a clause in contracts with suppliers, stating a common repudiation of commercial sexual exploitation of children.

4 To provide information to travellers by means of catalogues, brochures, inflight films, ticket-slips, home pages, etc.

5 To provide information to local 'key persons' at the destinations.

6 To report annually.

The signatory companies are required to report annually, and best practice experiences are shared via reporting on the code's website. The reporting provides useful examples of practice, with the added benefit of providing information and examples to other businesses. Information sharing and dissemination are important mechanisms for changing private sector behaviour. Although the code is a voluntary mechanism, the 'clan' (comprising UNICEF, WTO, ECPAT and a range of high-profile hotel chains) lends significant weight to the importance of becoming a signatory.

Source: *ECPAT 2005.*

Mixed instruments

Mixed instruments use a combination of measures, such as voluntary adoption of standards, regulation, subsidies and taxes, to achieve certain outcomes. Mixed instruments rely on the combined efforts of markets, civil society and governments to address shared tourism objectives. Mixed instruments include, for example, ecoaccreditation and ecolabelling programs such as Green Globe 21. In Green Globe 21 operators adopt a set of industry-wide standards for their operations and seek voluntary accreditation. Tourism operators voluntarily participate in a scheme to achieve ecoaccreditation and the right to use certain ecolabels on their advertising material. This ecoaccreditation supposedly gives operators the right to market and promote themselves as complying with a set of predetermined environmental standards, which in turn is perceived to give an edge in the marketplace. In some cases, the accreditation process is subsidised by local government, which seeks not only to help industry but also to raise both operator and market awareness. Self-implementation and self-monitoring by operators could conceivably make Green Globe 21 an effective management tool for governments whereby the costs of industry education, implementation and policing can be substantially reduced. In this way participation of industry, government and the public (i.e. tourism markets) is necessary for the success of the mixed instrument approach.

Moreover, in developing countries where there is little expertise in government and a lack of public resources, ecolabelling and ecoaccreditation can help by setting voluntary standards and monitoring procedures more quickly and efficiently than would be the case where government was left to its own devices to design and implement regulatory measures. The implementation of international ecoaccreditation programs can also help developing countries attract international development aid and grants by demonstrating their commitment to international standards.

Mixed instruments have been criticised on a number of levels. The World Wildlife Fund (2000) claims that ecolabels can promote confusion in the marketplace because a variety of logos are used and the consumer is unable to differentiate between a company seeking certification and a company that has achieved certification. Moreover, there is a problem with companies themselves setting the standards that they will achieve as opposed to a system in which companies have to achieve benchmarks and industry-wide standards (see also section 4.6). Mixed instruments should be treated with caution because compliance with any certification standards cannot be guaranteed, and penalties for failing to comply are generally a weak deterrent.

Compulsory instruments

Compulsory instruments, such as regulation and legislation, require government to proscribe solutions for addressing tourism issues and problems and penalties for non-compliance. Compulsory instruments are usually developed via public consultation and a rigorous legal drafting process. Such instruments can therefore claim to have a high degree of transparency, but their implementation and policing requires continuous commitment and resourcing by government. Moreover, implementation might well require the establishment of a separate agency and government structures and processes that did not previously exist. For example, the Great Barrier Reef Marine Park Authority (GBRMPA) was established by the Commonwealth Government under the *Great Barrier Reef Marine Park Act 1975* (Cwlth) 'to provide for the protection, wise use, understanding and enjoyment of the Great Barrier Reef in perpetuity through the care and development of the Great Barrier Reef Marine Park'. One of the principal functions of the authority is to prepare detailed policies, including zoning plans and regulations to manage the Reef. The Wet Tropics Management Authority (WTMA) is another example (see chapter 1, Planning in Practice: 'Wet Tropical rainforests, North Queensland', pp. 26–8) of a statutory authority created for the purpose of pursuing specific government objectives associated with managing and promoting the values of the World Heritage Area, including the management of tourism. However, the establishment of the agency itself is only part of the policy solution, the existence of which puts in train the development of processes, statutory planning instruments and policies that add an additional layer of complexity to the treatment of the issue.

Compulsory instruments usually address market failures or those problems that arise because of the market's inability to address the issue without government involvement. They are usually criticised as being heavy-handed and, because they are highly structured and inflexible, such solutions reduce opportunities for innovation (Hjalager 1996).

■ 5.2.2 Influences *on the choice of policy instrument*

Given the difficulty of itemising all the policy instruments available and, indeed, the questionable utility of such an exercise, recent attention has started to shift away from quantifying the number and classifying the characteristics of policy instruments available towards an understanding of how the choice of policy instrument is made. The Choice of Governing Instrument Conference (Government of Canada 2002) was a Canadian Government initiative that sought to examine the importance of choice in the policy formulation process. A number of important observations related to the choice of appropriate policy instruments emerged from this conference:

- Economic concerns alone are inadequate in informing instrument choices. Choice should primarily be a function of criteria devised from research and engagement with the communities of interest. Instrument choice based on (or even primarily about) cost, technical effectiveness or economic efficiency should be avoided.
- The legitimacy and acceptability of particular choices are bound up with political, legal, ethical, social and economic factors that operate across local, regional and global scales.
- Policy debates must move from individual instrument choice to instrument mixes and recognise that instruments are context-sensitive and rarely, if ever, designed or implemented in isolation.
- All instruments have important repercussions for the legitimacy and accountability of governments. Instruments that are perceived to address issues outside governments' range of concern are likely to lack legitimacy and be ignored by community and industry interests.
- Governance strategies, consultation and community engagement need to ensure both legitimacy and 'optimality' in instrument design and implementation.

Of course, choosing the right policy instrument is not simply a matter of 'rational' decision-making. When members of parliament engage in a dance of bargaining and negotiation in order to secure amendments in exchange for their support for a particular policy approach or instrument, persuasive political forces are often at work. Independent members and smaller political parties, such as the Greens and Democrats, tend to use this mechanism and can be influential in the choice of policy instruments as a result.

The above discussion can be reduced to four main factors that influence the choice of policy instrument:

1. *The disposition of the state.* The state brings with it a range of pre-existing conditions, ideas and cultures that influence choice of policy instrument. These factors include prevailing management philosophies, the resources available and the nature of the dominant political power at the time.

2. *Knowledge of policy instruments available.* Knowledge of available alternatives, the content and quality of policy research and the capacity of government, its bureaucrats, politicians and law-makers to develop innovative measures all influence the range of policy instruments available and the final choice.

3. *Current events.* Current events have an important influence on choice of policy instrument. The media has at times had a particularly strong influence on the identification of problems and the public acceptability of certain solutions or instruments. Moreover, at any one time, competing policy issues and the way they are cast within public attention have an important influence over which policy solutions are likely to be more acceptable.

4. *Knowledge of the consequences.* All instruments have consequences. Knowledge of the consequences of various instruments plays an important role in final choice; however, full and complete information about all policy instruments is not always available.

These above four factors influence which policy solutions are perceived to be available and are evaluated. Of course, the relative influence of these four streams depends on the policy problem itself and on the quality of policy expertise, advice and research available.

The choice of policy instruments therefore needs to take these factors into account and be evaluated along the following dimensions:

- the degree of effectiveness in addressing the particular policy problem(s)
- ease of implementation
- cost and other efficiencies
- equity among the community of stakeholders
- legitimacy in and acceptance by the community, and
- the level of political support.

The above discussion of the choice of policy instrument logically leads to questions of implementation. Even the most considered and careful selection of policy instrument can fail because of poor implementation structures and procedures.

𝓘MPLEMENTATION ....

■ *5.3.1* **What is** *implementation?*

A key activity of any democratically elected government is to deliver on its promises. By corollary, **implementation**, the process through which policy ideas and plans are translated into practice, should be a crucial aspect of government action (Mazmanian & Sabatier 1989). The challenge for policy-makers is to develop effective implementation methods for the delivery of government policy. In Mazmanian and Sabatier's (1989: 21) view the underpinning factor is the identification of those variables that are likely to affect the achievement of the policy objectives; that is, translating policy ideas into action is not a simple process. The complexity of government structures and processes and the dynamic interplay of social and economic factors complicate implementation (Bridgman & Davis 2004: 119). Implementation is further complicated by the fact that it is rarely executed in a single step by a single government agency. Responsibilities can be diffused among a range of actors and agencies, each operating under the influence of different factors. Mazmanian and Sabatier (1989) observe that implementation involves three spheres:

1. the centre — policy-makers directly involved in analysis, solution-building and implementation
2. the periphery — other actors and agencies that have a lesser role to play, and
3. the target group — those whose behaviour is to be changed or who will be affected by the implementation.

Implementation roles and responsibilities fall differently in all these spheres. Thus, implementation requires continuous political support and a keen awareness of possible conflicts in agency goals and actions. Moreover, understanding cause-and-effect relationships in a complex and dynamic social world is never clear-cut. A range of mitigating circumstances play out, unique to every case, so that it is nearly impossible to conclusively attribute responsibility for policy failure.

There is a large and fragmented body of research and theoretical development that attempts to understand the key ingredients contributing to the success or failure of implementation. This research is tempered by observations that pessimism exists about governments' ability to deliver, so it is not surprising that much of implementation research is critical of government (Mazmanian & Sabatier 1989). Moreover, some authors argue that any policy that seeks to change the status quo is exceedingly difficult to implement and that good policy implementation is more likely to involve small, incremental steps (Parsons 1995).

■ *5.3.2* **What** *influences implementation?*

A number of factors contribute to problems in implementation. First, the nature of problems and the way they are framed and analysed can influence the implementation approaches adopted. For example, where governments have interpreted the issue in terms of a need to 'enable' industry by building skills, business development programs and vocational training schemes are some of the solutions that might be chosen. What follows then is an implementation regime that reflects these values and is framed around creating a better business environment. If, on the other hand, the issue of tourism development is framed around the need to create an attractive and cohesive destination environment, then land use planning, urban design and architectural covenants could be implemented. Not surprisingly, different solutions will give rise to different implementation approaches and problems.

Second, policy problems are often complex and have multiple subissues. For example, the issue of managing the negative effects of holiday accommodation in residential areas is derived from many causes: land use planning frameworks, conflicting values, needs and expectations of residents, visitors and accommodation owners, and market mechanisms that result in holiday accommodation being more lucrative than residential tenancies. As a result, there is no single solution. Any single solution is likely to address only parts of the problem and will likely fall short of the objectives to reduce and manage conflicts (Howlett & Ramesh 1995).

Third, implementation rarely results in a direct and total resolution of the policy problem. Policy problems change as social, economic, technological, political and environmental conditions change. Where change is rapid or a time lag occurs between policy analysis and implementation, the solutions might no longer fit the original interpretation of the issue, and a mismatch between problem and solution could occur.

Fourth, implementation requires appropriate administrative support structures, resources and the management of the implementation process itself. Implementation procedures that are not sufficiently resourced, or that do not have the right administrative structures or expertise available, are more likely to encounter implementation problems. Moreover, implementation must be carried out by that agency with the expertise and the statutory power to do so. Allocating responsibility to an agency that does not have a clear and unambiguous interest in the issues will result only in a lack of commitment to the policy goals in question (Ham & Hill 1993). Implementation problems can emerge as a result of organisation of the implementation process itself. These problems could emerge as a result of organisational management or through poor management of conflicts of interests that arise during the implementation process (Cline 2000).

Fifth, the question of whether implementation should be top-down or bottom-up has been the subject of much debate and has been linked to implementation problems. Hogwood and Gunn (1984 in Hill 1997) identified 10 preconditions for perfect implementation from a managerial point of view (see Tourism Planning Breakthrough: 'Ten conditions for perfect implementation', p. 172). And, although Hogwood and Gunn concede that they are sympathetic to this top-down approach, they also acknowledge that 'implementation must involve a process of interaction between organizations, the members of which have many values, perspectives and priorities …' (p. 224). Others have argued that a bottom-up approach to implementation enables key actors and agencies to collaborate interactively, which can only improve implementation (Barrett & Fudge 1981; Sabatier 1997).

Source: *adapted from Hogwood & Gunn 1984 in Hill 1997.*

This discussion leads to a need to consider the role that coordination plays in implementation.

■ 5.3.3 **What** *is coordination?*

Some of the most challenging policy choices faced by government are those that cross the traditional boundaries between Cabinet ministers' portfolios and between the Australian, State and Territory levels of government ... [T]asks that run well beyond the remits of individual ministers ... are whole-of-government problems and their resolution requires a long-term strategic focus, a willingness to develop policy through consultation with the community and a bias towards flexible delivery that meets local needs and conditions. (Howard 2002.)

Governments rarely act without repercussions for other governments and non-government interests. The interconnectedness of policy domains, the overlapping nature of federal systems of government and the extent of shared roles and responsibilities have already been discussed (see the case study 'Inter-governmental relations and tourism in Australia' in chapter 2, pp. 63–5). Sometimes governments can have similar goals, but frequently governments can also have divergent and even conflicting goals that exacerbate difficulties in coordination and implementation. In other words, one government might seek to achieve certain policy outcomes but require partnership with another level of government to achieve these ends. This complexity underpins the importance of developing a framework for coordination and implementation that transcends government boundaries and party politics.

Coordination is the term used to denote efforts by government to minimise inconsistencies between the actions and inactions of other governments and non-government bodies for the purpose of implementing the government's goals. Governments include a coordination stage within their policy cycle because it is important to minimise incompatibility (Bridgman & Davis 2004: 93).

Incompatibility between the actions of different agencies and different levels of government can lead to ineffective implementation and resource wastage. It could also lead to a situation in which the positive outcomes of policy at one level of government are cancelled by policy at another level.

Coordination embraces institutionalised processes and structures that give explicit attention to the way government interactions can enhance policy outcomes and reduce conflicts. In recent years, governments have placed increasing emphasis on 'whole-of-government' approaches, which seek to coordinate government agencies and reduce the administrative, financial and political implications of policy conflicts. In this instance, information briefs to cabinet are an important instrument for facilitating inter-agency communication and assessment of possible conflicts.

■ 5.3.4 Towards coordination: *whole of government approaches*

> Whole of government denotes public service agencies working across portfolio boundaries to achieve a shared goal and an integrated government response to particular issues. Approaches can be formal and informal. They can focus on policy development, program management and service delivery. (Australian Public Service Commission 2004.)

The idea of coordination within the policy cycle is not new. In Australia, the division of roles and responsibilities embedded in the Constitution mean that overlapping policy actions can occur at different levels of government. Policies can be cancelled out or, at the very least, be less effective because of the actions of other levels of government. Historically, the challenge of coordination has been one of ensuring intergovernmental collaboration and has been met through institutionalised processes, routines and structures, such as the Loans Council or various ministerial councils (Bridgman & Davis 2004: 95). This structured approach has tended to be inflexible and unable to adapt quickly to new and urgent policy issues. In order to facilitate better coordination, in 1992 the Council of Australian Governments (COAG) was formed. COAG's role

> ... is to initiate, develop and monitor the implementation of policy reforms that are of national significance and which require cooperative action by Australian governments (for example, National Competition Policy, water reform, reform of Commonwealth and State/Territory roles in environmental regulation, the use of human embryos in medical research, counter-terrorism arrangements and restrictions on the availability of handguns). Issues may arise from, among other things: Ministerial Council deliberations; international treaties which affect the States and Territories; or major initiatives of one government (particularly the Australian Government) which impact on other governments or require the cooperation of other governments. (COAG 2005.)

However, intra-governmental relations are also an issue (i.e. where policy and actions of different agencies within the same level of government countervail each other). As a result, growing attention has been placed on the notion of **whole-of-government approaches** to coordination and implementation within each level of government. Whole-of-government approaches represent a departure from the coordinated structures and routines of the past. They seek to foster dialogue and information sharing across organisational boundaries and to promote supportive cultures and skill bases within the public service (e.g. Australian Public Service Commission 2004). In essence, then, whole-of-government approaches promote cultural change, flexibility and a breakdown in rigid departmental boundaries. The development of whole-of-government priorities are a manifestation of this whole-of-government approach.

From 1976 to 2005, the Tourism Ministers' Council was the mechanism set up to achieve intergovernmental coordination between state and federal governments in Australia. The main role of the council was to facilitate consultation and policy coordination, and this was achieved through the Australian Standing Committee on Tourism (ASCOT), which brought together senior officials at an operational level to discuss issues and make decisions that were then considered by the Ministers' Council. This framework was in operation from 1976 and provided an opportunity for the identification and discussion of policy coordination issues. As a result of recommendations made in the Tourism White Paper (2003), a Tourism Collaboration Intergovernmental Arrangement was developed, which provides a more detailed framework for cooperation. The main purpose of this arrangement is to identify how and where the parties can work in partnership with the driving objectives being to:

- provide a framework for intergovernmental collaboration in key areas that increase the contribution of tourism to Australia's economy, environment and society while maintaining respect for the organisational imperatives of the parties to this arrangement
- help clarify how and through what mechanisms the agencies will collaborate in areas of shared interest and responsibility
- develop long-term commitment by governments to provide the industry with a more stable environment that facilitates growth
- reduce duplication to maximise the resources available to create a conducive environment in which the industry can grow and develop, and
- identify further means and opportunities for productive collaboration, such as by developing bilateral agreements on specific issues (Commonwealth Government 2005, p. 7).

5.4   *E* VALUATION

5.4.1   What is *evaluation*?

Consult any text on policy analysis and you will find passages extolling the indispensability of program evaluation. It could hardly be otherwise, given that program evaluation is primarily about trying to figure out how successful a policy has been, whether it met its objectives, how far it fell short and what might be done to improve its impact. The same passages that extol evaluation, however, are usually complemented by ones that say evaluation is expensive, difficult, rarely conclusive and politically unpopular (Pal 1997: 233).

Evaluation is an increasingly important part of the policy process. **Evaluation** is defined as the disciplined and critical assessment of the consequences of government policy and actions (Hall & Jenkins 1995; Cameron 2000). Evaluation involves the systematic collection of qualitative and/or quantitative information, data and other outcomes of government policy for the purposes of analysing outcomes and for identifying improvements to policy. It is a highly creative and intuitive process that requires great skill and thorough understanding of the policy issues, the stakeholders and the nature of government roles and responsibilities; that is, evaluation experts must be careful to evaluate policy in the context of the legal and ethical roles of government. Evaluation that moves outside these parameters runs the risk of being irrelevant to the core business of making and improving governments' policy approach.

There are two broad approaches to policy evaluation grouped according to whether they employ quantitative data, statistical techniques and mathematical modelling or quantitative techniques, which explore themes and issues that are not readily quantified. Quantitative techniques such as cost-benefit analysis are frequently used to assist in decision-making about policy options and are based on projected or potential costs and benefits. Qualitative techniques are used in situations where there is a lack of quantitative data or where issues cannot be readily reduced to economic values or statistics. For example, evaluating the effect of tourism development policies on marginalised communities and cultures requires more than numerical analysis. Quantitative and qualitative techniques are not mutually exclusive and can be employed together in 'mixed methods approaches' to improve understandings of policy.

Traditionally, evaluation occurs at two main points in the policy process: (1) at the point where alternative policy solutions are evaluated and decisions made to adopt a particular approach and (2) at that point where implementation ends and the policy cycle starts again. For example, after a program or policy initiative has been implemented, there should be an opportunity to evaluate the outcomes and effects of that policy so that improvements can be made or the decision to axe the initiative taken. Evaluation is that point at which existing policy is assessed against other competitive policy issues and priorities. It is also the point at which decisions must be made about whether the current approach in dealing with a particular issue is the best way, or whether there are alternative and better ways of dealing with it.

In the past, the evaluation process was conducted in an ad hoc manner, at the convenience of government and with little structure or methodology. However, more contemporary approaches to policy evaluation in Australia have included an evaluation point in the middle of the program implementation and more rigorous frameworks of assessment being adopted. Evaluation is becoming a central part of the policy-making process, not an afterthought, and as such is receiving budgetary allocations. This makes sense since evaluation provides an opportunity to assess preliminary outcomes and adapt or refine further implementation. Evaluation can also improve government transparency, which is also becoming increasingly important in modern public management.

■ 5.4.2 The *changing nature of evaluation*

Although evaluation forms an important part of a reflective, responsive and adaptive policy approach, it has not always received as much attention as it should. Evaluation can be traced back to the nineteenth century when governments sought to better understand the effects of policy in a rapidly changing industrialising world. In particular, governments were experimenting with education and agricultural policy, and the purpose of evaluation was to better understand the effects of such initiatives. By the early twentieth century, there was a general expansion of bureaucracy, and the public service became a recognised and important career choice. As a result, expertise was built up within bureaucracy, and evaluation of certain policy initiatives was undertaken on a more regular basis.

From the 1930s to the 1960s, evaluation activities were characterised by a strong emphasis on the systematic analysis of quantitative data (Hughes 2003). Techniques such as cost-benefit analysis and **goals assessment** matrices lent a 'scientific' and supposedly rational framework to the analysis of public policies, which fitted with the Taylorist scientific management paradigm that dominated public administration at the time (see section 2.4.1). High levels of mathematical sophistication went into modelling the inputs and outputs of public policy, especially in complex policy arenas. However, the use of such modelling techniques involved the collating and structuring of data, the models were embedded with assumptions about cause and consequence, and decision rules about what was more or less important were applied (Hughes 2003). As a result, many values and assumptions were built into the cost-benefit models and applied without robust examination of their reliability or acceptability.

Cost-benefit analysis is one technique that has traditionally been used for evaluating planning policies. **Cost-benefit analysis** looks at whether the program has had a benefit and at what cost. It has traditionally been an appealing evaluative tool for planning because it simplifies complex policy outcomes by reducing them to an economic cost or benefit value, which can be used to guide decision-making and selection of the 'optimal' policy approach (Pal 1997). Popularised during the 1960s, cost-benefit analysis is again being reinvigorated because it fits well with neoliberal public management philosophies, which demand that public policy be efficient and accountable (Hughes 2003). More recent attempts at cost-benefit analysis have sought to incorporate social, cultural and other intangible effects. The notion of **triple bottom line accounting** (or sometimes quadruple bottom line where political sustainability is also included alongside social, environmental and economic issues) has emerged as a result and is a burgeoning area of contemporary research and practice. However, cost-benefit analysis still draws considerable criticism because it is difficult to value effects relative to each other and to reach an overall position. Hughes (2003: 122) argues that 'numbers are useful and provide information to decision-makers ... but [this type of modelling] gives them too much emphasis'. Too much reliance on rational, scientific evaluations is inappropriate because so much of policy-making depends on the political context (Patton & Sawicki

1986). Although a level of abstraction can be useful, it is imperative that evaluation recognises the inherently political and value-laden nature of policy-making (John 1998).

In the late twentieth century, there were increasing calls for evaluation to be made explicit and transparent. Evaluation, as a means of improving the actions of government and ensuring that resource use is optimised, remains an ever-present concern. However, the practice of policy-making reveals that it remains relatively common that policy choice, and hence outcomes, is subject to political influence. Evaluation activities must therefore draw from both qualitative and quantitative approaches and recognise the broader political context. Public participation and feedback therefore becomes an important aspect of the evaluation process.

TOURISM PLANNING BREAKTHROUGH
Tourism impact model for local government

The Tourism Impact Model (TIM) for Australian Local Government was prepared by the Commonwealth Government for the purpose of helping local government better understand the impact of tourism on their local community (Department of Industry, Tourism and Resources 2004). The model employs a cost-benefit analysis tool based on an Excel spreadsheet. Local government economic development managers, managers of corporate services and divisional managers add information to the model, and the output tables provide information on such aspects as:
• economic changes that would occur in the local government area if tourism were not present
• an estimate of the local government's share of visitor spending
• the effect of employment multipliers on different sectors of the local economy
• the effects of tourism on population, and
• the budgetary effects on councils of not having a tourism industry.

The information generated by the TIM can be used to inform debates about the level of local government support for tourism, the value of spending on local marketing and whether or not the costs and benefits of tourism are being shared among local councils where collaborative marketing is taking place. The TIM is highly quantitative in nature and is intended for use in the decision-making phase of local government's policy-making process. Its advantage is that, given the lack of local information and data on tourism, the model is useful in informing local policy-making by quantifying in dollar terms the local impact of tourism visitation and expenditure. The model's complexity and the lack of expertise and resources available in local government to adequately implement and interpret the modelling and its results are criticisms that have been recognised as impeding its adoption by local government.

Source: *adapted from Department of Industry, Tourism and Resources 2004.*

■ *5.4.3* **The** *practice of evaluation*

The practice of policy evaluation has predominantly been based on economic and other quantitative data. This is because this data is more readily available and is often able to be interpreted and compared more easily. Only in recent decades have criticisms surfaced about the inadequacy of relying solely on quantitative data, and a concerted effort has been made to collect and analyse qualitative data, such as interviews or testimonials. However, the analysis of qualitative data brings with it considerable challenges in terms of reliability, analysis and presentation.

Evaluation activities have different approaches and foci. These include:

- performance audits of organisations — evaluate how *organisations use their resources* and whether this use is economical, efficient and effective in meeting program objectives
- performance audits of policy outcomes — evaluate the *effects and outcomes of various programs* and activities. These activities might include, for example, cost-benefit analysis, benchmarking, state of the environment (SoE) reporting and monitoring activities
- stakeholder audits — evaluate the *effects of policies and programs on particular groups and individuals* in society. For example, social welfare policy evaluation might seek to evaluate the effects of policies on disadvantaged groups (low-income, single-parent families and so on), welfare services delivery organisations (e.g. Red Cross, Smith Family and so on)
- evaluations of the evaluation process — assess whether the *evaluation activities* themselves were fair and just.

Although evaluation is most often undertaken at the end of the implementation stage, it can be undertaken at any time during the policy formulation process. For example in each stage of the policy process, evaluation could take place by asking the following questions:

1. *Issue identification:* were the issues correctly identified? Were the issues correctly prioritised?
2. *Policy analysis:* were the methods and techniques of analysis appropriate? Was the analysis rigorous? Were there other approaches to analysis that might have revealed different issues and problems? Was the analysis reliable? Did the policy analysts have appropriate expertise?
3. *Policy instrument:* were all the available policy instruments assessed? Were some policy instruments or approaches not included in the analysis? Why?
4. *Consultation:* was the consultation process framed appropriately? Did it incorporate and engage all interests meaningfully?
5. *Coordination:* was coordination successful? What were the problems in coordination, and did these affect policy outcomes?
6. *Decision:* how was the decision made? Was it equitable and transparent? Was it the best decision to adopt this particular policy?
7. *Implementation:* was the strategy for implementation successful? What were the advantages and disadvantages of the implementation process? In what ways did the process of implementation affect the policy outcomes? How could implementation have been improved?

8. *Evaluation:* was the evaluation of the policy just and equitable to all interests? How was the evaluation framed? Was this the most appropriate approach? Why?

According Bridgman and Davis (2004: 137), there are obstacles to a full and robust evaluation of policy. These include:

- the level of uncertainty that exists over policy goals and their measurement
- the difficulty of determining what causes a particular outcome
- the diffuse and varied nature of policy impacts, which are quite often interrelated
- the difficulties of data acquisition and availability, especially social and other qualitative data types
- resistance to evaluation by politicians, public servants and interest groups
- perspectives, which are limited by time, expertise and the disciplinary or professional composition of the policy evaluation team.

Nevertheless, by drawing on the diverse implementation and evaluation literature it is possible to develop a broad framework for policy evaluation. This evaluation approach must move beyond the 'hard-edged' analytical frameworks of modern public administration to recognise the importance of 'soft', less tangible dimensions that make policy work, such as relationships, organisational culture, policy entrepreneurialism, leadership and trust. Evaluation of policy should cover the following aspects:

1. *The strategic vision, policy goals and objectives:* is the vision possible and appropriate? Were the goals and objectives realistic and achievable?
2. *The tasks:* were the tasks appropriate? Were the agencies with appropriate responsibilities identified?
3. *People:* were the people involved in implementation committed to the policy goals? Did they have sufficient training, and did they have the capacity to undertake the implementation tasks?
4. *Organisational structures:* were the organisational structures appropriate for the implementation of the policy? What were the constraints and opportunities of the organisational structures for implementation?
5. *Resources:* was the implementation of the program adequately resourced?
6. *Culture:* did the culture of the organisations responsible for delivery have a positive or negative influence on implementation? Was the change management process adequately managed?

Despite the best of intentions and even the most rigorous evaluation exercises, problems are inevitably encountered in measuring the consequences of tourism policies, plans and programs. In relation to the former Commonwealth Regional Tourism Development Program (see the case study in chapter 7, 'A critical assessment of the Regional Tourism Development Program, 1993–94', p. 259, for more details), Jenkins and Sorensen (1996) noted:

- the projects might have long-term effects
- the direct effects of some projects are likely to be quite small (this is not necessarily a defect of the programs or investment since most local economic development activities are low-key and incremental)
- the projects' indirect and induced multiplier effects might be difficult to measure

- the effects might also be in terms of morale: how communities perceive themselves, happiness and contentment (which are essentially unmeasurable) and general business management and leadership competencies. These might influence other development activities or possibilities over the longer term
- some grants will fail on their primary objectives but generate some positive benefits
- there might be demonstration effects whereby innovative ideas are adopted elsewhere
- local development is primarily influenced by a vast number of exogenous factors, many of which are beyond the control of any Australian government, and
- the opportunity costs arising from government programs are difficult to measure (and certainly they are rarely taken into account).

Evaluation, especially that undertaken by the very people who contribute to policy formulation, brings with it the potential for conflicts of interest. This conflict is founded in public servants' commitment to the pursuit of the common good versus their self-interest and survival in the bureaucracy (Mulgan 2001); that is, although bureaucrats are ostensibly committed to addressing public problems and finding solutions that will minimise negative consequences and maximise positive benefits, no bureaucrat wants their work to be judged as a failure. Accordingly, the way policy evaluation is framed and presented is also connected with the values and motivations of those who undertake and write the evaluation. Evaluation, therefore, can become a sensitive issue that brings with it political, administrative and budgetary implications. In order to address this issue and improve transparency, agencies can appoint evaluation teams that include internal and external representatives.

CHAPTER REVIEW

Governments achieve their objectives through the development and delivery of policy. This chapter has examined the nature and variety of policy instruments and issues associated with implementation and evaluation of tourism policy. Policy instruments are best understood as the tools and approaches used by governments to achieve outcomes and might be broadly classified according to the types of resources they use (e.g. information, money, government action and law). Tourism planners and policy-makers need to understand the potential benefits and disadvantages of these approaches in order to assist decision-makers choose appropriate courses of action. The context in which policy is developed will also make some instruments more appropriate than others, so it is important that policy instrument choice reflects the context. Of course, choosing the right policy instrument does not necessarily lead to perfect implementation and the realisation of a policy's objectives. Implementation refers to the steps that turn policy decisions into actions. Implementation of policy depends on a range of factors including the nature of the problem and how it is conceptualised; the complexity of the problem and its interrelatedness to other policy problems; the availability of appropriate institutional and administrative structures; and the skills, knowledge and values of those responsible for implementation.

Evaluation refers to the disciplined and critical assessment of a public policy for the purposes of informing and refining government approaches. The direct and indirect consequences of policy are often difficult to identify and assess, especially where there are cross-sectoral impacts. In this chapter the changing nature of evaluation and the advantages and disadvantages of quantitative and qualitative approaches were discussed. While consensus about the most appropriate evaluation techniques remains elusive, what is clear is that evaluation activities need to acknowledge the contributions of both quantitative and qualitative techniques. Moreover, the political influence on policy choice, implementation and evaluation needs to be acknowledged. Implementation and evaluation can be highly political, and strategic management of these processes is important.

Until relatively recently, implementation and evaluation were seen as ad hoc steps taken post-policy development. However, as calls for government transparency and accountability grow stronger, the importance of implementation strategies and evaluation of policy is becoming more obvious. Increasingly, governments are incorporating formalised implementation and evaluation strategies into their policy-making, and these aspects of policy-making are being more adequately funded. Some governments have also undertaken steps to 'objectify' evaluation by appointing independent review boards to assess the efficiency and effectiveness of policy and its delivery.

SUMMARY OF KEY TERMS

Compulsory instruments

Compulsory instruments include such approaches as legislation and regulation. They require government to proscribe and implement solutions to address certain policy issues and problems.

Coordination

Coordination is the term used to denote efforts by government to minimise inconsistencies between the actions and inactions of other governments and non-government bodies for the purpose of implementing the government's goals.

Cost-benefit analysis

Cost-benefit analysis is a specific technique that analyses how much economic benefit can be attributed to a particular policy change (e.g. economic growth, employment, foreign exchange earnings and revenue) relative to the costs of implementing that policy.

Evaluation

Evaluation is defined as the disciplined and critical assessment of government policy and actions. Evaluation involves the systematic collection of information, data and other outcomes of government policy for the purposes of analysing outcomes and for identifying improvements to policy.

Goals assessment

The process of assessing the level to which any given policy action achieves the goals and objectives it was designed to achieve. A 'goals assessment matrix' refers to a rational scientific evaluation process that assesses the achievement of policy goals. The process involves assigning a value that represents whether or not a particular goal has been achieved. The method has been criticised because it requires substantial value judgement on the part of the policy analyst.

Implementation

Implementation is the process through which policy ideas and plans are translated into government action.

Mixed instruments

Mixed instruments are those policy approaches and tools that employ a combination of methods to achieve a desired outcome. For example, environmental accreditation might be voluntarily sought by groups and individuals seeking to increase their market share and improve the practices and outcomes of their operations. Standards for ecoaccreditation might have been developed with government involvement so that they could be considered mixed instruments.

Policy instruments

Policy instruments are the means by which governments achieve their ends and include a wide range of instruments, programs, tools, approaches and techniques. Policy instruments exist on a continuum characterised by high government involvement (e.g. regulation) to local government involvement (e.g. voluntary measures).

Triple bottom line accounting

The expansion of traditional accounting procedures for measuring an organisation or government's success to include social, cultural and environmental criteria.

Voluntary instruments

Voluntary instruments are policies, approaches and actions that are voluntarily adopted by groups and individuals. They are designed to change the behaviour of industry and community groups in order to bring about a desired situation.

Whole-of-government approaches

The challenge of developing horizontal coordination (across the same level of government) and vertical coordination (between different levels of government) of policy directions and actions.

QUESTIONS

1 What are policy instruments?

2 Identify and give examples of different types of policy instruments in tourism.

3 Identify and discuss those factors that influence the choice of policy instrument.

4 Identify the types of government resources that can be used to address policy problems. Give examples in tourism.

5 What is implementation, and why is it important in the policy process?

6 What are the factors that influence policy implementation?

7 What is evaluation, and why is it important in the policy process?

8 Critically discuss broad approaches to policy evaluation and identify their advantages and disadvantages.

9 How has evaluation practice changed over time?

10 Discuss why policy evaluation can be politically and administratively sensitive.

EXERCISES

1 Find examples of codes of conduct for tourism. Try to find examples covering local, national and global levels that address different types of tourism activity. Examine the content of the codes, and compare and constrast the following aspects:

(a) Who are the codes directed at?

(b) What are the differences in the content and level of detail in the codes of conduct?

(c) In particular, is there a difference in the language of international codes and local codes? Why?

(d) Discuss how effective they might be in managing the consequences of tourism when applied.

(e) What is the value of having such a code?

2 Take Hogwood and Gunn's 10 preconditions for implementation (Tourism Planning Breakthrough, p. 172). Discuss whether these preconditions are realistic in the context of the Australian Government's National Tourism Policy. Identify and critically discuss where problems in implementation might emerge.

3 Examine a regional tourism plan of your choice. Examine the document and critically discuss the following questions:

(a) What sort of policy instruments are indicated in the plan? Why might these instruments have been chosen?

(b) Explain the implementation process that the plan went through. Critically discuss the factors that might have been influencing implementation.

(c) How might the plan be evaluated? Construct a list of evaluative questions that would form a framework for the assessment of the plan and its implementation.

FURTHER READING

Bridgman, P & Davis, G 2004, *The Australian Policy Handbook*, **3rd edn, Allen & Unwin, Sydney.** This book is a useful introductory text that provides an overview of policy instruments, implementation and evaluation and their relationship to the policy cycle.

Department of Industry, Tourism and Resources 2004, *Tourism Impact Model for Local Government*, **Tourism Division, DITR, Canberra.** This manual provides an overview of the Tourism Impact Model and provides a good, contemporary tourism-related illustration of the nature of cost-benefit analysis, the type of data required and the outputs from such an evaluation.

Howlett, M & Ramesh, M 1995, *Studying Public Policy: Policy Cycles and Policy Subsystems*, **Oxford University Press, Toronto.** This text contains a good discussion of policy instruments and the different ways in which instruments can be categorised. It discusses changing trends in use of instruments and those factors that influence instrument choice.

Restructuring the Scottish tourism industry

Tourism is an important sector of the Scottish economy, employing more than 215 000 people and generating more than £6.2 billion (about A$14.9 billion) in 2002. Although tourism revenues had been falling before 2002, strong growth was predicted as a result of increased mobility in European Union countries generally and growth in certain segments, such as the short break market. In 2003, an Ad Hoc Group of Ministers on Tourism was formed to review the tourism functions of government and the effectiveness of its existing policies in order to establish strategies to better capitalise on predicted growth. It was also realised that the marketplace would become increasingly competitive and that it was important to deliver consistently high-quality products and services to capture some of this growth.

It is important to note that this was not the first review of Scotland's tourism policies. Leading up to the appointment of the group, industry had become increasingly frustrated with the lack of strategic vision, coordination and leadership shown by the government (Kerr 2003). There were strained relationships and gaps between tourism and economic development functions. A structural overhaul of the delivery of tourism policy was needed. A number of reviews examining a range of agencies, responsibilities and funding arrangements were conducted in the period leading up the appointment of the Ad Hoc Ministers Group. During this period, traditional relationships and the status quo of existing power bases were being questioned, and considerable pressure was being exerted by the industry for wholesale change (Kerr 2003).

The public sector contributed in various ways to the development of tourism in Scotland until this time. This support was delivered through VisitScotland (which undertakes marketing, branding and booking functions), Enterprise Networks (which undertake business support, skill development and training functions), local authorities (which partially fund Area Tourism Boards and undertake other support activities) and Historic Scotland. Although these organisations were undertaking their functions well and contributing to tourism, the review considered that there were opportunities to improve and integrate the existing organisational structures. In particular, it was considered that new ways of encouraging training and improving service delivery were needed; more examples of best practice were needed; more champions and stronger leadership were needed; and enthusiastic ambassadors for the industry were needed. To this end, the review recommended that a more integrated support structure be developed (McAveety 2004).

The review also considered the role of the 14 Area Tourism Boards (ATBs), which function as regional tourism agencies and are funded through

(*continued*)

contributions by local authorities and tourism businesses. It was decided that the interests of Scottish tourism would best be served by a policy approach that replaced the existing ATBs with a single integrated network to deliver business services for the whole of Scotland. This approach reflected the observation that, as they currently operated, the ATB had different levels of skills and capacity to develop and promote tourism in their regions. The 14 existing ATBs would be replaced by 14 Local Tourism Hubs, which were to provide a more 'joined-up' delivery of government support for tourism than the existing and somewhat uneven capacity of the ATBs (McAveety 2004). However, the change was not simply a rebadging and a name change of the existing organisation but a refocusing of roles and relationships, about changing funding mechanisms, accountability and better meeting the needs of stakeholders. The traditional funding provided to the ATBs by local authorities would be discontinued, and in its place local authorities would negotiate directly with VisitScotland for tourism services they required for their area. Legislation was required to set up these new structures so, in the interim, Network Tourist Boards were set up as a 'stepping stone' to further implementation.

Stepping back for a moment then, it is possible to see that the Ad Hoc Group of Ministers conceptualised the issues and the challenges that lay ahead for Scotland in terms of the need to establish stronger, more robust businesses incorporating partnerships, synergy building, networking, information and experience sharing. In other words, the policy instrument chosen was a network organisation aimed at improving knowledge and skills — a learning and capacity-building network. However, its implementation required new structures, which needed to be established by legislation. This approach perhaps reflects dominant neoliberal management philosophies and is based on the notion that, although markets have a strong role to play in implementing policy solutions, the government's role is to facilitate, coordinate and provide leadership. It also illustrates that no single policy instrument can achieve this change. A range of policy instruments, including legislation, networks, voluntary mechanisms and incentives, is included in this approach. Ouchi's idea of clans (Ouchi 1980) is also important in this network approach, since it is the network clans who have a powerful role in influencing the ideas and adoption of initiatives in small business.

Implementation

The review recommended major structural change in the way the government delivered its support for tourism. The implementation of the recommendations required careful consideration since many stakeholders were involved and multi-agency support was needed. An implementation strategy was prepared following the release of the review, and the network was to be functional by March 2005. This Implementation Plan was based on consultation with all stakeholders. Clearly, in such a major restructure and a re-engineering of the way tourism support is delivered, there were some winners and some losers. Ham and Hill (1993) suggest that where changes to the status quo are proposed, implementation problems are more likely to emerge, and there is more likely to be resistance from those whose activities and resource streams are being affected. In previous review and evaluation activities conducted by the government, there had been continued problems and poor relations between some stakeholder groups. It was important that a strategy for the implementation of the proposed solution be developed, and changes needed to be carefully managed. The Implementation Plan identified the network's vision and current and proposed operating environment. It also identified a partnership approach and outlined funding arrangements. The plan defined the proposed roles of the stakeholders and how the network will be managed. An important component of this change management was the communication of proposed changes, initiatives and the clarification of questions. To this end a useful website was established to assist stakeholders through the process: www.scotexchange.net/tourism_organisations/to_new_scottish_tourism _network_main.

This case study illustrates that implementation is a continuous, dynamic process that has to be carefully managed and strategically conceptualised. In this case, the process of implementation was given strategic consideration and an inclusive and consultative approach was adopted.

Questions

1 What was the political and administrative context in which the review took place?

2 What were the policy instruments used in this case study, and why were they considered appropriate?

3 Why might implementation have been difficult?

4 How might this policy approach be evaluated in the future? Develop a broad framework for its evaluation.

References

Kerr, W 2003, *Tourism and the Strategic Management of Failure*, Pergamon Press, Oxford.
McAveety, F 2004, *Scottish Parliament Official Report*, 11 March 2004, www.scottish.parliament. uk/business/officialReports/meetingsParliament/or-04/sor0311-02.htm#Col6600.
VisitScotland 2005, VisitScotland Business Plan 2005–08, viewed 18 April 2005, www.lothian exchange.net/tourism_organisations/scottishlevel/visitscotland/vs_report/business_plan05-08.htm.

REFERENCES

Australian Public Service Commission 2004, 'Connecting government: Whole of government responses to Australia's priority challenges', viewed 29 March 2006, www.apsc.gov.au/mac/connectinggovernment1.htm.

Barrett, S & Fudge, C 1981, *Policy and Action: Essays on the Implementation of Public Policy*, Methuen, London.

Bridgman, P & Davis, G 2004, *The Australian Policy Handbook*, 3rd edn, Allen & Unwin, Sydney.

Cameron, W 2000, 'Program evaluation and performance auditing: Birds of a feather', presentation to the Australian Evaluation Society, 16 November, viewed 29 March 2006, www.audit.vic.gov.au/speeches/agspeech_03.html.

Cline, K 2000, 'Defining the implementation problem: Organisational management versus co-operation', *Journal of Public Administration Research and Theory*, vol. 10, no. 3, pp. 551–71.

Commonwealth Government 2005, 'Achievements by partnerships: Tourism collaboration intergovernmental arrangement', viewed 14 April 2006, www.industry.gov.au/content/itrinternet/cmscontent.cfm?objectID=CD36769B-65BF-4956-B5BD537275412B16.

Department of Industry, Tourism and Resources 2004, *Tourism Impact Model for Local Government*, Tourism Division, DITR, Canberra.

ECPAT 2005, 'The Code — Protection of Children from Exploitation in Travel and Tourism', viewed 29 March 2006, www.thecode.org.

Government of Canada 2002, 'Instrument choice in global democracies conference', McGill University, viewed 14 April 2006, http://policyresearch.gc.ca/page.asp?pagenm=law-droit_cr&langcd=E#2.

Great Barrier Reef Marine Park Authority 2005, 'Environmental management charge', viewed 29 March 2006, www.gbrmpa.gov.au/corp_site/permits/emc.html.

Greiner, R et al. 2000, 'Incentive instruments for the sustainable use of marine resources', *Ocean and Coastal Management*, vol. 43, no. 1, pp. 29–50.

Hall, CM & Jenkins, JM 1995, *Tourism and Public Policy*, Routledge, London.

Ham, C & Hill, C 1993, 'Towards implementation theory?', in *The Policy Process in the Modern Capitalist State*, 2nd edn, Harvester Wheatsheaf, New York.

Heywood, L 2005, 'Auditor to probe grants program', *Courier-Mail* (Brisbane), 26–27 November, p. 14.

Hjalager, A 1996, 'Tourism and the environment: The innovation connection', *Journal of Sustainable Tourism*, vol. 4, no. 4, pp. 201–18.

Hogwood, BW & Gunn, LA 1984, 'Why perfect implementation is unattainable', in M Hill (ed.), *The Policy Process: A Reader*, 2nd edn, Prentice Hall/Harvester Wheatsheaf, Hemel Hempstead, Herts, pp. 217–25.

Hood, C 1986, *The Tools of Government*, Chatham House, Chatham, NJ.

Howard, J 2002, 'Strategic leadership for Australia: Policy directions in a complex world', viewed 14 April 2006, www.dpmc.gov.au/speeches/pm/leadership/contents.cfm.

Howlett, M & Ramesh, M 1995, *Studying Public Policy: Policy Cycles and Policy Subsystems*, Oxford University Press, Toronto.

Hughes, O 2003, *Public Management and Administration: An Introduction*, 3rd edn, Palgrave, Basingstoke.

Jenkins, JM & Sorensen, AD 1996, 'Tourism, regional development and the commonwealth: A critical appraisal of the regional tourism development program', *Australian Leisure*, vol. 7, no. 4, pp. 28–35.

John, P 1998, *Analyzing Public Policy*, Pinter, London and New York.

Martyn, A 2004, Great Barrier Reef Marine Park Amendment Bill 2004, Commonwealth Department of Parliamentary Services, Bills Digest 98, 2003–04, Canberra.

Mazmanian, DA & Sabatier, P 1989, *Implementation and Public Policy*, University Press of America, Lantham, MD.

Mihalic, T 2003, 'Economic instruments of environmental tourism policy derived from environmental theories', in DA Fennel & RK Dowling (eds), *Ecotourism Policy and Planning*, CABI Publishing, Wallingford, UK, and Cambridge, MA, pp. 99–120.

Mulgan, R 2001, 'Public servants and the public interest', paper presented as a lecture in the Department of the Senate Occasion Lecture Series at Parliament House on 11 August 2000, viewed 28 March 2006, www.aph.gov.au/Senate/pubs/pops/pop36/c04.pdf.

O'Toole, L 2004, 'The theory-practice issue in policy implementation research', *Public Administration*, vol. 82, no. 2, pp. 309–29.

Ouchi, WG 1980, 'Markets, bureaucracies and clans', in G Thompson et al. (eds), *Markets, Hierarchies and Networks: The Co-ordination of Social Life*, Sage, London, pp. 246–55.

Pal, L 1997, *Beyond Policy Analysis: Public Issue Management in Turbulent Times*, International Thomson Publishing, Scarborough, Ont.

Parsons, W 1995, *Public Policy: An Introduction to the Theory and Practice of Policy Analysis*, Edward Elgar, Aldershot, UK.

Patton, CV & Sawicki, DS 1993, *Basic Methods of Policy Analysis and Planning*, 2nd edn, Prentice Hall, Englewood Cliffs, NJ.

Pressman, JL & Wildavsky, A 1984, *Implementation: How great expectations in Washington are dashed in Oakland: Or, why it's amazing that federal programs work at all, this being a saga of the economic development administration as told by two sympathetic observers who seek to build morals on a foundation of ruined hopes*, 3rd edn, University of California Press, Berkeley.

Sabatier, P 1997, 'Top-down and bottom-up approaches to implementation research', in M Hill (ed.), *The Policy Process: A Reader*, 2nd edn, Prentice Hall/Harvester Wheatsheaf, Hemel Hempstead, Herts, pp. 272–95.

Sabatier, P & Jenkins-Smith, HC 1993, *Policy Change and Learning: An Advocacy Coalition Approach*, Westview, Boulder, CO.

Simeon, R 1976, 'Studying public policy', *Canadian Journal of Political Science*, vol. 9, no. 4, pp. 558–80.

Tonge, R, Fletcher, S & Concept Tourism Consultants 2003, *Byron Shire Tourism Management: An Options Paper for Consideration*, Final Draft, Prepared for Byron Bay Shire Council and Tourism NSW.

Tourism White Paper 2003, viewed 10 October 2005, www.industry.gov.au/
content/itrinternet/cmscontentcfm?objectID=4E01EE73–65BF-4956-
B057EC96612BDDCB.

Westerhausen, K & Macbeth, J 2003, 'Backpackers and empowered local
communities: Natural allies in the struggle for sustainability and local
control', *Tourism Geographies*, vol. 5, no. 1, pp. 71–86.

World Wildlife Fund 2000, 'Tourism Certification: An Analysis of
GreenGlobe Certification and Other Certification Programmes', a report
by Synergy for WWF-UK, viewed 28 March 2006, www.wwf.org.uk/
filelibrary/pdf/tcr.pdf.

Dianne Dredge and
Meredith Lawrence

CHAPTER 6

Tourism *policy and planning processes*

LEARNING OBJECTIVES

After reading this chapter you will be able to:

1 discuss why it is important to understand tourism planning and policy processes, and identify the various perspectives that can be used to build insights

2 explain the policy cycle and discuss the advantages and disadvantages of the concept

3 identify and discuss alternative ways in which decision-making can take place in the policy process

4 discuss why issue identification is useful in understanding policy processes

5 explain the concepts of policy subsystems, advocacy coalitions and networks

6 identify and discuss the key features of good tourism planning and policy processes.

6.1 INTRODUCTION

> A good policy process is the vital underpinning of good policy development. Of course, good process does not necessarily guarantee a good policy outcome, but the risks of a bad process leading to a bad outcome are very much higher. (Keating 1996, p. 63.)

The policy process is a complex, multilayered process involving many institutions and actors; it is the process whereby issues are mediated and appropriate actions and interventions are identified. Therefore, and logically, good policy relies on a process of policy formulation that is rigorous, informed and grounded in its engagement with diverse stakeholders and communities of interest. It should also reflect and promote the ideals on which society is based. If this process or series of processes leading to policy formulation and implementation is flawed, then policy is more likely to be ineffective, inappropriate or unacceptable. A strategic understanding of the policy process is therefore essential for any effective policy agent.

In previous chapters, it has been noted that studies of policy processes are often concerned with a specific policy area (e.g. tourism) or single policy issue (e.g. a resort development or tourism developments in particular settings) and often focus on the policy process within an organisation or on the influences on policy within a particular community or society (Ham & Hill 1993). Understanding tourism policy processes requires one to step beyond a single issue or sector to develop an appreciation for the ways tourism policy affects other sectors, such as environmental management, and the ways other sectors, such as immigration policy, affect tourism. This chapter builds on the foundations established in previous chapters, especially chapter 1, to explore approaches to the analysis of tourism planning and policy processes. Following from this introduction, section 6.2 explores why a critical and reflective approach to understanding policy processes is important. Section 6.3 reviews traditional cyclic approaches to policy and planning. Section 6.4 outlines policy formulation as a decision-making process, and section 6.5 discusses policy formulation as a process of issue identification and agenda setting. Section 6.6 proposes a social constructionist approach to understanding the complexities of tourism policy and planning systems in specific tourism destination contexts. Finally, section 6.7 reflects on understandings developed throughout the chapter to identify principles that underpin good planning and policy processes.

6.2 UNDERSTANDING POLICY-MAKING

In chapter 1, tourism planning and policy-making was characterised as a dynamic, socially constructed activity that involves a wide range of agents and organisations with varying degrees of interest in and commitment to tourism. An understanding of planning and policy formulation processes needs to be socially constructed and take into account interactions between actors and agencies, their relationship with the institutional structures and processes, and the influence of both contemporary and historical ideas, theories and cultures (see section 1.5).

Understanding tourism planning and policy-making in this social constructionist context is important for two main reasons. First, interrogating how policy is made, and developing explanatory insights into how and why policy is formulated, can help to refine and improve the *substance* or content of policy. For example, understanding and explaining how and why some issues, such as the consequences of tourism for a community, are raised and debated within the policy process can inform us about which issues are more or less important and the subsequent emphasis they should receive in policy formulation. Second, insights into how policy is made can improve policy-making *practice*. For example, insights developed from examining how the policy process works can assist in designing and 'rolling out' other policy processes over time and across space. In this context, implementing the policy process becomes a strategic consideration and not simply a matter of adopting a standard 'how to develop policy' model.

The conceptual framework presented in chapter 1 (figure 1.1) provides the structure and broad principles for understanding policy formulation within a social constructionist perspective. This figure illustrates that the policy process is influenced at multiple levels: it is framed by the institutional context; it is influenced by past, present and future policy issues and problems; and it is shaped by actors and agencies and coloured by the dialogues that take place between them. References to figure 1.1 feature throughout this chapter as a basis for understanding policy processes.

In addition to the relevance of this framework, two important factors underpin interpretations of policy-making as they are presented in this chapter. First, policy formulation takes place within a system that is generally quite stable in terms of the macro environment, ever-changing at the middle and micro-levels, sometimes unpredictable and generally laced with conflict and compromise. The **systems approach** recognises that interactions occur between actors and agencies within a policy and planning system and between these actors and the institutional and environmental frameworks. This approach also acknowledges that policy development takes place both inside and outside government frameworks and that it involves diverse contributions from community, business and government. Individual actors and agencies do not exist in isolation but are part of a much larger interdependent system. In adopting a systems approach the analyst recognises that everything affects everything else, and it is necessary to understand all the parts in order to understand the whole system (Chadwick 1970; Mason 1997). **Meta-problems** or constellations of interrelated policy issues exist within the system and change in one issue necessarily affects all other issues.

Second, a wide range of **policy metaphors** and models lend themselves to describing planning systems and policy processes. Although useful to some extent, the limitations of models, as abstractions or representations of complex systems, must be appreciated; that is, abstract conceptions allow us to clarify and simplify but, at the same time, other factors deemed less important by the researcher will be minimised or ignored. Deciding just what model or metaphor to use is important. A different model or analytical perspective will significantly affect understandings of policy processes and the insights generated.

There is no single correct framework or approach for understanding policy and planning processes. This is an important point. Policy and planning analysts tend to adopt frameworks and approaches consistent with their own values, beliefs and ideas about policy, and these will tend to shape the understanding that emerges. For example, a policy researcher who views tourism policy as an industrial system is likely to generate a different understanding of policy formulation from one who adopts a social constructionist approach. In the former, tourism policy-making is framed around managing a series of inputs (e.g. capital investment, natural resources, attractions, visitors and investment) and outputs (e.g. visitation levels, tourist expenditure, length of stay) where the object is to maximise beneficial outputs. In the latter, social constructionists view policy development in terms of how policy issues are constructed and managed by a range of sociopolitical actors and agencies (Considine 1994). We will discuss this in more detail later. For now, it is sufficient to acknowledge that using multiple perspectives or viewpoints and hence drawing on diverse concepts and theories will produce more detailed and holistic understandings of policy formulation. Policy researchers, analysts and operators need to be aware that different perspectives exist.

The literature identifies a number of broad metaphorical perspectives to examine policy processes, and we discuss several of these in this chapter:
1. *Policy-making as a cycle.* Policy is a process or series of stages or decision-making points that shape the nature and outcomes of succeeding stages.
2. *Policy-making as decisions.* Policy formulation in this perspective is a process or series of processes principally geared towards decision-making about issues.
3. *Policy-making as issue identification and management.* Policy is a process in which issues are identified, and the way they are managed determines how the policy process plays out.
4. *Policy-making as a sociopolitical construction.* From this perspective, policy processes reflect the way policy percolates through multidimensional sociopolitical and economic contexts that shape government involvement and action.

These perspectives are not necessarily independent but can be simultaneously and collectively used to explain processes of planning and policy-making.

*P*OLICY-MAKING AS A CYCLE

6.3.1 **Development** *of the policy cycle*

The concept of a 'policy cycle' has traditionally been one of the most popular means of analysing public policy formulation. The policy cycle divides policy formulation into a series of sequential stages and substages whereby policy-makers move from one stage to the next in an orderly manner (Howlett & Ramesh 1995). In the modern policy sciences, 'stagist' models of the policy process first started to emerge in the 1950s. It is important to note, however, that simplified processes have long been advocated in planning, such as Lewis Mumford's 'survey — plan — analysis' formula (1899), and in administration studies, in Herbert Simon's 'Intelligence — design — choice' model (1947, in Parsons 1995).

Influenced by the growing adoption of scientific rationality in public administration and policy studies (see chapter 3), early models characterised policy-making as a sequence of stages comprising, for example:

1. intelligence gathering
2. recommendations
3. prescription
4. invocation
5. application
6. appraisal, and
7. termination (e.g. see Lasswell in Bridgman & Davis 2004).

At the time, the sociopolitical climate of many Western democracies was underpinned by ideas that governments were paternalistic, all-powerful and all-knowing. Conceptualisations of policy-making process were based on the notion that policy-making happened only within government. The rational scientific paradigm that dominated the social sciences at that time also contributed to this thinking (see section 3.4.2). This paradigm reinforced the notion that the policy process was easily compartmentalised into a number of logical, sequential stages and that there were clear 'cause-and-effect' relationships between problems and their solutions. For example, in the 1970s and 1980s financial and taxation incentives were often used to attract investment in tourism infrastructure and stimulate local economic development. The relationship between policy issue and solution was thought to be direct and clear-cut. However, history shows that such measures did not always attract the most appropriate investment. Moreover, the complexity of the problem meant that the chosen solution almost always had implications far beyond the immediate issue being addressed.

Dividing the policy process into stages could also help structure public administration practice. For example, each stage in the policy process would correspond to a particular administrative unit or process of government. As a result, it was not uncommon for problem identification and solution building (i.e. policy-making) to be separated from policy implementation and evaluation. The problem, as we shall see, is that the stages of the policy process are not so clear-cut and that what happens in one stage affects what happens at other points in the process. As a result, strategy development cannot be easily separated from implementation, and where they are, there are inevitable implementation problems because the strategy or policy solutions have not been grounded in the realities of practice.

This rational scientific model of policy-making was highly influential in the development of policy studies, provoking considerable discussion and refinement. However, critics rightly argue that this stagist model of the policy process gave limited consideration to the range of external factors that influence government behaviour and decision-making. This criticism led to the development of various models in the 1970s, such as that developed by Gary Brewer, which proposed a six-stage process:

1. invention/initiation
2. estimation
3. selection
4. implementation
5. evaluation, and
6. termination (Howlett & Ramesh 1995).

Brewer's version of the policy process, considered to be an improvement on earlier models, expanded the policy process beyond the confines of government to examine the process of problem recognition. More significantly, Brewer's model introduced the notion of feedback whereby the policy process was conceptualised as a continuous cycle. Other versions of the policy cycle emerged during the 1970s and 1980s and used a variety of stages to map the policy process (e.g. Jenkins 1978; Hogwood & Gunn 1984; Bridgman & Davis 2004). A generic policy cycle, which identifies the common elements or stages in these models, is shown in figure 6.1.

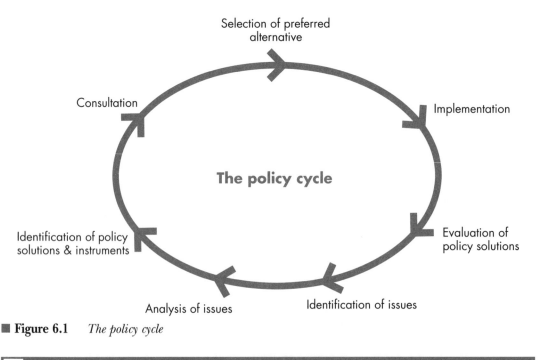

■ **Figure 6.1**   *The policy cycle*

In sum, the policy cycle is a model of applied problem-solving that is focused on achieving some goal or set of goals (Howlett & Ramesh 1995; Colebatch 2002). A range of problem-solving activities is associated with each stage of the policy process. Table 6.1 (p. 198) identifies the stages in the policy cycle and the associated problem-solving activities.

PLANNING IN PRACTICE

The tourism planning and policy cycle in park interpretation and education

Best practice guidelines set out by the Victorian Department of Natural Resources and Parks Victoria adopt a cyclic model for the planning of park interpretation and education that is integrated into the corporate management strategies of the agency (1999). In this model, shown in figure 6.2, best practice park interpretation and education is conceptualised as a cyclic process broadly comprising four stages. In the first stage, *definition*, the rationale for providing interpretation and education services is articulated and linked to the agency's mission and legislative roles and responsibilities. In the second stage, *development*, requires the identification of key results to be achieved within the corporate context. Third, *delivery*, requires that the roles and responsibilities for all stages of interpretation and education are clearly articulated, key performance indicators are identified and communication links between all suppliers are established. Fourth, *evaluation*, requires the systematic assessment of interpretation and education effectiveness, including the measurement of key performance indicators. In this model, park interpretation and evaluation is supported by a clear framework of procedures, training and communication strategies and occurs within an environment that integrates existing business systems operating in the organisation.

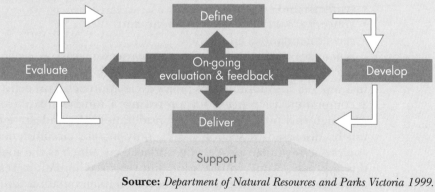

Source: *Department of Natural Resources and Parks Victoria 1999.*

■ **Figure 6.2** *Stages of best practice park interpretation and education*

■ Table 6.1 *The policy cycle and its applied problem-solving tasks*

STAGES IN POLICY CYCLE	PROBLEM-SOLVING TASKS	EXPLANATION
Agenda-setting	Problem scanning, identification and prioritisation	The process by which problems come to the attention of governments and are earmarked as deserving of government action
Policy formulation	Identification of alternative solutions	The process by which issues are analysed and policy options are formulated by government
Decision-making	Analysis and selection of preferred solution	The process by which governments adopt a particular course of action or non-action
Policy implementation	The identification of strategies and responsibilities for putting the solution into effect	The process by which governments implement policies
Policy evaluation	Monitoring results and effects of policy implementation	The processes by which results of policies are monitored by both state and societal actors

Source: *adapted from Howlett & Ramesh 1995: 11.*

In practice, the stages in the policy cycle may be labelled differently, but the basic approach remains the same. For example, the Victorian Department of Natural Resources and Parks Victoria adopted a cyclic model in a recent planning process relating to park interpretation and education activities (see Planning in Practice: 'The tourism planning and policy cycle in park interpretation and education', p. 197).

In tourism, cyclic models of tourism planning and policy-making began to emerge from the 1960s onwards, reflecting developments in policy studies literature described above. The strategic planning process described by Gunn and Var (2004) follows this model and includes five broad stages:

• setting objectives
• research and analysis
• synthesis and conclusions
• concept (or strategy) development, and
• recommendations and review.

Since this time, tourism planning processes, cast as cyclic systems, continue to be widely adopted (e.g. Getz 1986; McIntosh & Goeldner 1986; Inskeep 1987). Adopting this policy cycle approach, Inskeep (1991) sets out a comprehensive process for preparing a tourism plan (see figure 6.3). Although this process includes consideration of a wide range of issues (as will be discussed in section 6.3.2), only in rare circumstances can such a comprehensive plan process be undertaken, which is the main criticism of this approach. Time, information and resource limitations result in smaller, more bounded processes. Moreover, implementation and monitoring requires continuous political and financial commitment, which is often difficult to achieve. As a result, such processes are ideal but rarely achieved.

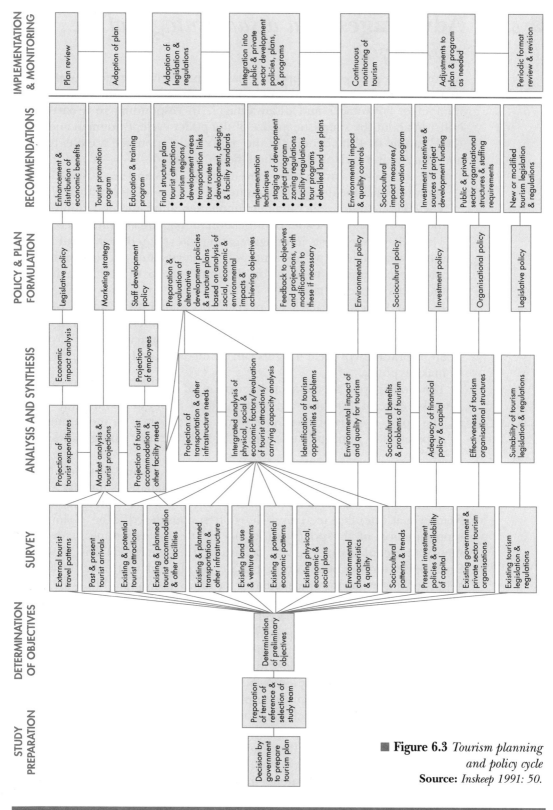

STUDY PREPARATION

Decision by government to prepare tourism plan

Preparation of terms of reference & selection of study team

DETERMINATION OF OBJECTIVES

Determination of preliminary objectives

SURVEY

External tourist travel patterns

Past & present tourist arrivals

Existing & potential tourist attractions

Existing & planned tourist accommodation & other facilities

Existing & planned transportation & other infrastructure

Existing land use & venture patterns

Existing & potential economic patterns

Existing physical, economic & social plans

Environmental characteristics & quality

Sociocultural patterns & trends

Present investment policies & availability of capital

Existing government & private sector tourism organisations

Existing tourism legislation & regulations

ANALYSIS AND SYNTHESIS

Projection of tourist expenditures

Economic impact analysis

Market analysis & tourist projections

Projection of tourist accommodation & other facility needs

Projection of employees

Projection of transportation & other infrastructure needs

Intergrated analysis of physical, social & economic factors/evaluation of tourist attractions/ carrying capacity analysis

Identification of tourism opportunities & problems

Environmental impact of and quality for tourism

Sociocultural benefits & problems of tourism

Adequacy of financial policy & capital

Effectiveness of tourism organisational structures

Suitability of tourism legislation & regulations

POLICY & PLAN FORMULATION

Legislative policy

Marketing strategy

Staff development policy

Preparation & evaluation of alternative development policies & structure plans based on analysis of social, economic & environmental impacts & achieving objectives

Feedback to objectives and projections, with modifications to these if necessary

Environmental policy

Sociocultural policy

Investment policy

Organisational policy

Legislative policy

RECOMMENDATIONS

Enhancement & distribution of economic benefits

Tourist promotion program

Education & training program

Final structure plan
• tourist attractions
• tourism regions/ development areas
• transportation links
• tour routes
• development, design, & facility standards

Implementation techniques
• staging of development
• project program
• zoning regulations
• facility regulations
• tour programs
• detailed land use plans

Environmental impact & quality controls

Sociocultural impact measures/ conservation program

Investment incentives & sources of project development funding

Public & private sector organisational structures & staffing requirements

New or modified tourism legislation & regulations

IMPLEMENTATION & MONITORING

Plan review

Adoption of plan

Adoption of legislation & regulations

Integration into public & private sector development policies, plans, & programs

Continuous monitoring of tourism

Adjustments to plan & program as needed

Periodic format review & revision

■ **Figure 6.3** *Tourism planning and policy cycle*
Source: *Inskeep 1991: 50.*

■ 6.3.2 **Advantages** *and disadvantages of the policy cycle*

Although the policy cycle approach has been widely adopted as a means of structuring the cyclic nature of policy development, the model has a number of advantages and disadvantages. In responding to a barrage of criticism about the simplistic nature of the policy cycle, Bridgman and Davis (2003) argue that the benefits of the policy cycle approach are plenty if the aim of using the cycle is clear. These benefits include:

1. The policy cycle conveys the movement of ideas and resources, the iteration of policy-making and a routine that does not finish with a decision. The cycle includes policy-making, implementation and evaluation, which then feeds back into issue identification and agenda-setting once again.
2. The policy cycle assists in disaggregating interrelated events and actions into manageable steps, allowing policy analysts and advisors, politicians and the community to focus on different aspects of policy-making and the needs of each phase.
3. In the policy cycle, each stage of the process aligns with a body of theoretical writings, which in turn facilitates the synthesis of existing knowledge about public policy with the concerns of practice. In other words, appropriate theoretical insights can be incorporated into the practice of making policy.
4. The policy cycle serves as a description of policy-making to assist and make sense of historical and contemporary policy development.
5. The policy cycle is normative, providing direction as to the sequence of steps or most appropriate way to approach the task (Bridgman & Davis 2003).

There are also several valid criticisms of cyclic models of policy formulation. First, the policy cycle does not provide explanations for why a policy issue develops in a particular way, nor why particular solutions emerge. Neither is it intended to. The cycle is often considered to be 'a simplified representation of the policy world, an aid to understanding', and not a theory that explains or predicts behaviour (Bridgman & Davis 2004: 10). Second, viewing the policy process as a cycle suggests that policy-makers go about solving problems in a systematic or linear fashion and that the policy process is self-contained and comprises a neat cycle of initial, intermediate and culminating events (Hogwood & Gunn 1984; Howlett & Ramesh 1995). Third, dividing policy-making into neat steps or cycles overemphasises the rational and sequential nature of policy-making. The policy process is 'not a conveyor belt in which agenda-setting takes place at one end of the line and implementation and evaluation occurs at the other end' (Parsons 1995: 79). Fourth, the policy cycle focuses on process as opposed to content. It misses the 'power plays' from which decisions emerge, and it does not sufficiently acknowledge that political and community pressures often have a stronger influence over the process than do bureaucratic processes (Everett 2003). Fifth, from an analytical viewpoint, the policy cycle does not provide any causal explanation of how policy moves from one stage to another. It is simply a descriptive framework that cannot be tested on an empirical basis (Sabatier & Jenkins-Smith 1993).

Parsons (1995: 80) sums up the criticisms in an amusing but scathing way: 'Frogs may have a life cycle, and living things may be regarded as "systems", but to imagine that public policy can be reduced to such over-simplified stages has more methodological holes than a sack-load of Swiss cheese.'

Together, these criticisms point to a need to understand policy not as a 'top-down' government-driven process, but one that acknowledges 'street-level' actors operating in a real world in which there are several levels of government, overlapping responsibilities, interacting cycles and diverse business and community interests. In the light of this discussion, it is important to return to figure 1.1 (p. 16). This figure and its accompanying discussion set the context for the policy cycle and illustrate that public policy is much more than a set of sequential phases through which governments move in a unidirectional manner; that is, the policy cycle alone cannot convey the richness of policy debates over time, across space and between different actors and agencies. Multiple and simultaneous cycles that address different but related issues might be taking place. Policy events coalesce and influence one another in a complex system. In this way, the way decisions are made and the consequences of those decisions also become a window into the policy-making process.

6.4 *P*OLICY-MAKING AS DECISION-MAKING

Policy formulation is also viewed as a process in which issues are identified, decisions are made (or not made) and events unfold as a result of those decisions (or non-decisions). In this perspective, the policy process is dependent on the unfolding of issues over time, the way these issues are processed by different interests and the influence of these interests on the politics of decision-making. Three broad streams for conceptualising policy formulation as decision-making are the rational comprehensive approach, incrementalism and public choice, all of which are described below.

■ 6.4.1 **Rational** *comprehensive*

The **rational comprehensive** approach proposes that policy-making is a rational and logical process based on the setting of goals, the identification and analysis of problems and the implementation of a 'best-fit' solution. Drawing from scientific method, rational comprehensive policy-making assumes that there is a clear causal relationship between problems and solutions and that simple decision rules are used to determine which policy solution will bring about maximum benefit (Lane 2000: 77). This rational comprehensive model supposedly offers a clear and accountable framework for policy development wherein policy issues are dealt with in a continuous process of plan implementation, monitoring and readjustment.

Although this perspective offers a clear, coherent and simple conceptualisation of the policy process, it has inherent problems. The main weakness of this conceptualisation of the policy process is that it lacks political reality. Goals are not always well defined, actors are not always rational and the 'best' solution is not always chosen. Information or the 'science' needed to support the decision-making process might also not be available. In other words, policy formulation is not necessarily rational or comprehensive. Planners and policy makers are bounded by a range of factors, including professional expertise, personal beliefs, organisational values and resource availability. These factors limit understandings of the problem and the identification of alternative policy options. Decision-makers are therefore choosing a 'best-fit' solution from a limited range of policy options. The solution usually attempts to satisfy as many goals as possible, but the selection of a solution is not necessarily objective or unbiased. Furthermore, rational comprehensive models of policy formulation sat well within the large, paternalistic bureaucracies of the 1960s and 1970s, but are less relevant today as a result of shifts towards public engagement, downsizing and outsourcing of policy formulation (see section 4.3).

■ 6.4.2 Incrementalism

Emerging from criticisms of the rational comprehensive view of policy-making comes the notion of incrementalism. **Incrementalism**, or the 'science of muddling through', was developed by Charles Lindblom in 1959 and is based on the idea that policy is the result of many incremental decisions being made over time, which are geared towards goals that are continuously being refined (Lindblom 1959). Incrementalism is an approach to public policy formulation that adopts a messy and complicated view of the world whereby historical events and the influence of external factors are given increased importance. In this view policy decisions are made on an incremental basis; actors do not necessarily act in a rational manner; and historical events and decisions weigh on current decisions. Although this perspective does offer a certain level of political reality, the main criticism of incrementalism is that it does not allow for long-term directions to emerge for consistent policy-making. It also leads to a lack of innovation and inertia (Dror 1968).

Influenced by criticisms of the rational comprehensive approach and incrementalism, Etzioni (1967) presents a model of policy-making called **mixed scanning**. Mixed scanning proposes that smaller decisions are made incrementally but that decisions of major directional importance provide the context for smaller decisions. Mixed scanning requires that decision-makers scan the field to develop an understanding of important issues. Decisions on these fundamental issues provide overall direction, and less critical decisions, made on an incremental basis, fit into the overall direction. Criticisms of this model raised the question: how do policy-makers know what critical and non-critical issues are? The short answer is that policy-makers make judgements about what are critical and non-critical issues on the basis of their own interpretations of factors and events, political influences and actor strategies. As a result, greater scrutiny has been placed on the role of values, beliefs and power relations in policy formulation.

In a field rich in metaphors, the garbage can has been used as a metaphor to explain policy-making as a process whereby policy problems and solutions are matched in an ad hoc manner. Problems and issues are generated simultaneously. The opportunity to make a decision about a policy issue, the identification of a viable solution and the actors able to make that decision all come together at a particular time. Timing is crucial to the ways in which problems, issues and solutions are matched. Policy-making takes place in a loose, unstructured manner as opposed to the rational, logical structures proposed in the policy cycle. Cohen explains the idea using the garbage can metaphor: 'Suppose we view a choice opportunity as a garbage can into which various problems are dumped by participants. The mix of garbage in a single can depends partly on the labels attached to the alternative cans; but it also depends on what garbage is being produced at the moment, on the mix of cans available, and the speed with which the garbage is collected and removed from the scene.' (Cohen, March & Olsen 1979: 26; quoted in Hogwood 1987: 23.) Some possible solutions that had been discarded might be produced later and considered worth implementing.

Kingdon (1984) also put forward the metaphor of 'policy streams'. In his view policy processes are characterised by three streams: the policy stream, the politics stream and the problem stream. In this view, there is a stream of continuous events in which policy problems are identified and come to the attention of decision-makers. The policy stream is a 'soup' of ideas and values from which important ideas float up to gain the attention policy analysis and decision-makers. All the other ideas and values fall to the bottom (Parsons 1995). The political stream is conceived as a series of critical events, environmental factors and a mix of actors and agencies that form the context of the policy-making activity. If all three streams come together, then an issue rises to the top and a politically and socially acceptable solution is found. In other words, policy solutions are found and implemented at that critical moment when politics, policy and problem streams come together (Parsons 1995).

6.4.3 **Public** *choice*

Public choice is another framework for understanding policy development, and it is based on the application of economic principles within a political policy-making environment. Public choice theorists observe that, just as individuals base their decisions on economic self-serving interest, governments and bureaucrats also are concerned with self-interest and seek to maximise their own, or their supporters', benefits (Parsons 1995). The focus of public choice theory is to explain why decisions are made and what solutions are likely to be adopted, given that individuals are often subject to incentives and interests that influence collective decision-making. (The observations of Machiavelli (see sections 1.2.1 and 3.3.3) are not lost here!) It follows, then, that public choice theory, when used to examine influences on decision-making, leads to conclusions that government decision-making leads to inefficient policy outcomes.

According to Michael (2001), the basic model proposes that policy-making is made up of interactions between the economy and the political institutions whereby decisions are made about issues sitting within a wider context that balances bureaucracy, government, voters and economy (see figure 6.4). The focus of public choice theory, then, is to give insights into why particular policy decisions are made and to explain the effect these decisions have on the community's collective interest. Public choice theory highlights important aspects of policy, including the scale and direction of government intervention, public interest and market failure.

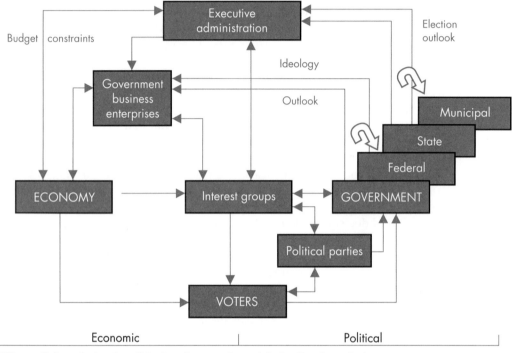

■ **Figure 6.4**   *A simple political and economic model of policy formulation*

6.5 𝒫OLICY AS ISSUE IDENTIFICATION AND MANAGEMENT

■ 6.5.1 **Issue** *identification*

Policy formulation is also conceptualised as a process of issue identification and management. One of the earliest such models was Richard Simeon's 'funnel of causality' (1976). In this model, planning and policy formulation is likened to a funnel through which policy and issues move. At the widest point of the funnel are societal issues and the broader context within which policy is made. Issues and problems are prioritised as they move through the funnel, and at its narrowest part those policy issues of most concern to stakeholders are identified and dealt with. This filtering process has important implications for the content and direction of policy debates and the level of resourcing that different issues receive. Although the funnel of causality is a useful metaphor for describing the filtering and issue selection process, the model is simplistic. It provides limited explanatory power of how issues are identified and moved forward; why issues are prioritised, or the relationship between the policy context and issue identification and prioritisation process.

Many models have since emerged that attempt to elaborate on the factors that influence agenda-setting processes. The **issue attention cycle** is one such model. It suggests that issues move through various stages of attention. For example, Downs (1972) suggests the following five stages:

1. *Pre-problem stage* — the issue is forming. Public interest is limited and patchy.
2. *Alarmed discovery* — the importance or severity of the issue is recognised.
3. *Realising the costs of significant progress* — the issue is examined, solutions are discussed, and action is taken or not taken.
4. *Gradual decline in public interest* — the importance of the issue begins to wane in the public sphere.
5. *Post-problem stage* — the issue subsides and the public focuses on other issues.

The main contribution of the issue attention cycle is that it acknowledges public attention is dynamic and that issues receive different levels of attention over time. But it is also a rather simplistic model. Many issues are simultaneously being identified, framed, prioritised and reprioritised at different spatial scales and locations. Issues are influenced by events, personalities, pressure groups and organisational and institutional success and failures. Issues change over time and across space and vary within different levels of government (see figure 1.2, p. 17); that is, a high priority issue for a local government in one destination might not have the same priority for a state government or, for that matter, an adjoining local government. Nor is it likely that the same issue will retain its priority over time as conditions and imperatives change.

An increasingly important view is that policy communities, or networks of interested stakeholders, play an important part in the development of issues and the way policy is formulated. All these factors work simultaneously — and sometimes in conflict — to emphasise certain issues over others. From this observation — that different and competing perceptions of issues have an important influence on the development and prioritisation of issues — the process of agenda-setting as a driver of policy formulation deserves attention.

6.5.2 Issues *and agendas*

Issue identification is an important dimension of the policy formulation process. Media and public opinion have a key role in shaping the importance of issues, the relative weight of those issues and the way they are dealt with (Parson 1995). Of course the media by itself does not directly drive policy formulation, but there are intricate relationships between the media, the development of public agendas and the way governments respond. The SARS outbreak in South-East Asia in 2003 illustrates the powerful influence the media can have (see Planning in Practice: 'The outbreak of SARS in South-East Asia, 2003').

The concept of an issue attention cycle is useful in understanding the way different stakeholders identify issues and the nature and extent to which issues are recognised and dealt with. Mahon and Waddock (1992) suggest broad stages or 'zones' of attention:

- *zone of rejection:* where issues are not considered relevant or important and are rejected as not deserving of government attention and resources
- *zone of indifference:* where issues are recognised as existing but not sufficiently important to warrant government attention or action
- *zone of symbolic action:* where issues are considered to be sufficiently important to warrant attention and some action but such attention and action are largely symbolic
- *zone of substantive action:* where the issues are recognised and given priority on government's agenda and substantive action is taken to address the situation.

PLANNING IN PRACTICE

The outbreak of SARS in South-East Asia, 2003

During the SARS outbreak in South-East Asia in 2003, the media flashed images across the world of people wearing protective masks going about their daily lives, tourists' temperatures being taken as they entered and left Hong Kong, condemned apartment buildings where multiple case of SARS had been identified, and mass killings of poultry. The media hype undoubtedly contributed to the efforts by governments in South-East Asia and elsewhere to halt the spread of the disease. In Thailand, tourists from affected areas were ordered to wear facemasks for the entire duration of their visit or face imprisonment, and airline passengers showing SARS-like symptoms would trigger quarantine for all passengers for two weeks. In Malaysia there was a travel ban on all tourists from SARS-infected countries. Singapore implemented an automatic 14-day quarantine period on returning residents who had visited infected countries. Taiwan imposed a 14-day quarantine period on incoming passengers. 'Media reports suggested that Asian tourists were denied entry to trade shows, hotels, and cruise ships and that some countries stopped issuing visas' (McKercher & Chon 2004: 717). This event illustrates that, although the media did not 'create' the issue, it had a powerful role to play the way issues were presented to the public and the way governments subsequently responded. Travel in and to affected countries dropped significantly as a result.

Importantly, stakeholders engage with issues in different ways and at different times. At any one moment, stakeholders can exhibit different levels of engagement with an issue. Issues are thrust on to political agendas for a myriad of reasons. Among these reasons, the issues are perceived by stakeholders to be important enough to warrant public attention because stakeholders possess the skills, information and strategies necessary to expose the issue and often because strategic alliances between disparate interests (e.g. media and stakeholders) create powerful synergies that pull issues into the spotlight, even against the will of politicians! Differences exist in the way stakeholders perceive issues and the relative power of stakeholders to influence the agendas of government. Frustration and even conflict can arise when stakeholders value issues differently. It follows then that policy formulation is a dynamic process of issue identification and agenda-setting, which leads seamlessly into the next approach used to understand policy-making: sociopolitical construction.

6.6 POLICY-MAKING AS SOCIOPOLITICAL CONSTRUCTION

The sociopolitical constructionist view of policy formulation processes embraces a discursive or communicative approach, whereby policy is conceptualised as a dynamic process resulting from interactions and contested dialogues among a multitude of actors and agencies. Problem definition, the identification of solutions and evaluation of them occur simultaneously. Actors and agencies continuously modify their behaviour and decisions on the basis of, among other things, events, decisions, information and behaviour of other stakeholders. In this view of policy-making, the focus is on how power, politics and **communities of interest** influence issue identification and action. The result is to depict policy processes as complicated series of events and actions that reflect the dynamic and communicative environment in which policy is formed (Levin 1997; Healey 1998). From this sociopolitical constructionist perspective, powerful organising concepts emerge that help to explain how and why policy is formed. These concepts include policy subsystems, advocacy coalitions and networks.

6.6.1 Policy *subsystems and advocacy coalitions*

Policy subsystems are systems of related policy issues around which actors and agencies operate to influence policy development. The policy subsystems approach recognises that policy formulation is organised around substantive issues and continuous relationships rather than in traditional political structures, such as political parties and government agencies. Policy subsystems are useful for the study of policy formulation for three main reasons. First, policy subsystems are made up of policy issues which share characteristics or commonalities that influence the way they are framed and dealt with. Second, policy subsystems are socially constructed and are not artificially defined. Policy susbystems therefore lend themselves to the analysis and explanation of policy development in a more holistic and organic manner than would be the case where a researcher adopts artificial boundaries around a policy issue. Third, policy subsystems are the domains in which individual policy actors and agencies undertake activities.

The earliest conception of the policy subsystem was the subgovernment, which was based on the observation that policy-making tended to occur in small subsystems of actors with mutual interests. Heclo (1978) proposed 'iron triangles', a metaphor that denotes the tight control interest groups, congressional committees and government agencies were perceived to have over policy-making at a time when public administration was heavily influenced by Taylorist principles (see section 3.4.2). Later it was observed that control was less tight and that other policy actors and agencies could also be influential. Iron triangles gave way to issue networks, which reflect a more open and less organised set of relationships between actors and agencies. On the basis of these observations, Sabatier (1988) developed the advocacy colation framework, which reflects the observation that actors and agencies developed allegiances and partnerships from which unequal power differentials emerge. These coalitions of interests work in diverse ways to influence policy formulation.

Over time, the 'policy subsystem' has become a powerful organising tool or metaphor lending itself to explanations of policy formulation. Pross (1992) argues that policy subsystems have two principle components:

- *Subgovernment:* the **subgovernment** is defined as small groups of people intimately connected with the core processes of policy formulation and implementation, and who usually occupy the top positions in their agencies and organisations. They can include federal and state ministers, local government councillors, senior public servants, chairpersons of advisory committees or executive boards of statutory agencies, key spokespersons for interest groups and private organisations.
- *Attentive public:* members of the **attentive public** include formal and informal groups, government agencies, peak agencies and producer groups and interested individuals who evaluate policies and identify their inadequacies. According to Pross (1992, cited in Homeshaw 1995), these groups are the main vehicles for policy innovation, and they move in and out of the policy community.

Homeshaw (1995) proposes another category: **executive core**, to denote actors in agencies of governments that do not make regular or routine decisions in a particular policy arena, but without whose agreement crucial decisions about that policy arena could not be made. In the context of a local tourism destination, the executive core might include state and regional agencies not directly involved in tourism but whose support is required. For instance, state environmental agencies, although not directly involved in tourism, have a powerful influence over the development and management of ecotourism activities.

■ 6.6.2 **Policy** *communities and networks*

Policy networks have emerged as powerful organising perspectives in efforts to understand policy-making (Milward & Walmsley 1984; Burstein 1991; Rhodes 1997; Dredge 2006a; see also section 8.5 of this book). **Networks** are sets of formal and informal relationships between actors and agencies that operate to influence policy debates and decision-making. They usually involve actors with a commitment to common goals and worldviews operating across government, industry and community boundaries to achieve particular outcomes. Networks can produce collaboration, collective learning and action, but they can also promote conflict and dissention where policy goals differ and actor commitment to those goals varies or is emotive.

Understanding networks provides insights into the ways policy develops, the ways policy actors learn and the ways policy systems innovate (Considine 1994: 104). Network theory therefore provides useful tools for exploring the way policy emerges from dynamic planning and policy-making processes that involve a myriad of actors and agencies among business, government and community sectors (Dredge 2006b). Closer examination of policy networks reveals the different levels at which policy discourses take place, decisions are made and action is taken. They acknowledge the complexity of the process and the multiple influences on policy formulation.

Although the network perspective acknowledges the overlapping and simultaneous manner in which policy issues are identified and debated, the main disadvantage is that network theory is little more than a metaphorical tool for conceptualising the interconnected nature of issues, problems, debates and actors. Networks and network theory therefore remain reliant on and interdependent on other explanations of policy development outlined in previous sections.

6.7 WHAT ARE THE PRINCIPLES OF GOOD TOURISM PLANNING AND POLICY PROCESSES?

It is useful at this point to return to figure 1.1 (p. 16). This figure provides a conceptual framework for the study of tourism planning and policy from a social-constructionist perspective and picks up many of the threads discussed in this and previous chapters. This figure outlines the context in which the policy formulation process takes place; that is, understanding the policy process requires an appreciation of the institutional context, the policy issues and problems present, the roles and strategies of actors and agencies involved and the dialogues taking place. In order to develop an appreciation of the policy process, it is necessary to understand relationships between these aspects over time and at different scales.

Drawing on the theoretical models and concepts discussed in this chapter and on the case study 'Tourism policy and planning in Byron Bay, New South Wales', on p. 215 (which is not atypical of the processes of tourism planning and management in destinations), a number of principles underpinning good planning and policy processes are identified:

- *Be strategic.* Planning and policy processes must be based on a strategic vision that combines understandings of past, current and future circumstances. The development of policy must also anticipate the interests and agendas of various policy actors within the policy subsystem.
- *Be flexible, adaptive and responsive.* Planning and policy processes must provide direction within a framework that is flexible and adaptive. Social, political and economic conditions change, and good processes should be able to adapt to current conditions so that strategic direction is not lost.
- *Promote active citizenry.* Planning and policy processes should foster engagement with communities of interested stakeholders. The process should enable participants to share information, ideas and knowledge in an effort to build a more robust shared vision.
- *Comprise of stages.* Planning and policy processes should be organised around a number of notional stages to facilitate administration and management. These stages should be flexible enough to adapt to change, and there should be the opportunity to provide iterative feedback at any stage. Stages will also assist in achieving transparency of the process.
- *Be accountable.* Planning and policy processes should be transparent and accountable, incorporating opportunities for public scrutiny as well as contributions. In particular, the values and interests operating to influence policy formulation should be identified and acknowledged.
- *Be equitable.* Planning and policy processes should promote equity of interests and embrace diversity of opinions and perspectives. Strategic use of networks can promote these values.
- *Be informed.* Planning and policy processes should be based on an informed appreciation of factors, events and information. This requires management of quantitative and qualitative information and knowledge of organisational histories. Attention to the collection, organisation and management of information is therefore a significant issue.

CHAPTER REVIEW

This chapter has explored various approaches to the analysis of tourism planning and policy processes. Section 6.2 explored why a critical and reflective approach to understanding policy processes is important, arguing that reflection highlights the strengths and weaknesses of the process. Section 6.3 reviewed traditional cyclic approaches to policy and planning and argued that, although they are important organising tools, there are important weaknesses in adopting a cyclic approach by itself. Section 6.4 outlined policy formulation as a decision-making process and discovered that there are certain merits in understanding the policy process as a series of interrelated decision-making points that frame future policy actions. Section 6.5 discussed policy formulation as issue identification and agenda-setting, highlighting that these aspects are significant drivers of policy processes. Section 6.6 proposed a social constructionist approach to understanding the complexities of tourism policy and planning systems within specific tourism destination contexts. The case study on Byron Bay (p. 215) explored tourism planning and policy formulation on the ground, illustrating that no single model or metaphor can be used to explain the process of policy formulation. All the models discussed so far hold some relevance, and policy formulation is depicted as dynamic and socially constructed. Finally, in the last section, drawing from the insights gained throughout the chapter, we identify a number of principles that should underpin good policy process.

SUMMARY OF KEY TERMS

Attentive public

Members of the attentive public include formal and informal groups, government agencies, peak agencies, producer groups and interested individuals who have an active interest in policy development.

Communities of interest

'Communities of interest' refers to the diverse constellations of individuals and agencies that exhibit shared values and interests on a particular issue or problem. Individuals and agencies could be members of more than one community of interest.

Executive core

Actors in government agencies in senior positions who are not involved in regular or routine decisions in a particular policy arena but whose support is crucial for policy decisions to be made.

Incrementalism

Incrementalism, also known as the 'science of muddling through', is a model of policy formulation based on the idea that policy is the result of many incremental decisions made over time.

Issue attention cycle

The dynamic process associated with the way issues are identified, given weight and dealt with by governments, the community, industry and other stakeholders.

Meta-problem

Meta-problem is a term used to denote the intractable problem sets that are not easily addressed by society. It is closely linked to systems thinking and the idea that a particular problem or issue has both forward and backward implications for other problems and issues. For example, the problem of high unemployment in peripheral regions, which could be solved through intense aquaculture, could conflict with environmental integrity and tourism.

Mixed scanning

A model of policy formulation which proposes that smaller decisions are made incrementally but that decisions of major directional importance provide the context for smaller decisions. Mixed scanning requires that decision-makers scan the field to develop an understanding of important issues. Decisions on these fundamental issues provide overall direction, and less critical decisions, made on an incremental basis, fit into the overall direction.

Network

A set of formal or informal social relationships between individuals and agencies who have common interests in a policy arena. A network spans civil society, public and private sectors, is non-hierarchical in nature and provides opportunities for dialogue and coordination of policy issues.

Policy metaphors

Terms used to describe abstractions or representations of complex systems. Policy cycles, networks and policy streams are examples of metaphors. They allow complex concepts and relationships to be conceptualised and simplified. Although they facilitate understanding of some aspects of policy-making, they can also minimise or ignore other aspects.

Policy subsystems

Actors and agencies organised around substantive issues and continuing relationships rather than in traditional political structures, such as political parties and government agencies.

Rational comprehensive

An approach to policy formulation which proposes that policy-making is a rational and logical process based on the setting of goals, the identification and analysis of problems and the implementation of the 'best' solution. Drawing from scientific method, rational comprehensive policy-making assumes that there is a clear causal relationship between problems and solutions.

Subgovernment

Small groups of people intimately connected with the core processes of policy formulation and implementation, and who usually occupy the top positions in their organisation.

Systems approach

The systems approach is based on the notion that interactions occur among actors and agencies within a policy and planning system and among these actors and the institutional and environmental frameworks. The approach also acknowledges that policy development takes place both inside and outside the frameworks of government and involves diverse community, business and government perspectives.

QUESTIONS

1 Explain what you might learn from an analysis of a previous tourism planning process.

2 Identify and explain five perspectives or approaches to understanding tourism planning and policy formulation.

3 What is the policy cycle? Identify and explain its advantages and disadvantages.

4 Briefly describe the rational comprehensive, incremental and public choice models of policy-making. What are the strengths and weaknesses of each?

5 Explain how the development of issues might influence tourism planning and policy processes. Give examples.

6 Discuss the role of the media in issue identification and agenda-setting. Give an example.

7 What are the main ideas that underpin the social constructionist approach to understanding policy formulation? What are its benefits over the rational scientific model of policy-making?

8 Consider your own values and beliefs. Which perspective of policy-making do you consider the most realistic and appropriate for explaining policy formulation? Why?

9 What are the principles that underpin good tourism planning and policy processes?

10 Outline a model of policy formation that you could use to guide the development of a local tourism strategy. Identify the steps and the activities that might be carried out in each.

EXERCISES

1 Imagine that you have just been invited to tender for the preparation of a local tourism strategy in a local government area of your choice. You are required to make a 15-minute presentation to Council explaining your proposed approach. Discuss what approach you intend to adopt and its advantages and disadvantages. Your aim is to win the tender. (Hint: remember who your audience is.)

2 Using mind-mapping techniques, map out the issue identification cycle for a destination of your choice. Identify zones of rejection, indifference, symbolic action and substantive action. You may use a newspaper data-base, such as Factiva, to help you identify the range of tourism-related issues in the destination over time.

FURTHER READING

Bramwell, B & Lane, B 2000, *Tourism Collaboration and Partnerships: Politics, Practice and Sustainability*, Channel View Publications, Clevedon, UK. This book contains an excellent collection of international case studies of tourism planning and policy development that illustrate the social constructionist view of policy-making. The focus of the case studies is on issue identification and stakeholder interactions, and the relationships between these and the broader social, economic and environmental context.

Davis, G & Wanna, J 2004, *The Australian Policy Handbook*, Allen & Unwin, Sydney. This text provides a useful introduction to the policy cycle, its advantages and disadvantages. Alternatives to the policy cycle are also briefly discussed. The authors are major proponents of the policy cycle as a tool for assisting policy formulation, and they explain each of the stages in depth.

Gunn, C & Var, T 2004, *Tourism Planning: Basics Concepts Cases*, 4th edn, Routledge, New York. Taking a predominantly spatial focus, this book examines tourism planning and policy development at different scales. It provides a thorough explanation of the tourism planning process and provides various case studies of the policy cycle approach.

Hall, CM 2000, *Tourism Planning: Policies, Processes and Relationships*, Prentice Hall, Harlow, UK. This book examines a range of conceptual issues and challenges associated with tourism planning and policy processes. It views planning and policy processes as being multi-scalar, cross-sectoral and highly political, and in this context examines the imperative of sustainability.

Tourism policy and planning at Byron Bay, New South Wales

Located on the north coast of New South Wales, Byron Bay is a significant domestic and international destination (see figure 6.1, p. 196). Boasting some of Australia's best beaches and coastal scenery, the township is also home to a sizeable 'alternative' community and a growing number of 'seachangers' and 'downshifters' seeking lifestyle change. In 2003 between 1.2 million and 1.75 million visitors arrived in Byron Bay (Tonge, Fletcher and Concept Tourism Consultants 2003). The estimated population of Byron Shire is currently 22 823 persons, of whom 4900 residents live in the township of Byron Bay and its immediate environs (ABS 2001).

Byron Bay emerged as a popular destination in the 1960s when surfers and campers were attracted to the area because of the excellent surfing and leisure experiences provided by Byron Bay's natural environment. Until the 1980s caravan and camping grounds were the most popular form of holiday accommodation. The momentum for increased tourism activity at the destination occurred from the late 1980s, and considerable tourism development activity occurred, including the establishment of backpacker hostels, B&Bs, luxury resort and apartment accommodation.

Various government, corporate and community stakeholders have been involved in tourism policy and planning issues and processes over this time (see table 6.2). Planning and policy development at Byron Bay has not been a seamless progression from planning to implementation and review as suggested by the generic policy cycle. Indeed, tourism planning and policy-making can be understood using each of the four broad frames identified and discussed earlier in this chapter.

A chronology of events (table 6.3, p. 218) provides an historical background to the various tourism planning and policy events that have shaped Byron Bay's development.

Issue drivers affecting the planning and policy process

Tourism planning and policy development in Byron Bay took place against a backdrop of events and circumstances that have shaped the issue identification and agenda-setting processes of government and the way public interest is formulated. In particular, the growing popularity of Byron Bay as a tourist destination has resulted in obvious strains on the town's infrastructure and service facilities and increased concern from residents about the effects of tourism on their community and lifestyle. The late 1980s and 1990s was an era of building for the town. Between 1992 and 1995 the number of new building applications received by Council increased by more than 300 per cent (Green 1997). In 1994 alone new development valued at $25 million was proposed, and by September 1995 a backlog of more than 240 development applications was

(continued)

■ **Table 6.2**   *Byron Bay stakeholders*

DESTINATION LEVEL	REGIONAL LEVEL	STATE LEVEL	FEDERAL LEVEL
EXECUTIVE CORE			
Byron Shire Council		NSW Tourism Minister	Federal Tourism Minister
		NSW Planning Minister	
		NSW Local Government Minister	
		NSW Minister for the Environment	
SUBGOVERNMENTS			
Byron Shire Council (BSC)	Northern Rivers Regional Development Board (NRRDB)/Invest Northern Rivers	NSW Department of Tourism, Sport & Recreation	Department of Industry, Tourism & Resources
	Tourism New South Wales, Regional Manager	Tourism New South Wales (TNSW)	Tourism Australia/ See Australia
	Northern Rivers Regional Tourism Organisation (NRRTO)	Department of Infrastructure, Planning & Natural Resources (DIPNR)	
		Department of State and Regional Development (DSRD)	
OTHER ATTENTIVE PUBLICS			
Byron Shire Tourism Association (BSTA)	National Parks and Wildlife Service, Northern Rivers Region	Coastal Council of NSW	
Byron Bay Chamber of Commerce (BBCC)	Department of Infrastructure, Planning & Natural Resources (regional office)		

DESTINATION LEVEL	REGIONAL LEVEL	STATE LEVEL	FEDERAL LEVEL
Byron Environment and Conservation (BEACON)	Southern Cross University		
Byron Environment Centre (BEC)	Nature Tourism Taskforce Northern Rivers NSW		
Byron Visitor Centre Management Board			
Byron Shire Businesses for the Future (BSBF)			
Other communities of interest	Other communities of interest	Other communities of interest	Other communities of interest

Note: *Government agencies and departments have had different names during the period. For the purposes of this table, names current in 2004 have been used.*

awaiting Council consideration, a record for New South Wales (Green 1997). Most of these development applications were associated with tourism, including a landmark application submitted by Club Mediteranee Pty Ltd in 1993. This development application proposed an $80 million resort two kilometres north of the Byron Bay township. From 1993 to 1995 Council was kept busy with this development application and a subsequent New South Wales Land and Environment Court appeal initiated by the pressure group Byron Businesses for the Future (BSBF).

Owing to the limitations imposed by the capacity of the sewerage system, in 1995 a moratorium on all new medium-density development was put in place until a new sewage treatment plant could be developed. The development moratorium was lifted in late 2005 when the new sewage treatment plant opened. Whether or not its existence initiates a further wave of development remains to be seen.

In addition to these pressures, from 1995 onwards Byron Shire Council experienced considerable financial strain as a consequence of inheriting a $3 million debt from an earlier Council. Owing to these financial constraints, Council made a decision in 1996 to withdraw funding from visitor information services in Byron Bay. The growth in tourism activity and development in Byron Bay is explained by Westerhausen and Macbeth (2003) as having evolved as a result of external pressure placed on a very small community that has operated in an unregulated environment, without significant community consultation and with an eager, pro-development Council. Furthermore, Council continued to approve development far beyond the capacity of the shire's existing infra- structure and displayed a lack of concern for the long-term social and environ- mental costs of such development.

(continued)

■ Table 6.3   *Chronology of tourism planning and policy in Byron Bay*

YEAR	EVENT OR ISSUE
1988	Tourism strategy prepared for Byron Shire by Tourism Commission NSW in partnership with Byron Shire Council.
1989	Strategic marketing manager employed by Council to implement plan.
1991	Strategic marketing manager position rescinded owing to election of new Council and change in Council priorities.
1992	Byron's building boom gains momentum.
1993	Club Med development application initiates substantial community action against the proposed development.
1995	Byron Shire Council's financial situation becomes apparent after inheriting a $3 million debt from previous Council. Moratorium on development.
1996	Council withdraws funding for visitor information services.
1997	Byron Bay Chamber of Commerce and Byron Shire Tourism Association (BSTA) take over operation of the visitor information centre.
2000	Mayor collaborates with Tourism New South Wales, Department of State and Regional Development and BSTA to prepare an application for the preparation of a tourism plan under the Commonwealth Regional Tourism Program (the application was unsuccessful).
2002	Tourism NSW funds Tourism Management Options Paper in partnership with Byron Shire Council. Other principal stakeholders included Northern Rivers Regional Development Board and Northern Rivers Tourism.
2004	Tourism industry association re-formed: Tourism Byron.
2004	Council proposes to take action to manage holiday-letting issue by amending its planning scheme.
2005	Moratorium on development to be lifted when new sewerage treatment plant opens.

From this background it is evident that a range of issue drivers have had important implications for tourism planning and policy formulation in Byron Bay. They were interconnected, and many of the same stakeholders were involved in the development of these issues and in the formulation of policy responses. In the case of Byron Bay, the identification of principal stakeholders in the system and analysis of their roles, activities and interactions provide a means of understanding the processes of tourism policy and planning formulation.

Figure 6.5 plots significant tourism issues emerging in Byron Bay between 1988 and 2004 to illustrate the process of policy formulation. Using the zones of rejection, indifference, symbolic action and substantive action, the position of each stakeholder is plotted at various stages of policy formulation.

Stakeholder participation, agendas and policy

Stakeholder participation in tourism planning and policy development in Byron Bay has historically been patchy. Table 6.2 identifies the stakeholders involved in tourism planning and policy development in Byron Bay between 1988 and 2004. Stakeholders have moved in and out of participation in tourism planning and policy formulation, influenced by a range of internal and external factors. Moreover, there have been times when lack of commitment has led to a tourism planning and policy vacuum. Government stakeholders at local and state levels demonstrated substantive collaborative action in the late 1980s with the development of the Byron Bay Tourism Strategy. The preparation of this strategy adopted a cyclic approach but, in the end, lack of political commitment and financial resourcing by Council meant that the strategy's recommendations were abandoned a short time later.

The 1990s was a time of indifference for most stakeholders. For example, during the decade Tourism New South Wales (TNSW) appears to have been focused on marketing and promotional efforts rather than on contributing to policy and planning processes for the destination. Only since 2000 have these stakeholders taken substantive action in addressing tourism policy and planning issues.

Drawing from Mahon and Waddock's (1992) issue identification cycle (see section 6.5.2), Byron Shire Council's commitment to tourism policy, planning and destination management fell into a 'zone of symbolic action' when Council withdrew support for implementation of the 1988 Tourism Strategy's recommendations, but continued to fund visitor centre operations. In 1996 Council withdrew funding for managing and operating the Byron Bay Visitor Information Centre and entered a period of 'rejection', followed by a period of 'indifference' when the Byron Shire Tourism Association and Byron Bay Chamber of Commerce worked collaboratively to operate and manage the centre from 1997. Around 2000, Council planners contributed 'symbolic action' to the application process for funding to develop a tourism plan through the Federal Government's Regional Tourism Program. However, the political arm of Council demonstrated indifference to tourism policy by its decision not to provide financial support for this application process. In 2002 Council again began to demonstrate 'substantive action', providing support for the development of a Tourism Management Options Paper. Council has also demonstrated 'substantive action' in efforts to deal with increasing community concerns regarding holiday-letting of properties in residential areas through proposed changes to land-use planning instruments from 2004.

Pressure groups and interest networks have been largely responsible for leading the issue development process in Byron Bay. They have framed issues, offering the first interpretation of events and making the first call for attention in the media. For example, the Byron Shire Tourism Association (BSTA) and the Byron Bay Chamber

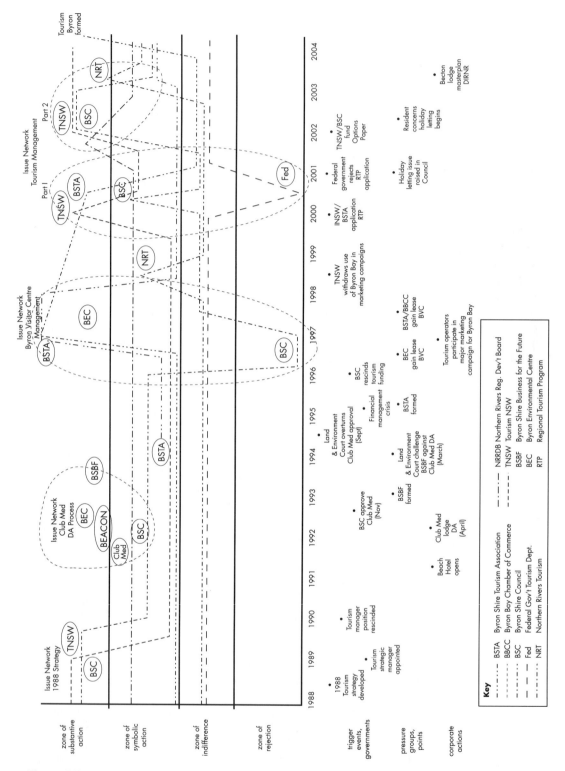

■ Figure 6.5   *Byron Bay tourism planning and policy processes 1988–2004*

of Commerce (BBCC) demonstrated 'substantive action' and collaboration in 1997, to gain the lease of the Byron Visitor Centre and to operate and manage the centre from this time. Issue networks have also formed in relation to other significant destination policy, planning and destination management issues. For example, the Byron Environment Centre (BEC), the Byron Environmental and Conservation Organisation Incorporated (BEACON), the Byron Businesses for the Future (BSBF) and the Bay Residents Against Community Erosion (BRACE) have been active in issue identification and agenda-setting processes, which in turn have resulted in planning and policy action by local government.

Discussion

As shown by plotting the actions of principal stakeholder groups to the system (see figure 6.5), a number of significant issue networks have emerged in relation to tourism policy, planning and management issues in Byron Bay. This figure illustrates that there have been a number of key policy and planning actors with an active presence within the system. It is also evident that these actors and agencies move in and out of the policy and planning arena depending on the nature and perceived importance of particular policy, planning and destination management issues at the time. As a consequence policy formulation takes place as a result of the substantive actions of stakeholders. Interestingly, it also appears that when Council has exhibited 'rejection' of the policy issue, an issue network formed to take 'substantive action'. It also appears that an issue network requires at least two stakeholder groups demonstrating substantive action to influence the development of policy.

Evidence of collaboration has been apparent only since 2000. As shown in figure 6.5, a 'tourism management' issue network first emerged in the system with the collaborative efforts of TNSW, the BSTA, DSRD and Council planners in 2000 to develop an application for Regional Tourism Program funding. The rejection of this application by the Federal Government appears to have been a trigger that stimulated collaborative action among a broader group of system stakeholders to develop local tourism policy and planning initiatives. Since this time, stakeholder groups active in the system have begun the collaborative process of sharing ideas and information and are starting to find a common platform on which to negotiate and move forward.

This case study demonstrates how theories of policy networks and issue identification can be used together to better understand how policy processes work. It demonstrates that various models of the policy processes have explanatory power and that no single model of the policy process provides all the answers. In Byron Bay, the generic policy cycle was adopted in the 1988 Tourism Strategy, and its weaknesses soon became apparent. Tourism planning and policy does not move unidirectionally through a process independent of its context. As a result, the importance of a social constructionist approach to understanding the policy process becomes evident.

(continued)

Questions

1 Review the different perspectives or viewpoints used to explain policy processes. Which of them best fits your understanding of the tourism planning process occurring in Byron Bay? Why?

2 Why do you think the 1988 Tourism Strategy had little influence on the development and management of tourism in Byron Bay?

3 Is the policy cycle an appropriate model of policy development in destinations like Byron Bay, which are characterised by strong and often conflicting networks of interest?

References

Australian Bureau of Statistics 2001, *Census of Population and Housing Byron — New South Wales*, ABS, Canberra.

Green, R 1997, 'Community perception of town character: A case study', PhD thesis, School of Planning, Landscape Architecture and Surveying, Queensland University of Technology, Brisbane.

Tonge, R, Fletcher, S & Concept Tourism Consultants 2003, *Byron Shire Tourism Management: An Options Paper for Consideration*, Final Draft, Prepared for Byron Bay Shire Council and Tourism NSW.

Westerhausen, K & Macbeth, J 2003, 'Backpackers and empowered local communities: Natural allies in the struggle for sustainability and local control', *Tourism Geographies*, vol. 5, no. 1, pp. 71–86.

REFERENCES

Bridgman, P & Davis, G 2003, 'What use is a policy cycle? Plenty if the aim is clear', *Australian Journal of Public Administration*, vol. 62, no. 3, pp. 98–102.

—— 2004, *The Australian Policy Handbook*, Allen & Unwin, Sydney.

Burstein, P 1991, 'Policy domains: Organisation, culture, and policy outcomes', *Annual Review of Sociology*, vol. 17, pp. 327–50.

Chadwick, GA 1970, *A Systems View of Planning: Towards a Theory of the Urban and Regional Planning Process*, 2nd edn, Oxford University Press, Oxford.

Colebatch, HK 2002, *Policy*, Open University Press, Buckingham.

Considine, M 1994, *Public Policy: A Critical Approach*, Macmillan, Melbourne.

Department of Natural Resources and Parks Victoria 1999, *Best Practice in Park Interpretation and Education*, Melbourne.

Downs, A 1972, 'Up and down with ecology: The issue attention cycle', *Public Interest*, vol. 28, pp. 38–50.

Dredge, D 2006a, 'Policy networks and the local organisation of tourism', *Tourism Management*, vol. 27, no. 2, pp. 269–80.

—— 2006b, 'Networks, conflict and collaborative communities', *Journal of Sustainable Tourism* (forthcoming).

Dror, Y 1968, *Public Policy Reexamined*, Chandler Publishers, San Francisco.

Easton, D 1965, *A Systems Analysis of Political Life*, John Wiley & Sons, New York.

Etzioni, A 1967, 'Mixed-scanning: A "third" approach to decision-making', *Public Administration Review*, vol. 27, no. 5, pp. 385–92.

Everett, S 2003, 'The policy cycle: Democratic process or rational paradigm revisited?', *Australian Journal of Policy Administration*, vol. 62, no. 2, pp. 65–70.

Getz, D 1986, 'Models in tourism planning: Towards integration of theory and practice', *Tourism Management*, vol. 7, no. 1, pp. 21–32.

Gunn, C & Var, T 2004, *Tourism Planning: Basics Concepts Cases*, 4th edn, Routledge, New York.

Ham, C & Hill, M 1993, *The Policy Process in the Modern State*, Harvester Wheatsheaf, Hemel Hempstead, Herts.

Healey, P 1997, *Collaborative Planning: Shaping Places in Fragmented Societies*, Macmillan, London.

—— 1998, 'Building institutional capacity through collaborative approaches to urban planning', *Environment and Planning* A30 1531–46.

Heclo, H 1978, 'Issue networks and the executive establishment', in A King (ed.), *The New American Political System*, American Enterprise Institute, Washington, pp. 87–124.

Hogwood, BW 1987, *From Crisis to Complacency? Shaping Public Policy in Britain*, Oxford University Press, Oxford.

Hogwood, BW & Gunn, LA 1984, *Policy Analysis for the Real World*, Oxford University Press, Oxford.

Homeshaw, J 1995, 'Policy community, policy networks and science policy in Australia', *Australian Journal of Public Administration*, vol. 54, no. 4, pp. 520–32.

Howlett, M & Ramesh, M 1995, *Studying Public Policy: Policy Cycles and Policy Subsystems*, Oxford University Press, Toronto.

Inskeep, E 1987, 'Environmental planning for tourism', *Annals of Tourism Research*, vol. 14, no. 1, pp. 118–35.

— 1991, *Tourism Planning: An Integrated and Sustainable Development Approach*, Van Nostrand Reinhold, New York.

Jenkins, WI 1978, *Policy Analysis*, Martin Robertson, Oxford.

Keating, M 1996, 'Defining the policy advising function', in J Uhr & K Mackay (eds), *Evaluating Policy Advice*, ANU Federalism Research Centre and Commonwealth Department of Finance, Canberra.

Kingdon, JW 1984, *Agendas, Alternatives and Public Policies*, Harper Collins, New York.

Lane, J 2000, *The Public Sector: Concepts, Models and Approaches*, Sage, London.

Levin, P 1997, *Making Social Policy: The Mechanisms of Government and Politics and How to Investigate Them*, Open University Press, Buckingham, UK.

Lindblom, CE 1959, 'The science of muddling through', *Public Administration Review*, vol. 19, no. 2, pp. 79–88.

Mahon, J & Waddock, S 1992, 'Strategic issues management: An integration of issue life cycle perspectives', *Business & Society*, vol. 31, no. 1, pp. 19–32.

Mason, GL 1997, 'A conceptual basis for organisational modelling', *Systems Research Behavioural Science*, vol. 14, pp. 331–45.

McIntosh, RW & Goeldner, CR 1986, *Tourism: Principles, Practices and Philosophies*, John Wiley & Sons, New York.

McKercher, B & Chon, K 2004, 'The over-reaction to SARS and the collapse of Asian tourism', *Annals of Tourism Research*, vol. 31, no. 3, pp. 716–19.

Michael, E 2001, 'Public choice and tourism analysis', *Current Issues in Tourism*, vol. 4, nos 2–4, pp. 308–30.

Milward, HB & Walmsley, GL 1984, 'Policy subsystems, networks and the tools of public management', in R Eyestone (ed.), *Public Policy Formulation*, JAI Press, Greenwich, CT, pp. 3–25.

Parsons, W 1995, *Public Policy: An Introduction to the Theory and Practice of Policy Analysis*, Edward Elgar, Aldershot.

Pross, P 1992, *Group Politics and Public Policy*, 2nd edn, Oxford University Press, Toronto.

Rhodes, RAW 1997, *Understanding Governance: Policy Networks, Governance, Reflexitivity and Accountability*, Open University Press, Buckingham.

Sabatier, P 1988, 'An advocacy coalition framework of policy change and the role of policy-oriented learning therein', *Policy Sciences*, vol. 21, pp. 129–68.

Sabatier, P & Jenkins-Smith, HC 1993, *Policy Change and Learning: An Advocacy Coalition Approach*, Westview, Boulder, CO.

Simeon, R 1976, 'Studying public policy', *Canadian Journal of Political Science*, vol. 9, no. 4, pp. 558–80.

7

National *tourism policy and planning*

LEARNING OBJECTIVES

After reading this chapter you will be able to:

1 describe the responsibilities of national governments in national tourism policy and planning

2 describe the key principles and themes evident in national tourism strategies and policies in Australia since the 1960s

3 explain important public policy issues, perspectives and interests affecting the development of national tourism policies in Australia

4 identify and elaborate on some key trends in national tourism policy

5 critically engage with the aims and content of Australian federal tourism policy since the 1960s.

This chapter directs its attention to national tourism administration and policy in Australia. Tourism public policy reflects government ideology and priorities but, by and large, national tourism plans and policies are geared towards the economic development of tourism in ways that are touted as exceeding or at least building on previous governments' efforts. Australia now has an impressive collection of past and present tourism policies, although the early 1990s was perhaps the most intensive period of policy development seen anywhere in the world. A comprehensive review is impossible, so some key decisions, actions and events are discussed and a wide range of resources are listed for students who wish to deepen their knowledge of national tourism policy.

After a brief overview of the Commonwealth Government's responsibilities concerning tourism (section 7.2), the development of national tourism policies and plans since the 1960s is traced in sections 7.3 to 7.6. The discussion is divided into changes in government and differences in party political ideology.

7.2 *O*VERVIEW OF THE COMMONWEALTH'S TOURISM RESPONSIBILITIES ·····················

The federal division of responsibilities in Australia and the distribution of responsibilities for policy and planning among many public sector institutions and different levels of government have led to problems of policy coordination in almost every policy and planning arena: transport, environmental conservation, communications, mineral resources, water, energy, forestry, urban affairs, Aboriginal affairs, urban planning and taxation. Tourism has been no exception. Tourism is not explicitly mentioned in the Australian Constitution, so the responsibilities of various levels of government for tourism have developed disjointedly under the divisions of powers that directly and indirectly affect tourism (Hall 1998).

The lack of specific powers to deal with tourism under the Constitution has resulted in the duplication of government responsibilities and, therefore, disagreement between the states and between the states and the Commonwealth (Hall 1998). For example, in a submission to the Commonwealth's Senate Standing Committee on Environment, Recreation and the Arts (1992: 248), the Northern Territory Government argued that it 'does not see a significant role or need for the coordination of foreign tourist development between the States, including the Northern Territory, by the Commonwealth Government'. Such disagreements have not been unusual, despite the **Tourism Ministers' Council** Agreement of 1976, which encapsulates the responsibilities of the Commonwealth and state governments and the responsibilities of the **Australian Standing Committee on Tourism** (ASCOT). There is no clear divide between the roles and responsibilities of the Commonwealth, state and territory governments. State, as well as regional and local, tourism organisations undertake domestic and overseas marketing and promotion, and do not always agree or comply with Commonwealth decisions and actions. The Commonwealth Government is now investing substantial resources in domestic campaigns and supports regional development programs, which are also vital functions of the states and territories.

Effective coordination of tourism policies and programs at the national, state and regional levels has been attempted through various mechanisms, especially in marketing and promoting Australia, but agreement and compliance will never be universal in what has become an increasingly competitive market. Coordination is a difficult task, in part because issues concerning tourism (e.g. the structures, roles and functions of tourism agencies) are often highly political and laced with administrative and historical legacies (see chapters 2, 3 and 4). There is a potentially volatile mix of government ideology, values and interests and hence conflict among the states, territories and the Commonwealth, especially when governments of different political persuasions — Coalition/Liberal/National Party and Australian Labor Party — are in power at different levels.

PLANNING IN PRACTICE

Partnership Australia

Comprehensive tourism policy integration (e.g. in marketing and promotion) in Australia has met with little success despite the release of Australia's first comprehensive National Tourism Strategy by the federal Labor government in July 1992 and its 'successors', such as the Tourism White Paper discussed later in this chapter. The continuing fragmentation of responsibility for industry planning, development, marketing and promotion continues to lead to overlapping policy goals and instruments. However, an initiative that went some way to alleviating the problems of overlap in state and Commonwealth marketing and promotion was the Partnership Australia program, launched by the Labor Federal Government in 1994. Partners included the Australian Tourist Commission (ATC), state and territory marketing organisations or authorities and private industry. Partnership Australia was devised to overcome coordination problems in the way Australian tourism was developed and marketed overseas. The principal objectives of Partnership Australia were to:

- coordinate Australia's international tourism marketing and promotional efforts to improve efficiency and effectiveness (thereby eliminating costly duplication and fragmentation in marketing)
- develop a wider range of tourism product for international markets

(continued)

- provide information to overseas consumers and industry to generate more sales and extend product distribution, and
- motivate and train the overseas trade to sell Australia better (Pearce et al. 1998: 230; Australian Tourist Commission 1993: 1; see also ATC 1995).

The Partnership Australia program had some initial problems with members disagreeing about the constitution of the ATC board and the direction of marketing activities and proportional representation of states in such programs. However, the program eventually met with some success and much recognition, leading to the establishment of Aussie Helplines in Europe, North America, Asia, Japan and New Zealand. Travel counsellors, who staffed the telephone lines in 1994–95, answered 398 000 trade and consumer inquiries about Australian tourism, and industry partners spent approximately $26.7 million on short-term advertising campaigns overseas (ATC 1995).

Nevertheless, the ATC was still confronted with the problems concerning where and how to market and to brand products without upsetting its state and territory partners. Moreover, despite the praise or the criticisms levelled at the ATC, no-one has ever really known or been able to measure precisely what influence it has had in encouraging international visitors to Australia. For this reason alone the ATC has been confronted with major inquiries and several restructures since its establishment in 1965.

The above discussion has briefly described some important structural constraints in Australia's **federal system** of government and highlighted the lack of clarity and coordination in government roles and responsibilities with respect to tourism. These matters aside, recent rethinking of the role of the state in modern capitalist society has led to interesting developments in the ways in which governments set up tourism administrations to market and promote destinations, develop policy, conduct research, establish partnerships and networks and implement programs. We now turn our attention to these matters as they affected national tourism policy in Australia and trace some of the key administrative and policy developments from the 1960s.

7.3 PUBLIC ADMINISTRATION AND POLICY, 1960–83

The period from the 1960s to the late 1970s or early 1980s was an important period of tourism policy development in many countries. In the 1960s policies focused greatly on increasing tourist travel flows, and emphasis was given to international marketing and promotion as tourism became a mass phenomenon (Jeffries 2001: 77). National tourism authorities, generally statutory authorities, were not well equipped 'to deal with new problems posed by the boom in tourism'. Moreover, 'the very bodies which should have been directing tourism policies had to contend with a growing compartmentalisation of policy' (OECD, in Jeffries 2001: 78). National governments had invested heavily in transport and services infrastructure, and in promoting tourism had reached a point where concerns about the excessive speed of tourism development and growing levels of visitation and consequences of tourism were being raised but were dealt with inadequately.

The OECD identified four main concerns for OECD countries in 1972:

1. growing sensitivity to the pressures of rapid growth of tourism, which could be addressed by better information provision and public participation in planning processes
2. the need to consider the costs of tourism development in relation to the environment and people's quality of life
3. the need to plan simultaneously for recreational and tourist use of resources, and
4. increasingly prominent policies to ensure that recreational and tourism resources are available for 'more sectors of the population' (OECD 1973: 12).

Of course, along with these themes there were the usual foci on marketing and promotion, collection of data on domestic and international visitors and matters dealt with largely outside the auspices of tourism administrations (e.g. visas, transport and communications and other infrastructure). However, even in the marketing sphere there were noted developments to stimulate tourism through 'conventions' and 'incentives', 'special interest groups' and 'automobile clubs' (OECD 1973: 29). These themes, along with several others, have remained at the forefront of many national plans, and their recognition as important elements of niche marketing clearly existed much sooner than many authors either were aware of or have been willing to acknowledge.

The economic and travel figures for tourism in the early 1970s before the recession of 1974–76 were impressive (although they have since been criticised as gross overestimates). In 1972 it was estimated that Australia received about 425 000 visitors, who spent approximately A\$139 million during their visit. The Australian National Travel Association (ANTA) estimated that the industry generated A\$2.4 billion, or 8 per cent of Australia's Gross National Income, and was labour intensive, employing 10 per cent of the Australian workforce. Between 1970 and 1979 international visitor arrivals fluctuated; for example, there were solid increases from 1971 to 1974 and in 1978–79 but a decrease during the recession, when oil prices and inflation surged (BTR 1989; ABS 1990).

In 1973, the newly elected Labor government, led by Prime Minister Gough Whitlam (see table 7.1, p. 230), appointed Australia's first federal Minister for Tourism and Recreation and created the Department of Tourism and Recreation (DTR). These moves signalled the greater importance being attached to tourism as an aspect of government activity, partly driven by a need to develop and promote tourism domestically and internationally. In *Development of Tourism in Australia* (1973), DTR unveiled many innovative ideas for tourism, some of which were a long time in gestation. The department prefaced the document with the claim: 'This paper is the first step in formulating a comprehensive national plan for the development of tourism in Australia' (DTR 1973). However, almost twenty years would pass before such a plan was actually developed, released and implemented, but this was a potentially fruitful and ambitious beginning.

■ **Table 7.1**
Australia's prime ministers and their political parties

PRIME MINISTER	POLITICAL PARTY	TERM OF OFFICE
Sir Robert Menzies	Liberal	19 December 1949 – 26 January 1966
Harold Holt	Liberal	26 January 1966 – 19 December 1967
Sir John (Jack) McEwen	Country Party	19 December 1967 – 10 January 1968
Sir John Gorton	Liberal	10 January 1968 – 10 March 1971
Sir William McMahon	Liberal	10 March 1971 – 5 December 1972
(Edward) Gough Whitlam	Labor	5 December 1972 – 11 November 1975
(John) Malcolm Fraser	Liberal	11 November 1975 – 11 March 1983
Robert Hawke	Labor	11 March 1983 – 20 December 1991
Paul Keating	Labor	20 December 1991 – 11 March 1996
John Howard	Liberal	11 March 1996 – continuing

Leisure and tourism were important policy areas for the Whitlam Government. As Leader of the Opposition in the 1960s, then as Prime Minister, Gough Whitlam had long argued the importance of leisure in contemporary society (see Tourism Planning Breakthrough: 'It's time for leadership'). His government had a strong and committed social democratic agenda.

TOURISM PLANNING BREAKTHROUGH
It's time for leadership

Extract from Australian Labor Party policy speech 1972 delivered by Gough Whitlam at Blacktown Civic Centre on 13 November

THE QUALITY OF LIFE
There is no greater social problem facing Australia than the good use of expanding leisure. It is the problem of all modern and wealthy communities. It is, above all, the problem of urban societies and thus, in Australia, the most urbanised nation on earth, a problem more pressing for us than for any other nation on earth. For such a nation as ours, this may very well be the problem of the 1980s; so we must prepare now; prepare the generation of the '80s — the children and youth of the '70s — to be able to enjoy and enrich their growing hours of leisure.

TOURISM

The quality, accessibility and cheapness of Australian leisure should be incomparable in the world. The tourist industry is one of Australia's largest sources of overseas income and regional employment. We will make grants, loans, tax concessions and other inducements, as recommended by the Australian Tourist Commission, to ensure that Australian cities and tourist centres are provided with accommodation and amenities of international standard.

Following the early passage of the Territorial Sea and Continental Shelf Bill, we will declare the Great Barrier Reef a national park. Townsville, the gateway to the Reef, will be made an international airport.

We will set up a national parks service to administer national parks in the ACT, Jervis Bay and the Northern Territory. We would also work in cooperation with the New South Wales and Victorian Governments for a National Park in the Australian Alps and with the New South Wales and South Australian Governments to develop a Central Australian wilderness area.

We will encourage Australia's airlines to provide as cheap holidays within Australia as Australia's overseas airline has been able to do for overseas travel.

We will vest the Australian Tourist Commission with the Commonwealth's full constitutional powers to engage in business activities appropriate to tourism, such as the licensing of overseas and interstate travel agents.

Source: *Whitlam 1972*

In the 1970s, as we saw in chapters 2 and 4, there was an increasing shift towards master planning, supply-driven tourism planning and policy development, while relationships between government and civil society became more prominent. DTR considered tourism to be developing 'haphazardly' but saw its wider community benefits. The department regarded tourism as a 'nationally important industry' and argued that 'a planned and coordinated approach is essential to achieve a balanced relationship in the development of destination areas' and tourism sectors, such as attractions, transportation and accommodation. Such an approach needed to be coupled with domestic promotion programs and well-conceived marketing and promotion in overseas markets (DTR 1973: 1–2).

The importance of tourism to job creation, foreign exchange earnings and regional development was recognised (DTR 1973). Specific attention was directed to tourism's social and cultural significance, potential for employment creation and decentralisation, contribution to public revenues and earnings from foreign exchange, multiplier effects, Aboriginal participation and relationships with the environment. With regard to the latter, sustainability (although not by that name) was evident in the Whitlam Government's tourism agenda: 'Planned and balanced tourism development in association with interpretive programmes can in fact provide the means of educating man to appreciate Australia's unique characteristics of scenery, flora and fauna' (DTR 1973: 11). The department recommended more flexible working hours, four-day working weeks, the establishment of a research framework and arm, the development of a domestic campaign (Go See Australia, perhaps a forerunner to the recent See Australia; see below) and greater cooperation between states and territories and the Federal Government. These were initiatives based on a fundamental principle that 'To savour the life and history around us is a natural pleasure and an undeniable right … What we are speaking of is called recreation. A recharging of the spirit, the mind and the body to enable us to occupy usefully the growing hours of leisure and to face more confidently the increasing pressures of the daily working life' (p. 55).

This was the first and last time writings of this kind would appear in Australia's national tourism policy documents. Labor's commitment to tourism was domestically grounded, backed by a commitment to overseas promotion and strongly linked to people's leisure and quality of life and to social cohesion. Recreation and tourism were regarded as 'pursuits which can contribute significantly to the community's standards of physical and mental health'. DTR also described how Australians' understanding of other cultures and the development of global perspectives could be enhanced through tourism (DTR 1973: 7–8).

The Whitlam Government lasted only three years in office. By November 1975, when it was dismissed by the Governor-General in controversial circumstances, few of its tourism plans had come to fruition, but the seeds had been scattered. Despite the prominence given to tourism — recognition it had previously lacked — the bureaucratic network for tourism was limited, there was no defined research branch for the collection and dissemination of industry-related information, and no university in Australia offered a specific tourism program (Carroll 1991; Richardson 1999). The development of a comprehensive national tourism strategy or plan was always on tenuous ground as several factors were lacking. These factors included experience in the bureaucracy and private sector in tourism planning and policy-making at this level and well-developed networks and partnerships and industry associations to foster discussion, debate and argument about policy. Financial resources were also under pressure. Even during Labor's term of office, a report by Coombs (1973), which reviewed program expenditure commitments of government agencies, recommended large reductions in funding to the ATC for the following year and ultimately its abolition. The report argued that persisting with the ATC for a short time 'would give the industry an opportunity to assess whether it wished to finance the activities of the Australian Tourist Commission from its own resources and, if so, to make the necessary arrangements'. The ATC's funding was briefly reduced, but the agency lived on, thanks in part to a major submission by the Department of Tourism and Recreation, which argued the central place and critical role of the ATC in international marketing and promotion.

The cuts in ATC funding need to be set against developments in the wider socioeconomic and political environments. The Whitlam Government's term coincided with the oil crisis, inflation and growing unemployment while the government was embarking on unprecedented education, health and welfare packages. The Whitlam Government was in fact an important change agent for social progress, Aboriginal rights, sexual equality, racial equality and economic justice (Whitford et al. 2001: 153). Indigenous involvement in tourism had been recommended by Harris, Kerr Forster (1965) in their widely publicised report *Australia's Travel and Tourist Industry* (see Whitford et al. 2001), and it had taken several years for the Federal Government to engage with some of its more culturally sensitive recommendations. DTR stated: 'the development of tourism can provide an opportunity for many Aboriginal Australians to engage in worthwhile economic activities and increase their self-reliance.' The department envisaged developing partnerships with the Department of Aboriginal Affairs and other agencies 'to encourage appropriate training programmes and employment opportunities so that Aborigines could gain maximum benefits from participation in tourism projects' (DTR 1973: 11). Again, it was a long time before these initiatives were addressed in any decisive manner.

Ultimately, for all its promise, DTR lacked a strong departmental base and was responsible to a junior minister. Tourism interests were divided in their opinions about the government's strategies in its early years. State governments 'were generally unsympathetic'. In brief, in these circumstances, 'Federal Government policy in regard to tourism began to stagnate in 1974 and 1975' (Carroll 1991: 74–5). The early momentum had been lost.

The Coalition Government, led by Malcolm Fraser, which came into power in November 1975, stated that even greater emphasis would be given to tourism. However, as was usual for Coalition governments until the 1990s, tourism was a minor issue of little economic importance and was generally relegated to a minor portfolio. DTR and grants for the development of tourist attractions were abolished (Carroll 1991). Tourism was relegated to a branch in the Department of Industry and Commerce. The government sought to reduce the size of the public service (also see section 2.3) and to pursue its **new federalism** agenda, which involved divesting itself of responsibilities (or at least minimising its activities) in areas that could be addressed by the states (Leiper 1980). Cutting domestic tourism promotion by the ATC was one avenue, although a minor one, for achieving this goal. Along with these actions, Leiper (1980: 158) believed that 'abolishing a department of "leisure" helped strengthen the new Government's image as a propagator of the work ethic'. As Prime Minister Malcolm Fraser told Australians, 'Life wasn't meant to be easy'! (Perhaps if, in using a piece of George Bernard Shaw's message, he had also included Shaw's moderating statement: 'but take courage, my child, it can be delightful', this comment would never have become a constant refrain during and after his term of office.)

A series of fortuitous and deliberately initiated events probably saved the ATC from a fate similar to DTR. The predicted resources boom of the early 1980s never eventuated. The proportion of Australians working in manufacturing had been falling steadily. Conversely, the tertiary sector had been expanding, save for a brief period of stagnation just after World War II, when immigration and industrialisation were strongly encouraged by government. By 1980 tertiary industries accounted for about 70 per cent of total employment. Tourism was a service industry showing strong signs of growth and was being supported by an increasingly effective lobby group, the Australian Tourism Industry Association (ATIA). The Australian Bicentennial Authority, set up in 1979, was charged with the responsibility to coordinate a national program of celebrations and was run by a board of directors comprising members nominated by the Commonwealth, state and Northern Territory governments. One of the authority's key objectives was 'to project Australia to the world and invite international participation with the aim of strengthening relationships with other nations'. Opportunities for tourism were considered 'very significant' (ABS 1986), and the states were making serious moves in the tourism policy arena.

In Queensland, Joh Bjelke-Petersen (Premier from 1967 to 1989) was aware of the potential for Queensland to become a popular destination for international and domestic tourists. Tourism was a key driver of his 'developmental ethos' (Craik 1991a: 194; 1991b), the like of which has been subsequently seen only in Western Australia under Premier Richard Court during the 1980s and in Victoria under Premier Jeff Kennett in the 1990s.

In 1979, the Queensland Government established the Queensland Tourist and Travel Corporation, which was headed by Sir Frank Moore, who also headed ATIA. The QTTC was set up as a statutory corporation to 'Upgrade and streamline government's involvement in tourism' and to 'revitalise and rejuvenate' the tourism industry (Parliament of Queensland 1979b: 111, 118–20, in Craik 1991: 183). Large-scale events and resorts were high on the government and corporation's agendas as means to help fuel the Queensland development engine. The corporation was equipped with powers to be a key facilitator of tourism development in Queensland and, reflecting its leaders' agendas, was aggressive and unyielding in its approach. The 1982 Commonwealth Games was another international activity with substantial potential tourism benefits that also had the support of the Federal Government.

In 1979, South Australia set up a Department of Tourism, and every other state was also to follow in the footsteps of the QTTC's more aggressive and entrepreneurial approach to tourism development (see section 4.5). QTTC became a benchmark. The Federal Government was under considerable pressure in the Tourism Ministers' Council and from ATIA to maintain a prominent and decisive presence, particularly in international marketing, export market programs and research and national leadership. Moreover, tourism regained some status in the government's administrative arrangements and financial allocations after a reduction in ATC funding in 1976–77. The committee recommended that the Department of Industry and Commerce be abolished and replaced by the Department of Industry, Commerce and Tourism. A series of other recommendations flowed from the report, including the conduct of research into tourism's economic significance, incentives to encourage tourism's development and promotion by the private sector and finding means of addressing concerns about fragmentation in the industry (see Leiper 1980).

Along with strong aggregate growth in domestic and international travel in the early 1980s, the industry benefited from extensions of eligibility for Export Market Development Grants, income tax deductions for depreciation on tourist accommodation, increased funding for ATC marketing and promotion, and international aviation agreements designed to open up the skies to more foreign airlines, reduce fares and lessen controls on charter flights (Department of Industry and Commerce 1976, 1977; Carroll 1991). The stage was set for what was still an infant industry to begin a phase of rapid growth and, it was hoped, national recognition and maturity, encouraged by a growing developmental and entrepreneurial ethos in government.

7.4 TOURISM POLICY AND ADMINISTRATION, 1983–91

Visitor arrivals for people whose primary purpose of visit was going on holidays grew dramatically between the late 1970s and 1987. Visitor numbers in this period rose by 239 per cent in total, while holiday visitor numbers had grown by 467 per cent (BTR 1989; ABS 1990). Between 1980 and 1987, short-term arrivals of overseas visitors rose from 904 600 to 1 784 900 and, for the first time since the early 1970s, these arrivals outnumbered the short-term departures of Australian residents. Numbers declined marginally in 1989, but strong growth resumed in 1990–91, as arrivals increased by 7 per cent as opposed to growth in world travel arrivals of 1.5 per cent (DoT 1992). These relatively high rates of growth over the period 1983–91 could be attributed to the rapid decline in the value of the Australian dollar after it was floated in 1983, increased travel activity from Asia, improved transport links and technology, overseas investors' interest in Australia, exports of Australian produce, Australia's political stability, marketing campaigns of the ATC and the drive to stage large-scale events (Hall 1998; Carroll 1991; Faulkner 1990). Domestic tourism had also been growing, but of course all travel to and within Australia slowed dramatically after the major events coinciding with the stock market crash of 1987, while the Bicentenary of Australia and the 1988 World Expo had brought forward people's travel plans, which would inevitably affect future visitor numbers (Faulkner 1990). They were further disrupted domestically by the 1989 air pilots' dispute (see section 7.4.1).

The Labor Party was returned to government in 1983 with Bob Hawke as Prime Minister. In 1985 the tourism branch was relocated to a Department of Sport, Recreation and Tourism. DSRT was headed by an energetic and enigmatic minister, John Brown, who wielded considerable influence in government. In *Tourism gets Australia Going*, launched on World Tourism Day 1983, Brown outlined a series of policy developments for tourism (see table 7.2). Brown argued: 'It is time now to promote tourism as an accelerator to assist in providing the boost that the Australian economy needs ...

Increased domestic and international tourism will provide jobs for Australians in all walks of life, in all parts of Australia' (p. 2).

In 1983–84, the ATC received $17.5 million (a 75 per cent increase in funding on the $10 million granted in 1982–83) and $13 million for the Paul Hogan overseas promotion campaigns. This was on the back of an aim of doubling 'the number of overseas visitors to Australia by 1988 and substantially increasing domestic tourism' (Brown 1983: 3). ATIA's interest and influence in policy-making was indicated when Brown stated that the importance of the above aim 'to the industry was recognised by the Australian Travel Industry Association (ATIA) in its valuable strategy document released in September 1982 — which the Tourism Ministers' Council envisages being developed, in consultation with ATIA, into a National Tourism Policy Statement' (p. 3). Brown painted a rosy picture of tourism and gave weight to his claims and visions with a myriad of policy statements and promises to initiate actions.

■ Table 7.2
John Brown's
tourism
promises in
Tourism gets
Australia
Going

• Increase ATC activity in the US, Asia, Europe, the UK, New Zealand
• promote Australia as a convention destination
• undertake joint promotions with overseas airlines servicing Australia
• promote and increase awareness of domestic travel opportunities
• remove sales taxes on cruise vessels
• give $5 million to the Tasmanian government to develop tourist facilities in the south-west
• provide an operating subsidy of $2.5 million for the sea passenger service between Tasmania and the mainland
• increase road grants funding coinciding with the Bicentenary of Australia (1988)
• provide $5 million for preliminary planning for a proposed Alice Springs to Darwin railway
• support capital injections for Qantas and Trans Australian Airlines (TAA)
• allocate funding to natural and historic attractions such as the Great Barrier Reef
• provide almost $0.5 million for tourism industry training committees in addition to the establishment of a Townsville School of Catering and Hospitality ($1.14 million)
• support various Bicentenary projects
• establish a National Tourism Awards scheme to promote excellence in the industry, and
• ensure Australia's commitment to international programs, agencies and partnerships (e.g. World Tourism Organization, Pacific Area Travel Association).

The government also elected to pump-prime tourism through financial support to and promotion of mega-events such as the Adelaide Grand Prix, the 1982 Commonwealth Games in Brisbane, the Brisbane World Expo '88 and Australia's Bicentenary celebration.

Other policy developments not specifically directed to tourism had tremendous influence on it. Such developments included the imposition of a fringe benefits tax and the removal of entertainment expenses as a tax deduction. These policies of course affected business entertainment and discretionary expenditure (Carroll 1991). The phasing out of the Two Airlines Agreement and relaxation of controls on foreign investment (which saw the Queensland Government attract huge amounts of Japanese investment and controversy in the mid- to late 1980s) were part of the policy mix designed to open and deregulate the Australian economy.

In the late 1980s, after another administrative reshuffle, tourism was merged with other departments to form the Department of the Arts, Sport, the Environment, Tourism and Territories (DASETT). The tourism aspect of the portfolio had four key areas:

1. Policy and program support by the department had the objective of '[maximising] the contribution of tourism to the economy by ensuring that Government policy formulation takes account of the interests of the industry to the extent that they will contribute to this end; and to ensure the activities of the Tourism Program are conducted efficiently and effectively through the provision of program support services' (DASETT 1989: 37).

2. The Tourism Development and Special Events Branch of the department had the objective of fostering 'closer economic, social, cultural and political relationships with overseas countries and to attract tourists to Australia through participation in World Expositions; and to enhance national pride through the celebration of Australia Day and other significant national and historic events' (DASETT 1989: 48).

3. The Bureau of Tourism Research had the objective of '[enhancing] the development of the tourism industry in Australia by disseminating sound, timely and comprehensive statistics and analyses which are appropriate to the needs of the industry and which facilitate the formulation of appropriate policies by Commonwealth and State Governments' (DASETT 1989: 54).

4. The Australia Tourist Commission's objectives were 'To enhance awareness of Australia overseas and market internationally the attractiveness of Australia as a destination; to facilitate coordination of and bring to focus the efforts of the tourism industry and the States and to increase the number of foreign visitors, enhance awareness of the tourism industry and achieve the best possible returns from tourism to Australia' (DASETT 1989: 58).

Some key events in 1983–91 that affected tourism included the Australian air pilots' dispute, the development of the environmental lobby, the increasingly muddied waters in business–government relations and large-scale public inquiries into tourism.

■ 7.4.1 The *air pilots' dispute*

The air pilots' dispute was triggered in July 1989 when the Australian Federation of Air Pilots lodged a claim on behalf of more than 1600 pilots for a 29.5 per cent pay increase. The airlines promptly rejected this claim. Originally limiting services to the hours of 9am to 5pm, this dispute then dragged on for 11 months after pilots resigned on 24 August. The government supported domestic travel by releasing RAAF aircraft and by recruiting pilots from Australia and overseas (Faulkner 1990). Some airlines including Qantas recruited pilots from other industries, such as agriculture (i.e. crop duster pilots), and trained them. Soon after, in October 1990, the Commonwealth Government deregulated the airline industry and opened the market to private competition (see Richardson 1999: 197–8) as recommended in the IAC report (1989), but with mixed success.

The ATC received an additional $18.5 million to help the industry re-establish itself in the aftermath of the pilots' dispute. However, it took time for the industry to recover. International and domestic travel had been greatly affected as people changed their travel plans to seek other destinations, to use alternative forms of transport or, in the case of Australians, to travel outside of the country at the expense of domestic providers. Remote regions such as North Queensland, the Northern Territory, Western Australia and Tasmania experienced devastating declines in visitor numbers (Faulkner 1990).

■ 7.4.2 The *environment*

The environment attracted much attention in the 1980s. The establishment of World Heritage Areas, the rapid growth in the numbers of national parks and tourism development in fragile areas (such as coastal and alpine areas), the prominence of the Green Party in Tasmania and gradual recognition of tourism's environmental consequences brought nature-based tourism and environmental protection to centre stage. These developments concerning individual and collective rights in land in Australia were subjected to increasingly complex and extensive intervention from government, especially during the 1980s, which reflected a growing community concern about land and a changing attitude towards land that has been of direct relevance to the development of tourism and other industries. Gilpin (1980: 119) attributed that intervention to the 'increasing recognition that the free market does not always allocate [or manage] land in socially desirable ways ... the market cannot adequately reflect the ecological, economic, social and environmental externalities resulting from its development'.

Since the 1960s, the conservation and environmental movements have developed into strong, although not always coherent, land management lobbies. Campaigns to end the degradation of Australia's land base from all manner of uses 'have multiplied and intensified as the membership of Australia's environmental groups has grown from 100 000 in 1974, to 500 000 in 1982, to 700 000 in 1991' (Bonyhady 1993: ix; see also Grinlinton 1990 and Mercer 1991). As these groups grew in size, they also became better organised, better financed and more skilful in voicing their concerns.

In Australia, since the mid-1970s, the environmental movement has significantly influenced the course of environmental debates and, indeed, several state and federal elections (Mercer 1991; Bonyhady 1993). Their influence in tourism policy-making is now unarguable, and environmental planning legislation requires much greater consideration of environmental and social consequences and extensive environmental impact statements before it is considered at local and state government levels.

■ 7.4.3 Big business *and government*

The federal Labor government (headed by Bob Hawke and then Paul Keating in the period 1983–96) also fostered close ties with big business. 'Under the adversarial system of government in Australia, business is generally linked with the conservative coalition and the unions linked with labor' (Horgan 1991: 2). That said, Labor governments were greatly influenced by the increasing local and international pressures of globalisation from the mid-1970s. So, by the time the federal and state Labor governments came to power in the early 1980s, Australia had entered a phase of widespread economic restructuring as it adapted from a regulated economy to the perspective of Asia–Pacific and global trade with changing patterns of industrial development, economic deregulation, reduced protectionism, flourishing multinational corporations and fewer trade barriers (for more detailed discussions see Fagan & Webber 1994: 1–26; Hall et al. 1997: 26–30).

Interestingly, business and pressure groups like ATIA, TCA and TTF themselves (see chapter 4) became less and less party political. It makes little sense for industry groups to alienate themselves from a particular major political party and hence from government purely because of ideological differences. In any case, the differences between the Labor and Liberal parties appear to be diminishing as increasingly influential neoclassical economic paradigms have infiltrated policy-making. Moreover, not all business leaders vote for the same party.

■ 7.4.4 Inquiries *in tourism*

There have been several detailed and extensive inquiries into travel and tourism in Australia (see table 7.3).

■ **Table 7.3**
Commonwealth-level inquiries into tourism

YEAR	BODY
1986	Joint Committee on the Australian Capital Territory (Hospitality in the ACT)
1986	Australian Government Committee of Inquiry into Tourism
1987–88	Committee of Inquiry into Tourism Shopping in Australia (Department of the Arts, Sports, Tourism and Territories)
1988–89	Industries Assistance Commission Inquiry into Tourism
1989	Senate Select Committee on Certain Aspects of the Airline Dispute

Source: *Hall 1998.*

The Australian Government Committee of Inquiry in Tourism (1986) had a direct bearing on national policy development. The Bureau of Tourism Research was established, the Australian Tourist Commission's corporate structure was reviewed and its identity reimaged, and the Commonwealth Government's roles and responsibilities were evaluated. In September 1988 the Federal Government released a discussion paper, *Directions for Tourism*, which was designed to generate debate on goals and objectives for government policy. During this time, the idea of a national tourism strategy and a separate department gained momentum, and the Treasurer persuaded the government of the need for an inquiry into the travel and tourism industries.

Following close on the heels of this inquiry was the Industries Assistance Commission Inquiry into Tourism (1988–89). This inquiry was held for three reasons: first, to identify factors constraining tourism's development and how to 'allow tourism to develop to its full potential' (p. 3); second, because of concerns about tourism's rapid growth, it was 'important to consider whether tourism is developing in the best interests of the community' (p. 3); and third, to review the government's role in tourism. The inquiry found that the 'main impediments to the development of tourism and its contribution to the Australian economy lie in the provision of transport services' (p. 4). Transport industries, and particularly air transport, were considered the highest priority areas for change (p. 5). Indeed, the report criticised government ownership of carriers, regulation of competition and infrastructure provision. Air transport needed to be opened up to more carriers and greater competition generally. These proposed reforms were echoed by ATIA (1990).

The growth of tourism and the increasing recognition of its economic, environmental and social effects had stimulated much public sector debate about tourism and the development of strategic directions.

7.5 *T*OURISM POLICY AND ADMINISTRATION, 1991–96

The ATC's budget was reduced by approximately 3 per cent from approximately $38.2 million (1988–89) to $36.9 million (1989–90). However, soon after, the tourism industry received good news when the Commonwealth Department of Tourism was created in December 1991. The department was established in order to advise the Minister for Tourism. It worked to formulate and implement government policies and programs that would 'encourage the tourism industry to take up opportunities for industry development; and reduce constraints on and impediments to, industry development' (DoT 1992: 3). At the same time and for the next four years, the Commonwealth Government discharged direct responsibilities for tourism, via the Minister for Tourism, through three main administrative units: the Department of Tourism, the Bureau of Tourism Research (BTR) and the Australian Tourist Commission (ATC). These bodies had different roles and functions and varied considerably in the length of time they had been established.

■ 7.5.1 The *Australian Tourist Commission*

The Australian Tourist Commission was established as a department by the Commonwealth Government in 1967. It became a statutory authority, established under the Australian Tourist Commission Act, in 1987. Its prime task was to market Australia overseas as a tourist destination. The ATC was governed by a board of directors from private enterprise and was directly responsible to the Minister for Tourism. Over the course of its life, the ATC's board usually comprised 7 to 10 members appointed by the minister.

After the Australian Government Inquiry into Tourism (widely referred to as the Kennedy Inquiry) in 1986, the ATC's charter was revised to specify the following mission: 'to market Australia overseas for the economic benefit of all Australians in a way that enhances the quality of the visitor experience and preserves Australia's natural and social environment (ATC 1992: 10). That mission was later revised to: 'We promote Australia internationally to become the chosen destination for overseas visitors for the economic and social benefit of all Australians' (ATC 1999). The ATC's principal objectives were:
• to increase the number of visitors to Australia
• to maximise the benefits to Australia from overseas visitors, and
• to ensure that Australia is protected from adverse environmental and social impacts of tourism.

By the late 1990s, the ATC promoted Australia in more than 40 countries from its Sydney head office and offices in Los Angeles, Hong Kong, Singapore, Taipei, Shanghai, Seoul, Tokyo, London, Frankfurt and Auckland. The ATC's marketing activities focus on consumer advertising on television and in print, the Internet, consumer promotions, public relations (e.g. a visiting journalists' scheme), information programs and customer servicing, and the coordination of Australian industry participation in international trade events. The ATC played a lead role in trade marketing development and retail travel agent education programs and contributed to government and industry policies affecting tourism. Most recently, the ATC has focused on maximising tourism opportunities related to such major events as the Sydney 2000 Olympic Games by way of media programs and alliances with global marketing partners (ATC 1999). Table 7.4 (pp. 242–3) highlights the objectives, strategies and outcomes concerning ATC activities for 1998–99.

■ **Table 7.4** *The ATC's objectives, strategies and outcomes, 1998–99*

STATUTORY OBJECTIVES	OUTCOME INDICATORS	STRATEGIES	OUTCOMES
To increase the number of visitors to Australia from overseas	Change in number of visitor arrivals Change in Australia's market share in all countries where the ATC is actively marketing	Reinforce and expand the positioning of Australia through the development of Brand Australia, integrated public relations, promotional activities and tactical campaigns Convert interest in Australia into actual travel through a range of conversion programs including referrals, tactical programs and publications	Visitor arrivals increased by 1.6 per cent to 4.3 million in 1998–99 Australia gained market share in 17 of 25 countries or regions where the ATC is actively marketing
To maximise the benefits to Australia from overseas visitors	Change in total visitor expenditure in Australia by overseas visitors Change in average visitor expenditure in Australia by overseas visitors Change in total visitor nights in Australia by overseas visitors Change in geographic dispersal of overseas visitors	Utilise Partnership Australia as a vehicle for segment and market development and a mechanism for achieving dispersal and yield objectives Incorporate new destinations and new products that match market needs into tactical and other activities Access and target new or changing market segments that produce greater yield and/or dispersal of tourists throughout Australia. Inform, encourage and assist identified decision-makers in the Meetings, Incentives, Conventions and Exhibitions (MICE) segment to promote Australia as a desired MICE destination	Total visitor expenditure by overseas visitors rose by 7.3 per cent since 1997 to more than $16 billion An increase of 10.5 per cent in average visitor expenditure by overseas visitors over 1997 More than 100 million visitor nights in Australia by overseas visitors, representing an annual increase of 9.3 per cent Decrease in geographic dispersal (travel beyond the top eight tourist regions) of overseas by 0.4 per cent between 1997 and 1998

STATUTORY OBJECTIVES	OUTCOME INDICATORS	STRATEGIES	OUTCOMES
To ensure that Australia is protected from adverse environmental and social effects of international tourism	Level of awareness by overseas visitors of the need to care for Australia's natural environment

Level of acceptance by the Australian community of international tourist arrivals

Change in Australians' attitudes to tourism as measured by on-going quantitative research | Responsible strategic marketing that gives consideration to the impact of the tourism marketing strategy on the natural and social environment

Contribution, in partnership with industry and government, to the development of a national approach to the management of the relationship between tourism and the environment in Australia

Education and awareness-raising about tourism and the environment

Working with a range of government agencies and industry partners to raise the level of awareness by overseas visitors of the need to care for Australia's natural environment | The number of environment-related pages accessed on the ATC's internet site (australia.com) increased by 521 per cent between 1997–98 and 1998–99.

A 93 per cent level of acceptance by the Australian community of the desirability of international tourists visiting Australia

A 94 per cent level of recognition of the net benefits of inbound tourism as measured by on-going quantitative research

With industry partners, produced tour operator, travel agency and tour wholsaler environment manuals, *Being Green Keeps You Out of the Red* and *Being Green is Your Business* |

Source: *ATC 1999: 5–6.*

From the 1970s, concerns had been raised about the ATC's activities and outcomes. Indeed, government support for the ATC was also challenged during the 1989 Industries Assistance Commission inquiry. In its draft report, the IAC suggested that government funding be withdrawn and that the tourist industry assume responsibility for promoting Australia internationally. The former Australian Tourist Industry Association responded with the claims that:

> Should government funding be withdrawn from the ATC, there would be substantial under-promotion of Australia as a tourist destination. Moreover, the problem of lack of contributions from industry cannot be overcome by imposing levies as in the case of wool, coal and other products. In addition to the practical difficulty of identifying 'tourism producers', industry levies are only feasible where the products are single, identifiable products. In contrast, the tourist industry provides thousands of different services for purchase by tourists. (Grey et al. 1991: 62.)

Dwyer and Forsyth (1992) supported such claims. They indicated that net benefits to Australia would arise from additional expenditure by government on overseas marketing and promotion by the ATC. Their findings, however, were 'highly tentative given uncertainty regarding impacts of promotion expenditure on tourism flows and tourism expenditure' (pp. 24–5). The fact is that existing concepts and theories were — and indeed remain — inadequate for addressing this uncertainty.

These earlier reports, coupled with the ATC's more rigorous accounting procedures and reporting of its objectives, strategies and outcomes, lent considerable justification to government funding of the commission.

In 1998, the Federal Government announced an increase of $50 million in additional funding to the ATC for the period 1998–99 to 2001–02, taking the total investment in that period to $359 million. This funding allowed the commission to explore and enter new markets, to undertake additional activities in existing markets and to increase its alliance with Olympic-related strategies. In 1998–99 the ATC received $89 million, which was complemented by other sources of funding, including $38.3 million in direct investment and $41.2 million from other alliances. Table 7.5 (p. 246) provides a list of some of the new and intensified activities undertaken by the ATC in 1998–99.

■ 7.5.2 The *Bureau of Tourism Research*

The Bureau of Tourism Research (BTR) was established in 1987 in accordance with the recommendations of the Australian Government Inquiry into Tourism. BTR was an agency administered through the Commonwealth Department of Tourism, funded jointly by Commonwealth and state and territory governments. It also derived revenue from data and publications sales and consultancy services provided to a range of clients. BTR's mission was 'to provide independent, accurate, timely and strategically relevant statistics and analyses to the tourism industry, government and the community at large in order to enhance the contribution of tourism to the wellbeing of the Australian community'. Its objectives were:

• to provide a national focus for the collection, analysis and dissemination of tourism and related data

- to provide relevant, timely and high-quality tourism statistics
- to analyse and distribute tourism data in such a way as to encourage their widespread and effective use in tourism industry development
- to undertake or coordinate research on priority issues in the tourism field
- to promote an understanding and awareness of the role of tourism research in the development of Australian tourism.

BTR reported directly to the Minister for Tourism and the Tourism Ministers' Council. An advisory council provided advice on research directions. BTR was now better resourced but still not adequately. The private sector was not in a position to — or did not yet see the worth of — undertaking and coordinating research, which is expensive and restricted, if undertaken by private agencies, and which requires long-term commitment. Projects undertaken by BTR included the International Visitor Surveys (IVS), the Domestic Tourism Monitor, labour force surveys, research into economic impacts of tourism and forecasting international visitor arrivals. It also published such documents as conference proceedings and working papers on a variety of tourism subjects.

■ 7.5.3 The *Commonwealth Department of Tourism*

The Commonwealth Department of Tourism had four broad goals necessary to guide the balanced development of the industry:
- *Economic goal:* to optimise the tourism industry's contribution to national income, employment growth and the balance of payments by creating a favourable economic environment for industry development
- *Environmental goal:* to provide for sustainable tourism development by encouraging responsible planning and management practices consistent with the conservation of our natural and cultural heritage
- *Social goal:* to enhance access to quality tourism experiences and ensure favourable outcomes of tourism by diversifying the product base, raising industry standards and protecting the public interest
- *Support goal:* to provide and encourage the necessary promotional, planning, coordination, research and statistical support to assist the industry's development (Department of Tourism 1992: 3).

For the Department of Tourism: 'A balanced approach to the achievement of these goals is necessary. For example, it would be undesirable to concentrate on attaining high economic returns from industry growth at the expense of long-term environmental degradation of natural attractions. Similarly a preoccupation with protecting the public interest may result in an over-regulated industry structure that stifles economic performance' (Department of Tourism 1992: 3).

The establishment and support of the above three agencies were perhaps the most significant actions of the Commonwealth with regard to tourism since the establishment of the ATC itself almost 25 years earlier. In the *One Nation* statement, the Prime Minister, Paul Keating, announced that 'tourism was one of the economic stars of the '90s' and that 'tourism represented the best opportunity to provide immediate jobs across all skill levels for young Australians' (ATC 1992: 4). He endorsed these comments in the 1993 budget.

■ **Table 7.5**
*New and
intensified
activities of
the ATC,
1998–99*

- Cemented working relationships to gain benefits from Australia's hosting of the 2000 Olympic Games. Alliances generated additional publicity for Australia, estimated to be worth more than $60 million.

- Launched new $150 million Brand Australia promotional campaign, in order to build depth and dimension in the way the world sees Australia. The television campaign associated with this branding will be seen by an estimated 300 million people in 11 countries over three years. Qantas Airways, Ansett Airlines, Singapore Airlines, various sectors of the tourism industry and state tourism authorities have joined the ATC as partners in the campaign. In addition, the ATC and state partners are working together towards cohesive co-branding strategies to ensure that all global communications reflect the shared vision.

- Australia became the first Western nation to be granted Approved Destination Status by China. An ATC office was opened in Shanghai.

- Further development of marketing activities in India and Latin America.

- IT (information technology) identified as central to the future of tourism promotion. After extensive research and planning, the ATC developed a significant and technologically advanced presence on the Internet and is integrating the online environment with all traditional marketing. The ATC appointed its first chief information officer to help in developing and using innovative technology to promote Australia. In 1999 use of the ATC's consumer internet site increased by 161 per cent from 1998. Almost nine million pages of information were delivered to users in 212 countries, an increase of 144 countries in 1998–99. The ATC site is attracting audiences by integrating the website address (www.australia.com) into TV, print and cinema advertising, publications and collateral distributed around the world.

- Appointed a manager to oversee the ATC's worldwide promotion and development of Indigenous tourism.

- Established Team Alliance, an alliance between the ATC and 13 of Australia's convention and visitors bureaux to better promote Australia as a destination for meetings, incentives, conferences and exhibitions.

- ATC's visiting journalists program generated coverage worth an estimated $1 billion in leading newspapers, magazines, radio and television programs. The number of journalists sponsored under the program increased by 36 per cent to 1453 in 1998–99.

- The Australian Tourism Exchange (ATE), a specialist travel trade workshop, is at the forefront of Australian marketing activities, both in Australia and in principal markets overseas. The main aim of ATE is to familiarise international buyers with a vast array of Australian inbound tourism product and to provide the opportunities for existing and new products to be included in overseas tour programs. More than 550 Australian tourism product organisations will be represented at the 2001 ATE. The Australian delegation will be selected to represent a balanced and wide cross-section of organisations with products suitable for the international tourist market. It is expected that approximately

750 international buyers plus overseas representatives of tourism authorities and domestic and international airlines will attend. Fifty leading travel writers representing all market areas will attend ATE and undertake product familiarisation.

- Traveller's Guides are the ATC's primary consumer publication for trade shows and presentations. They highlight the diverse range of holiday opportunities throughout Australia. The guides are used to satisfy responses to the ATC's television, website, radio and press advertising. They are also distributed through travel agents, airline offices, Australian embassies, high commissions and consulates in each market region. More than a million copies a year are distributed, in six separate editions and in 13 languages.

- Trade direct marketing and advertising: the ATC has developed extensive networks of travel agents and wholesalers in all regions with a particular interest in Australia and Australian product. These contacts are available to operators wishing to mail their material directly. Periodic mailings to these lists are also made by the ATC so operators not wanting to do their own mailing have the opportunity to have their brochures included in exclusive ATC brochure collections.

- The 'Tourism Source' is a comprehensive and easy-to-use resource. It is a publication that reaches the key markets of the USA, Europe, the UK, Asia, China, India, South Africa, the South Pacific and the Middle East. It allows agents to access and provide up-to-date information and design complete itineraries clients. It provides a constant, reliable reference for agents and gives Australian operators continuous exposure to major industry players around the globe.

Source: *adapted from ATC 1999: 5–6.*

The 1992 National Tourism Strategy (*Tourism — Australia's Passport to Growth*) had three aims:
1. to provide all levels of government, the industry and other interest groups with a clear statement of the Commonwealth Government's objectives for the future development of the tourism industry
2. to provide a sound basis for the formulation of government tourism policy and industry planning during the 1990s, and
3. to enhance community awareness of the economic, environmental and cultural significance of the tourism industry.

The establishment of an autonomous government department, whose staffing prospered in numbers and experience over a short period, supported by BTR in particular and headed by a highly regarded minister, led to a flurry of policy activity unheralded in Australian tourism. In a period of two to three years the following strategies and programs were launched in direct response to broader Commonwealth goals and responsibilities: Sites of National Tourism Significance Program, National Ecotourism Strategy (and associated National Ecotourism Program), Regional Tourism Development Program (see case study 'A critical assessment of the Regional Tourism Development Program, 1993–94', p. 259), National Rural Tourism Strategy (and associated

Rural Tourism Program), Forest Ecotourism Program, Backpacker Program and Strategy, National Cruise Shipping Strategy, Indigenous Tourism Strategy and Initiatives, Financial Management Manuals (see DoT 1994a).

The Labor Government had embarked on a range of policies and programs to address major industry issues and was prepared to back its priorities with considerable funding. It recognised the importance of addressing the effects of tourism as well as promoting the industry's growth and supported industry-based ideas for self-regulation (see for example the discussion in section 4.6). All looked rather rosy for those working in this increasingly prominent policy arena. The industry was now being consulted on a more regular basis, and close partnerships and networks were developed among the department, BTR, ATC and such interest groups as Tourism Council Australia and Tourism Task Force (later renamed Tourism and Transport Forum).

However, this policy-making activity was soon curtailed.

7.6 TOURISM ADMINISTRATION AND POLICY, 1996–2005

The Department of Tourism was abolished after the Keating Labor Government was defeated at the March federal election. The new Coalition (Liberal–National Party) Government, led by Prime Minister John Howard, has been a committed agent for the privatisation of government business enterprises and the reduction of staffing of many government agencies. This situation is not uncommon and, indeed, the US Government abolished its national tourism agency in that same year (see Planning in Practice: 'Tourism departments live and die and are reborn').

PLANNING IN PRACTICE

Tourism departments live and die and are reborn

On occasion, governments have withdrawn aspects of industry support by abolishing entire tourism departments and corporations (e.g. the Swedish Tourist Board in 1992) or by reducing or terminating their funds (e.g. the United States Travel and Tourism Administration [USTTA] in 1995). Then, as circumstances change, as states and governments revise their roles, or if there is a change of government, the nature or extent of intervention will change. So the discussion of Australia is not an unusual 'case study'. This brief discussion of the USA provides some interesting comparisons.

The US National Tourism Act (1996) alluded to some of the reasons for the abolition of USTTA: lack of resources, a failure to increase the US share of international travel and the idea that the private sector could more effectively manage international travel and tourism promotion at far less cost to taxpayers (Jeffries 2001). The Act nonetheless authorised the Secretary of Commerce to continue several vital federal functions through the National Tourism Office (then Tourism Industries Office). The Act specified the purposes of the new body as to:

- seek and work for an increase in the US share in the global tourism market
- work in conjunction with federal, state and local agencies to develop and implement a coordinated US travel and tourism policy
- advise the President, the Congress and the domestic travel and tourism industry on the implementation of the national travel and tourism strategy and on other matters affecting travel and tourism
- operate travel and tourism promotion programs outside the USA in partnership with the travel and tourism industry in the USA
- establish a travel and tourism data bank to gather and disseminate travel and tourism market data
- conduct market research necessary for effective promotion of the travel and tourism market, and
- promote US travel and tourism, including international trade shows and conferences (United States Code as of 26 January 1998, Section 2141a: United States National Tourism Organization; see also Jeffries 2001: 183–4).

Various functions and resources of the USTTA were therefore transferred to the International Trade Administration in the Department of Commerce, within which the Tourism Industries office was established. The mission of this office was 'to foster an environment in which the US travel and tourism industry can generate jobs through tourism exports' (Gouldner et al. 2000: 109). It was originally staffed by only 12 employees under a Deputy Assistant Secretary and organised into three groups: (1) Deputy Assistant Secretary for Tourism Industries, (2) Tourism Development and (3) Tourism Policy Coordination, including the Tourism Policy Council, which comprises 'nine Federal agencies and the President of the US National Tourism Organisation' (Gouldner et al. 2000: 110–11).

The terrorist attacks of 11 September 2001 severely disrupted international and domestic travel in the USA. Subsequently, there were rushed and determined efforts to recharge the tourism industry. The Tourism Policy Council was revitalised on 29 October 2001. 'The TPC coordinates national policies and programs related to travel and tourism, recreation and national heritage resources that involve federal agencies. The TPC also provides a forum to ensure that US government agencies work together to enhance consumer confidence in the safety and security of travel, while taking into account the needs of tourists and business travellers' (Baker 2002: 3). The US Government, then, dramatically revised its interventionist role because of threats to the industry's sustainability; threats with which the market itself could not cope.

As with previous versions of the tourism portfolio under a Coalition government, the Office of Tourism (akin to a branch), buried within the Department of Industry and Science and then Industry, Science and Tourism (and now Industry, Tourism and Resources), was dramatically restructured (DIST 1997). In 1996–97 the new office had an estimated staff of 88 (compared with 120 in 1995–96), and total outlays had fallen from $23.4 million to $16 million. The Office of National Tourism, responsible for the DIST 'SubProgram' of Tourism, had the objective 'To improve the international competitiveness of Australia's tourism industry by assisting in the development of an economically viable, environmentally sustainable and socially responsible tourism industry' (DIST 1997: 43). Tourism: A Ticket to the 21st Century: National Action Plan for a Competitive Australia was launched by DIST in 1998. The commitment was to a more competitive tourism industry for Australia. The plan's objectives were to:

- optimise tourism employment and investment growth
- develop the potential of new and emerging markets through targeted marketing strategies
- maximise tourism opportunities from major events, such as the Sydney 2000 Olympic Games, the Centenary of Federation and international expositions
- remove unnecessary regulatory and other impediments to industry growth
- encourage the development of efficient and competitive transport networks
- foster regional tourism development
- enhance industry standards and skill levels
- encourage the conservation of Australia's unique natural and cultural heritage
- encourage diversification of the industry's product base, and
- reinforce Australia's image as a safe and friendly destination.

Hall (1998: 93) has argued that 'the general thrust of the Commonwealth role has been consistent since the inquiry into tourism in the mid-1980s. The inquiry argued that the roles for the Commonwealth should be to encourage and improve the range of tourism opportunities in Australia, develop a viable and efficient industry and conserve the natural and cultural environments.' Although Hall offered DIST's objectives as a centre-piece to demonstrate these links and similarities, the argument holds little water and sheds little light. Objectives are one thing, but how these objectives are interpreted and implemented or sought are indeed another. The Coalition Government has embarked on a scheme for tourism policy-making and implementation somewhat different from that of its predecessor, the Hawke and Keating Labor Government.

■ 7.6.1 The *White Paper*

In 2003–04, the Australian Government published the Tourism White Paper, a document that spelled out profound structural public administration shifts for national tourism policy and planning. The paper began with the usual planning refrain: tourism's economic significance, its importance to regional development, the need for sustained growth and the promise of government commitment. The key administrative reforms were the abolition of former agencies (Australian Tourist Commission, See Australia (recall the Go See Australia campaign of the 1970s — see section 7.3), the Bureau of Tourism Research and the Tourism Forecasting Council) and their merging to create Tourism Australia.

PLANNING IN PRACTICE

The Tourism White Paper

The new strategy for tourism in Australia developed by the Howard Government was part of its 2001 election commitment. The first stage in the development of the strategy was the release of a discussion paper, *The 10-year Plan for Tourism*, on 2 May 2002. More than 55 000 copies of the plan were distributed to interested parties. After its release, extensive consultations were held with public and private sector stakeholders. More than 275 submissions were received.

The subsequent Green Paper was launched on Thursday 5 June 2003. The Green Paper was developed to maximise tourism's long-term contribution to Australian society, and it was argued that the industry needed to develop in an environmentally sustainable manner while meeting the needs of local communities, including Indigenous Australians.

The main vision of the Green Paper was 'to have an internationally competitive and sustainable tourism industry that utilises the rich diversity of our land and people, to the benefit of all'. The key themes that guided the Tourism Green Paper were:

- diversification of Australia from a travel destination to a lifetime experience
- diversification of the Australia tourism product
- focus on business yield and niche markets
- enhancing business profitability to better position the industry against volatility and global uncertainty, and
- improving asset utilisation and coordination across public and private sectors.

A major strategic objective of the Tourism Green Paper was to increase both domestic and international tourism. Domestic travel in Australia currently comprises about 80 per cent of regional tourist flows, and it was forecast that inbound travel to regional areas would also increase. Hence it was considered vital that effective marketing strategies and suitable infrastructure and facilities be made available to domestic and international visitors to regional areas. The strategic options proposed in this Green Paper had a strong focus on tourism growth in rural and regional Australia.

The Tourism Green Paper also employed the Platinum Plus (or primary destination/product) concept. A Platinum Plus destination was defined as a destination that has high-quality tourism products, able to compete with the best in the world. Not only were these products valuable destinations or icons but also they could value add to niche markets such as education-based travel, Indigenous

(continued)

tourism, special interest tourism, ecotourism and cultural tourism. A Platinum Plus approach was considered necessary to achieve sustainable growth in the tourism sector, to diversify tourism product and experiences, to encourage growth and support niche markets and to facilitate effective international and domestic branding, marketing and promotion.

Perhaps most significantly, the Tourism Green Paper proposed a major reform of Australia's tourism institutional arrangements and administrative frameworks. It proposed to:

- merge the Australian Tourism Commission and See Australia to enhance promotional partnerships and improve coordination between international and domestic marketing activities, and
- call the new unit Australian Tourism, within which there would be a tourism events group, Australian Tourism Events (ATE). ATE would provide opportunities for Australian Tourism to promote and use strategic events to offset seasonal variations in demand and promote return visits. Amalgamating See Australia and the Australia Tourism Commission could provide an opportunity to develop more coordinated and comprehensive contingency plans and strategic directions when unexpected events such as terrorist attacks or natural disasters affected tourism activity.

Following the release of the Tourism Green Paper, feedback was obtained from 19 consultation sessions held around the country as well as 155 written responses from diverse interests, including private industry interests, the conservation lobby, academics, government departments and state and territory tourism authorities.

On 20 November 2003 the Australian Government launched its Tourism White Paper: *A Medium to Long Term Strategy for Tourism*. The Prime Minister himself was heavily engaged in the launch. The government's new investment in tourism amounted to funding of more than $500 million over four and a half years. The government announced the much-anticipated establishment of Tourism Australia, which encompassed the functions of the Australian Tourism Commission, See Australia, the Tourism Forecasting Council and the Bureau of Tourism Research. Tourism Australia was established by the *Tourism Australia Act 2004* and the *Tourism Australia (Repeal and Transitional Provisions) Act 2004*. Within Tourism Australia, two new units were created: Tourism Events Australia and Tourism Research Australia. The main mission of Tourism Australia was to boost international marketing, stimulate growth in domestic tourism, particularly in regional areas, and pursue structural initiatives to assist in the growth of tourism in Australia over the next 10 years. This new agency:

will vigorously market a revitalised Brand Australia in key global markets. It will leverage international and domestic promotion of Australia through strategic partnerships with State and Territory marketing bodies and industry. It will also assist in the attraction of major events to Australia and assist growth of business tourism. It will conduct an expanded range of research and analysis tailored to meet government and market needs. It will focus resources on analysing and disseminating trends in global and domestic tourism to help with strategic planning, including for regional tourism. It will develop strategies to promote growth in the domestic tourism industry and encourage regional dispersal of international tourists. (Australian Government 2003: ix.)

While continuing with traditional international promotion activities of the ATC, Tourism Australia has also been charged with substantial domestic tourism responsibilities, including helping to stimulate growth in domestic tourism. It is interesting that Tourism Australia's functions include working with regional and local tourism operators to support regional tourism marketing and development when the states already do so, and indeed many provide substantial funding to regional organisations. Regional tourism organisations are state-based institutions, which could be terminated at a state government's whim by withdrawal of funding (see Jenkins & Dredge 2000). The duplication of responsibilities in this regard will be an aspect of tourism policy worth observing in the next few years.

Finally, it is perhaps worth noting that the name of Tourism Australia was not at all new. Recommendation 17 in the Report of the Australian Government Inquiry into Tourism (1986: 8) stated: 'That the formal title "Australian Tourist Commission" be retained but that the title "Tourism Australia" be adopted as a trading name for all commercial activities' (also see p. 113). Old ideas are sometimes presented as new ones, but often history is repeated in some interesting ways, which just goes to show that the 'garbage can model of policy-making' is alive and well in the field of tourism (see section 6.4.2). Incidentally, the Australian Government paid $201 000 ($175 000 plus GST and other costs) to Graeme Haycraft, a former Australian Tourism Export Council and ATC employee, for the tourismaustralia.com domain name. Haycraft had registered the name in 2000.

Source: *John Jenkins and Nicole Travis*

Immediately after the release of the Tourism White Paper, the Tourism and Transport Forum, a key interest group (see table 2.1 and section 4.7), agreed with the proposed changes to the government policy and administration and worked closely with the Department of Tourism in the successful implementation of the White Paper and the Tourism Australia Bill that followed (see Tourism Australia www.tourism.australia.com/AboutUs.asp?lang=EN&sub =0304 for up-to-date information on the Tourism White Paper and its implementation). Generally, it seems, the tourism industry (based on submissions over the last few years) has a high regard for Tourism Australia as a new administrative arrangement for federal tourism policy-making. However, if history is any guide, it will not be too long before there is an inquiry into its structures, functions and operations.

Whole-of-government approaches to tourism are a feature of the Tourism White Paper. Getting departments and other agencies to 'speak to each other' and coordinate their activities is a critical issue in efficient and effective use of government resources. One example of this approach is the Memorandum of Understanding (MoU) between the Australian Trade Commission (Austrade) and the ATC. Austrade provides an avenue for greater exposure and penetration into markets where the ATC would not normally direct promotional efforts. In this way, Austrade attempts to attract overseas business for Australian products and so reduce 'the time, cost and risk involved in selecting, entering and developing international markets' (Vaile & Hockey 2004).

The 1986 Australian Government Inquiry into Tourism lamented the lack of a 'coordinated tourism framework which would encourage an integration of the efforts of a wide range of tourism related interests' and stated that the 'concept of a national tourism policy is not a new one' (Report of the Australian Government Inquiry into Tourism 1986: 58–9). A recommendation (no. 8, on p. 7) in the Report of the Australian Government Inquiry into Tourism (1986) stated: 'That the Commonwealth develop and adopt as a matter of immediate priority, a National Tourism Policy after consultation with State/Territories, industry and relevant Government departments to provide a strategic, coordinated framework to maximise industry growth and to resolve constraints to that growth while developing a quality tourism product' (see also p. 60). It took 25 years of jostling and dancing among stakeholders before the 1992 National Tourism Strategy was launched, yet for all the effort and resources invested it lasted four years. Australia has now had three markedly different strategies initiated in little more than a decade (1992–2003, with various discussion papers and Green Papers in between), which raises questions about policy learning and policy continuity amid changing government priorities. Funding to tourism has been inconsistent and often reactive, and the commitment to consolidated institutional arrangements and administrative frameworks for tourism has wavered. Governments still struggle to address the complexity of the tourism arrangements and the unique nature of policy-making in a federal system. The constant state of flux here should attract greater research attention. The issue of coordination remains elusive, while environmental management and the cultural and social effects are now neglected aspects of tourism planning and policy-making by tourism agencies as their foci has turned to economic growth. The present Commonwealth Government has a now well-established history of meddling in state and local development affairs and supporting projects that clearly impact negatively on sensitive environments.

The future for government support of the tourism industry in the short term is quite promising from research and marketing and promotion perspectives. The Federal Government also funds the Sustainable Tourism Cooperative Research Centre (STCRC), based at Griffith University and involving a partnership of many universities and industry-based collaborators across Australia, although questions must surely soon emerge about the value, relevance and effectiveness of some of its programs and publications.

The Howard Government has allocated enormous resources to 'the industry' (public sector agencies, Sustainable Tourism CRC, reactive measures to mitigate the effects of international events) and provided many avenues and programs for its development. However, for all this funding, the question must be raised of whether this government is adequately fulfilling important roles in the area of market failure in tourism discussed earlier in this book (e.g. in section 4.6). Choy (1991: 328–9) sees three major types of market failure relevant to tourism planning and policy: collective consumption of parks, highways, beaches and historic sites; the external effects on persons not directly involved in an activity (e.g. aircraft noise, congestion, pollution, crowding, resort construction, which impedes local residents' access to coastlines and other resources); benefits and costs 'which are not reflected in market prices such as the value of open space, costs of social impacts and benefits of environmental preservation' (p. 329). Given the discussion in earlier chapters (e.g. self-regulation, accreditation, privatisation, deregulation), there are valid concerns that the Howard Government is neglecting many key aspects of market failure in pursuit of international free trade, economic growth and efficient use of resources.

SUMMARY OF KEY TERMS

Australian Standing Committee on Tourism

Australian Standing Committee on Tourism (ASCOT) is the administrative framework through which senior tourism officers discuss tourism operations matters. Any decisions taken by ASCOT must be forwarded to TMC. ASCOT meets twice a year, and its aim 'is to improve co-operation and coordination of Government policies and activities as they affect tourism'. ASCOT's membership includes Australian federal, state and territory representatives, the New Zealand Minister for Tourism, and Tourism Australia and Tourism Research Australia representatives.

Federal system

Federal systems of government are those in which sovereignty is constitutionally divided between at least two levels of government and no single level has power over the other levels. Examples of federal systems include Australia, Canada, the United States, Germany and Switzerland.

New federalism

In the Australian context, 'new federalism' refers to efforts to work more closely and cooperatively and to address overlapping and countervailing policy initiatives between sovereign levels of government.

Tourism Ministers' Council

Tourism Ministers' Council was established in 1976 as a means of coordinating and facilitating the development of tourism policy. It meets once annually and includes the relevant portfolio ministers from Australia's federal, state and territory governments as well as the New Zealand Government. Norfolk Island and Papua New Guinea representatives have an observer status.

QUESTIONS

1 Why might developing a national tourism policy be so difficult for federal governments?

2 Why do national tourism policies lead such short lives?

3 What was the main thrust of the Whitlam Government's commitments to tourism? What do you think of the leisure-based thrust that Whitlam gave to tourism?

4 What were the key themes in the 1992 National Tourism Strategy?

5 Why might we speculate that the Howard Government is priming the tourism industry for its intentions to shed responsibility for Tourism Australia and seek to privatise that agency or abolish it altogether?

6 Select one of the national tourism strategies or policies launched in 1992 or 2003. Critically assess the content of that policy. What are its key themes, priorities and areas for action?

7 To what extent should governments meddle in (a) domestic marketing and promotion and (b) international marketing and promotion? Should the Australian Government leave international tourism promotion to private industry and abolish the ATC?

8 Discuss the major positive and negative externalities that you have observed in a tourist destination of your choice.

EXERCISES

1 Refer to the Tourism Australia website: www.tourism.australia.com/AboutUs.asp?lang=EN&sub=0354. List the board members of Tourism Australia, profile them and research their backgrounds. Does anything about their political or industry backgrounds strike you as being important or noteworthy? Is a former Labor government minister ever likely to be appointed to a position similar to that filled by the former Deputy Prime Minister, Tim Fischer, under a Coalition government?

2 Parliamentarians such as John Brown and Bruce Baird have occupied senior ministerial portfolios with respect to tourism (Baird has in fact been a member of Coalition governments at state and federal levels). Trace their backgrounds through media and Internet searches. Discuss other roles they have filled, particularly with regard to their associations with tourism industry associations and pressure groups.

chapter review

Australian Government 2003, *A Medium to Long Term Strategy for Tourism: The Future View of Australian Tourism,* **Tourism White Paper, viewed 7 April 2006, www.tourism.australia.com/AboutUs.asp?sub=0304.**

Carroll, P et al. 1990, *Tourism in Australia,* **Harcourt Brace Jovanovich, Sydney.** This book contains a series of excellent discussions concerning Australian tourism policies in the 1970s and 1980s. Highly recommended.

Craik, J 1991a, *Resorting to Tourism: Cultural Policies for Tourist Development in Australia,* **Allen & Unwin, St Leonards, NSW.**

—— **1991b,** *Government Promotion of Tourism: The Role of the Queensland Tourist and Travel Corporation,* **Research Paper No. 20, Centre for Australian Public Sector Management, Griffith University, Brisbane.** Each of these sources provide compelling accounts of tourism policy and planning in Queensland.

Department of Industry, Tourism and Resources 2003, *A Medium to Long Term Strategy for Tourism,* **Tourism Green Paper, viewed 7 April 2006, www.industry.gov.au/content/itrinternet/cmscontent.cfm?objectid= 6CAA3E62-D2DF-4340-9F4AA9CC6563504C&searchID=74517.**

Department of Industry, Tourism and Resources, viewed 1 November 2005, www.industry.gov.au/content/itrinternet/cmsindexpagecfm?objectid= 48A3400C-20E0–68D8-ED0D0548296A04E7.

Department of Tourism 1992, *Tourism — Australia's Passport to Growth: A National Tourism Strategy,* **DoT, Canberra.**

Hall, CM 1998, *Introduction to Tourism in Australia: Development, Dimensions and Issues,* **3rd edn, Longman, Melbourne.** This text or any of its predecessors and later editions will provide useful overviews of contemporary government and public policy issues in Australia This is one of the leading introductory texts.

Jeffries, D 1999, *Governments and Tourism,* **Butterworth Heinemann, Oxford.** This book places Australian policy developments in a broader international context than can be done here.

Jenkins, JM & Sorensen, AD 1996, 'Tourism, regional development and the Commonwealth: A critical appraisal of the regional tourism development program', *Australian Leisure,* **vol. 7, no. 4, pp. 28–35.** This article (on which the chapter's case study is based) also discusses the issue of pork-barrelling as governments invest resources in an effort to sway voters.

Parliament Australia, www.aph.gov.au/parl.htm, and **Australia Now, www.dfat.gov.au/facts/sys_gov.html (both viewed 28 April 2006).** Excellent descriptions of the structure and features of Australian government, from the Constitution to relations between governments to disclosure of donations to political parties.

Richardson, J 1999, *A History of Australian Travel and Tourism,* **Hospitality Press, Melbourne.** Contains some excellent historical material for case studies but is a little thin on conceptual and theoretical interpretations of policy and planning.

Whitfield, M, Bell, B & Watkins, M 2001, 'Indigenous tourism policy in Australia: 25 years of rhetoric and economic rationalism', *Current Issues in Tourism*, **vol. 4, no. 2–4, pp. 151–81.** Provides an extensive account of national and Queensland ATSI tourism policy initiatives in the period 1979 to 1995.

chapter review

A critical assessment of the Regional Tourism Development Program, 1993–94

As part of its commitment to regional Australia, the former Federal Labor Government (1983–96) established a number of programs, including the Regional Tourism Development Program (RTDP), to ensure that the community as a whole benefited from the growth in the tourism industry (Department of Tourism 1993a, 1993b, 1994a). The department's program was representative of wider government industry policies that place increasingly less reliance on resource industries and seek to capitalise on the 'transition from a "goods producing economy" to a "service-providing" one' (Jones 1983: 34; Craik 1991b). The traditional promotion of secondary and resource industries had given way to the promotion of service industries, including tourism, in state and federal industry policies (Warhurst 1986, in Craik 1991b).

In the 1993–94 federal budget, the Federal Government allocated $23 million over four years to the RTDP as part of a wider $42 million strategy to improve the capacity and ability of regional Australia to attract international and domestic tourists (DoT 1993a, 1993b, 1994a). The Department of Tourism asserted that responsible planning and management practices can assist regional areas to develop tourism opportunities that guarantee long-term employment and sustainable tourism businesses. Grants under the RTDP aimed to assist such efforts and, simultaneously, diversify the product base, raise industry standards and protect the public interest (DoT 1993b).

Only local governments, regional tourism associations and regional development organisations were eligible to apply for RTDP funding. In an attempt to measure program performance, successful applicants were required to forward management and accounting reports to the department during the project. On completion of the project and for three years thereafter, grant recipients were required to demonstrate the effectiveness of their projects with respect to rates of tourist visitation and tourist spending and the effects on tourism employment and investment in the region. The program guidelines required that projects should have 'the capacity to become self-supporting' (DoT 1993b).

In the 1993–94 (first) round of the RTDP, the DoT received 524 applications, of which 119 were eliminated because the organisation applying for the grant was considered ineligible (which reflected poor skills and knowledge in applying for grants, and the department sought to address this problem in later rounds and years). The department reviewed internally the remaining applications over a three-month period (November 1993 to February 1994). The

(continued)

applications were never made available for public scrutiny as they were submitted as 'commercial in confidence'. According to one DoT officer, as part of the department's attempt to 'assess the economic viability of the projects, we [the Department of Tourism] did ask applicants to provide us with any sort of statistics they could on multiplier effects of the project ... That's a difficult thing for them to do; not many people were geared up to do it. *In fact, only one application in 524 last year did that to any degree of satisfaction* [author's emphasis] ... it was successful' (anon. pers. comm., Officer A, DoT 1995).

The final decision concerning funding recipients rested with the Minister for Tourism, who was furnished with a list of 'Highly Recommended' applications (27 applications were allocated to this category), 'Medium Recommended' (44), 'Lowly Recommended' (108) and 'Not Recommended' (226) (anon. pers. comm., Officer A, DoT 1995). All 27 'Highly Recommended' applications and 22 of 44 from the 'Medium Recommended' list received funding. 'We had to ... agree on a suitable comparative merit assessment short-listing and we did that in consultation with the minister' (anon. pers. comm., Officer A, DoT 1995). For example, where projects were of equal merit, higher priority was afforded that project with the higher proportional outside funding, whether in cash or in kind (anon. pers. comm., Officer A, DoT 1995).

Projects favoured were:

- projects that contributed to attracting to regions a larger share of the international market or contributed to diverting outbound tourists to the domestic market
- projects in regions where there was demonstrated tourism growth potential, with preference being given to regions outside capital cities
- projects that had a demonstration effect or that provided regional tourism development models with potential national application, and particularly those that included:
  - integrated planning and development, and
  - innovative approaches to planning and development, where new types of practices, products and technology could be trialled to assess their effectiveness
- projects that would provide benefits beyond their immediate locality, were part of a regional strategic plan and/or involved cooperation of a number of local areas within an identified region
- projects with the capacity to become self-supporting
- projects with significant cooperative contributions in cash or in kind (DoT 1993b).

The RTDP greatly expanded the scope for Commonwealth involvement with all sorts of local infrastructure and facilities and muddied the division of responsibilities between the Commonwealth and the states. The Commonwealth was funding regional development strategies, walking tracks, tourist information centres, viewing platforms, trails and regional signage (DoT 1994b). Obvious infrastructure projects of national significance or benefit where the Commonwealth has a legitimate role include the national rail network, satellite systems, the national power grid and the telephone network. What national benefits arise from walking tracks, signposting and regional tourism development strategies? As a matter of principle these limited projects are best left to the states and the community concerned.

It seems also that the Commonwealth expected several of the projects to fail. One senior DoT officer (anon. pers. comm., Officer A, DoT 1995) commented: 'Not all projects will be as successful as we'd like, but we're working pretty hard to make sure they at least get over the line.'

There are many problems associated with programs like the RTDP. However, such programs probably appeal to government for several reasons, including:

- They are relatively cheap (they ranged from about $15 000 to around $500 000, but many were in the range of $30 000 to $150 000). This is just as well if their outcomes are problematical. Thus governments cannot be accused of wasting much money.
- Such key political constituencies as environmental groups can be assuaged by targeting environmentally sensitive areas for interpretation and other programs.
- They have moderate political visibility in that (1) politicians make announcements that are widely reported and (2) communities get the impression of significant activity (even if there is very little).
- Community leaders have a fair chance of landing a funded project, which keeps them reasonably happy. They are also kept busy making grant applications.
- Funds expended can be magnified through matching funds raised at the community level. Governments could therefore get more credit than they deserve.
- It might be preferable to allocate funds to economically successful localities through a bidding process. Such places are less likely than economically static or declining regions to waste the funding or could well yield a higher return on public investment.

Of course one might question whether the cost of the process outweighs the funding distributed. The administrative complexity of the RTDP suggests that it costs more to administer some projects than the money received.

Source: *Jenkins & Sorensen 1996.*

Questions

1 Briefly describe the RTDP and compare it with the more recent regional development programs of the Commonwealth Government.

2 Should federal governments be concerned with the development of minor tourist infrastructure such as walking tracks and road signage?

3 In your view, is it fair to say that governments invest resources in some regions because they might be able to help attract votes, especially in marginal seats?

4 List and describe three major infrastructural projects in which the Commonwealth Government could invest to the benefit of the tourism industry.

5 Why might departmental officers involved in assessing grant applications and dispensing funding to applicants believe that some projects will inevitably fail?

References

Craik, J 1991, *Government Promotion of Tourism: The Role of the Queensland Tourist and Travel Corporation*, Research Paper No. 20, Centre for Australian Public Sector Management, Griffith University, Brisbane.

Department of Tourism 1993a, *Talking Tourism*, Sept–Oct, DoT, Canberra.

—— 1993b, *Regional Tourism Development Program 1993–94*: Guidelines, Application Form, Conditions of Grant, DoT, Canberra.

—— 1994, *Tourism Assistance Guide: Commonwealth Government Programs and Initiatives for the Tourism Industry*, September, DoT, Canberra.

REFERENCES

Australian Bureau of Statistics 1986, *Year Book of Australia*, ABS, Canberra.

—— 1990, *Overseas Arrivals and Departures*, Cat. No. 340200, ABS, Canberra.

Australian Government Committee of Inquiry into Tourism 1986, *Report of the Australian Government Inquiry into Tourism*, vol. 1, AGPS, Canberra.

Australian Tourist Commission 1992, *Annual Report 1991/92*, ATC, Sydney.

—— 1993, *Australia*, ATC, Sydney.

—— 1995, *Partnership Australia: Information for Australian Tourism Operators*, ATC, Sydney.

—— 1999, *Annual Report, 1998/99*, ATC, Sydney.

Australian Tourism Industry Association 1990, *ATIA's Strategy for the 1990s*, ATIA.

Baker, D 2002, 'Helping the tourism industry recover', Export America, viewed 7 April 2006, www.export.gov/exportamerica/NewOpportunities/no_tourismrecov.pdf.

Bonyhady, T 1993, *Places Worth Keeping: Conservationists, Politics and Law*, Allen & Unwin, St Leonards, NSW.

Brown, J 1983, *Tourism gets Australia Going*, Address by the Honourable John Brown, Minister for Sport, Recreation and Tourism, to the National Press Club, 26 September, AGPS, Canberra.

Bureau of Tourism Research 1989, *Tourism Data Card*, BTR, Canberra.

Carroll, P 1991, 'The Federal Government and tourism', in P Carroll et al. (eds), *Tourism in Australia*, Harcourt Brace, Sydney, pp. 68–81.

Choy, D 1991, 'Tourism planning: The case for "market failure" ', *Tourism Management*, December, pp. 313–30.

Coombs, HC 1973, *Review of the Continuing Expenditure of the Previous Government* (Report of the Task Force Appointed by the Prime Minister), June, AGPS, Canberra.

Craik, J 1991, *Resorting to Tourism: Cultural Policies for Tourist Development in Australia*, Allen & Unwin, St Leonards, NSW.

Department of the Arts, Sport, the Environment, Tourism and Territories 1989, *Annual Report 1988–89*, vol. 1, DASETT, AGPS, Canberra.

Department of Industry and Commerce 1976, *Annual Report*, DIC, AGPS, Canberra.

—— 1977, *Annual Report*, DIC, AGPS, Canberra.

—— 1978, *Annual Report*, DIC, AGPS, Canberra.

Department of Industry, Science and Tourism 1997, *Commonwealth Department of Industry, Science and Tourism Annual Report, 1996–97*, DIST, Canberra.

—— 1998, *Tourism: A Ticket to the 21st Century*, DIST, Canberra.

Department of Tourism 1992, *Tourism: Australia's Passport to Growth*, A National Tourism Strategy, DoT, Canberra.

—— 1994, *Regional Development Branch 1993–94 Grants by State* (internal document), DoT, Canberra.

Department of Tourism and Recreation 1973, *Development of Tourism in Australia*, DTR, Canberra.

Dwyer, L & Forsyth, P 1992, *The Case for Tourism Promotion: An Economic Analysis*, Discussion Paper No. 265, Centre for Economic Policy Research, Australian National University, Canberra.

Fagan, RH & Webber, M 1994, *Global Restructuring: The Australian Experience*, Oxford University Press, Melbourne.

Faulkner, HW 1990, 'Swings and roundabouts in Australian tourism', *Tourism Management*, March, pp. 29–37.

Gilpin, A 1980, *Environment Policy in Australia*, University of Queensland Press, St Lucia.

Gouldner, C, Brent Ritchie, JR & McIntosh, RW 2000, *Tourism: Principles, Practices, Philosophies*, John Wiley & Sons, New York.

Grey, P, Edelman, K & Dwyer, L 1991, *Tourism in Australia: Challenges and Opportunities*, Longman Cheshire, Melbourne.

Grinlinton, D 1990, 'The "environmental era" and the emergence of "environmental law" in Australia: A survey of environmental legislation and litigation 1967–87', *Environmental Planning and Law Journal*, vol. 7, pp. 74–105.

Hall, CM 1998, *Introduction to Tourism in Australia: Development, Dimensions and Issues*, 3rd edn, Longman, Melbourne.

Hall, CM, Jenkins, JM & Kearsley, GW (eds) 1997, *Tourism Planning and Policy in Australia and New Zealand: Cases, Issues and Practice*, Irwin/ McGraw-Hill, Sydney.

Hansards (Senate: Economics Legislation Committee) 2004, Budget Estimates, 31 May, viewed 4 November 2005, www.aph.gov.au/hansard/ senate/committee/S7638.pdf.

Harris, Kerr, Forster & Stanton, Robbins & Co. 1965, *Australia's Travel and Tourist Industry*, Australian National Travel Association, Sydney.

Horgan, J 1991, 'The private sector and government: WADC an agenda for change', in A Peachment (ed.), *The Business of Government: Western Australia 1983–1990*, Federation Press, Leichhardt, NSW.

Industries Assistance Commission 1989, *Travel and Tourism*, Report No. 423, 29 September, AGPS, Canberra.

Jeffries, D 2001, *Governments and Tourism*, Butterworth-Heinemann, Oxford.

Jenkins, J & Dredge, D 2000, 'Away from the city', *Australian Leisure Management*, vol. 19, no. 1, pp. 60–2.

Jenkins, JM & Sorensen, AD 1996, 'Tourism, regional development and the commonwealth: A critical appraisal of the regional tourism development program', *Australian Leisure*, vol. 7, no. 4, pp. 28–35.

Jones, B 1983, 'Industry and development', in J Reeves & K Thomson (eds), *Labor Essays 1983*, Drummond, Blackburn, Vic.

Leiper, N 1980, 'An interdisciplinary study of Australian tourism: its scope, characteristics and consequences, with particular reference to government policies since 1965', unpublished Master of General Studies thesis, University of New South Wales, Kensington, NSW.

Mercer, DC 1991, *A Question of Balance: Natural Resources Conflict Issues in Australia*, Federation Press, Leichhardt, NSW.

Organization for Economic Co-operation and Development 1973, *Tourism Policy and International Tourism in OECD Member Countries*, OECD.

Pearce, PL, Morrison, AM & Rutledge, JL 1998, *Tourism: Bridges Across Continents*, McGraw-Hill, Sydney.

Richardson, J 1999, *A History of Australian Travel and Tourism*, Hospitality Press, Melbourne.

Senate Standing Committee on Environment, Recreation and the Arts 1992, *The Australian Environment and Tourism Report*, Senate Standing Committee on Environment, Recreation and the Arts, Parliament of the Commonwealth of Australia, AGPS, Canberra.

Vaile, M & Hockey, J 2004, joint media release, 'Austrade and ATC agree on integrated tourism plan', 17 March, viewed 1 February 2006, www.trademinister.gov.au/releases/2004/mvt_joint_hockey_170304html.

Whitford, M, Bell, B & Watkins, M 2001, 'Indigenous tourism policy in Australia: 25 years of rhetoric and economic rationalism', *Current Issues in Tourism*, vol. 4, no. 2–4, pp. 151–81.

Whitlam, G 1972, 'It's time for leadership: Australian Labor Party policy speech delivered at Blacktown Civic Centre',13 November, viewed 4 October 2005, www.whitlam.org/collection/1972/1972_alp_policy_speech/index.html.

United States Code, Section 2141a: United States National Tourism Organization, 26 January 1998, viewed 7 April 2006, www.washington watchdog.org/documents/usc/ttl22/ch31A/sec2141a.html.

Christof Pforr

CHAPTER 8

Regional *tourism policy and planning*

LEARNING OBJECTIVES

After reading this chapter you will be able to:

1 discuss the sociopolitical and economic changes that have refocused attention on the regional sphere and their implications for regional tourism policy and planning

2 discuss why regions are so difficult to define

3 critically assess the role of tourism in broader regional planning and development contexts

4 understand the responsibilities, roles and influence of stakeholders in regional tourism policy and planning and appreciate the importance of collaboration and negotiation processes for regional governance

5 critically discuss whether and how tourism can contribute to the sustainable future of a region.

8.1 INTRODUCTION

The role of tourism in the economic and social development of regions has been widely promulgated in government publications and the media. Tourism has been promoted as a mechanism for rejuvenating regional and rural areas that have experienced dramatic changes in their industrial structures and functions, access to services, employment opportunities and demography. However, the underpinnings of regional approaches to tourism planning, development and marketing (especially branding) are coming under greater scrutiny, especially in a climate of globalisation, economic restructuring and uncertainty. This chapter critically examines the context and challenges associated with regional tourism planning and policy. Section 8.2 introduces the rather elusive concept of a region. Regional tourism and its capacity to promote regional development is then outlined in section 8.3. Section 8.4 presents the governance implications of these changes for regional tourism policy and planning, and discusses the need for more collaborative, participative and communicative approaches. Section 8.5 introduces policy networks as a new mode of regional governance. Section 8.6 then discusses existing approaches to regional tourism policy and planning. Finally, section 8.7 examines how tourism policy making can contribute to more sustainable regional outcomes. In this chapter, Australia is used as an example of current practices in regional tourism policy and planning.

8.2 WHAT IS A REGION?

Since the 1980s, the significance of tourism to regional areas has grown substantially. Many of Australia's unique tourist attractions (e.g. Uluru, Kakadu, Great Barrier Reef and Monkey Mia) are based on natural and cultural resources dispersed throughout regional areas. It is therefore no surprise that regional tourism represents around 60 per cent of all tourism activity and accounts for 6.8 per cent of rural and regional employment (Commonwealth of Australia 2003: 34). Regional tourism is often regarded as a means of supporting and developing regional economies, particularly when many regions are experiencing a decline in traditional industries (e.g. agriculture, forestry and fishing) and are finding it difficult to adjust to global processes of economic and social restructuring.

Regional areas often face higher levels of unemployment and shortages of new employment opportunities. They frequently experience population decline, particularly as younger and skilled people migrate towards capital cities and larger urban centres in search of education and employment opportunities, to travel or to access social and cultural resources unavailable in smaller regional centres. This gradual reduction in a vibrant economy and social structure subsequently results in ever-diminishing provision of services and a lack of new development opportunities. Where present, these complex socioeconomic matters present an increasing array of challenges to regional policy-making, planning and development.

In the search for economic and employment alternatives, tourism has often been embraced by governments at all levels as a new driving force for regional development. There have been high expectations that tourism can drive and diversify regional economic activities by offering new business opportunities, create employment and income growth, and facilitate investment and new infrastructure developments (e.g. Commonwealth of Australia 2003; Prosser 2001). One of the key government responses to the crisis in the regions has been regional development programs and policies specifically targeted at the tourism industry. But these have not always delivered positive outcomes for regional development. Driven by an overly enthusiastic and optimistic attitude to tourism's potential, top-down government responses have often taken a narrow, tourism-centric focus and have been characterised by policy and decision-making based on inadequate, outdated or unreliable data and information. Consequently, instead of contributing solutions, government policies and plans have, in many cases, reinforced existing regional disparities.

■ 8.2.1 Defining *the region*

The stronger emphasis of '**regioness**' as a re-emerging level of spatial planning and development is a response to economic and sociopolitical structural changes taking place since the 1970s. In particular, the emergence and endorsement of neoliberal economic and social agendas and policies by Western governments, political and administrative reforms, devolution of responsibilities from central to local levels, fiscal constraints, globalisation and associated competitive pressures for communities, the emergence of new forms of technology, and the need to pursue sustainable development are all planning and policy challenges that have shifted attention to the regional level in an attempt to improve governance capacity. Consequently, the concepts **region**, **regionalism** and **regionalisation** have been extensively discussed in recent years.

The shift towards regional planning and policy development can be traced to the structural changes in sociopolitical systems that occurred in Western societies following World War II and contributed to societies becoming increasingly fragmented. Following a progressive expansion of state responsibilities, governments found it difficult to formally implement public policy and deliver public services and so began to share their powers with non-state actors (e.g. profit-making firms and non-profit private organisations). These changes reflect a general belief that governments should begin to share responsibility and roll back their functions through a new commitment to individualism and market forces. Consequently, policy-making began to rely less on the political and administrative machinery with its formal processes and more on collaboration among business, government and other interests drawing on pluralist and corporatist models of government (Thompson & Pforr 2005). Indeed, in the light of the changing role of the state and the redefinition of its functions the discussion is now shifting from government to governance, a trend that is also expressed in approaches such as 'civic regionalism' (Lane 2005) and the concept of **new regionalism**, seen as an alternative model of regional development with less top-down and free market and more democratic and inclusive approaches (e.g. Rainnie & Grobbelaar 2005; Smyth et al. 2005). This discourse has caused a reappraisal of the region, which is no longer seen as only a concept of spatial classification but more as a unit of socioeconomic activities and structures, including tourism.

So what are the core elements of the current, lively debate on regioness? Based on the global/regional dichotomy, it is argued on the one hand that the regional level has lost autonomy and governing capacity. In the context of tourism Weiermair (1995: 11), for instance, points out that one of the structural problems that many regions face is 'the increasing international-isation and globalisation of service sectors including tourism, the associated expansion of activities of multinational firms in these sectors and at the same time the inability of the small business sector to face either of these structural changes'. Others, however, point to increased opportunities and therefore advocate a more active and powerful role for a region in man-aging its own affairs (e.g. Rainnie & Grobbelaar 2005).

This discussion has considerable spatial implications and wide-ranging consequences for regional tourism policy and planning, which will be elaborated later in this chapter. Before that, however, attempts to define the terms 'region', 'regionalism' and 'regionalisation' are presented in this section as they are all fundamental to this debate.

Although the use of the terms 'regionalism', which can be described as a bottom-up process, and 'regionalisation', its top-down equivalent (Morgan 2005), has grown rapidly in academic literature, no succinct and uniform definitions have yet emerged. Consequently the concepts have remained diffuse and unclear (e.g. Tosun & Jenkins 1996).

Generally, regions can be defined, for instance, in the form of adminis-trative and political boundaries or are based on physical features or classified as urban or non-urban. Bätzing (2001) argues that definitions of regions have several dimensions. They can be classified by a single dominating attribute, such as a particular physical feature, for instance geology, climate, soil or vegetation. But there are also linguistic, cultural, economic, tra-ditional or historical regions delimited by anthropogenic attributes as well as political and administrative units defined by clear boundaries. In political terms regions are, for instance, often regarded as subnational entities, such as the Australian states and territories, the German Bundesländer or the Swedish Läns. From an economic perspective, on the other hand, regions can also form mega-economic spaces as is seen in the case of the European Union or ASEAN (Association of South-East Asian Nations). In all cases, boundaries are set for specific reasons. Thus, regions are very much an anthropogenic construct based on function, purpose and task and consti-tuted by political, economic and sociocultural actions (Moose & Brodda 2002; Fürst 2002). Regions are therefore demarcated from the perspective of those who define, for example, their spatial boundaries. So, to be able to comprehend the definition of a region, it is important to understand who prescribes its boundaries and for what reason. Figure 8.1 illustrates this point by showing various perspectives on regioness, which were taken into consideration in drawing up new regional boundaries for tourism in Western Australia. As can be seen in the case study 'From tourism regions to tourism zones in Western Australia' (p. 291), iconic clusters and major touring routes influenced the final decision-making process in the realignment of tourism boundaries in Western Australia in 2003–04.

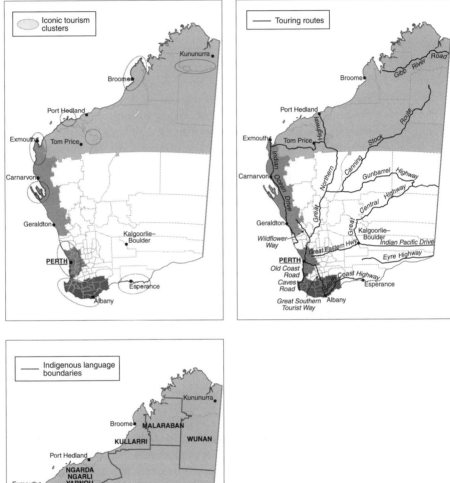

■ **Figure 8.1**

Regional perspectives of Western Australia, 2003–04

Source: *Tourism WA 2003d.*

In reality, however, demarcating regions is difficult. Understanding the making of a region requires knowledge of the interplay of the social, cultural, economic and physical features of a place. A region is a complex and multidimensional geographical and/or political administrative unit, and there is no generally accepted agreement on how to delineate conceptional and practical boundaries. Given the difficulty of defining regions and drawing their boundaries, Jenkins (2000: 188) suggests, 'the concept of a region, however it is defined, forms meaningful, but not always appropriate, divisions of space, and its application to tourism is widely accepted but rarely questioned'.

Various attempts have been made to conceptualise 'regioness'. Smith (1995: 175) for instance, defines a region as 'a contiguous area that has been explicitly delineated by a researcher, planner or public agency as having relevance for some aspects of tourism planning, development or analysis'. He identifies three types of regions, so-called *a priori* **regions**, where boundaries (e.g. political) already exist, **homogenous regions** sharing a common internal similarity and *functional* **regions** with a high degree of interrelational constellations. Referring to Smith (1995) and Richardson (1978), Jenkins (2000) outlines three similar categories: *homogenous*, *nodal* and *planning* regions, whereby the first can be defined by a unifying attribute, such as the economy (e.g. industry), sociocultural aspects (e.g. language) and physical features (e.g. climate, soil) but also in an integrative mix. Nodal regions are defined similarly to Smith's (1995) functional regions and planning regions constructed for political and administrative purposes.

■ 8.2.2 Defining *tourism regions*

In the field of tourism, the idea of a region has been discussed by various authors (e.g. Gunn & Var 2002; Murphy & Dore 2000; Tosun & Jenkins 1996; Pearce 1995, 1989, 1980; Smith 1995; Inskeep 1991; Hall & Page 2002; Jenkins 2000; Dredge & Jenkins 2003; Dowling 1993). For Pearce (1989: 262), 'tourist regions identified at the national level will usually be defined in terms of the spatial association of attractions and associated facilities, or possibly in physical terms … or administrative ones, especially where tourism forms part of an overall regional strategy'. In the general debate the term 'tourism region' is often used synonymously with 'tourism destination' (e.g. Smith 1995; Inskeep 1991; Gunn 1994), yet the two concepts are far from identical. Tosun and Jenkins (1996: 520) suggest that 'for subnational tourism planning purposes, they should be distinguished and defined'. Common to both, in any case, is the fact that they are unclear concepts characterised by considerable complexity.

A **tourism destination** refers to a geographical location that is distinct from a traveller's origin and in which the activity of tourism is conducted and tourism products and services are consumed. Hall (2005: 162) refers to this concept as a location of tourism consumption. A tourism destination is defined by the mobility characteristics of tourists themselves, and it can exist at a variety of scales from national to regional to subregional.

Alternatively, a **tourism region** refers to the geographical location in which common characteristics and synergies exist between tourism products and services, and the term is also associated with a politico-administrative framework in which tourism planning and policy is delivered. Tourists can visit multiple tourism destinations within a tourism region.

The Northern Territory — a unique region

The Northern Territory of Australia has become internationally renowned since the 1970s as an attractive tourist destination, home to such famous Australian landmarks as Uluru in the Uluru Kata-Tjuta National Park and the Kakadu National Park, widely known through the legendary movie Crocodile Dundee. 'You'll never never know if you never never go' has been a marketing slogan of the tourism industry to capitalise on the Territory's natural and cultural assets. Remoteness, vast distances, spectacular scenery, distinctive landscapes with rich and diverse flora and fauna, wilderness experience, the sparsely populated outback as well as the unique Aboriginal culture are key aspects of the NT's appeal as a tourist destination.

Yet these self-same characteristics are often seen and experienced by those who live there — 'Territorians' as they are wont to call themselves — in a quite different light. Many non-Indigenous Territorians, like most Australians from other parts of the country, see the Territory in much the same way 'as it has seemed throughout its recorded history, a vast, remote, harsh, and largely unknown part of the continent' (Heatley 1979: 1). Although written more than twenty-five years ago, Heatley's observation remains at least partially valid today. Isolation, great distances and physical adversity still dominate non-Indigenous perceptions of the NT, often reinforcing its image as a difficult and unattractive environment. The Territory is characterised by its extremes of geography and climate. Within this challenging environment Europeans have fashioned political and economic infrastructures, the operation of which are also shaped by the complex sociocultural factors of a multiracial and multiethnic society. The Territory is therefore a unique region. It often stands as — indeed represents itself as being — both unique and different from the rest of Australia.

Many of the interrelated factors noted above significantly affect and influence the form and dynamics of tourism policy and planning and demonstrate the importance of the specific policy environment as one parameter to comprehend policy processes. Thus, tourism public policy in the Northern Territory shapes and is shaped by a specific set of local characteristics, an amalgamation of distinct political, socioeconomic and physical factors.

The concept of a region shows many facets and perspectives in theory and practice. It is characterised by intense disciplinary discourse in geography, economics, tourism and political science, where, for instance, the focus is on varying aspects of scale, function and administration (Murphy & Dore 2000). Sorensen (1995: 624) summarises the elusive concept of a region as follows: 'On one level we can try to identify reasonably homogeneous regions on the basis of a single distinctive attribute like lifestyle, culture, economy or political sentiment. Alternatively, we can attempt to identify regions in which such attributes interact with each other and the physical environment to create a distinctive and integrated landscape.' Here the latter approach, whereby the region is defined as an amalgamation of distinct political, socioeconomic and physical factors that yield a 'distinctive and integrated landscape', is advocated.

As seen in Planning in Practice 'The Northern Territory — a unique region', the Northern Territory encapsulates this multifaceted and diverse nature of regioness. In this region, different and contradictory perspectives of the region emerge, which reinforces the notion that it is never a single attribute that makes a region but a contextual mix.

8.3 TOURISM AND REGIONAL DEVELOPMENT

■ 8.3.1 The *regional development imperative*

As mentioned earlier, for many regions the tourism sector plays an important role in the traditionally socioeconomically focused concept of regional development. The main goals of **regional development**, according to Müller (1995), are appropriate settlement in peripheral regions, reduction of undesirable disparities between agglomerations and rural areas (especially those of declining prosperity) and improvement of the general living conditions, in the sense of the quality of life of the local population. In the Australian context it can be argued that the degree of disparity between regions appears to be less pressing despite 'considerable physical, economic, social, political and technological diversity' (Jenkins 2000: 183). Nevertheless, regional inequalities — in particular between coastal and outback regions — and problems do exist, and it is therefore important to assess whether tourism can reduce regional imbalances and disparities. Hence tourism's capacity to contribute positively to the development of a region must be cautiously assessed.

The region has always been the basis for tourism development and, as Hall et al. (1997: 264) state, regionalism is 'now providing an overarching framework for tourism planning, policy, development and marketing'. But Telfer (2002: 113) adds that, since 'regions are so diverse ... the viability and the appropriateness of any tourism development needs to be considered within the parameters of local socioeconomic, geographic and political conditions'. Therefore, in the context of tourism, regional development requires careful consideration of the often diverse and disparate natural and cultural resources of a region. As Hall et al. (1997: 265) point out: 'For a region to develop in a sustainable way, the development of tourism may need to be restrained, as part of selecting the most appropriate industry mix for the future an area wants. It is therefore vital that tourism "fits in" to the local economy, culture and environment rather than an automatic assumption being made that tourism is the best development alternative.'

Accordingly, an integrated approach to regional development and careful consideration of tourism's role in the wider regional context is required. The focus on integrated regional policy and planning is a powerful tool for ensuring that such regions really experience the development that is most appropriate and viable in the long term. Integrated regionalism across economic, environmental and sociopolitical objectives and actions is imperative. However, to understand regional tourism policy and planning it is also important to think across scales. The capacity for regional planning and policy initiatives to institute change is often interlinked with the objectives and actions of other tiers of government (e.g. Lane 2005). Commitment to regional initiatives and actions by governments also change over time, so that an awareness of historical issues and influences is also important (e.g. Dredge 2005). In this context, readers are referred to the importance of figure 1.1 (p. 16) in setting the overall context for understanding regional tourism planning and policy development.

8.3.2 Regional *tourism organisations*

In Australia, multiple regional organisations operate to develop and influence regional planning and policy. The limited size and capacity of local government to deal with issues that extend beyond its boundaries has stimulated federal and state or territory policy directives that establish such regional organisations. These organisations are often supported by combined federal, state and local government financial assistance, which might be supplemented by industry memberships and funding. At any one time multiple regional organisations with different roles and responsibilities could be undertaking similar, overlapping activities. Among these are regional tourism organisations (RTOs), regional development organisations (RDOs), area consultative committees (ACCs) and regional organisations of councils (ROCs).

These regional organisations are important conduits for drawing together disparate local government initiatives, building partnerships among sub-regional public and private sector agencies and organisations with similar goals and objectives, and applying higher levels of policy to local issues. However, regional organisations have also been accused of adding an extra layer of policy complexity (e.g. Rainnie & Grobbelaar 2005).

In this context, regional tourism organisations (RTOs) have emerged since the 1960s as important tools and sites of tourism planning and policy development in Australia. Whereas state or territory RTO policy approaches are inspired by historical legacies and reflect the local peculiarities of contemporary issues and problems, the main objective of RTOs is to assist in regional tourism development via marketing, product development and management activities. The extent to which RTOs emphasise these various activities varies. Most RTOs are in the business of marketing place identity (Dredge & Jenkins

2003); that is, they see themselves principally as marketing agencies that seek to differentiate and brand their regional product, making it more recognisable and competitive in the marketplace. Unfortunately, less emphasis is generally given to equally important activities such as product development, stakeholder collaboration, governance and integration with policy development in related sectors. Lack of expertise, leadership and understanding of these tasks has resulted in RTOs not engaging as thoroughly as they perhaps should in these activities, although there is a growing interest in regional governance and partnerships as a result of the ideological shifts in public administration discussed earlier (see sections 4.3 and 4.4).

8.4 REGIONAL GOVERNANCE

Recently, there has been a strong trend for regions to be characterised by networks of social relations motivated by functional aspects, which often exceed traditional regional boundaries. As functional networks increase in importance, it appears that territorial references for actors and their (inter)actions decrease at the same time; spatial alienation as a response to globalisation, individualised lifestyles, high mobility and importance of economic networks creates tension between functional and territorial perspectives, which has implications for regional policy and planning (Fürst 2002). There is a reorientation in regional governance, which focuses on endogenous capacities of a region supported by institutional arrangements with new and expanded responsibilities for regional development. At its core stronger participation of local actors and agencies and cooperation within the region is encouraged. These changing perspectives on a region link back to new regionalism, which is often described as a bottom-up, proactive and process-oriented approach that is socially integrated, economically viable and environmentally responsible.

As a response to the structural and ideological changes taking place in the way governments undertake their business, there has been a shifting 'downwards' and an outsourcing of government functions to subnational governance structures such as regions, communities, volunteer groups, the private sector or NGOs. Driving this process of regionalisation are two key political strategies: decentralisation of government functions and cooperation between government and non-government sectors. These strategies have led to mixed forms of governance (e.g. Ribot 2002; Rose 2000). Thus, a new, more cooperative, participative and communicative policy style has emerged, which transcends the traditional divide between public and private sector roles and responsibilities. The main aim is to mobilise the development of endogenous potential and all relevant stakeholders of a region, to combine initiatives and capacities to improve regional development through synergies of networks and collaboration (Hall 2005).

Collaborative and partnership approaches have been frequently discussed in tourism analysis in recent years. Bramwell and Lane (1999: 180), for instance, argue that 'collaborative arrangements for sustainable tourism are part of the conflict resolution, problem solving and capacity building processes that are central to sustainable development'. The literature on collaborative arrangements is characterised by great diversity in its terminology and encompasses such terms as coalitions, alliances, task forces, networks and public–private partnerships (Bramwell & Lane 2000). Here, the term 'collaboration' refers to the involvement of all relevant stakeholders in dialogue structures and information networks with the aim of negotiating a regional strategy based on common objectives and through consensual agreement. This is regarded as an important and powerful tool for developing sustainable regions.

Despite the benefits of collaborative arrangements in regional tourism policy and planning, a successful collaboration of all relevant stakeholders is rarely found. 'Perhaps the most startling point in many regions', as Pipkin (1996: 796) remarks, 'is how often people who care about the region's destiny have simply never sat together and talked about where the region was going, what changes they would like to see, or what tools are available to shape the future.' There are certain problems associated with a collaborative approach, which often result from existing conventional power structures and political processes. For example, entrenched business and government alliances can negatively influence the inclusiveness of policy networks (see also Planning in Practice: 'Tourism policy-making in the Northern Territory of Australia', p. 277). This often neglects stakeholders representing sociocultural and environmental community needs. Selin (1999: 271), in a more critical review, states that 'it will take a concerted effort from many sectors to ensure that current and emerging tourism partnerships contribute to the sustainable future of the field'. The appropriate inclusion of all relevant stakeholders in the policy-making process forms the basis for consensus and shared decision-making, which in turn leads to a greater legitimacy of political decisions, democratic empowerment and equity and therefore fulfils aspects of the social dimension of sustainability (Hall 2000). Collaboration is therefore an important mechanism 'for achieving sustainable outcomes and is symbolic of new ways of working' (Robinson 1999: 393).

However, some questions still remain unanswered (Ryan 2002; Jenkins 2001; Hall 1999): how can the process of consensus-building best be organised? Who is allowed to participate, and who gives that permission? What happens to those who are not allowed to participate for one reason or another? How is the process entrenched in existing political structures? Hence, the debate about collaboration in tourism policy and planning at the regional level is inherently political and illustrates the distribution of power that shapes regional tourism development.

In this context, the new regionalism discourse, which encapsulates many of the above outlined elements, promises a different quality of politics with alternative forms of policy and decision-making. An expression of this new regional governance is, for instance, the emergence of policy networks (Kilper 1998). They can be regarded as a way to enhance the efficiency and legitimacy of complex and dynamic policy-making processes, thus representing a new pattern of political exchange and conflict management beyond traditional forms of governance.

Börzel (1997: 2) defines policy networks in general terms 'as power relationships between the government and interest groups, in which resources are exchanged'. However, the policy network concept in the field of public policy and administration comprises a number of specific approaches emerging from two different schools of thought: the *interest intermediation school* and the *governance school* (see especially Börzel 1998). The so-called governance school conceives policy networks specifically as an alternative form of governance to that of hierarchy and market (see section 2.5.2). Analysts from this school of thought are of the view that because societies have become increasingly differentiated and fragmented since the end of World War II many kinds of policy network have emerged in response to these changes. The governance school thus regards policy networks as specific forms of interaction between the state and civil society that are based on non-hierarchical forms of coordination (Thompson & Pforr 2005).

In essence, policy network research acknowledges that policy-making is complex, diffuse and non-rational; a plethora of actors participate in often informal arrangements. As a consequence, the ability of government to shape processes of policy-making has weakened, indicating a shift in the distribution of political power and influence. Thus, in theory, policy networks can disperse political powers through cooperative arrangements by engaging civil society in policy and decision-making processes. To assess their effectiveness, however, it is important to better understand the meaning of 'governance' and to develop clear expectations of the role of policy networks instead of falling back on rhetorical terms such as 'modern', 'better' or 'good' governance.

The term 'governance', discussed in chapter 2 (especially section 2.5.2), broadly means all forms of producing and steering social order (see Börzel & Risse 2005). For example, the state does not have a governance monopoly as steering functions can also be taken over by markets and, indeed, by policy networks. When viewed in this light, policy networks may be conceived as being bound, determined and controlled by formal institutions. Here, however, governance is understood more specifically as 'governance without government', or as a mode of governing that is more in line with the cooperative rather than the interventionist state in which state and non-state actors participate in mixed public and private policy networks (Mayntz 2002). In other words, policy networks cut across formal institutional arrangements and highlight the importance of informal, decentralised processes and relationships in policy-making.

In practice, however, stakeholder engagement at any level is often difficult to achieve and requires a comprehensive debate and overview about how policies and decisions are made. In an ideal situation, policy networks as a form of good governance will be democratic if all members of the network are afforded equal opportunities to participate in, and control, political decisions through consensus and compromise. Of course, in reality, this occurs rarely, if at all (Thompson & Pforr 2005), as is illustrated in Planning in Practice: 'Tourism policy-making in the Northern Territory'.

Tourism policy-making in the Northern Territory

To illustrate the complex nature of the interaction between various stakeholders in the tourism system at the subnational level, the development of the first Northern Territory Tourism Development Masterplan (TDMP) will be used as a case study from Australia's Northern Territory (Pforr 2006, 2002, 2001). The discussion focuses on issue-specific reputation, communication and collaboration networks, which underpinned the development of that tourism plan. In essence, the main focus is directed to the questions: who were the core actors and what was the nature of their interaction? Generally, in network analysis relational configurations can represent the involved actors' communications, participation, resource exchange, sociopolitical support, or perceived influence (Pforr 2006). Here the focus is set on three main types of interaction: on reputational ties, on cooperation and on information exchange (i.e. communication), which measures mutual relevance, the way the core tourism stakeholders take each other into account in their actions.

A summary of the extent of mutual relevance in the case study is presented in figure 8.2 in the form of a three-dimensional scattergram. The relative position of each tourism stakeholder demonstrates its overall performance in the development of the NT tourism masterplan. When the scattergram is analysed from a functional perspective, the dominant position of political and administrative actors in the process becomes apparent. Other stakeholders who were allowed access to this exclusive political and administrative circle were mainly those bodies representing the tourism industry (i.e. the regional tourism associations). For the NT this was a typical partnership between political and business interests. Stakeholders from outside this alliance were almost completely excluded from the policy process; neither community-based interest groups nor the environmental lobby played any significant role. Hence figure 8.2 presents a close network of political and economic stakeholders, an unbalanced and top-down structure, one that mostly ignored interests other than those of key concern for the tourism industry. Tourism policy-making at the subnational level was therefore clearly subordinated to political and industry priorities. The strong control over this policy development by the central political power base is also evidence for a lack of mechanisms to direct responsibilities to the subordinate local tiers. As can be seen in figure 8.2, these actors did not have any significant influence in the development of the TDMP, which is mirrored, for instance, by the lack of influence of the NT local government authorities, as indicated by the scores of relatively close to zero on all three axes.

With this network analysis, it can be demonstrated that the specific set of policy actors involved in the NT masterplan development and their relational constellation did not reflect appropriate mechanisms of collaboration and coordination in regional policy and planning. To be more sympathetic to

(continued)

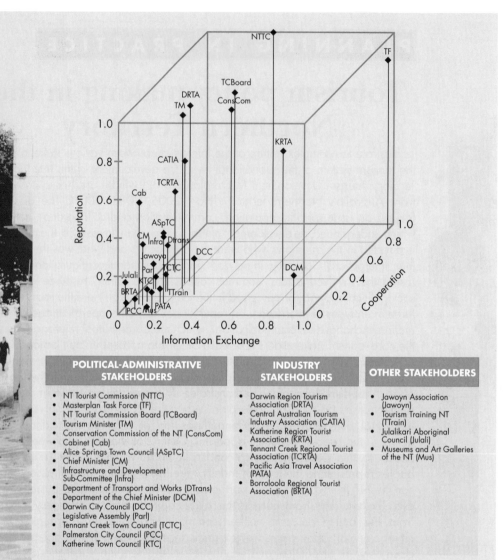

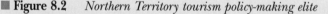

POLITICAL-ADMINISTRATIVE STAKEHOLDERS	INDUSTRY STAKEHOLDERS	OTHER STAKEHOLDERS
• NT Tourist Commission (NTTC) • Masterplan Task Force (TF) • NT Tourist Commission Board (TCBoard) • Tourism Minister (TM) • Conservation Commission of the NT (ConsCom) • Cabinet (Cab) • Alice Springs Town Council (ASpTC) • Chief Minister (CM) • Infrastructure and Development Sub-Committee (Infra) • Department of Transport and Works (DTrans) • Department of the Chief Minister (DCM) • Darwin City Council (DCC) • Legislative Assembly (Parl) • Tennant Creek Town Council (TCTC) • Palmerston City Council (PCC) • Katherine Town Council (KTC)	• Darwin Region Tourism Association (DRTA) • Central Australian Tourism Industry Association (CATIA) • Katherine Region Tourist Association (KRTA) • Tennant Creek Regional Tourist Association (TCRTA) • Pacific Asia Travel Association (PATA) • Borroloola Regional Tourist Association (BRTA)	• Jawoyn Association (Jawoyn) • Tourism Training NT (TTrain) • Julalikari Aboriginal Council (Julali) • Museums and Art Galleries of the NT (Mus)

■ **Figure 8.2** *Northern Territory tourism policy-making elite*

Source: *adapted from Pforr 2004c.*

the idea of new regional governance as outlined earlier, the NT tourism master-plan should have been the outcome of broad consultation and participation of all interested parties and individuals in an open and democratic manner. This would have ensured a continuous commitment to tourism's sustainability by the wider community as well as by government and industry. The analysis of the NT tourism masterplan, in contrast, highlighted the problematic nature of the much-promoted public and private partnerships as an exclusive network structure between government and industry. But it is not only a matter of opening policy networks to a wider range of stakeholders. It is also necessary to demonstrate willingness to share decision-making powers to enable community needs and

In Australia, the public sector has developed a variety of region-specific institutions, programs, policies, strategies and plans. However, since the 1980s there has been a dramatic shift from a traditional public administration model that sought to implement government policy for a perceived public good to a corporatist model that emphasises efficiency, investment returns, the role of the market and the relations with stakeholders, usually defined as industry (Hall 1999: 274). Hence the commitment to destination marketing, the streamlining of government organisations primarily towards marketing functions and the promotion of partnerships between government and industry have been key features of government's increasingly commercial dealings with tourism. This reflects the withdrawal of direct involvement by central governments in many areas of public policy and a shift towards public–private partnerships (see section 2.5). In most cases, illustrated also in Planning in Practice: 'Tourism policy-making in the Northern Territory', these have entailed only a very narrow understanding of the term 'partnership', one that includes mainly key public sector agencies (e.g. national tourism organisations) and peak industry bodies such as regional tourism associations; these are political and business alliances that often neglect sociocultural and environmental community interests.

In Australia, responsibility for regional development is spread among a number of departments and agencies from all three tiers of government. Although there is much overlap, federal intervention in regional development policy and planning has been minimal (Jenkins & Sorensen 1996). In 2001, for instance, the Liberal-National Coalition Government developed a strategy to foster regional development in Australia, termed Stronger Regions: A Stronger Australia, which included such goals as 'strengthening regional economic and social opportunities, sustaining productive natural resources and environment, delivering better regional services and adjusting to economic, technological and government-induced change' (Commonwealth of Australia 2001: 3). These objectives for Australia's regions have been implemented through various government initiatives, such as the Sustainable Regions Programme. They all have the advancement of economic development at the regional level as their key motivation.

In this context, tourism is regarded as a core component in regional development strategies. A Tourism White Paper states: 'Tourism is an important driver for regional development. Ensuring the sustainability and viability of the regional tourism industry is vital to the economic diversification of regional Australia' (Commonwealth of Australia 2003: 33). The key aims and objectives outlined in the White Paper are to ensure stronger regional economic growth, including enhanced opportunities for indigenous economic development; the generation of new employment opportunities; and the provision of better regional infrastructure and standards. To achieve these targets, the Commonwealth Government has developed a set of programs, such as the Regional Tourism Program (replaced in 2004 by the Australian

Tourism Development Program) and the Regional Partnerships Program (Commonwealth of Australia 2003: 34). However, despite this federal intervention, regional affairs are mainly dealt with at the subnational level; that is, the 'states and territories, because of their powers relating to town and city planning, land use and environmental protection (and indeed other areas left to them under the Constitution) have the responsibility for the regulation of tourist development, and the marketing and promotion of state attractions' (Jenkins & Hall 1997: 40).

According to Dredge and Jenkins (2003: 388), the 'formal and informal institutional environment in which tourism planning and policy-making occurs varies spatially and temporally'. Each state and territory has its own key government agency, which is normally a statutory authority often under the portfolio of a Minister for Tourism and governed by a board of commissioners. These agencies are mainly responsible for developing and marketing tourism at the subnational level. Furthermore, in each state and territory (except the ACT) numerous regional and local tourism organisations that represent tourism industry interests (see table 8.1). Generally, regional tourism associations (RTAs) or regional tourism organisations (RTOs) are the tourism industry's peak bodies and the most influential voice representing regional industry interests. Although their function has changed in recent years to include, for instance, product development and destination management, their traditional role is to service the needs of their members, promote the region, attract visitors and develop services for tourists. They are normally headed by a board or executive committee and receive funding from state and local governments as well as from membership fees. 'Regional or subnational organisations have emerged as an important feature in the public sector organisation of tourism in many countries, including Australia.' (Dredge & Jenkins 2003: 389.)

■ Table 8.1
State and territory tourist organisations, 2005

JURISDICTION	KEY GOVERNMENT AGENCY	NUMBER OF RTAS/RTOS
Australian Capital Territory	Australian Capital Tourism	0
New South Wales	Tourism New South Wales	14
Northern Territory	Northern Territory Tourist Commission	4
Queensland	Tourism Queensland	14
South Australia	South Australian Tourism Commission	12
Tasmania	Tourism Tasmania	3
Victoria	Tourism Victoria	12
Western Australia	Tourism Western Australia	5

Opinions differ as to the effectiveness of these diverse regional tourism structures. The current Federal Government, for instance, promotes less regional representation, claiming that the 'large number of regional and local tourism organisations and local government associations can sometimes lead to fragmented planning and effort on tourism and serve to build rivalries between regions, rather than encourage synergies for creation of new growth opportunities' (Commonwealth of Australia 2003: 34). On the other hand, the Australian Regional Tourism Network, an unincorporated association consisting of a steering committee with representation from each state and territory tourism authority, Commonwealth departments and various regional tourism organisations, recommends an increase in the number of associations as 'these can ensure a voice for small and isolated operations in regional and state organisations and improve the effectiveness of communication and networking chains throughout the tourism industry' (Kelly & Taylor 2004: 21).

Institutional arrangements for managing regional tourism are mostly defined by political and administrative units, which have traditionally been based on geographical areas imposed from above. However, in recent times there has been a strong move away from the geography of government administration as a framework for promoting, developing and planning regional tourism. In its place there has been growing emphasis on units of administration that recognise networks and constellations of interests that cannot necessarily be defined by geographical boundaries. These changes in the regional organisation of tourism reflect a clear policy direction for enhancing international competitiveness by proactive destination marketing. Dredge and Jenkins (2003: 386) highlight that 'in an increasingly competitive global tourism marketplace, destinations are under increasing pressure to construct and promote distinct identities in order to position themselves competitively in the global context'. In an attempt to better tap into not only international but also interstate markets, Western Australia, for instance, recently reduced its eleven tourism regions with ten RTAs to only five tourism zones with five RTOs (see the case study 'From tourism regions to tourism zones in Western Australia', p. 291).

Similarly, the Northern Territory is also currently implementing a new model for regional tourism, the so-called 'Destination Model' whereby tourism regions are defined not so much by government boundaries as by tourism characteristics. The Northern Territory Tourist Commission argues that current regional boundaries are artificial and mean little to tourists as they 'tend to select destinations to visit regardless of what region they are in' (NTTC 2002: 23). Key features of this new destination approach are to focus on local resources to meet tourist demands, to foster tourism development in remote destinations, and to better respond to local marketing and development needs. In turn, this focus is aimed at empowering destinations and enhancing ownership and commitment to tourism development on a micro level. One of the key arguments in the Northern Territory for implementing this Destination Model is that it is more suitable in geographically remote areas. However, four RTAs based on tourism regions associated with the Territory's main population hubs — Darwin, Katherine, Tennant Creek and Alice Springs — are not yet obsolete, since the new Destination Model is seen to 'complement and enhance the regional framework of Regional Tourism Associations which supports the Northern Territory's tourism industry' (NTTC 2004: 2).

In conclusion, regional tourism structures and approaches are currently under review in Australia, as can be seen from the above examples of Western Australia and the Northern Territory, and elsewhere (e.g. New Zealand and United Kingdom). Since there appears to be no consistent answer to the question of how tourism can best contribute to regional development, a level of uncertainty and instability exists in tourism policy and planning at the regional level. Hence there will always be different approaches to tourism planning and management at the subnational level in response to the dynamic challenges facing regions. In this context, the role of tourism in sustainable regional development is considered in the next section.

8.7 SUSTAINABLE REGIONAL DEVELOPMENT

8.7.1 The *regional challenge*

Sustainable development in general can be described as a target triangle, balancing the three, often seemingly conflicting, dimensions of the environment, society and economy. These three elements must be applied to tourism development to promote ecologically responsible, economically efficient and socially sensitive tourism. Thus, to contribute to sustainable development, it is important to interlink the often overriding economic goals of regional development (including tourism) with ecological and social concerns. Regional and local levels offer an appropriate frame for operationalising the concept of sustainable development because, at these lower levels, the often vague global agenda can be turned into something more meaningful and spatially tangible. However, although dedication to the sustainability paradigm has been overwhelming, clarification as to how it can be applied has not been forthcoming.

Naturally, regions have diverse economic, ecological and social resources, interests, concerns and aspirations. This means that sustainable regional development has to accommodate different regional development perspectives, one of which might be tourism, which itself consists of multiple interests. Thus, the sustainability triangle reflects complex, diverse and differentiated sets of social, environmental and economic interests, such that sustainable tourism development must be cast as a political process of negotiation and conciliation.

The search for a sustainable approach to tourism development in the regions is a sociopolitical challenge, in which different interests and values determine the meaning of sustainable development and its route to implementation. To ignore these interactions and power structures at play would be to ignore the highly political context of sustainable regional tourism. It is this context that governs the way regional sustainable development is defined and translated into action or non-action (Pforr 2004a, 2004b).

Planning in Practice: 'The Australian situation: ecologically sustainable development' illustrates the challenges of implementing sustainable development at a regional level.

The Australian situation: ecologically sustainable development

Ecologically sustainable development (ESD) has been defined as 'using, conserving and enhancing the community's resources so that ecological processes, on which life depends are maintained, and the total quality of life, now and in the future, can be increased' (Commonwealth of Australia 1990: 6). By signing the Rio Declaration (1992) Australia formally committed itself to the main principles of sustainable development and to implementing the so-called ecologically sustainable development process. This commitment led to the development of a national strategy for ESD, the National Strategy for Ecologically Sustainable Development (NSESD) (Commonwealth of Australia 1992). The ESD strategy acted as a mechanism for coordinating policy diffusion from the Commonwealth level and set out 'the broad strategic and policy framework under which governments will co-operatively make decisions and take actions to pursue ESD in Australia' (ESD Steering Committee 1992: 17). In the development of this strategy, approximately 500 recommendations were made by various working groups. The key working groups came from manufacturing, mining, agriculture, forests, fisheries, energy production, energy use, tourism and transport.

In the 1990s, ecologically sustainable development became a popular political and social goal. Based on the broad policy directions of the NSESD, the principles of ESD (see figure 8.3) have since flowed on into a number of other, more specific strategies, plans and policies. This strategic policy approach has

- Decision-making processes should effectively integrate both long and short-term economic, environmental, social and equity considerations.
- Where there are threats of serious or irreversible environmental damage, lack of full scientific certainty should not be used as a reason for postponing measures to prevent environmental degradation.
- The global dimension of environmental impacts of actions and policies should be recognised and considered.

- The need to maintain and enhance international competitiveness in an environmentally sound manner should be recognised.
- Cost effective and flexible policy instruments should be adopted, such as improved valuation, pricing and incentive mechanisms.
- Decisions and actions should provide for broad community involvement on issues which affect them.

■ **Figure 8.3**   *The guiding principles of ecologically sustainable development (ESD)*

Source: *Commonwealth of Australia 1992: 8.*

(continued)

emerged as the preferred mechanism for implementing the sustainability agenda at all three tiers of government and in various sectors, including tourism. On the basis of this sectoral approach adopted in the NSESD, several objectives for tourism were identified (see figure 8.4) (Pforr 2004d).

- To ensure tourism strategies developed at all levels of government are based on ESD principles and provide effective mechanisms for industry and community input
- To examine the most appropriate use of regulatory mechanisms to ensure tourism development is ecologically sustainable
- To encourage environmentally appropriate tourist operator and visitor behaviour through the production and adoption of codes of environmental behaviour and practice and to improve tourist awareness of ESD principles.
- To develop a greater understanding of the economic and environmental impacts of tourism developments, including monitoring of tourism trends, such as ecotourism.

■ **Figure 8.4** *National Strategy for Ecologically Sustainable Development Goals for the Tourism Sector, 1992* **Source:** *ICESD 1996.*

There was, however, no legal requirement for the implementation of the NSESD in any Australian jurisdiction. This situation draws attention to the lack of policy coordination in Australia's federal system of government and demonstrates the frag-mentation of tourism and related environmental responsibilities (Pforr 2000, 2004d). As discussed in the case study 'Intergovernmental relations and tourism in Australia' (chapter 2, pp. 63–5), the split of responsibilities between the three tiers of government creates complex and often confusing arrangements. Since the Constitution is silent about tourism, these policy domains are most often left to the states and territories as residual powers and there is a consequent danger of a fragmented and little coordinated government approach. Consequently, the subnational level has an important function in policy-making and in the implemen-tation of ESD principles in the tourism system, a role that, compared with the national level, has so far received only limited attention in academic debate (Pforr 2004d).

This uncertainty continues to undermine the ESD implementation as the different tiers of government often pursue conflicting interests and objectives. The sub-national level has responded with various localised approaches to define and conceptualise ESD principles, which leads to challenges in synchronising policy both vertically between different levels of government and horizontally among agencies operating at the same level. As Jenkins and Hall (1997: 46) highlight, 'within the Australian federal system the emphasis on state rights has meant that even when state and federal governments are all of the same political persuasion, unanimous agreement on policies is extremely difficult to achieve'.

Despite the fragmented political environment, complex networks of actors and a lack of consultation and communication between the many players, a number of initiatives at the state and territory level in the past reflects an attempt to trans-late ESD principles into positive action. In the early 1990s ESD was a key driver for the development of tourism plans by setting a particular focus on ecotourism as a facilitator for a more sustainable approach to tourism. This is, for instance, evident at the subnational level in the release of the Victorian Ecotourism Strategy,

Ecotourism: A National Strength of Victoria (Department of Conservation and Environment 1993), *The Queensland Ecotourism Plan* (Department of Tourism Sport and Racing 1997; Tourism Queensland 2002), the South Australian initiative, *Ecotourism: A Natural Strategy for South Australia* (South Australian Tourism Department and Tourism Commission and the Department of Environment and Natural Resources 1995), the Tasmanian discussion paper on nature-based tourism, *Ecotourism: Adding Value to Tourism in Natural Areas* (Department of Tourism, Sport and Recreation 1994), *The Nature in Tourism Plan* in New South Wales (Tourism NSW 2004) or the Western Australian *Nature Based Tourism Strategy* (WA Tourism Commission and the Department of Conservation and Land Management 1997, 2004). These plans all reflect initiatives to implement components of the four NSESD tourism objectives at the state and territory level (see figure 8.4).

ESD principles receive widespread recognition in a vast number of tourism policies, programs and strategies in Australia, many of which focus on protected areas. However, Preece et al. (1995: 19) remarked that although most 'give strong positive support to the principles of ESD and environmental responsibility, ... the translation into action is rarely evident'. A similar conclusion is drawn by Butler (1998: 26), who writes: 'In some traditional tourist destination countries, while sustainable development and sustainable tourism may be officially promoted, rarely [it] is more than lip service paid to the application of the concept.'

■ 8.7.2 Framing *and implementing sustainable tourism development*

There are many difficulties in implementing sustainable development when the main drivers of regional development are economic considerations. Furthermore, there is little policy coordination at the subnational level and limited cross-sectoral harmonisation of tourism policy and planning. This situation is clearly counterproductive to policy innovation and policy transfer. There is also a noticeable lack of cooperation and collaboration between key stakeholders, such as government agencies, the tourism industry and community groups. Thus, in common with many regions around the world, Australia's states and territories have also experienced difficulties in transforming the principles of the sustainability agenda into action at the subnational level (Pforr 2004d).

The application of sustainable tourism development principles and practices at regional and local levels is lacking. Obstacles include the complex nature of tourism policy and planning and the limited awareness and understanding of those involved in related dialogues. The framework for sustainable regional tourism development can serve only as a guiding concept. It needs to be adapted and framed in the specific context of a region. Strong political leadership and sound strategies are needed. Unfortunately, governments have become extremely canny in reproducing the sustainable development rhetoric without actually effecting fundamental policy shifts at a regional level. Nonetheless, despite the great diversity and even contradictory nature of various approaches to realise sustainability, the notion itself remains a positive, even common-sense perspective within which to frame the different attempts to deliver a better future for a region. In pursuit of this goal, politics, as we have seen throughout this book, has a crucial role to play. Max Weber (1973: 185) once described the political process as 'a strong and slow boring of hard boards'. Indeed, it is only through political processes that sustainable tourism development can be realised at regional and other levels.

CHAPTER REVIEW

This chapter discussed regional tourism policy and planning in the context of the pressures and changes regions have experienced in recent times. In particular, in the light of increasing economic globalisation and associated competitive pressures, these challenges have led to a refocusing of policy activity at the regional level. As a corollary, the unique qualities and internal potential of regions to maintain and expand autonomy and governing capacity have been emphasised. This shift to the subnational level has not only caused uncertainties and instability for regional policy and planning but also created new opportunities for regional development. In this context, regional tourism has often been promoted, particularly by government and industry interests, as the backbone of regional economic development. Such a predominantly economic, top-down and tourism-centric perspective is, however, not without problems as it frequently minimises the socioeconomic and environmental complexity and dynamics of a region. It is argued in this chapter that in future regional tourism should no longer be considered in isolation but regarded as an integral part of the wider planning and development context of a region.

Furthermore, regional tourism policy and planning needs to better acknowledge the influence of networks of stakeholders, often with conflicting interests, expectations and priorities, on the way policy emerges. Lane (2005: 7), for instance, highlights that the geometry of planning has changed: 'Instead of solutions being imposed (vertically) from above, they must instead be negotiated (horizontally).' It is therefore crucial to improve methods of consultation and communication, and to mediate between the faultlines of regional conflict. It is also important to better harmonise regional tourism policy and planning vertically within the hierarchy of planning and horizontally between regions and sectors by acknowledging policy-making and planning also as a multisectoral and multilevel activity. Such an approach has the potential to create a better balance between global competitiveness and the sustainable regional development.

SUMMARY OF KEY TERMS

A priori regions

A *priori* regions are those areas where boundaries have been predetermined by others external to the planning and policy-making process.

Functional regions

Functional regions refer to destinations determined by a set of functional interactions that regularly take place. These interactions could be based on economic characteristics, social interactions or similar.

Homogeneous regions

Homogeneous regions refer to destinations where the boundaries have been set according to some set of internally consistent social, physical, environmental and economic characteristics that make it distinguishable from other regions.

New regionalism

New regionalism is an alternative model of regional development that is characterised by less 'top-down' intervention from central government and greater participation at the grassroots level. In principle, new regionalism is based on more localised and inclusive approaches to policy development that reflect unique qualities and strengths of regions. However, the power of interest clusters and networks can operate to exclude some interests, especially community and environmental concerns.

Region

A region is an amalgamation of political, socioeconomic and physical factors that yield a distinctive and integrated landscape.

Regional development

Regional development refers to development strategies and processes that aim to secure appropriate economic and social development in peripheral and generally non-urban regions. Regional development also aims to reduce undesirable disparities between urban and rural areas and to improve the general living conditions and quality of life of the local population.

Regionalisation

Regionalisation refers to a rescaling of politics and policy-making to the regional level, and is often referred to as a 'bottom-up' or organic process of defining and managing regional affairs.

Regionalism

Regionalism refers to a 'top-down' approach to regional development. Regionalism is characterised by delegation of responsibilities from central government to the subnational levels (decentralisation). Levels of policy intervention and coercion from upper levels of government can be high, and levels of commitment and ownership of policy at the local level can be low.

Regioness

Regioness refers to the unique economic, sociopolitical and environmental characteristics of a region, the commonalities and synergies of which make it distinct from its surrounding context. The term refers to intangible qualities, such as cultural characteristics and belongingness and, as such, it extends beyond a spatial interpretation.

Tourism destination

A tourism destination refers to a geographical location, distinct from a traveller's origin, in which the activity of tourism is conducted. A destination is defined by the mobility characteristics of tourists themselves, and it can exist at a variety of scales from national to regional to subregional.

Tourism region

A tourism region refers to the geographical location in which common characteristics and synergies exist between tourism products and services, and the term is also associated with a politico-administrative framework in which tourism planning and policy is delivered. Tourists can visit multiple tourism destinations within a tourism region.

QUESTIONS

1 What is a tourism region? What factors contribute to the definition of tourism regions?

2 Why is tourism often promoted as a mechanism for rejuvenating regional and rural areas?

3 Can tourism be an effective means for regional development? What are the arguments for and against the use of tourism as a tool for regional development?

4 What are the advantages and disadvantages of planning for a destination region compared with the more holistic, multisectoral approach to regional development?

5 Why are collaboration, coordination and communication among stakeholders essential for the successful planning and management of tourism at the regional level?

6 What are the principles underpinning regional governance?

7 What are policy networks, and why are they useful in improving the regional governance of tourism?

8 Discuss the changing nature of government involvement in regional tourism policy-making and planning.

9 Do national and state governments still have a role to play in regional tourism policy and planning?

10 Discuss the relationship between sustainable tourism and scale. Is the region an appropriate level for securing more sustainable outcomes?

EXERCISES

1 As is indicated in table 8.1, there are various structures for and approaches to managing tourism at the regional level. Summarise the way regional tourism is organised in the various states and territories. What are the differences and similarities? Is there a common trend in Australia?

2 Select a regional tourism plan and outline its structure, the key stake-holders involved and the planning process that was adopted. What are the key aims and objectives for the region? Are issues of sustainability and partnership considered? If so, how are they addressed?

FURTHER READING

Bramwell, B & Lane, B (eds) 2000, *Tourism Collaboration and Partnerships: Policy, Practice and Sustainability*, Channel View Publications, Clevedon, UK. This book contains a diverse collection of case studies that illustrate the challenges associated with tourism planning and policy development at different scales.

Hall, CM 2005, *Tourism: Rethinking Social Science of Mobility*, Pearson, Harlow, UK. This book discusses a range of key concepts and issues associated with tourism, including globalisation, localisation and identity, and their influence on regional tourism planning and policy.

Rainnie, A & Grobbelaar, M (eds) 2005, *New Regionalism in Australia*, Ashgate, Aldershot, UK. This book contains a collection of articles that outline the shifts taking place in approaches to regional planning and policy-making. The book critically discusses new regionalism as a response to processes of globalisation and identifies strengths and weaknesses in current theoretical debates.

Smith, SLJ 1995, *Tourism Analysis: A Handbook*, 2nd edn, Longman, Harlow, UK. This text provides a useful discussion of the concept of the 'region' and the different viewpoints used to define regions and for what purposes.

Telfer, DJ 2002, 'Tourism and regional development issues', in R Sharpley & DJ Telfer (eds), *Tourism and Development: Concepts and Issues*, Channel View Publications, Clevedon, UK, pp. 112–48. This chapter critically discusses important concepts and issues associated with definitions of regions and regional development.

Tosun, C & Jenkins, CL 1996, 'Regional planning approaches to tourism development: The case of Turkey', *Tourism Management*, vol. 17, no. 7, pp. 519–31. This article provides a useful discussion of the vexed concept of the region and its application in planning, policy and research.

....

From tourism regions to tourism zones in Western Australia

In a Sustainable Tourism Cooperative Research Centre project conducted in 2004, Western Australia was selected as a case study for exploring issues associated with regional tourism planning. The purpose of this study was to investigate how effectively tourism stakeholders work together at a regional level in Western Australia in the transition phase from 11 tourism regions to five tourism zones (see figures 8.5a and 8.5b). One of the five newly established tourism zones, Australia's South West (ASW), an amalgamation of the two former Western Australian tourism regions South West (SW) and Great Southern (GS), was selected as a case study.

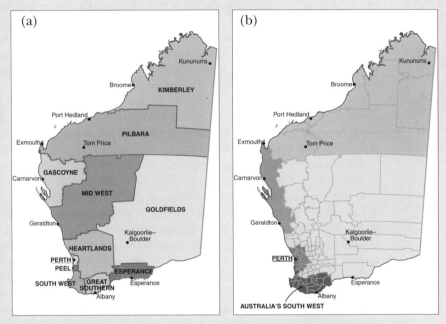

■ **Figure 8.5**   *Western Australia: from regions to zones. (a) Western Australia's former eleven tourism regions; (b) Western Australia's new five tourism zones*

Source: *Western Australian Tourism Commission 2003c, 2003e. Copyright © Tourism WA; used with permission.*

Background

A review of the Partnership 21 document (P21)[1] by the Western Australia Tourism Commission (WATC), which was a five-year planning framework for the state's tourism industry (2000–05), was conducted in 2002 with

(continued)

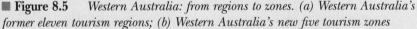

wide-reaching implications for tourism in the state (WATC 2002). It facilitated a debate, which led to the development of a new vision for the future of the state's tourism industry. The initiation of a new approach for regional tourism in Western Australia has been a key component of this strategic plan. During the P21 review various concerns directly related to regional tourism in Western Australia were identified and a number of recommendations calling for greater tourism marketing synergies and for prioritising resource needs at the regional level were made. Furthermore, the importance of delineating regional boundaries in line with travel routes and tourism experiences in the state was also highlighted (see figure 8.1). The main purpose of this realignment of tourism boundaries was to enhance regional marketing efforts to create smaller, more memorable and marketable packages, geared at international and interstate markets. However, in ASW, for example, these markets constituted only 5 per cent and 8 per cent respectively of total visitors to the region (Tourism WA 2004). It was argued that this marketing approach better reflected travel patterns, visitor expectations, product availability and iconic experiences. Moreover, the new approach also aimed to create more efficient and effective administrative arrangements for Western Australia's tourism with greater control and responsibilities being devolved to the regional level (e.g. intrastate marketing and funding arrangements). The efficiency of this approach was justified through the reduction of the existing eleven regions with ten regional tourism associations (RTAs) to five tourism zones with new organisational structures called regional tourism organisations (RTOs) (WATC 2003c).

However, such a major reshuffle of tourism at the regional level was occasionally problematic in its implementation. Some of the contentious issues were, for example, related to the boundaries of the five new tourism zones and to funding and human resource issues.

The amalgamation of two former tourist regions, South West (SW) and Great Southern (GS), formed Australia's South West (ASW) tourism region. ASW is now the second most visited tourism region in Western Australia, receiving 2.14 million visitors in 2002–03, for example (Tourism WA 2004). Although ASW might better reflect visitor expectations and experiences and streamline regional marketing efforts, it brings together two very different destinations. The former SW region can be seen as rather powerful as it had been the second most popular tourist destination in 2002, accounting for 19 per cent of Western Australia's overall tourism market share (after Perth with 36 per cent). In comparison, despite having ranked fourth in the former regional tourism structure, the former GS region had only a 6 per cent market share (WATC 2003a). This imbalance in performance as a tourist region is not only a reflection of the relative proximity of the SW region to Perth as a gateway but might also mirror different interests and development stages of the tourism industry in each of the former regions.

Several individuals and groups in the former SW and GS tourism regions opposed the amalgamation from two regions to one tourism zone for two main reasons. Most notably, some mistrusted the State Government's ability to look after the interests of the regions, and some argued that the previous arrangements for regional tourism at the local level had been working quite well.

Nevertheless, the merger was received favourably across the state (WATC 2003d). Support was strongest in ASW with almost two-thirds (64 per cent) of stakeholders being in favour of the realignment of the tourism regions. However, by disaggregating this support into those from the former SW and those from the former GS tourism region, a more detailed picture emerges. The SW strongly supported this new arrangement (78 per cent in favour) whereas respondents' support from the former GS region amounted to only 27 per cent. This contrast in responses might be explained by the differences in the regions outlined earlier. According to Tourism WA research, the two most contentious issues were tourism zoning and funding arrangements; concerns mainly being about size, membership and lack of equity between the two regions (WATC 2003d).

Progress at the regional level

When comparing and contrasting the specific views of individuals from each former tourism region, differences of opinion as to the effectiveness of the merger began to emerge more clearly. For example, there was the feeling among stakeholders of the former South West region that the merger had not been necessary in the first place. It was also seen as a clear top-down initiation by Tourism WA — stakeholders in the regions had little choice but to accept. However, in the former SW region it is now widely accepted that ASW has the potential to create future benefits for both regions, particularly in managing and marketing the new ASW tourism zone. The view was also expressed that previously existing joint marketing efforts in the regions were now formally acknowledged through the merger. Moreover, stakeholders from the former SW anticipate a future increase in funding and more effective and efficient use of resources (i.e. financial, physical and human). However, some major concerns were also raised, including the size of the new region and the large number of tourism businesses, which it was feared might create some difficulties in promoting the new ASW zone effectively. A proposed shift away from the current intrastate market (87 per cent) towards international and interstate marketing efforts was met with reservations as this might create uncertainties and risks, particularly for smaller operations, whereas bigger tourism businesses might find it easier to capitalise on the interstate and international markets.

This concern of 'small versus big' is also mirrored in comments made by stakeholders from the less prominent and more remote former Great Southern tourism region. Among its stakeholders there was widespread concern that the larger single ASW tourism zone could swallow up their businesses and their power to shape directions within ASW. The perception was that communication and collaboration between tourism stakeholders in the larger zone might become less effective. Stakeholders perceive that they are 'lost in the system' and hence there is little hope of gaining advantages from the merger — so why bother? This anticipation of lack of fairness and equity between former regions in the new tourism zone (i.e. membership base and funding arrangements) is at the core of disapproval of the new ASW zoning expressed by stakeholders of the former GS region.

Moreover, stakeholders from the SW and GS regions felt that the former regional tourism associations worked well and had been able to form an effective

(continued)

network of partnerships within their boundaries. The new organisational arrangements might create a power imbalance that favoured certain interests (including those who were simply more charismatic and able to use the media well) and disadvantage less prominent players. They might also lead to disproportionate allocation of funds for marketing tourist hot spots within the ASW zone.

Conclusion

The study shows that despite generally positive responses to the amalgamation, there was a perception, predominantly from the former Great Southern tourism region, that they have little role to play in the new tourism zone. Feelings of powerlessness were identified despite the efforts by Tourism WA to communicate and to promote the benefits of the merger and to assist through the transition phase. This suggests that communication and collaboration to date might not have been effective enough for a successful operation after the merger. The study has, for instance, shown that working together on issues relevant to tourism in the new regional tourism zone appears to be dominated by members from the former South West tourism region. On the other hand, members of the former Great Southern region still prefer to collaborate within their traditional regional structure.

Tourism WA's intention to realign the management of regional tourism into five tourism zones in order to focus on growth in the interstate and international markets might not have given adequate consideration to the processes of collaboration, networking and consensus-building associated with such a major reform. To better implement the new regional concept for tourism in Western Australia much more attention should be paid in the future to the complex sets of interrelationships that often occur at the regional and local levels. These interrelationships form webs of consensus and conflict. Leadership contests, local politics, funding, conflicts between shires, personalities, jealousies, vested and business interests, pride, ownership, territoriality and a shared sense of place are difficult dimensions to manage. This Western Australian case study sheds light on some of these issues and highlights the need for improved consultation and collaboration with all stakeholders to develop ways to work towards common goals and objectives in the new ASW tourism zone.

. . . .

[1] Since replaced by the new strategy *Pathways Forward — Strategic Plan 2003–2008* (WATC 2003b).

Questions

1   Critically discuss the advantages and disadvantages of Western Australia's move to reduce the number of tourism regions.

2   Imagine you work for Tourism WA. What advice would you give to the Great Southern and South West tourism regions to assist in the amalgamation and in the management of change?

References

Tourism WA 2004, *Australia's Coral Coast Tourism Perspective 2003*, Tourism WA, Perth.

Western Australian Tourism Commission 2002, 'Review of Partnership 21 Terms of Reference', accessed 13 December 2004, www.touras.com.au/html/p21_review.html.

—— 2003a, *Australia's South West Tourism Perspective 2003*, WATC, Perth.

—— 2003b, *Pathways Forward: Strategic Plan 2003–2008*, WATC, Perth.

—— 2003c, *The New Concept for State Tourism: A Zone Strategy for Western Australia*, WATC, Perth.

—— 2003d, unpublished data from the consultation process of discussion and position papers, WATC, Perth.

—— 2003e, *Western Australian Tourism Product and Infrastructure Development Plan 2003–2012*, WATC, Perth.

ACKNOWLEDGEMENT

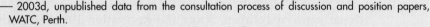

The author would like to thank Graham Thompson for his contribution to the discussion on policy networks and governance as well as for his work as research assistant in the STCRC project on regional tourism in Western Australia.

REFERENCES

Bätzing, W 2001, 'Zum Begriff und zur Konzeption von "Region" aus der Sicht der Geographie', in R. Sturm (ed.), *Die Region in Europa verstehen: Konzepte und Ideen in der wissenschaftlichen Debatte*, pp. 33–8, Zentralinstituts für Regionalforschung, Erlangen.

Börzel, TA 1997, 'What's so special about policy networks?', *European Integration Online Papers*, vol. 1, no. 16, pp. 1–24.

—— 1998, 'Organising Babylon: On the different conceptions of policy networks', *Public Administration*, 76, pp. 253–73.

Börzel, TA & Risse, T 2005, 'Public–private partnerships: Effective and legitimate tools of international governance?', in E Grande & LW Pauly (eds), *Complex Sovereignty: On the Reconstitution of Political Authority in the 21st Century*, University of Toronto Press, Toronto, pp. 195–216.

Bramwell, B & Lane, B 1999, editorial, *Journal of Sustainable Tourism*, vol. 7, nos 3–4, pp. 179–81.

—— 2000. *Tourism Collaboration and Partnerships: Policy, Practice and Sustainability*. Channel View Publications, Clevedon, UK.

Butler, RW 1998, 'Sustainable tourism: Looking backwards in order to progress?', in CM Hall & A Lew (eds), *Sustainable Tourism: A Geographical Perspective*, Longman, Harlow, UK, pp. 25–34.

Commonwealth of Australia 1990, *Ecologically Sustainable Development: A Commonwealth Discussion Paper*, APGS, Canberra.

—— 1992, *National Strategy for Ecologically Sustainable Development*, APGS, Canberra.

—— 2001, *Stronger Regions: A Stronger Australia*, APGS, Canberra, viewed 3 May 2006, www.dotars.gov.au/regional/statement/contents.aspx.

—— 2003, *Tourism White Paper: A Medium to Long-term Strategy for Tourism*, APGS, Canberra.

Department of Conservation and Environment 1993, *Ecotourism: A National Strength of Victoria*, DCE, Melbourne.

Department of Tourism, Sport and Racing 1997, *The Queensland Ecotourism Plan*, DTSR, Brisbane.

Department of Tourism, Sport and Recreation 1994, *Ecotourism: Adding Value to Tourism in Natural Areas*, DTSR, Hobart.

Dowling, R 1993, 'An environmentally based planning model for regional tourism development', *Journal of Sustainable Tourism*, vol. 1, no. 1, pp. 17–37.

Dredge, D 2005, 'Local versus state-driven production of "the region": Regional tourism policy in the Hunter, New South Wales, Australia', in A Rainnie & M Grobbelaar (eds), *New Regionalism in Australia*, Ashgate, Aldershot, UK, pp. 301–19.

Dredge, D & Jenkins, JM 2003, 'Destination place identity and regional tourism policy', *Tourism Geographies*, vol. 5, no. 4, pp. 383–407.

Ecologically Sustainable Development (ESD) Steering Committee 1992, *National Strategy for Ecologically Sustainable Development*, APGS, Canberra.

Fürst, D 2002, 'Region und Netzwerke: Aktuelle Aspekte zu einem Spannungsverhältnis', viewed 9 April 2006, www.diezeitschrift.de/12002/region_und_netzwerke.htm.

Gunn, CA 1994, *Tourism Planning*, 3rd edn, Taylor & Francis, Washington, DC.

Gunn, CA & Var, T 2002, *Tourism Planning*, 4th edn, Routledge, New York.

Hall, CM 1999, 'Rethinking collaboration and partnership: A public policy perspective', *Journal of Sustainable Tourism*, vol. 7, nos 3–4, pp. 274–88.

—— 2000, *Tourism Planning: Policies, Processes and Relationships*, Prentice Hall, Harlow, UK.

—— 2005, *Tourism: Rethinking Social Science of Mobility*, Pearson, Harlow, UK.

Hall, CM, Jenkins, J & Kearsley, G (eds) 1997, *Tourism Planning and Policy in Australia and New Zealand: Issues and Cases*, Irwin Publishers, Sydney.

Hall, CM & Page, S 2002, *The Geography of Tourism and Recreation*, 2nd edn, Routledge, New York.

Heatley, A 1979, *Government of the Northern Territory*, University of Queensland Press, St Lucia, Qld.

Inskeep, E 1991, *Tourism Planning: An Integrated and Sustainable Development Approach*, Van Nostrand Reinhold, New York.

Intergovernmental Committee for Ecologically Sustainable Development (ICESD) 1996, *Report on the Implementation of the National Strategy for Ecologically Sustainable Development 1993–1995*, APGS, Canberra.

Jenkins, JM 2000, 'The dynamics of regional tourism organisations in New South Wales, Australia: History, structures and operations', *Current Issues in Tourism*, vol. 3, no. 3, pp. 175–203.

—— 2001, 'Statutory authorities in whose interests? The case of Tourism New South Wales, the Bed Tax, and "the Games" ', *Pacific Tourism Review*, vol. 4, pp. 201–18.

Jenkins, JM & Hall, CM 1997, 'Tourism policy and legislation in Australia', in CM Hall, JM Jenkins & G Kearsley (eds), *Tourism Planning and Policy in Australia and New Zealand: Cases, Issues and Practice*, Irwin, Sydney, pp. 37–48.

Jenkins, JM & Sorensen, AD 1996, 'Tourism, regional development and the Commonwealth: A critical appraisal of the Regional Tourism Development Program', *Australian Leisure*, vol. 7, no. 4, pp. 28–35.

Kelly, I & Taylor, A 2004. *Australian Regional Tourism Handbook: Industry Solutions 2003*, Centre for Regional Tourism Research, Southern Cross University, Lismore, NSW.

Kilper, H 1998, *Regionalisierung: Prinzipielle Überlegungen und Denkanstöße aus der internationalen Bauausstellung Emscher Park*, Institut Arbeit und Technik, Gelsenkirchen, Germany.

Lane, MB 2005, 'Regional environmental governance: The critical questions', unpublished paper, Geographical & Environmental Studies, University of Adelaide, Adelaide, SA.

Mayntz, R 2002, 'Common goods and governance', in A Héritier (ed.), *Reinventing European and International Governance*, Rowman & Littlefield, Lanham MD, pp. 15–27.

Moose, I & Brodda, Y 2002, 'Regionalentwicklung, Regionalisierung, regionale Identität: Perspektiven für die Region', paper presented at 5 Südharz-Symposium 11–12 October, Bad Sachsa, Germany.

Morgan, K 2005, 'Sustainable regions: Governance, innovation and sustainability', in A Rainnie & M Grobbelaar (eds), *New Regionalism in Australia*, Ashgate, Aldershot, UK, pp. 27–48.

Müller, H 1995, 'Nachhaltige Regionalentwicklung durch Tourismus: Ziele—Methoden—Perspektiven', in A Steinecke (ed.), *Tourismus und Nachhaltige Entwicklung: Strategien und Lösungsansätze*, Europäisches Tourismus Institut, Trier, Germany, pp. 11–18.

Murphy, PE & Dore, LR 2000, 'A conceptual framework for regional tourism and training', in E Michael (ed.), *Peak Performance in Tourism and Hospitality Research*, La Trobe University, Bundoora, Vic, pp. 153–64.

Northern Territory Tourist Commission 2002, *The Northern Territory Strategic Plan 2003–2007*, NTTC, Darwin.

—— 2004, *Destination Development Strategy*, NTTC, Darwin.

Pearce, DG 1980, 'Tourism and regional development: A genetic approach', *Annals of Tourism Research*, vol. 7, no. 1, pp. 69–81.

—— 1989, *Tourist Development*, Longman, Harlow, UK.

—— 1995, *Tourism Today: A Geographical Analysis*, 2nd edn, Longman, Harlow, UK.

Pforr, C 2000, 'Ökotourismus in Australien: Echte Alternative oder nur Alibi? Eine tourismuspolitische Perspektive', *ÖKOZIDjournal*, vol. 19, no. 1, pp. 11–18.

—— 2001, 'Tourism policy in Australia's Northern Territory: A policy process analysis of its Tourism Development Masterplan', *Current Issues in Tourism*, vol. 4, nos 2–4, pp. 275–307.

—— 2002, 'The "makers and shapers" of tourism policy in the Northern Territory of Australia: A policy network analysis of actors and their relational constellations', *Journal of Hospitality and Tourism Management*, vol. 9, no. 2, pp. 134–51.

—— 2004a, 'Policy-making for sustainable tourism', in FD Pineda, CA Brebbia & M Mugica (eds), *Sustainable Tourism*, WIT Press, Southampton, UK, pp. 83–94.

—— 2004b, 'Sustainable development: A dynamic process', in P Sauer, A Nankervis & S Mensik (eds), *Sustainability in Global Services: Selected Essays*, Prague University of Economics, Prague, pp. 1–15.

—— 2004c, 'Sustainable tourism: Governance through policy networks', in R MacLellan et al. (eds), *Tourism: State of the Art II*, Conference Proceedings, 27–30 June, University of Strathclyde, Glasgow.

—— 2004d, 'On the road to sustainable tourism? Policy diffusion of sustainable development principles', in C Cooper et al. (eds), *Creating Tourism Knowledge*, CAUTHE Conference Proceedings, University of Queensland, Brisbane.

—— 2006, 'Tourism policy in the making: An Australian network perspective', *Annals of Tourism Research*, vol. 33, no. 1, pp. 87–108.

Pipkin, J 1996, 'Biological diversity conservation: A public policy perspective', *Environmental Management*, vol. 20, no. 6, pp. 793–7.

Preece, N, Van Oosterzee, P & James, D 1995, *Two-Way Track. Biodiversity Conservation and Ecotourism: An Investigation of Linkages, Mutual Benefits and Future Opportunities*, Department of the Environment, Sport and Territories, Canberra.

Prosser, G, 2001, 'Regional tourism', in N Douglas, N Douglas & R Derrett (eds), *Special Interest Tourism*, John Wiley & Sons, Brisbane, pp. 86–112.

Rainnie, A & Grobbelaar, M (eds) 2005, *New Regionalism in Australia*, Ashgate, Aldershot, UK.

Ribot, JC 2002, *Democratic Decentralization of Natural Resources: Institutionalizing Popular Participation*, World Resources Institute, Washington, DC.

Richardson, H 1978, *Regional and Urban Economics*, Penguin, Harmondsworth, UK.

Robinson, M 1999, 'Collaboration and cultural consent: Refocusing sustainable tourism', *Journal of Sustainable Tourism*, vol. 7, no. 3–4, pp. 379–97.

Rose, N 2000, 'Community, citizenship and the Third Way', *American Behavior Scientist*, vol. 43, no. 9, pp. 1395–411.

Ryan, C 2002, 'Equity, management, power sharing and sustainability: Issues of the "new tourism" ', *Tourism Management*, vol. 23, no. 1, pp. 17–26.

Selin, S 1999, 'Developing a typology of sustainable tourism partnerships', *Journal of Sustainable Tourism*, vol. 7, nos 3–4, pp. 260–73.

Smith, SLJ 1995, *Tourism Analysis: A Handbook*, 2nd edn, Longman, Harlow, UK.

Smyth, P, Reddel, T & Jones, A (eds) 2005, *Community and Local Governance in Australia*, University of New South Wales Press, Kensington, NSW.

Sorensen, T 1995, 'Regionen und Regionalismus in Australien', *Geographische Rundschau*, vol. 47, no. 11, pp. 616–24.

South Australian Tourism Department and Tourism Commission and the Department of Environment and Natural Resources 1995, *Ecotourism: A Natural Strategy for South Australia*, South Australian Tourism Commission, Adelaide.

Telfer, DJ 2002, 'Tourism and regional development issues', in R Sharpley & DJ Telfer (eds), *Tourism and Development: Concepts and Issues*, Channel View Publications, Clevedon, UK, pp. 112–48.

Thompson, G & Pforr, C 2005, *Policy Networks and Good Governance: A Discussion*, SOM Working Paper Series (01/2005), Curtin University of Technology, Perth, WA.

Tosun, C & Jenkins, CL 1996, 'Regional planning approaches to tourism development: The case of Turkey', *Tourism Management*, vol. 17, no. 7, pp. 519–31.

Tourism NSW 2004, *The Nature in Tourism Plan*, Tourism NSW, Sydney.

Tourism Queensland 2002, *Queensland Ecotourism Plan 2003–2008*, Tourism Queensland, Brisbane.

Tourism WA 2004, *Australia's Coral Coast Tourism Perspective 2003*, Tourism WA, Perth.

Weber, M 1973, 'Der Beruf zur Politik' in H Winckelmann (ed.), *Max Weber: Soziologie—Universalgeschichtiche Analysen—Politik*, 5th edn, Kröner, Stuttgart, pp. 167–85.

Weiermair, K 1995, 'Structural changes in the tourism industry and the adaptation of occupational and vocational training systems: Problems and prospects', *Zeitschrift für Fremdenverkehr*, vol. 50, no. 3, pp. 11–17.

Western Australian Tourism Commission 2003a, *Australia's South West Tourism Perspective 2003*, WATC, Perth.

—— 2003b, *Pathways Forward: Strategic Plan 2003–2008*, WATC, Perth.

—— 2003c, *The New Concept for State Tourism: A Zone Strategy for Western Australia*, WATC, Perth.

—— 2003d, unpublished data from the consultation process of discussion and position papers, WATC, Perth.

Western Australian Tourism Commission and Department of Conservation and Land Management 2004, *A Nature Based Tourism Strategy*, WATC & CALM, Perth.

Dianne Dredge

CHAPTER 9

Local *destination planning and policy*

LEARNING OBJECTIVES

After reading this chapter you will be able to:

1 discuss why 'local' is sometimes difficult to define but is nevertheless an important scale of tourism planning and policy development

2 discuss the institutional context in which local destination planning and policy development occurs

3 explain the changing role of local government and how it has influenced tourism

4 identify and discuss the influences on local government in local destination tourism policy and planning

5 outline and discuss what is meant by strategic planning, spatial master planning and issues-based planning in the context of local tourism planning and policy.

9.1 INTRODUCTION ···

This chapter places local tourism planning and policy within its broader economic, social and political contexts and explores the institutional settings and challenges that shape its development. In doing so, much of the chapter focuses on local government as an important arena for destination planning and policy. However, it is emphasised that it is not the only space in which local planning and policy development takes place. Regional tourism organisations, local and regional economic development agencies and state development and planning agencies also have significant but often indirect influences on local tourism planning and policy.

Section 9.2 examines the concept of 'local' tourism policy and planning. Section 9.3 examines local government roles and responsibilities, as local government provides the institutional context for much local tourism planning and policy. Section 9.4 identifies and explores influences on local government tourism planning and policy development. Section 9.5 identifies various approaches that local government has taken to address tourism policy and planning and argues for an integrated and holistic approach that incorporates elements of each approach.

9.2 CONCEPTUALISING LOCAL TOURISM PLANNING AND POLICY ·························

Not surprisingly, *local* tourism policy and planning is undertaken at a *local* level. Yet defining just what is 'local' can be quite problematic. Local destinations do not necessarily conform to local government boundaries, and this can lead to quite disparate views of the **local destination** by different actors and agencies involved in tourism planning and policy development (Dredge 2005). Local tourism planning and policy formulation requires an understanding of the diverse influences shaping destination development and the way they play out to make a destination unique. No two destination planning and policy approaches can be the same. Any number of conditions, such as different spatial scales (destination size), geography (including topography and climate), local economic conditions, social and cultural values and political orientations combine to produce different issues and outcomes.

So what is the local scale at which tourism planning and policy applies? According to Gunn (1993, 2002), a destination is conceptualised as a geographical area the limits of which are defined by complex sets of relationships among community, attractions and travellers. For Gunn, a destination is difficult to define because it is perceived by travellers and defined by travellers' movements among attractions, accommodation and services. In other words, destinations have a cognitive dimension and can be defined by tourists' perceptions of what makes up the destination, their mobility characteristics and their interactions with services and attractions.

The notion of the **tourist gaze** embodies the idea that destinations are made up of symbols to which tourists give meaning (Urry 1990). The particular combination of symbols and their relationship to each other determine how destinations are perceived and understood (Urry 1990). Moreover, there may be multiple, overlapping destinations, which are viewed from the perspectives of culture, ethnicity, age, gender and lifestyle (Urry 2003). Different tourists perceive and experience their destination in different ways; they generate and accumulate different types of knowledge, engage with different aspects and have different levels of spatial engagement with the location (e.g. Walmsley & Jenkins 1992). In this way, tourism planners and policy-makers need to be aware of the different ways in which destinations are understood, perceived and defined.

Destinations are frequently defined at different spatial scales from national to regional to local, depending on the objectives of the planning or policy exercise and the agency undertaking the planning exercise. For example, a national government interested in boosting foreign income from tourism might conceptualise an entire country as one destination. Alternatively, a local agency interested in managing the effects of tourism on a particular local protected area might conceptualise the destination as a small discrete area encompassing a local government area or part thereof. This multiscaled nature of destinations presents certain challenges for tourism planning because the issues addressed at each scale will vary. Further, destinations do not necessarily correspond to government or other administrative boundaries. Some destinations overlap with other destinations. As a result, various local destination planning and policy initiatives overlap and, in some cases, countervailing planning and policy initiatives emerge that can cancel each other out.

Local destinations therefore exist in conceptual, ambiguous and imprecise ways and can be defined using geographical, politico-administrative or cognitive boundaries. Nevertheless, it is important to draw boundaries because public policy, being a product of government, applies to geographically defined areas or jurisdictions over which government has authority. Responding to this practical need for definition, and as previously discussed in section 8.2.1, Smith (1995) observes that there are three ways in which local destinations can be delineated:

1. *A priori* regions — where the boundaries are defined by someone external to the planning and policy exercise and are accepted by the researcher.
2. *Homogeneous* regions — where local destinations are drawn according to a set of internally consistent social, economic and cultural characteristics that are distinguishable from other regions
3. *Functional* regions — where local destination boundaries are determined by a set of functional interactions.

In practice, local planning and policy usually adopts a combination of these approaches to define the destination. Planners and tourism officers working for local government usually adopt *a priori* administrative boundaries. However, they might also divide destinations into subregions on the basis of localised *homogeneous* tourism characteristics or spatial clusters of tourism activities, attractions and services that *function* together. For the purposes of this chapter, local destinations are geographical units defined by the unique social, economic, environmental and cultural qualities that give a destination identity; they are characterised by the functional integration of tourist attractions and services. The destination comprises many interrelated parts, including tangible features, such as attractions, services and communities, and intangible features, such as a sense of place and community goodwill (Gunn 2002). Destinations overlap and are functionally intertwined.

Most local tourism planning and policy development exercises are undertaken by or on behalf of local governments. Local industry associations and community groups are increasingly involved (see section 2.5). For this reason it is important to consider the changing nature of local government and the challenges associated with its involvement in tourism planning and policy-making.

9.3 LOCAL GOVERNMENT AND LOCAL TOURISM PLANNING AND POLICY

Responsibility for the development and management of tourism falls more and more to local government. Local government undertakes a number of important policy functions, such as land use planning, environmental management, infrastructure provision and economic development, that influence the achievement of sustainable tourism development (Dredge 1998; UNEP 2003). Local governments, often acting within national and regional policy frameworks, are partners in a range of local development and resource management dialogues that influence tourism (Hall 1994; Elliott 1997). In these dialogues local government has a potentially important role in negotiating and mediating among business, community and government interests and can provide effective leadership in sustainable tourism development (UNEP 2003).

According to the New Zealand Government (2001), the roles that local government plays in tourism include:
• provision and operation of tourism facilities and services
• provision of funds for tourism marketing and services
• community facilitation
• regulation of land use, public health and other functions related to tourism
• provision of basic infrastructure, services and facilities.

New Zealand is among the first national governments to acknowledge the importance of local government and has developed a national approach, published as *Postcards from Home: The Local Government Tourism Strategy 2003*.

In developing countries, however, local governments often do not have sufficient resources, expertise or political power to undertake tourism planning and local policy development. In such cases, provincial or national government undertake local planning and policy development on their behalf. The case of the Mexican Government's involvement in local destination planning and design, discussed in Planning in Practice: 'Local planning and policy by national government — Cancún, Mexico' (p. 323), provides a good example of a national government driving local tourism planning and policy for the national benefit. Nevertheless, it is important to understand something of the historical underpinnings and institutional cultures that shape local government approaches to tourism as this level of government remains an important player in local destination planning in most countries.

■ 9.3.1 **Historical** *influences*

Local government has a significant role in destination planning and policy development, but it is subject to a range of influences that shape its capacity to deal with tourism, its level of involvement and its general approach (Dredge 2001a). In Australia, the establishment of local government can be traced back to the nineteenth century struggle to service rapidly growing urban areas that emerged as a result of the Industrial Revolution (Marshall 1997; Dredge 2001a). Legislation prepared and reworked during the mid-nineteenth century established local government and defined its powers and responsibilities as those predominantly associated with basic infrastructure provision and servicing of local communities. This legislation also provided a set of procedures, rules and routines for the election of local representatives. Under colonial rule governments generally took a paternalistic and technocratic approach to planning and policy-making, and local government legislation remained relatively intact throughout the twentieth century. In the 1990s, however, major reviews of legislation in most states and territories were undertaken and the role and nature of local government began to change significantly. As a result, in many countries, including Australia and the United Kingdom, local government legislation has been completely rewritten to recognise local government's role in achieving sustainable development, in building a community's capacity and wellbeing (Marshall 1997; Keen & Scase 1998). These ideas reflect growing commitment to sustainable development and recognition that local government has a powerful role in shaping development and resource use dialogues at the level at which decisions are made (UNEP 2003).

■ 9.3.2 **Statutory** *roles and responsibilities*

Traditionally, the powers given to local governments in Australia were aimed at servicing local communities and protecting local community interests. These powers were divided into two groups:

1. *mandatory powers* and responsibilities enshrined in (a) local government legislation and (b) secondary legislation. These responsibilities include

the provision of basic services, such as waste collection, roads, water and electricity supply

2. *permissive powers* or those that local government could opt to undertake in addition to mandatory powers. These include powers to declare and manage recreation reserves and the provision of bathing facilities. Tourism and local economic development are permissive powers.

The operation, roles and responsibilities of local government and participants in Australia's local government system are set out in the relevant state and territory legislation. In general, this legislation gives local government powers to make and enforce local laws, develop and implement policy and undertake all the necessary administration to fulfil its legislated obligations.

In addition to this local government legislation, secondary legislation sets out roles and responsibilities for local government in a range of areas including planning, building, environment and health. Planning legislation in Australian states and territories, for example, sets out local government roles and responsibilities in relation to managing land use change, in developing planning strategies and assessing development applications. Public health legislation sets out roles and responsibilities for local government in, for example, the licensing of eating establishments. Secondary legislation is diverse, resulting in a situation in which local government has a wide range of roles, responsibilities and functions that directly and indirectly affect the planning, delivery and management of tourism products and services within a destination.

Local government undertakes many planning processes as a result of these powers. Traditionally, land use planning, open space planning, infrastructure planning and social planning were all carried out as separate tasks under separate divisions within council. Now, as a result of the recent shifts taking place in local government described above, it is more common for multisectoral planning to take place as a council-wide planning process, which is then tied into council corporate plans. Nevertheless, council formulates policy in a wide range of areas, and local government has significant responsibilities with respect to the way tourism develops and is managed at the destination level. The relationship between council planning and policy development and tourism is outlined in table 9.1.

These responsibilities are derived from legislation that sets out roles, responsibilities and duties of local government; that is, although local government can choose to address a certain issue, it must be satisfied that it has the power under legislation to do so. In order to further understand existing and potential roles and responsibilities of local government, a brief overview of the institutional environment in which local government operates is necessary.

9.3.3 The *changing role of local government*

In Australia, the main role of local government has historically been as a service provider focusing on the three Rs: roads, rates and rubbish (Marshall 1997). The logic behind the creation of local government was

■ Table 9.1
*Local
government
roles and their
influence on
tourism*

LOCAL GOVERNMENT ROLES	POTENTIAL INFLUENCE ON TOURISM
Infrastructure provision and maintenance	Transport infrastructure can shape access to the destination and travel patterns within the destination Basic infrastructure capacity (e.g. water and sewerage) can shape the destination's capacity to absorb tourists and might limit development
Land use planning	Development assessment and strategic land use planning influences on the built character of the destination and the spatial integration of the destination
Environmental management	Protects and preserves unique environmental features of a destination
Open space planning and management	Protects and conserves open space, influences the character and amenity of the destination, helps create a 'sense of place'
Public health and safety management	Protects and enhances visitor satisfaction, destination image and quality
Local economic development	Encourages synergetic economic activity, the development of appropriate tourism business and support activities
Education, training and employment	Influences quality in the delivery of tourism services and facilities
Tourism promotion and marketing	Fosters branding and destination image development
Arts and cultural development	Encourages the development of unique and positive sense of community and belongingness attractive to tourism
Community development	Encourages a community supportive of tourism activity and enterprise
Human services	Encourages positive attitudes and improved service delivery

that another level of government closer to the people was needed. Colonial governments were unable to devote adequate resources and attention to local needs when there were many 'big picture' issues associated with servicing the rapidly growing colonies. The logic went that, through the election of local representatives and the establishment of local government, local community needs could be better addressed in the rapidly developing colonies (Larcombe 1961; Painter 1993).

Colonial governments held a paternalistic view about the population and this influenced the way local governments were set up. The dominant view was that the government 'knew best'. In Australia at that time there were also a large number of pardoned convicts and free settlers with limited education, which contributed to a belief that the colonial governments had to keep a tight reign on these new local governments and their elected representatives, dictating not only their roles and responsibilities but also how they went about their activities. Moreover, colonial governments required that local councils raise part of the revenue they needed through a limited range of sources, including land taxes and other charges. The limited financial position of local government also acted to ensure that it maintained a fairly narrow range of concerns (see the discussion of fiscal imbalance in the case study 'Intergovernmental relations and tourism in Australia' in chapter 2, pp. 63–5).

More recently, roles and responsibilities have expanded significantly. The sustainable development imperative, technological advances in transport and communication, changing lifestyle aspirations, increased environmental awareness and globalisation have all contributed to a growing range of issues that challenge local government (Dredge 2001a). Australia's constitutional division of roles and responsibilities is evolving to respond to these emerging conditions. In these new circumstances, local government now finds itself involved in a range of activities that extend well beyond the traditional provision of roads, collection of rates and rubbish. This expanded range of activities includes social servicing, the protection of community wellbeing, environmental management and economic development.

Changes in the way local government has undertaken its business first became evident in the 1980s. The rise of neoliberal economic management philosophies has profoundly influenced the way local government undertakes its planning activities (Imrie & Thomas 1995; Healey 1997). Strong centralised planning processes, often with an overt spatial emphasis, and direct infrastructure and service provision were replaced with a range of fragmented planning and policy processes often based on single issues. Policy solutions frequently sought to offset the responsibilities of government through outsourcing to the private sector, transferring responsibility to industry through such measures as self-regulation, and through incentives designed to empower business to help itself (see section 4.6). As a result, these days many planning activities are undertaken by consultants, and decision-making is undertaken by boards that comprise community, industry and local government representatives. Local government is no longer the all-powerful central agent in local planning and policy development.

These changes have resulted in an increase in community and business groups involved in destination planning and policy-making and a fracturing of the institutional landscape into multi-actor networked policy settings based on issues and short-term problem solving (Hall 2000; Dredge 2006). Strategic planning became less important from the 1980s onwards and has started to re-emerge only since the turn of the century.

Since 2000, ageing infrastructure, land use and growth management issues, economic restructuring and social marginalisation and other community issues in many urban areas have stimulated growing calls for more sustainable and comprehensive planning and cross-sectoral management. Redland Shire, discussed in the case study, 'Local planning and policy by local government —

Redland Shire, Australia' (p. 330), is a good example of a local government that has undertaken a comprehensive approach to its planning and policy development. Strategic planning and visioning have re-emerged as important tools to combat the failures of laissez-faire approaches adopted since the 1980s. Many large-scale planning and management projects spanning mega-urban regions, and major infrastructure planning are being undertaken. Such projects involve multiple government agencies, community groups, industry partners and NGOs. In this context, the development of local destination tourism planning and policy is increasingly being integrated within a more elaborate institutional framework and is seen less frequently as a stand-alone exercise. The time, energy and focus of destination tourism planning and policy development therefore will depend on where tourism fits into local social, political and economic development agendas of government ministers and agencies, businesses, communities, pressure groups, researchers, advisers and other interests.

Of course, this expanded consultation, the increased number of actors and agencies involved and the diffusion of decision-making and planning among different sectors means that planning and policy development has become more elaborate and informed. Expanded responsibilities and scarce resources mean that there is often strong competition for council attention and resources between the traditional service functions of local government, such as water, sewerage and roads, and the more recently defined roles, such as tourism and local economic development. Corporate planning processes, the onerous requirements of statutory planning processes (i.e. those the council has an obligation under legislation to undertake) and the professional characteristics of staff can result power struggles between various sections or departments within council. Decision-making is often based on narrow sectoral interests rather than broader concerns about social, economic and environmental sustainability. The perceived importance of tourism in the community, and a council's relationship with tourism operators and the broader community, has important implications for the way in which tourism is valued and managed. Further, these relationships can have important effects on the way local government perceives its role with respect to tourism and what resources are allocated for tourism planning and management.

9.4 INFLUENCES ON LOCAL GOVERNMENT TOURISM PLANNING AND POLICY

In order for local tourism planning and policy-making to be grounded in the special qualities and dynamics of place, an appreciation of the factors influencing local tourism development and the dynamics of local processes are important. These include:
• processes of globalisation and its impact on the local government area
• ideological influences impacting upon local government management

- economic, political, sociocultural and environmental influences
- institutional arrangements
- unique features and qualities of the destination
- community attitudes to and involvement in tourism
- local characteristics of tourism.

Each of these influences will be discussed in turn.

■ 9.4.1 Globalisation

The term 'globalisation' encapsulates a range of sociocultural and economic processes characterised by, among other things, global movement of capital, economic integration and cultural homogenisation (Appadurai 1996). These complex, dynamic forces shape local economies. Many heavy industrial areas, such as Broken Hill and Newcastle in New South Wales, have seen their local economies severely affected by factory closures and high unemployment as a result of, for example, differentiation and specialisation within mass markets and the moving of factories to countries with cheaper labour and less onerous laws. In these situations, tourism is frequently mooted as a tool for local economic development and a panacea for employment growth and economic diversification (Milne 1998; Dredge 2001b).

At the same time, advances in communication and information technology have changed how and where people live and their patterns of work. Many people are gravitating towards the seachange and treechange communities to fulfil lifestyle aspirations. Tourism contributes to these changing patterns of mobility, and these patterns of mobility contribute to changing patterns of tourism (Hall 2005).

As a result of these and other changes, globalisation has brought with it a restructuring of relationships between urban and rural areas. It has also stimulated the emergence of contrasting landscapes of economic production (e.g. urban economic powerhouses characterised by strong diversified production) and consumption (e.g. landscapes dominated by tourism and leisure). As a result, increasing competition has emerged between urban regions to attract investment, and roles and responsibilities of local government have shifted considerably in attempts to adjust (Dredge & Jenkins 2003). Rural areas, finding it increasingly difficult to compete, are searching for economic replacement activities that can help to stem out-migration and activities that can assist in reaffirming a sense of community and civic pride (Carson & Macbeth 2005). Under these conditions associated with globalisation, local government involvement in tourism is often framed.

The initiatives contained in **Local Agenda 21** have also acted as powerful incentives for local government involvement in many new sectors. Local Agenda 21 originally emerged as a response to the Earth Summit in 1992. Its intention is to provide a local framework for implementing 'big-picture' sustainability objectives espoused by the international community in the Rio Declaration. The Australian Government, as signatory to the Rio Declaration, has adopted the Local Agenda 21 initiative and has sought to develop a range of programs, research, frameworks and practice directions to assist in the local implementation of sustainable development (Cotter & Hannan 1999). Commonwealth funding has been made available for various implementation initiatives. It is not surprising that many councils across Australia, either from ethical considerations or as a result of financial incentive, have sought to implement Local Agenda 21 initiatives. The management of tourism is seen as an important issue within this agenda (Cotter & Hannan 1999).

As a result of the above forces, local government has shifted away from its narrowly defined role in servicing and infrastructure provision to embrace a more active role in achieving sustainable development, economic prosperity and community wellbeing. The nature and extent of local government involvement in tourism is increasingly considered as part of a broader and more holistic view of local government's role in creating livable, vibrant, prosperous, innovative and sustainable communities (Carson & Macbeth 2005). The development and management of a viable tourism industry can contribute to the broader development and maintenance of community wellbeing and livability in tangible and non-tangible ways. For example, employment generated from tourism activity has a direct benefit for the economic wellbeing of the community. Indirect benefits accruing from increased employment include civic pride, a heightened sense of community belonging and a positive view of the future. Although these benefits might be intangible, they nevertheless contribute to perceived wellbeing and prosperity.

9.4.2 Ideological *influences*

Ideological influences refer to deeply embedded values, ideas and behaviour of different stakeholders and individuals that influence their engagement in and contribution to local tourism planning. These ideas, values and behaviour are driven by:

• the level and nature of commitment to sustainable development and its interpretation
• relationships between local government, tourism businesses and the community
• the perceived level and type of government involvement most appropriate for tourism, and
• whether tourism should be developed and, if so, how tourism should best be managed at the destination.

These ideological influences shape, often covertly, debates about how tourism should be developed, promoted and managed and the appropriate extent and style of government involvement. These influences also shape the way the policy process unfolds, the behaviour of and strategies adopted by individuals and agencies, the level and quality of policy debates that occur and the creation and maintenance of networks of interests. These ideological influences can be so deeply embedded in the individuals and agencies involved that they are often difficult to identify. Nevertheless, reflection and a critical perspective on the values, ideas and ethical positions of actors has important benefits in making the tourism planning and policy approach more transparent and accountable (Macbeth 2005).

■ 9.4.3 Economic, *political, social and environmental influences*

As previously discussed, broad social, economic and environmental trends influence the way tourism is perceived by and valued in a local community and, in turn, how it is addressed. Tourism is frequently identified as a tool of local economic development, employment generation and investment attraction. More recently it has been argued that tourism can also be a tool for improving community wellbeing. The interplay of social, economic and environmental conditions can have a profound effect on the perceived importance of tourism and the relative power of different interest groups at the destination (e.g. Dredge 2001a). A range of factors inevitably influences local tourism planning, including:

• the effects of globalisation and economic restructuring on local communities
• population migration, demographic and socioeconomic characteristics of the local community and its attitudes towards tourism
• the political importance of tourism in the local context
• the nature and sociocultural significance of environmental assets from which tourism draws
• the availability of public funding and support for tourism.

How these influences develop and change over time provides an important historical dimension that influences current thinking, sometimes indirectly. A thorough investigation of these issues must underpin the development of an effective local tourism planning and policy approach.

The way tourism is framed politically has important implications for the way tourism is managed and the type of government involvement that might be considered appropriate. Traditionally, tourism has been conceptualised as a tool for local economic development and has been located within the economic development units of councils. Such activities as investment attraction, small business development, marketing and promotion have been the natural consequences of locating tourism in the economic development unit. Moreover, since processes of globalisation have stimulated a restructuring of local and regional economies, tourism has increasingly been seen as an economic replacement activity in many industrial and agricultural centres now facing economic and population decline. The industrial centres of Newcastle, Wollongong and Broken Hill in Australia are notable examples.

In a study of Victorian local governments, Carson, Beattie and Gove (2003) found that the economic conception of tourism dominated. Among their key findings it was noted that:

1. Most local governments considered tourism to be a legitimate area of concern. Tourism units were generally located in the local economic development division of councils, indicating that tourism was primarily perceived to be a driver of economic development.

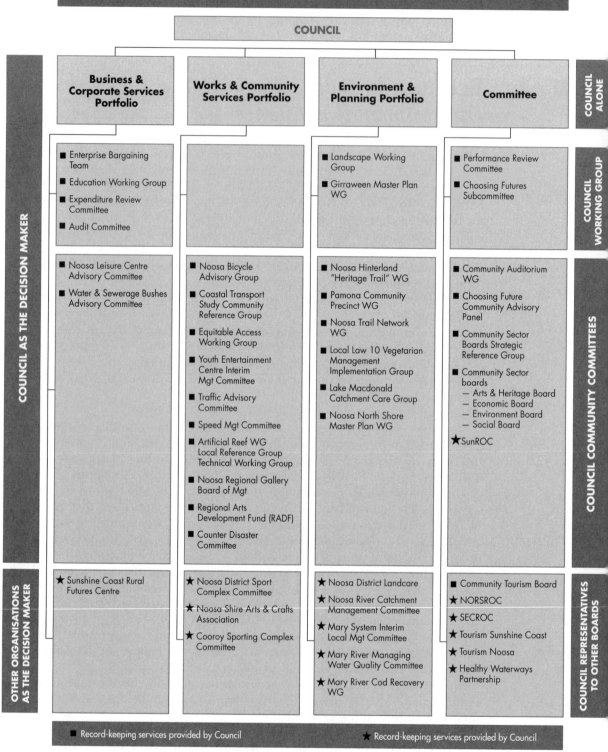

■ Figure 9.1   *Noosa Shire Council's organisational structure*

Source: *Noosa Shire Council Corporate Plan 2003–07.*

2. Integration of tourism within the wider business of council is generally limited. A third of councils responding to the survey claimed that tourism did not feature in any council plans.

3. A large majority of councils indicated that they had a tourism strategy, indicating a commitment to tourism. However, there appeared to be a lack of integration and understanding about how tourism fitted with other council roles and responsibilities outside economic development.

Despite the dominance of the economic framing of tourism, Richins (2000) found that councillors were the most influential actors in local government decision-making about tourism and that they tended to give more weight to community issues. Vexed and politically contentious tourism issues meant that councillors needed to give particular attention to the positive and negative effects of tourism, which include economic benefits.

To reflect the need for collaborative decision-making about tourism (and to offset direct responsibility for an often-contentious area) some councils have removed tourism as an internal function of council. The supporting argument is that industry should have some ownership and a stronger influence on debates and policy development. In such cases, councils support (wholly or in part) a statutory corporation or incorporated association, which in turn is charged with responsibility for tourism. A council's organisation structure provides important information as to how tourism is conceptualised and managed and who makes decisions about tourism. For example, figure 9.1 illustrates the way tourism is framed by Noosa Shire Council. This figure illustrates that, while Noosa undertakes a range of planning and policy activities (and tourism would be taken into account as part of these), the council also participates in tourism planning and policy-making activities external to council.

■ 9.4.4 Institutional *arrangements*

The institutional frameworks that provide the structures and processes for local tourism planning and policy are complex and multidimensional. These frameworks are characterised by the coalescing of various planning processes that occur in different sectors within the same level of government. These can include the planning of land use, infrastructure, open space, cultural and local economic development. Different planning processes might also occur at different levels of government. In Australia for example, state and territory governments have a range of responsibilities, including protected area management and development and investment programs, which also have an impact at the local level. Tourism planners and policy practitioners working at this level need to appreciate the overlapping nature of some of these planning and policy frameworks and the particular challenges and complexity of the local institutional framework for tourism planning and policy.

The National Competition Policy (1995) is such an example, in which Commonwealth policy has had a profound effect on the structure of local government and the way it conducts its business (see Planning in Practice: 'Australia's National Competition Policy').

Australia's National Competition Policy

The Commonwealth Government introduced the National Competition Policy (1995) with the intention of reforming laws that restrict market competition in the provision of government services and address concerns about the government inefficiency. The policy requires that governments introduce competitive practices within their sphere in order to increase efficiency with the ultimate aim of improving community benefit. This policy has had a significant influence on the structure and operations of local government in particular. Competitive tendering and contracting out have been introduced and many councils restructured to reflect a split in local government functions between provider and purchaser (Worthington & Dollery 2002). The most commonly contracted-out services include recycling, garbage collection, cleaning, drainage, operation of childcare centres and elder care services (Evatt Research Centre in Worthington & Dollery 2002).

The way tourism is treated within local government has also been affected by the National Competition Policy. In many local government areas, the running of visitor information centres has come under scrutiny. Before the policy's introduction, many local councils operated their own visitor information centres with input from the local tourism association (if there was one). Increasingly, however, local governments have been examining their operations and have sought to outsource operations that might be run more efficiently by external providers. The contracting out of visitor information centre (VIC) services and some local economic development functions, such as event organisation, has resulted. In many local governments where there is a large, robust and relatively mature industry, the tourism industry itself is better able to manage VIC services. It is also assumed that the industry is better able to deliver VIC services that meet the needs and expectations of the local industry as opposed to local government, which has a broader public mandate. However, it is still the case that smaller local government areas, which are often characterised by more limited expertise, the VIC services continue to be run by council.

In sum, the National Competition Policy was developed by the Commonwealth Government to achieve ideological goals that are aligned with neoliberalism. These included greater efficiency and increased competition. The policy has had profound implications for the functions and organisation of government at all levels, including local government. The provision and delivery of tourism services at the local level has not escaped change. This case demonstrates the complex institutional environment in which local destination tourism planning and policy takes place.

References

Commonwealth of Australia 2003, 'Australia's National Competition Policy: Its evolution and operation', viewed 9 April 2006, www.aph.gov.au/library/intguide/econ/ncp_ebrief.htm.

Worthington, AC & Dollery, BE 2002, 'An analysis of recent trends in Australian local government', *International Journal of Public Sector Management*, vol. 15, no. 6, pp. 496–515.

■ 9.4.5 Unique *features of the destination*

Local tourism planning and policy development is one of the most fascinating scales at which to work and to research because a range of global and national influences intersect with the daily lives, routines and concerns of local inhabitants. The very nature of tourism is that tourists travel to destinations that offer attractions and experiences generally not available in their place of origin. The particular combination of environmental, sociocultural and economic conditions contributes to a unique sense of place that attracts visitors and shapes the experiences offered at a destination (Gunn & Var 2002; Ashworth & Dietvorst 1995). But destinations are much more than a particular combination of circumstances. Cartier (2005) argues that destinations, or touristed landscapes, are subjectively defined through an individual's sensory engagement with their environment and their experience thereof. Destinations and experiences are therefore culturally defined and viewed through 'cultural filters' (Williams 1998: 173). The implications for policy and planning are clear: namely, that unique features of a destination are perceived differently and that planning and policy formulation must acknowledge, protect and enhance the multiplicity of experiences, qualities and features that make destinations attractive. In figure 9.2 the Noosa visitor experience is conceptualised as connections among a range of features or clusters. New products are those that are consistent with and build on these existing attributes.

Although unique features might be easy to identify, the protection of these attributes is sometimes difficult. For example, the coherence and unity of the unique architectural features of a small country town might be placed at risk by standardised building structures associated with a global restaurant chain like McDonald's or KFC. Supermarket complexes, cinemas and other large structures can also intrude into architecturally significant historical landscapes and jeopardise a localised sense of place. In other words, the challenge of protecting and enhancing the unique qualities of place is vexed. Local governments are eager to attract investment and stimulate development, but at the same time they need to actively engage in defining and shaping the type of place the destination will become in the future through daily decision-making in a range of activities, including development assessment, building controls and infrastructure provision. Planning in Practice: 'Douglas Shire's role in protecting visitor experiences north of the Daintree River' (p. 317) provides an example of a local council's approach to coping with the demands of tourism growth.

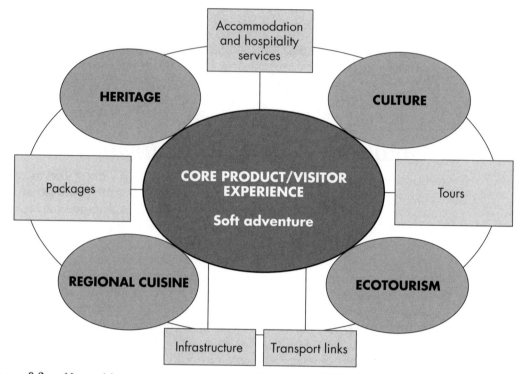

■ **Figure 9.2**   *Noosa visitor experience and unique qualities, Noosa Shire, Queensland*

Source: *Noosa Tourism Community Board 2002.*

■ *9.4.6* **Community** *attitudes and involvement*

A destination's unique sense of place is intimately tied to communities and communities to destinations. According to Hall (2000: 33), sustainable tourism planning and policy development is founded on the objective of 'providing lasting and secure livelihoods which minimise resource depletion, environmental degradation, cultural disruption and social instability'. Studies in both developing and developed countries indicate that the success of a destination will largely depend on the support and engagement of the local community. Not only do local communities provide human and social capital to service tourism activity but also the community contributes to the unique qualities of place, the culture and the tourist experience. Often it is the cultural qualities, attitudes to tourism and other non-tangible qualities that attract tourists to a destination.

However, after 20 years of neoliberalism and a general emphasis on self-interest, increasing concern has been voiced about the declining integrity and cohesiveness of the social fabric in many developed countries, including the USA (Putnam 2000) and in Australia (Eckersley 1998). People are also searching for a sense of belonging and have a desire to secure a place in a new socially networked world (Gleeson 2004). As a result, many governments have been increasingly concerned with strengthening social ties and developing social cultural and political capital (Macbeth 2005).

Douglas Shire's role in protecting visitor experiences north of the Daintree River

Douglas Shire has demonstrated a commitment to identifying and protecting the unique qualities that make the destination unique (Dredge & Humphreys 2003). In the late 1980s debates emerged over the possible development of a bridge linking the more developed southern part of the shire with the pristine wilderness World Heritage Areas north of the Daintree River. The bridge offered advantages of reducing congestion of the small vehicular ferry that linked the two parts of the shire, it would increase tourist flows to the World Heritage Area, and it would improve residents' access to the shire's services. The disadvantages were identified as a reduction in the sense of wilderness by allowing more tourists to travel to the area and the fact that further urban development would inevitably take place and potentially destroy the unique wilderness qualities and visitor experiences north of the Daintree River. The small vehicular ferry was thought to offer a unique gateway experience to tourists' World Heritage experience. The decision was eventually made not to build a bridge, although ferry capacity was upgraded and the road north of the river was eventually widened. This debate illustrates the important role the local government can play in identifying and maintaining unique qualities. Moreover, this issue also illustrates that a decision about infrastructure provision can have important flow-on consequences for tourism.

Under the rubric of sustainability, community engagement and collaboration have become increasingly important cornerstones for tourism planning and policy (Healey 1997; Bramwell 2004). As a result, new forms of collaboration and partnership building are receiving experimentation, and local tourism planning and policy has not escaped these shifts. Local tourism planning and policy development has direct and indirect influences on people's lives, their wellbeing and sense of community and, as such, consistency between community aspirations, values and beliefs and tourism planning is important.

However, developing frameworks for community collaboration and engagement must be based on an analysis of the particular characteristics of the community. Reed (2000) draws attention to the impact that change, uncertainty, complexity and conflict can have on establishing frameworks of collaboration. In emergent tourism settings, where shifts are taking place, perhaps from traditional economic bases towards tourism and leisure-oriented activities, there might be a lack of clarity about whom to involve and in what capacity and how to organise inter-organisational relationships. Collaboration, partnership building and learning require an adaptive and flexible approach (Reed 2000).

■ 9.4.7 **Knowledge** *and expertise*

Within local government, expertise for tourism policy and planning comes from two main groups: local government public servants and the community. First, local government officers might be appointed to undertake tourism planning and policy development on behalf of the local council and to facilitate networking and partnership development with the local industry. McKercher and Ritchie's (1997) study of local government tourism officers in Australia found that local government tourism officers were predominantly young, inexperienced graduates and that the politically charged environment of local government is difficult to deal with. They found that there was often high turnover of staff and that high levels of stress were associated with the position.

Second, expertise for tourism planning and policy is also found in the local community, particularly industry and some community members. However, volunteer fatigue is a problem among some industry and community members whose contribution is heavily relied upon and who participate over long periods. Volunteer fatigue is generally associated with an inability of the local community and industry to facilitate learning and share expertise so that new people can be groomed for leadership roles.

■ 9.4.8 **Local** *characteristics of tourism*

The characteristics of tourism have an important influence on local tourism planning and policy formulation. In particular, the issues shown in table 9.2 can influence the issues identified and the way debates develop.

■ **Table 9.2**
Characteristics of tourism

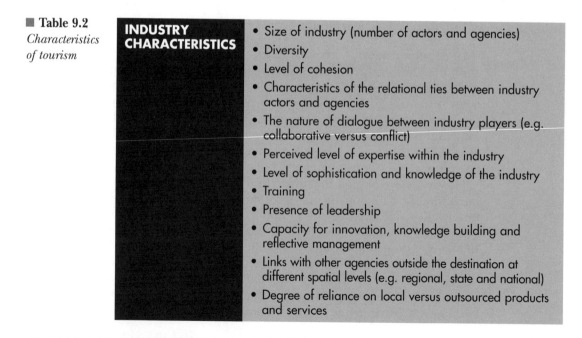

INDUSTRY CHARACTERISTICS	• Size of industry (number of actors and agencies) • Diversity • Level of cohesion • Characteristics of the relational ties between industry actors and agencies • The nature of dialogue between industry players (e.g. collaborative versus conflict) • Perceived level of expertise within the industry • Level of sophistication and knowledge of the industry • Training • Presence of leadership • Capacity for innovation, knowledge building and reflective management • Links with other agencies outside the destination at different spatial levels (e.g. regional, state and national) • Degree of reliance on local versus outsourced products and services

DESTINATION CHARACTERISTICS	• Level of destination development (i.e. developing to developed) • Diversity of tourism products, attractions and services • Complementarity of tourism products, attractions and services or opportunities for packaging • Geography, topography, climate and weather • The spatial arrangement of tourism services and facilities (e.g. clustered versus dispersed) • Level of brand development (e.g. weak to strong) • Extent of established markets • Accessibility • Infrastructure
COMMUNITY CHARACTERISTICS	• Level of community involvement in tourism (e.g. low to high) • Community ownership and control over tourism • Level of community support for tourism (e.g. low to high) • Nature and extent of positive and negative effects of tourism on the community

Table 9.3 identifies a number of inquiring questions that can be posed in order to develop an appreciation of the dynamic context in which local tourism and planning takes place. These questions can be used to scope and develop an appreciation of the complexity and dynamism of local tourism and its interconnectedness with processes and events occurring at different scales.

■ **Table 9.3**

Appreciating the context of local tourism planning and policy

- What is the unit (i.e. spatial unit, administrative unit or other) I am planning for?
- What scale is being planned for? Are there any subscales?
- What are the globalising influences on the destination, and how do these affect tourism development?
- Who are the stakeholders?
- What are the agencies with a direct or indirect interest in the planning and policy process?
- What are the roles and responsibilities of the agency undertaking the planning exercise? How does this planning/policy exercise align with these roles and responsibilities?
- What other planning processes are currently being undertaken and may this influence this planning and policy exercise?
- What is the ideological approach driving this planning and policy development process?
- Where is tourism situated within the political, economic and social content of the destination relative to other issues and interests?
- What are the unique features of the destination? How can it be differentiated from it competitors?
- What are the attitudes of the community towards tourism and the local council of involvement sought?
- What broad approach and level of intervention is going to be most acceptable to the local council?
- Where is the expertise? How can I access it? How can I foster its further development?

𝒜 STRATEGIC AND SUSTAINABLE APPROACH TO LOCAL PLANNING AND POLICY

A number of approaches to destination planning and policy development since the 1960s can be distinguished in the literature. These approaches are discussed in section 3.6. They are not independent or mutually exclusive. In reality, there are traces of each approach in most local destination planning exercises, with the emphasis depending on the objectives of the exercise, the nature of the issues to be addressed and the expertise of the people involved. Each tradition has its advantages and disadvantages, and none can claim to be superior to the others. Each approach lends important direction to the development of an integrated and holistic approach to local destination planning and policy development. Today, most local tourism planning and policy development exercises combine these approaches and are integrated into wider planning processes and founded on the rubric of sustainability. The different traditions outlined below represent the different emphases that local planning and policy solutions can take.

■ 9.5.1 Strategic *tourism planning*

The strategic approach to tourism planning and policy development embraces a forward-looking and anticipatory style of tourism planning and policy-making. The strategic plan is a document that guides future directions, activities, programs and actions (Hall 2000). The aims and values embedded in strategic planning can vary depending on the organisation undertaking the exercise, and different 'genres' of strategic plans have emerged. For example, strategic business planning focuses on enhancing competition and improving business development outcomes through the identification of business clusters, market differentiation and synergy building. The main foci of these exercises are on growing tourism markets, on improving the alignment between supply and demand and on enhancing competitiveness and investment potential.

Strategic tourism plans embody a number of qualities:
- They are based on an analysis and evaluation of the strengths, weakness, opportunities and threats facing a destination's development.
- They identify incorporate directions for enhancing local tourism competition.
- They seek to match tourism product supply with demand now and in the future.
- They are prepared in consultation with a wide range of stakeholders.
- They contain a long-term vision and short-term measures to achieve it.
- They anticipate and address uncertainty.

The emphasis on strategic economic development is evident in tourism policy across Australia where, for example, the emphasis has been on enabling and facilitating business and industry interests and marketing and promotion to improve destination competitiveness. Policy and planning have taken an economic and financial focus, and the preparation of master plans or spatial policies is a rare occurrence. Unfortunately, branding, marketing and facilitation alone cannot create the sense of place necessary for a vital tourism industry. Spatial strategies are also needed to promote destination cohesion, a sense of unity and uniqueness, and cognitive understanding of the destination.

■ 9.5.2 Spatial *destination planning*

The destination spatial master planning tradition emerged during the 1960s and was popularised by, among others, Clare Gunn's seminal texts *Vacationscape* (Gunn 1972) and *Tourism Planning* (1988, 1993 and with Var 2004). This approach incorporates destination site analysis and facility planning. This approach was generally consistent with the dominant technocratic and centralised approaches to planning at the time. The destination was conceptualised as a spatial planning unit comprising a number of elements (as shown in figure 9.3) and included:

- a *gateway* that marks entry and exit to the destination region
- a *community* that services and supports the destination region
- *access routes* or linkage corridors that facilitate movement throughout the region and connections to other regions, and
- *attraction complexes*, which comprise a range of features and unique experiences that draw tourists to the region.

Spatial planning exercises draw most criticism from their difficulty in implementation. In most cases, implementation depends on the agreement and goodwill of private sector investors. It also requires close alignment between private sector goals and interests and the spatial plan. In other words, the heavy hand of bureaucracy cannot make the destination develop in accordance with a spatial plan.

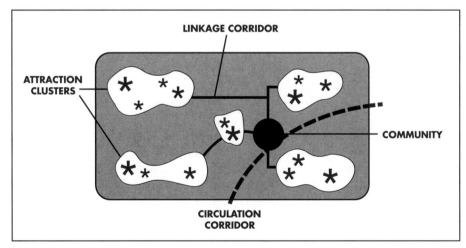

■ **Figure 9.3**   *Gunn's destination concept*

Source: *Gunn 1988: 192.*

Planning critics observe that spatial planning has received little attention since the 1980s (Gleeson 2003). Instead, planning has been focused on issues and places and has been outcome-oriented. Tourism planning in particular has focused on empowering industry, on marketing and on being consultative. As a result, the focus has not been on the future but on process, on service delivery and on benchmarking and measurement. Long-term, big-picture issues about the way destinations develop, their spatial synergies and their sense of uniqueness have not gained the attention they deserve.

Land-use planning can greatly assist in shaping the spatial qualities of the destination and in creating and maintaining a unique sense of place. More-over, spatial planning can foster private sector investment in appropriate locations. Land-use planning regulations can also be used to protect environmental and landscape amenity and shape such aspects as architectural integrity, landscaping and urban design.

■ 9.5.3 Issue-based *planning*

Issues-based planning and policy development draws its inspiration from incremental approaches to planning and policy development (see section 6.4.2). In this approach tourism planning and policy is driven by the issues that emerge from time to time and the search for solutions to those issues. These issues are dealt with incrementally and, although there might be a general approach to tourism management, issues are not necessarily linked or seen to form part of a broader framework for management. Such local-ised issues could include:

• holiday letting and its effect on local residential communities
• minimising the impact of events and festivals
• regulating bed and breakfast accommodation
• managing consequences of coastal development
• preservation of scenic quality and landscape amenity, and
• tourism signage.

The difficulty of managing tourism on an issue basis is exacerbated by the fact that tourism is multisectoral and related or similar issues can emerge in different sectors and departmental units of a local council. Unless communication channels within council are good, these issues might be dealt with quite independently. For example, the management of caravan parks, as a business function of council, could be dealt with by one section, yet strategic land-use and tourism marketing issues could emerge from time to time in other sections of council.

Although the importance of dealing with issues in a timely manner is recognised, this issues-based approach, if not coordinated and held together by a strategic plan that provides overall vision and direction, can be quite fragmented. Sometimes it makes sense for a national government to have a coordinated response to the development of tourism because capacity does not exist at the local level. The case of Cancún, Mexico, is a case in point.

Local planning and policy by national government — Cancún, Mexico

In the 1970s, the Mexican Government embarked on an ambitious program of integrated destination planning and development. During the late 1960s Bank of Mexico studies assessing the potential benefits of tourism highlighted increased foreign earnings, employment benefits and economic growth in underdeveloped regions (Jiminez 1990). These findings suggested that Mexico could reap substantial economic benefits as a result of its proximity to US and Canadian tourism markets but that new, high-quality product was required to meet the demands of an emerging mass tourism market.

On the basis of these arguments, in 1974 the Mexican Government set up FONATUR (Fondo Nacional de Formento al Turismo) as the statutory corporation charged with the responsibility for promoting Mexico's international tourism potential and turning this potential into economic development. A Five-Year Plan for Tourism Development (1969–73) was formulated, which was an ambitious state-driven economic development program that focused on investment attraction and the development of tourism infrastructure in five principle locations: Cancún, Bahías de Huatulco, Ixtapa, Loreto and Los Cabos. Today these destinations account for 40 per cent of all foreign visits and 54 per cent of foreign income earned by tourism. A feature of this approach was government-driven development of high-quality infrastructure, including roads, water supply, sewerage and telecommunications, to create the right conditions for attracting international investment in hotels and attraction infrastructure (Clancy 2001). Economic benefits were expected to flow on to local fishing and agricultural communities as a result of the economic synergies developed from tourism.

Since its inception, FONATUR's role has been to undertake background studies and prepare master plans for the development and consolidation of tourism destinations. The agency is also responsible for the subdivision, selling and leasing of land and buildings. This infrastructure and destination planning exercise has combined a strong physical and spatial planning approach with an aggressive economic development and investment strategy.

FONATUR's master planning and development has resulted in significant growth in tourism since the 1970s. Initially, international visitation to Mexico grew strongly throughout the 1970s despite global economic and economic conditions that impeded the development of tourism more generally. For example, a global economic recession and transport price increases, brought about in part by a global oil shortage, slowed global tourism growth. Nevertheless, during the 1970s significant economic benefits of tourism were evident in underdeveloped regions, such as Cancún in Quintana Roo, and investment in tourism infrastructure, services and attractions expanded.

(continued)

By the late 1970s, the Mexican Government began to scale back its active and direct investment in tourism, which was being criticised as a drain on national economic resources, seeking to address other, more pressing domestic economic issues. In turn, the government sought to transfer the burden of infrastructure investment to the tourism industry itself through the adoption of the 'megaproject' concept. 'Megaprojects' refer to the integrated development of all tourism services, accommodation, attractions and infrastructure. Although previous developments were 'integrated', the government had provided the land and infrastructure. In the megaproject, the developer was made responsible for the improvement of the land, including the construction of roads, telecommunications infrastructure, water supply and sewerage reticulation.

Cancún

Cancún is located in the eastern state of Quintana Roo. This state was traditionally one of the poorest and least developed in Mexico, and only 14 families lived on the narrow coastal spit that has since become the resort destination of Cancún. In 1974 when Cancún commenced its first stage of operation there were approximately 1300 rooms in 14 hotels. Today there are 27 200 hotel rooms in 146 accommodation establishments. In 2004 an estimated 2.3 million international visitor nights were spent in Cancún and 1 million nights were spent by domestic visitors (FONATUR 2004). Estimates put the number of permanent inhabitants at around 500 000 people. This data tends to undervalue tourism because it does not include visitors staying in condominiums, second homes, timeshares or private homes (Clancy 2001). Visitation could, therefore, be much higher. The state of Quintana Roo is now fourth in terms of national GDP, which indicates the economic success that can be attributed to this government-driven destination planning and policy approach.

The destination of Cancún from the outset was a highly planned resort development. This planning took a number of different forms. The government set out to plan and develop the resort as an export commodity and, in doing so, assumed many of the entrepreneurial risks and costs that usually fall to business (Clancy 2001). The government also adopted a strong spatial planning focus. The master plan was designed around three core elements: a resort tourist zone, a residential zone for permanent residents and an international airport. The traditional community was relocated from the spit to a settlement near the airport. The preparation of the resort area was a massive task that required 240 square kilometres of topsoil and the clearing of 372 000 square metres of mangroves to improve flow between the sea and the lagoon. Thirty kilometres of water pipes and 100 kilometres of sewerage pipes were laid for the township.

The economic success of FONATUR's integrated destinations led to the opening up of mass markets, which in turn resulted in an explosive growth in visitation. However, environmental costs have been high with Cothran and Cothran (1998) arguing that Cancún exhibits all the classic signs of an overbuilt mass tourism destination. Bosselman (1978) identified environmental impacts associated with overdevelopment of the delicate sand spit during the first stage of Cancún's development far back as 1978. Since then sewerage problems, water pollution, coastal erosion, urban congestion and loss of biodiversity have become considerable environmental issues. Issues identified in land use and environmental impact studies have been minimised or disregarded in decisions about the continued development and promotion of Cancún (Pi Sunyer & Thomas 1997 in Clancy 2001). There has been growing criticism of the inadequate attention given to accommodating the transient population in search of employment and the resultant informal urban growth on the fringes of the Cancún township. There is also growing division between the tourist and local populations and the breakdown of the traditional *ejidal* (farming cooperative) community. The tourist space has become known as 'Gringolandia' (Torres & Momsen 2005). It has lost its cultural identity and offers inauthentic tourism products and activities catering to mass US and Canadian markets. Jimenez (1990: 205) argues that there is a crisis afoot in Mexico, which has largely resulted from the concentration of tourism policy and planning activities on promotion and marketing, on the development of tourism infrastructure and in the spatial and economic development of tourism destinations.

References

Bosselman, F 1978, *In the Wake of the Tourist: Managing Special Places in Eight Countries*, Conservation Foundation, Washington, DC.

Clancy, M 2001, *Exporting Paradise: Tourism and Development in Mexico*, Pergamon, Amsterdam.

Cothran, D & Cothran, C 1998, 'Promise or political risk for Mexican tourism', *Annals of Tourism Research*, vol. 25, no. 2, pp. 477–97.

FONATUR 2004, 'Estadísticas sobre turismo', viewed 10 April 2006, www.fonatur.gob.mx/ index_estadisticas.html.

Jiminez, A 1990, *Turismo: Estructura y desarrollo*, McGraw-Hill/Interamericana de Mexico, Mexico City.

Torres, RM & Momsen, JD 2005, 'Gringolandia: The construction of a new tourist space in Mexico', *Annals of the Association of American Geographers*, vol. 95, no. 2, pp. 314–55.

CHAPTER REVIEW

This chapter has examined local tourism planning and policy and has focused principally on the roles, responsibilities and influences on local government. The term 'local' is often difficult to define because it is largely a question of scale. For our purposes we interpreted local tourism planning and policy as taking place at the scale that reflects local relationships between governments, business and communities. However, planners and policy-makers need to be aware that local destinations can be interpreted differently by stakeholders and that sensitivity to these interpretations is essential.

Local government is an important player in local tourism planning and policy development, although the extent of its engagement with tourism varies considerably. Processes of globalisation, ideological influences, economic, social and environmental influences, and the unique qualities and characteristics of destinations all influence local government approaches to tourism. These approaches can be broadly identified as a strategic approach, a spatial approach and an issues-based approach to tourism planning and policy development. A well-developed and responsible approach will necessarily involve all three approaches and be guided by broad sustainable development objectives.

In sum, local tourism policy and planning is heavily influenced by the unique characteristics of the place, its tourism industry and its people. Local government operates in an environment in which some issues and certain sectors are important and some are less important. Tourism is multisectoral and, as such, tourism interests can permeate many council planning and policy-making activities. It is important that tourism planners and policy-makers are aware of these connections and the interplay between issues so that tourism can be appropriately addressed.

SUMMARY OF KEY TERMS

Local Agenda 21

The United Nations Conference on Environment and Development (UNCED), also known as the Earth Summit, developed Agenda 21 as a blueprint for action to achieve sustainable development. Chapter 28 of the blueprint nominated local councils as having a particularly important role in working towards sustainable development, and Local Agenda 21 was developed to provide specific direction, local awareness and more focused activities.

Local destinations

Local destinations are defined by the unique social, economic, environmental and cultural qualities that give a destination identity; they are characterised by the functional integration of tourist attractions and services. Local destinations are the smallest geographical unit for tourism planning and policy but can encompass more than one local government area.

Mandatory powers

Mandatory powers are those powers that governments have been given under legislation and which they have an obligation to undertake.

Permissive powers

Permissive powers are those powers that local government has been given under legislation and which they may undertake but are not obligated to do so.

Tourist gaze

Tourism gaze is a term originally coined by sociologist John Urry. It refers to the way tourists scan and perceive a destination, the symbols to which they attach meaning in a destination and the way the destination is interpreted. The tourist gaze means that destinations are individually interpreted and given meaning, and it problematicises the scale and politico-administrative boundaries associated with destination planning.

QUESTIONS

1 Explain why 'local destination' is so hard to define. Identify and discuss three ways a local destination might be defined for the purpose of tourism planning and policy-making.

2 Explain the way local government roles and responsibilities have changed between the inception of local government and the present day.

3 Why is tourism planning and policy now a concern of local government?

4 Identify and briefly explain five responsibilities of contemporary local governments. How might tourism affect these responsibilities, and how might these responsibilities influence tourism? Give examples.

5 Identify and briefly discuss the various influences that influence local government tourism planning and policy.

6 What local characteristics of tourism need to be taken into account in local tourism planning and policy?

7 Explain what is meant by strategic planning, spatial planning and issues-based planning. Why are all three necessary for local tourism planning and policy?

8 Explain Gunn's destination concept. What might be the advantages and disadvantages of applying only this approach to local tourism planning?

9 What are the advantages and disadvantages of using an issues-based approach to tourism planning and policy?

10 Explain reasons for and against central government-driven local tourism planning. Where might central government local tourism planning be best undertaken?

EXERCISES

1 Prepare a class debate using the following topics:

(a) A national approach to local tourism planning is best.

(b) Local government is the best level for preparing local tourism plans and policy.

(c) Definitive boundaries can be drawn around local destinations.

(d) Local tourism planning exercises are best undertaken by national governments.

2 Choose a local government you are familiar with. Describe and discuss this council's approach to tourism planning and policy. Examine the corporate plan, planning schemes, any available discussion papers and tourism plans. Your review should cover at least some of the following aspects:

(a) Where does tourism fit within council's organisational structure?

(b) What are council's overall goals and objectives?

(c) Are there any goals and objectives in the corporate plan that relate to tourism?

(d) What were the aims of the tourism planning and policy exercise?

(e) What was the predominant approach taken in the development of the plan and the ideology influencing its development?

(f) What were the roles of government, industry and the community?

FURTHER READING

Commonwealth Department of Environment and Heritage 2004, *Steps to Sustainable Tourism,* **DEH, Canberra, viewed 10 April 2006, www.deh.gov.au/heritage/publications/sustainable-tourism/index.html.** This government publication provides a step-by-step guide for planning a sustainable future for tourism. It demonstrates how local tourism planning and policy is developed in practice and the type of practical considerations that are needed.

Gunn, CA with Var, T 2002, *Tourism Planning,* **4th edn, Routledge, New York.** This is a classic text that provides a thorough overview of tourism planning. It emphasises the spatial dimension of tourism planning and provides an excellent range of international case studies.

Macbeth, J 2005, 'Towards an ethics platform for tourism', *Annals of Tourism Research,* **vol. 32, no. 4, pp. 962–84.** This theoretical paper describes different perspectives that frame tourism scholarship and, as a corollary, shape tourism policy, planning and development. The paper stimulates thought and raises awareness of the need to identify and consider the ethical judgements and values embedded in local tourism planning and policy.

United Nations Environment Program 2003, *Tourism and Local Agenda 21: The Role of Local Authorities in Sustainable Tourism,* **International Council for Local Environmental Initiatives, Paris, viewed 10 April 2006, www.uneptie.org/pc/tourism/library/local-agenda21.htm.** This is an excellent resource that outlines the role of local governments in achieving sustainable development. The report outlines typical objectives for the implementation of sustainable development and explores international case studies of local government approaches to sustainable tourism development.

Local planning and policy by local government — Redland Shire, Queensland

Redland Shire is located south-east of Brisbane and encompasses mainland coastal areas and a number of Moreton Bay islands. The shire has a well-developed urban area that acts as a dormitory to Brisbane, the state capital. Large tracts of land on both the mainland and the islands have high nature conservation and recreational value, and contain significant social and indigenous cultural resources. The location of the shire on Moreton Bay, the natural environmental attributes of the area, particularly North Stradbroke Island, and its proximity to Brisbane have made Redland Shire a desirable residential, daytripper and tourism destination.

In 2004 the population of Redland Shire was 128 000 persons (ABS 2004). Over the period 1986–2004 the shire's population grew 6.8 per cent per annum, making it one of the fastest-growing areas in Australia. Although the average age of the population is 37 years, it is expected that the average age will increase significantly in the next decade in accordance with Australia-wide trends and because it attracts a high proportion of retirees from Brisbane. Approximately 95 per cent of residents live on the mainland, and the majority of the remainder (5 per cent) reside on the islands, where tourism activity is concentrated. This population distribution has significant implications for the relative importance of tourism to the community and, by corollary, on council's agenda; that is, although tourism is an important economic driver on the islands, it is economically important to only a small number of residents and is relatively unimportant on the mainland.

The shire's approach to tourism planning and policy and the nature of dialogues taking place among industry, community and local government are influenced by a range of factors. First, the political importance of tourism is, overall, relatively low given that not many residents are directly involved in tourism. However, there are some locations, such as the islands, where almost all residents are involved in tourism. As a result, it is difficult to raise the profile of tourism on council's agenda where it is seen to be important to only a marginalised set of interests. Second, although most of the shire acts as a residential dormitory for Brisbane, the islands offer unique but largely undeveloped ecotourism and indigenous tourism opportunities close to the capital city. Third, those parts of the shire with the highest tourism potential are also the most difficult to access. Opening up access and reducing barriers to visitation would likely have a negative impact on the quality of the resources, given the mass market at the doorstep. The tourist experience would be denigrated, and local residents' lifestyle and retirement aspirations could be negatively affected. Fourth, the business environment is conducive to tourism, being close to a major international gateway and with good access to the range of services and facilities Brisbane has to offer. However, many businesses are based on lifestyle and not commercial objectives so that growing synergies and development opportunities is difficult. Fifth, residents include many lifestyle refugees and seachangers who oppose the development of tourism, which results in the politicisation of tourism issues.

Redland's tourism planning and policy approach

Redland Shire Council has undertaken a comprehensive multisectoral planning exercise based on an overarching commitment to a 'quadruple bottom line', which addresses four fundamental platforms: environmental sustainability, social sustainability, economic sustainability and good governance. Direction for the way tourism will be planned and managed is contained in two main council strategies: council's Corporate Plan 2002–06 and the Redlands Planning Scheme (2006). These are official documents with statutory significance. The Corporate Plan espouses an economic focus for tourism, with objectives and targets relating to growing tourism demand, visitation, and marketing and visitor expenditure (Redland Shire 2002). The Redlands Planning Scheme (RPS) deals with land-use implications of tourism, specifically bed and breakfast establishments, tourist accommodation and tourist parks. The RPS defines these uses and identifies zones where these tourism land uses may be appropriate. It also identifies a range of criteria used to assess such tourist development proposals, including location, site size, layout and design, visual privacy, landscaping, access and parking, pedestrian paths and access, services, disabled access, waste collection, communal facilities and signage.

These official plans help to guide and justify incremental decision-making and daily actions about tourism. In other words, these plans are not definitive. Redland Shire has demonstrated a strong commitment to sustainable tourism through its commitment to be a pilot project for Green Globe 21, an international certification and benchmarking program. It also supports the visitor information centre and the regional tourism organisation and undertakes local economic development programs to strengthen business and build tourism synergies. These activities fall outside the official planning and policy document but can nevertheless be considered part of council's overall approach to and support for developing sustainable tourism in the wider context.

The statutory plans are supported by a range of non-statutory documents and studies that help to understand the basis for and justification of the council's official policy approach. These include:

- *Redland Shire Community Vision (2001)*. This plan embraced the principles of *Local Agenda 21* in developing a living plan for the Redlands community based on an integration of environmental, social and economic goals and outcomes.
- *Draft Sustainable Tourism Strategy (2003)*. This strategy was designed to embrace the principles of ecologically sustainable tourism development in the shire.

(continued)

- *Redlands Economic and Tourism Development Marketing Plan (2004)*. The overriding goal of the plan was to encourage economic growth in the shire while maintaining the quality of life for residents, businesses and visitors.
- *Sustainable Tourism Action Plan 2004–05* developed by the Tourism Development Unit.

From this overview, it is possible to make a number of important observations about Redland Shire's local tourism planning and policy:

1 Local tourism planning and policy is underpinned by the rubric of sustainability, and in particular, the 'quadruple bottom line'.
2 Tourism is increasingly being integrated into more complex institutional framework of local government-wide planning and management.
3 Although tourism planning and policy development exercises provide important and specific guidance, no single document provides overarching direction. Redland's approach has emerged as a result of various studies directly and indirectly related to tourism, which now form a web of strategic and specific guidance for tourism.
4 The distribution of tourism development and tourism interests within the shire is spatially uneven. Tourism planning and policy development seeks to foster tourism in appropriate areas only.
5 Sense of place and the unique qualities of the local destination are recognised as important, and council seeks to protect and enhance these qualities.
6 Tourism competes against a range of other issues on council's agenda and, although it is important for Stradbroke Island residents, it is of lesser importance on the mainland. This understanding provides the political context in which tourism planners and policy-makers must operate.
7 Tourism planning and policy is embedded in objectives about local economic development.

Dianne Dredge and Narelle Beaumont

Questions

1 Identify and discuss the broad social, economic, cultural and environmental factors influencing council's approach to tourism. Explain how these influences shape the way tourism is framed politically.

2 Why might it be difficult to raise the profile of tourism on council's agenda?

3 Council's planning and policy directions for tourism are elaborated on in different documents. Discuss the advantages and disadvantages of this approach.

References

Australian Bureau of Statistics 2004, *Regional Population Growth, Queensland (at 30 June 2004) and Revised Median Ages (at 30 June 2003)*, Catalogue no. 3218.0, ABS, Canberra.
Redland Shire Council 2002, *Redland Shire: Our Redlands Our Future. Corporate Plan*, Redland Shire Council, Cleveland, Qld.
— 2006, *Redlands Planning Scheme*, Redland Shire Council, Cleveland, Qld.

REFERENCES

Appadurai, A 1996, *Modernity at Large: Cultural Dimensions of Globalization*, University of Minnesota Press, Minneapolis.

Ashworth, G & Dietvorst, A 1995, *Tourism and Spatial Transformations*, CAB International, Wallingford, UK.

Bramwell, B 2004, 'Partnerships, participation, and social science research in tourism planning', in A Lew, CM Hall & A Williams, *A Companion to Tourism*, Blackwell, Oxford.

Carson, D et al. 2003, *Tourism Management Capacity of Local Government: An Analysis of Victorian Local Government*, CAUTHE 2003, Southern Cross University, Coffs Harbour, NSW.

Carson, D & Macbeth, J 2005, *Regional Tourism Cases: Innovation in Regional Tourism*, Common Ground Publishing, Altona, Vic.

Cartier, C 2005, 'Introduction: Touristed landscapes/seductions of place', in C Cartier & A Low (eds), *Seductions of Place: Geographical Perspectives on Globalization and Touristed Landscapes*, Routledge, Abingdon, UK, pp. 1–20.

Cotter, B & Hannan, K (Environs Australia) 1999, *Our Community Our Future: A Guide to Local Agenda 21*, Commonwealth of Australia, Canberra.

Dredge, D 1998, 'Land use planning policy: A toll for destination place management. The approach of Douglas Shire, North Queensland', *Australian Journal of Hospitality Management*, vol. 5, no. 1, pp. 41–50.

—— 2001a, 'Local government tourism planning and policy-making in New South Wales: Institutional development and historical legacies', *Current Issues in Tourism*, vol. 4, nos 2–4, pp. 355–80.

—— 2001b, 'Leisure lifestyles and tourism', *Tourism Geographies*, vol. 3, no. 3, pp. 279–99.

—— 2005, 'Local versus state-driven production of "the region": Regional tourism policy in the Hunter, New South Wales, Australia', in A Rainnie & M Grobbelaar (eds), *New Regionalism in Australia*, Ashgate, Aldershot, UK, pp. 301–19.

—— 2006, 'Policy networks and the local organisation of tourism', *Tourism Management*, vol. 27, no. 2, pp. 269–80.

Dredge, D & Humphreys, J 2003, 'Local government, world heritage and ecotourism: Policy and strategy in Australia's tropical rainforests', in DA Fennell & RK Dowling (eds), *Ecotourism Policy and Planning*, CABI Publishing, Wallingford, UK, pp. 121–40.

Dredge, D & Jenkins, J 2003, 'Destination place identity and regional tourism policy', *Tourism Geographies*, vol. 5, no. 4, pp. 383–407.

Eckersley, R 1998, *Measuring Progress: Is Life Getting Better?* CSIRO Publishing, Collingwood, Vic.

Elliott, J 1997, *Tourism: Politics and the Public Sector*, Routledge, London.

Gleeson, B 2003, 'The difference that planning makes: That was then, this is now', *Environment & Planning A*, vol. 35, no. 5, pp. 765–9.

—— 2004, 'Deprogramming planning: Collaboration and inclusion in new urban development', *Urban Policy and Research*, vol. 22, no. 3, pp. 315–22.

Gunn, C 1972, *Vacationscape: Designing Tourist Regions*, University of Texas, Austin.

—— 1988, *Tourism Planning*, Taylor & Francis, New York.

—— 1993, *Tourism Planning: Basics, Concepts and Cases*, Taylor & Francis, Washington, DC.

Gunn, CA with Var, T 2002, *Tourism Planning*, 4th edn, Routledge, New York.

Hall, CM 1994, *Tourism and Politics: Policy, Power and Place*, John Wiley & Sons, Chichester, UK.

—— 2000, *Tourism Planning: Policies, Processes and Relationships*, Prentice Hall, Harlow, UK.

—— 2005, *Tourism: Rethinking the Social Science of Mobility*, Pearson, Harlow, UK.

Healey, P 1997, *Collaborative Planning: Shaping Places in Fragmented Societies*, Macmillan, London.

Imrie, R & Thomas, H 1995, 'Changes in local governance and their implications for urban policy evaluation', in R Hambleton & H Thomas (eds), *Urban Policy Evaluation: Challenge and Change*, Paul Chapman Publishing, London, pp. 123–255.

Jiminez, A 1990, *Turismo: Estructura y Desarrollo*, McGraw-Hill/ Interamericana de Mexico, Mexico City.

Keen, L & Scase, R 1998, *Local Government Management: The Rhetoric and Reality of Change*, Open University Press, Buckingham, UK.

Larcombe, FA 1961, *The Development of Local Government in New South Wales*, FW Cheshire, Melbourne.

Macbeth, J 2005, 'Towards an ethics platform for tourism', *Annals of Tourism Research*, vol. 32, no. 4, pp. 962–84.

Marshall, N 1997, 'Introduction: Themes and issues in Australian local government', in B Dollery & N Marshall, *Australian Local Government: Reform and Renewal*, Macmillan Education Australia, Melbourne, pp. 1–14.

McKercher, B & Ritchie, M 1997, 'The third tier of public sector tourism: A profile of local government tourism officers in Australia', *Journal of Travel Research*, vol. 36, no. 1, pp. 66–72.

Milne, SS 1998, 'Tourism and sustainable development: Exploring the global–local nexus', in CM Hall & A Lew (eds), *Sustainable Tourism: A Geographical Perspective*, Longman, Harlow, UK, pp. 35–48.

New Zealand Government 2001, *New Zealand Tourism Strategy 2010*, Wellington.

—— 2003, *Postcards from Home: The Local Government Tourism Strategy 2003*, Wellington.

Noosa Tourism Community Board 2002, *Tourism New Product Development Project: Final Report*, November, Noosa, viewed 28 April 2006, www.noosa.qld.gov.au/docs/KPMG-FinalReport31March03.pdf.

Noosa Shire Council n.d., *Noosa Shire Council Corporate Plan 2003–07*, Noosa, viewed 28 April 2006, www.noosa.qld.gov.au/index120.php.

Painter, M 1993, 'Local government', in R Smith (ed.), *Politics in Australia*, 2nd edn, Allen & Unwin, Sydney, pp. 165–75.

Putnam, R 2000, *Bowling Alone: The Collapse and Revival of the American Community*, Simon & Schuster, New York.

Reed, M 2000, 'Collaborative tourism planning as adaptive experiments in emergent tourism settings', in B Bramwell & B Lane (eds), *Tourism Collaboration and Partnerships: Policy, Practice and Sustainability*, Channel View Publications, Clevedon, UK, pp. 247–71.

Richins, H 2000, 'Influences on local government tourism decision-making: A study of authoritative opinion', *Journal of Tourism Studies*, vol. 11, no. 2, p. 2.

Smith, SLJ 1995, *Dictionary of Concepts in Recreation and Leisure Studies*, Greenwood Press, New York.

United Nations Environment Program 2003, *Tourism and Local Agenda 21: The Role of Local Authorities in Sustainable Tourism*, International Council for Local Environmental Initiatives, Paris.

Urry, J 1990, *The Tourist Gaze: Leisure and Travel in Contemporary Societies*, Sage, London.

—— 2003, *Globalising the Tourist Gaze*, Department of Sociology, Lancaster University, Lancaster, UK, viewed 10 April 2006, www.lancs.ac.uk/fss/sociology/papers/urry-globalising-the-tourist-gaze.pdf.

Walmsley, DJ & Jenkins, JM 1992, 'Tourism cognitive mapping of unfamiliar environments', *Annals of Tourism Research*, vol. 19, no. 2, pp. 268–85.

Williams, S 1998, *Tourism Geography*, Routledge, London.

Worthington, AC & Dollery, BE 2002, 'An analysis of recent trends in Australian local government', *International Journal of Public Sector Management*, vol. 15, no. 6, pp. 496–515.

James Higham and
Harry Maher

CHAPTER 10
Protected *lands*

LEARNING OBJECTIVES

After reading this chapter you will be able to:

1 discuss the principles of policy and planning for protected lands

2 explain the three fundamental components of any regulatory management system for protected lands

3 describe the historical development of New Zealand's designated protected areas and the philosophies underpinning the development of this system of protected lands

4 examine contemporary policy directions and planning frameworks for New Zealand's system of protected lands

5 discuss the policy development and planning challenges associated with the commercialisation of nature-based tourism.

*I*NTRODUCTION

It is increasingly recognised that tourism management systems in **protected areas** around the world generally share a number of common elements. These include a sound legislative framework, a management planning system and the implementation of a range of management actions to deliver on the goals and objectives of the planning system (e.g. IUCN 1991). It is also acknowledged that an important element of tourism policy and planning for protected lands is a stated link between the activities of tourists, the values and attributes of the sites where that activity occurs and the effects of visitor activities (Eagles & McCool 2002). However, these elements are not always present or effective. Hence it is critical to examine and understand visitor management systems for protected areas in terms of protected area management theory and practice.

Section 10.2 examines the context in which protected lands management takes place and, in particular, the connections between legislation, management and actions. Section 10.3 contextualises the previous discussion by examining New Zealand's system of protected lands management, which is long established. Section 10.4 examines the historical development of New Zealand's protected lands policy and planning approaches in managing tourism and recreation. Section 10.5 discusses institutional arrangements underpinning New Zealand's protected lands management. Section 10.6 examines contemporary policy and planning approaches for New Zealand's protected areas. Section 10.7 explores policy approaches that have shaped the commercial development of nature in New Zealand, and section 10.8 concludes with a discussion of the search for sustainable ecotourism.

*L*EGISLATION, MANAGEMENT AND ACTION

Tourism management systems in protected areas around the world generally share one or more of three key features: (1) a sound and binding **legislative foundation**, (2) a system of **management planning** that creates goals and objectives for management and (3) the use at sites of a series of actions by **protected area managers** that are designed to deliver on the requirements of the legislative framework and achieve the goals and objectives identified by the planning system (e.g. IUCN 1991; Eagles, McCool & Haynes 2002; Pedersen 2002). Another common element of tourism policy and planning for protected lands is the linkage between the activities of tourists, the values and attributes of the sites where that activity occurs and the **visitor impact** (potential and actual, as well as immediate and cumulative) that results from activities and management responses to that impact. Mathieson and Wall (1982) initially and a number of scholars subsequently (see for example Hammitt & Cole 1998; Eagles & McCool 2002; Eagles, McCool & Haynes 2002; Pedersen 2002; Newsome, Moore

& Dowling 2002) all discuss these linkages and the importance of understanding these elements of tourism in managing protected lands.

In order to examine and understand **visitor management systems** for any protected area, it necessary to examine, at least at a general level, how these key features interact in protected area management theory. This chapter presents and discusses the various planning approaches that have been developed for the management of tourism and recreation activities in protected lands. The discussions that follow examine planning and policy developments for tourism in protected areas in New Zealand.

This chapter discusses tourism management models only as they apply to the management of protected lands. A large number of tourism management models are designed to address a wide variety of tourism issues and situations. Many of these models and approaches relate, for example, to urban planning situations. This chapter focuses on protected areas, the values and attractions of tourist sites within protected area designations and the activities carried out at those sites. There are many commonalities linking policy and planning for protected areas, such as national parks, in the international context and many distinctions separating visitor management initiatives in protected and non-protected areas. For this reason, only those models that have been designed for protected areas are relevant to this discussion.

■ *10.2.1* **The** *building blocks of visitor management in protected lands*

In many protected areas visitation, tourism and recreation are treated as quite different activities, and there is much debate in the literature over definitions of 'tourist' and different types of tourist. In protected area contexts, such as the Antarctic, all visitors (including scientists and base personnel) are from another country and the vast majority (such as scientists, base staff, commercial tourists, government representatives) are involved in recreational pursuits and visits to sites of special scientific importance (SSSI). Hence, in some contexts, the distinction between tourist, recreationist and visitor in reality is quite meaningless. However, in other planning contexts, particularly in protected areas located close to urban areas, the activities, values and needs of tourists, day visitors and local residents might be quite distinct (e.g. in terms of facilities, group composition, length of stay and requirements for visitor services). Many of the management models discussed in the literature, for example Davis's (1999) discussion on the application of the 'Limits of Acceptable Change (LAC)' model, are actually models for managing recreation, not tourism per se, in which case recreation models relating to visitor management can be considered just as valid as tourism models.

Many of the approaches, particularly those used in the North American, New Zealand and Australian protected areas systems, have a broad content that relates to managing visitor satisfaction (e.g. the Visitor Experience and Resource Protection Framework, or VERP; USDA 1997). In the situations where these approaches have been developed and implemented there exists a legal framework that requires the protected area agency to manage for visitor satisfaction. This is certainly the situation in New Zealand where visitor management in national parks and other protected lands is governed by the *New Zealand Conservation Act 1987*. Section 6(e) of this Act requires the Department of Conservation (DoC) to 'foster the use of natural and historic resources for recreation'. Once again, the situation in Antarctica offers a valuable contrast. No such legal imperative to manage for visitor satisfaction exists for Antarctica. The Antarctic Treaty System (ATS) provides only for the peaceful use and protection of Antarctica (Articles 1–1 and IX-1(f)) and does not require the protection or provision of experiences for tourists. Some researchers (e.g. Maher, Steel & McIntosh 2003) have undertaken research into this area but, although it is accepted that assessing the benefits to tourists of their Antarctic experiences might have value in terms of justifying tourism as a valid activity, in terms of discussing and designing a regulatory and management system, visitor satisfaction is part of the policy and planning frameworks.

A number of valuable overviews of the history and application of policy and planning frameworks for tourism in protected areas are available. Chief among these are Hammitt and Cole (1998), Eagles and McCool (2002), Eagles, McCool and Haynes (2002) and Newsome, Moore and Dowling (2002), all of which provide in-depth and contemporary examinations of both policy and planning processes and management actions with respect to tourism in protected lands. These authors confirm that one of the fundamental aspects of management of visitors to protected lands is having both a robust planning framework and the ability and intent to act on the results of that planning. Eagles, McCool and Haynes (2002) in their report for the IUCN, *Sustainable Tourism in Protected Areas*, note (p. 159):

> These guidelines suggest that national and international organisations need to encourage governments to make improvements (in the management of protected areas) in the following critical areas:
> - Support for effective legislation, with adequate resources for implementation
> - Creation of national policies on protected areas and management of tourism (as well as education about the environment and conservation), and
> - Development of a management plan for each protected area, covering all activities, including tourism, to ensure that objectives are achieved and resources are well used.

These principles are reinforced in the United Nations Educational, Scientific and Cultural Organisation (UNESCO) manual *Managing Tourism at World Heritage Sites* (Pedersen 2002) and in the Australia and New Zealand Environment and Conservation Council report *Commercial Management — Processes in the Delivery of Park Services* (ANZECC 1999). A sound legislative framework, good planning systems and the use of a range of management tools to achieve desired outcomes are fundamental requirements for the management of protected lands. Certainly the protected areas jurisdictions of New Zealand, the USA, Canada and Australia all have, or are endeavouring to develop, these fundamental elements of their regulatory systems. In most cases this framework takes the form of a hierarchical system, as illustrated in figure 10.1.

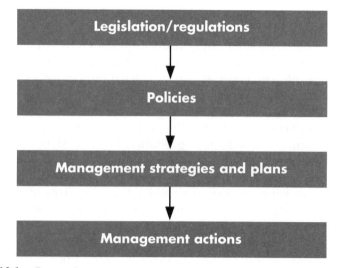

Legislation/regulations

↓

Policies

↓

Management strategies and plans

↓

Management actions

■ **Figure 10.1**   *Protected area management: heirarchy of management instruments*

Source: *adapted from Maher 2006.*

Legislation

The first important aspect of the theoretical model is the grounding in a sound legislative framework (Eagles, McCool & Haynes 2002). This theme is a common thread to the literature on visitor management in protected areas. A robust and clear legal foundation for managing tourism in protected areas is critical. The goals and objectives that are developed as an early step common to all of the models will inevitably have their basis in the objectives of the jurisdictional legal framework. The legal framework for protected lands varies significantly in the international context. Biocentric (natural) and scientific values prevail in some contexts (e.g. Antarctica), but anthropocentric (human) and recreational values prevail in many others. Furthermore, although the legal framework for tourism in protected lands is clear, in others this is not the case. The planning and policy framework for tourism in Antarctica is uncertain and poorly defined (e.g. Joyner 1998). The situation in Antarctica is different in many ways from those of sovereign nations elsewhere, but the legislation governing tourism is unclear and the regulations that apply to those visiting sites in Antarctica are lacking.

Policies

Many international management models use formal policies as a means to interpret the relevant legislation in the context of the situation at hand (Pedersen 2002). An example of this is the New Zealand *General Policy for National Parks* (NZCA 2005) and the 'Conservation General Policy' (DoC 2005a). Both these documents provide guidance for managers and public (and industry participants) regarding such matters as the siting of accommodation facilities and the provision of recreational opportunities. In most cases these policies formally inform management plans and strategies and provide valuable guidance to management participants.

Management strategies and plans

Newsome et al. (2002: 147) describe **planning for visitors** as being 'the process of setting goals and then developing the actions needed to achieve them' and, further, 'the basic task of planning is to visualise the area, that is, the product, as visitors and managers wish it to be in the future'. The development and existence of a wide variety of visitor management systems has occurred largely in North American protected areas since the 1970s (Eagles & McCool 2002). These various models have been developed in an attempt to provide managers of protected areas with planning tools that enable them to produce management plans and other statements of desired goals, objectives and outcomes, on which management actions can be based. A variety of approaches exist; both Eagles and McCool (2002) and Newsome et al. (2002) noting and analysing at least six different models. Examples include the LAC model (Stankey et al. 1985) and the Visitor Experience and Resource Protection Framework (VERP; USDA 1997). All of the models have been applied in part or in whole in various protected areas around the world with varying levels of acceptance and success.

This chapter does not seek to provide an in-depth analysis of each of the models, nor to compare or contrast them to each other. This has been undertaken thoroughly elsewhere and does not need to be repeated (see Dearden & Rollins 1993). It is sufficient to state here that an integrated and comprehensive tourism management system for protected lands should include the use of a planning model with attributes that are generally acceptable and applicable in this context. In general the models that are analysed in the literature are largely derivative of each other and focus significantly on the management of visitor experiences (Boyd & Butler 1996; Newsome et al. 2002).

Generally there are two types of model: those that can be said to be generally '**anthropocentric**' or focused on human outcomes, such as visitor satisfaction, and those that can be considered '**biocentric**' or '**ecocentric**'; that is, environment focused. The VERP and Recreational Opportunity Spectrum (ROS) approaches are typical anthropocentric models, while of the many models it appears that the LAC model is possibly the most 'ecocentric' (Eagles & McCool 2002). Again, the applicability of different management models is likely to vary with context. Protected areas situated in an urban or peri-urban context, where visitor demands are likely to be high, should perhaps more appropriately be subject to anthropocentric models governing the management of tourism, recreation and visitation (e.g. TOMM, ROS and VERP). By contrast, given that the 'legal' mandate for the management of tourism in Antarctica does not include an objective of managing visitor experiences, and given that the sites where tourism occurs are often highly susceptible to environmental damage (Hoffmann & Jatko 2000), it is likely that the LAC model could be most suited to an Antarctic tourism management system.

Management actions

The development and application of planning frameworks is only part of the picture with respect to managing tourism in protected areas. The other part is the issue of the interaction between the planning frameworks and management actions. Hammitt and Cole (1998) make a significant point of this, describing the relationship between the formulation of goals and objectives for protected areas and the management actions required to achieve those goals. Newsome et al. (2002) and Eagles and McCool (2002) also examine this issue. This is an important issue in that it links the planning for outcomes and the achievement of those outcomes through a regulatory regime. Maher (2004) argues that planning for protected areas must inextricably be linked to decisions about how those goals and objectives will be realised through action.

Newsome et al. (2002) summarise the possible types of regulatory or management reaction to planning outcomes into two main streams (p. 185):

1. **site** or **visitor management**, whereby site management focuses on actions at the sites (e.g. track hardening) and visitor management focuses on managing the visitors themselves (e.g. regulation, information)
2. **direct** or **indirect management**, whereby direct management actions restrict individual choice (e.g. regulation of access) and indirect management actions seek to influence visitors (e.g. information).

It is possible to describe the potential actions of managers as occurring along a continuum, from reasonably 'soft' and indirect interventions, such as information and advocacy, through to 'hard' or direct actions, such as physical site works or restrictions on access to various sites. Managers are able to choose various actions in order to achieve certain outcomes that result from the application of the aforementioned planning frameworks, depending on the circumstances of the case. It is also possible for a regulatory system to involve 'movement' along the continuum of intervention choices, choosing other 'harder' interventions should the previously tried 'soft' interventions fail to achieve the intended outcomes (Newsome et al. 2002).

Some consider that there is a distinct relationship among the activities of tourists or recreationists, the attributes of the sites involved, the degree of vulnerability of the site and the appropriate management response required. Hammitt and Cole (1998) structure their book on this subject in exactly this way, and Eagles and McCool discuss the linkages among these elements extensively. Newsome et al. (2002) also refer to this linkage and present the two main approaches with respect to management response in a diagrammatic form (see figure 10.2).

Hence, the management of tourism in protected areas requires the presence of three fundamental components in the regulatory system:

1. appropriate and binding legislation and the resources to implement it
2. the use of applicable plan/ning approaches to develop goals and objectives for the management of the places where tourism occurs
3. a range of direct and indirect management techniques that can be used to manage the impact of visitors and achieve the goals and objectives as developed by the planning processes and as envisaged by the legislation.

It is also clear that linkages between site values, tourism activities and impact and the management responses to the activities and impacts are required. Some sites are more vulnerable than others, and some activities have more potential for impact than others. Management responses to activities and impacts therefore need to be set in the context of the sites where the activities occur.

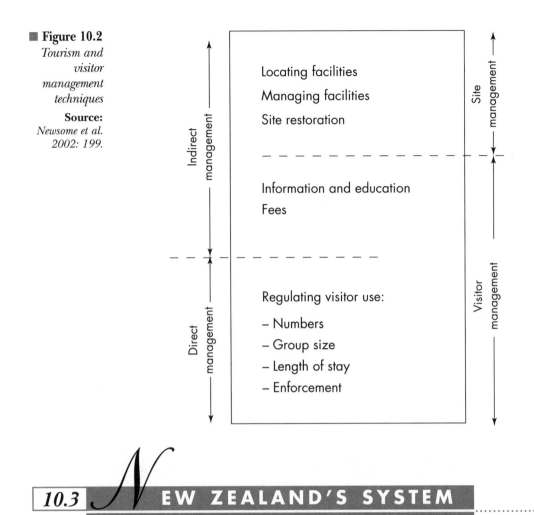

Indirect management

Site management

Locating facilities

Managing facilities

Site restoration

Information and education

Fees

Direct management

Visitor management

Regulating visitor use:

– Numbers

– Group size

– Length of stay

– Enforcement

10.3 NEW ZEALAND'S SYSTEM OF PROTECTED LANDS

The unrestricted enjoyment of New Zealand's protected lands is a corner-stone of the New Zealand way of life (DoC 2005a). However, the development of this system has always been complicated by two quite contrasting philosophies on nature conservation. One philosophy sees wild lands as 'barren and sterile' until modified for utilitarian use or served with facilities for tourism and recreational purposes (Hall 1992). The other values nature for its intrinsic worth. The Department of Conservation (2005a, n.p.) acknowledges that 'New Zealand's earliest attempts to legislate for the protection of natural resources reflected this philosophical ambivalence'. Both views were accommodated in early efforts to protect New Zealand's natural areas. In terms of the former, the designation of New Zealand's first national parks, as in North America and Australia, was intended to ensure the protection and enjoyment of national parks in perpetuity. By contrast, the Romantic view of nature led to the protection of such places as Resolution Island (1891) and Little Barrier Island (1894), in the interests of scientific rather than recreational values (DoC 2005a).

10.3.1 **The** *genesis and continuing development of a system of protected areas*

The development of an extensive system of national parks in New Zealand dates from 1887. In that year Paramount Chief Te Heuheu Tukino of the Ngati Tuwharetoa gave the summits of three tribal mountains near Lake Taupo (central North Island; see figure 10.3 on p. 346) to the Crown as a gift. These three peaks, steeped in oral tradition and highly sacred to the Maori people, provide the nucleus of Tongariro National Park. Tongariro is New Zealand's first national park (the fourth designated national park in the world), which occupies 79 598 hectares (Statistics New Zealand 1995). The actions of Chief Te Heuheu Tukino provided 'the first steps towards preserving vast tracts of [New Zealand's] most magnificent territory' (Watkins 1987: 201). Today there are fourteen New Zealand national parks; the most recent, Rakiura National Park, which occupies 85 per cent of Steward Island, being gazetted in 2003 (see table 10.1).

■ Table 10.1
New Zealand national parks
Source:
adapted from DoC 2005b.

NORTH ISLAND		
PARK	**ESTABLISHED**	**AREA (HA)**
Urewera	1954	212 675
Tongariro	1887	79 598
Egmont	1900	33 543
Whanganui	1986	74 231
Total		400 047
SOUTH ISLAND		
Abel Tasman	1942	22 541
Kahurangi	1995	400 000
Nelson Lakes	1956	101 753
Paparoa	1987	30 560
Arthur's Pass	1929	114 357
Mount Cook	1953	70 728
Westland	1960	117 547
Mount Aspiring	1964	355 531
Fiordland	1952	1 251 924
Rakiura	2003	157 000
Total		2 621 941

The anthropocentric philosophy is evident in the *National Parks Act 1952*, which states that the purpose of national parks is to 'preserve in perpetuity ... for the enjoyment of the public, areas of New Zealand that contain scenery of such distinctive qualities or natural features so beautiful or unique that their preservation is in the national interest'. In doing so the Act allows for public rights of access so that visitors may 'receive, in full measure, the inspiration, enjoyment, recreation and other benefits that may be derived from mountains, lakes and rivers'.

The *National Parks Act 1980* succeeded that of 1952. Section 4 (2), (a)–(e) of the Act outlines the specific purposes of the Act. Under legislation these areas are to be maintained in their natural state. This involves the protection of indigenous species of plant and animal and the removal of introduced species. Archaeological and historic sites are to be preserved in context. Water, soil and forest resources in national parks are to be maintained. Freedom of access to national parks is conditional on restrictions deemed necessary to safeguard the distinctive qualities of the park.

Thus, the *National Parks Act 1980* required a balancing of the need to protect the distinctive character of conservation lands with 'public access and enjoyment'. The provision for recreational use of the conservation estate necessitated the delineation of 'specially protected areas' and 'wilderness areas'. The Department of Conservation dictates entry into 'specially protected areas' through the issuing of permits. Activities conducted in designated wilderness areas are also governed by the department. A series of 10 wilderness areas lie at the core of New Zealand's national and forest parks system. Wilderness areas in New Zealand comply with a highly purist legislated definition of wilderness based on a phenomenal definition of 'wilderness' (Kliskey 1992) established by the Wilderness Advisory Group (WAG) in 1983 and adopted by the Minister of Conservation in 1989.

In addition to the two million hectares of national parks, the Department of Conservation also administers approximately five million hectares of other protected lands, the majority of which (4.7 million hectares) is 'stewardship areas' held under the *Conservation Act 1987*. Stewardship areas are held under section 25 of the Act to be managed so that their natural and historic resources are protected. Stewardship areas include 20 forest parks (fourteen in the North Island and six in the South Island) that collectively occupy an area of more than 1.8 million hectares (see figure 10.3). Forest parks are designated primarily to protect forested mountain catchments but also provide a 'less restricted range of recreational activities than national parks ... including tramping, camping, fishing and shooting for a variety of game' (Statistics New Zealand 1995). Reserve lands, which consist primarily of approximately 1200 scenic reserves, occupy a further 300 000 hectares. These include areas of scenic interest including native flora, limestone features, thermal areas, glow-worm caves and waterfalls (Statistics New Zealand 1995). Additional reserve designations include scientific, historic, recreation and wildlife reserves. New Zealand's system of protected areas includes an expanding series of marine reserves and three World Heritage sites listed in the UNESCO World Heritage Convention, Te Waipounamu (South-west New Zealand), Tongariro National Park and a World Heritage area that incorporates New Zealand's peri-Antarctic islands.

The most recent significant additions to the conservation estate have been an extensive series of former high country sheep stations. In more recent years high country areas (typically alpine tussock grasslands that have historically been heavily grazed under a Crown lease system) have been subject to tenure review. The Department of Conservation has participated in the review of Crown pastoral leases and occupation licences under the *Crown Pastoral Lands Act 1998* and the *Land Act 1949* (DoC 2000, 2001). Under tenure review many former high country sheep stations, predominantly in the central South Island, have been incorporated into the conservation estate. More than 127 000 ha of high country pastoral land, mostly in the Otago conservancy, had been added to the conservation estate up to the end of 2005, through 66 tenure reviews of pastoral land (DoC 2005a). This figure excludes the transfer of the 180 476 hectare Molesworth Station to the Department of Conservation in 2005. Much of this land includes snow tussock and alpine herb fields. New holdings have been transferred to the department, including lands in the Remarkables Range, as well as areas in the Old Man, Old Woman and Rock and Pillar ranges of Central Otago. These designations are located in the upland zones that fall between the more populated parts of the country and the more remote alpine national parks. As such these additions to the conservation estate potentially offer significant implications for recreation and tourism, particularly tourism in the rural communities adjacent to new conservation designations.

■ **Figure 10.3**
New Zealand's protected area system
Source: *DoC 2005a, www.doc.govt.nz /About-DOC/ 001~Overview/ Map-Showing-Public-Conservation-Land.asp.*

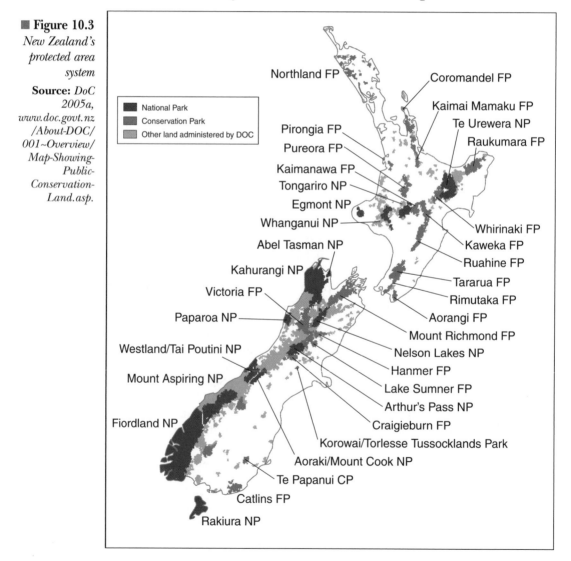

Thus, in overview, the conservation estate consists primarily of:

- an extensive series of national parks centred on the southern alps of the South Island and volcanic cones of the central North Island
- a large area of stewardship land with lower use levels and more remote values
- a scattered series of small reserves with greater proximity to the population centres of the North Island and eastern coastline of the South Island
- an expanding series of high country parks in the South Island situated in between.

New Zealand's system of protected areas is illustrated in figure 10.3.

10.4 TOURISM AND RECREATION IN NEW ZEALAND'S PROTECTED AREA SYSTEM

Lands with high value for conservation and recreation have been visited by New Zealanders and overseas visitors for more than a century. Maori played a leading role in the development of tourism associated with the geothermal attractions of Rotorua (Watkins 1987). 'The first Hermitage Hotel was built at Mount Cook in 1884; the Milford Track was opened in 1890; by the 1890s the Whanganui River was known to visitors as the "Rhine of New Zealand" and glacier guiding was available on the Franz Josef and Fox glaciers' (DoC 2005a, n.p.). These remain some of the earliest manifestations of tourism in New Zealand. By 2001 two million international tourists were visiting New Zealand annually, an increase of 85 per cent since 1990 (Cessford & Thompson 2002). Hence levels and patterns of use of protected areas have changed as the mix of visitors (and the experiences that they seek) has evolved. In reference to international visitors, Department of Conservation (2005a, n.p.) states that 'their rapid growth in numbers, generally lower level of backcountry skills and desire for higher quality facilities in the front country, has highlighted the tension between "protection" and "visitor use" that has always been there in our legislation'. (Visitor use of protected areas is conveniently described as 'frontcountry' — day use — and 'backcountry' — areas that require at least one night to be spent in a hut or designated camping area.)

■ 10.4.1 The *historical relationship between tourism and protected areas in New Zealand*

The relationship between tourism and protected lands in New Zealand has always been close. New Zealand's 'clean and green' image is an essential element of its attractiveness as an international tourism destination. Although New Zealand's rural environment, based on images of sheep grazing on rolling green hills, is an important contributor to this image, it is primarily based on perceptions of clear rivers and lakes, alpine areas and forest wilderness that centre on the extensive system of conservation lands described in section 2.1 (Higham 1996; Hall et al. 1997). The following discussion adopts an historical perspective and outlines the way in which previous sets of institutional arrangements and values have established environmental management regimes that influence subsequent policy settings and actions. Hall and Higham (2000) identify four main periods of institutional arrangements that can be identified with respect to the management of protected lands in New Zealand. These four periods provide the structure for the following discussion.

Utilitarian conservation, 1870s–1940s

The history of New Zealand's protected lands highlights the role of a utilitarian conservation ethic in the development of the national and forest parks. The nucleus of present-day Tongariro National Park, although given to the Crown in 1887, was not in actual fact legally designated until 1894. This considerable delay reflected the government's concern that only 'worthless' land would be incorporated in the park. 'There had to be absolute certainty that land being added to the park had no economic value' (Harris 1974). The 'worthless lands' view of national parks, so characteristic of early attitudes towards parks in Australia, Canada and the USA (Runte 1972, 1973, 1979; Hall 1988a, 1992), was also dominant in New Zealand (Hall 1988b; Hall & Shultis 1991). For example, in discussing Tongariro National Park, the Hon. John McKenzie, Minister for Lands, was reported as telling parliament that 'anyone who had seen the portion of the country … which he might say was almost useless so far as grazing was concerned would admit that it should be set apart as a national park for New Zealand' (New Zealand 1894: 579). In a similar fashion to Canada and the USA, the New Zealand Government saw national parks as a means of economically developing areas through tourism, the aesthetic value of such regions being the attraction to tourists.

The introduction of exotic species into the national parks of New Zealand is a recurring theme in the history of New Zealand's protected lands. Sheep were not the only introduced species to create problems of land degradation. The introduction of deer for hunting purposes brought considerable damage to extensive upland protected areas. By the 1880s many Canterbury rivers were stocked with trout. Trout were subsequently introduced to the catchments of Lake Taupo, the Rotorua Lakes and the Southern Lakes and quickly became a major tourism attraction. They remain so today, and considerable debate currently surrounds whether or not international visitors should pay more for fishing licences and/or be subject to different licence conditions (e.g. catch and release only) than their domestic counterparts. By 1900 the acclimatisation movement had progressively introduced many exotic animals for game sport (e.g. trout and Himalayan thar), many of which have become serious conservation pests (e.g. deer). Nevertheless, despite the emergence of a positive ecological viewpoint towards the role of the national parks in the 1920s, it should be noted that they were still seen primarily in economic terms. Indeed the grazing of valley systems in southern New Zealand national parks (e.g. the grazing of cattle in the Dart Valley, Mount Aspiring National Park and sheep in the Eglinton Valley, Fiordland National Park) continued until remarkably recently.

The creation of a New Zealand national parks system, 1950s–60s

By 1952, four national parks has been established under a variety of Acts, and each park was managed separately. They included Tongariro (1887), Egmont (1900), Arthur's Pass (1929) and Abel Tasman (1942). These parks were created because of their cultural values and/or spectacular scenery. The parks contained examples of New Zealand's unique fauna and flora as well as introduced plant and animal species, such as deer, pigs, goats and opossums, which caused enormous damage to forested and grassland ecologies (Veblen & Stewart 1982). The lack of a coordinated and systematic approach to national park planning was criticised by a number of groups and individuals in the interwar years, including the director of Kew Gardens, Dr Arthur Hill (Thompson 1976; Fleming 1979). These criticisms had little influence on government policy towards conservation; however, the recreational perspectives of tramping associations and mountaineering clubs did have a significant influence on park policy. Through a comparison of overseas initiatives in park planning a subcommittee of the Federated Mountain Club (FMC; formed in 1931) decided 'to put forward suggestions for more systematic general control, based upon the successful and businesslike examples of the United States and Canada' (Thompson 1976: 9). The lobbying of the FMC appeared to have some influence on the New Zealand Government, but the reorganisation of the parks had to wait until after World War II.

A burgeoning demand for outdoor recreation began after World War II and led to the formation of many new tramping, hunting and skiing clubs throughout New Zealand. At the same time, the need for better administration of public lands for outdoor recreation was recognised. In line with US perspectives, an anthropocentric philosophy underpinned the *National Parks Act 1952* in which New Zealand's designated protected areas were seen as being recreational in character. The recreational importance attached to New Zealand's national parks was demonstrated in the 1952 Act, which, following North American national park legislation, defined the purpose of the parks to be for the benefit and enjoyment of the public (see section 10.3.1). There followed an intense period of park designation in which Fiordland (1952), Mount Cook (1953), Urewera (1954) and Nelson Lakes (1956) national parks were gazetted in quick succession.

The *National Parks Act 1952* and its successor, the *National Parks Act 1980*, while stressing that parks were to be preserved in perpetuity, also recognised that 'the public shall have freedom of entry and access to the parks, so that they may receive in full measure, the inspiration, enjoyment and other benefits that may be derived from mountains, forests, sounds, sea coasts, lakes, rivers and other natural features'.

By the mid-1960s, this public interest in both protection and recreation had been recognised by the formation of 10 national parks, including Westland (1960) and Mount Aspiring (1964). The first of 19 forest parks, Tararua, was set up under the *Forests Act 1949*, a statute that had been amended to place greater emphasis on multiple use and the provision of opportunities for outdoor recreation. The numbers of deer in New Zealand's protected areas had built up alarmingly during the 1940s and 1950s. This led to the development, during the 1960s and early 1970s, of an extensive network of huts and tracks throughout the protected forests and forest parks managed by the Forest Service. Many of today's backcountry huts, tracks and bridges date to this period. So, too, does the development of the adventure tourism industry, which is derived from the transition in deer hunting to fixed-wing and, latterly, helicopter-based hunting and deer recovery for export.

Wilderness preservation, 1970s–80s

Legal recognition of the wilderness concept in New Zealand first occurred under the *National Parks Act 1952*, with the first wilderness area being established under the Act in 1955. The *National Parks Act 1980* has similar provisions that repeat the 1952 Act. Provision for wilderness areas was also made in the *Reserves and Domains Act 1955*, which was subsequently revised as section 47 of the *Reserves Act 1977*. However, no wilderness area was actually established in the reserves system. Section 14 of the *National Parks Act 1980* referred to the creation and management of wilderness areas, which were defined as 'an area whose predominant character is the result of the interplay of purely natural processes, large enough and so situated as to be unaffected, except in minor ways, by what takes in the non-wilderness around it. In order that the enjoyment of a completely natural unspoilt environment may be experienced, access to and within a wilderness area will be by foot only' (National Parks Authority 1978: 3.2).

In 1981, following the fiftieth jubilee Wilderness Conference organised by the Federated Mountain Club (FMC), the Minister of Lands and Forests established a Wilderness Advisory Group (WAG) to advise the minister 'on policy for wilderness establishment and use, on the identification and assessment of potential wilderness and on priorities for action' (Department of Lands and Survey 1984: C.1). At the Wilderness Conference the FMC proposed 10 wilderness areas, which were examined by the WAG (Hall 1988b). WAG consisted of representatives from both government and public interest organisations. According to WAG (1985: n.p.), 'wilderness areas are wild lands designated for their protection and managed to perpetuate their natural condition and which appear to have been affected only by the forces of nature, with any imprint of human interference substantially unnoticeable'.

Wilderness areas in New Zealand should meet the following criteria:
1. they will be large enough to take at least two days' foot travel to traverse
2. they should have clearly defined topographic boundaries and be adequately buffered so as to be unaffected, except in minor ways, by human influence
3. they will not have such developments such as huts, tracks, bridges, signs or mechanical access (WAG 1985: n.p).

Provision for wilderness areas on Forest Service land was made by a 1976 amendment to the *Forest Act 1949*. The first state forest park wilderness area, Raukumara (see figure 10.3), was established in June 1986. At the beginning of 1987 two further wilderness areas had received ministerial approval and approval-in-principle respectively. They were the Tasman wilderness area (91 000 ha) in the North West Nelson State Forest Park (now Kahurangi National Park) and the Paparoa wilderness (35 000 ha) in the Paparoa Range (now Paparoa National Park) (New Zealand Forest Service 1986a: n.p.). However, wilderness preservation advances made in the late 1970s and early 1980s slowed in the late 1980s with the development of new institutional arrangements for the conservation estate. This transition in policy priorities coincided with a period of rapid and sustained growth in international tourism.

New economic conservation, 1987–present

Environmental administration in New Zealand was overhauled by the fourth Labour Government (1984–90) (Crabtree 1989). Environmental reform under the Labour government was initiated by the *Environment Act 1986* (Palmer 1990). The enactment of this legislation established the Ministry for the Environment (MfE) and the position of Parliamentary Commissioner for the Environment, described by Palmer (1990) as 'an independent guardian to protect the environment'. The third major reform to environmental administration in New Zealand was the creation of the Department of Conservation, the organisation responsible for the conservation estate, which came into existence at the start of the financial year, 1 April 1987.

The creation of the Department of Conservation was the result of a restructuring of the Department of Lands and Survey and the New Zealand Forest Service. The department was established on a four-tier structure consisting of Head Office (Wellington), eight regional offices, 34 district offices and numerous suboffices or field centres. The *Conservation Act 1987* reiterated the validity of recreational use of most lands managed by the department, providing that conservation values were safeguarded. The *Conservation Act 1987* Part II, section 6(e) states: 'To the extent that any use of any natural or historic resource for recreation or tourism is not inconsistent with its conservation, to foster the use of natural and historic resources for recreation and to allow their use for tourism.' Thus, the department was charged primarily with the management of the conservation estate, including all national parks, and was obliged to foster recreational use of heritage resources and allow tourism (Cahn & Cahn 1989). In addition, the management of reserves, forest parks and other state forests, wildlife and native plants, historic foreshores, seabeds, lakes and rivers, marine resources and marine mammals were drawn together under the department's umbrella (Molloy 1993).

The importance of protected areas to contemporary economic development in New Zealand was confirmed by the publication of *New Zealand Conservation Estate and International Visitors* in 1993 by the Department of Conservation and the New Zealand Tourism Board (now Tourism New Zealand), which is responsible for the promotion of New Zealand to international tourists (DoC/NZTB 1993). The trends emerging from this policy document included the doubling or tripling of international tourist arrivals to New Zealand and increases in demand for forest and national park recreation resources commensurate with this goal. These trends were described by Boas (1993) as 'disturbing' given the absence at that time of a framework for environmental management.

The 'new economic conservation' philosophy was pursued despite concerns over the capacities of sites within the conservation estate to cope with projected tourist demand (DoC/NZTB 1993). *New Zealand Conservation Estate and International Visitors* (DoC/NZTB 1993) identified that levels of use at many forested sites, such as the Routeburn, Milford, Rees-Dart, Dusky and Copland tracks as well as Great Barrier Island, were at or beyond their capacities to cope. Some tracks were considered capable of accommodating increased levels of use. These included the Abel Tasman, Kepler, Greenstone and Stewart Island tracks. Others, including some of New Zealand's most significant backcountry tracks, the Caples, Wilkin-Young and Hollyford, were considered capable of accommodating double the levels of use that they were then receiving, in order to meet projected levels of demand.

The management of visitors to protected areas (both terrestrial and marine areas) became a live issue in the 1990s. New Zealand's protected areas have attracted an unprecedented number of international visitors. Their impact is especially felt on the Great Walks like the Routeburn Track and Abel Tasman coastal walk and in key scenic areas like Milford Sound, Mount Cook, Cape Reinga and South Westland's glaciers. A significant number of these overseas visitors are seeking 'ecotourism' experiences. Provision of the expected visitor services — information centres, education on wildlife and conservation, safe visitor facilities (e.g. huts, tracks and bridges, picnic areas, toilets and short walks), advice on personal safety and appropriate care for the environment — has fallen on the Department of Conservation.

10.5 INSTITUTIONAL ARRANGEMENTS RELATING TO NEW ZEALAND'S PROTECTED AREAS

Institutional arrangements provide a set of rules and procedures that regulates how and where demands on public policy can be made, who has the authority to take certain decisions and actions, and how decisions and policies are implemented. The study of institutional arrangements has long been regarded as a significant aspect of resource and environment management (e.g. Mitchell 1989). For example, O'Riordan (1971: 135) observed that:

> One of the least touched upon, but possibly one of the most fundamental, research needs in resource management is the analysis of how institutional arrangements are formed and how they evolve in response to changing needs and the existence of internal and external stress. There is growing evidence to suggest that the form, structure and operational guidelines by which resource management institutions are formed and evolve clearly affect the implementation of resource policy, both as to the range of choice adopted and the decision attitudes of the personnel involved.

More recently, the study of institutional arrangements has been seen as critical to understanding the conditions by which sustainable development may be encouraged (e.g. Ostrom 1986). However, although the study of institutional arrangements is fundamental to the context in which environmental and resource management occurs, little consideration has been given to the role that institutional arrangements play with respect to tourism and environmental management (Hall & Jenkins 1995). There is therefore relatively little understanding of the way the institutional context has influenced the environmental management of tourism.

The Department of Conservation is charged with the management of New Zealand's protected lands. As a government department, the department is subject to laws passed by parliament. The *Conservation Act 1987* sets out the majority of the department's responsibilities and roles. The department administers 25 Acts of Parliament and has functions under several other Acts (DoC 2005a). It can function only in accordance with legislation and in doing so reports ultimately to the Minister of Conservation.

Under the Act, the Department of Conservation has a number of functions. These include the management for conservation purposes of land and natural and historic resources, conservation advocacy, the provision of educational and promotional conservation information, the provision of advice to the Minister for Conservation and fostering recreation and allowing tourism on conservation land, providing the use is consistent with the conservation of the resource. In doing so, the department places emphasis on protecting biodiversity and minimising biodiversity risks, protecting historic and cultural values, promoting appropriate recreation and public enjoyment of protected lands, engaging the community in conservation and promoting effective partnerships with Tangata Whenua ('People of the Land'; i.e. Maori).

These are the functions and policy priorities of the Department of Conservation as they exist in 2006. However, it should be noted that with the growth and diversification of tourism the department has also been required to function in collaboration with an increasing number of tourism stakeholders.

10.6 CONTEMPORARY POLICY AND PLANNING FOR NEW ZEALAND'S PROTECTED AREAS

As noted previously in this chapter, management of protected areas is subject to a 'hierarchy' of institutional arrangements, being legislation, national policy or strategy and local or regional management plans and strategies. Below the level of legislation, the planning and management requirements of the department are guided and informed by a series of policies and strategies that have been developed, with consultation, in accordance with the Conservation Act. These policies and strategies clearly articulate the department's strategies and plans and, with relevance to the management of tourism, are listed on the following page.

- General Policy for National Parks
- Conservation General Policy
- *Visitor Strategy*, 1996 (DoC 2005b).

The management of the conservation estate vis-à-vis recreation and tourism is primarily addressed in the *Visitor Strategy* and the Statement of Intent (SOI; DoC 2005c), which provides guidance for the department's planning and management relating to visitor services. The two general policies also refer to the management of recreation and tourism, providing policies on ski areas, aerial cableways (including gondolas) and aircraft use. The department's *Visitor Strategy* was developed following extensive consultation (e.g. with Royal Forest and Bird Protection Society, Federated Mountain Clubs, New Zealand Tourism Board, the Ministry of Commerce Tourism Policy Group, New Zealand Tourism Industry Association and the New Zealand Conservation Authority) and public comment. The *Visitor Strategy* directly addresses five key goals (see table 10.2). It signals a commitment to a holistic approach to visitor planning, and it articulates a commitment to such matters as the protection of natural and historic values, working with Maori, the delivery of a wide range of recreational opportunities, appropriate and safe visitors' facilities and services, and development and maintenance of relationships with communities, recreation and conservation groups (DoC 1996).

■ **Table 10.2**   *Department of Conservation Visitor Strategy: issues and goals*

GOAL	POLICY STATEMENT
Goal 1: Protection	To ensure that the intrinsic natural and historic values of areas managed by the department are not compromised by the impact of visitor activities and related facilities and services. (This links closely with other key department strategic initiatives, such as the biodiversity action plan and the historic heritage strategy.)
Goal 2: Fostering visits	To manage a range of recreational opportunities that provide contact with New Zealand's natural and historic heritage, and provide a range of recreational and educational facilities and services consistent with the protection of the intrinsic natural and historic values of department-managed areas.
Goal 3: Managing tourism concessions on protected lands	In managing a range of recreational opportunities, to allow the private sector to provide visitor facilities and services where they do not compromise the intrinsic natural and historic values of areas managed by the department and do not compromise the experiences or opportunities of other visitors.
Goal 4: Informing and educating visitors	To share knowledge about our natural and historic heritage with visitors, to satisfy their requirements for information, deepen their understanding of this heritage and develop an awareness of the need for its conservation. (This goal operates alongside 'Conservation Connections', the department's public awareness strategy.)
Goal 5: Visitor safety	To provide visitors with facilities that are safe and are located, designed, constructed and maintained in accordance with all relevant legislation and sound building practices to meet appropriate safety standards. To raise visitor awareness of the risks present in department-managed areas and the level of skill and competence they will require to cope with these risks.

Source: *DoC 1996.*

More recently, the SOI (DoC 2005c) for the period 2005–08 has demonstrated further refinement of these concepts since 1996. The SOI provides the strategic 'umbrella' for the work of the department. In this document, the department's work is generally said to be for either 'Protection' or 'Appreciation'. The two outcomes are not unrelated, with the SOI noting (DoC 2005c: 13): 'the inter-relationship between the Protection and Appreciation outcomes can be described in this way: New Zealand's heritage needs to be preserved and protected so people can enjoy and benefit from it, while people's support for conservation is linked to their appreciation and valuing of our heritage.'

The proposed initiatives for the management of tourism in protected areas include working closely with the tourism industry and private enterprises to ensure that the integrity of conservation values is not compromised (concessions management system) and upgrading facilities to improve the quality of infrastructure.

The delivery of visitor services is also addressed in the regional conservation management strategies as well as the management plans for national parks. These strategies and plans must be consistent with overlying policies and strategies, including the General Policy and *Visitor Strategy.*

10.6.1 **Managing** *visitor infrastructure, recreational opportunities and tourism businesses*

The Department of Conservation provides for tourism is three primary ways: (1) through the provision of government-funded visitor infrastructure of walking tracks, roads, huts and campsites, amenity areas and visitor centres; (2) through visitor information and services such as maps, brochures and staff interpretation and information at visitor centres and (3) by way of the 'concessions system' for management of private sector-provided tourism activities in public conservation areas. The role of DoC in tourism is recognised through the *New Zealand Tourism Strategy 2010* (TNZ 2000), which notes that DoC has a key role in sustainable tourism in protected areas by way of monitoring visitor impact on the protected environment and intervening to manage it using tools such as booking systems and one-way routes for popular tracks and by investing in maintenance of the existing network of recreational services and facilities and developing new ones, to support increased visitor growth without damaging the environment.

The management of visitor infrastructure is a considerable challenge, one that effectively serves all visitor use of protected areas in New Zealand (Cessford & Thompson 2002). In the year ending 30 June 2005 the department spent approximately NZ$104m on the provision of recreational opportunities (DoC 2005a). This represented just over 43 per cent of the total expenditure in that year. In facilitating this task the Department of Conservation has implemented a Visitor Asset Management Programme (VAMP), based on three main management-defined components. They are visitor groups, visitor sites and visitor assets, discussed on pages 358–9.

RECREATION FEATURES	VISITOR GROUP						
	SHORT-STOP TRAVELLERS	DAY VISITORS	THRILL SEEKERS	OVERNIGHTERS	BACKCOUNTRY COMFORT SEEKERS	BACKCOUNTRY ADVENTURERS	REMOTENESS SEEKERS
SETTINGS AND ACCESSIBILITY	Roadside travel breaks or attraction visits for up to 1 hour.	Across most of ROS, often coastal/lake/river sites. Road access, often long travel times.	Natural/spectacular sites across ROS. Access by vehicles (land/sea/air), or short well-built tracks.	Rural/Backcountry drive-in and boat-in to camps or other overnight facilities.	Backcountry walk-in, good transport links to high-use walking tracks, some boat/air options.	Backcountry walk-in and Remote. Variety of less-developed tracks, boat/air options uncommon.	Remote/Wilderness. Basic track access to edges, no tracks, facilities, signs or boat/air options within.
NATURE OF VISIT AND ACTIVITIES	Passive viewing and short easy walks in casual sightseeing recreation.	Day at a site/day doing a specific activity. Facilities allow casual visitors.	Exciting/extreme activity. If more than 1 day, then Backcountry Adventurers.	Camping main use, base for variety day activities. 1 night to 1+ weeks. Often regular holiday spot.	Mostly tramping well developed tracks (Great Walks). 2–5 days, with 1 night at each hut/camp.	Tramping/backcountry activity, high self-reliance. 2–7 days or longer. Some specialised day visits.	Tramping/backcountry activity, total self-reliance. 3–7 days or longer.
EXPERIENCE SOUGHT	Convenience or easy visit to attractions, scenic or of historical, cultural, natural significance.	Social group visit or specific activity in outdoor natural setting. Sense of space and freedom.	Managed risk in exciting outdoors. Attractive and natural setting desirable.	Traditional NZ family summer holiday. Mainly overnight stays, associated outdoor activities.	Backcountry walking in managed safe conditions. Often first introduction to NZ backcountry settings.	Traditional NZ experience in backcountry, challenge, sense of freedom, accept some risk/difficulty.	Activities with purist wilderness experiences, challenge, freedom, accept much risk/difficulty.

RECREATION FEATURES	SHORT-STOP TRAVELLERS	DAY VISITORS	THRILL SEEKERS	OVERNIGHTERS	BACKCOUNTRY COMFORT SEEKERS	BACKCOUNTRY ADVENTURERS	REMOTENESS SEEKERS
FACILITIES SOUGHT	Quality carparks, toilets, interpretation and information facilities and short tracks catering for most abilities and ages.	Quality road access, toilets, carparks, picnic sites, good access to tracks and waterways important.	Specialised facilities (e.g skifields, bungy ramps) or key natural features (e.g cliffs, rapids, caves). Often commercial agents.	Basic camp facilities (toilets, water) and high activity facility standards. Some seek developed sites. Activity information important.	Quality tracks, bridges, huts, camps, signs. Often hut wardens. All-weather access. Some commercial provision of opportunities.	Basic facilities, varying standards of huts, tracks, route-marking, limited signs and key bridges. Access often subject to weather/environment.	No facilities once in remote/wilderness areas. Access totally subject to weather/environment.
VISITOR TYPES AND NUMBERS	NZ and overseas visitors. High numbers if sites at scheduled stops or key attractions.	NZ and overseas, med-high numbers. Sites for local repeat users or non-local one-off visits.	Young and affluent. Low numbers if independent activity, high numbers if commercial operation.	NZ family groups stay longer, independent overseas mostly 1 night while touring country. High peak summer use.	Often mostly overseas aged 20–40. NZ ages wider. Inexperienced relative to other NZ backcountry visitors.	Experienced, fit, young, male, NZ in low numbers. Fewer overseas, lack required knowledge, experience, opportunity.	Experienced, fit, young, male, NZ in very low numbers. Overseas rare, lack required knowledge, experience, opportunity.
PROJECTED USE	Rapid overseas visitor growth, pressure around main tourism highways and attractions.	Growth rapid for overseas visitors and slow for NZ. Pressure on sites used mainly by non-locals.	Demand in activities popular with overseas visitors. Supply pressures may intrude on other sites.	Slow increase, where most visitors NZ, pressure at key sites 'discovered' by overseas visitors.	Rapid increase in overseas numbers. NZ numbers static, or even declining (crowding displacement).	Slow increase as most from NZ. Displacement from busy tracks may lead to growth in some areas.	Slow increase as most from NZ. Overseas visitor growth limited by current management conditions.

		FRONTCOUNTRY FOCUS				BACKCOUNTRY FOCUS	

Source: *Cessford 2001, developed from Visitor Strategy categories (DoC 1996).*

Visitor groups

The Recreation Opportunity Spectrum (ROS) management framework was adopted by the Department of Conservation in 1993 (DoC 2005). The ROS is a system that enables land managers to inventory, plan for and protect opportunities for recreation. The system was developed in the USA and was adapted for use in New Zealand by the Department of Conservation, in consultation with key recreation groups. In adapting this US planning approach to New Zealand a seven-fold user classification system was developed. This system classifies visitors according to their facility and service needs; their setting, activity and experience preferences; and the degree of risk accepted in their activity. The Department of Conservation ROS recognises seven recreational groups as follows:

- Short-stop Travellers
- Day Visitors
- Thrill Seekers
- Overnighters
- Backcountry Comfort Seekers
- Backcountry Adventurers
- Remoteness Seekers (DoC 1996).

Defining these groups is the critical first step towards planning for a spectrum of recreational opportunities, each with unique facility and service requirements (see table 10.3).

Visitor sites

Cessford and Thompson (2002) describe visitor sites as 'spatially defined places managed to provide visitor services for priority visitor groups and can include locations of huts and campsites, road-ends, viewpoints and sections of track'. Visitor sites typically comprise a number of visitor assets in combination.

Visitor assets

The Department of Conservation maintains recreational facilities (including huts, tracks, boardwalks and bridges, among many others), each of which is referred to as a visitor asset, through the VAMP process. This process, as described by Cessford and Thompson (2002), includes:

- definition of the visitor sites at which the assets are located
- an accurate inventory of all visitor assets
- development of legal and service standards for asset groups (e.g. tracks, huts and so on)
- inspection programs for all assets against the specified standards
- application of lifecycle modelling for each asset, to predict maintenance and replacement costs and specify work schedules
- specification of other key management information relating to each site (e.g. key natural and cultural values, impact issues, priority visitor groups, management plan specifications, publication resources and so on)
- a site-scoring process incorporating public consultation processes, to indicate the importance of each visitor site and the related priorities for funding the asset management and maintenance at each

- incorporation of all site and asset data in a centrally managed Visitor Asset Management System (VAMS) database accessible to DoC managers and rangers.

The Department of Conservation's extensive VAMP system consisted, as at June 2005, of 3700 visitor sites and more than 35 000 visitor assets, including approximately 992 huts, 148 campsites, 12 800km of tracks, 2200km of roads, 550 carparks, 1500 signs, 1680 toilets, 13 464 structures (such as bridges, boardwalks, jetties and boat-ramps), 400 amenity areas (such as carparks, picnic areas and viewpoints) and 1100 other buildings (such as shelters and shower blocks) (DoC 2005b). This overview of visitor assets managed by the department confirms the importance of this government department's role as an agency of tourism management in New Zealand.

Visitor information

The Department of Conservation is a significant provider of visitor information to the tourism industry. Its 2004–05 Annual Report (DoC 2005b: 73) notes: 'Information is the other (in addition to visitor facilities) main ingredient provided to enable people to enjoy the large network of protected areas ...' The department manages thirteen 'icon' visitor centres at such locations as Mount Cook, Franz Josef, Punakaiki and Whakapapa, as well as seven regional visitor centres (DoC 2005a). It also provides interpretation services through such actions as guided talks, audiovisual displays, interpretive signs, maps, publications and website material.

The concessions system

A concession is an authorisation to conduct a commercial activity within an area of public conservation land. In 2006, approximately 1600 tourism concessions were operating in New Zealand. The Department of Conservation's concessions system consists of an inter-related system of planning for appropriate use of areas (by way of conservation management plans and strategies), the allocation of concessions to applicants and the subsequent monitoring of those activities.

■ **Figure 10.4**
Department of Conservation concessions management framework
Source: *adapted from DoC 2004.*

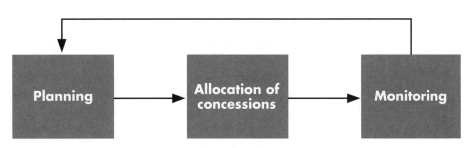

By way of the concessions system, tourism operators are able to provide visitors' products and services in protected areas. Most of the 'iconic' New Zealand tourism products are conducted under concessions. Examples include Milford Sound, Mount Cook Village, Waitomo Caves and most of the country's ski areas. In 2004 the Department of Conservation completed a review of the concession system (DoC 2004), which noted that concessions management essentially consisted of a series of inter-related management actions, such as monitoring, planning, quality standards, relationship management, data management and contractual matters. The review findings noted among other improvements the need for clearer and more explicit planning, greater use of proactive allocation approaches, the need to improve monitoring of the effects of tourism and the potential for tourism operators to contribute positively to the management of conservation areas (and the appreciation of visitors).

10.7 THE COMMERCIAL DEVELOPMENT OF NATURE

The rapid growth in tourism that has occurred in New Zealand since the late 1980s has had many consequences for conservation and the management of protected areas. One of these consequences has been the commercial development of nature. That this course of development has occurred should be no surprise, given the almost exclusive international marketing of New Zealand as a '100% Pure' destination that offers visitors unparalleled nature experiences. The commercial development of nature-based tourism has had several implications for the Department of Conservation. One has been a role in the management of commercial ecotourism businesses operating outside the conservation estate, but in association with such resources as marine mammals (as per the *Marine Mammal Protection Act 1978*) or protected bird species.

10.7.1 The *emergence of an ecotourism industry*

A significant commercial ecotourism sector has evolved in recent years from relatively humble origins. In the 1970s nature-based recreation and tourism in New Zealand was served by a small number of local trusts and conservation groups. The last twenty years has witnessed the large scale development of commercial ecotourism businesses, many based outside the system of protected areas. Indeed, Dickey (2005) confirms that much of the development of commercial ecotourism has taken place in coastal and marine contexts and in or adjacent to wildlife reserves often situated close to urban areas. This course of development has raised a new range of policy and planning challenges, as well as opportunities for conservation advocacy and the education of visitors through their involvement in conservation projects.

Pukaha Mount Bruce
National Wildlife Centre

Pukaha Mount Bruce is the National Wildlife Centre for the conservation of some of New Zealand's most endangered wildlife, including Kiwi, Kokako and Kaka. It is also a centre for environmental education and an ecotourism attraction. Pukaha Mount Bruce is operated by the Department of Conservation and is located in one of the few remaining areas of native lowland forest in New Zealand that is set within a wider agricultural landscape. This is a habitat that, along with many species of native lowland birdlife, was systematically and extensively cleared to make way for agriculture in the nineteenth century (King 1984).

Pukaha Mount Bruce is situated alongside national State Highway 1 (SH1) providing ease of access for visitors travelling north from Wellington. The convenience of the site ensures a high rate of casual visitation. This, then, is an example of a large-scale, highly accessible visitor operation. The Pukaha Mount Bruce visitor centre is set alongside an extensive carpark providing access for visitors of all levels of mobility. This spacious facility includes a lecture and audiovisual theatre, interactive and static interpretation displays, indoor/outdoor tea rooms and public convenience facilities. Access to the visitor centre is free. Conservation funds are generated through a small fee for entering the forest reserve, the sale of souvenirs from a shop alongside the reception desk and by donation in a donation box in the foyer of the reception centre. All donations and a proportion of all souvenir shop purchases are designated towards the conservation projects that visitors are able to observe and experience.

The Pukaha Mount Bruce forest reserve provides varied walking opportunities, access to aviaries and complete freedom from time constraints. Information and visitor guidelines for successful bird viewing are presented to visitors on a site map (brochure), which is available to visitors at reception and in various interpretive panels. The site map advises visitors to remain on marked tracks and not to feed the birds and educates them on conservation methods employed at Pukaha Mount Bruce. It also invites visitors to help with research by recording birds observed and/or heard. Prominently featured on the map are the sites and times at which two interpretation programs involving endangered native species are presented by conservation staff.

Interpretation programs are delivered by scientific staff employing personal, field-based interpretation. Both programs employ rare wildlife species to focus visitor attention on environmental issues of regional and national significance. The first addresses the native New Zealand river eel during a regular daily feeding program. This interpretation program deliberately challenges widely held perceptions of eels as slimy unattractive creatures and focuses on the longevity of the species and breeding migrations across the Pacific Ocean, which take place in the last year of an eel's life. Environmental issues relating to the

(continued)

damming of rivers and the implications for migratory river species such as the native eel are highlighted. Visitors are able to observe and converse informally with interpreters during the interpretation program.

The second interpretation program takes place in a forest clearing at which Kaka (native parrot) feeding stations are located. The secluded setting serves the purpose of minimising possible outside distractions during the interpretation program. Bait traps and nesting boxes are displayed for visitors in the Kaka feeding area to provide insight into methods used for the Kaka breeding program and predator control at Pukaha Mount Bruce. Kaka feeding allows interpretation to take place while demonstrating the multiple benefits of Kaka feeding in the interests of scientific research (recording the presence of individual birds), breeding success (providing energy-rich food sources) and visitor education.

Source: *www.mtbruce.org.nz/index.htm (viewed 11 April 2006).*

10.8 THE SEARCH FOR SUSTAINABLE ECOTOURISM

Various policy and planning efforts have been aimed at sustainable tourism development in New Zealand. In 2000 the Tourism Industry Association of New Zealand (TIANZ) initiated the introduction of Green Globe 21 (GG21) to the New Zealand tourism industry through the development of an environmental plan (EP). This coincided with the development of quality tourism standards (QTS) in 2003, which TIANZ claims provides a client-focused, cost-effective quality standard for providers of tourism products (TIANZ 2004). These standards cover a number of fields, including the eco- or nature tourism sector (TIANZ 2004), and are administered, marketed and accredited through Qualmark, which is a government–private sector partnership that licenses tourism businesses to use the Qualmark logo. The Qualmark system is designed to assess the components that contribute to the delivery of high-quality visitor experiences. The most prominent element of Qualmark has hitherto been the star grading of the accommodation sector. These initiatives and other attempts to establish environmental certification for commercial ecotourism businesses have been supported by the Department of Conservation. However, although well intended, there has been some debate over the effectiveness of environmental certification programs in terms of ecotourism planning and management. Such concerns have arisen over ecotourism certification programs in Australia and elsewhere (see section 4.6).

CHAPTER REVIEW

Environmental management policy and planning directions can change and, indeed, must be responsive to changing and dynamic demands. This is certainly the case in New Zealand where the institutional arrangements and priorities that surround the management of protected lands have shifted over time. This chapter has argued that the management of recreation and tourism in protected lands is greatly determined by the institutional arrangements in which they are set. From this discussion it emerged that protected area designations are genuinely protected, in a visitor management sense, only if they are subject to a sound and binding legislative foundation, a planning system that creates goals and objectives for management and management actions that achieve the goals of the existing legislative framework and planning systems. This chapter explored the policy and planning directions of the New Zealand Department of Conservation, which illustrates the dynamic nature of legislative and policy settings as well as recreational preferences and the demands of a dynamic tourism industry. These are some of the challenges that exist in the realm of policy and planning for protected lands.

SUMMARY OF KEY TERMS

Anthropocentric

Visitor planning and management approaches that are focused on human outcomes, such as visitor satisfaction.

Biocentric (or ecocentric)

Visitor planning and management approaches that are focused on environmental outcomes, such as the protection of diverse ecological systems or the preservation of rare or engendered species.

Direct management

Management actions that restrict individual choice, such as regulation of access.

Indirect management

Management actions that seek to influence visitors rather than directly regulate access, such as provision of information to inform a range of choices.

Legislative foundation

A sound and binding legislative foundation comprising government policies that provide the legal basis for the management of protected natural areas.

Management planning

This involves the clear statement of goals and objectives for management and the use at sites of a series of actions by protected area managers that are designed to deliver on the requirements of the legislative framework.

Planning for visitors

The process of setting goals for visitor management and developing and implementing the actions required to meet those goals.

Protected area

An area designated primarily for conservation. In many parts of the world these areas are also to be used for recreation and tourism insofar as such uses do not comprise the goal to preserve in perpetuity.

Protected area manager

One who is charged with the task of implementing management planning processes in order to meet the legislative requirements governing the management of protected natural areas.

Site management

Management actions, such as track hardening, at recreational and tourist sites.

Visitor impact

The impact, both potential and actual, as well as immediate and cumulative, that result from activities and management responses to that impact.

Visitor management

Management action that focuses on managing visitors themselves, such as regulation and information.

Visitor management systems

Visitor planning and management frameworks that are designed and implemented to provide guidance on the visitor management in protected natural areas.

QUESTIONS

1 What are the fundamental components of any regulatory management system for protected lands?

2 What is meant by the term 'institutional arrangements'?

3 Discuss the changing nature of legislation as it relates to the management of protected lands in New Zealand.

4 What are the major goals of the Department of Conservation *Visitor Strategy* (1996)?

5 What are the Recreation Opportunity Spectrum and Visitor Activities Management Process, and to what degree are the two integrated?

6 In reflecting on your own values and interests in terms of nature-based recreation and tourism, how would you fit into the Department of Conservation's seven-fold classification of visitors to protected areas in New Zealand?

7 Describe the Department of Conservation's concession system. What might be its relative strengths and weaknesses?

8 What is an environmental certification scheme? What has been the response of commercial tourism operators to environmental certification, and what factors explain this response?

EXERCISES

1 Access the Department of Conservation policies, plans and reports online at www.doc.govt.nz/about-doc/policies-plans-and-reports/index.asp and review the department's current policy directions.

2 What is the Romantic view of nature, and how does it contrast anthropocentric values associated with nature conservation? Having answered this question, consider the following exercises in relation to protected lands in your country, state or region:

(a) To what degree have recreation and tourism interests been to the fore in the development of a system of protected lands?

(b) Review the relative merits of biocentric and anthropocentric values as they relate to the historical designation of protected lands.

(c) Review the relative merits of these views as they relate to contemporary policies and planning directions for protected lands.

FURTHER READING ···

Cessford, G & Thompson, A 2002, 'Managing tourism in the New Zealand protected area system', *Parks,* **Special Issue on Tourism and Protected Areas, vol. 12, no. 1, pp. 26–36.** Cessford and Thompson provide a comprehensive review of the management of tourism in New Zealand's protected natural areas and the planning and management of tourism in ways that protect and enhance natural and cultural heritage values.

Department of Conservation 2005, 'Policies, plans and reports', viewed 11 April 2006, www.doc.govt.nz/about-doc/policies-plans-and-reports/ index.asp. This document provides a comprehensive overview of the New Zealand Department of Conservation's policies, plans and reports relevant to the management of tourism and recreation in protected natural areas.

Hall, CM 1992, *Wasteland to World Heritage: Preserving Australia's Wilderness,* **Melbourne University Press, Carlton, Vic.** Hall provides the first comprehensive history of wilderness preservation in Australia and, in doing so, documents the creation of Australia's system of protected natural areas.

Newsome, D, Moore, S & Dowling, R 2002, *Natural Area Tourism: Ecology, Impacts and Management,* **Channel View Publications, Clevedon, UK.** This book explores the ecology of natural areas and the environmental impact of tourism before providing a comprehensive analysis of planning and management approaches for tourism in natural areas. Discussions are illustrated with a wide range of case studies.

Rowe, T & Higham, JES 2006 (in press), 'Ecotourism certification in New Zealand: Operator and industry perspectives', in R Black & A Crabtree (eds), *Ecotourism Certification and Quality Control,* **CABI, Wallingford, UK.** This book chapter draws on Rowe's original research into the development of voluntary codes and certification programs to oversee the management of ecotourism in and adjacent to protected natural areas in New Zealand. It provides insights into operator and industry perspectives on the management of ecotourism.

Ecotourism operator perspectives on environmental certification schemes

In 2003 Rowe (2004) sought to quantify the extent to which New Zealand ecotourism operators currently use environmental certification schemes and assess their awareness and perceived value on different aspects of environmental certification. The term 'environmental certification scheme' was defined by Honey and Rome (2001: 17) as any 'voluntary procedure that assesses, monitors and gives written assurance that a business, product, service or management system conforms to specific requirements. A marketable logo or seal is awarded to those that meet or exceed baseline standards.'

Rowe's (2004) research was conducted using a questionnaire that was primarily designed to profile New Zealand ecotourism businesses and analyse operator perspectives on environmental certification. The research utilised an existing database of New Zealand ecotourism operators (Higham et al. 2001), which identified that in 1999 there were approximately 230 ecotourism businesses in New Zealand. The database was updated in August 2003 employing the same criteria developed by Higham et al. (2001). All operators that appeared in the 2003 ecotourism database were invited to complete an online survey. The questionnaire, which was password protected, generated a total response rate of 36 per cent.

Rowe's (2004) analysis showed that small operators, defined as those with fewer than three employees, were less likely to be members of an environmental certification scheme ($\chi2 = 16.015$, df = 5, $p \leq 0.007$). Another significant factor for operator membership status was the longevity of the business. Eighty-one per cent of environmental certification scheme members had been in operation for more than 10 years, whereas businesses that had been operating less than 4 years represented only 6.3 per cent of members ($\chi2 = 8.006$, df = 2, $p \leq 0.018$). Ninety-four per cent of operators who were members of an ECS indicated that they had a predominantly international visitor base ($\chi2 = 8.519$, df = 3, $p \leq 0.036$). Almost all members of environmental certification schemes were also Department of Conservation concession holders (94 per cent) ($\chi2 = 7.757$, df = 1, $p \leq 0.005$).

Responding operators viewed membership fees (60 per cent) and the perceived time involved in completing the required paperwork (64 per cent) as barriers to joining an environmental certification scheme (see table 10.4). Those who were not members of an environmental certification scheme were most likely to consider membership fees a barrier to joining (70 per cent). Operators were largely undecided whether they would be willing to absorb the membership costs of an environmental certification scheme (44 per cent); however, a significant proportion (51 per cent) of operators who were members of

(continued)

environmental certification schemes agreed that they would be willing to absorb the cost of membership ($\chi2 = 10.678$, df $= 2$, p ≤ 0.005). Thirty-nine per cent felt that the consumer should absorb the financial costs associated with environmental certification schemes.

Responding operators provided various insights into perceptions of environmental certification schemes (see table 10.4). The majority of New Zealand ecotourism operators agreed with the statements that environmental certification schemes could improve relationships with the local community (57 per cent) and help with public relations (56 per cent) and that customer demand for environmentally certified business is increasing (74 per cent). However, despite this many operators were undecided whether environmental certification schemes would actually increase the credibility of their ecotourism operation. Forty-one per cent of operators remained undecided on the marketing benefits of environmental certification schemes, and many operators (49 per cent) were undecided whether the benefits of being environmentally certified would outweigh the costs. Similar results were found around perceptions that media publications (travel guides or brochures) were more effective means of market communication than being a member of an environmental certification scheme.

■ **Table 10.4** *New Zealand ecotourism operator perceptions of environmental certification schemes (%), n = 66*

VARIABLE	1	2	3	4	5	M	STD DEV.
Increase profitability	3	8	51	38	—	3.24	0.725
Increase customer satisfaction	2	18	48	24	8	3.18	0.875
Increase employee satisfaction	3	21	42	30	3	3.09	0.872
Improve relationships with the local community	3	54	29	11	3	2.56	0.844
Help with public relations	14	42	29	11	4	2.50	1.011
Increase a business's credibility as an ecotourism provider	11	26	48	12	3	2.71	0.924
Marketing advantage over competitors	3	27	41	23	6	3.02	0.936
Customer demand for environmentally certified businesses is increasing	23	51	23	3	—	2.06	0.762
Endorsements by media, publications and travel guides are more powerful marketing than most ECS	8	20	38	27	7	3.08	1.042
Most ecotourists are aware of ECS	—	3	33	41	23	3.83	0.815

1 = strongly agree, 2 = agree, 3 = undecided, 4 = disagree, 5 = strongly disagree.

Source: *Rowe 2004.*

By contrast, it was found that 88 per cent of businesses were operating in accordance with a code of best practice (only 9 per cent indicated that they were not). New Zealand ecotourism operators who had been in business for more than 10 years were more likely to follow a code of conduct, compared to those who had been in business for 5–9 years and 4 years and under ($\chi2 = 11.817$, $df = 4$, $p \leq 0.019$). Also significant was the number of operators (64 per cent) who followed a code of best practice and perceived most ecotourists to be unaware of environmental certification schemes ($\chi2 = 10.397$, $df = 4$, $p \leq 0.034$). In terms of value, most operators perceived there to be some value in joining environmental certification schemes (57 per cent), although more than a quarter (26 per cent) saw no value in environmental certification whatsoever.

Rowe's (2004) research provides valuable insights into operator perceptions of the relative merits of environmental certification programs. The perception widely held by New Zealand ecotourism operators is that most ecotourists are generally not aware of environmental certification schemes. Nonetheless, most operators agreed that customer demand for environmentally certified businesses is increasing (74 per cent). New Zealand ecotourism operators, however, indicated that demand for environmentally certified businesses in New Zealand is not strong. Further marketing of environmental certification schemes could potentially influence tourist and operator awareness. Although operators agreed that levels of customer demand are increasing, 38 per cent were undecided whether endorsements by media and travel publications are more powerful marketing tools than environmental certification. Hence, there appears to be a necessity for the industry to contemplate approaches that will increase levels of awareness of environmental certification schemes on the part of ecotourism operators as well as tourists.

Certification at any level involves a time commitment by the staff of a business, and meeting the costs of operating environmentally sustainable businesses perhaps explains why larger-scale operations are more likely to commit to certification programs (Sasidharan & Font 2001; Font 2004). New Zealand operators were critical of the fee structure of most programs, which highlights the perception of high costs and fees as a barrier to considering — let alone pursuing — membership (Rowe 2004). Recent research suggests that sustainable tourism certification criteria can lead to short-term returns on investment through 'eco-savings', reportedly to be up to 30 per cent savings (energy and water savings) (Sanabria et al. 2003). Regardless of these views, scepticism in the New Zealand industry towards the relative merits, costs and savings of the programs is indeed a barrier (Cheyne & Barnett 2001). At present operating in accordance with a code of best practice remains the preferred option in terms of demonstrating a commitment to the environment.

Questions

1 What potential benefits might ecotourism business operators derive from being environmentally certified?

2 What factors influence the likelihood that commercial ecotourism businesses are environmentally certified?

(continued)

3 What are the barriers to joining an environmental certification scheme as perceived by commercial ecotourism business operators?

4 What are the relative advantages and disadvantages or strengths and weaknesses associated with environmental certification in the ecotourism sector?

References

Cheyne, J & Barnett, S 2001, 'Environmental certification schemes: A New Zealand case study of operator perceptions', in M Joppe (ed.), *Optimising Your Destination: Finding a Balance*, Travel Tourism Research Association Conference, Niagara Falls, Ontario, October.

Font, X 2004, 'Sustainability standards in the global economy', in W Theobald (ed.), *Global Tourism*, 3rd edn, Butterworth-Heinemann, Oxford.

Higham, JES 1996, 'Wilderness perceptions of international visitors to New Zealand: The perceptual approach to the management of international tourists visiting wilderness areas within New Zealand's conservation estate', unpublished PhD thesis, University of Otago, Dunedin, New Zealand.

Honey, M & Rome, A 2001, *Protecting Paradise: Certification Programs for Sustainable Tourism and Ecotourism*, Institute for Policy Studies, October.

Rowe, T 2004, 'New Zealand ecotourism operators' perception of environmental certification schemes', unpublished Master of Tourism thesis, University of Otago, New Zealand.

Sanabria, R et al. 2003, *Sustainable Tourism Stewardship Council: Raising the Standards and Benefits of Sustainable Tourism and Ecotourism Certification*, Rainforest Alliance, New York, viewed 11 April 2006, www.rainforest-alliance.org/programs/tourism/initiatives/stewardship-council.html.

Sasidharan, V & Font, X 2001, 'Pitfalls of ecolabelling', in X Font & RC Buckley, *Tourism Ecolabelling: Certification and Promotion of Sustainable Management*, CABI Publishing, Wallingford, UK.

ACKNOWLEDGEMENTS

The historical review presented in section 10.4.1 was originally developed and published by Professor C. Michael Hall and Dr James Higham (University of Otago). The data presented in the case study 'Ecotourism operator perspectives on environmental certification schemes' (p. 367) is adapted from T Rowe & JES Higham 2006, 'Ecotourism certification in New Zealand: Operator and industry perspectives', in R Black & A Crabtree (eds), *Quality in Ecotourism*, CABI Publications, Wallingford, UK, and included with permission. Table 10.3 is used with the permission of Gordon Cessford (Department of Conservation).

REFERENCES

Boas, A 1993, 'Tourism', letters to the editor, *Otago Daily Times*, 15 September, p. 14.

Boyd, SW & Butler, RW 1996, 'Managing ecotourism: An opportunity spectrum approach', *Tourism Management*, vol. 17, no. 8, pp. 557–66.

Cahn, R & Cahn, PL 1989, 'Reorganising conservation efforts in New Zealand', *Environment*, vol. 31, no. 3, pp. 18–20, 40–5.

Cessford, G & Dingwall, P 2001, 'Wilderness and recreation in New Zealand', in G Cessford (ed.), *The State of Wilderness in New Zealand* (special issue), Science Publications, Department of Conservation, Wellington, New Zealand; www.doc.govt.nz/publications/004~Science-and-Research/Miscellaneous/PDF/wilderness.pdf.

Cessford, G & Thompson, A 2002, 'Managing tourism in the New Zealand protected area system', *Parks*, Special Issue on Tourism and Protected Areas, vol. 12, no. 1, pp. 26–36.

Crabtree, PSJ 1989, 'A nature conservancy for New Zealand: The Department of Conservation — its genesis', unpublished essay submitted in partial fulfilment of the Postgraduate Diploma in Political Studies, University of Otago, Dunedin.

Davis, P 1999, 'Beyond guidelines: A model for Antarctic tourism', *Annals of Tourism Research*, vol. 26, no. 3, pp. 516–33.

Dearden, P & Rollins, R 1993, *Parks and Protected Areas in Canada: Planning and Management*, Oxford University Press, Toronto.

Department of Conservation 1996, *Visitor Strategy*, DoC, Wellington, New Zealand, viewed 10 April 2006, www.doc.govt.nz/About-DOC/Policies-Plans-and-Reports/Visitor-Strategy/index.asp.

—— 2004, *Concessions Review Project: Final Report*, Wellington, NZ.

—— 2005a, 'Policies, plans and reports', viewed 14 June 2005, www.doc.govt.nz/about-doc/policies-plans-and-reports/index.asp.

—— 2005b, *Annual Report for the Year Ended 30 June 2005*, Wellington, New Zealand.

—— 2005c, *Statement of Intent 2005–2008*, Wellington, New Zealand.

Department of Conservation and New Zealand Tourism Board 1993, *New Zealand Conservation Estate and International Visitors*, DoC & NZTB, Wellington, New Zealand.

Department of Lands and Survey 1984, *Report of the Department of Lands and Survey for the Year Ended 31 March 1984*, Government Printer, Wellington, New Zealand.

Dickey, A 2005, 'The development of commercial ecotourism in New Zealand: A spatio-temporal analysis', unpublished Master of Tourism thesis, University of Otago, Dunedin, New Zealand.

Eagles, P & McCool, S 2002, *Tourism in National Parks and Protected Areas: Planning and Management*, CABI Publishing, Wallingford, UK.

Eagles, P, McCool, S & Haynes, C 2002, *Sustainable Tourism in Protected Areas*, IUCN, Cambridge, UK.

Egan, P 1999, *Commercial Management Processes in the Delivery of Park Services*, ANZECC Standing Committee on National Parks and Protected Areas Management.

Fleming, C 1979, 'The history and future of the preservation ethic', pp. 54–64 in *National Parks of New Zealand: Proceedings of the Silver Jubilee Conference of the National Parks Authority of New Zealand, Lincoln College, 5–8 July 1978*, National Park Series No. 14, National Parks Authority of New Zealand, Department of Lands and Survey, Wellington.

Hall, CM 1988a, 'The geography of hope: The identification and conservation of Australia's wilderness', PhD thesis, Department of Geography, University of Western Australia, Nedlands, WA.

—— 1988b, 'Wilderness in New Zealand', *Alternatives: Perspectives on Science, Technology and the Environment*, vol. 15, no. 3, pp. 40–6.

—— 1992, *Wasteland to World Heritage: Preserving Australia's Wilderness*, Melbourne University Press, Carlton, Vic.

Hall, CM & Higham, JES 2000, 'Wilderness management in the forests of New Zealand: Historical development and contemporary issues in environmental management' in X Font & J Tribe (eds), *Forest Tourism and Recreation: Case Studies in Environmental Management*, CABI Publishing, Wallingford, UK.

Hall, CM & Jenkins, J 1995, *Tourism and Public Policy*, Routledge, London.

Hall, CM, Jenkins, J & Kearsley, G (eds) 1997, *Tourism Planning and Policy in Australia and New Zealand: Issues and Cases*, Irwin Publishers, Sydney.

Hall, CM & Shultis, J 1991, 'Railways, tourism and worthless lands: The establishment of national parks in Australia, Canada, New Zealand and the United States', *Australian–Canadian Studies*, vol. 8, no. 2, pp. 57–74.

Hammitt, W & Cole, D 1998, *Wildland Recreation: Ecology and Management*, 2nd edn, John Wiley & Sons, New York.

Harris, WW 1974, 'Three parks: An analysis of the origins and evolution of the national parks movement', unpublished MA thesis, Department of Geography, University of Canterbury, Christchurch, New Zealand.

Higham, JES, Carr, A & Gale, S 2001, 'Ecotourism in New Zealand: Profiling visitors to New Zealand ecotourism operations', Research Paper No. 10, Dunedin, New Zealand. Department of Tourism, University of Otago.

Hoffman, R, & Jatko, J 2000, 'Assessment of the possible cumulative environmental impacts of commercial ship-based tourism in the Antarctic Peninsula Area', Proceedings of a workshop held in La Jolla, June 2000, National Science Foundation, Washington, DC.

IUCN 1991, *A Strategy for Antarctic Conservation*, IUCN, Gland, Switzerland.

Joyner, C 1998, 'Recommended measures under the Antarctic Treaty: Hardening compliance with soft international law', *Michigan Journal of International Law*, vol. 19, pp. 401–27.

King, C 1984, *Immigrant Killers: Introduced Predators and the Conservation of Birds in New Zealand*, Oxford University Press, Melbourne.

Kliskey, AD 1992, 'Wilderness perception mapping: A GIS approach to the application of wilderness perceptions to protected areas management in New Zealand', unpublished PhD thesis, University of Otago, Dunedin, New Zealand.

Maher, H, 2004, 'The management of tourism operations on public conservation lands through concessions', unpublished dissertation, University of Otago, New Zealand.

—— 2006, 'Managing tourism in Antarctica: A framework for the future', unpublished Masters of Tourism thesis, University of Otago, New Zealand.

Maher, P, Steel, G & McIntosh, A 2003, 'Examining the experiences of tourists in Antarctica', *International Journal of Tourism Research*, vol. 5, pp. 59–67.

Mathieson, A & Wall, G 1982, *Tourism: Economic, Physical and Social Impacts*, Longman Scientific and Technical, Harlow, UK.

Mitchell, B 1989, *Geography and Resource Analysis*, Longman Scientific and Technical, Harlow, UK.

Molloy, LF 1993, 'The interpretation of New Zealand's natural heritage', in CM Hall and S McArthur (eds), *Heritage Management in New Zealand and Australia: Visitor Management, Interpretation and Marketing*, Oxford University Press, Auckland.

National Parks Authority 1978, *New Zealand's National Parks: National Parks Authority General Policy*, National Parks Series No. 9, Department of Lands and Survey for the National Parks Authority, Wellington, New Zealand.

Newsome, D, Moore, S & Dowling, R 2002, *Natural Area Tourism: Ecology, Impacts and Management*, Channel View Publications, Clevedon, UK.

New Zealand 1887, *Parliamentary Debates*, vol. 57, p. 399.

—— 1894, *Parliamentary Debates*, vol. 86, p. 579.

New Zealand Forest Service 1986a, *Proposed Tasman and Paparoa Wilderness Areas*, Document No. FS 36/4/1 6/0/12 (24245E), 11 July, New Zealand Forest Service, Wellington.

—— 1986b, *Recommendations for the Proposed Raukumara Wilderness Area*, Document No FS 6/0/12 (1615E), New Zealand Forest Service, Wellington.

O'Riordan, T 1971, *Perspectives on Resource Management*, Pion, London.

Ostrom, E 1986, 'An agenda for the study of institutions', *Public Choice*, vol. 48, pp. 3–25.

Palmer, G 1990, *Environmental Politics: A Greenprint for New Zealand*, John McIndoe, Dunedin, New Zealand.

Pedersen, A 2002, *World Heritage Manual — Managing Tourism at World Heritage Sites: A Practical Manual for World Heritage Managers*, UNESCO, Paris.

Runte, A 1972, 'Yellowstone: It's useless, so why not a park', *National Parks and Conservation Magazine*, vol. 46 (March), pp. 4–7.

—— 1973, ' "Worthless" lands — our national parks: The enigmatic past and uncertain future of America's scenic wonderlands', *American West*, vol. 10 (May), pp. 4–11.

—— 1979, *National Parks: The American Experience*, University of Nebraska Press, Lincoln, NE.

Stankey, G et al. 1985, *The Limits of Acceptable Change (LAC) System for Wilderness Planning*, USDA Forest Service Intermountain Research Station, Ogden, Utah.

Statistics New Zealand 1995, *New Zealand Official Yearbook*, Auckland, New Zealand.

Thompson, J 1976, *Origin of the 1952 National Parks Act*, Department of Lands and Survey, Wellington, New Zealand.

Tourism Industry Association of New Zealand 2004, 'Quality tourism standards', www.tianz.org.nz, viewed 12 December 2004.

Tourism New Zealand 2000, *New Zealand Tourism Strategy 2010*, Wellington, New Zealand.

US Department of Agriculture 1997, *VERP — The Visitor Experience and Resource Protection (VERP) Framework: A Handbook for Planners and Managers*, National Park Service, Denver, CO.

Veblen, TT & Stewart, GH 1982, 'The effects of introduced wild animals on New Zealand forests', *Annals of the Association of American Geographers*, vol. 72, no. 3, pp. 372–97.

Watkins, L 1987, *Billion Dollar Miracle*, Inhouse Publications, Auckland, New Zealand.

Wilderness Advisory Group 1985, *Wilderness Policy*, Department of Lands & Survey and New Zealand Forest Service, Wellington, New Zealand.

Carl Cater and Erlet Cater

CHAPTER 11

Protected *marine areas*

LEARNING OBJECTIVES

After reading this chapter you will be able to:

1 describe the highly complex nature of planning and policy development in the marine environment

2 discuss the role and responsibilities of various agencies in planning and regulating marine tourism

3 explain the variety of policy scales that affect marine tourism activities

4 identify the place of government and non-government entities in marine tourism planning

5 explain the importance of stakeholder involvement in the marine planning context and identify methods for achieving it.

Planning for sustainable marine tourism is considerably more complicated than that of the terrestrial environment examined in chapter 10. We are faced not only with conflicting sectoral interests but also with a number of other complicating issues. In particular these relate to the open nature of the marine environment. Access to this environment is largely free to all; it is commonly conceived as **common property**; it is highly dependent on activities that take place on the adjacent land mass; and there might be multiple jurisdictions working alongside one another. The sea is a highly mobile resource itself, and likewise its utilisation might be significantly 'footloose'. Cruise ships are an excellent example, being able to travel pretty much as their operators wish, often making limited contributions to local economies. Hall (2001: 605) goes so far as to suggest that cruise ships are emblematic of a deterritorialisation of boundaries and a true manifestation of 'globalisation at sea'. A growing number of **marine protected areas** (MPAs) worldwide have become the focus of a booming marine tourism industry. In this chapter we shall take a look at some of the agencies and policies that underpin the planning and management of tourism in marine protected areas. However, it is vital that we understand these policies in a broader marine regulation framework for the highly interdependent nature of this environment dictates a holistic perspective.

Tourism has received only slight and incidental attention in the literature of marine policy as a whole. This can be attributed, in part, to the fact that, as Miller and Auyong (1991: 75) write:

> [tourism] has been dominantly driven by private sector interests, rather than government regulatory policies, and that much tourism takes place on the land of the coastal zone. Furthermore, the problems of tourism do not fall squarely within a single subdomain of marine affairs, or within the purview of a single discipline … tourism transcends the realm of environmental pollution and protection. It is also pertinent to the policies of ports authorities and local governments and to those of fishery management, national park and coastal management agencies; not to mention the recreational practices of individuals.

However, navigating this web of interests is important if we are to engage with tourism planning in a marine context. An understanding of this policy realm of rules and regulations, which relies on a vast number of agencies, jurisdictions, protocols and laws, is vital for the long-term sustainability of marine tourism. As Hall (2000: 602) suggests, 'there is a clear need to gain a better understanding of the institutional and policy dimensions of integrated coastal and marine management in order to better incorporate the significance of tourism as a component of coastal and ocean development'. In many ways, the ebb and flow of the ocean reflects the dynamic policy context in which marine tourism planning takes place and further justifies the dialectical approach to tourism planning that this book advocates.

INTERNATIONAL MARINE PLANNING

As described in earlier chapters of this book, and especially section 3.4.4, contemporary neoliberalist political beliefs and market-driven economic policy have advocated a minimalist role for the state (Scheyvens 2002). However, a simultaneous concern with the health of marine environments in recent years has led to an increased role for government in the planning, regulation and management of marine spaces at a variety of scales. Although not all engage explicitly with marine tourism, there are obvious implicit implications for sustainable outcomes, given that initiatives will shape the overall context of the seas and oceans in which it is set as a process.

■ 11.2.1 International *conventions and organisations*

A bewildering array of international conventions and organisations govern, or attempt to govern, ocean use. Kimball (2001) views ocean agreements as an interlocking web, exerting 'push and pull' effects on one another. A new policy can often serve as a model for subsequent developments in other forums. Conversely existing policies can exert a 'drag' effect as obligations under one treaty might influence the achievement of goals in another. Kimball cites the case of the UN Convention on the Law of the Sea (UNCLOS; see Planning in Practice: 'The United Nations Convention on the Law of the Sea'), Article 194(5), which requires states to take pollution control measures that 'include those necessary to protect and preserve rare or fragile ecosystems as well as the habitat of depleted, threatened or endangered species and other forms of marine life', which will obviously reinforce area and species protection established under other conventions. This has important ramifications for marine tourism resources.

Kimball (2001: 81–2) lists the important roles of conventions as being those of providing information and assessment initiatives; influencing sustainable ocean development initiatives and international support; and promoting accountability. Another major international marine environmental initiative is the Global Programme of Action on Protection of the Marine Environment from Land-Based Activities (GPA). It is estimated that run-off and land-based discharges contribute 44 per cent of all marine pollution. Concern over the costs at the national level of deterioration in coastal environments led to the promotion of the GPA by UNCED in 1995. Although it is in itself non-binding, the role of the GPA is to push for global, legally binding instruments for the reduction and/or elimination of deleterious emissions and discharges (Kimball 2001).

The Convention on Biological Diversity also has the potential for an important role in the conservation and sustainable use of marine and coastal biodiversity. It calls on states to conserve and sustainably manage biodiversity, taking necessary measures to protect threatened species, including the establishment of marine and coastal protected areas. It is significant, as Kimball

(2001) suggests, for its emphasis on sustainable use, thus recognising the role of socioeconomic values in conservation (including knowledge of indigenous people), as well as acknowledging local and national concerns. It provides the key international framework on the ecosystem approach, incorporating and entailing a number of key principles. These include decentralisation of resource management, incorporating stakeholder engagement, and a need to understand and manage the ecosystem in an economic context that is compatible with conservation and sustainable development.

PLANNING IN PRACTICE

The United Nations Convention on the Law of the Sea

UNCLOS is the first comprehensive, enforceable international environmental law. As such, it is held to be the most important international achievement since the approval of the UN Charter itself in 1945 (UN 2002). Promulgated in 1982, it came into force in 1994. UNCLOS serves as an umbrella for numerous other existing international agreements covering the oceans, including international fisheries agreements and regional initiatives. Canada was the 144th country to ratify the convention in 2003. Although the USA was expected to follow in 2004, being the last industrialised nation to act, this now seems unlikely following intensive conservative lobbying on the grounds of risk to national security.

The Law of the Sea Convention sets down the rights and obligations of states and provides the international basis on which to pursue the protection and sustainable development of the marine and coastal environment. It defines five offshore zones (Kimball 2001): internal waters, which are landward of the baseline (normally the low-water line), forming part of a state's territory; a territorial sea of up to 12 nautical miles (nm) in which the state exercises full sovereignty; a contiguous zone that extends up to 24 nm from the baseline, in which the coastal state may prevent and punish infringements of its laws and regulations (such as customs); an exclusive economic zone (EEZ), which may not extend beyond 200 nm, in which the state has sovereign rights over natural resources and other economic uses as well as jurisdiction over marine scientific research and marine environmental protection; and the continental shelf, which may extend up to 350 nm from the baseline, where the state exercises sovereign rights over natural resources and jurisdiction over marine scientific research. All states have the same rights and obligations on the high seas beyond these zones.

UNCLOS lays down strong and binding obligations for marine environmental protection and preservation, including rare or fragile ecosystems, marine species' habitats and conservation of living marine resources. It endorses a marine ecosystems approach to marine biodiversity conservation, again exerting a strong 'drag' effect on other conventions and agreements.

There are also various conventions governing protected species, which obviously include marine species. These include the Convention on International Trade in Endangered Species of Wild Fauna and Flora (CITES), which aims to avoid unsustainable harvesting and commerce in wild species, as well as the Convention on the Conservation of Migratory Species of Wild Animals. As far as marine tourism is concerned, the role of CITES in controlling trade of coral and tropical fish is significant as depletion in these species has obvious ramifications for destination attractiveness. Among other activities, the latter convention has obvious significance for marine mammal viewing, as well as for turtle watching and the observation of migratory sea birds.

There are three global instruments that define geographic areas for special protection, all of which relate to the territorial sea zone (Kimball 2001). The Wetlands (or Ramsar) Convention aims to develop and maintain an international network of wetlands important for global biodiversity conservation and sustainable livelihoods. Nearly a third of the thousand wetlands designated by Ramsar have a marine or coastal component, including mangroves, seagrass beds, coral reefs, intertidal zones and estuaries, all of which have considerable marine ecotourism potential. The World Heritage Convention covers both natural and cultural areas of outstanding value, which again include marine and coastal areas. More than 30 natural sites thus designated have a marine or coastal component; they include the Great Barrier Reef of Australia (see the case study 'Great Barrier Reef, North Queensland', p. 396) as well as Belize's Barrier Reef, both of which are significant tourist attractions. The Man and the Biosphere Reserve Programme (MAB) of UNESCO, although not a legally binding convention, identifies national and international priorities and provides guidance. About a third of MAB reserves globally have a marine or coastal component.

Another international convention that has a significant bearing on marine tourism is that of the International Convention for the Regulation of Whaling of 1946. This convention established the International Whaling Commission (IWC); membership being open to any country that formally adheres to the convention. In 1975 the IWC adopted a new management policy for whales, which is designed to bring all stocks to the levels that provide the greatest long-term harvests by setting catch limits for individual stocks below their sustainable yields. However, because of uncertainties in the scientific analyses, the IWC decided that there should be a moratorium in commercial whaling on all whale stocks, effective from 1986. This pause in commercial whaling does not affect aboriginal subsistence whaling, which is permitted from Denmark (Greenland fin and minke whales), the Russian Federation (Siberia gray whales), St Vincent and the Grenadines (humpback whales) and the USA (Alaska bowhead and, occasionally off Washington, gray whales). Since the moratorium came into effect, Japan, Norway and Iceland have issued scientific permits as part of what they declare to be research programs. There have been accusations that such permits have been issued merely as a way around the moratorium decision; these have been countered by claims that the catches are essential to obtain information necessary for rational management and other important research needs.

All proposed permits have to be submitted for review by the Scientific Committee following guidelines issued by the IWC (IWC 2004). However, the ultimate responsibility for issuing them lies with the member nation, and much adverse publicity surrounded Iceland's catch of 36 minke whales in the summer of 2003 (Parsons & Rawles 2003). Given that there is also lack of international consensus as to whether the moratorium covers small cetaceans, with many states maintaining that they are subject to national jurisdiction within the EEZ (Kimball 2001), its efficacy must be questioned. This is all the more surprising in the light of the fact that the revenue from whale watching is worth many times that from commercial whaling. The Icelandic economy, for example, benefited by US$13.8 million from 60 000 whale watchers in 2001 (Cetacean Society International 2003), a figure that is expected to increase to more than US$20 million by 2006 (Parsons & Rawles 2003).

Of the international initiatives specifically aimed at consumers of marine resources examined by Kimball (2001), the World Bank's Marine Market Transformation Initiative (MMTI) has the most relevance for marine tourism as one of its four areas of concern is specifically to link marine tourism with coral reef conservation. The MMTI will 'support changes largely in private sector operations through policy reforms, alternative technologies, economic instruments, targeted investments, consumer education and eco-labeling and marketing' (Kimball 2001: 60). The UN Commission on Sustainable Development (CSD7) endorsed a work program on tourism in 1999, and the secretariat will collaborate with the World Tourism Organization in establishing a working group to promote sustainable tourism development. It invited the parties to the Convention on Biological Diversity to contribute to international guidelines for sustainable tourism development, including in vulnerable marine and coastal ecosystems, protected areas and habitats of major importance for biodiversity (Kimball 2001: 77).

There are bound to be gaps in the international agencies involved in oceans governance described above but, to add to the list, the **IUCN**, which was accorded status of observer at the UN General Assembly in 1999, together with WWF, developed a global marine policy, *Creating a Sea Change*. This policy has the goals of maintaining the biodiversity and ecological processes of marine and coastal ecosystems; ensuring that any use of marine resources is both sustainable and equitable; and restoring marine and coastal ecosystems where their functioning has been impaired (IUCN 1998).

■ *11.2.2* **Multilateral** *and bilateral funding*

It is interesting to reflect that, until the early 1990s, tourism was seen as an inappropriate avenue for donor finance. With increasing recognition of the conservation–development nexus and a growing engagement with the need to enhance local livelihoods through sustainable resource utilisation, ecotourism captured the attention of international funding bodies as a funding avenue. In 1992, for example, the International Resources Group prepared a report for USAID on ecotourism as a viable alternative for the sustainable management of natural resources in Africa (IRG 1992). Since then both multilateral and bilateral funding has been increasingly directed towards ecotourism projects. The Global Environmental Facility (GEF) of the World Bank is a financial mechanism that provides grants and concessional funds to recipients from developing countries and countries in transition for projects and activities that aim to protect the global environment. A number of GEF-funded projects have had a marine tourism component ranging from the global through to the local. For example, GEF is continuing to develop a global project on best practices for integrating biodiversity considerations into the tourism sector (Kimball 2001: 77); it has supported a Marine Resource Management Project in the Egyptian Red Sea, which aimed to address coastal marine-related tourism and conservation; and its small grants program has promoted marine tour guide training in five coastal communities in Belize (GEFSGP 2004).

The main underlying problem with the GEF is the fact that the World Bank manages the fund (it is implemented by UNDP and UNEP). Yet the World Bank itself is simultaneously a massive promoter of energy and forest projects and operates without adequate environmental safeguards. It has been criticised for failing to address the macro root of many global environmental problems. This criticism extends to suggestions that the GEF has been used to mitigate environmental problems arising from new projects funded by the World Bank and other institutions as well as reducing existing environmental problems (Down to Earth 2001). In Pakistan, the building of dams and barrages under the Indus Basin Project, funded by contributions from the World Bank and other donors, necessitated the wholesale relocation of a considerable number of settlements and disrupted the distinctive livelihoods of the Indus boat people. GEF Small Grants Projects funds have been allocated to an ecotourism initiative at Taunsa barrage to create alternative livelihoods for these boat people in a sanctuary for the Indus River Dolphin (GEFSGP 2004).

The European Union's European Regional Development Fund part-funded the Marine Ecotourism for the Atlantic Area (META) project, which was a collaborative exercise between Torbay Council; the Marine Institute, Dublin; MBA Escuela, Gran Canaria; and the University of the West of England, Bristol (META-Project 2000). Bilateral funding has also been increasingly directed towards marine conservation and marine tourism. The Canadian International Development Agency (CIDA) assists developing countries with the protection of their ocean environment for sustainable trade, shipping and tourism. Among projects supported by the German overseas development agency, GTZ, are the Chumbe Island Coral Park, Zanzibar — global winners of the 2001 British Airways Tourism for Tomorrow Award, and the establishment of marine protected areas in Negros Oriental, Philippines. The New Zealand Official Development Assistance Programme has provided technical and financial assistance to develop ecotourism accommodation and activities at Marovo Lagoon in the Solomon Islands, which provide alternative sources of livelihood and resource use to the local people as well as securing a World Heritage listing for the lagoon (Halpenny 1999).

■ *11.2.3* **Effectiveness** *of international marine governance*

It is not surprising, given the plethora of international agencies involved in one way or another with ocean governance, that the effectiveness of such agencies is characterised — and thus seriously compromised — by competition and duplication of effort. Valencia (1997), for example lists the multiplicity of UN (UNEP and UNDP) and other specialised UN agencies and organisations participating in the GPA (ranging from FAO to the World Health Organization) as a prime illustration of this fact. This situation has been described as a meta-problem. Hall (2000: 145), citing Ackoff, describes the tourism meta-problem as being characterised by highly interconnected planning and policy 'messes' that 'cut across fields of expertise and administrative boundaries and, seemingly, become connected with almost everything else'. Yankov and Ruivo (1994) point to the fact that, despite the large number of global and regional institutions with competence in marine issues and the number of legal instruments dealing with various aspects of ocean affairs, the absence of an appropriate coordinating global forum acts as a serious impediment to the identification of issues, priorities and strategic planning needs. Such a forum could also promote intra- and interregional cooperation and mobilise funding.

Given the potential of UNCLOS as a comprehensive, enforceable, international environmental law, it is disappointing not only that the USA is conspicuous by its absence as a signatory but also that uptake of UNCLOS has been selective across the globe. Nicol (undated), for example, describes the situation in the Caribbean, where the weaknesses of existing environmental law and policy frameworks, lack of resources and political will, together with the problem of overlapping maritime zones, hamper its effective implementation. Furthermore, UNCLOS proceeds on the clear premise that competent international organisations have vital roles to play in the implementation of its provisions in many crucial areas. However, as Mensah (1994) suggests, the effective discharge of these roles will entail institutional and procedural changes both within and without these organisations, as well as implications for resource allocation and a readiness to forge cooperative relationships with states and other organisations.

A further barrier to effective planning and implementation is the absence of adequate baseline information, as well as a well-organised system of databases on the potential and actual impact of activities, in different types of marine ecosystems. As Kimball (2001) notes, baseline information is critical if we are to hope to measure progress in managing resources. This baseline information needs to include more than just introductions of new activities and should cover assessments of the distribution and impact in socioeconomic and environmental terms. Once an inventory of such activities has been achieved for sites in the coastal and marine realm, it is important that further elaboration takes place at higher regional or global scales so that an accurate overview of impact is achieved. From this process comprehensive codes of conduct can be articulated. Voluntary compliance with such a code could be reinforced if it were endorsed pursuant to one or more relevant conventions (e.g. regional marine or wetlands). Certain measures might even be adopted as binding rules. In the Arctic, Principles and Codes of Conduct for Arctic Tourism, developed through a WWF project, helped change operational procedures in certain tourism enterprises cooperating in pilot projects, for example through recycling and more intensive education of clients (Kimball 2001: 66, 77).

However, there are a number of weak links that hamper the realisation of a comprehensive inventory. The first and weakest, Kimball suggests, is the ability to collect, organise and disseminate knowledge and experience across the globe in order to solve site-specific problems. Second is the need to strengthen knowledge and capabilities at local, national and regional levels. The third is the need to foster a collective understanding of the causes and impact of and solutions to shared ocean problems. Kimball describes how these weak links have been compounded by the late realisation of the fact that extension of the EEZ to 200 nm offshore spread impact to ever-larger segments of society and coastal and marine ecosystems that transcend national boundaries.

Added to the above problems are those of the imposition of external agendas on local societies, which is particularly the case when donor funding is added into the picture. Mowforth and Munt (2003: 60) voice this concern, suggesting that environmental conditions and caveats placed on Western loans and grants promote a greening of social relations that could be viewed as an adjustment that requires Third World people to take on First World thinking.

11.3 REGIONAL MARINE PLANNING

It is evident from the above discussion on international governance that a considerable problem of collaboration and coordination of efforts exists at that level. However, although it is essential to recognise the international dimensions of the marine environment, it is clear that there is a need to reconcile the needs of human society as a whole with those of communities dependent on marine ecosystems and to reconcile the sector-specific thread of international legal instruments with the more comprehensive, ecosystem-based approach necessary to diagnose complex problems. Kimball (2001: 81) suggests that logical ecosystem-based units of ocean management converge with international institutional arrangements at the subregional and regional levels. This is because the international dimensions of the marine environment mean that local and national knowledge needs to be assembled at the regional level to improve understanding and effective responses.

Launched in 1974, the Regional Seas Programme of UNEP was revitalised by the adoption of the GPA in 1995. More than 140 countries participate in the 13 regional programs in the Black Sea, Caribbean, East Africa, East Asia, the Kuwait Convention region, Mediterranean, North-East

Pacific, North-West Pacific, Red Sea and Gulf of Aden, South Asia, South-East Pacific, South Pacific and West and Central Africa (Adler 2003). Each program is tailored to the specific needs of its constituent states, but contains an action plan for cooperation on the management, protection, rehabilitation, development, monitoring and research of coastal and marine resources; an intergovernmental agreement of framework convention (not necessarily legally binding as, although the conventions are presented under the UNEP Regional Seas Programme umbrella, they are independent and separate juridical entities); and detailed protocols dealing with particular environmental issues, such as protected areas. In addition to the participating regions, there are five partner programs for the Antarctic, Arctic, Baltic Sea, Caspian Sea and North-East Atlantic.

A global effort in the form of the Large Marine Ecosystems Strategy is also underway by IUCN, the Intergovernmental Oceanographic Commission of UNESCO (IOC), other UN agencies and the US National Oceanic and Atmospheric Administration (NOAA) to improve the long-term sustainability of resources and environments of the world's Large Marine Ecosystems and linked watersheds. Recognising the transboundary implications of marine resources, pollution and critical habitats, the Large Marine Ecosystems Strategy defines relatively large regions of the order of 200 000 square kilometres. Sixty-four Large Marine Ecosystems have been designated to date, many of which are receiving GEF support.

Individual regional marine programs can include specific tourism-related measures, for example three training manuals on Water and Solid Waste Management for the Tourism Industry, Integrated Coastal Area Management and Tourism and Siting and Design of Tourist Facilities are being developed through the Caribbean regional marine program for use by educational and training institutions and individuals involved in the tourism industry (Kimball 2001: 77).

■ 11.3.1 Effectiveness *of regional marine governance*

Although the Regional Seas Programme has had several positive outcomes, in particular increasing developing countries' capacity to participate in regional marine environmental protection, many criticisms have been levelled at it. These point to the need for restructuring and a new perspective. It is particularly criticised for its failure to involve the private sector, unions and general public as well as to address those agencies responsible for pollution, such as energy and tourism (Valencia 1997).

Furthermore, particular concern has been voiced regarding the enactment of UNCLOS embodied in the Regional Seas Programme, particularly with respect to developing nations. For example, in the Caribbean, Nicol (undated) highlights the challenge of increasing poverty and environmental degradation among the developing countries of the region. She points to the difficulty of applying international law in the Caribbean for many reasons, such as the balkanised nature of marine contexts, lack of funds, the increasing role of tourism in national economies, the special vulnerability of the region to natural hazards and the outdated political and legal infrastructures as a result of colonialism. Many of the regional decision-makers are therefore rejecting UNEP's regional seas programme for the Caribbean (the Cartagena Convention), which is based on UNCLOS and its regime of conventions. They criticise it as a fragmented application that crosscuts the region and relies on extra-territorial organisation and structure for implementation.

For these reasons, regional institutions within the Caribbean have defined the Caribbean Sea as a Patrimonial Sea, or common source of sustenance and identity for all regions. They call for the region to be designated, instead of a regional sea, as a 'Special Area in Context of Sustainable Development' (a regionally organised conservation regime that relies on existing capacity for implementation). This geographical basis defines functional space and a common identity that traverses linguistic, cultural and political divisions. It is argued that such designation will be more effective in arriving at a consensus on environmental agendas as it acts as a unifying concept as well as being a powerful metaphor.

11.4 NATIONAL MARINE PLANNING

As seen above, a considerable number of environmental policies and regulations have been promoted for the marine environment since the 1980s. However, these have mostly been reactive responses to specific issues and generally derive from outside the nation state. In the light of increasing realisation of the value of the marine environment and of the accelerating pressures on it, national governments are at last waking up to the need for a strategic, coordinated approach that provides proactive mechanisms to manage marine biodiversity (DEFRA 2002a). As Borgese (1994) describes, 'At the national level, the incorporation of integrated ocean policy into national development plans is gradually taking place, altering traditional approaches to social and economic development.'

As will be seen presently, the overall picture with regard to national ocean affairs is that of a fragmented, haphazard approach. However, some governments have considered the advantages of more stable and efficient mechanisms on an intersectoral basis (Yankov & Ruivo 1994). For example Australia's Oceans Policy, launched in 1998, has several objectives, including the protection of Australia's marine biodiversity and the ocean environment and ensuring that the use of oceanic resources is ecologically sustainable within its Exclusive Economic Zone. In 1999 the National Oceans Office was formed as an executive agency to coordinate the overall implementation and further development of Australia's Oceans Policy, which is to be implemented through regional marine plans. Canada's Oceans Act of 1997 establishes obligations for the Minister for Fisheries and Oceans for the management and conservation of Canadian waters. It also establishes the legal framework for a national strategy for the management of estuarine, coastal and marine waters within Canadian jurisdiction. India established its Department of Ocean Development as early as 1981. Despite the fact that DEFRA (2002b: 15) does not believe that a stakeholder body is needed to cover all marine and coastal policies in the UK, the very creation of the Department for Environment, Food and Rural Affairs in the UK in 2001 brought together interests in marine science to support conservation, environmental protection, fisheries and coastal management objectives (DEFRA 2002a). This has led the UK Government to adopt an ecosystems-based approach for marine management to better integrate marine protection objectives with sustainable social and economic goals (DEFRA 2002a).

So, what forms can government intervention take with regard to sustainable coastal and marine tourism? Hall (2001) identifies five policy measures aimed at the development of coastal and marine tourism:

1. regulatory instruments (regulations permits and licenses that have a legal basis)
2. voluntary instruments actions or mechanisms that do not require substantial public expenditure (e.g. the development of information and interpretive programmes)
3. direct government expenditure to achieve policy outcomes, including the establishment of protected areas such as marine and national parks
4. financial incentives, including taxes, subsidies, grants and loans, which are incentives to undertake certain activities or types of behaviour
5. non-intervention where the government deliberately avoids intervention, especially with respect to allowing market forces to determine policy outcomes (however, Hall (2000) suggests that this last measure is relatively amoral as it allows individuals to be immoral).

Hall (2001) stresses that there is no universal 'best way' and that each locality needs to choose an appropriate policy mix to address local requirements. However, he laments the fact that little research has been done on how to achieve the ideal, place-specific mix and that there is often minimal monitoring and evaluation of policy measures.

■ *11.4.1* **Effectiveness of** *national marine governance*

It remains an unfortunate fact that the general approach to marine conservation has been one of non-intervention in comparison to the active management framework for conservation increasingly promoted on land. In the UK, despite DEFRA's call for an ecosystems-based approach, there remains a fundamental concern that marine governance should be coupled with reforms to the law protecting the UK's diverse marine life and cultural heritage while providing sustainable solutions for marine industries and activities (Wildlife and Countryside Link 2004). Not surprisingly, a similar scenario exists for coastal and marine tourism, which are heavily dependent on a healthy marine environment. As stated by Hall (2001: 614):

Unfortunately there is usually little or no coordination between programmes that promote and market tourism and those that aim to manage coastal and marine areas ... Implementation strategies often fail to recognise the interconnections that exist between agencies in trying to manage environmental issues, particularly when, as in the case of the relationship between tourism and the environment, responsibilities may cut across more traditional lines of authority ... one of the greatest challenges facing coastal managers is how to integrate tourism development within the ambit of coastal management and thus increase the likelihood of long-term sustainability of the coast as a whole.

Why has government involvement in coastal and marine tourism been relatively unsuccessful to date? First, it has been characterised by a fragmented, and therefore often uncoordinated, approach, hampered by intersectoral competition for resources. This is still common with regard to tourism planning, whereby agencies and stakeholders are more likely to seek achievement of a narrowly defined set of goals rather than aiming for broader, collaborative approaches. Unfortunately, this traditional sectoral approach continues to dominate national administration of ocean affairs, despite increasing and intensive multiple use of the oceans and growing difficulties of management (Yankov & Ruivo 1994). Furthermore, as Vallejo (1994) has pointed out, policy-making at the sectoral level is predominantly reactive and does not have the luxury of interagency consultation. Consequently, marine policies often have conflicting objectives, resulting in at best ineffective implementation or at worst in increased environmental damage. Fragmented decision-making and frequent duplication of procedures are evident; overlap and competition between agencies are common. This is the most common scenario across the globe. Saharuddin (2001) describes the situation in Malaysia where the organisational structures governing the ocean for policy implementation are present but are fragmented and uncoordinated. As a result, sectoral and intersectoral management problems have been created, such as multiple-use conflicts, overlapping of jurisdiction and duplication of efforts. Inevitably the manifest results are that ocean management is, as Lubchenco et al. (2002) describe for the USA, 'haphazard, piecemeal and ineffective in the face of declining ocean conditions'.

Second, as Vallejo (1994) also suggests, in the majority of cases ocean affairs often come lower down in the pecking order of political importance. Such policy-making usually takes place at a lower level in the government hierarchy and is often pushed into more powerful agencies whose primary remit is not that of marine affairs. An example is the common situation whereby fisheries are part of the Ministry of Agriculture. This usually translates into limited personnel and lower levels of funding than terrestrial resource allocation.

Third, largely as a result of the above, government decision-making is consequently ad hoc and characterised by reactive rather than proactive decision-making (Hall 2001).

Fourth, at the implementation level, the major problem is the absence of coordination between the planning and operational levels (Vallejo 1994).

This occurs not only horizontally, between sectors and agencies, but also vertically, between different levels. Scheyvens (2002) describes how the Costa Rica Government collects tourist taxes and entrance revenues at the sea turtle nesting site in the Ostional Wildlife Refuge. However, it has not been proactive in enhancing the capacity of the local community to benefit from the increasing numbers of tourists visiting the site. Similarly, in Baja California, Mexico, two principal federal agencies are both tasked with conducting the monitoring of tourism activity around grey whales and enforcing laws governing such activity. However, as Young (1999) describes, both are overcentralised, with decision-makers in Mexico City being far removed from the local context and having little understanding of local ecological and social conditions. As a result, what should be an effective umbrella of regulatory policy is hampered by distant government obstacles.

It follows, from the above considerations, that an improved understanding of the policy process and institutional arrangements by which coastal and ocean areas are managed is essential in order for a better integration of tourism development in coastal communities and marine ecosystems to be achieved without due negative consequences (Hall 2001).

11.5 PROVINCIAL MARINE PLANNING

Although it is not dedicated to marine tourism, the fact that institutionalisation of coastal management increasingly occurs at the provincial level has obvious implications for improved integration of tourism development within coastal communities and ecosystems while mitigating adverse effects. In Australia, the Queensland Government Environmental Protection Agency is preparing regional coastal management plans that focus on integrated coastal zone planning and management and incorporate ecologically sustainable use and development. In the USA, several states have advanced oceans programs, for example Oregon's Territorial Sea Plan and Hawaii's Ocean Resource Management Plan. Under the auspices of the former, the community at Cape Arago has formulated policies to strike a balance between growing recreational and tourist use of the rocky shore environment and the protection of marine life and habitats (Hershman 1999). Massachusetts established its Ocean Management Initiative in 2003, to establish a more proactive process for managing ocean resources within state waters (Massachusetts Government 2004).

11.5.1 Effectiveness of provincial marine governance

As at other levels of governance, provincial initiatives are vulnerable to political and leadership changes. Of four American initiatives examined by Hershman (1999), only Oregon maintains steady progress as it is firmly established in a respected program activity of the executive branch. A further complication arises when there are conflicts over jurisdiction between different levels of governance. Meinhold (2003: 29–31), for example, cites the case of whale-watching management in the Robson Bight Ecological Reserve, British Columbia. Here the Canadian Government has jurisdiction over its marine waters, whereas BC Parks has jurisdiction over the land portion, rubbing beaches and seabed. BC Parks lacks the mandate to enforce the Marine Mammal Protection Regulations and therefore depends on the Canadian Department of Fisheries and Oceans for effective enforcement.

A similar situation has developed on the Gold Coast in Australia, where controversy surrounded the development of a number of new whale-watching operators in 2005. Previously, under Queensland government policy, no whale-watching operators were to be granted licenses below 27 degrees south, west of Moreton Island (Department of the Environment 1997), which has long been regarded as an important migration corridor for the cetaceans. However, because state waters extend only three nautical miles offshore, the state was powerless to stop boats from conducting tours in the Commonwealth zone as long as they had federal permits to do so.

11.6 LOCAL GOVERNANCE

The overall picture regarding local marine governance is that of a top-down process, beset with now-familiar problems of being reactive rather than proactive, of fragmentation and of competition for financial resources and expertise. However, there are some examples across the globe of the initiative from the bottom up. At Ulugan Bay, in the Philippines, the councils of the five local *barangays* (together with ancestral domains) proposed their own community-based sustainable tourism initiatives, which were integrated with broader conservation and development issues as well as with long-term strategic planning in the wider municipality within which Ulugan Bay is located. The draft plan was submitted to wider stakeholders before being sub-mitted as a final draft to the municipal authority and back to the local author-ities for endorsement. Once endorsed, implementation of the action plan commenced, which included both training and capital works initiatives prioritised for implementation in each community area. These activities are supported by a rolling program of community consultation and participation, which functions as a monitoring mechanism (Felstead, undated).

In China, in theory, local coastal governments should be in a position to play an important role in protecting the marine environment. This is because decentralisation has granted local governments jurisdictional rights in handling local political and social problems, including environmental problems, together with local financial autonomy and better information than central government agencies. However, faced with the constraints of limited finance, lack of institutional and technical capacity and the dilemma of reconciling economic development with environmental protection, it is suggested that the international community should develop partnerships at the local level to enhance technical, financial and institutional capacity (Chen & Uitto 2004).

■ *11.6.1* **Effectiveness** *of local marine governance*

As Vodden (2002) suggests, local capacity is a crucial factor in determining the success of local marine governance. Local networks rarely have the financial or organisational resources to cope with an increasingly complex policy nexus. Higher levels of governance, which might have such resources, are slow to appreciate this shortfall when planning responsibility transfer. To redress this shortfall, major international non-governmental organisations (INGOs) are increasingly becoming engaged in the types of partnership as suggested by Chen and Uitto (2004) above. This is particularly because they are often brought in as the implementation partners in projects funded by international donor agencies.

11.7 NON-GOVERNMENTAL ORGANISATIONS

■ *11.7.1* **International** *NGOs*

In the same way that marine conservation and, in turn, marine tourism have become increasingly popular targets for multilateral and bilateral funding from supra-national and national donor agencies, so, too, have international NGOs focused on projects that promote the conservation of the marine environment while simultaneously enhancing coastal livelihoods. Frequently, as described above, these INGOs might be the channels through which donor funding is channelled.

World Wildlife Fund (WWF) is purportedly the world's premier conservation organisation. Thematically, WWF has chosen to work on oceans and coasts as one of its three target biomes; on Marine Turtles and Great Whales as two of the list of flagship species on which it is concentrating; on the spread of toxic chemicals and on the threats of climate change. It is clear, therefore, that the work of WWF is relevant to marine tourism, and several of its projects have a declared marine tourism component. For example, WWF has facilitated the production of a shared management plan for the Sulu Sulawesi Marine Ecoregion (SSME) by the three nations of the Philippines, Indonesia and Malaysia. SSME is home to around 35 million people who are directly or indirectly dependent on coastal and marine areas for their livelihoods, and a major objective is to develop operational, sustainable and conservation-linked livelihood systems. Towards this end, immediate actions include the development of model marine tourism sites (WWF 2004).

Conservation International (CI), an influential non-profit organisation based in Washington, DC, operates in more than 30 countries worldwide.

CI has strong links with the World Bank, and its corporate partners include Bank of America, Ford Motor Company, McDonalds Corporation and ExxonMobil. CI's activities in marine tourism include the creation of a new marine protected area in southern Belize to protect the whale sharks that congregate in the area and to generate revenue for local communities through ecotourism (CI 2004a). CI's Marine Rapid Assessment Programs, which establish baseline biodiversity information on selected coral reef areas and analyse this information in tandem with social, environmental and other ecosystem information, are undertaken in 'a time frame suited to managers and decision-makers' (CI 2004b).

The world's richest environmental group, with assets of $3 billion, The Nature Conservancy (TNC) is a not-for-profit organisation that boasts of a million members worldwide. Members of its corporate forum, the International Leadership Council, include Boeing, Delta Airlines, ExxonMobil, Monsanto and Proctor & Gamble. TNC's Global Marine Initiative complements the more than a hundred marine projects that TNC has around the world. In Komodo National Park, Indonesia, TNC is working with fishermen using destructive practices, such as cyanide, to divert them to sustainable fishing and marine ecotourism (Kirkpatrick & Cook, undated).

An INGO with a specific ecotourism remit is that of The International Ecotourism Society (TIES), which changed its name from The Ecotourism Society in 2000. TIES is a much smaller INGO in terms of both membership and assets. Nonetheless it exerts considerable influence around the world in disseminating information on how to do ecotourism right (albeit set in existing power relationships, as Mowforth and Munt (2003) suggest). Among TIES's marine ecotourism initiatives is the publication of *Marine Ecotourism: Impacts, International Guidelines and Best Practice Case Studies* (Halpenny 2003) as well as guidelines on how to be a marine ecotourist (TIES 2003).

■ *11.7.2* **National** *and local NGOs*

As with most of the INGO examples above, conservation might be the primary mandate of many national and local NGOs, but many have adopted ecotourism as a form of development that is complementary to the goals of conservation (Halpenny 2003). Countering the criticism that NGOs tend to have narrow, specialist, frequently Western-centric views and ignore the public good, Halpenny suggests that this phenomenon is becoming less evident as levels of professionalism mount and points to the positive roles that NGOs perform in marine tourism in terms of financing conservation, establishing tourism standards, education and research.

A number of environmental, educational and scientific organisations offer nature, adventure, study and service tours to their members, which increasingly also incorporate ecotourism principles. The Whale and Dolphin Conservation Society's Out of the Blue holidays, for example, give people the opportunity to see and learn about whales and dolphins, and all profits are devoted to whale and dolphin conservation.

Some non-profit organisations are specifically geared to recruit paying volunteers to work on conservation projects. Since 1986 the non-profit organisation Coral Cay Conservation (CCC) has recruited paying volunteers to survey tropical reefs in several locations across the globe. The data and information collected on reef ecosystems not only enhances local knowledge and understanding of the fragility of such systems but also furnishes an all-important base-line to inform future decision-making. In countries with limited capacity to carry out such research, this becomes vital in the development of marine protected areas and the future management of tourism. For example the data furnished by Coral Cay was instrumental in the designation of the Belize Barrier Reef as a World Heritage Site in 1996 and in its subsequent management. In the Philippines, three years after CCC joined forces with the Philippine Reef and Rainforest Conservation Foundation to survey the coral reefs of Danjugan Island, Negros, the island became a world-class marine reserve.

Active community involvement and outreach in these volunteer programs has meant that they epitomise bottom-up tourism planning and are characterised by broad stakeholder involvement. For example the organisation recognises the importance of including all resource users of a region within an environmental education and awareness program. CCC targets a diverse range of audiences including local schoolchildren, village community leaders, resort guests, dive instructors and tourism guides. This ensures that the knowledge gained during the project phase is actively put into communities, rather than staying purely within the policy realm.

■ 11.7.3 The *role of research institutes*

The role of research institutes in supporting the development of sustainable marine ecotourism is not inconsiderable. The Smithsonian Tropical Research Institute (STRI) undertakes marine environmental monitoring at the Galeta Marine Laboratory, Panama, which also acts as an educational site for local and international visitors. A management plan for the use of the adjacent area for research, education and ecotourism is being developed to allow joint use by STRI, local universities, members of the local community and visitors.

The Irish Marine Institute produced a Marine Research, Technology, Development and Innovation Strategy for Ireland in 1998, which provided an economic profile of the marine tourism sector and identified prioritised R&D requirements. These priorities have since been addressed via the implementation of various activities, which included developing a framework for the development of special interest marine tourism in the West Clare Peninsula (which was to provide the foundation for the inclusion of that area in the meta-project as discussed in section 11.2.2).

CHAPTER REVIEW

From the above analysis it would appear that, for a multitude of reasons, marine policy and, in turn, the context for planning for sustainable marine tourism can be regarded as a prime — if not the most glaring — example of a meta-problem. This is hardly surprising, given the fact that each of its components, sustainability, the marine environment and tourism, are in themselves meta-problems. The interconnected nature of the marine realm creates planning and policy 'messes' that transgress areas of expertise and administration. Equally, sustainability and the health of the marine environment are set in this enormously complicated and confusing scenario. The dilemma is how to make sense of this conundrum. The call must be to develop a coordinated approach. This might occur through the creation of new organisations or the allocation of new responsibilities to existing ones. However, given the plethora of already existing organisations and conventions and their problems when translated to place-specific contexts (for example the Regional Seas program in the Caribbean as described in section 11.3), such a response would not by itself solve the problem of bringing various stakeholders and interests together. In the USA, there has been a shift towards the implementation of an 'ecosystem management' approach among government natural resource management agencies whereby it might be possible for different agencies to discover a common or public interest.

It is encouraging that a marine ecosystems approach is now being advocated at many levels by different agencies across the globe: for example by UNCLOS; by the IUCN, other UN bodies and agencies and the US NOAA in the worldwide Large Marine Ecosystems Strategy; by the Community Marine Strategy of the European Community; by WWF UK in its Living Seas program; in the regional marine ecosystems of Australia's Ocean Policy; and as declared by DEFRA for the UK (DEFRA 2002b). Concern still remains, however, as to whether such a holistic, process-based approach will be adequately backed by effective legislation in order to achieve sustainable outcomes.

SUMMARY OF KEY TERMS

Common property

Environmental resources that are (or could be) held or used collectively by communities. This concept is particularly relevant to the marine environment for, unlike the land, there are very few examples of individuals 'owning' space.

IUCN

The International Union for the Conservation of Nature and Natural Resources, also known as the 'World Conservation Union'. Founded in 1948, the IUCN is the world's largest and most important conservation network, with a membership of 82 states, 111 government agencies, more than 800 NGOs and about 10 000 scientists and experts.

Marine protected area

Definitions of marine protected areas (MPAs) vary depending on the level of use and protection that is envisaged. For example, some might see MPAs as sheltered or reserved areas where little, if any, use or human disturbance should be permitted. Others see them as specially managed areas designed to enhance ocean use. IUCN defines MPAs as 'any area of the intertidal or subtidal terrain, together with its overlying water and associated flora, fauna, historical and cultural features, which has been reserved by law or other effective means to protect part or all of the enclosed environment' (IUCN 1998).

QUESTIONS

1 How might marine tourism planning be an example of a meta-problem?

2 What are the major challenges facing the protection and management of tourism in marine protected areas?

3 Identify and briefly describe the institutional frameworks that provide for the protection and management of marine areas.

4 How effective have international policies been at protecting the marine environment? Could you identify any examples of conflicting values in such policies?

5 Why is an appreciation of scale particularly important in a marine planning context?

6 Identify and discuss which pressure groups have an interest in the protection and management of marine resources. How effectively do they pursue these interests in planning and policy debates?

7 What activities do you enjoy in the marine environment? How might these be governed or restricted by some of the policies outlined in this chapter?

8 Identify and briefly discuss stakeholders' interests in the protection and management of tourism in a marine protected area familiar to you.

9 What is zoning, and how is it applied in marine protected areas to manage tourism?

10 What methods could be used to involve marine stakeholders in the planning process at a local scale? How might these methods encourage sustainable goals?

EXERCISES

1 Find a local example of a marine protected area. What is the history of this park or region, when was it established and how has it changed since then? Identify all relevant stakeholders and how their interests might have changed over time. How is tourism managed in this area, and what mechanisms exist for stakeholder involvement in the planning process?

2 Examine the planning documents associated with a marine protected area of your choice. Using mind-mapping techniques, identify and briefly describe the hierarchy of policy directions, instruments and tools that contribute to creating the framework for management of tourism in this area.

FURTHER READING

Cater, C & Cater, E 2006, *Marine Ecotourism*, **CABI, Wallingford, UK.** A comprehensive text that looks at the growth of marine ecotourism from a wide range of angles, including resources, motivations, management and planning.

Garrod, B & Gössling, S (eds) 2006, *Diving Tourism: Experiences, Sustainability, Management*, **Earthscan, London.** A book that examines the issues facing this important marine ecotourism sector.

Hall, CM 2000, *Tourism Planning: Policies, Processes and Relationships*, **Prentice Hall, Harlow, UK.** An important tourism planning text that emphasises the value-laden and political nature of the process.

Higham, J & Lück, M (eds) 2006, *Marine Wildlife and Tourism Management*, **CABI, Wallingford, UK.** A forthcoming book that discusses the management of marine wildlife tourism and the minimisation of adverse impacts.

Orams, M 1999, *Marine Tourism: Development, Impacts and Management*, **Routledge, London.** One of the first books to look at the growth of and issues for sustainable marine tourism.

....

Great Barrier Reef, North Queensland

As the largest biological feature on earth, the Great Barrier Reef is arguably the world's most famous marine tourism attraction, stretching more than 2300 km along the north-east coast of Australia from the northern tip of Queensland to just north of Bundaberg. Aside from the coral reefs, the region also contains a wide variety of other habitats and an extraordinary diversity of plant and animal species. Its popularity as a destination has increased in parallel with political and scientific interest in the marine environment since the 1950s. Technological advances that enabled access to this environment, particularly the invention of the aqualung, had no small part to play in significant increases in visitors throughout the 1970s and 1980s. At this time forecasts were being made of continued growth for the foreseeable future, and therefore a concern with the potential impact of these tourists lead to the founding of the Great Barrier Reef Marine Park Authority (GBRMPA) in 1975 and to World Heritage Listing in 1981. The rapid increase in numbers of tourists and development of tourism infrastructure development on the Reef, which caused great concern in the 1980s, has stabilised since 1995.

As befits such a destination as the Great Barrier Reef, the scope and range of tourism activity within its boundaries is truly diverse. Figures suggest that tourism is far and away the largest commercial activity in the Great Barrier Reef region, generating more than A\$4.228 billion per annum (PDP Australia 2003). As a consequence, the marine tourism industry is a major contributor to the local and Australian economy. In 2004 approximately 730 tourism operators and 1500 vessels and aircraft were permitted to operate in the park. Tourism attracts approximately 1.8 million visitors each year (GBRMPA 2004). Recreational use of the GBR region by coastal residents is also high and, in many circumstances, the impact of recreational users can be impossible to separate from that of commercial tourism activities (Harriott 2002). Some of the principal tourist activities in the marine park include boat trips, snorkelling, scuba-diving, fishing, whale-watching, island resorts and cruise ships. Harriott (2002) takes a structural approach to the division of tourism facilities operating in the park, listing the major sectors of the Great Barrier Reef marine tourism industry as being:

- *Structure-based tourism operations.* Tourist pontoons are used as a base for day passengers. Other structures include underwater observatories and a floating hotel that operated briefly in the 1980s. Larger daytrip operations to pontoons represent the largest single component of the industry.
- *Vessel-based tourism operations.* These carry from less than 10 to more than 400 passengers; they might be site-specific or roving and might operate to islands or moorings.

- *Extended vessel-based tourism operations.* Vessels carry 6–160 passengers on trips of several days to weeks, generally stopping at more than one destination.
- *Bareboat charter.* Primarily based in the Whitsunday Islands, yachts are available for charter with or without crew for operation within a restricted area.
- *Cruise ships.* Large cruise ships (i.e. those of more than 10 000 tonnes) pass through and anchor overnight in the marine park.
- *Aircraft-based operations.* Conventional aircraft, seaplanes and helicopters are used for sightseeing and transfers.
- *Resort- and shore-based operations.* There are 27 island-based resorts in the marine park and a number of mainland resorts adjacent to it.

However, it is important to note that this tourism activity is highly concentrated. Eighty-five per cent of all visits take place within the Cairns and Whitsunday sections of the park, which represent less than 7 per cent of the total area (CRC Reef 2003). Data from EMC returns (see below) suggests that visitation to the Great Barrier Reef from Cairns has been largely static since the mid-1990s. In stark contrast to the Cairns planning area, the Whitsundays region has seen significant growth in visitation. Although the region seems to have suffered a slight stagnation and downturn in visitors in the late 1990s, the four years from 1999 to 2002 saw an increase in visitation from 335 459 to 687 436 total visitor days, a growth of 105 per cent (Cater 2004).

Managing tourism to the Great Barrier Reef

Managing tourism activity in this huge area (the park is bigger than the area of the UK, Switzerland and the Netherlands combined) is far from simple. Under the World Heritage listing the Australian Government is responsible for ensuring a delicate balance between reasonable human use and the maintenance of the World Heritage Area's natural and cultural integrity. As a UNESCO report states: 'the enormity of this task is compounded by the sheer size of the GBRWHA [Great Barrier Reef World Heritage Area], its economic importance, the political and the jurisdictional complexities determined by Australia's system of Federalism, the close proximity of rural and urban populations to the coast, the range of users and interest groups whose use patterns frequently compete and displace each other, the need for equity and fairness in access to resources and the ecological diversity of the region' (2002: 10). Management has been achieved primarily using a spectrum of multiple-use zones ranging from General Use Zones, where most reasonable activities can occur, through to National Park Zones (no-take zones that provide opportunities to see and enjoy the diversity of the Reef but where no fishing or collecting are allowed), to Preservation Zones (reference areas that are off limits to virtually everyone except for limited scientific research).

The Great Barrier Reef Marine Park Authority takes the lead role in day-to-day management of the region in conjunction with Queensland Parks and Wildlife Service. This activity is funded by both the Commonwealth and State governments, which provide matching funds primarily for enforcement, surveillance, monitoring and education and interpretation. In order to provide additional funds for these activities, an Environmental Management Charge (EMC) was introduced in mid-1993, which is payable by all visitors to the Reef

(continued)

on commercial operations. In 2006 the charge for individual visitors was $4.50. EMC logbooks and charging returns are provided by the GBRMPA to all commercial operators at the beginning of each calendar year or when a new permit is granted. Operators are required to keep a logbook of operations and supply charging returns on a quarterly basis. Penalties exist for commercial operators who do not maintain records or pay the required EMC. EMC data from the logbooks is used for the purposes of charging but also provides valuable data to the GBRMPA relating to tourism use of the marine park.

Policy context

The policy context in which the Great Barrier Reef exists is almost as diverse as the Reef itself. In addition to the World Heritage Convention, a number of other international conventions discussed in this chapter apply to the GBRWHA or parts of it, for example the 1971 Ramsar Convention; the Convention on International Trade in Endangered Species of Wild Fauna and Flora (CITES 1973); the Convention on Conservation of Migratory Species of Wild Animals (Bonn Convention 1979); the Convention on the Law of the Sea (UNCLOS 1982); the International Convention for the prevention of pollution at sea (MARPOL); and the Convention on Biological Diversity (CBD 1992) (UNESCO 2002).

At a national level the most important legislation is of course the Great Barrier Reef Marine Park Act, which was enacted in 1975 'to provide for the protection, wise use, understanding and enjoyment of the Great Barrier Reef in perpetuity'; in other words, to protect the area's outstanding biodiversity while providing for reasonable use. However, a plethora of other Commonwealth Acts are also relevant to its management, for example the *Environment Protection and Biodiversity Conservation Act 1999* and the *Environment Protection (Sea Dumping) Act 1981*. Queensland legislation is also relevant. For example, almost 50 per cent of the state islands within the GBRWHA are national parks under the *Nature Conservation Act 1992* (Qld). In some areas within the GBRWHA, the tidal lands and tidal waters are declared state marine parks under Queensland legislation (*Marine Parks Act 1982*) to complement the provisions of the adjoining Commonwealth marine park. Additional Queensland legislation that is important include:

- *Coastal Protection and Management Act 1995*
- *Environmental Protection Act 1994*
- *Integrated Planning Act 1997*
- *State Development and Public Works Organisation Act 1971*
- *Fisheries Act 1994*
- *Transport Infrastructure Act 1994*.

In 2003–04 the Great Barrier Reef Marine Park was rezoned as a result of implementing the Representative Areas Program. The rezoning was instigated by a recognition that the previous zoning of no-take or green zones, which made up less than 5 per cent of the park, did not adequately protect the entire range of plants and animals and should be revised. In addition, there were a number of inconsistencies between the management of state waters, which extend to three nautical miles offshore, and the federal zone beyond. As a result, a selection of

70 bioregions was identified, being 'representative' examples of all of the different habitats and communities in the GBRWHA. Each bioregion contains plant and animal communities, together with physical features, that are significantly different from the surrounding areas and the rest of the GBRWHA (GBRMPA 2005). A high degree of public consultation was encouraged throughout the planning process. These representative areas join the existing network of green zones in forming a greater area that restricts extractive activity. Approximately a third of the total area of the park is now afforded this higher level of protection. Many non-consumptive tourism activities, such as swimming and snorkelling, are still permitted within these zones.

By and large the planning and management of tourism to the Great Barrier Reef has been successful. In many cases the region is upheld as an example of world-class planning practice, with significant recognition being given to the issues of connectivity and consultation relevant to such a large natural area. It is important that this planning is adaptive to future threats and opportunities, especially that of global warming and resultant coral bleaching, which occurred on a significant scale in 1998 and 2002. In addition certain commentators have suggested that the Commonwealth and State governments see the Great Barrier Reef as a tourism 'cash cow' (Mules 2004). Without fair reinvestment of the significant returns from tourism to the region, adequate planning for the future could be jeopardised.

Questions

1   How does the Great Barrier Reef embody the principles of the World Heritage Convention?

2   How is day-to-day management of tourism to the Great Barrier Reef coordinated?

3   What was the rationale behind the recently introduced representative areas program?

References

Cater, C 2004, 'The Great Barrier Reef Marine Tourism Industry: A review prepared for Queensland Tourism Industry Council', viewed 12 April 2006, www.qtic.com.au/documents/Marine TourismIndustryReviewDraft.doc.

CRC Reef 2003, Marine Tourism on the Great Barrier Reef: Current State of Knowledge, CRC Reef, Townsville.

Great Barrier Reef Marine Park Authority, www.gbrmpa.gov.au.

—— 2004, 'Tourism on the Great Barrier Reef', viewed 29 August 2004. www.gbrmpa.gov.au/corp_site/key_issues/tourism/tourism_on_gbr.html.

—— 2005, 'Representative areas in the Marine Park', viewed 25 October 2005, www.gbrmpa.gov.au/corp_site/key_issues/conservation/rep_areas/index.html.

Harriott, VJ 2002, Marine Tourism Impacts and Their Management on the Great Barrier Reef, CRC Reef Research Centre, Technical Report No. 46, CRC Reef Research Centre, Townsville.

Mules, T 2004, 'The economic contribution of tourism to the management of the Great Barrier Reef Marine Park: A review prepared for Queensland Tourism Industry Council', viewed 12 April 2006, www.qtic.com.au/documents/Finaleconomiccontribution.doc.

PDP Australia 2003, *An Economic and Social Evaluation of Implementing the Representative Areas Program by Rezoning the Great Barrier Reef Marine Park*, Report on the Revised Zoning Plan, PDP Australia, Sydney.

UNESCO 2002, *Australian National Periodic Report, Section II: Report on the State of Conservation of Great Barrier Reef*, viewed 12 April 2006, http://whc.unesco.org/archive/periodic reporting/cycle01/section2/154.pdf.

UNESCO World Heritage Centre, http://whc.unesco.org.

REFERENCES

Ackoff, RL & Emery, FE 1972, *On Purposeful Systems*, Tavistock Publications, London.

Adler, E 2003, 'A world of neighbours: UNEP's regional seas programme', viewed 28 April 2006, www.unep.ch/regionalseas/pubs/f.adler.html.

Borgese, EM 1994, 'Global governance and the four problem areas', in PB Payoyo (ed.), *Ocean Governance: Sustainable Development of the Seas*, UN University Press, Tokyo.

Cetacean Society International 2003, 'It's a wonder the International Whaling Commission survives', *Whales Alive*, vol. 12, no. 2, viewed 12 April 2006, http://csiwhalesalive.org/csi03204.html.

Chen, S & JI Uitto 2004, 'Governing marine and coastal environment in China: Building local government capacity through international cooperation', China Environment Series 6, viewed 28 April 2006, www.wilsoncenter.org/topics/pubs/6-feature_5.pdf.

Conservation International 2004a, 'New marine protected area to safeguard world's largest fish', viewed 28 April 2006, www.conservation.org/xp/news/press_releases/2004/021104.xml.

—— 2004b, homepage, www.conservation.org/xp/CIWEB/home.

Department of the Environment 1997, *Conservation and Management of Whales and Dolphins in Queensland 1997–2001*, Brisbane.

Department for Environment, Food and Rural Affairs 2002a, *Safeguarding Our Seas*, DEFRA, London.

—— 2002b, *Seas of Change*, DEFRA, London.

Department of the Environment, Transport and the Regions 2001, *Review of Marine Nature Conservation: Interim Report*, DETR, London.

Down to Earth 2001, 'The global environmental facility', Down to Earth IFI Factsheet 18, viewed 18 April 2006, http://dte.gn.apc.org/Af18.htm.

Felstead, ML (undated), 'Coastal resources management, Ulugan Bay, Palawan Island, The Philippines', 12 April 2006, www.unesco.org/csi/act/ulugan/ulugan4.htm.

Global Environment Facility Small Grants Programme 2004, 'Promoting marine tour guide training in communities that impact the Belize barrier reef reserve system', viewed 12 April 2006, www.gefsgp.org/2.html.

Hall, CM 2000, 'Rethinking collaboration and partnership: A public policy perspective', in B Bramwell & B Lane, *Tourism Collaboration and Partnerships*, Channel View Publications, Clevedon, UK.

—— 2001, 'Trends in ocean and coastal tourism: The end of the final frontier', *Ocean and Coastal Management*, vol. 44, pp. 601–18.

Halpenny, E 1999, 'The state and critical issues relating to international ecotourism development policy', paper presented at 1999 Ecotourism Australia meeting, viewed 28 April 2006, http://210.193.176.101/service/confproc/ecotourism99/section_3.pdf.

—— 2003, 'NGOs as conservation agents: Achieving conservation through marine education', in B Garrod & J Wilson, *Marine Ecotourism: Issues and Experiences*, Channel View Publications, Clevedon, UK.

Hershman, MJ 1999, 'Building capacity for ocean management: Recent developments in US West Coast states', viewed 12 April 2006, www.oceanservice.noaa.gov/websites/retiredsites/natdia_pdf/19hershman.pdf.

International Resources Group 1992, *Ecotourism: A Viable Alternative for Sustainable Tourism Management of Natural Resources in Africa*, Agency for International Development, Bureau for Africa, Washington, DC.

International Whaling Commission 2004, 'IWC information', 28 April 2006, www.iwcoffice.org/commission/iwcmain.htm.

IUCN 1998, 'Creating a sea change: A WWF/IUCN vision for our blue planet', viewed 12 April 2006, www.iucn.org/themes/marine/pdf/seachang.pdf.

Kimball, LA 2001, *International Ocean Governance: Using International Law and Organizations to Manage Marine Resources Sustainably*, IUCN, Gland, Switzerland.

Kirkpatrick, H & Cook, C (undated), 'The nature conservancy programme', viewed 12 April 2006, www.spc.int/coastfish/News?LRF/2/8TNC.htm.

Lubchenco, J, Davis-Born, R & Simler, B 2002, 'The need for a new ocean ethic', *Open Spaces*, vol. 5, no. 1, pp. 10–19.

Massachusetts Government 2004, Massachusetts Ocean Management Initiative, viewed 28 April 2006, www.mass.gov/czm.oceanmanagement/index.htm.

Meinhold, SL 2003, 'Designing an education program to manage the undesirable effects of whale watching', MA thesis, Royal Roads University, Victoria, BC, Canada.

Mensah, TM 1994, 'The competent international organizations: Internal and external changes', in PB Payoyo (ed.), *Ocean Governance: Sustainable Development of the Seas*, UN University Press, Tokyo.

META-Project 2000, *Marine Ecotourism for the Atlantic Area (META-): Baseline Report*, University of the West of England, Bristol.

Miller, ML & Auyong, J 1991, 'Coastal zone tourism: A potent force affecting environment and society', *Marine Policy*, vol. 15, no. 2, pp. 75–99.

Mowforth, M & Munt, I 2003, *Tourism and Sustainability: Development and New Tourism in the Third World*, Routledge, New York.

Nicol, HN (undated), 'The Caribbean as an environmentally sensitive area: Are new regimes required?', viewed 28 April 2006, http://ru.nl/html/files/nichol-paper.doc.

Parsons, ECM & Rawles, C 2003, 'The resumption of whaling by Iceland and the potential negative impact in the Icelandic whale-watching market', *Current Issues in Tourism*, vol. 6, no. 5, pp. 444–8.

Saharuddin, A H 2001, 'National ocean policy: New opportunities for Malaysian ocean development', *Marine Policy*, vol. 25, no. 6, pp. 427–36.

Scheyvens, R 2000, 'Promoting women's empowerment through involvement in ecotourism: Experiences from the Third World', *Journal of Sustainable Tourism*, vol. 8, no. 3, pp. 232–49.

The International Ecotourism Society (2003), *Marine Ecotourism: How to be a Marine Ecotourist*, Washington, DC, viewed 20 November 2003, www.ecotourism.org.

United Nations 2002, 'Oceans and law of the sea', viewed 12 April 2006, www.un.org/Depts/los/index.htm.

Valencia, MJ 1997, *A Maritime Regime for Northeast Asia*, Oxford University Press, Oxford.

Vallejo, SM 1994, 'New structures for decision-making in integrated ocean policy: Introduction', in PB Payoyo (ed.), *Ocean Governance: Sustainable Development of the Seas*, UN University Press, Tokyo.

Vodden, K 2002, 'Governance for sustainability: Lessons from Canada', viewed 12 April 2006, www.sfu.ca/coastalstudies/voddenparis.doc.

Wildlife and Countryside Link 2004, 'A future for our seas', viewed 12 April 2006, www.wcl.org.uk/downloads/2004/WCL01_Governance_BP5_19Apr04.pdf.

World Wildlife Fund 2004, 'Sulu and Sulawesi Seas conservation results', viewed 12 April 2006 www.worldwildlife.org/wildplaces/ss/results.cfm.

Yankov, A & Ruivo, M 1994, 'An ocean assembly', in PB Payoyo (ed.), *Ocean Governance: Sustainable Development of the Seas*, UN University Press, Tokyo.

Young, EH 1999, 'Balancing conservation with development in small-scale fisheries: Is ecotourism an empty promise?', *Human Ecology*, vol. 27, no. 4, pp. 581–620.

Heather Zeppel

CHAPTER 12

12 Indigenous *tourism*

LEARNING OBJECTIVES

After reading this chapter you will be able to:

1 define the terms 'Aboriginal tourism' and 'Indigenous tourism' and key products in this sector

2 describe the policy environment and policy arena for Indigenous tourism

3 identify and discuss the social and political factors influencing Indigenous tourism planning and policy

4 explain the objectives of Aboriginal/Indigenous tourism strategies and ecotourism plans that include Indigenous issues

5 discuss the significance of cultural heritage and nature conservation for Indigenous tourism planning and policy.

This chapter describes and reviews Indigenous tourism planning and policy in Australia from 1995 to 2004. It considers Indigenous participation in tourism and the changing roles of Indigenous people in tourism policy-making and state-based plans for developing Aboriginal tourism or ecotourism. The extent and effectiveness of Indigenous participation in tourism policy and planning by state or federal agencies is also evaluated. The roles of Indigenous people in Australian tourism now include native title holders, traditional owners, land managers, business investment, park rangers, tourism operators and guides. Section 12.2 defines Aboriginal or Indigenous tourism in Australia, and section 12.3 reviews Indigenous involvement in cultural tourism or ecotourism ventures. Section 12.4 reviews research on Indigenous tourism, including Indigenous tourism planning and policy. Section 12.5 goes on to describe the tourism policy-making process and policy environment for tourism and Indigenous people. In section 12.6 various Aboriginal tourism and Indigenous tourism strategies are reviewed with reference to the Indigenous contribution and roles in tourism. Section 12.7 examines the policy and management roles for Indigenous people in nature-based tourism strategies and ecotourism plans. A case study highlights the role of rainforest Aboriginal people in policy-making and tourism strategies prepared for the Wet Tropics World Heritage Area of North Queensland. Finally, section 12.8 suggests that tourism policies and plans address Indigenous cultural heritage and environmental relationships, but have limited means for Indigenous participation in the control and management of tourism as native title holders and traditional owners of land.

12.2 $\mathcal{D}$EFINING ABORIGINAL TOURISM AND INDIGENOUS TOURISM

Aboriginal tourism has been defined as 'a tourism product which is either: Aboriginal owned or part owned, employs Aboriginal people, or provides consenting contact with Aboriginal people, culture or land' (SATC 1995: 5). It includes cultural heritage, rural and nature-based tourism products or accommodation owned by Indigenous operators. The *National Aboriginal and Torres Strait Islander Tourism Industry Strategy* defined Indigenous tourism as 'All forms of participation by Aboriginal and Torres Strait Islander people in tourism: as employers, as employees, as investors, as joint venture partners, providing indigenous cultural tourism products and providing mainstream tourism products' (ATSIC 1997a: 4). Attractions based on Indigenous culture that are owned and operated by Indigenous people represent 'culture controlled' or **Indigenous cultural tourism** while other service-based tourism ventures that are controlled by Indigenous people (such as resorts, boat cruises and camping grounds) represent **diversified Indigenous tourism** (Hinch 1996). **Indigenous tourism** involves **Indigenous people** and is sensitive to the presentation of Indigenous culture. Most tourism agencies consider Indigenous tourism, along with cultural tourism, nature-based tourism or ecotourism, as niche or special interest areas of tourism. Although the term 'Indigenous tourism' is now used by federal and most state tourism agencies, the term **Aboriginal** is still mainly used for tourism marketing purposes. This chapter uses the term 'Indigenous tourism', with a key focus on Indigenous-owned tourism ventures. Section 12.2.1 reviews Indigenous tourism and a range of Indigenous cultural or ecotourism ventures in Australia.

■ *12.2.1* **Defining** *Indigenous ecotourism and Indigenous cultural tourism*

Ecotourism Australia (EA 2006) defines ecotourism as 'Ecologically sustainable tourism with a primary focus on experiencing natural areas that fosters environmental and cultural understanding, appreciation and conservation'. There is a primary focus on the natural environment and a secondary emphasis on cultural heritage, including Indigenous cultures. Indigenous ecotourism, however, involves nature-based attractions or tours owned by Indigenous people as well as Indigenous interpretation of the natural and cultural environment. Indigenous ecotourism ventures operate on Aboriginal lands or protected areas.

The Wilderness Society defines Indigenous cultural tourism as 'responsible, dignified and sensitive contact between indigenous people and tourists which educates the tourist about the distinct and evolving relationship between indigenous peoples and their country, while providing returns to the local indigenous community' (Wilderness Society 1999). Indigenous cultural attractions and tours are located on traditional country and in urban areas.

It includes Aboriginal people on their traditional land sharing culture (cultural tourism) and Aboriginal people, not on their own land, speaking about culture (interpretive experience) (Ellis 2003). These tourism ventures include cultural centres, tours and art and craft galleries.

12.3 *I*NDIGENOUS INVOLVEMENT IN TOURISM

Aboriginal-owned tourism ventures have been a growing segment of the Australian tourism industry since the 1990s (DISR 2000; Elder 2005; Office of Northern Development 1993; Department of Tourism 1994a; Sykes 1995; Aboriginal and Torres Strait Islander Commission 1997a; Pitcher, van Oosterzee & Palmer 1999; Zeppel 1998a, 1998b, 1998c, 1998d, 1999, 2001; Singh et al. 2001; Crawshaw 2005). The range of Aboriginal-owned tourism products includes cultural tours, art and craft galleries, cultural centres, accommodation, boat cruises and other visitor facilities. Well-known Aboriginal tourist ventures include the Tjapukai Aboriginal Cultural Park in Cairns (QLD), which is 50 per cent owned by the local Djabugay people, and Tiwi Tours on Bathurst and Melville Islands (NT), which has been fully owned by the Tiwi Tourism Authority since 1995. Aboriginal culture has mainly been promoted in the Northern Territory, North Queensland and the Kimberley (Western Australia), but other states (e.g. New South Wales, South Australia and Victoria) are also developing Indigenous tourism products and attractions.

There are around 200 Indigenous tourism businesses in Australia, and recent estimates indicate that Aboriginal cultural tourism earned approximately A\$5 million a year while mainstream Aboriginal tourism enterprises generated A\$20–30 million (ATSIC 1997a). In the Northern Territory, Aboriginal landowners also derive income from licensing, leasing, renting and tourism concessions operating on Aboriginal lands (Sykes 1995; Pitcher, van Oosterzee & Palmer 1999). In the remote Kimberley region of Western Australia, Aboriginal communities on the Dampier Peninsula, north of Broome, provide accommodation and charge access fees for tour groups and private vehicles (WATC 1999). National parks such as Uluru, Kakadu and Nitmiluk (Northern Territory) and Mutawintji (New South Wales), jointly managed with Aboriginal landowners, also provide a variety of Aboriginal-owned tours (Mercer 1994; Sutton 1999). Most nature-based Indigenous tourism ventures are located on Aboriginal lands in rural areas or jointly managed national parks in northern and Central Australia.

12.3.1 **Indigenous** *cultural tourism ventures*

Indigenous cultural tourism ventures are tourism products based on an Indigenous culture, heritage site or experience. They include culture centres, art and craft galleries, Indigenous dance or music festivals, rock art sites, didgeridoo workshops and cultural tours. Indigenous cultural centres are found mainly in urban areas, national parks or tourist locations and usually represent the history and culture of one local Indigenous group. Cultural tourism ventures typically involve Indigenous ownership or joint venture enterprises that emphasise Indigenous interpretation, cultural authenticity and cultural maintenance. Indigenous people control the presentation and interpretation of Indigenous culture to tourists in the tours or attractions. Culture-based Indigenous tourism ventures are found throughout Australia.

12.3.2 **Indigenous** *ecotourism ventures*

Indigenous ecotourism ventures include boat cruises, nature-based accommodation, cultural ecotours and wildlife attractions operating on Aboriginal lands, national parks and in traditional tribal areas (see table 12.1). These Indigenous-owned ecotourism enterprises present unique Indigenous perspectives of the natural and cultural environment, promote nature conservation and provide employment for local Indigenous people (ANTA

2001). Hence, these Indigenous products meet the key criteria of eco-tourism as nature-based tourism with environmental education and ecological sustainability or conservation supporting tourism (Blamey 1995). Indigenous nature conservation or 'caring for country' involves traditional land owners and custodians 'looking after the environmental, cultural and spiritual well being of the land' (ATA 2005). Looking after Aboriginal sites, landscapes or natural resources and educating visitors about 'country' often motivates Indigenous conservation ethics in ecotourism or land management. Nganyintja, a Pitjantjatjara elder working with Desert Tracks, stated that 'carefully controlled ecotourism has been good for my family and my place, Angatja' (cited in James 1994: 12). Most Aboriginal nature tours are marketed as cultural tours rather than ecotours, emphasising the links between Indigenous operators and their traditional lands.

■ **Table 12.1**

Indigenous tourism ventures in Australia

BOAT TOURS	Yellow Water Cruises, Kakadu, NT[a] Guluyambi Aboriginal Cultural Cruise, Kakadu, NT[a] Nitmiluk Cruises, Katherine, NT[a] Darngku Heritage Cruises, Geikie Gorge, Kimberley, WA[a]
ACCOMMODATION	Gagudju Lodge, Kakadu, NT[b] Seisia Resort and Campground, Cape York, Qld[b] Kooljaman at Cape Leveque, Kimberley, WA[b]
CULTURAL ECOTOURS	Tiwi Tours, NT[b] Umorrduk Safaris, Arnhem Land, NT[b] Manyallaluk, NT[b] Anangu Tours, Uluru, NT[a] Wallace Rockhole, NT[b] Desert Tracks, Pitjantjatjara Lands, SA[b] Camp Coorong, SA Iga Warta, SA[b] Karijini Walkabouts, WA[a] East Gippsland Wilderness Tours, Vic Harry Nanya Tours, NSW Mutawintji Heritage Tours, NSW[a] Tobwabba Tours, NSW Umbarra Cultural Tours, NSW Native Guide Safari Tours, Qld Munbah Aboriginal Culture Tours, Qld[b] Kuku-Yalanji Dreamtime Walks, Qld[b]
CULTURAL ATTRACTION	Tjapukai Aboriginal Cultural Park, Qld Yarrawarra Aboriginal Cultural Centre, NSW[b] Brambuk Living Cultural Centre, Vic
WILDLIFE ATTRACTION	Whale Watching, Yalata Aboriginal Land, SA[b]

Notes:

[a] *Indigenous-owned cruises or tours operating in Aboriginal-owned and/or jointly managed national parks.*

[b] *Nature-based accommodation, cultural tour or wildlife attraction located on Indigenous land.*

Indigenous ecotourism ventures focus on Indigenous relationships with the land and the cultural significance of the natural environment, which includes Indigenous use of bush foods and traditional medicine, rock art, landscape features with Dreamtime significance, creation stories, totemic animals, traditional artefacts and ceremonies and contemporary land use. Such tours educate visitors on Indigenous environmental values, sustainable use of natural resources and 'caring for country'. As Tom Trevorrow, an Ngarrindjeri operator of Camp Coorong, noted: 'We have to look after the environment and we teach visitors the importance of this' (cited in ATSIC 1996: 29). Indigenous interpretations of nature are important for the maturing ecotourism market (Office of National Tourism 2001). Aboriginal operators, however, resent 'outsiders' setting up tours in their traditional area. They resent the issuing of permits to visit sites in their own country and ecotourism certification whereby 'Aboriginal "accreditation" involves approval from elders' (Bissett, Perry & Zeppel 1998: 7). These key issues for Indigenous ecotourism ventures receive little exposure in state-based plans and strategies for ecotourism.

12.4 *R*ESEARCH ON INDIGENOUS TOURISM

Research on Indigenous issues in tourism includes sustainable development of Aboriginal tourism (Burchett 1992; Altman & Finlayson 1993; AIATSIS 2004); environmental impacts of tourism (Ross 1991; Miller 1996); Aboriginal heritage sites and cultural interpretation (Bissett, Perry & Zeppel 1998); and Aboriginal tourism in national parks (Mercer 1994; Pitcher, van Oosterzee & Palmer 1999; Sutton 1999). Research on industry issues includes ecotourism education and training for Aboriginal people (ANTA 2001; Weiler 1997); Aboriginal tourism strategies (Zeppel 1998a, 1998b, 2001); Aboriginal control of tourism (Pitcher, van Oosterzee & Palmer 1999); Indigenous involvement in Australian ecotourism (Dowling 1998); and Aboriginal nature-based tourism products (Zeppel 1998d). Other research has reviewed Indigenous wildlife tourism in Australia (Muloin, Zeppel & Higginbottom 2000, 2001); and cultural interpretation by Aboriginal tour guides at Mutawintji National Park (Howard, Thwaites & Smith 2001). International research has addressed the benefits of ecotourism for Indigenous communities (Zeppel 1997, 1998c), especially women (Scheyvens 1999, 2000) and potential conflicts between ecotourism and Indigenous hunting or use of natural resources (Grekin & Milne 1996; Hinch 1998). Most of the research has focused on product development or delivery of Indigenous tourism.

12.4.1 Research *on planning and policy*

There has been limited research assessing tourism policies or tourism planning for Indigenous people (Pitcher, van Oosterzee & Palmer 1999) or the implementation of Aboriginal tourism plans (Zeppel 2001). Whitford, Bell and Watkins (2001) reviewed 72 federal and Queensland government tourism and Aboriginal development policies produced from 1975 to 1999. These policy and planning documents had a strong **economic rationalism** approach based on financial outcomes and the commercialisation of Indigenous culture and heritage for tourism. Apart from the *National Aboriginal and Torres Strait Islander Tourism Industry Strategy* (ATSIC 1997a), a content analysis of 17 policy documents and plans found an average 2.7 per cent of the content was dedicated to Indigenous tourism issues. A Federal government access and equity plan for tourism produced in 1993 had 20 per cent content devoted to Indigenous tourism. Common themes addressed in the policy and planning documents were supporting Indigenous employment and Indigenous tourism businesses and using Indigenous culture and natural heritage for tourism. The tourism policies and plans were produced by government agencies in response to wider Indigenous social and economic issues. Economic concerns dominated these policies and plans, with Indigenous tourism providing a competitive edge for international tourism marketing of Australia (Whitford, Bell & Watkins 2001).

Zeppel (2003) reviewed 17 federal and state plans prepared for Aboriginal tourism and Indigenous issues included in ecotourism or nature tourism strategies from 1995 to 2002. The focus was on Indigenous involvement in ecotourism policy and planning in Australia. Key issues addressed in the Aboriginal tourism or ecotourism plans included cultural integrity and interpretation, access to Aboriginal land and Indigenous joint management of national parks. Social values and community attitudes towards Indigenous people and their ties with the land influenced public policy-making and planning for Aboriginal tourism and ecotourism. These tourism policies and plans addressed Indigenous cultural heritage and environmental relationships, but had limited means for Indigenous participation in the control of tourism.

Wearing and Huyskens (2001) also found that cross-cultural approaches to joint management of national parks and policies based on ecotourism and community ownership of tourism were mainly a political means to meet legal requirements under the *Native Title Act 1993* (Cwlth).

Nielsen (2005) interviewed Aboriginal respondents in north-west New South Wales about their attitudes towards regional tourism planning. Qualitative analysis of the semi-structured, in-depth interviews conducted by Nielsen identified three main themes and eleven other subthemes about Aboriginal views on tourism planning and policy processes. The main themes were recognising and understanding Aboriginal people in regional areas, Aboriginal interest in entering the tourism industry and the need for tourism planning to be led by Aboriginal people, rather than white-dominated tourism planning from government tourism agencies. An Aboriginal-driven tourism planning process involved meaningful participation and involvement. Nielsen suggests that a participatory approach to regional tourism planning, one that involves Aboriginal people, will lead to more sustainable outcomes for Indigenous tourism ventures.

Ellis (2003) reviewed the extensive consultations undertaken with Indigenous tourism operators and Aboriginal communities in preparing the new Northern Territory *Indigenous Tourism Strategy*.

Indigenous groups were often still overlooked in land-use planning and decision-making processes, despite owning most of the land where Northern Territory tourism icons were located (e.g. Uluru, Kakadu). Aboriginal cultural responsibilities, service-based training, business mentoring and accreditation were other key issues. Business support, seed capital for basic infrastructure and a lead agency (NTTC) were seen as essential requirements for developing Northern Territory Indigenous tourism ventures. Section 12.5 addresses the **policy environment** and policy arena influencing tourism planning for Indigenous people in Australia.

12.5 POLICY ENVIRONMENT FOR AUSTRALIAN TOURISM AND INDIGENOUS PEOPLE

The Australian policy environment for tourism and Indigenous issues reflects social values and community attitudes towards Indigenous people and public policy-making for tourism. In Australia, tourism policy is largely a public policy-making or government activity. Tourism policies guide government actions, decision-making, funding and planning for tourism (see chapters 1 and 2 for more detailed discussions) and reflect the interests of government agencies, pressure groups (e.g. conservation groups), tourism industry associations, community leaders, significant individuals, bureaucrats and politicians and, more recently, Indigenous groups.

Key elements in **tourism policy-making** include:
- *the policy environment:* power arrangements, values and institutional arrangements
- *the policy arena:* interest groups, institutions and their leadership, important individuals
- *specific policy issues:* demands, decisions, outputs (products) and outcomes (or impacts) (Hall, Jenkins & Kearsley 1997).

Table 12.2 (p. 412) outlines key features of the policy environment and the **policy arena** shaping Indigenous involvement in ecotourism and Aboriginal tourism. In Australia, Indigenous people have been included in tourism policies only since the 1990s (Whitford, Bell & Watkins 2001; Zeppel 1997, 2001, 2002). Greater government recognition of the real need for Aboriginal economic and social advancement mainly stemmed from the recommendations contained in the 1991 Royal Commission into Aboriginal Deaths in Custody report. This report led, in 1997, to the development of tourism, rural and cultural industry strategies for Aboriginal and Torres Strait Islander (ATSI) people as three key areas for Indigenous economic progress. The other crucial factor was legislation recognising Indigenous rights to land, the *Aboriginal Land Rights (Northern Territory) Act 1976* and the *Native Title Act 1993* (Cwlth). These laws recognise Aboriginal or **native title** rights and interests over traditional land areas and use of natural resources (e.g. fauna, flora) in Crown lands and national parks.

12.5.1 Tourism *industry and environmental policies for Indigenous tourism*

In response to public policy-making, relevant tourism policies are also developed by the tourism industry and by non-government environmental agencies. The former Tourism Council Australia's statement on Indigenous tourism focused on industry issues and training needs (TCA 1999; see section 4.7 for a discussion of TCA). It supported Aboriginal Tourism Australia as the key industry body for Indigenous tourism, providing Indigenous involvement in marketing and tourism policy development (ATA 2005). The recently established Commonwealth statutory corporation, Tourism Australia (see section 7.6.1), has no policy on Indigenous tourism but conducts market research on visitor interest in Indigenous experiences (TA 2003). Two of the key environmental organisations in Australia, the Wilderness Society and Australian Conservation Foundation, have specific policy documents on tourism and on Indigenous rights and interests in wilderness areas as well as land and water management (Wilderness Society 1999; ACF 2000). These policies support consultation and partnerships with Indigenous people for tourism on Indigenous lands and Indigenous involvement in national park management.

Ecotourism Australia (EA) has no policy document on tourism and Indigenous people. Instead, EA manages the Eco Certification or Nature and Ecotourism Accreditation Program (NEAP), which certifies genuine ecotour operators. This NEAP document (EA 2005) includes a cultural component recognising Indigenous consultation, interpretation and employment in ecotourism. Of 297 products accredited by December 2000, Tobwabba Tours (New South Wales) was the sole Aboriginal business certified by the NEAP. Tobwabba Tours and Desert Tracks (South Australia) were listed in the *Australian Ecotourism Guide 2001*. No Indigenous tourism businesses were listed in the EA *Directory of EcoCertified Products in Australia 2004/2005*. The EA executive or committee also has no Indigenous members. At the 2000 EA conference, an Aboriginal keynote speaker, Gatjil Djerrkura, wanted 'Aboriginal enterprises to be given the opportunity to play contemporary roles in Australia's burgeoning ecotourism industry' (*Ecotourism News* 2000: 6). The next section reviews Indigenous roles in Aboriginal tourism strategies and plans for nature tourism or ecotourism.

12.6 ABORIGINAL TOURISM STRATEGIES

From 1995 to 1998, Aboriginal tourism strategies were produced for Australia as a whole (ATSIC 1997a), for three states (South Australia, Northern Territory, Victoria) and for one region (Kimberley, Western Australia). Aboriginal cultural links to the environment and Indigenous issues relevant to ecotourism were outlined in most of these strategies (see table 12.3). The

■ Table 12.2
*Australian
policy
environment
for tourism
and
Indigenous
peoples*

POLICY ENVIRONMENT	
Power arrangements (government)	Dept of Industry, Tourism and Resources, state/territory tourism commissions
	Environment Australia, state/territory national park and World Heritage agencies
	ATSIC,* state/territory Aboriginal affairs departments
Legislation	*ATSI Heritage Protection Act 1984*
	World Heritage Properties Conservation Act 1983
	Native Title Act 1993
	Environment Protection and Biodiversity Conservation Act 1999
	State/territory Aboriginal heritage and Aboriginal land acts
	State/territory national parks and nature conservation acts
Institutional arrangements (industry)	Aboriginal Tourism Australia, Ecotourism Australia
	Indigenous Business Australia, Indigenous Stock Exchange
	Sustainable Tourism, Tropical Savannah and Desert Knowledge CRC
	Other tourism industry associations; Interpretation Australia Association
	ATSI Commercial Development Corporation, Indigenous Land Corporation
	ATSI cultural heritage and cultural custodians (consultation, negotiation)
Social values (attitudes towards Indigenous people)	ATSI affinity with natural environment (ecological and spiritual relationships)
	ATSI native title landholders and traditional landowners (partnerships, control)

POLICY ARENA		
Interest groups	Tourism industry associations, ecotourism and Aboriginal tourism operators	
	Aboriginal land councils, native title landholders, Indigenous communities	
	Non-government environmental agencies (e.g. ACF, Wilderness Society, WWF)	
Institutions and institutional leadership	As above — government and industry	
	Tourism education and training providers (e.g. TAFE, university)	
Significant individuals	Politicians (federal/state ministers for tourism, environment or Aboriginal affairs)	
	Aboriginal leaders (e.g. Noel Pearson, Cape York)	
	Environmental leaders (e.g. Peter Garrett, ACF)	
	Aboriginal tourism operators/officers (e.g. Joe Ross, WA; Trudi Ridge, Indigenous Business Australia)	

Notes

ACF: Australian Conservation Foundation; ATSI: Aboriginal and Torres Strait Islander; ATSIC: Aboriginal and Torres Strait Islander Commission; CRC: Cooperative Research Centre; WWF: World Wide Fund for Nature (formerly World Wildlife Fund)

* ATSIC was the peak federal Indigenous agency from 1990 to 2004. The Office of Indigenous Policy Coordination, a National Indigenous Council and 30 Indigenous coordination centres now focus on ATSI policy implementation and service delivery.

Indigenous issues included cultural integrity, interpretation, access to Aboriginal land, developing Aboriginal tourism, and consultation or partnerships with Aboriginal people. The South Australian strategy noted that 'Aboriginal communities live in or have cultural ties to [diverse natural] environments' (SATC 1995: 6), with semi-traditional Aboriginal lifestyles being a strong attraction in the Pitjantjatjara Lands, an area with restricted visitor entry. Aboriginal culture was also associated with the Flinders Ranges, Murray River and Coorong regions. Key aspects for tourism were Indigenous cultural integrity, tour guides 'who can legitimately speak about Aboriginal history and culture or show sites' (SATC 2000: 9) and gaining consenting contact with Aboriginal people or land. This strategy recommended tourism training with ecoawareness seminars and the development of Aboriginal tourism products within strong and sustainable tourism niche areas, such as ecotourism and cultural tourism.

■ Table 12.3

Indigenous
tourism issues
in Australian
Aboriginal
tourism
strategies

ABORIGINAL TOURISM STRATEGY, AREA, YEAR	INDIGENOUS TOURISM ISSUES
Aboriginal Tourism Strategy, SA, 1995[a]	Cultural integrity, consent, Pitjantjatjara lands
Aboriginal Tourism Strategy, NT, 1996	Land access, partnerships, interpretation
Kimberley Aboriginal Cultural Tourism Strategy, WA, 1996[b]	Control and manage tourism, copyright, joint management (national parks), cultural integrity, protect sites and landscapes
Indigenous Tourism Product Development Principles, NSW, 1997	Consultation, interpretation, protocols, cultural integrity, intellectual property
National Aboriginal and Torres Strait Islander Tourism Industry Strategy, Australia, 1997	Cultural interpretation, permits, employment, national parks, ecotourism operators
National Aboriginal and Torres Strait Islander Cultural Industry Strategy, Australia, 1997	Indigenous arts and crafts, tourist sales, souvenirs, performing arts, cultural centres
National Aboriginal and Torres Strait Islander Rural Industry Strategy, Australia, 1997	Recreational fishing and safari hunting; access to and travel through Indigenous land
Aboriginal Tourism Industry Plan, Vic, 1998	Business skills, cultural centre and trail
An Aboriginal Tourism Marketing Strategy for WA, WA, 2004	Promoting export-ready Aboriginal tourism, training, mentors, partnerships, business support
Indigenous Tourism Strategy, Qld, 2004	Mainstream tourism, business partnerships
NT Indigenous Tourism Strategy, NT, 2004	Market and develop Indigenous tourism, access

Notes:

[a] *South Australia was preparing a new Indigenous Tourism Strategy in 2004–05.*

[b] *Non-government strategy prepared by Global Tourism and Leisure for the Kimberley Aboriginal Tourism Association, WA.*

The Northern Territory strategy focused on developing partnerships between Aboriginal groups and the Northern Territory tourism industry. The task force for this strategy included the tourism industry, Aboriginal land councils, tourism operators and government agencies (e.g. ATSIC, Office of Aboriginal Development). It noted that Aboriginal people 'control large tracts of land [i.e. 50 per cent of NT], largely in a natural state and that they have control over access to those tracts of land' (Northern Territory Tourist Commission (NTTC) 1996: 10). The opportunities identified for nature-based tourism were wilderness camps, tourism accommodation and development of natural attractions on Aboriginal land. It further noted that 'Aboriginal owned National Parks in the Northern Territory [e.g. Uluru, Kakadu] already play a crucial role in the tourist industry' (NTTC 1996: 12). Aboriginal interpretive material was to be included in cultural centres in such parks. Aboriginal tourism opportunities in national parks included nature interpretation, cultural tours and joint management roles. One key aim of the NT strategy was to develop models of access to Aboriginal land or sea by tour operators through a system of permits and licences. Tourism ventures on Northern Territory Aboriginal lands are negotiated with the Aboriginal land councils.

A non-government strategy for the Kimberley region was developed 'primarily to enable Kimberley Aboriginal people to control and manage tourism on their land' (Global Tourism and Leisure 1996). The strategy was prepared for the Kimberley Aboriginal Tourism Association and included actions for product development, cultural integrity and environmental issues. To this end, the strategy focused on protecting Aboriginal knowledge and cultural integrity, gaining access to traditional lands and seeking greater involvement in management, operation and tourism joint ventures in national parks. This strategy emphasised the cultural relationship between Aboriginal people and their land and Kimberley Aboriginal communities deriving economic benefits from tourism. Specific programs for managing tourism on Kimberley Aboriginal land were not outlined in the strategy.

In New South Wales, the Indigenous Tourism Product Development Principles (Tourism NSW 1997) were based on consultations with Indigenous communities. These principles aimed to protect Aboriginal heritage and cultural integrity by setting out key protocols for tourism industry operators. No specific mention was made of Aboriginal involvement in ecotourism. The strategy particularly stated that 'Government policy strongly supports the interpretation of Aboriginal culture by Aboriginal people' (Tourism NSW 1997: 4). It also recommended consultation and negotiation with New South Wales Aboriginal land councils and tribal elders about access to and interpretation of Aboriginal heritage sites.

A Tourism Industry Advisory Committee, including four Indigenous members involved in tourism, guided the Australian *National Aboriginal and Torres Strait Islander Tourism Industry Strategy* (ATSIC 1997a). The strategy included a section on 'links with nature-based tourism' that focused on Indigenous interpretation of the natural environment. It noted that obstacles to Aboriginal involvement in nature-based tourism were a lack of commercial permits for Aboriginal tour operators and 'uncertainty on the part of ecotourist operators about how to involve Indigenous people' (ATSIC 1997a: 25). This strategy highlighted the training and employment of Indigenous people as interpreters in national parks, nature reserves and Aboriginal lands with conservation significance. It suggested that it was more feasible to develop Indigenous tourism where an enterprise could 'be linked to an area of spectacular environmental quality' (ATSIC 1997a: 22).

This national strategy included three specific actions aimed to assist Indigenous people in presenting their culture to visitors. These were allocating permits for Indigenous environmental tours in protected areas, Indigenous employment in national parks and nature-based tour operators employing Indigenous people as environmental and cultural guides or interpreters (ATSIC 1997a). The strategy, however, did not mention government environmental or national park agencies as key stakeholders in Aboriginal nature-based tourism. Of 172 submissions received for the draft strategy, 30 were from Aboriginal cultural or community organisations and another 30 were from Indigenous individuals. The strategy had a strong cultural emphasis and had few specific suggestions for developing Indigenous tourism ventures. Appendix D of the strategy, however, reviewed an Indigenous tourism venture, Karijini Walkabouts, in Karijini National Park in the Pilbara region.

The *National Aboriginal and Torres Strait Islander Cultural Industry Strategy* (ATSIC 1997b) focused on Indigenous arts and crafts, tourist sales, artist-in-residence programs at resorts, souvenirs, Indigenous performing arts and cultural centres for gaining economic benefits from tourism. The *National Aboriginal and Torres Strait Islander Rural Industry Strategy* (ATSIC 1997c) reviewed rural tourism opportunities for Indigenous communities. These options included recreational fishing and trophy hunting on Aboriginal lands but not Indigenous ecotourism. Environmental agencies were not mentioned as potential Aboriginal tourism partners, but controlling tourist numbers and impact on Aboriginal lands or communities was addressed. This rural strategy also noted the need to 'develop policies and programs which will manage travel through Indigenous owned lands' (ATSIC 1997c: 36).

In Victoria, the Aboriginal Tourism Industry Plan simply noted that Aboriginal tourism appealed to visitors seeking 'quality experiences of nature and culture' (Tourism Victoria 1998). The plan focused on developing Aboriginal business skills and tourism industry networks. Aboriginal Tourism Australia and Aboriginal government agencies were included as partners in the plan. Specific actions were to upgrade visitor access and interpretation at Brambuk Cultural Centre in the Grampians and an Aboriginal cultural trail for the Murray Outback region of western Victoria.

The *Aboriginal Tourism Marketing Strategy for Western Austraia* (WATC 2004a) focused on developing and promoting Western Australian Indigenous tourism products in partnership with the Western Australian Indigenous Tourism Operators Committee (WAITOC, established in 2002) and key government agencies (e.g. Office of Aboriginal Economic Development, ATSIS, Conservation and Land Management). The main focus was assisting **export-ready** Aboriginal tourism products to get into the marketplace. This marketing plan was part of an overall Western Australia Indigenous tourism strategy. Further training and mentoring aimed to build Indigenous ventures into marketable products. There were 60–70 Indigenous tourism products in Western Australia, with some Indigenous ventures being packaged and sold by large tour companies such as AAT Kings and Australian Pacific Tours. This Aboriginal tourism marketing program was expected to cost $3.2 million over five years.

■ *12.6.1* **Indigenous** *tourism strategies*

In 2004, Indigenous tourism strategies were prepared for the Northern Territory (Ellis 2003; NTTC 2004) and for Queensland (TQ 2004). The Queensland strategy was an internal policy document providing a framework for Tourism Queensland to facilitate Indigenous involvement and participation in mainstream tourism rather than just cultural tourism products (e.g. art, crafts, and dance performances). This strategy defined Indigenous tourism as 'all tourism activities that involve Australian Indigenous people and are sensitive to Indigenous culture' (TQ 2004: 3). Key principles were involving Indigenous people in all aspects of tourism, generating community benefits, better business planning and integration with the wider tourism industry. This strategy supported the need for more Indigenous tourism enterprises, increased participation by Indigenous people in all areas of tourism, access to Indigenous heritage sites and partnerships between tourism operators and Indigenous people or communities. Key concerns were reconciliation, alcohol, native title, core aspects of traditional Indigenous culture and limited market interest by Australians in Indigenous tourism experiences. The action steps focused on community tourism plans, business partnerships and cultural protocols. Consultations were held with nine government agencies (two Aboriginal), two Aboriginal corporations on Cape York Peninsula and the Queensland Tourism Industry Council. Funding for Indigenous tourism training and business development was linked to existing government programs.

The *Northern Territory Indigenous Tourism Strategy* (NTCC 2004) updated the 1996 *Aboriginal Tourism Strategy*. The new strategy acknowledged the competitive advantage of Aboriginal cultural tourism with more training and support required for financially viable Indigenous businesses. Cultural revival and economic benefits were linked to community benefits from Indigenous tourism. Indigenous people comprise a third of the Territory's population and own nearly 50 per cent of its land. Key issues were tourism training, protecting and utilising Aboriginal land for tourism, and Indigenous groups securing investment or operational funding. Key principles guiding this strategy were cultural and ecological sustainability, financial viability and other community benefits (e.g. cultural revival, education, employment, esteem), as well as overall quality and integrity in the promotion of Indigenous people, culture and heritage.

This included joint management of all Northern Territory national parks with traditional owners, Indigenous employment as park rangers, a signage program with Indigenous place names and their cultural significance, and new Indigenous tourism or business opportunities in parks. Increasing Indigenous employment in the mainstream tourism industry was also addressed.

Consultations in the Northern Territory
Indigenous Tourism Strategy

Indigenous tour operators and communities participated in developing the Northern Territory Indigenous Tourism Strategy (NTCC 2004). The Northern Territory Tourist Commission followed a two-stage process of community and industry consultation in preparing this new strategy. The first phase of consultation sought responses from Indigenous tourism stakeholders, using case studies of successful Indigenous tourism operators in the Territory. These consultations were held by NTTC staff in the field and in the communities of Indigenous operators (Ellis 2003). Most of the Indigenous stakeholders preferred to use the term 'Indigenous', but Indigenous tourism operators also realised that the term 'Aboriginal' is more recognised by Australian and international tourists when marketing the NT.

The Indigenous operators supported the marketing of Indigenous tourism products by the NTTC but sought more cooperation and commitment from the mainstream tourism industry. The marketing of 'Aboriginal experiences' also needed to fit visitor expectations of Aboriginal culture. The Indigenous stakeholders differentiated between Aboriginal cultural tourism (i.e. Aboriginal people on their traditional land sharing culture) and Aboriginal interpretive experiences (i.e. Aboriginal people, not on their own country, speaking about culture). These interpretive experiences, including talks by non-Indigenous guides, took place at museums, art galleries, cultural centres and sites not on the traditional country of tour guides (Ellis 2003). Some people also wanted the Indigenous ownership of a tourism business to be stated.

The second stage of consultation involved feedback from other broad stakeholders involved in the Northern Territory tourism industry, at art centres and Northern Territory Government agencies. Other written responses from interested groups and the consultations guided the key principles and overall direction of this strategy in fostering Indigenous tourism enterprises. The processes for consultations and the implementation of key action plans were coordinated by the NTTC and guided by an Indigenous tourism reference group, which included representatives from Indigenous organisations, Northern Territory Government agencies and tourism groups. Twice a year, the strategy was to be updated and republished by NTTC, listing the achievement of action steps and outlining further steps in developing Indigenous tourism. Indigenous tourism development officers from the NTTC and similar positions at the Northern and Central Aboriginal land councils also assisted in implementing this strategy.

A proposed Northern Territory Aboriginal Tourism Association would have a mentoring role in sharing Indigenous business knowledge and experience with other Indigenous people or groups starting tourism ventures. An Indigenous tourism representative was also needed for all government planning processes.

The strategy listed action steps for cultural sustainability (9), ecological sustainability (7), financial viability and community benefit (13) and quality/integrity (9, with 7 on marketing).

Key outcomes were new marketing campaigns for Indigenous tourism products that targeted international and domestic visitors and promoted these core products on the NTTC website.

■ 12.6.2 **Aboriginal** *economic development strategies and tourism*

From the mid-1990s, Indigenous tourism was included in various Aboriginal economic development strategies prepared by state agencies in Western Australia, Queensland and the Northern Territory (see table 12.4). These strategies focused on tourism opportunities for Indigenous groups, who form a significant part of the regional or remote population of northern Australia. Other southern states (e.g. New South Wales, Victoria) also now have Aboriginal or Koori business development units.

■ **Table 12.4**
Indigenous tourism issues in Aboriginal economic development strategies

ABORIGINAL ECONOMIC STRATEGY, AREA, YEAR	INDIGENOUS TOURISM ISSUES
Aboriginal Economic Development in WA, WA, 1997	Developing Aboriginal tourism enterprises Kimberley, Pilbara, national parks (e.g. Karijini)
Building a Better Territory: Economic Development Strategy, NT, 2002 (Indigenous economic development)	Indigenous tourism and Indigenous arts strategies Market Indigenous tourism Access to NT parks
Cape York Partnerships Economic Development Policy Framework, Qld, 2004	Facilitate new tourism enterprises and employment Community-based cultural and ecotourism projects

A strategy for Aboriginal Economic Development in Western Australia (Office of Aboriginal Economic Development 1997) outlined government support for developing Aboriginal tourism businesses, focused on the

Kimberley region and national parks. A key principle of this strategy was Aboriginal participation in national parks and tourism development. There was a strong focus on Aboriginal involvement in national parks and 'enabling visitors to experience Aboriginal heritage in the natural environment' (OAED 1997: 8). The strategy noted that the Aboriginal Tourism Unit in the Department of Conservation and Land Management was training Aboriginal people and developing Aboriginal heritage and tourism enterprises on Western Australia's national park lands. It also promoted Indigenous partnerships with the tourism sector and developing tourism projects on Aboriginal land.

Indigenous economic development was a key part of the Northern Territory *Economic Development Strategy* (OTD 2002). The strategy focused on improving economic outcomes for Indigenous people from Indigenous tourism and arts, with training and enterprise support. These sectors were to be developed through partnership agreements and joint ventures between the private sector and Indigenous organisations and with business mentoring. The tourism section of this strategy sought to increase the number of Indigenous tourism ventures and to establish Indigenous cultural centres in major towns and Indigenous training in tourism. Increased marketing of Indigenous tourism products and working with traditional owners to maintain access and tourism opportunities in Territory parks were also part of this strategy. Of 15 priority actions for tourism, five related to Indigenous tourism development in the Northern Territory.

The Cape York Partnerships Economic Development Policy Framework outlines cooperative steps between government agencies and Aboriginal communities to facilitate new tourism enterprises, business mentoring and Indigenous training and employment in tourism and hospitality (DSD 2004). The focus is on developing community-based Indigenous arts, cultural and ecotourism projects in regional hubs such as Lockhart River, Weipa, Laura, Lizard Island and Mossman Gorge. This included tourism infrastructure, small businesses and other community opportunities to generate economic development through tourism on Cape York Peninsula, where large areas of land are owned by Indigenous groups. Business development for Indigenous people was supported through community enterprise hubs. Section 12.7 reviews Indigenous involvement in nature tourism or ecotourism strategies and plans.

12.7 AUSTRALIAN ECOTOURISM STRATEGIES AND INDIGENOUS INVOLVEMENT

From 1994 to 2000, various ecotourism and nature-based tourism strategies were devised in Australia. Indigenous tourism issues and roles were addressed in ecotourism plans for Australia and Queensland and in nature-based tourism strategies for Western Australia and the Wet Tropics of North

Queensland (see table 12.5). These key ecotourism issues included Indigenous nature interpretation, intellectual copyright, consultation with Indigenous people, developing Indigenous ecotourism and ecotourism assets on Aboriginal lands.

■ **Table 12.5**
Indigenous issues in Australian nature-based/ ecotourism strategies

NATURE/ECOTOURISM STRATEGY, AREA, YEAR	INDIGENOUS ISSUES IN ECOTOURISM
National Ecotourism Strategy, Australia, 1994	• Consultation and negotiation with ATSI communities • Recognise ATSI intellectual property rights • Minimise social and cultural impact on ATSI sites
Ecotourism: Adding Value to Tourism in Natural Areas, Tasmania, 1994	• Aboriginal products, heritage sites, consultation
Ecotourism: A Natural Strategy for South Australia, SA, 1994	• Increase in Aboriginal operators, Aboriginal lands
Nature Based Tourism Strategy for WA, WA, 1997	• Aboriginal involvement in tourism, Aboriginal lands—natural and cultural assets, interpretation
Keeping It Real: A Nature Based Tourism Strategy for Western Australia, WA, 2004	• Support Aboriginal tourism development and marketing • Cultural affinity, business skills, accreditation
Queensland Ecotourism Plan, Qld, 1997	• ATSI cultural perspectives of natural environment
Queensland Ecotourism Plan, Qld, 2003–08	• Foster ATSI involvement in Qld ecotourism
Wet Tropics Nature-Based Tourism Strategy, 2000; Wet Tropics Walking Strategy, Qld, 2001	• Partnerships, management of nature-based tourism • Cultural values, tourism employment and training

Note:
No Indigenous involvement in ecotourism is mentioned in *Nature-Based Tourism in Tasmania 1998–99 Update* (May 2000), *Nature-Based Tourism Strategy* (SA 2000), *Nature-based Tourism: Directions and Opportunities* (VIC 2000) or *Ecotourism: A Natural Strength for Victoria—Australia* (1992).

The *National Ecotourism Strategy* (Department of Tourism 1994b) included a section on the 'Involvement of Indigenous Australians' (section 5.10, pp. 42–5) in ecotourism. It recognised opportunities for the involvement of Aboriginal people and Torres Strait Islanders (ATSI) in ecotourism as 'land owners, resource managers and tourism operators' (1994b: 3) and as 'site and intellectual property custodians' (1994b: 8). Two (of seven) key actions to enhance opportunities and encourage Indigenous involvement in Australian ecotourism were as follows:

- '*Action 1:* include ATSI communities and organisations in development and implementation of ecotourism programs', and
- '*Action 4:* encourage ATSI to participate across the full range of ecotourism development, planning, management, decision-making, regulation and implementation' (1994b: 44).

Specific measures to include ATSI people in ecotourism programs were not addressed, although the strategy recognised that 'many potential indigenous tourism products will be ecotourism based' (Department of Tourism 1994b: 44). However, the entire Indigenous contribution to the National Ecotourism Strategy consisted of just 10 comments or submissions (out of 252) from four Aboriginal agencies and one Aboriginal tour operator, Desert Tracks. The strategy also received input from an ATSI Tourism Resource Steering Committee. This 1994 ecotourism strategy, however, is no longer Federal Government policy.

The ecotourism strategy for South Australia sought to increase the number of Aboriginal tourism operators, noting that 20 per cent of the state was held as Aboriginal freehold land. It featured Aboriginal culture and heritage as a key ecotourist attraction and included comments by ecotour operators. For example, Tom and George Trevorrow, the Aboriginal managers of Camp Coorong, stated: 'true ecotourism needs the meaningful involvement of Australia's indigenous people' (SATC 1994). However, specific programs to involve Aboriginal people in ecotourism were not outlined. In Tasmania, a discussion paper on ecotourism addressed the need for more Aboriginal heritage products and consultation with Aboriginal communities about tourism. It included a section on the 'Involvement of Tasmanian Aboriginals', focused on the needs of Aboriginal people in tourism and other issues in presenting Aboriginal heritage sites to visitors (Foley 1994).

In Queensland, Aboriginal interests and links with natural areas were recognised in the *Queensland Ecotourism Plan* (DTSBI 1997; TQ 2002). This included the Indigenous cultural significance of natural areas and Aboriginal guided tours interpreting Indigenous heritage in the natural environment. The plan included sections on Indigenous involvement in ecotourism and land management and Indigenous people as stakeholders in ecotourism. It recognised that Indigenous people could be involved in ecotourism as 'operators … guides and trainers, or as participants in ecotourism planning, management and operation' (DTSBI 1997: 33). Indigenous people were listed ninth of 10 key stakeholders in Queensland ecotourism. The plan emphasised the development of Indigenous ecotourism ventures and producing materials to support Indigenous involvement in ecotourism. It highlighted the opportunities for ecotours with an Indigenous cultural focus on Indigenous lands and national park areas. In this plan, Indigenous people were considered 'integral to all stakeholder groups' for ecotourism (DTSBI 1997: 52). However, Indigenous contributions to the ecotourism industry, government agencies and as natural resource managers were not specified.

Aboriginal cultural links with the natural environment and the benefits of Aboriginal involvement in ecotourism were also recognised in the *Nature-Based Tourism Strategy for Western Australia* (WATC 1997). The strategy included sections on Aboriginal tourism and Aboriginal community involvement in nature-based tourism. It particularly noted that Aboriginal knowledge of the environment would 'provide an enormous resource for the development of nature-based tourism products' (WATC 1997: 14). The strategy acknowledged the unique relationship between Aboriginal people and the land. It further recognised that Aboriginal lands contained cultural and nature-based assets of great interest to ecotour operators. However, practical methods for involving Aboriginal communities in nature-based tourism planning and activities or in Western Australia's national parks were not outlined. *Keeping It Real*, the revised and updated nature-based tourism strategy for Western Australia (WATC 2004b), supported Aboriginal tourism development and marketing, the need for Indigenous business skills, accreditation of Aboriginal operators and their cultural affinity with nature.

In contrast, Aboriginal involvement in rainforest-based tourism was central to the *Wet Tropics Nature-Based Tourism Strategy* (WTMA 2000). This tourism strategy for the Wet Tropics World Heritage Area (WHA) of North Queensland aimed to 'facilitate Aboriginal involvement in [nature] tourism and tourism management' (WTMA 2000: 3). It also acknowledged the native title rights of rainforest Aboriginal people and their role as participants and partners in managing nature tourism in the Wet Tropics WHA. The strategy included policy statements on 'Rainforest Aboriginal people's rights and interests', including the cultural responsibilities of native title holders, visitor site management involving traditional Aboriginal owners and Aboriginal involvement in nature-based tourism. The strategy outlined Aboriginal participation, employment and training in tourism, interpretation of natural and cultural values, and partnerships in tourism, such as Aboriginal cultural tours at Mossman Gorge. The Bama Wabu Rainforest Aboriginal Association was listed as a key partner in Wet Tropics marketing guidelines, monitoring visitor sites and setting accreditation levels for tour operators but not with tourism permits. (See Tourism Planning Breakthrough 'Indigenous tourism in protected areas'.)

TOURISM PLANNING BREAKTHROUGH
Indigenous tourism in protected areas

Participation of Indigenous people in tourism as park rangers and tour operators is a feature of national parks jointly managed with Aboriginal landowners, such as Uluru, Kakadu and Nitmiluk (Northern Territory), Mutawintji (New South Wales) and the Wet Tropics World Heritage Area (North Queensland). The traditional owners determine the cultural information or sites shared with visitors at cultural centres, interpretive signs and on Aboriginal-guided tours or ranger

(continued)

talks. Kakadu National Park is jointly managed with the Bininj/Mungguy traditional owners who comprise a majority (10 of 15) on the board of management. Half of Kakadu is Aboriginal land leased back as a national park with the remaining park areas being under land claims. Lease agreements with three Aboriginal land trusts provide for traditional uses, lease payments, a share in park revenue, Aboriginal employment and training, supporting Aboriginal enterprises and a licensing and induction system for all tour operators. More than 120 companies operate land-based tours, boat tours, canoeing and sport fishing in Kakadu. The park receives around 200 000 visitors a year, although there has been a decline since 1994; 50 per cent of visitors arrive between June and August (DEH 2005).

Parks Australia employs Aboriginal rangers and guides on Kakadu nature walks, art site talks and cultural activities in the dry season. Aboriginal groups own Yellow Water Cruises and Guluyambi Cruise in Kakadu, with the latter employing Aboriginal guides. The Gagudju Hotel in Jabiru is owned by Aboriginal organisations and employs Aboriginal people. Some tour or sport fishing operators also employ local Aboriginal guides. Park income for traditional owners was reduced in 2004, when entry fees to Kakadu were abolished. Aboriginal participation in tourism and Aboriginal culture is a key feature of the new strategy document *Walking to the Future ... Together: A Shared Vision for Tourism in Kakadu National Park* (Morse, King & Bartlett 2005). Traditional owners wanted new job opportunities for young Aboriginal people in tourism and government assistance with business skills and venture capital for Indigenous tourism ventures in Kakadu. Other aspects were managing the impact of tourism at popular rock art or waterfall sites, a stronger tourism focus in park management, business investment by the tourism industry and providing new visitor experiences or facilities in Kakadu based on Aboriginal heritage and the unique landscape. Aboriginal storytelling on guided tours and the unique six seasons of Kakadu in the Aboriginal calendar were to be featured in the tourist marketing and promotion of Kakadu.

Kakadu National Park has been jointly managed with traditional owners since 1979 (see Wearing & Huyskens 2001 for a review of joint management policy regimes in Australian national parks to 2000). The new tourism strategy for Kakadu promotes the economic development of Aboriginal communities through new businesses and joint ventures. The Indigenous cultural and natural values of Kakadu were also supported in this strategy, along with sustainable tourism. These tourism initiatives were to be included in the fifth Kakadu Plan of Management, 2004–11. Consultations with traditional owners, the tourism industry, parks staff, Aboriginal organisations and government tourism agencies contributed to this new strategy for Kakadu. This planning process provides a model for other jointly managed national parks in developing tourism opportunities and employment for Indigenous groups living in the area.

Social values and attitudes towards Indigenous people and Indigenous relationships with the land influence public policy-making for tourism. The current need for partnerships or consultation with Aboriginal people about national park management and tourism ventures have been driven mainly by federal legislation for Aboriginal land rights and native title. Both community values and legislation are reflected in the policy arena for ecotourism and nature-based tourism, for Aboriginal economic development and in strategies prepared for Indigenous tourism in Australia. Public tourism policies address Indigenous cultural heritage and environmental relationships, but have limited means for Indigenous participation in the control and management of ecotourism (see table 12.6). Tourism policies for industry bodies (e.g. Ecotourism Australian, Tourism Council Australia) and Aboriginal tourism strategies for southern states (i.e. New South Wales, Victoria, South Australia) still focus on Aboriginal people as cultural heritage custodians instead of as landowners. They mainly discuss consultation and negotiation processes with Indigenous people about cultural heritage, site management and appropriate use of Aboriginal culture in tourism. Other tourism policy focuses on Indigenous knowledge of the natural environment (including ecological and spiritual relationships), which is recognised as a prime asset in nature interpretation for ecotourists. Ecotourism and nature tourism strategies for Australia, Queensland and Western Australia mainly present Aboriginal people in terms of their affinity with the natural environment. They also include Aboriginal groups as stakeholders in ecotourism.

■ **Table 12.6** *Community values and policies for Aboriginal tourism and ecotourism*

Cultural heritage (consultation): Aboriginal heritage sites, cultural copyright	Aboriginal/Indigenous tourism strategies (NT, NSW, SA, Vic, WA, Kimberley—WA, Qld) *National ATSI Tourism Industry Strategy 1997* Ecotourism Australia; Interpretation Australia Association Heritage Council Australia
Natural environment (ecological relationship): environmental knowledge, interpretation	*National Ecotourism Strategy 1994* Ecotourism (Qld), nature tourism (WA) Aboriginal Tourism Australia Department of Industry, Tourism and Resources
Native title holders/ traditional owners (partnerships): Aboriginal lands, national parks	Aboriginal tourism (NT), Aboriginal economic development (WA, NT, Cape York Peninsula, Qld) *Wet Tropics Nature Based Tourism Strategy 2000 and Wet Tropics Walking Strategy 2001* (Qld) Wilderness Society, Australian Conservation Foundation, WWF Aboriginal land councils/corporations

Note:
ATSI: Aboriginal and Torres Strait Islander; WWF: World Wide Fund for Nature (formerly World Wildlife Fund).

Policies for non-government environment agencies (i.e. Australian Conservation Foundation, Wilderness Society) and Aboriginal land councils, however, recognise Indigenous people as landowners and native title holders with special rights and interests in land. Such policies promote Indigenous partnerships in national park management and Indigenous people controlling tourism on their lands. They recognise Indigenous people as key managers of land areas rather than just heritage sites. Strategies for Aboriginal tourism (Northern Territory) and Aboriginal economic development (Western Australia) address the need for beneficial tourism joint ventures with Indigenous landowners. In North Queensland, the nature tourism strategy for the Wet Tropics WHA has specific policies and legislation regarding the involvement of traditional landowners in site management and tourism. Eighty per cent of the Wet Tropics WHA is claimable under the Native Title Act. Public land policies recognising native title rights and tourism industry positions are required if Indigenous people are to have contemporary roles in Australian ecotourism. Indigenous members of ecotourism committees and on permit-granting bodies for protected areas are also needed.

CHAPTER REVIEW

This chapter has evaluated Indigenous tourism planning and policy in Australia between 1995 and 2004. It considered Indigenous participation in tourism and the changing roles of Indigenous people in tourism policy-making and government plans for developing Indigenous tourism or ecotourism. The policy environment for tourism and Indigenous people was analysed with reference to the level of Indigenous involvement and management roles in various tourism strategies.

Most Indigenous tourism ventures are located on Aboriginal lands or jointly managed national parks in northern and Central Australia. These enterprises included cultural tours, boat cruises, accommodation, cultural centres, crafts, ecotours and wildlife attractions. Indigenous tourism included unique Indigenous perspectives of the natural and cultural environment and provided economic benefits for local Indigenous people. These ventures, however, remained peripheral to the mainstream tourism industry. Southern Australian states (i.e. South Australia, Victoria, New South Wales and Tasmania) still have little Indigenous involvement in tourism. In the Northern Territory, Western Australia and Queensland, Aboriginal land rights and the *Native Title Act 1993* (Cwlth) have been the main policy influences on tourism strategies, including Indigenous groups as landowners and tourism partners.

Since the mid-1990s, Indigenous opportunities for tourism development have been included in Indigenous tourism strategies, some economic development strategies and in plans or strategies for nature tourism and ecotourism. Most of these plans focused on the economic and social benefits of Indigenous tourism, along with access to Indigenous heritage sites and national parks. Indigenous consultation was a key feature of new tourism plans prepared for the Northern Territory, Kakadu National Park and the Wet Tropics rainforest of North Queensland. This chapter suggests that tourism policies and plans address Indigenous cultural heritage and environmental relationships, but have limited means for Indigenous participation in the control and management of tourism as native title holders and traditional owners. Few Indigenous people are employed by state or federal tourism agencies, and involvement of Indigenous people in public tourism planning and policies is very limited.

SUMMARY OF KEY TERMS

Aboriginal

The native or original peoples of mainland Australia, Tasmania and offshore islands. The people descended from and recognised by Aboriginal groups; also Koori, Murri and Noongar.

Aboriginal tourism

Tourism product that is Aboriginal owned or operated, employs Aboriginal people and/or provides consenting contact with Aboriginal people, culture or land.

Diversified indigenous tourism

Tourism ventures such as transport, accommodation and visitor services that are controlled by Indigenous people but do not have Indigenous culture as their main theme.

Economic rationalism

An economic model in which monetary value or financial gain dominates in selling goods or services for profit.

Export ready

A tourism product that has a commission fee for agents included in the wholesale price, can be purchased in tourism export markets (international or domestic) and is reliably available in the destination area.

Indigenous cultural tourism

Cultural tourism product based on an Indigenous culture, heritage site or experience (e.g. culture centre, festival, rock art, arts and crafts). Typically involves Indigenous ownership or joint venture enterprise that emphasises Indigenous interpretation, cultural authenticity and cultural maintenance.

Indigenous ecotourism

Nature-based attractions or tours owned by Indigenous people as well as Indigenous interpretation of the natural and cultural environment on cultural ecotours.

Indigenous people

The native groups or original inhabitants of the land, such as Aboriginal people and Torres Strait Islanders. Indigenous people have continuous cultural, spiritual and environmental ties to the land.

Indigenous tourism

All forms of participation by Aboriginal and Torres Strait Islander people in tourism: as employers, as employees, as investors, as joint venture partners, providing indigenous cultural tourism products and providing mainstream tourism products.

Native title

Native title recognises traditional owners and Indigenous rights of access, use, possession or occupation of Crown lands and pastoral leases in Australia, under the *Native Title Act 1993* (Cwlth).

Policy arena

The interest groups, institutions and key individuals that influence the process of making policies.

Policy environment

The political power, economic and social values and institutional arrangements that determine the process of policy-making.

Tourism policy-making

The process of government agencies and industry bodies devising and implementing tourism policy.

QUESTIONS

1 What is meant by the term 'Indigenous tourism'?

2 What is Indigenous tourism planning?

3 Discuss the changing nature of Indigenous involvement in tourism policy-making. In the context of this chapter, is this a form of 'public policy-making'?

4 What is the economic rationalism approach to Indigenous tourism policy?

5 Identify and discuss the key factors that influence Indigenous tourism planning and policy development.

6 Reflect on your cultural values and interests. How might they affect the ways in which you might address an Indigenous tourism policy issue? Give examples.

7 Why are cultural heritage and nature conservation important for Indigenous tourism? Provide an example of a tourism development issue that clashes with Indigenous values for heritage sites and natural areas.

EXERCISES

1 Locate and copy 10–15 articles on Indigenous tourism issues from an Aboriginal newspaper (e.g. *Koori Mail, Murri Views, The Aboriginal, Land Council News*). Identify the key tourism planning and policy issues covered in Indigenous media. What are the Indigenous perspectives on these tourism planning and policy issues? Identify overlaps with general tourism planning and policy development.

2 Locate two or three of the Indigenous tourism strategies or plans reviewed in this chapter. Find the definition of Aboriginal or Indigenous tourism and the objectives or aims listed in each of these tourism plans or reports. Complete the following exercises:
(a) Compare and contrast the way Aboriginal or Indigenous tourism has been defined.
(b) Decide whether the objectives or aims are focused on economic, cultural or environmental outcomes of tourism for Indigenous peoples.
(c) Which government agency developed the plan? Discuss what might be the dominant interests driving Indigenous tourism planning in each report (e.g. economic development, growing visitor markets, managing tourism impact, cultural revival, access to Indigenous land).

FURTHER READING

Aboriginal Tourism Australia 2005, *ATA Key National Programs,* **ATA, Melbourne, viewed 12 April 2006, www.ataust.org.au/ about.asp?data=010C07064D4C4F497557584C434D4C.** Marketing programs and business development activities of the national industry association promoting Aboriginal tourism across Australia.

Butler, R & Hinch, T (eds) 1996, *Tourism and Indigenous Peoples,* **International Thomson Business Press, London.** The first book on Indigenous involvement in tourism; it reviews cultural products and diversified Indigenous tourism ventures and includes case studies on Pacific islands, Australia, the USA, Indonesia, Nepal and Thailand.

Buultjens, J, Waller, I, Graham, S & Carson, D 2002, *Public Sector Initiatives for Aboriginal Small Business Development in Tourism,* **Occasional Paper No. 6, Centre for Regional Tourism Research, Southern Cross University, Lismore, NSW.** Review of Australian government funding and assistance programs for developing and supporting Aboriginal tourism businesses.

Department of Industry, Science and Resources 2000, *National Indigenous Tourism Forum: Tourism an Indigenous Opportunity, 2–4 June,* **DISR, Canberra, viewed 4 May 2006, www.industry.gov.au/assets/documents/ itrinternet/IndigenousForum2000Communique.pdf.** Conference papers by government, tourism industry and Aboriginal people on opportunities and obstacles for developing Indigenous tourism.

Department of Industry, Tourism and Resources 2004a, 'Demand for nature-based and Indigenous tourism product: Findings on Indigenous

product', viewed 4 May 2006, www.industry.gov.au/assets/documents/
itrinternet/5_Findings__Indigenous_products20041110165259.pdf.
National survey of Australian tourist demand for Indigenous tourism
products, activities and experiences.

——2004b, Research result summary demand for Indigenous tourism
product, 'What are tourists looking for in Indigenous tourism?', DITR,
Canberra, viewed 12 April 2006, www.industry.gov.au/assets/documents/
itrinternet/survey_indigenous_ART20041110152059.pdf. Market
research report on visitor demand for Indigenous tourism products,
activities and experiences.

Pitcher, M, van Oosterzee, P & Palmer, L 1999, *Choice and Control: The
Development of Indigenous Tourism in Australia*, Centre for Indigenous Natural
and Cultural Resource Management & CRC for Sustainable Tourism,
Darwin, NT. Assessment of cultural, environmental, land tenure and
business issues for Aboriginal groups to control and benefit from tourism.

Ryan, C & Aicken, M (eds) 2005, *Indigenous Tourism: The Commodification
and Management of Culture*, Elsevier, Oxford. Critical review and analysis
of Indigenous culture as a tourism product and controlling tourism on
Indigenous land; includes case study chapters on the USA, Canada,
China, Indonesia, Africa, Scandinavia, Australia and New Zealand.

Singh, S et al. 2001, *Aboriginal Australia and the Torres Strait Islands: Guide to
Indigenous Australia*, Lonely Planet, Footscray, Vic. First travel guide to
profile Indigenous tourism products around Australia, linked with
traditional Aboriginal tribal or clan territories.

Tourism Australia 2003, 'Market research intelligence on Aboriginal
tourism', *Segment Insights Pack, March 2003*, Australian Tourist
Commission, Sydney, viewed 12 April 2006, www.tourism.australia.com/
content/Research/aboriginal_research_0303.pdf. Industry market
research on international visitor demand for Aboriginal tourism
products.

Tourism Queensland 2002, 'Indigenous tourism', Special Interest Fact
Sheets, viewed 12 April 2006, www.tq.com.au/tq_com/dms/
50E01489E86C4131684C06571E25C4A5.pdf. Research review of visitor
market segments, product gaps and key issues for the emerging
Aboriginal tourism sector.

Zeppel, H 2001, 'Aboriginal cultures and indigenous tourism', in N Douglas,
N Douglas & R Derrett (eds), *Special Interest Tourism: Context and Cases*,
John Wiley & Sons Australia, Brisbane, pp. 232–59. Profiles Indigenous
culture as a special interest area of tourism; includes an overview of
Aboriginal tourism products, cultural issues, marketing and training
needs for Indigenous people involved in Australian tourism.

—— 2003, 'Sharing the country: Ecotourism policy and Indigenous peoples
in Australia', in DA Fennell & RK Dowling (eds), *Ecotourism Policy and
Planning*, CABI, Wallingford, UK, pp. 55–76. Critical review of Australian
government plans for developing Aboriginal tourism and Indigenous
culture within ecotourism and nature-based tourism.

Indigenous tourism in the Wet Tropics

Rainforest Aboriginal people ('Bama') are key stakeholders in tourism planning and policy for the Wet Tropics World Heritage Area (WHA) of North Queensland, Australia. Aboriginal consultation and involvement is required in legislation, management plans and policies, with 80 per cent of the Wet Tropics WHA being claimable under native title. Strategies for nature tourism and walking tracks include site management, presenting Aboriginal cultural heritage values and developing Aboriginal tourism ventures in the Wet Tropics.

Rainforest Aboriginal people

There are 18 to 19 Rainforest Aboriginal groups living within the Wet Tropics WHA, comprising around 20 000 people. The rainforest provides food, medicine and tools, and social practices; cultural sites and spiritual beliefs link Aboriginal groups to rainforest areas (WTMA 2005a). The Wet Tropics Management Authority (WTMA) assists Rainforest Aboriginal groups in managing their traditional country, with administrative support, funding and facilities for cultural tourism such as interpretive signs, walking tracks, cultural centres and tours (WTMA 2005b). Native title interests, Indigenous land use agreements (ILUA) and management agreements are also negotiated with Rainforest Aboriginal groups to resolve use of land and natural resources. Some 26 453ha of land in the Wet Tropics WHA is under Indigenous management with Aboriginal communities at Wujal Wujal, Mona Mona (near Kuranda) and Yarrabah. By 2004, 16 native title claims had been lodged over 32 per cent of land (282 966ha) in the Wet Tropics WHA (WTMA 2004a). In December 2004 the Djabugay people won their native title claim over 92 per cent of the 2800ha Barron Gorge National Park between Cairns and Kuranda. Other agreements are being negotiated with the traditional owners of Gadgara State Forest, Wooroonooran National Park, Yarrabah and Buru (China Camp) in the Daintree. Aboriginal cultural heritage values and native title interests are also included in the *Wet Tropics Conservation Strategy* (WTMA 2004b).

Wet Tropics tourism

Rainforest-based nature tourism and ecotourism is a major activity in the Wet Tropics WHA. In 1998 more than 210 commercial tour operators had permits to operate in the Wet Tropics region, and the Wet Tropics received 2.8 million visitors per year (WTMA 2000). Tourism in the Wet Tropics WHA directly generates A$179 million, and flow-on tourism expenditure in the local region was around A$753 million in 1993 (Driml 1997). Visitor spending in the Wet

Tropics now exceeds A$2 billion annually with tourism accounting for 35–40 per cent of regional income and employment (WTMA 2003). At present, Rainforest Aboriginal groups do not receive any licensing income from tourism operations in the Wet Tropics nor do visitors pay park entry fees at popular rainforest sites, such as waterfalls, lakes and rainforest boardwalks. Apart from consulting with traditional owners about site management, there is limited Aboriginal participation in the planning and management of tourism in the Wet Tropics WHA (Driml 2000; Zeppel 2002).

Aboriginal tourism enterprises in the Wet Tropics include Kuku-Yalanji Dreamtime Walks in Mossman Gorge (Sofield 2002); Native Guide Safari Tours conducted by Hazel Douglas in the Daintree; the Walker sisters' guided tours at Wujal Wujal; Tjapukai Aboriginal Cultural Park in Cairns; didgeridoo making and playing with M & J Aboriginality (Babinda); Waroo Tours to Yarrabah, Mossman and Wujal Wujal; and guided rainforest walks at Malanda Falls with Ngadjonji elder Ernie Raymont. Aboriginal cultural tours and craft activities are offered at three resorts in the Daintree area. Rainforest Aboriginal groups also give dance performances and cultural talks at Rainforestation (Kuranda) and since 2003 at Paronella Park (Innisfail). Other Aboriginal participation in Wet Tropics tourism includes arts and crafts, cultural centres, constructing boardwalks and cultural interpretation signs in national parks (WTMA 2001). In 2002 Johnstone Shire Council signed an agreement with Ma:Mu Aboriginal people for a new rainforest canopy tower to be built near Innisfail. This agreement involved protection of cultural heritage and Aboriginal employment opportunities in construction and cultural tourism at the new canopy tower (JSC 2002).

Institutional context for Indigenous involvement

The involvement of Rainforest Aboriginal communities is set out in Queensland and Commonwealth Wet Tropics WHA legislation (1993–94), the *Wet Tropics Management Plan 1998* (section 62) and in the key policy document *Protection through Partnerships*. This involvement includes the need to consult Rainforest Aboriginal people on cultural sites, land use and permits. Formal protocols guide these consultations. There is an Aboriginal member on the WTMA board of directors and two Aboriginal members on the Community Consultative Committee, but no Aboriginal operator on the Tourism Industry Liaison Group. The WTMA Aboriginal Resource Management Unit employs three Aboriginal community liaison officers on a contract basis. These Aboriginal staff members liaise with traditional owners in the northern, central and southern Wet Tropics region on land management issues, including tourism. They help provide Aboriginal views and contributions to Wet Tropics planning and policies for nature tourism, walking tracks and conservation. The new Aboriginal Rainforest Council and formerly the Bama Wabu Association also represent Wet Tropics native title holders on all land and cultural heritage management issues. In April 2005, 18 Rainforest Aboriginal groups, WTMA and the Queensland and

(continued)

Federal governments signed a new Wet Tropics Regional Management Agreement to involve traditional owners effectively in rainforest management (WTMA 2004a).

Since the mid-1990s Rainforest Aboriginal people have sought to have the Wet Tropics officially relisted for its Indigenous cultural values in order to manage the WHA jointly. With this official cultural recognition or heritage listing, 'they would become equal partners rather than seen simply as "stakeholders" ' in Wet Tropics management, including tourism (WTMA 2005a).

Indigenous tourism planning and policy

Aboriginal involvement in rainforest tourism was addressed in the *Wet Tropics Nature Based Tourism Strategy* (WTMA 2000). This strategy promoted Aboriginal cultural heritage values and Aboriginal participation in nature tourism. 'Tourism use should contribute to the conservation and understanding of Aboriginal cultural heritage and help Aboriginal people as tourism industry participants to achieve economic and social benefits' (WTMA 2000). ATSIC, Bama Wabu and local Indigenous groups contributed to policies and principles for nature tourism. Consultation with traditional owners about site planning and management was required for most of the popular visitor areas in the Wet Tropics. Rainforest Aboriginal interests in tourism or cultural interpretation were also mentioned for 18 sites, including Mossman Gorge, Cathedral Fig Tree, Lake Barrine, Lake Eacham, Tully Gorge and five scenic waterfalls. Other sites were under review with traditional Aboriginal groups about tourism use (e.g. Roaring Meg Falls, Bare Hill, North Johnstone rafting sites and Lamins Hill Lookout). The strategy noted the need for assessment of the impact of tourism on Aboriginal cultural landscapes in the Wet Tropics. Unfortunately, it did not address the programs, funding or training required for developing Aboriginal tourism ventures at key sites.

The *Wet Tropics Walking Strategy* identified 145 managed walks in the WHA region. It acknowledged the Aboriginal cultural significance of walking trails; many being based on traditional trading routes through rainforest areas. The Indigenous cultural setting was one of four key criteria used to assess walk experiences, focusing on Indigenous history, use, perceptions, names, cultural associations and stories about walkways. The strategy also highlighted opportunities for Aboriginal groups in track construction, maintenance and cultural tourism. Walking track management by community rangers and Indigenous cultural walks were identified for key rainforest areas, such as Malanda Falls, Bare Hill, Wabunga Wayemba, Echo Creek Falls, Barron Gorge and Murray Falls (WTMA 2001). Other key issues were walking track routes, permits and funding for track construction.

The Wet Tropics WHA has specific legislation, policies and plans regarding the involvement of traditional Aboriginal landowners in site management and tourism. The nature tourism and walking strategies for the Wet Tropics promote Aboriginal cultural heritage values and Aboriginal participation in tourism. These tourism strategies need the support of government agencies, Aboriginal groups and the commercial sector to manage cultural sites effectively. This case study illustrates that Aboriginal consultation on land management and cultural heritage is the main outcome of tourism planning and policy for the Wet Tropics WHA.

Questions

1 List all the key agencies involved in Aboriginal tourism planning and policy in the Wet Tropics WHA.

2 What are the main types of Aboriginal tourism venture in the Wet Tropics WHA? How does the Wet Tropics Management Authority support Aboriginal tourism?

3 What are the key economic, social or cultural goals for Aboriginal tourism in the Nature Tourism Strategy and the Walking Strategy for the Wet Tropics WHA?

4 Explain the importance of native title and land management agreements for Aboriginal tourism. Identify any possible conflicts between culture and tourism.

References

Driml, S 1997, *Towards Sustainable Tourism in the Wet Tropics World Heritage Area*, Report to the Wet Tropics Management Authority, Cairns, WTMA.
—— 2000, 'Ecotourism—opportunities and threats', in G MacDonald & M Lane (eds), *Securing the Wet Tropics*, Federation Press, Leichhardt, NSW, pp. 200–18.
Johnstone Shire Council 2002, 'MaMu Canopy Walk heads of agreement (20 March 2002)', JSC, Innisfail, Qld, viewed 12 June 2006, www.atns.net.au/biogs/A000396b.htm.
Sofield, THB 2002, 'Australian Aboriginal ecotourism in the Wet Tropics Rainforest of Queensland', *Australia Mountain Research and Development*, vol. 22, no. 2, pp. 118–22.
Wet Tropics Aboriginal Plan Project Team 2005, 'Tourism', in *Caring for Country and Culture: The Wet Tropics Aboriginal Cultural and Natural Resource Management Plan*, Rainforest CRC & FNQ NRM Ltd, Cairns, pp. 93–8, viewed 4 May 2006, www.rainforest-crc.jcu.edu.au/publications/research%20reports/NRMSeries/AboriginalPlan/preliminaryPages.pdf.
Wet Tropics Management Authority 2000, *Wet Tropics Nature-Based Tourism Strategy*, WTMA, Cairns, viewed 4 May 2006, www.wettropics.gov.au/mwha/mwha_pdf/Strategies/naturebased_tourism.pdf.
—— 2001, *Wet Tropics Walking Strategy*, WTMA, Cairns, viewed 4 May 2006, www.wettropics.gov.au/mwha/mwha_pdf/Strategies/Walking%20Strategy.pdf.
—— 2003, 'Tourism and recreation', in *Annual Report 2002–2003*, WTMA, Cairns, pp. 48–50, viewed 8 June 2006, www.wettropics.gov.au/mwha/mwha_pdf/annual_reports/2003a_report.pdf.
—— 2004a, 'Aboriginal interests in land', in *Annual Report and State of the Wet Tropics Report 2003–04*, WTMA, Cairns, pp. 30–3.
—— 2004b, 'Aboriginal cultural heritage values' and 'Aboriginal interests', in *Wet Tropics Conservation Strategy Summary*, WTMA, Cairns, pp. 4, 10.
—— 2005a, 'Rainforest Aboriginal Heritage', viewed 12 April 2006, www.wettropics.gov.au/rah/rah_cult_tourism.html.
—— 2005b, 'Cultural tourism', viewed 12 April 2006, www.wettropics.gov.au/rah/culture_tourism.htm.
Zeppel, H 2002, 'Indigenous tourism in the Wet Tropics World Heritage Area', *North Queensland Australian Aboriginal Studies*, Special Issue: Australian Indigenous Heritage Tourism, 2002/2, pp. 65–8.

ACKNOWLEDGEMENTS

Staff at state tourism organisations kindly forwarded copies of Aboriginal tourism and nature tourism and ecotourism strategies. Sue Muloin provided helpful comments on a draft of this chapter.

REFERENCES

Altman, J & Finlayson, J 1993, 'Aborigines, tourism and sustainable development', *Journal of Tourism Studies*, vol. 4, no. 1, pp. 38–50.

Australian Conservation Foundation 2000, 'ACF policies', www.acfonline.org.au/asp/pages/policy.asp.

Australian Institute of Aboriginal and Torres Strait Islander Studies 2004, 'Innovation and sustainability in indigenous tourism', abstracts, AIATSIS Conference, 22–25 November, Canberra, viewed 8 June 2006, www.aiatsis. gov.au/research_program/events2/conferences_and_workshops/conf 2004_papers/abstracts#Bennett.

Australian National Training Authority 2001, 'Indigenous ecotourism toolbox', www.dlsweb.rmit.edu.au/toolbox/Indigenous/ ecotourismtoolbox/home.html.

Aboriginal and Torres Strait Islander Commission 1996, *On Our Own Terms: Promoting Aboriginal and Torres Strait Islander Involvement in the Australian Tourism Industry*, ATSIC, Canberra.

—— 1997a, *National Aboriginal and Torres Strait Islander Tourism Industry Strategy*, ATSIC & Office of National Tourism, Canberra.

—— 1997b, *National Aboriginal and Torres Strait Islander Cultural Industry Strategy*, ATSIC & Department of Primary Industries and Energy, Canberra.

—— 1997c, 'Rural tourism', in *National Aboriginal and Torres Strait Islander Rural Industry Strategy*, ATSIC & Department of Primary Industries and Energy, Canberra.

Aboriginal Tourism Australia 2005, 'Cultural protocols', www.ataust.org.au/ indigenousasp?data=0608000A4D4C4F497D5B535050545E5D414A17625 45F435951494B.

Bissett, C, Perry, L & Zeppel, H 1998, 'Land and spirit: Aboriginal tourism in New South Wales', in S McArthur & B Weir (eds), *Australia's Ecotourism Industry: A Snapshot in 1998*, Ecotourism Association of Australia, Brisbane, pp. 6–8.

Blamey, RK 1995, *The Nature of Ecotourism*, Occasional Paper No. 21, Bureau of Tourism Research, Canberra.

Burchett, C 1992, 'Ecologically sustainable development and its relationship to Aboriginal tourism in the Northern Territory', in B Weiler (ed.), *Ecotourism Incorporating the Global Classroom*, Bureau of Tourism Research, Canberra, pp. 70–4.

Crawshaw, I 2005, *Aboriginal and Indigenous Australia: An Owner's Manual*, Cactus Media, Sydney.

Department of the Environment and Heritage 2005, 'Tourism issues in Kakadu', *Kakadu National Park Management Plan 2004–11*, www.deh.gov.au/parks/publications/kakadu-tourism.html.

Department of Industry, Science and Resources 2000, 'National Indigenous Tourism Forum: Tourism—the Indigenous opportunity', DISR, Canberra, www.industry.gov.au/assets/documents/itrinternet/IndigenousForum 2000Communique.pdf.

Department of State Development 2004, *Cape York Partnerships Economic Development Policy Framework*, Cape York Partnerships Unit, Department of State Development, Brisbane, www.sdi.qld.gov.au/dsdweb/v3/guis/ templates/content/gui_cue_doccfm?id=4014.

Department of Tourism 1994a, *A Talent for Tourism: Stories about Indigenous People in Tourism*, Department of Tourism, Canberra.

—— 1994b, *National Ecotourism Strategy*, AGPS, Canberra.

Department of Tourism, Small Business and Industry 1997, *Queensland Ecotourism Plan*, DTSBI, Brisbane.

Dowling, R 1998, 'The growth of Australian ecotourism', in J Kandampully (ed.), *Advances in Research: Proceedings of New Zealand Tourism and Hospitality Research Conference 1998*, Part 1, Lincoln University, Canterbury, New Zealand.

Driml, S 1997, *Towards Sustainable Tourism in the Wet Tropics World Heritage Area*, Report to the Wet Tropics Management Authority, Cairns, WTMA.

Ecotourism Australia, 2006, 'What is ecotourism?', EA, viewed 8 June 2006, www.ecotourism.org.au/index.asp.

—— 2005, 'Eco-Certification Program', EA, Brisbane, www.ecotourism.org.au/eco_certification.asp.

Ecotourism News 2000, 'Aborigines offer ecotourism more than just the didgeridoo', *Ecotourism News* (EAA), Spring 2000, p. 6.

Elder, B 2005, 'Feel the spirit', *Sydney Morning Herald*, 30 April–1 May 2005, pp. 1, 6–7.

Ellis, A 2003, 'Indigenous tourism strategy', *Seizing our Economic Future: Indigenous Economic Forum 2003*, forum papers, transcripts, speech notes and summaries, www.indigenousforums.nt.gov.au/dcm/indigenous_ policy/forums/pdf/Anthony%20Ellis.pdf.

Foley, J 1994, *Ecotourism: Adding Value to Tourism in Natural Areas*, A Discussion Paper on Nature-Based Tourism, July 1994, Department of Tourism, Sport and Recreation, Hobart.

Global Tourism and Leisure 1996, *Kimberley Aboriginal Cultural Tourism Strategy*, Kimberley Aboriginal Tourism Association.

Grekin, J & Milne, S 1996, 'Towards sustainable tourism development: The case of Pond Inlet, NWT', in R Butler & T Hinch (eds), *Tourism and Indigenous Peoples*, International Thomson Business Press, London, pp. 76–106.

Hall, CM, Jenkins, J & Kearsley, G 1997, *Tourism Planning and Policy in Australia andNew Zealand: Cases, Issues and Practice*, McGraw-Hill, Sydney.

Hinch, T 1998, 'Ecotourists and Indigenous hosts: Diverging views on their relationship with nature', *Current Issues in Tourism*, vol. 1, no. 1, pp. 120–4.

Howard, J, Thwaites, R & Smith, B 2001, 'Investigating the roles of the indigenous tour guide', *Journal of Tourism Studies*, vol. 12, no. 2, pp. 32–9.

James, D 1994, 'Desert tracks', in *A Talent for Tourism: Stories about Indigenous People in Tourism*, Department of Tourism, Canberra, pp. 10–12.

Mercer, D 1994, 'Native peoples and tourism: Conflict and compromise', in WF Theobald (ed.), *Global Tourism: The Next Decade*, Butterworth Heinemann, Boston, pp. 124–45.

Miller, G 1996, 'Indigenous tourism: A Queensland perspective', in H Richins, J Richardson & A Crabtree (eds), *Ecotourism and Nature-based Tourism: Taking the Next Steps*, Ecotourism Association of Australia, Brisbane, pp. 45–57.

Morse, J, King, J & Bartlett, B 2005, *Walking to the Future … Together: A Shared Vision forTourism in Kakadu National Park*, Department of the Environment and Heritage, Canberra, www.deh.gov.au/parks/publications/kakadu/tourism-vision/index.html.

Muloin, S, Zeppel, H & Higginbottom, K 2000, 'Indigenous wildlife tourism in Australia: Issues and opportunities', *4th New Zealand Tourism and Hospitality Conference*, Auckland University of Technology, Auckland, viewed 2 August 2005, http://online.aut.ac.nz/conferences/NZTHRC/conf.nsf/programme?OpenView.

—— 2001, *Indigenous Wildlife Tourism in Australia: Wildlife Attractions, Cultural Interpretation and Indigenous Involvement*, CRC for Sustainable Tourism, Gold Coast.

Nielsen, N 2005, 'The need for Aboriginal-driven tourism planning in regional NSW', in P Tremblay & A Boyle (eds), *Sharing Tourism Knowledge*, CAUTHE 2005 Conference Proceedings, Charles Darwin University, Darwin, NT, pp. 331–43.

Northern Territory Tourist Commission 1996, *Aborginal Tourism Strategy*, NTTC, Darwin.

—— 2004, *Northern Territory Indigenous Tourism Strategy*, NTTC, Darwin, viewed 8 June 2006, www.tourismnt.com.au/nt/nttc/industry/strategies/indigenous.html.

Office of Aboriginal Economic Development 1997, *Aboriginal Economic Development in Western Australia: A Strategy for Responsive Government Services and Programs*, OAED, Department of Commerce and Trade, Perth.

Office of National Tourism 2001, *Ecotourism*, Tourism Facts No. 15, Department of Industry, Science and Resources, Canberra.

Office of Northern Development (ed.) 1993, *Indigenous Australians and Tourism: A Focus on Northern Australia*, ATSIC & Office of Northern Development, Darwin.

Office of Territory Development 2002, *Building a Better Territory: The Economic Development Strategy for the Northern Territory*, Northern Territory Government, Darwin, viewed 8 June 2006, www.nt.gov.au/dcm/publications/policies/20020226EconomicDevStrategy.pdf.

Pitcher, M, van Oosterzee, P & Palmer, L 1999, *Choice and Control: The Development of Indigenous Tourism in Australia*, Centre for Indigenous Natural and Cultural Resource Management & CRC Tourism, Darwin.

Ross, H 1991, 'Controlling access to environment and self: Aboriginal perspectives on tourism', *Australian Psychologist*, vol. 26, no. 3, pp. 176–82.

Scheyvens, R 1999, 'Ecotourism and the empowerment of local communities', *Tourism Management*, vol. 20, no. 2, pp. 245–9.

—— 2000, 'Promoting women's empowerment through involvement in ecotourism: Experiences from the Third World', *Journal of Sustainable Tourism*, vol. 8, no. 3, pp. 232–49.

Singh, S et al. 2001, *Aboriginal Australia and the Torres Strait Islands: Guide to Indigenous Australia*, Lonely Planet, Footscray, Vic.

South Australian Tourism Commission 1994, *Ecotourism: A Natural Strategy for South Australia*, SATC, Adelaide.

—— 1995, *Aboriginal Tourism Strategy*, SATC, Adelaide.

—— 2000, *Nature Based Tourism Strategy*, SATC, Adelaide.

Sutton, M 1999, 'Aboriginal ownership of National Parks and tourism', *Cultural Survival Quarterly*, vol. 23, no. 2, pp. 55–6.

Sykes, L 1995, 'Welcome to our land', *Geographical Magazine*, vol. 67, no. 10, pp. 22–5.

Tourism Australia 2003, 'Market research intelligence on Aboriginal tourism', *Segment Insights Pack, March 2003*, Australian Tourist Commission, Sydney, viewed 12 April 2006, www.tourism.australia.com/content/Research/aboriginal_research_0303.pdf.

Tourism Council Australia 1999, *Policy and Research—Indigenous Tourism*, TCA, Sydney.

Tourism New South Wales 1997, *Indigenous Tourism Product Development Principles*, Tourism NSW, Sydney.

Tourism Queensland 2002a, 'Indigenous tourism', Special Interest Fact Sheets, viewed 2 August 2005, www.tq.com.au/tq_com/dms/50E01489E86C4131684C06571E25C4A5.pdf.

—— 2002b, *Queensland Ecotourism Plan, 2003–2008: Sustainable Tourism in Queensland's Natural Areas*, Tourism Queensland, Brisbane, viewed 4 May 2006, www.tq.com.au/tq_com/dms/F3DDBA55A064F3695E27649C38F1D755.pdf.

—— 2004, 'Indigenous tourism strategy: Including Indigenous people in tourism', August, Tourism Queensland, Brisbane, viewed 26 May 2006, www.tq.com.au/tq_com/dms/E37CFAEA0126F22A07512E1C9910C3F5.pdf.

Tourism Victoria 1998, *Aboriginal Tourism Industry Plan*, Melbourne, Tourism Victoria.

Wearing, S & Huyskens, M 2001, 'Moving on from joint management policy regimes in Australian national parks', *Current Issues in Tourism*, vol. 4, nos 2, 3, 4, pp. 182–209.

Weiler, B 1997, 'Meeting the ecotourism education and training needs of Australia's indigenous community', in W Nuryanti (ed.), *Tourism and Heritage Management*, Gadjah Mada University Press, Yogyakarta, Indonesia, pp. 304–16.

Western Australian Tourism Commission 1997, *Nature Based Tourism Strategy for Western Australia*, WATC, Perth.

—— 1999, *Guide to Kimberley Aboriginal Product Experiences*, WATC, Broome.

—— 2004a, *An Aboriginal Tourism Marketing Strategy for Western Australia: A Discussion Paper*, Perth, WATC.

—— 2004b, *Keeping It Real: A Nature Based Tourism Strategy for Western Australia*, Perth, WATC.

Wet Tropics Management Authority 2000, *Wet Tropics Nature-Based Tourism Strategy*, WTMA, Cairns, www.wettropics.gov.au/mwha/mwha_pdf/nature.pdf.

—— 2001, *Wet Tropics Walking Strategy*, WTMA, Cairns, veiwed 4 May 2006, www.wettropics.gov.au/mwha/mwha_pdf/Strategies/Walking%20Strategy.pdf.

—— 2002, 'Rainforest Aboriginal heritage—people of the rainforest', WTMA, Cairns, www.wettropics.gov.au/rah/rah_default.html.

Whitford, M, Bell, B & Watkins, M 2001, 'Indigenous tourism policy in Australia: 25 years of rhetoric and economic rationalism', *Current Issues in Tourism*, vol. 4, nos 2, 3, 4, pp. 151–81.

Wilderness Society 1999, *Tourism in Natural Areas*, Policy 16, May 1999, www.wildernessorgau/member/tws/projects/General/tourismhtml.

Zeppel, H 1998a, 'Selling the Dreamtime: Aboriginal culture in Australian tourism', in D Rowe & G Lawrence (eds), *Tourism, Leisure, Sport: Critical Perspectives*, Hodder Headline, Sydney, pp. 23–38.

—— 1998b, 'Beyond the Dreaming: Developing Aboriginal tourism in Australia', in J Kandampully (ed.), *Advances in Research: Proceedings of New Zealand Tourism and Hospitality Research Conference 1998*, Part 1, Lincoln University, Canterbury, New Zealand.

—— 1998c, 'Land and culture: Sustainable tourism and indigenous peoples', in CM Hall & A Lew (eds), *Sustainable Tourism: A Geographical Perspective*, Addison Wesley Longman, London, pp. 60–74.

—— 1998d, 'Tourism and Aboriginal Australia', *Tourism Management*, vol. 19, no. 5, pp. 485–8.

—— 1999, *Aboriginal Tourism in Australia: A Research Bibliography*, CRC Tourism Research Report Series, Report 2, CRC for Sustainable Tourism, Gold Coast, Qld.

—— 2000, 'Ecotourism and Indigenous peoples. Issues', *All Australian Educational Magazine*, vol. 51, July. Special Issue: Ecotourism.

—— 2001, 'Aboriginal cultures and indigenous tourism', in N Douglas, N Douglas & R Derrett (eds), *Special Interest Tourism: Context and Cases*, John Wiley & Sons Australia, Brisbane, pp. 232–59.

—— 2002, 'Indigenous tourism in the Wet Tropics World Heritage Area', *North Queensland Australian Aboriginal Studies*, 2002/2, pp. 65–8.

—— 2003, 'Sharing the country: Ecotourism policy and Indigenous peoples in Australia', in DA Fennell & RK Dowling (eds), *Ecotourism Policy and Planning*, CABI, Wallingford, UK, pp. 55–76.

Dianne Dredge and
John Jenkins

CHAPTER 13

Conclusion:
challenges and issues

LEARNING OBJECTIVES

After reading this chapter you will be able to:

1 discuss the relationships between tourism policy and planning research and practice

2 identify the challenges of tourism policy and planning research

3 identify the challenges of tourism policy and planning practice

4 discuss the skills, knowledge and characteristics of reflective tourism policy and planning practitioners.

13.1 INTRODUCTION

> Generally, one should not permit oneself to be bound too rigidly or too dogmatically to a particular model ... the explanation of political behaviour, rather than the validation of a given theoretical approach, should be the main purpose of political inquiry and analysis. (Anderson, 1984: 25.)

Anderson's quote raises an interesting conundrum about what policy researchers ought to aspire to do. Anderson challenges us to see the world in different ways than we normally might and, more explicitly, to accept that one theoretical approach cannot adequately explain policy and planning processes. This approach underpins this book. Its main thrust is to present theoretical frameworks, ideas, concepts, methods and approaches that can be used to build critical and reflective understandings of tourism policy and planning. The aim of this book is to help readers develop and enhance their skills and knowledge of tourism policy and planning processes, contexts and settings.

Of course, good policy research does not stand alone. It should not be research for the sake of research. Policy and planning research should be the conduit between theory and practice that provides insights and a balanced and critical view of decisions, actions, events, opportunities and effects, and problems. But most importantly it should inform the practice of policy-making and simultaneously advance theory. Practitioners devoid of the insights provided by theoretical frameworks are less likely to be strategic and entrepreneurial. They are more likely to be ineffectual, if not callous and conflictual.

In this final chapter, drawing on the previous chapters and the theoretical and practical understandings developed, an overview of tourism policy is presented (section 13.2). We then go on to examine the challenges for research and theoretical development of tourism policy and planning (section 13.3), and an overview of the challenges for tourism policy and planning practice (section 13.4). We conclude in section 13.5 with reflections on the nature of practice and the skills and knowledge required for critical and reflective tourism planning and policy practitioners.

13.2 OVERVIEW

In a modern, capitalist system, tourism policy-making is a complex process characterised by diverse, competing values, interests, perceptions and choices. There are continuous struggles between interests, but power with respect to a particular public policy arena changes over time. New policy directives derived from organisational adaptation rely on the ability of an organisation's staff to perform tasks according to the expectations of the government of the day, the organisation's staff and the public. We generally assume that public administrators have the responsibility 'for carrying out the work of the government' and that in the 'course of their everyday work administer the law of the land and carry out the civil dictates of society' (Harmon & Mayer 1986: 5). Such a responsibility carries the outdated assumption that organisations are in and of themselves capable of carrying out civil dictates or are completely committed to do what they are supposed to do in a reliable and consistent way (Harmon & Mayer 1986). Indeed, much public policy literature challenges such assumptions.

In order to unravel the complexity of policy and planning processes, we began in chapter 1 by progressing to a definition of policy as being a position, strategy, action or product adopted by government and arising from contests between different ideas, values and interests. Planning was identified as a traditional and basic human activity, which, in its simplest form, is about identifying appropriate steps to achieve some predetermined goal. Planning was identified as dialogue between overlapping or complementary and competing interests, communicative action, collaboration and partnership building, and capacity building. These ideas about planning alert us to linkages and synergies between government, community and business and the building of social, intellectual and institutional capacity. However, planning is political; planning is all about politics. Planning is the activity and process of policy development and relationship-building between various actors, agencies and interests. The links between policy and planning are unmistakable. It is practically impossible to talk about one without the other at the very least lurking in the background. These comments link nicely with those of Linda Richter (1989: 210), who was writing in a markedly different context:

> Studying tourism policies is more than a way of comparing strategies of tourism development. It is also a way of exploring local, national, and international politics, and of examining strengths and weaknesses in the policy process of various societies. It is a way of studying political culture and social values and assessing theories of development and ideological assumptions. It is also a way of dissecting the actual as opposed to the rhetorical freedom of manoeuvre of individuals and groups within the political process.

To understand the political process, then, one must grasp the concept of the state and the role of the state. Hence, in chapter 2 we explained the role of the state and the nature of the institutional environment for tourism planning and policy-making. We reviewed several theories of the state and how these theories, if applied to the same policy and planning issue, would cause us to look at different aspects of the policy and planning process. Ultimately, by plying our trade with different theoretical orientations we would arrive at different explanations of events concerning the same issue and perhaps also different views about what the public interest is and how it is defined and interpreted by government. We saw, too, that the role of the state has in fact changed a great deal in less than a generation. Globalisation and governance structures seeking to establish partnerships between civil society, interest groups and the state have become particularly salient. How governments get business done has changed dramatically since the 1970s and continues to change.

In chapter 3, we attempted a summary of some of the important shifts in the social sciences and public administration ideology that have served to shape tourism policy and planning thought, theory and practice. The point we wanted to make is that history is important. There can be no argument that to understand any event requires historical knowledge. Curiously, however, 'history' is an aspect of tourism that has only recently attracted research attention, with integration of history and politics sadly limited. We are, therefore, a long way from any coherent political economy of tourism. So we hope the discussion in chapter 3 inspires a greater research emphasis on the critical analysis of historical events that substantially influence tourism planning and policy in Australia and elsewhere.

Among other things, chapter 4 highlighted the increasingly blurred boundaries between the public and private sectors, and critically examined some important themes in tourism development, including self-regulation and accreditation schemes, statutory corporations, pressure groups and the power of multinational corporations. We believe the drive to self-regulation is an ideological one, which, at least in the context of tourism, has not been demonstrated to be more efficient or effective than traditional forms of government regulation. We are concerned about the extent to which governments such as Australia's federal and state governments are deregulating the economy for short-term economic gain when impending social problems (e.g. failure to endorse universal service obligations; unemployment from job losses after corporatisation or privatisation; inadequate health care; inadequate care for the aged; increased costs of higher education; and health problems and low life expectancies for Indigenous Australians) and prospects of market failure remain unresolved. Moreover, for some observers, these problems might seem only remotely linked to tourism planning and policy, but as more and more people live longer, health and social welfare will remain salient aspects of people's leisure, travel and quality of life.

Governments achieve their objectives through the development and delivery of policy. Chapter 5 discussed policy implementation tools and evaluation and saw them as integral components in policy development. Put simply, it is little use developing policy that looks good on paper but which has little or no hope of implementation, or which contains no measurable (or inadequate) objectives.

Chapter 6 explored many different approaches to the analysis of tourism planning and policy processes. A critical and reflective approach to understanding policy processes was described and given substantial support, because reflection highlights the strengths and weaknesses of the process. All the models discussed were considered to hold some relevance because policy-making is a dynamic process, socially constructed and often unpredictable. Notwithstanding these aspects of policy-making, in the last section, drawing from the insights gained throughout the chapter, several important principles for policy-making were prescribed.

With these ideas in mind, we refer you to the case study of the Cuban missile crisis of 1962, an early investigation into a public policy and planning issue that had the potential to disrupt world 'peace'. Graham Allison's investigation of the crisis presents us with a practical and valuable example of how we, as individuals, possess the skills and knowledge to address a situation and understand it from different perspectives or different viewpoints. One 'incident' can be interpreted in many different ways depending on the approach one adopts.

PLANNING IN PRACTICE ....

Graham Allison's analysis of the Cuban missile crisis

The days of 16–28 October 1962 are long remembered as a period when the Cold War nearly escalated to nuclear war between the Soviet Union and the United States. The Soviet Union had installed nuclear missiles in Cuba, and these were discovered by a US reconnaissance flight. Eventually, Nikita Kruschev, President of the Soviet Union, ordered the dismantling of the nuclear weapons. Precisely what happened during those 13 days has been a source of longstanding conjecture.

Essence of Decision: Explaining the Cuban Missile Crisis was written by Graham Allison and published in 1971. The book was rewritten in 1999 after additional government documents became available. The title of the book actually draws from a speech by the former US President John F. Kennedy, who said: 'The essence of ultimate decision remains impenetrable to the observer — often, indeed, to the decider himself.' The book is regarded as a classic reference for looking at a subject from different perspectives. What follows is a brief summary of Allison's work.

Allison was critical of 'rational models' of decision-making, whereby governments and decision-makers evaluate information and weigh up their options before deciding how to act. This was in fact the first unit of his analysis. Allison employed the 'rational actor model or paradigm' such that the government, as a central actor, examines its goals against options and the consequences of pursuing particular options. The government might employ cost-benefit analysis and select the option that maximises its net benefits. What we know for certain, however, is that actors do not always act in rational ways.

So, Allison examined the crisis from the perspective of the 'organizational process model or paradigm'. Before Allison's work, several authors, such as Herbert Simon (see section 6.3.1), had already highlighted the critical role of organisations in decision-making and especially the way the bureaucracy comprises a cast of thousands of individuals, develops organisational cultures and reacts in given ways to a problem or issue. The ways organisations do things can be easily predicted, and organisations operate to preserve and protect themselves, as do government officials. So, because of red tape, hierarchical structures, staff training and recruitment, there is little variation in the way an organisation reacts to a problem. Time is limited, and so are resources. Perfect information is not available. Organisations seek to find answers to problems in traditional ways. Many questions cannot be answered. Officials and then leaders 'satisfice' (reach an agreed rather than an optimal position) by pursuing a solution or option that best fits the problem, often with only a short-term view of the consequences of their action. As Peter Hall (1980: 193) explained, 'government is an established conglomerate of organizations, each with goals and programmes; change will be marginal and incremental, and long-range planning will be disregarded; solutions will not be adopted, indeed they may not be considered, if they depart from existing programmes or demand cooperation with other rival organizations'.

Allison also saw merit in the governmental politics model or paradigm because the organisational paradigm failed to account for the conflicts, compromises, debate and argument that might arise between individuals and agencies and even within agencies themselves. Individuals take positions — government ministers, senior and lower-level bureaucrats, the media all have their positions and all seek to influence decision-making. Power is a vital element. Actors in an organisation do not always implement policy in ways intended or instructed by senior executives. People perceive problems in different ways, do not communicate their decisions or non-decisions, and their responses to problems might be rushed. Put simply, the policy and decision-making processes are a long way from rational, and the perspectives we use to critically examine a problem or issue will greatly affect our understanding. Adopting a rational process paradigm is fraught with risk because it perhaps more than any other paradigm fails to reflect movement and dynamic environments. It is perhaps useful only as a means of control — suggesting how people ought to act and decide. It does not help us much in understanding how or why people and organisations and institutions act the way they do.

Sources: *Allison 1971; Hall 1980.*

In contrast to Allison's coverage of a near-nuclear disaster (well, perhaps — we don't know for sure!) is Doug Pearce's (2001) 'Tourism, trams and local government policy-making in Christchurch, New Zealand' in which he conducted a detailed analysis of the policy-making process underpinning the development of the tramway, which returned to the streets of Christchurch after an absence of 40 years. Focusing on local government and skilfully blending primary and secondary sources, Pearce's narrative account unravels a complex policy process and explains why and how a tourist tramway was developed in Christchurch. Pearce recommends the importance of developing a detailed chronology of events, of focusing on key factors and events, and of seeking explanation through the use of multiple data sources and diverse frames of reference.

His analysis was revealing in a number of ways, but one of the paper's highlights was the way it amply demonstrated some important aspects of local government policy-making: the fuzziness in distinguishing formulation and implementation; 'the shaping of policy by council officers and the coming together of officers and councillors close to the workface ... the overlapping interests of key individuals, particularly of some council officers who were also members of the THS [Tramway Historical Society]' and, who according to the press, enthusiastically pushed the proposal along beyond their advisory roles.

So the relative importance of the issue to national or international politics is not critical. Insights can be gained from looking at the small-scale policy-making and planning processes. This should encourage readers to study matters of great interest to them and from which social and environmental benefits are derived.

The substantive case studies presented in chapters 7 to 12 addressed a plethora of issues. Each author explained aspects of their designated theme (national tourism policy, protected marine areas and so on) with considerable freedom. The authors were requested to include broad conceptual and theoretical introductions to policy and planning in their respective arenas and to give practical insights through case studies and examples from environments and settings with which they were familiar. Clearly, the ways the authors addressed their themes varied, but one gap that is particularly evident is discovering why people (or individuals rather than organisations) make the decisions they do. There is still a great need in tourism studies for researchers to peel back the skins of organisations and look at their internal workings, the ways they relate to one another, how they perceive the world.

13.3 CHALLENGES AND ISSUES

■ 13.3.1 Theoretical *scaffolding*

Over the course of more than a century, systems of tourism planning and policy-making in different jurisdictions have evolved and changed dramatically in terms of their structures, processes, themes, geographical extent and form. The actions of governments, the values embedded in political decision-making and the quality of policy analysis on which tourism policy and planning are founded have, however, received only limited critical attention. This is gradually changing as the field widens and interdisciplinary scholarship emerges. However, as Jenkins (2001) notes, the field is still quite fragmented and the diversity of frameworks, ideas, methods, concepts and theories not only exacerbates but also enriches the development of a coherent body of tourism policy and planning literature. In particular, the tourism studies field exhibits a lack of attention to:

1. detailed historical understandings of tourism policy-making in Australia and many other countries, regions and localities
2. understandings of relationships between tourism planning and policy at horizontal (i.e. intra-government) and vertical (inter-government) scales
3. incisive theoretical frameworks of tourism planning and policy that have been tested empirically and which deal with such matters as personal

and organisational values, perceptions and choices, power, policy development, pressure groups, public interest, law and the state, and

4. case studies of tourism policy, planning and organisations that show how such research in a complex public policy arena might be accomplished.

The early chapters of this book presented a schema for the study or analysis of tourism policy and planning. Clearly, the study of tourism policy and planning is something of an art as well as a science. The researcher is an artisan, given a canvas that can be coloured in myriad ways. How we view the world affects our analytical perspective and the pictures we paint. Take the issue of tourism statutory corporations and their structures, functions and operations. One could study them in a number of ways and all would enhance our knowledge of them: the influence of pressure groups on tourism research, plans and marketing and promotion; links between statutory corporations and big business; the roles of significant individuals in tourism policy-making and planning; organisational culture and how statutory authorities conduct their business and make day-to-day decisions; shifts in administrative frameworks; and inter-organisational relations. Each theme is probably just as important as any other, but telling the complete story (or painting the canvas to capture every internal and external detail over time) would be a task probably beyond any individual, especially when an organisation's origins goes back several decades in various guises, and when its genesis is not at all obvious from without.

So, we must accept that our knowledge of policies, organisations, the state and its institutions will always be limited, if not piecemeal. Even people working within an organisation are not able to grasp its structures, functions and operations in their entirety, and this is one of the reasons why, for example, organisations contain several administrative units and hierarchical reporting mechanisms. Gradually, however, a piecemeal approach is enhancing our knowledge of complex planning and political 'systems'. We confidently claim that the tourism policy models introduced in the 1970s and 1980s (see section 3.6) are now defunct and were remarkably weak anyhow given what had evolved in public policy theory before the time of their writing.

Mill and Morrison, for example, fail to capture the political essence of tourism policy and planning. Tourism planning and policy-making are first and foremost political, value-laden activities, and the field of tourism studies should give greater recognition and resources to their study. Tourism planning and policy does not proceed along any neat rational and predictive route. Put simply, 'policies must be, and be seen to be, politically feasible, all are equally constrained in some measure by antecedents from past experience, and all must in time meet the tests of popular satisfaction and cost-effectiveness, if they are to persist unchanged or even to persist at all' (House 1983: 4).

Herein lies an important challenge for tourism policy and planning researchers. Researchers adopt certain frames, values and ethical positions in their research. They have certain ways of looking at the world that are inevitably informed by, among other things, education, experience and organisational culture. These values, ideas and ethical positions will affect the way research is conducted, the policy alternatives investigated and recommendations made. It is important that these values and frames are openly acknowledged so that planning and policy research can be evaluated, if not compared, on a more informed basis.

■ 13.3.2 **What** *type of policy and planning research?*

Another challenge for tourism policy and planning research concerns the relationships between description, explanation and prescription. Descriptive research is the lowest common denominator. **Descriptive research** offers little more than a description of issues and events, at times adopting theoretical models from the literature (although at times we question whether the right theoretical frame has been adopted). There have been voluminous descriptive contributions to knowledge of tourism policy and planning. Explanatory research is higher up the chain in terms of its theoretical rigour and value. **Explanatory research** describes and analyses an issue or event positing cause and consequence relationships. From this, a courageous researcher may offer 'policy implications'. Few offer recommendations. Preferred courses of action are almost unheard of. Recent advances in the social sciences encourage researchers to acknowledge the value of multiple frames of knowing and the benefits of alternative solutions. This leads to a situation in which academic policy and planning researchers do not feel comfortable prescribing solutions to particular policy issues and problems (Forester 2001). But more about this later.

Paradoxically, prescriptions for sustainable tourism planning and policy are still forthcoming at an astonishing rate. The main aim of **prescriptive research** is to prescribe what *ought to be done* and might include prescribing courses of action, or standards to be achieved such as benchmarks and performance criteria. Much of this prescriptive research is used to inform government action, yet its engagement with the reality and messiness of tourism policy and planning is often, at best, superficial. A good example is Inskeep's (1994) *National and Regional Tourism Planning: Methodologies and Case Studies*, which prescribes a rational model of planning. This kind of benchmarking 'research' is becoming increasingly popular. It is appealing to governments and industry organisations or associations as means to measure and evaluate their performance in dealing with particular issues or to offer blueprints. It is based on the collection and compilation of various indicators, yet the barriers and opportunities of government to the implementation of these benchmarks do not appear to be a major concern. In other words, there is a huge gap between benchmarking research that informs government policy and action and the way policy is actually made and implemented. Consequently, it is important that tourism policy and planning researchers engage more closely with the nature of benchmark research and their role as advocates and change agents in that research and its use (Coplin, Astrid & Bourdeaux 2002).

◼ 13.3.3 Academic *vs practitioner research*

The distinction between academic policy research and practitioner research was raised earlier and is returned to now. Wildavsky (1979) reminds us that policy research 'speaks truth to power', but the relationship between the policy researcher and the political decision-maker has never been less clear. The general position is that policy research seeks to provide informed, reliable advice to decision-makers, but the role and values of the researcher must also be taken into account. Most academic policy research is cast within an intellectual tradition. The academic researcher is neither pacifier nor consensus builder (Said 1996 in Mintrom 2003) and maintains a critical distance from the policy-making process, its decision-makers and institutions. Researchers are, ultimately, accountable to themselves and the university that demands their academic outcomes.

The practitioner or policy analyst is, on the other hand, an employee of or consultant to government. The values and agendas of analysts will be quite different. The policy analyst practitioner will be sensitive to the interests of government, will be wary in the timing of advice and attuned to windows of opportunity for encouraging both conflict and consensus. At difficult moments in the policy process, the analyst will seek opportunities to voice damning research evidence privately. At other moments the analyst will promote dialogue and consult strategically with powerful individuals and agencies.

The task of an academic policy researcher is to apply intellectual rigour and to promote and inform public commentary and critical analysis. The task of the policy analyst practitioner is to ensure that policy alternatives are based on reliable research and that alternative solutions are capable of being implemented (Mintrom 2003). On balance, however, both academic and practitioner policy and planning research has a role. Good tourism policy and planning research is a forerunner of good practice. It is this subject to which attention is now turned.

13.4 *P*OLICY AND PLANNING IN PRACTICE

◼ 13.4.1 Deliberative *practitioners*

The preceding chapters have sought to review a range of theories, concepts, methods and ideas that help improve understandings of the complex and value-laden world of tourism planning and policy. 'But why is this relevant to me?' ask those who have little interest in pursuing a career in tourism policy or planning. The answer is simple. All jobs in tourism involve, to some extent, engaging in policy and planning. Indeed, life's journey will ensure that you become involved in many different types of planning and policy. Operating a bed and breakfast requires knowledge of local planning regulations and participating in a local or regional tourism association, which is subject to institutional rules and routines. Submitting a proposal to extend a licensed eating area requires understanding of planning, building, public health and food and beverage laws. Holding an event requires familiarity with government incentive and funding programs and local government application processes. These are just a few examples.

The real challenge for policy and planning practitioners is to operate effectively in a complex world in which there are multiple views and interests. Forester (2001, p. 247) puts it succinctly: 'planning and policy practitioners have to go where their academic colleagues have been trained not to go: into the prescriptive world of making good judgements about what to do'. Insightful practitioners draw from their theoretical understandings, they reflect on their experience, and they develop a keen sense of political survival and people management.

Forester (2001) encourages planners and policy practitioners to adopt **deliberative practice**. Deliberative practice is about listening closely to the fears, worries and interests of others while reflecting on theoretical literature. It is about embracing policy and planning processes as unique learning and problem-solving exercises that assist in building capacity within the individuals and agencies involved. It requires planners and policy practitioners to navigate the uncertainties and ambiguities of policy problems about which there is a lack of full information and knowledge and to make considered judgements. On this basis, it is useful to consider the skills and knowledge needed by tourism policy and planning practitioners to operate effectively.

■ 13.4.2 **Skills** *and knowledge*

In a Canadian study, Pal (1997) asks policy and planning practitioners what sorts of skills are necessary to operate effectively in the contemporary policy and planning context. Paraphrased from the words of these practitioners, the findings are summarised in table 13.1.

On a practical level, these skills suggest that policy and planning practitioners are individuals with diverse interpersonal and analytical skills. Yet there is a deeper set of capabilities that sets good policy practitioners apart. According to Forester (2001), policy and planning practitioners build bridges, negotiate and mediate all at the same time. They work to encourage informed public debate. They try to understand the world and its many interrelated policy problems through the eyes of multiple actors. They appreciate the historical underpinnings of problems yet always have an eye on the future. Policy and planning practitioners also anticipate change and reflect on what solutions are feasible and practically viable; what is acceptable to whom. They are both visionaries and pragmatists. These are personal qualities that go to the very heart of the ethics and integrity of policy and planning practice.

- Interpersonal skills — getting along with others, being attentive and understanding
- an ethical and responsible approach
- the ability to deal with concepts, find patterns and make connections
- the ability to appreciate historical connections and international comparisons
- political sensibility — seeing beyond the facts and interpreting the research in a political light
- the ability to have a broad reach — someone who can cross boundaries, maybe has two degrees and has interwoven perspectives
- breadth of experience
- creativity — to take a model and mould it to the policy issue
- innovation — not just incremental thinking
- ability to describe the problem in a concise way and substantiate it
- ability to sift out the extraneous matter and get to the core issues
- communication, consultation and teamwork skills
- ability to couch technical work so that is can be read by lay people
- patience
- generic skills
- ability to understand implementation — the do-ability of a solution
- cognizant of political forces
- the ability to think ahead and understand the consequences downstream.

■ *13.4.3* **Ethics**

Ethical considerations are a growing concern in policy-making and planning, especially in modern public administration where roles and responsibilities are increasingly blurred, policy analysis is outsourced, and planning and decisions are made by collections of individuals from within and without government. Pal (1997) identifies four dimensions of integrity that underpin planning and policy practice:

1. *Integrity of persons* refers to the way in which policy analysis and planners conduct themselves in the policy process. The integrity of policy and planning practitioners can be understood in terms of respect for the duties and responsibilities of one's office; having regard for the truth; responsibility for one's actions; and acting with civility and sympathy.

2. *Integrity of process* refers to the integrity of policy and planning processes. Corruption is not black and white, and political debate is often marred by innuendo, threats and misinformation. Take for instance the process whereby the city hosting the Olympic Games is selected. In the late 1990s

corruption of certain voting officials was exposed and, as a result, a shadow of doubt was cast over the integrity of previous selection processes. It extended to the officials and the cities, including Sydney and Athens. Jennings in *The New Lords of the Rings: Olympic Corruption and How to Buy Gold Medals* (1996) also sheds much light on the modern Olympics.

3. *Integrity of government* refers to the integrity of the government and the way it conducts its business. Increasingly, governments are adopting business models in which citizens are consumers and the focus is on profit and economic efficiency. In this climate it is important to acknowledge that governments also have an important role in protecting the public interest and in facilitating democratic participation.

4. *Integrity of purpose* refers to values that are embedded in policy and planning and which are much wider than sectional interests or immediate gains. In tourism, policy and planning activities that embrace higher-order values, such as sustainability, wellbeing, equality and diversity, are not focused only on immediate short-term gains; and have integrity of purpose.

The above represent broad integrity considerations in policy and planning processes. However, ethical considerations are also linked to the moral and personal qualities of individuals and how these influence the process. Planners and policy practitioners do much work before decision-makers make decisions (Forester 2001). How they approach and fulfil these tasks, the way they behave, the strategies they employ, and their ethical and moral positions are worthy of reflection.

A practitioner's ethical position can influence policy processes and outcomes in many ways, including the following:

- in framing, conceptualising and interpreting information in a certain way
- by making inferences about causes, consequences, relationships between variables and actors and agencies, and prioritising some issues more than others
- by applying values and interests to cast a preferred solution
- in making decisions, either as moral judgements or calculated reason, about the scope of policy and planning research
- to pursue consultation with some and not other stakeholders
- by valuing and prioritising some interests and issues over others
- by interpreting institutional roles and routines in certain ways and emphasising some tasks over others
- by applying disciplinary expertise, methods and ways of knowing, and
- by making practical judgements about the problem and what is important to decision-makers.

Clearly, then, practitioners do not have a silver bullet. There is no magical solution and no template for tourism planning and policy development. Although they might not make final decisions or control budgets and resources, policy and planning practitioners exercise their power in diverse ways on a regular basis inside and outside the formal policy-making arena. Entrepreneurial practitioners will be aware of their influence and balance it with a depth and breadth of theoretical knowledge and astute reflection.

To close, it is useful to reflect on what is good planning and policy. The journey taken through previous chapters has encouraged an appreciation of different viewpoints from which to view policy and planning and acceptance that tourism policy and planning is not easy. The question: what is good policy? has been posed by many researchers and practitioners eager to draw some normative guidance from what seems like a messy field of theory and practice. Planning in Practice: 'What is good policy? An on-line discussion' (p. 456) summarises the results of one discussion held in Australia.

Finally, Bridgman and Davis (2004) offer a similar point of view, identifying principles that should be kept in mind:

1. *Policy is public.* Policy advice and development is a public service activity. Although outsourcing, external consultants and governance structures are removing some control of government, policy is nevertheless a function of government. Policy-making must therefore maintain the integrity of the institutions of government and the public interests they serve.

2. *Contestable.* Policy should be open to scrutiny, be consultative and developed by more than one perspective or set of interests.

3. *Not be captured.* Policy should be based on reliable information and rigorous analysis. It must draw on the information provided by stakeholders but not be captured by that information. Policy should be balanced and not be captured by the interests of a particular individual, group or agency.

4. *Flexible and responsive.* Policy needs to be flexible enough to accommodate change in broader social, economic and environmental conditions and in staff changes.

5. *Proactive.* Policy processes need to proactively anticipate change. Policy needs to respond to opinions and reflect the latest development in the field.

6. *Enhance the skills of others.* Policy needs to enhance understanding and awareness of different stakeholders who have an interest in the issue.

7. *Build networks.* Policy should emerge from information sharing, negotiation and compromise between interested parties.

What is good policy?
An on-line discussion

In Australia, an on-line discussion of 'what is good policy' took place on 12 February 2002 (Curtain 2002). High-ranking academics, senior politicians, former public servants and ministerial advisers all contributed to the discussion, although, interestingly, no currently employed public servants contributed. Vexed issues emerged. According to one researcher, an important measure of good public policy advice was the minister's acceptance of that advice. Another scathingly added that this was a 'damning indictment of our accountability indicators' (Roskam in Curtain 2002). Ministers or elected representatives should not be the sole arbiters of what makes good policy. Other tests of good policy included logic and consistency, implementability and outcomes consistent with the aims of that policy. Colebatch (in Curtain 2002) added that good policy is not simply about outcomes. Drawing attention to the quality of the process, he argued that policy is what is done 'in the right way'.

Conversely, when participants were asked what makes bad policy, the following definitions were offered:
- policy that is based on unrealistic assumptions
- policy that is at variance with its goals
- policy that has no demonstrable positive impact, and
- policy that is not coordinated or is even contradictory (Scherer in Curtain 2002).

The question was then posed: what criteria define good public policy? A range of responses emerged:
- Policy must incorporate long-range thinking
- Policy must be collaborative with an agreed set of priorities on cross-cutting issues
- Policy must be timely and anticipate political exigencies
- Policy must be based on systematic data collection and analysis
- Policy must use and triangulate all available evidence and open that evidence to scrutiny
- Policy must encourage involvement of all stakeholders
- Policy must acknowledge the constraints of policy-making and take these into account in the design of solutions
- Policy must be politically and economically feasible
- Policy must make values explicit.

Source: *adapted from Curtain 2002.*

CHAPTER REVIEW

The benefits of policy analysis are far-reaching. At the very least the study of politics and political theory 'should make us more defensive and more sceptical of the justifications of the system which nourish our compliance, and more willing to contemplate alternative political and social forms' (Goodwin 1997: 15). At best, it might force us to rethink and recast theories and models or change policy and policy processes. As we debate the merits of particular theories and approaches, we should not be at all surprised that there is no dominant or coherent approach in public policy studies generally and with respect to tourism specifically. Every paradigm, model or theory is open to question. Every interpretation and dissection of any decisions, actions, policies and plans is swayed by the viewpoint we employ. The real or whole truth might be hard to find or to discern, but we will get a greater sense of society. As individuals we then have a greater opportunity to confront reality. As John Ralston Saul (1997: 39) put it: 'This evening I have simply been exercising my right as a citizen — my Socratic right — to criticize, reject conformity, passivity and inevitability. What encourages me in this process is the "delight" that I take in the human struggle.'

In some ways, there is a link between Anderson's suggestion (in section 13.1) that we shake off ideological constraints and Saul's suggestion that we delight in understanding the human struggle. In this way, the study and practice of tourism policy and planning can be truly fascinating. Question tourism policies and plans. Question corporatist ideology. Question public administration practice. Confront reality (however reality is perceived by you and others).

SUMMARY OF KEY TERMS

Deliberative practice

Deliberative practice is about listening closely to the fears, worries and interests of others while reflecting on theoretical literature. It is about embracing policy and planning processes as unique learning and problem-solving exercises that assist in building various types of expertise.

Descriptive research

Descriptive research involves the description of issues and events that frequently (although not always) adopt theoretical models from the literature as a scaffold for description.

Explanatory research

Explanatory research describes and analyses an issue or event positing cause and consequence relationships. Explanatory research usually, but not always, draws from and reflects and refines the theoretical literature.

Prescriptive research

Research that prescribes what ought to be done including, for example, identifying preferred courses of action and standards to be achieved, such as benchmarks and performance criteria.

QUESTIONS

1 Explain the research challenges facing tourism policy and planning practitioners.

2 What is a deliberative planning and policy practitioner? What skills might such a practitioner possess?

3 How might a practitioner's ethical position influence tourism planning and policy? Give examples.

4 Discuss why the values of an academic policy researcher might be different from those of a policy practitioner. Whose advice would you value more: the academic policy researcher or the policy practitioner? Why?

5 Discuss the characteristics of 'good' policy. By corollary, what might be 'bad' policy?

6 Make some personal reflections. What have you learned about tourism policy and planning? Has it changed your opinion about the field of policy and planning studies? How?

7 How interested are you in analysing tourism policy and planning processes and outcomes? Why?

8 Evaluate your own skills and knowledge. What are the skills you already possess, and what skills will you need to develop to become a deliberate practitioner?

EXERCISES

1 Using the policy cycle explained in chapter 6 (especially section 6.3), take one stage in the policy cycle (e.g. issue identification, agenda setting, analysis and so on) and identify five skills that a policy and planning practitioner might need at this stage of the process. Give examples as they apply to tourism.

2 Examine a tourism planning and policy issue you are familiar with. Describe the position and behaviour of the tourism practitioner. Discuss the values, ideas and ethics that appear to have influenced their position in this issue.

REFERENCES ....

Allison, G 1971, *Essence of Decision: Explaining the Cuban Missile Crisis*, 1st edn, Little, Brown, Boston.

Allison, G & Zelikow, P 1999, *Essence of Decision: Explaining the Cuban Missile Crisis*, 2nd edn, Longman, New York.

Anderson, JE 1984, *Public Policy-Making*, 3rd edn, Holt, Rinehart & Winston, New York.

Bridgman, P & Davis, G 2004, *The Australian Policy Handbook*, 3rd edn, Allen & Unwin, Sydney.

Coplin, W, Astrid, M & Bourdeaux, C 2002, 'The professional researcher as change agent in the government-performance movement', *Public Administration Review*, vol. 62, no. 6, pp. 699–711.

Curtain, R 2002, 'What is good public policy?', Report on the inaugural online discussion of the Australian Public Policy Research Network, unpublished report, Australian Public Policy Research Network, Melbourne.

Forester, J 2001, *The Deliberative Practitioner: Encouraging Participatory Planning Processes*, MIT Press, Cambridge, MA, and London.

Goodwin, B 1997, *Using Political Ideas*, John Wiley & Sons, Chichester, UK.

Hall, P 1980, *Great Planning Disasters*, University of California Press, Berkeley.

Harmon, MM & Mayer, RT 1986, *Organization Theory for Public Administration*, Scott, Foresman & Co., Glenview, IL.

House, J 1983, 'The policy arena', in J House (ed.), *United States Public Policy: A Geographical View*, Clarendon Press, Oxford.

Jenkins, J 2001, 'Editorial', *Current Issues in Tourism*, Tourism Policy Making: Theory and Practice (special issue), vol. 4, nos 2–4, pp. 69–77.

Jennings, A 1996, *The New Lords of the Rings: Olympic Corruption and How to Buy Gold Medals*, Pocket Books, London.

Mintrom, M 2003, *People Skills for Policy Analysts*, Georgetown University Press, Washington, DC.

Pal, L 1997, *Beyond Policy Analysis: Public Issue Management in Turbulent Times*, International Thomson Publishing, Scarborough, Ont.

Pearce, D 2001, 'Tourism, trams and local government policy-making in Christchurch, New Zealand', *Current Issues in Tourism*, vol. 4, nos 2–4, pp. 331–54.

Richter, L 1989, *The Politics of Tourism in Asia*, University of Hawaii Press, Honolulu.

Saul, JR 1997, *The Unconscious Civilization*, Penguin, London.

Wildavsky, A 1979, *Speaking Truth to Power: The Art and Craft of Policy Analysis*, Little, Brown, Boston.

A priori **regions:** *A priori* regions are those areas where boundaries have been predetermined by others external to the planning and policy-making process p. 270.

Aboriginal: The native or original peoples of mainland Australia, Tasmania and offshore islands. The people descended from and recognised by Aboriginal groups; also Koori, Murri and Noongar p. 405.

Aboriginal tourism: Tourism product that is Aboriginal owned or operated, employs Aboriginal people and/or provides consenting contact with Aboriginal people, culture or land p. 404.

Agencies: 'Agency' (agencies) refers to government departments and other bodies created to perform a government or quasi-government function. For the purposes of this book, agencies can include statutory corporations, ministries, departments and government research organisations p. 2.

Anthropocentric: Visitor planning and management approaches that are focused on human outcomes, such as visitor satisfaction p. 341.

Attentive public: Members of the attentive public include formal and informal groups, government agencies, peak agencies, producer groups and interested individuals who have an active interest in policy development p. 208.

Australian Standing Committee on Tourism: Australian Standing Committee on Tourism (ASCOT) is the administrative framework through which senior tourism officers discuss tourism operations matters. Any decisions taken by ASCOT must be forwarded to TMC. ASCOT meets twice a year, and its aim 'is to improve co-operation and coordination of Government policies and activities as they affect tourism'. ASCOT's membership includes Australian federal, state and territory representatives, the New Zealand Minister for Tourism, and Tourism Australia and Tourism Research Australia representatives p. 227.

Biocentric (or ecocentric): Visitor planning and management approaches that are focused on environmental outcomes, such as the protection of diverse ecological systems or the preservation of rare or engendered species p. 341.

Bureaucracy: Bureaucracy denotes the administrative or organisational arm of government and is characterised by an organised hierarchical structure, permanent employees and a set of procedures and routines that are used to support the legislature in its law-making p. 43.

Cabinet: Cabinet refers to the ministers who have executive powers over a particular area of policy. In Australia's parliamentary system, ministers are members of parliament, and they are accountable to parliament and, by default, the people. In presidential systems, ministers can be appointed from the legislative body or from other positions. They are removed from the legislative body when they become ministers p. 34.

Capacity building: 'Capacity building' refers to ability to develop, enhance and maintain different capabilities, skills, knowledge and expertise necessary for tourism planning and policy development p. 9.

Civil society: Civil society denotes a broad range of self-organising communities of common interest, which could be formal or informal. It includes such organisations as registered charities, non-governmental organisations, community groups, women's organisations, faith-based organisations, professional associations, trades unions, self-help groups, social movements, business associations, coalitions and advocacy groups p. 44.

Collaborative planning and policy-making: 'Collaboration', and 'collaborative planning and policy-making' in particular, refers to cooperation, support and mutual assistance between actors and agencies in the pursuit of common interests p. 6.

Common property: Environmental resources that are (or could be) held or used collectively by communities. This concept is particularly relevant to the marine environment for, unlike the land, there are very few examples of individuals 'owning' space p. 376.

Communicative action: 'Communicative action' is a term originally derived from the works of the German philosopher Jürgen Habermas to denote the process of expressing, appreciating and processing others' views in an effort to arrive at an agreed solution or course of action p. 9.

Communitarianism: An ideology that emerged in the late twentieth century and criticises classical liberalism and capitalism. It emphasises notions of civil society, the individual's responsibility to the community and the importance of the family to society. Communitarian philosophy asserts the importance of social capital and human rights p. 83.

Communities of interest: 'Communities of interest' refers to the diverse constellations of individuals and agencies that exhibit shared values and interests on a particular issue or problem. Individuals and agencies could be members of more than one community of interest p. 207.

Compulsory instruments: Compulsory instruments include such approaches as legislation and regulation. They require government to proscribe and implement solutions to address certain policy issues and problems p. 167.

Constitution: A constitution is a document or set of documents that sets out the fundamental principles by which the state operates, including the form, character and powers of governments and the desired relationship between the people and the legislature, executive and judiciary p. 34.

Coordination: Coordination is the term used to denote efforts by government to minimise inconsistencies between the actions and inactions of other governments and non-government bodies for the purpose of implementing the government's goals p. 172.

Corporate planning: Corporate planning is a process in which decisions are made systematically with reference to their costs, associated risks and effects. Corporate planning implies that decision-making has a carefully devised and ordered structure and that the performance of any decisions, actions and programs are thoroughly monitored and evaluated in a timely manner p. 113.

Corporatism: Corporatism is a theory of the state that recognises the bargaining between different interests in the policy process and that corporate interests have particular influence with the state p. 38.

Cost-benefit analysis: Cost-benefit analysis is a specific technique that analyses how much economic benefit can be attributed to a particular policy change (e.g. economic growth, employment, foreign exchange earnings and revenue) relative to the costs of implementing that policy p. 176.

Deliberative practice: Deliberative practice is about listening closely to the fears, worries and interests of others while reflecting on theoretical literature. It is about embracing policy and planning processes as unique learning and problem-solving exercises that assist in building various types of expertise p. 452.

Descriptive research: Descriptive research involves the description of issues and events that frequently (although not always) adopt theoretical models from the literature as a scaffold for description p. 450.

Direct management: Management actions that restrict individual choice, such as regulation of accessp. 342.

Diversified Indigenous tourism: Tourism ventures such as transport, accommodation and visitor services that are controlled by Indigenous people but do not have Indigenous culture as their main theme p. 405.

Economic rationalism: An economic model in which monetary value or financial gain dominates in selling goods or services for profit p. 409.

Ecotourism: Ecologically sustainable tourism with a primary focus on experiencing natural areas, which fosters environmental and cultural understanding, appreciation and conservation p. 132.

Elite theory: Elite theory is a theory of the state based on the premise that power (political and/or economic) is concentrated in a minority of the population and that public policy reflects the values of the governing elite p. 36.

Enlightenment: The Enlightenment, also known as the 'Age of Reason', was an intellectual movement that occurred in Europe and spanned much of the fifteenth to nineteenth centuries. The term is generally used to denote a rejection of religious explanations of the world in favour of increasingly rational and scientific explanations of natural and physical worlds p. 73.

Evaluation: Evaluation is defined as the disciplined and critical assessment of government policy and actions. Evaluation involves the systematic collection of information, data and other outcomes of government policy for the purposes of analysing outcomes and for identifying improvements to policy p. 175.

Executive: The executive, also known as the cabinet or ministry, is those individuals charged with delivering and administering the law p. 42.

Executive core: Actors in government agencies in senior positions who are not involved in regular or routine decisions in a particular policy arena but whose support is crucial for policy decisions to be made p. 208.

Explanatory research: Explanatory research describes and analyses an issue or event positing cause and consequence relationships. Explanatory research usually, but not always, draws from and reflects and refines the theoretical literature p. 450.

Export ready: A tourism product that has a commission fee for agents included in the wholesale price and can be purchased in tourism export markets (international or domestic) and is reliably available in the destination area p. 416.

Federal system: Federal systems of government are those in which sovereignty is constitutionally divided between at least two levels of government and no single level has power over the other levels. Examples of federal systems include Australia, Canada, the United States, Germany and Switzerland p. 228.

Federalism: A system of government in which the central government is stronger and more powerful than the weaker provincial governments, such as in Australia p. 64.

Functional regions: Functional regions refer to destinations determined by a set of functional interactions that regularly take place. These interactions could be based on economic characteristics, social interactions or similar p. 270.

Globalisation: Globalisation is the transformation of the economic system and its consequent effects on political and social systems. It is characterised by the deregulation of financial markets and the increased flightiness of global capital to the point where governments' ability to manage their own affairs have been undermined p. 53.

Goals assessment: The process of assessing the level to which any given policy action achieves the goals and objectives it was designed to achieve. A 'goals assessment matrix' refers to a rational scientific evaluation process that assesses the achievement of policy goals. The process involves assigning a value that represents whether or not a particular goal has been achieved. The method has been criticised because it requires substantial value judgement on the part of the policy analyst p. 176.

Governance: Governance involves the establishment and maintenance of new relationships between the state, civil society and economic interests, and it embodies a less state-centric conception of the role of state in society. It also reflects a more active citizenry and a proliferation of interest groups engaging with more open and transparent government p. 54.

Homogeneous regions: Homogeneous regions refer to destinations where the boundaries have been set according to some set of internally consistent social, physical, environmental and economic characteristics that make it distinguishable from other regions p. 270.

Implementation: Implementation is the process through which policy ideas and plans are translated into government action p. 170.

Incrementalism: Incrementalism, also known as the 'science of muddling through', is a model of policy formulation based on the idea that policy is the result of many incremental decisions made over time p. 202.

Indigenous cultural tourism: Cultural tourism product based on an Indigenous culture, heritage site or experience (e.g. culture centre, festival, rock art, arts and crafts). Typically involves Indigenous ownership or joint venture enterprise that emphasises Indigenous interpretation, cultural authenticity and cultural maintenance p. 404.

Indigenous ecotourism: Nature-based attractions or tours owned by Indigenous people as well as Indigenous interpretation of the natural and cultural environment on cultural ecotours p. 406.

Indigenous people: The native groups or original inhabitants of the land, such as Aboriginal people and Torres Strait Islanders. Indigenous people have continuous cultural, spiritual and environmental ties to the land p. 405.

Indigenous tourism: All forms of participation by Aboriginal and Torres Strait Islander people in tourism: as employers, as employees, as investors, as joint venture partners, providing indigenous cultural tourism products and providing mainstream tourism products p. 405.

Indirect management: Management actions that seek to influence visitors rather than directly regulate access, such as provision of information to inform a range of choices p. 342.

Institutional arrangements: Institutional arrangements are the complex and overlapping webs of formal and informal structures, laws, rules, conventions, relationships, behaviour, values, ideas and processes. Institutional arrangements transcend organisational units and particular governments; they are ways of practice, values and ideas that are embedded in society and are carried forward, re-evaluated and modified over time p. 33.

Institutions of government: The term 'institutions of government' refers to organisational structures set up by government to achieve certain objectives. Institutions of government are often resilient because they have a long tradition and have established strength in their practices and routines. Institutions can change as a result of political pressures and shifting government philosophies; however, change is generally slow p. 6.

Institutions of the state: Institutions of the state are the organisational structures and practices that allow societies to make policy and pursue society's objectives p. 53.

Interest groups: Interest groups are formal or informal collectives of non-governmental actors and agencies organised around common interests p. 49.

Intergovernmental relations: Intergovernmental relations refer to the relationships and nature of exchange between different governments. Intergovernmental relations can exist between different levels of government in a federal system or between nation states. In Australia, state and federal governments are sovereign entities, and intergovernmental relations refer to the full range of formal and informal mechanisms through which governments relate to one another p. 34.

Issue attention cycle: The dynamic process associated with the way issues are identified, given weight and dealt with by governments, the community, industry and other stakeholders p. 205.

Issue drivers: 'Issue drivers' are those internal and external factors that 'push' problems on to political agendas for resolution. The rise of the environmental movement, for example, has seen the mobilisation of conservation as a key political concern. Similarly, tourism issue drivers such as the World Tourism Organization or, in Australia, the former Tourism Council Australia, have been able to influence the political agendas of elected governments p. 18.

IUCN: The International Union for the Conservation of Nature and Natural Resources, also known as the 'World Conservation Union'. Founded in 1948, the IUCN is the world's largest and most important conservation network, with a membership of 82 states, 111 government agencies, more than 800 NGOs and about 10 000 scientists and experts p. 380.

Judiciary: The judiciary, made up of the courts and its officers, has responsibility for interpreting the law as required p. 42.

Legislative foundation: A sound and binding legislative foundation comprising government policies that provide the legal basis for the management of protected natural areas p. 337.

Legislature: The legislature is the institution given responsibility for making laws. The legislature is formed in different ways depending on the system of government adopted. In democratic systems, the legislature comprises representatives elected by popular vote who debate and make laws p. 41.

Local Agenda 21: The United Nations Conference on Environment and Development (UNCED), also known as the Earth Summit, developed Agenda 21 as a blueprint for action to achieve sustainable development. Chapter 28 of the blueprint nominated local councils as having a particularly important role in working towards sustainable development, and Local Agenda 21 was developed to provide specific direction, local awareness and more focused activities p. 309.

Local destinations: Local destinations are defined by the unique social, economic, environmental and cultural qualities that give a destination identity; they are characterised by the functional integration of tourist attractions and services. Local destinations are the smallest geographical unit for tourism planning and policy but can encompass more than one local government area p. 301.

Management planning: This involves the clear statement of goals and objectives for management and the use at sites of a series of actions by protected area managers that are designed to deliver on the requirements of the legislative framework p. 337.

Mandatory powers: Mandatory powers are those powers that governments have been given under legislation and which they have an obligation to undertake p. 304.

Marine protected area: Definitions of marine protected areas (MPAs) vary depending on the level of use and protection that is envisaged. For example, some might see MPAs as sheltered or reserved areas where little, if any, use or human disturbance should be permitted. Others see them as specially managed areas designed to enhance ocean use. IUCN defines MPAs as 'any area of the intertidal or subtidal terrain, together with its overlying water and associated flora, fauna, historical and cultural features, which has been reserved by law or other effective means to protect part or all of the enclosed environment' (IUCN 1998) p. 376.

Marxism: Marxism is a theory of the state that is concerned with who gets what in society and the role of the state in regulating and perpetuating class relations. In Marxism the state is considered to work largely on behalf of the capitalist class in fostering capital accumulation and supporting the exploitation of workers. The state's role is to address only the worst excesses of capitalism to give it a 'human face' p. 37.

Mechanistic systems: Mechanistic systems are stable systems of a hierarchical and well-defined order in which authority flows through predetermined lines, usually from the top down p. 116.

Meta-problem: Meta-problem is a term used to denote the intractable problem sets that are not easily addressed by society. It is closely linked to systems thinking and the idea that a particular problem or issue has both forward and backward implications for other problems and issues. For example, the problem of high unemployment in peripheral regions, which could be solved through intense aquaculture, could conflict with environmental integrity and tourism p. 193.

Mixed instruments: Mixed instruments are those policy approaches and tools that employ a combination of methods to achieve a desired outcome. For example, environmental accreditation might be voluntarily sought by groups and individuals seeking to increase their market share and improve the practices and outcomes of their operations. Standards for ecoaccreditation might have been developed with government involvement so that they could be considered mixed instruments p. 166.

Mixed scanning: A model of policy formulation which proposes that smaller decisions are made incrementally but that decisions of major directional importance provide the context for smaller decisions. Mixed scanning requires that decision-makers scan the field to develop an understanding of important issues. Decisions on these fundamental issues provide overall direction, and less critical decisions, made on an incremental basis, fit into the overall direction p. 202.

Modernity: Modernity denotes a period in the history of Western culture when traditional societies were transformed from small, religious, authoritarian communities by the growth of the science and rationality associated with the Enlightenment. The modern period generally includes the seventeenth to late nineteenth centuries and traverses the Renaissance to the Industrial Revolution p. 78.

Native title: Native title recognises traditional owners and Indigenous rights of access, use, possession or occupation of Crown lands and pastoral leases in Australia, under the *Native Title Act 1993* (Cwlth) p. 410.

Neoliberalism: A contemporary interpretation of economic liberalism that emerged in the 1970s. Neoliberalists argue that government interventions results in market inefficiencies and can impede market development and economic growth. They support free trade and open markets as measures to improve corporate efficiencies p. 84.

New federalism: In the Australian context, 'new federalism' refers to efforts to work more closely and cooperatively and to address overlapping and countervailing policy initiatives between sovereign levels of government p. 233.

Network: A set of formal or informal social relationships between individuals and agencies and who have common interests in a policy arena. A network spans civil society, public and private sectors, is non-hierarchical in nature and provides opportunities for dialogue and coordination of policy issues p. 209.

New regionalism: New regionalism is an alternative model of regional development that is characterised by less 'top-down' intervention from central government and greater participation at the grassroots level. In principle, new regionalism is based on more localised and inclusive approaches to policy development that reflect unique qualities and strengths of regions. However, the power of interest clusters and networks can operate to exclude some interests, especially community and environmental concerns p. 268.

Organic systems: Organic systems are systems of management that allow people to deal with matters as they arise. People are not limited to highly specialised tasks and move fluidly between tasks of sometimes a markedly different nature p. 116.

Organisational culture: Organisational culture is a catch-all term that describes the way things are done in a work environment. It is commonly applied to indicate that the way people do things has a pattern that has developed over time. So it can encompass such matters as standards of dress, ways of addressing people, lines of responsibility, record-keeping and file management, inductions and codes of behaviour p. 118.

Organisational theory: Organisational theory is concerned with the best way to structure and manage organisations. In organisational theory several schools of thought trace the origins of organisations and explain inter-relationships among components of an organisation and its outside environment and hence arrange them into some coherent collective, chronologically and/or thematically p. 114.

Permissive powers: Permissive powers are those powers that local government has been given under legislation and which they may undertake but are not obligated to do so p. 305.

Planning: 'Planning' is defined as strategic activity comprising a number of stages that lead to the determination of a course of action to meet pre-determined goals. Planning is concerned with the future; is devoted to acquiring knowledge and identifying appropriate courses of action; is about anticipating change, developing a strategic vision and facilitating political decision-making; and is value-laden and political p. 8.

Planning for visitors: The process of setting goals for visitor management and developing and implementing the actions required to meet those goals p. 341.

Pluralism: Pluralism is a society-centred theory of the state that sees the state as a more or less neutral body that arbitrates between competing interests of society p. 36.

Policy: 'Policy' is defined as being a position, strategy, action or product adopted by government and arising from contests between different ideas, values and interests p. 7.

Policy actors: 'Policy actors' refers to individuals as active agents operating within planning and policy processes to pursue individual goals and objectives p. 2.

Policy arena: The interest groups, institutions and key individuals that influence the process of making policies p. 410.

Policy environment: The political power, economic and social values and institutional arrangements that determine the process of policy-making p. 410.

Policy instruments: Policy instruments are the means by which governments achieve their ends and include a wide range of instruments, programs, tools, approaches and techniques. Policy instruments exist on a continuum characterised by high government involvement (e.g. regulation) to local government involvement (e.g. voluntary measures) p. 160.

Policy metaphors: Terms used to describe abstractions or representations of complex systems. Policy cycles, networks and policy streams are examples of metaphors. They allow complex concepts and relationships to be conceptualised and simplified. Although they facilitate understanding of some aspects of policy-making, they can also minimise or ignore other aspects p. 194.

Policy subsystems: Actors and agencies organised around substantive issues and continuing relationships rather than in traditional political structures, such as political parties and government agencies p. 207.

Political realism: Political realism gives prominence to power and the role of the nation state. Nation states are principally concerned with the 'national interest' and hence with such matters as its political autonomy and ability to defend itself and to compete with other nation states. The national interest could also include concerns about cultural, economic, environmental and political resources and hence decisions and actions concerning expansion of the nation state or enhancing quality of life in existing territorial regimes p. 4.

Politics: 'Politics' has been defined in many ways. According to Heywood (1997: 410), politics is the 'activity through which people make, preserve and amend the general rules under which they live'. According to Davis et al. (1988: 61), 'Politics is the process by which the structure, process and institutions are brought to a decision [including non-decisions] or outcome. It is an endless activity; while politics operates, all decisions [and non-decisions and actions] are provisional.' So politics means that no decision or action is final. All decisions and actions of a government or institution of the state are open to question, debate and argument and are, ultimately, subject to change p. 8.

Positivism: Positivism denotes a commitment to rational scientific explanations of cause and effect and the belief that a single, real and objective truth exists p. 80.

Postmodernism: Postmodernism is characterised by a rejection of overarching theoretical foundations in favour of free-floating and pragmatic approaches to understanding social change. It recognises that there are multiple ways of framing social issues and building understandings and that there is no single overarching truth p. 82.

Pragmatism: Pragmatism is understood as a process of problem-solving in which solutions are developed and tested, and empirical knowledge is in turn fed into the process of change for societal progress and betterment p. 82.

Prescriptive research: Research that prescribes what ought to be done including, for example, identifying preferred courses of action and standards to be achieved, such as benchmarks and performance criteria p. 450.

Pressure group: Pressure groups (also known as lobby or interest groups) are associations or organisations that represent particular interests and seek to influence policy and planning processes. These groups might be large and have lengthy histories, or they might rise in response to specific development or other issues and hence have specific foci and lead a short life p. 136.

Protected area: An area designated primarily for conservation. In many parts of the world these areas are also to be used for recreation and tourism insofar as such uses do not comprise the goal to preserve in perpetuity p. 337.

Protected area manager: One who is charged with the task of implementing management planning processes in order to meet the legislative requirements governing the management of protected natural areas p. 337.

Public interest: Public interest is a complex and controversial term generally used to denote the aggregate interests of a society, which are to be enhanced or protected by some form of government intervention. However, the notion of public interest sits in opposition to observations that societies are characterised by a range of competitive interests and values such that there can be no aggregation of individual needs and expectations p. 40.

Rational comprehensive: An approach to policy formulation which proposes that policy-making is a rational and logical process based on the setting of goals, the identification and analysis of problems and the implementation of the 'best' solution. Drawing from scientific method, rational comprehensive policy-making assumes that there is a clear causal relationship between problems and solutions p. 201.

Region: A region is an amalgamation of political, socioeconomic and physical factors that yield a distinctive and integrated landscape p. 267.

Regional development: Regional development refers to development strategies and processes that aim to secure appropriate economic and social development in peripheral and generally non-urban regions. Regional development also aims to reduce undesirable disparities between urban and rural areas and to improve the general living conditions and quality of life of the local population p. 272.

Regionalisation: Regionalisation refers to a rescaling of politics and policy-making to the regional level, and is often referred to as a 'bottom-up' or organic process of defining and managing regional affairs p. 267.

Regionalism: Regionalism refers to a 'top-down' approach to regional development. Regionalism is characterised by delegation of responsibilities from central government to the subnational levels (decentralisation). Levels of policy intervention and coercion from upper levels of government can be high, and levels of commitment and ownership of policy at the local level can be low p. 267.

Regioness: Regioness refers to the unique economic, sociopolitical and environmental characteristics of a region, the commonalities and synergies of which make it distinct from its surrounding context. The term refers to intangible qualities, such as cultural characteristics and belongingness and, as such, it extends beyond a spatial interpretation p. 267.

Responsible government: Responsible government, also known as the parliamentary system, has the executive drawn from and accountable to the legislature. This contrasts with the presidential system whereby the executive and legislature are separate p. 42.

Scientific management: Scientific management is a school of management theory and approaches first developed by Frederick Winslow Taylor to facilitate factory production. The work environment is designed in a manner that promotes efficient resource use and task specialisation to maximise output while reducing staff effort p. 114.

Scientific rationality: Scientific rationality is founded on rational and logical notions of cause and consequence. In this view, it is possible to anticipate and measure policy outcomes and choose courses of action on the basis of their expected outcomes. This thinking later gave rise to a rational logic approach, which was used to evaluate the different courses of action open to decision-makers p. 76.

Self-regulation: Self-regulation can take many forms and is evident in many policy and planning arenas. Self-regulation, in theory, seeks to encourage people to meet a non-enforced set of standards, operational criteria or processes. It involves the assumption that people and groups can work together. Non-government organisations often set up codes of behaviour and standards for industry, but there is no compulsion for individuals or companies to comply with them p. 131.

Site management: Management actions, such as track hardening, at recreational and tourist sites p. 342.

State: The state refers to the full collection of political institutions through which control is exercised and societal change is regulated. The state includes the legislature, various arms of the bureaucracy, the judiciary, military, police, regulatory authorities, government business enterprises and a full range of rules, regulations, laws, conventions and policies p. 33.

Statutory corporations or agencies: Statutory corporations or agencies are not part of the conventional public service, but they do fall within ministerial portfolios. In brief, they are more independent of cabinet control than are departments and are established by legislation to function independently of government departments p. 125.

Strategic planning: Strategic planning involves a process of preparing short- to long-term strategies to meet business and corporate objectives. Strategic plans typically define an organisation's mission and values; critically examine its strengths, weaknesses, opportunities and threats; analyse the human and other resources available to an organisation; indicate the organisation's potential strategic directions — objectives and key result areas — after consultation with stakeholders; indicate possible options; ensure a program of implementation, monitoring and evaluation exists; and presents scenarios based on estimates of change in factors influencing an organisation p. 120.

Subgovernment: Small groups of people intimately connected with the core processes of policy formulation and implementation, and who usually occupy the top positions in their organisation p. 208.

Sustainable development: The term 'sustainable development' was coined in the Brundtland Report, *Our Common Future* (World Commission on Environment and Development 1997) and is used to denote the idea that development should meet the needs of current population within the ecological limits of the earth without compromising the needs of future generations p. 14.

Systems approach: The systems approach is based on the notion that interactions occur among actors and agencies within a policy and planning system and among these actors and the institutional and environmental frameworks. The approach also acknowledges that policy development takes place both inside and outside the frameworks of government and involves diverse community, business and government perspectives p. 193.

Tourism destination: A tourism destination refers to a geographical location, distinct from a traveller's origin, in which the activity of tourism is conducted. A destination is defined by the mobility characteristics of tourists themselves, and it can exist at a variety of scales from national to regional to subregional p. 270.

Tourism Ministers' Council: Tourism Ministers' Council was established in 1976 as a means of coordinating and facilitating the development of tourism policy. It meets once annually and includes the relevant portfolio ministers from Australia's federal, state and territory governments as well as the New Zealand Government. Norfolk Island and Papua New Guinea representatives have an observer status p. 226.

Tourism policy-making: The process of government agencies and industry bodies devising and implementing tourism policy p. 410.

Tourism region: A tourism region refers to the geographical location in which common characteristics and synergies exist between tourism products and services, and the term is also associated with a politico-administrative framework in which tourism planning and policy is delivered. Tourists can visit multiple tourism destinations within a tourism region p. 271.

Tourist gaze: Tourism gaze is a term originally coined by sociologist John Urry. It refers to the way tourists scan and perceive a destination, the symbols to which they attach meaning in a destination and the way the destination is interpreted. The tourist gaze means that destinations are individually interpreted and given meaning, and it problematicises the scale and politico-administrative boundaries associated with destination planning p. 302.

Triple bottom line accounting: The expansion of traditional accounting procedures for measuring an organisation or government's success to include social, cultural and environmental criteria p. 176.

Utilitarianism: Originally advocated by Jeremy Bentham, utilitarian is the belief that achieving the greatest happiness of the greatest number should guide government decisions p. 76.

Values: 'Values' are the beliefs, ideas and principles that underpin groups, societies and individuals. Values can be deeply embedded and unexpressed, or they can be overt. Actors and agencies in planning and policy use their value systems to determine which issues are deemed to be problems, which issues require attention and which issues do not p. 18.

Visitor impact: The impact, both potential and actual, as well as immediate and cumulative, that result from activities and management responses to that impact p. 337.

Visitor management: Management action that focuses on managing visitors themselves, such as regulation and information p. 342.

Visitor management systems: Visitor planning and management frameworks that are designed and implemented to provide guidance on the visitor management in protected natural areas p. 338.

Voluntary instruments: Voluntary instruments are policies, approaches and actions that are voluntarily adopted by groups and individuals. They are designed to change the behaviour of industry and community groups in order to bring about a desired situation p. 165.

Whole-of-government approaches: The challenge of developing horizontal coordination (across the same level of government) and vertical coordination (between different levels of government) of policy directions and actions p. 174.

legislation, 33, 34, 35, 41, 42, 54, 86, 125, 127, 130, 304, 305, 308, 337, 339, 340, 342, 344–5, 349–50, 353, 376, 378, 382, 398, 410, 412, 425, 433, 434
legislative foundation, 337, 364
legislature, 33, 34, 41–2, 43, 60, 130
leisure, 11, 12, 38, 78, 79, 87, 230–1, 232, 317, 445
levies, 158–9, 163, 164, 165, 244
licences, 163, 164, 386, 389, 406, 415, 424
lifestyle, 121, 143, 307, 309, 331
'Limits of Acceptable Change' model, 338, 341
Little Barrier Island (NZ), 343
living conditions, 9, 272
lobby groups, 33, 51, 52, 136–42, 145, 234
    see also interest groups; pressure groups
Local Agenda 21, 309–10, 327, 331
local characteristics of tourism, 318–19, 452
local communities, 2, 9, 13, 97, 132
local destination planning and policy, 301
    conceptualisation of, 301–3
    influences on, 308–19
    local government and, 303–19, 322, 330–2
    strategic and sustainable approach to, 320–5
local destinations, 301–3, 327
local economies, 143, 179, 309, 376
local government, 34, 40, 43, 45, 63, 64, 65, 87, 92, 96, 167, 177, 205, 208, 259, 273, 280, 301, 302, 303–19, 322, 330–2, 376, 389, 447

Malaysia, 387, 390
Man and the Biosphere Reserve Programme, 379
management:
    actions, 337, 339, 340, 341–3
    authoritarian, 116
    direct, 342, 343, 363
    indirect, 342, 343, 363
    mechanistic systems of, 116–17, 144
    models of, 341
    organic systems of, 116, 145
    planning, 337, 339, 340, 341, 353, 364, 392
    strategies, 340, 341, 342–3
mandatory powers, 304–5, 327
mangroves, 379
Maori people, 344, 347, 354
marine areas, protected, 375–402
marine ecosystems, 378, 379, 380, 382, 383, 388
Marine Ecotourism of the Atlantic Area project, 381, 392
marine environment, 377, 378, 384, 385
    see also marine ecosystems
marine governance, 382–3, 384–5, 386–90
marine mammal viewing, 134, 135–6, 164, 379, 380, 388, 389, 391, 407
Marine Market Transformation Initiative, 380
Marine Parks Act 1982 (Qld), 398
marine parks/reserves, 345, 351, 386, 392, 398
    see also marine protected areas
marine planning, 376, 377–89
marine protected areas, 375–402
    see also marine parks/reserves
marine resources, 378, 384
marine scientific research, 378, 379
marine species, 377, 378, 379
    see also marine mammal viewing
maritime zones, 382

market awareness, 167
market building, 96–8
market competition, 314
market concentration, 38
market differentiation, 320
market-driven approach, 97
market economies, 77
market efficiency, 98
market failure, 124, 125, 168, 204, 445
market forces, 164, 267, 386
market interests, 49
market management, 83
market planning and policy, 90
market segments, 242
market share, 143, 292
marketing, 46, 228, 229, 250, 251, 266, 273, 274, 280, 281, 292, 293, 303, 306, 311, 320, 321, 322, 360, 411, 417, 418, 420, 423, 449
    international, 227, 231, 232, 234, 237, 241, 244, 252, 253
    trade direct, 247
markets, 83, 90, 164, 166, 250, 276, 279
MARPOL, 398
Marxism, 37–8, 60, 75, 78, 80
mass markets, 309, 323, 325, 330
mass production, 78, 79
master planning/plans, 91, 106, 231, 277, 278, 321
media, 205–6
Meetings, Incentives, Conventions and Exhibitions segment, 242
mega-events, 237
Melville Island (Qld), 406
mergers, 142, 143
meta-problems, 193, 212, 382
Mexico, 304, 323–5, 388
microeconomic reform, 39
ministry see executive
mixed instruments, 165, 166–7, 182–3
mixed scanning, 202, 212
modernisation, 80, 94
modernity, 78–84, 91, 100, 103
money (policy instrument), 161, 163
monopolistic advantages, 143
Mount Aspiring National Park (NZ), 346, 349
Mount Cook National Park (NZ), 346, 349
multinational corporations, 5, 36, 37, 120, 142–3, 239, 268, 445
multiplier effects, 231, 260
Mutawintji National Park (NSW), 406, 407, 408, 423

National Competition Policy (1995), 313–15
National Cruise Shipping Strategy, 248
National Ecotourism Accreditation Program, 132, 133–4
National Ecotourism Program, 247
National Ecotourism Strategy, 247, 421–2, 425
national interest, 42, 43
National Oceanic and Atmospheric Administration (US), 384
National Oceans Office, 385
national parks, 85, 86, 132, 164, 197, 231, 238, 339, 343, 344, 345, 346, 347, 348, 349–50, 351, 355, 376, 386, 397, 406, 408, 409, 410, 411, 412, 415, 416, 419, 420, 422, 423–4, 425, 426, 433

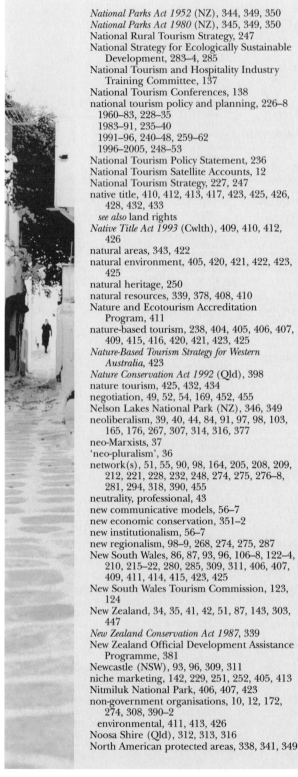